Wales

The principal sights:

< Lift flap for map

Peter Sager

Wales

PALLAS GUIDES

Front Cover: Cader Idris (Photograph: Alexander Fyjis-Walker) © Pallas Athene 1991
Inside Front Cover: Augustus John: Dylan Thomas in 1936 (Photograph: National Museum of Wales, Cardiff)
Back Cover: Roadsign (Photograph: Peter Sager)
Inside Back Cover: In Aberfan (Photograph: Peter Sager)
Inside Flaps: Maps by Ted Hammond © Pallas Athene 1991
Frontispiece: Thomas Rowlandson: The Artist's Journey in Wales (Self-Portrait) Aquatint, 1799 (National Museum of Wales, Cardiff)

ENGLISH VERSION PREPARED BY DAVID HENRY WILSON

German edition first published by DuMont Buchverlag GmbH & Co., Cologne 1985.
English edition published by Pallas Athene, 59 Linden Gardens, London 1991.
© DuMont Buchverlag, Köln, 1985
Translation and revision © Pallas Athene 1991

ISBN 1 873429 00 2

Typeset by Nene Phototypesetters Ltd, Northampton

Printed in Singapore

Contents

For Elle and Laura

Foreword

I set out to write a small book about a small country, but to my surprise (and to the anguish of my publisher) it turned into this weighty tome. I can only hope that the reader will finish up by sharing my view that Wales, far from being simply part of England, is a many-sided and fascinating country in itself.

The text wanders freely from south to north, and there are times when my descriptions are governed more by historical than by geographical links. Ultimately, we all travel with our own compasses and our own predilections.

George Borrow was an Englishman who loved Wales, and whose 'Wild Wales' I consider to be a classic travel book because it communicates not only information but also sheer enjoyment of country and people, capturing the present just as vividly as the past, and planting the author's own enthusiasms and criticisms into the reader. In 1862 he wrote what I repeat here without the slightest reservation: 'Wherever I have been in Wales I have experienced nothing but kindness and hospitality, and when I return to my own country I will say so.'

I should like to thank the poet R. S. Thomas, the grand old man of Welsh literature, as one of many Welsh people whose readiness to talk about their country has helped me to gain a deeper insight into it. Special thanks are due to Robert Koenig of the British 'Zentrale für Fremdenverkehr' in Frankfurt and the British Tourist Authority in London, to Barbara Fyjis-Walker who has chased many errant quotations as well as to David Henry Wilson, who has translated with a fine mixture of care and flair.

My greatest debt, however, is to my wife Else Maria, whose helpful criticism has accompanied this book through all its stages.

Books live with their readers, and some may also grow with their readers: all suggestions will be welcome.

PS

Wales and the Welsh – Nation or State?

> *Wales's greatest tragedy is that she is so far from God and so near to England*
>
> *(Council of the Free Church of North Wales, 1981)*

Borderline Cases – Where Does Wales Begin?

A man travels to Wales. He leaves the train at *Chester* because, since this is his first visit, he wants to cross the border on foot like a pilgrim. He has taught himself Welsh by reading Milton's 'Paradise Lost' twice in Welsh. After a ten-mile walk he reaches *Wrexham* around midday. 'Are you Welsh?' he asks some people in the street. 'Yes, sir, presumably, as we're called Welsh.' 'So do you speak Welsh?' 'No, sir, the only word we all know, or rather want to know, is *Cwrw da.*' And that means 'good beer'. What else did George Borrow expect in summer 1854, when he first encountered 'Wild Wales'? A proper border, something foreign, something totally un-English? Not until that evening in *Llangollen*, when a harpist accompanied his dinner in the Hand Hotel, did he really feel: 'I am in Wales!'

Where does a country begin? With the music accompanying the meal, or with what's on the plate? South of Llangollen, I stopped in 'The Lion' in *Llanymynech*. 'Half in England – Half in Wales' says the sign. The bar is divided by the border, and each side claims it drinks more than the other; they're probably both right. Not so long ago one half of the pub was dry on Sundays, and the other wet, until with the last referendum (they take place every seven years) the Welsh section of Llanymynech voted to join forces with the Sunday sinners of the English section. 'Welsh Sunday', the Lord's dry day, came to an end, and with it a national institution. After the drinks referendum of 1982, only two out of 37 districts, *Ceredigion* and *Dwyfor*, sided against the Satanic bottle. 'We must hold onto something if we are to keep our self-respect as a nation,' cried 'Y Faner' ('The Banner'), 'and respect for the Welsh Sunday is one of the foundation stones of our Welshness.' The shared pleasures of Llanymynech's pub continue, as befits a village on the border, right to the end in Llanymynech's cemetery. Some, it is said, even lie buried half in Wales and half in England, 'with their heads in heaven while their feet dance with the devil'.

Where does a country begin? With its law and folklore? In its pubs and cemeteries? Or in the diary of a Victorian country parson? On November 18 1870, the Reverend Francis Kilvert tells of a birth in the border village of *Brilley*, in a house that is half in England and half in Wales. In order that the child may have the best possible start in life, it is to be born in England. 'Stand here, Betsey, in this corner,' says the midwife, and the mother gives birth to the child standing in the right English corner. So much for nationalist gynaecology. But this borderline case of 1870 is also interesting for another reason: 1870 sees the birth of the Education Act, imposing the English educational system on all Welsh people. Henceforth, anyone speaking Welsh in school is to be punished. There, then, is a real, political border: the language.

And so the occasional incursions by the English authorities are not territorial acts of violence – they are linguistic, though in Welsh eyes this is no less reprehensible. Thus, for instance, Lake Vyrnwy Hotel in *Llanwddyn* suddenly found itself transferred postally to a neighbouring country: Shropshire SY10 0LY. Its prospectus now informs all clients that the official address is misleading, and the hotel is actually in Wales, in the county of Powys. Such high-handed British bureaucracy offers the national party Plaid Cymru abundant evidence of how Westminster treats Wales as 'England's backyard' (Dafydd Williams).

Y ddraig goch: A Little Welsh Dragonology

Where does a country begin? Is it perhaps with the appearance of a mythical beast? The Welsh dragon is red, and he greets you at the border: *'Croeso i Cymru'* – Welcome to Wales. Wherever you go, you'll find him – only in China will you find more dragons than in Wales. He's on signs, T-shirts, buttons, beer cans, coats of arms, advertisements and official emblems (colour plates 44–51). The dragon is the nation's trademark, and the domestic pet of the Welsh soul. As a symbol of sovereignty, the dragon may not be the most convincing of creatures, since in most mythologies he usually comes off second best. One need only think of Perseus, or Siegfried – not to mention St George. But the Welsh dragon seems to be indestructible. Where does he come from, and why is he red?

When the legendary Celtic King Vortigern wanted to build a fortress to repel the Anglo-Saxon invaders in the 5th century, every night the earth kept swallowing the stones that had been brought for that purpose. The king summoned his wizard. Beneath the earth, said Merlin, there are two dragons, one white and one red. King Vortigern had the place dug up, and the two dragons were found; they fought each other, and the red dragon won. According to Merlin, that meant the Celts would defeat the Saxons. But it was only in the mountains of Wales that Vortigern's people were able to prevail. And so ever since, they have kept the red dragon as their emblem, and wait for him to drive the Anglo-Saxons away. But King Arthur sleeps still in Avalon.

The long wait of the Welsh led to a wild proliferation of dragons. A nation without power tends to develop legends that are all the more powerful. The fruitfulness of the dragon-seeds was ensured by heraldry and by the bards. After King Arthur – and here we enter historical territory – it was Owain Glyndwr, the heroic freedom-fighter, who in 1400 waged war on the English in the name of the dragon. Generations later, in 1485, the Red Dragon triumphed in London, when Henry Tudor became the first Welshman to mount the English throne (illustration, page 21). At his coronation, Henry VII wore a jerkin in the same colours as the victorious Welsh bowmen had worn at the Battle of Crécy (1346) during the Hundred Years' War: green and white, the Welsh national colours.[1] He named his first son Arthur, thus setting an example to all patriotic British fathers, and immediately made him Prince of Wales, thereby fulfilling Merlin's prophecy without bloodshed, closing the circle and making the myth come true.

When in 1536 his son Henry VIII united Wales and England, the supporting lion in the royal coat-of-arms was joined by a dragon who appeared to have equal rights. In fact, though, this was the moment when he lost his power. When James I began a new dynasty in 1603, a new beast was to take the heraldic honours, for the Stuarts' Scottish unicorn drove off the Welsh dragon. Yet once again it was the English lion that did the taming.

Powerless in London, helpless at home, the Red Dragon was out of the reckoning. Well, not quite: he was given one crumb of comfort, an ornamental niche in the Prince of Wales's coat-of-arms, next to the three feathers. Thus the Celtic dragon took his place on the substitutes' bench of the British royal family, where from then on he has been used and abused, patted, petted and pitied. The dragon is dead, long live the panto-dragon. Thus the collective subconscious of the nation consoles itself for lost hopes. When nowadays the English travel cheerfully round the Kingdom of the Red Dragon, that does not mean that they do not understand the signs they see. But their latest invasion, the invasion of the tourists, has led to the inflation of the dragon, for now the symbol of Welsh sovereignty is a souvenir. The myth is once more an all-powerful motif – for the photographer. No, the dragon-killers have nothing to fear now, for after all St George is patron saint of England – history's ironic twist to Anglo-Welsh relations.

Another ironic twist is to be seen in the emblem of the Welsh Language Society: it is the dragon's tongue. The amputated tongue is as much a symbol of amputation as it is of language.

Taffy was a Welshman: Neil Kinnock and Other Clichés

The Red Dragon has two tongues. He speaks Welsh and English, as is made abundantly clear at the border: 'Croeso i Cymru – Welcome to Wales' – a friendly, emotional greeting with national aspirations. The English neighbours are more succinct with their county borders: perhaps instead of signs that merely announce 'Cheshire' or 'Gloucestershire', they should greet their Welsh neighbours with 'Welcome to England'. National differences

1   The Red Dragon on a green and white background has been the official Welsh flag since 1959. The common Welsh motto – e.g. of Cardiff – 'Y ddraig goch ddyry cychwyn' (the Red Dragon is our inspiration) also goes back to Henry VII: it stems from a poem written for the king in 1485 by the bard Deio ap Ieuan. The East India Company flagship that first sailed to India in 1601 was also called 'Red Dragon'. Today it symbolizes anything from the rock group 'Draig Goch' to the computer firm 'Dragon Data' in Port Talbot.

in language and temperament are already clear from names: the Welsh call themselves Cymry, 'compatriots', whereas the Anglo-Saxons used to call them and all the other original inhabitants of Britain 'wealeas', 'foreigners': and out of this came the word 'Welsh'. When Romanic tribes occupied the previously Celtic Gallia, the original meaning of the term was extended: since then the French-speaking Swiss have been known as 'Welsche', and in Belgium there are the Walloons, who share with the Welsh not only their etymology but also their language problem.

Cymru, land of compatriots. Does Wales begin, then, with the first foreign word over the border? Or does it already begin at home, with the clichés locked in the brain? Land of rain and rugby, churches and chapels, coalmines, great castles and little railways, land of sheep and Dylan Thomas, Snowdon and Eisteddfod, land of the unpronounceable. Clichés they may be, but they somehow do not add up to a publicity campaign. The Welsh, wrote John Cowper Powys with undisguised relief, are undoubtedly 'the least advertised race on earth' – a nation in the slipstream of publicity. Wales: geographically and historically peripheral seen through English eyes, and even more so through continental. How happy the tour operators would be if only the Welsh had something typical like kilts or bagpipes, or a pint of Guinness. But they have to make do with the advertising symbol from Buckingham Palace, the Prince of Wales. And who is he to compete with the Loch Ness Monster?

Where, then, does a country begin? With its people, perhaps? With names we know but have never associated with Wales? Rolls, partner of Royce; Stanley, who presumed to find Dr Livingstone; Sir George Everest, who gave his name to the mountain; the MP Benjamin Hall, after whom 'Big Ben' was named; the Tudor Kings Henry V and VII; Tory ministers and rebels Michael Heseltine and Geoffrey Howe; Mary Quant, inventor of the mini-skirt; Robert Recorde, inventor of the equals sign; Richard Burton, Tom Jones, Margaret Price, Gwyneth Jones, Shirley Bassey – they all came or come from Wales. Does this make them Welsh? When I asked people whether they were Welsh, I was frequently told. 'I'm English' or – sometimes proudly, and sometimes diplomatically – 'I'm British.' Anyone who would then indignantly cry: 'They're not Welsh' was certainly Welsh.

People are Welsh by birth, out of conviction, or with mixed feelings. Kyffin Williams, a painter from Anglesey, says Wales is his fatherland, and English his mother tongue. There are English-speaking and Welsh-speaking Welsh people, and it is the latter who claim they are the only true Welsh. But the outside world thought the opposite when they took Dylan Thomas, who spoke not a word of Welsh, for the archetypal Welshman. And he, incidentally, saw himself in the same light (colour plate dust cover; plate 15). Some say you find the best Welsh folk in London, for there's many a professional patriot who will do anything for Wales except live there. There are Welsh isolationists, internationalists, separatists and loyalists. And there's also the 'Dic Sion Dafydd', who upon crossing the Severn becomes so English that he makes English people feel like foreigners. There are also professional Welshmen who fight for a state that does not yet exist, and there are folklore

Welshmen who show the world a country that has long since passed away. Somewhere in between all these you will find Wales.

It's a small country living next to Big Brother England. And how the Welsh have hated, admired, attacked and imitated their neighbour. Most have learnt to live with him, many believe that they need him, and some believe that he needs them even more. For too long there has been a feeling of superiority on the one side and dependence on the other. Has the national inferiority complex really disappeared now? They have not been enemies for a long time, but they have not been friends either. They are neighbours who have grown old squabbling over the garden fence and still not quite knowing each other. One feels strong because he remembers all his defeats and knows they are finished; the other is stronger because he forgets what is no longer relevant. I have often been asked quite innocently by English people in Wales: 'How do you like it here in England?' For native Welsh people, this is a perfidious ignorance, or an ignorant perfidy.

What is Welsh about the Welsh? Take Neil Kinnock, for instance (picture, page 21). When, as a left-winger, he was elected leader of the Labour Party in 1983, the Press went to town on his Welsh origin and temperament, his gift of the gab, his singing voice, and his rugby-style politics – not averse to the occasional foul. It's not a bad image: the miner's son from the valleys, an angel in the choir, a tough guy on the pitch. Is Neil Kinnock a typical Welshman? Or just another cliché? There are many such clichés, like the Taffy that generations of English children have sung about in a slanderous little song: 'Taffy was a Welshman, Taffy was a thief:/Taffy came to my house and stole a piece of beef.' Thus the folk who live near the River Taff are branded as cattle thieves; scarcely more flattering than this piece of 18th century ridicule is the portrait the Oxford historian John Bowle draws of the original inhabitants of Wales as being talkative and touchy, and always ready to bring their own (or other people's) sheep out of the cold. There they are, ruffians, rebels in the Wild West, trouble-makers in Westminster. Plus ça change.

The desire to pinpoint the Welshness of the Welsh is as tempting and as futile as all attempts at national typology. National characters can change, and even if there are national stereotypes which after a while imprint themselves on other people's minds, they remain stereotypes. But the smaller the nation, the greater the need for a special profile, and the greater also the temptation to find a national common denominator, epitomized perhaps by the great individual who embodies all the virtues and the vices of his people. It might be Dylan Thomas, for instance, the drunken soul from Swansea, who defied the Puritanical image of his compatriots in a welter of images; or David Lloyd George (picture, page 21), the political firebrand who could charm the bark off the trees. Welsh archetypes? Yes, both of them, the poet and the politician, each fêted from London to New York as 'Welsh wizards', modern Merlins, weaving their magic spells with their mastery of language. And that is indeed a Welsh characteristic – not simply confined to the poets and politicians, whom one expects to have the gift of the gab, but to be found even in the man in the street: they are born talkers. They love to talk, not only in the pub but anywhere, and once they have started, they take some stopping; and the images grow more and more fantastic, the sentences more and more labyrinthine, and every story never-ending. In Richard Llewellyn's novel 'How Green Was My Valley', Welshmen have 'tongues a yard long' – but otherwise they have nothing in their heads, because they need the rest of the space to roll their tongues up in. They speak with the whole body, using mime and gesture with far less reserve and far more emotion than their English neighbours. Perhaps it's part of the Celtic heritage. The Welsh, like the Irish, have a long oral tradition – it's a culture of the word rather than the picture. With a few exceptions, painting and architecture play little part in Welsh culture. In a country that was always poor, and whose aristocrats swiftly emigrated to England, there were no patrons for the fine arts. But poets and singers always found willing ears among the people, even if they did not always find willing purses.

'Put two Welshmen together and you always get three points of view.' People who like talking also like arguing. As far back as the 12th century, the outspoken church dignitary and chronicler Giraldus Cambrensis boasted of his countrymen's rhetorical gifts, from the lowest to the highest, their love of puns, their quick-wittedness, and their boldness with language. The verbal wit is often expressed in the nicknames they give to people – a Welsh speciality: an old man with just one front tooth left in his mouth was called 'Dai Central Eating'; a well-known communist rejoiced in the name of 'Emlyn Kremlin', The journalist Wynford Vaughan-Thomas, who for many years was the Voice of Wales for most British people, once suggested: 'Perhaps talk is the real national industry.' Coal and steel may go downhill, but nothing will close the mouthworks. Historically this is even reflected in people's employment: most of the entrepreneurs in Wales came or have come from England. The Welsh have seldom been businessmen, industrialists or managers. But anything connected with language – whether spoken, written or sung – they have seized on avidly, blossoming forth and duly reaching the top. Teachers and preachers – these were the classic Welsh professions in the 19th century. Anyone who wasn't a farmer or a miner became a teacher or a preacher. And many of the latter were poets, singers, bards of the pulpit, Celtic Druids in Protestant cassocks. The Methodist spirit and a non-conformist upbringing, with a passionate mixture of Protestantism, spirituality and political radicalism all this had a far more intense and durable effect on the Welsh than on the English. But perhaps we are getting too close again to our clichés. It would be as absurd to call the Welsh a nation of teachers and preachers as it is to call the English a nation of shopkeepers.

John Cowper Powys, born an Englishman but styling himself a Welshman (picture, page 21) called his beloved nation 'a bookish people'. A people of the word, and the word was the Bible, and the Bible was the book of the people – and often their only book. Thanks to Bishop Morgan's translation of 1588, God did not speak English to them, but Welsh – the one language which they all understood at that time. And this biblical Welsh word was spread and sung and preached in sermons, hymns and rhapsodies, resounding forth from the chapels and the pulpits into the very heart of the community. 'The great rhythms had rolled over me from the Welsh pulpits,' wrote Dylan Thomas, recalling his childhood, when these rhythms made a far greater impact on him than his father's attempts to teach him an accent-free English. The language of the Bible, with all its rich imagery and rhetorical power found a congenial medium in the musical cadences of Welsh. 'Musical' is the right epithet, for one word flows harmoniously into the next, and one image grows out of another: *Llanhaeadr-ym-Mochnant* – the holy place on the waterfall of the pigstream. Such a place-name is seductively Welsh – it meanders poetically along in stark contrast to the laconic names the English give their towns.

'The words seem to have something of that strange elemental rhythm,' wrote John Cowper Powys on reading the Welsh Bible, 'that I catch in Homer, seem indeed to be nearer than ours to the primeval voices of hill and forest and river and moorland, the very consonants changing in their musical mutation like the rushing of the wind itself.' The metamorphoses of sounds and objects, the magical bond between language and Nature, the mythical landscape and the heroic history, all these constituted the Welshness which, after years of wandering round the world, Powys was to embrace, declaring Wales to be his chosen home, and calling himself – the pastor's son from Derbyshire – an 'Aboriginal Welshman'. He did not regard himself as a literary man, but as a 'talker' and an 'orator'. He called the speaker's platform his bed, his battlefield, his gallows, and his throne, and with his magical words he cast a Celtic spell over the New World much as Dylan Thomas did on his American lecture tours.

Choirs: Gardener Wanted, Tenor Preferred

The Welsh love of talking is only exceeded by their love of singing. 'I loved a man whose name was Harry, / Six feet tall and sweet as a cherry,' sings Polly Garter, and the Reverend Eli Jenkins cries out in delight: 'Praise the Lord! We are a musical nation.' Since the BBC first broadcast 'Under Milk Wood' in 1954, just three months after Dylan Thomas's death, the play has been regarded all over the world as a kind of symphony to the Welsh soul. I would consider this to be a misunderstanding, though a very beneficial one for Wales. For Willy Nilly the postman, Organ Morgan, Dai Bread with his two wives (one for the day and one for the night), and all the other eccentric inhabitants of Llareggub (which, for those who don't know, is 'bugger all' spelt backwards) have done more for the image of Wales than all the Princes of Wales put together. It is the most Welsh play in the English language, which in this century has never sounded more melodious or colourful. And anyone who has ever heard Dylan Thomas himself read his play for voices – enchanting, exulting, whispering, thundering – would think that here was the revivalist preacher par excellence, revelling in the glory of the '*hwyl*', the speech-song.

During his trip to Wales in 1763, the Methodist John Wesley was present at one such community song. After the sermon, each singer began one verse of the hymn, singing it 'over and over with all their might, perhaps above thirty, yea, forty times. Meanwhile the bodies of two or three, sometimes ten or twelve, are violently agitated; and they leap up and down, in all manner of postures, frequently for hours together.' One can sense the reserved Englishman's discomfort in the face of this Welsh fervour. These hymns with their quite literally entrancing *hwyl* were gospel for the Welsh Non-Conformists, who were an oppressed minority in those days. With prayer they strengthened their faith, but only through song did they free themselves completely, though it was only an inner freedom that could change nothing in the outer misery. The choirs of miners in the 19th century could not bring revolution to the mining valleys of South Wales, but through their songs they bore the grim conditions with heads held high. During the strike of 1893, the Rhondda Glee Society inspired the demonstrators with 'Cambria's Song of Freedom', and yet shortly afterwards the same choir was proudly singing its British heart out in front of Queen Victoria in Windsor Castle. Even in Red Rhondda, Marxism never had a chance against Methodism. Why change society when the community was so united? When choirs and chapels could boast a solidarity that was unknown to the working classes in Manchester? But even the socialism of the English working classes was more Non-Conformist than Marxist. 'Sing then. Sing, indeed, with shoulders back, and head up so that song might go to the roof and beyond to the sky' is the message in Richard Llewellyn's mining novel 'How Green Was My Valley' (1939). 'Singing, Singing until life and all things living are become a song. O, voice of man, organ of most lovely might.'

'Praise the Lord! We are a musical nation.' Where else, apart from Wales, would the songs of the artisan Joseph Parry have aroused such enthusiasm that a collection was made to bring him back from his exile in America and live as an honoured composer in his homeland? Where else would a choirmaster have a monument built to his memory, as was done for Griffith Rhys Jones in *Aberdare*? There he stands in bronze outside the Black Lion, a violin at his feet, the most famous conductor in all the valleys. With his choir of 456 he won the choral competition in London's Crystal Palace two years running, in 1872 and 1873. Caradog, which was his bardic name, was a smith by trade, and he used to say that it was his hammer and anvil that had developed his feeling for music.

In *Gregynog Hall* I heard of an advertisement which could not have been more Welsh: Gwendoline and Margaret Davies, two art-loving sisters, used to run their own choir on their country estate before the war. It was made up from members of their staff, and so one day they advertised as follows: 'Gardener wanted. Tenor preferred.'

Ever since the days of the Tudor kings, the Welsh, even if they have not exactly set the tone, have nevertheless made music at the court in London. Thus it was that in 1981, at the wedding of the Prince of Wales to Lady Diana, the most prominent Welsh composer of the day, William Mathias, contributed the official hymn: 'Let the people praise thee, O God.' But where, alas, is the Prince's harpist? This royal post, which traditionally went to a Welshman, has been struck off the list – as indeed has the post of official Scottish bagpiper. Yet the first singer to be ennobled by the Queen was neither an Englishman nor a Scotsman, but a Welshman – Sir Geraint Evans. He was born a miner's son in the valley village of *Cilfynydd*. At the age of 17 he sang Elias in Mendelssohn's oratorio at a working men's club; at 26 he triumphed as the Night Watchman in 'The Mastersingers' at Covent Garden; and for more than 30 years the voice of the Welsh Papageno cast its spell all over the world. The famous Mozart tenor, Stuart Burrows came from the same mining village, just a few houses away. Why are there so many outstanding singers in Wales? In his autobiography Geraint Evans suggests that it is due to the language, with all its open vowels. At home in his singing valley he and all his family spoke Welsh. Perhaps this is why London's Sadler's Wells found itself nicknamed 'Sadler's Welsh'.

But the epitome of Welsh musicality is not its international stars like Sir Geraint, Dame Gwyneth Jones or Margaret Price; it is the choirs. These are what make up the great reservoir of talent that offer so many performances of such astonishing quality for so small a country, and these are the true voice of the people. At the beginning of this century, every chapel had its own choir and its own amateur theatre and there was scarcely a village that could not boast at least four chapels, or even as many as a dozen. Every community, every district and every county held its own regular Eisteddfod – a contest for singers and poets, the winners being honoured with chairs, crowns or miniature harps. And even when the religious fires of Methodism were dampened, the singing continued. The chapels became empty, but the choirs remained. Then they, too, began to dwindle, and now there are problems: 'Young people today are more interested in pop music than in real art,' complains the general secretary of the famous Cwmbach Male Voice Choir. And in the most legendary of all the Rhondda choirs, the Pendyrus Male Voice Choir, which once consisted only of miners, there is not one single pitman left, for all the collieries have closed. The quality of the valley choirs has diminished, claim the cynics, because the clerks and managers and all the other new singers lack the special timbre of coaldust in the lungs.

But even today there are still more than 300 choirs in Wales. They have long since lost their original, religious purpose, but they follow their own ritual. Their second and scarcely less important social function of knitting the community together is one which they have also, to a large extent, lost. And although they are still amateurs, they have a thoroughly professional business sense these days. They may all go their own way, but they are also part of the tourist industry and are a cultural export. They are one of Wales's myths.

Rugby: How the Welsh take Revenge for Llywelyn

The most passionate of all Welsh choirs is to be found neither in chapel nor at the Eisteddfod, but at Cardiff Arms Park:

Sing a song of rugby,	When the match is over,
Buttocks, booze and blood,	They're at the bar in throngs,
Thirty dirty ruffians	If you think the game is filthy,
Brawling in the mud.	Then you should hear the songs.

(Harri Webb)

Together with singing, rugby is the national passion. Its stars are like gods, and great names from the past, like Barry John, Gareth Edwards, J. P. R. Williams, live on as legends in the valleys. 'There are no heroes like rugby heroes,' wrote *The Times* when yet again the Anglo-Saxons bit the dust in Cardiff. Beating England at rugby is history's consolation, revenge for Llywelyn. '*Mae Hen Wlad Fy Nhadau*', they sing – 'Land of my Fathers', the Welsh national anthem - and '*Sospan Fach*', 'the little frying pan',[1] and the mighty stadium echoes with the massed voices of the mighty choir. This special atmosphere is so intoxicating and so unique, with its hymns and choirs and cheers, that it has even been captured on a record: 'The Sound of Welsh Rugby'. And he who has a ticket has a treasure beyond price. A popular joke tells of an empty seat at an international. A man in the row behind can't believe it, and taps the shoulder of the man next to the empty seat. 'Who's seat's that?' he asks. – 'My wife's.' – 'Then where is she?' – 'Dead.' – 'What, man, couldn't you have given the ticket to her brother?' – 'I did, but the idiot insisted on going to her funeral today.'

In England rugby is a game, but in Wales it's a national drug. Yet rugby originated in the English town of Rugby – in fact, at the public school there, in 1823, when William Webb Ellis during a football match suddenly picked up the ball, breaking all the rules, and ran across the goal-line with it. At least, so legend says. The Welsh, never at a loss for a story, especially if it's a story that will put them one up on the English, tell a different tale. In his 'Description of Pembrokeshire', the chronicler George Owen describes a ballgame played in 1603 between two villages, with each side using every means possible to stop the other from carrying the ball into their own village. The battle raged for hours over hill and dale, hedge and stream, and then at last both sides would go home in their hundreds, 'with broken heads, black faces, bruised bodies, and lame legs, yet laughing and merrily jesting at their harms.' The name of the game was *cnapan*,[2] and the Welsh have no doubt that this was primal rugby.

Whoever it was that started the great punch-up, the fact remains that the Welsh see the origins in a game played between peasants out in the open fields, while the English attribute it to the upper-class pupils of a public school. It's the social class that matters, not the date. And while some regard the sophisticated refinements of cricket as being

---

1 'Sospan Fach' comes from Llanelli, the steelworkers' town where frying pans were produced. The Llanelli Rugby Football Club actually has two frying pans on its goalposts.

2 'Cnapan' was the name given to the ball, which was originally made of wood and boiled in fat to make it slippery.

England's national sport, there is no doubt that the blood and thunder of rugby is that of Wales – which makes it doubly ironic that the game should be named after an English boarding-school. Rugby was a sport that could easily catch on in a relatively poor country like Wales: a contact sport tailor-made for miners and steelworkers, its technical requirements are few and inexpensive – little more than a field, a ball, and a set of posts. The mining communities of South Wales swiftly took it to their hearts, this brawl that roused the old warrior spirit and allowed their patriotic fervour to express itself on new, less dangerous battlefields. Meanwhile, in the north of England, parallel to the public school tradition, the working classes developed their own form of rugby – 13 men instead of 15, professional and not amateur, rugby league as opposed to rugby union. These were social differences that did not apply to the game in Wales.

If 'Englishness' is typified, as J. B. Priestley suggests, by an inborn class consciousness, can the lack of it be regarded as typical of 'Welshness'? If only national characteristics were so distinct, and national differences so simple, perhaps there would be less misunderstanding between nations. Wales does not, of course, have a classless society. But social differences are not so marked as in England, and they play a very minor role. In England you can still judge a man by his accent, whereas in Wales the accents are regional, not social: workers and professors, farmers and managing directors all speak the same Welsh. There are historical reasons for this. After union in 1536 most of the Welsh aristocracy moved to the court in London, and the landlords who remained all became anglicized sooner or later. They had little in common with the ordinary people: they spoke English and not Welsh, belonged to the High Church and not to the Non-Conformist, and were Tories, not Radicals. The people found their new leaders in their own ranks: preachers, teachers and poets – a spiritual aristocracy that knew how to advance their aspirations politically as well as intellectually, and not only through opposition to England.

No, it's not class differences that make Wales Welsh. So is it other distinctions? Between North and South Wales? Between Welsh and English speakers? Between desk clerks in Cardiff and miners in the valleys? Between the industrial worker in Port Talbot, the hill-farmer in Snowdonia, and their sons in London? They're all different, and they're all Welsh. Polarization would be as futile as the search for a common denominator. Is 'Welshness' simply an imaginary dimension, a melting pot of national stereotypes and lost hopes, an empty space in national consciousness, or a political postulate?

Eisteddfod: Festival of the Welsh Soul

For me, Welshness is above all a personal experience, and a particular one too: the Royal National Eisteddfod. Once a year the Arch-Druid of Wales has his big moment. '*Oes Heddwch?*' he cries amid the circle of standing stones. He pulls his gigantic sword half out

King Henry VII (1457–1509)

Reverend Christmas Evans (1776–1838)

William Williams Pantycelyn (1717–91)

David Lloyd George (1863–1945)

Neil Kinnock (born 1942)

Gwynfor Evans (born 1912)

John Cowper Powys (1872–1963)

Saunders Lewis (1893 1985)

R. S. Thomas (born 1913)

of its sheath. *'Heddwch!'* comes the muffled reply from the crowd. Three times the bizarre ritual is repeated: 'Is there peace?' – 'Peace!' Well, let's pretend anyway.

Year after year there are strange goings-on in another stone circle (colour plates 61, 62; plate 58). Figures stand all around, wrapped in billowing robes of white, blue, and green – the three orders of the Gorsedd. Trumpeters fanfare to the four corners of the earth, harpists serenade, bards sing, and barefoot elfin children dance the flower-dance. The Arch-Druid drinks the wine of welcome out of the horn of Hirlas, while we – natives and visitors alike – stand and watch in this Celtic open-air theatre that has no equal anywhere. For the whole thing is an ingenious fraud. The 'Gorsedd Beirdd Ynys Prydain' – the assembly of the bards of the British Isles – is an historic fiction just like the Gaelic Ossian (1760). Emulating his Scottish contemporary James Macpherson, the Welshman Edward Williams invented legends, poems and chronicles which he passed off as evidence of earlier Eisteddfods, in order to endow the bards of his region with older traditions and richer ceremonies. Iolo Morganwg, as he called himself after his home county of Glamorgan, was a stone mason, a self-taught writer and a passionate archaeologist. Above all he was an eccentric. If sheep and cows can eat grass, then so can people, he said once, and spent a whole day on hands and knees grazing in a meadow. He did not revolutionize our eating habits, but he certainly enriched Welsh folklore. At the first British assembly of bards in 1792, on Primrose Hill in London, he held the first of his Druid ceremonies.[1] By the time of the Eisteddfod in *Carmarthen* in 1819, the ritual was perfect, with white, blue and green armbands as insignia of the Gorsedd. And in the garden of the Ivy Bush Hotel, whose bar contains a glass window commemorating Iolo, his Stonehenge trick had its world premiere: he took a few stones out of his pocket and laid them in a circle on the ground. Where there are no prehistoric monuments, you have to do-it-yourself. Since then, every major Welsh venue for the Eisteddfod has boasted its own mini-Stonehenge, and the number increases every year.

The Gorsedd is a strange but, in the eyes of many Welshmen, a necessary fiction. The Arch-Druid James Nicholas, Her Majesty's Schools Inspector in Wales, told me that, along with the Eisteddfod, it was the only pure Welsh institution. 'We have no state of our own that can give decorations,' he said, 'but the Gorsedd does.' So instead of thistles and garters and other London orders, the Gorsedd bestows green, blue, and – highest of the high – white robes on those whose contribution to Welsh language and culture has merited them. And their numbers are evidently on the increase: in 1927 the Gorsedd had 460 members, and now it has well over 1,300. They include some of the most prominent Welsh citizens: TV stars, bishops, rugby players, mayors, officials from the Welsh Office and their most vehement opponents, such as the protest singer Dafydd Iwan (plate 30). And although they don't speak Welsh (otherwise a strict condition of admittance), the Queen

---

1 'The Most Ancient Order of Druids' was founded in 1717 on Primrose Hill by one John Toland. Once a year, on Midsummer Night, the members of the 'Order of Bards, Ovates and Druids' still meet there.

and Queen Mother are honorary members. The Royal Eisteddfod enjoys the loftiest patronage, and in turn the Royal Family enjoy as much loyalty from the Welsh as they get from the English. But that does not prevent the occasional contretemps. When the librarian Sion Aled, whose protests had already led to several previous convictions, was crowned bard at Machynlleth in 1981, he refused a place in the Gorsedd because he objected to there being a crowned member from Buckingham Palace. The Queen's realm ends at the Severn, say Sion and other members of the Welsh Language Society. As far as they are concerned, the last legitimate King of Wales was Llywelyn the Last, and he died in 1282.

Current and anachronistic – those are the problems of the Welsh and of associations like the Gorsedd. Its Arch-Druids, by no means the museum-pieces they may seem to be, see themselves as the conscience of the nation, like the bards of old. They stand guard not only over the purity of poetic metres and dubious ceremonies, but also over matters of political concern, such as the nuclear waste disposal sites in Snowdonia. And they campaign for a Welsh TV Channel. Not for nothing is their Druid motto: '*Y gwir yn erbyn y byd*' – The Truth Against The World. The Gorsedd is the most spectacular, though certainly not the most important element of that Welshest of Welsh institutions, The Royal National Eisteddfod.

Year after year, like salmon pressing on to their spawning beds, the Welsh throng to their Eisteddfod. They come from Abergavenny and Abu Dhabi, Harlech and Hong Kong, Nant Gwynant and New Zealand, by car, by plane, by wheelchair, 100,000 and more from here, there and everywhere. In order not to miss this highlight of the Welsh year, they close their shops, put off their holidays, postpone conferences, weddings and deaths. During this first week of August, nothing, but nothing is more important than the Eisteddfod. This is Mecca, Woodstock and the Grand National all rolled into one. For the outsider, according to the English journalist Trevor Fishlock, the whole thing is like a folkloric mist, in which part of the Welsh nation disappears amid strange noises.

Of all European festivals, it is the oldest, the most poetic, and the most political. The first Eisteddfod dates from the year 1176, and was held in *Cardigan Castle*. The word means literally a sitting. It was a gathering of poets much like the medieval German 'Meistersinger', with precise rules and extraordinary prizes – namely, chairs. In the middle of the 15th century the Eisteddfod, by command of Queen Elizabeth I, served as a sort of test for poets, so that the good ones could be separated from the bad, the self-styled verse-smiths. And so, with various interruptions, the national festival gradually evolved, and since 1860 it has been held regularly, announced at least a year and a day in advance, the week-long festivities alternating yearly between North and South Wales.

What is the reason for all the to-ing and fro-ing? Why do they carry their bulky pavilion of culture from north to south, up and down like hill farmers with their cattle, summer in the mountains, winter in the valleys? Are they all shepherds at heart? The change of venue – burdensome though it may be in terms of organization and finance – is an essential part of the festival's success and of its Welshness. Culture must come from the people, and not from some centralized institution; each of the different regions must impart its own particular tone to the Eisteddfod. This is part of the nature and the history of Wales. In contrast to England, where successful culture has to be London culture, Wales has always been a nation of regions, decentralized, split up by its rugged mountains and its tribalism. This is one reason why invaders always had trouble with the Welsh, and the Welsh always had trouble with themselves and with the concept of unity. But a peripatetic festival binds them together, as well as creating new focal points. It functions rather like a sprinkler, spreading Welshness evenly across the land. And this is all the more essential for a nation that long had no national institutions of its own, and did not even have a capital city or, rather, an administrative centre until the middle of the 20th century. Every town where the Eisteddfod is held becomes for one week the cultural capital of Wales.

The Eisteddfod, then, is a travelling circus of culture, the most poetic in Europe. Where else will you find so many poets and singers? Where else will you find academics and farmers, amateurs and professionals all under one roof, competing with the oldest and most difficult verse forms their language can produce? Where else will you hear such wittily improvised rhymes with such trenchant judgments passed as in the 'Babell Len', the literature tent? There I met one Dic Jones: 'Some people like to go bowling, but I like to write verse.' Dic Jones, farmer and poet from Cardigan, has twice won the bardic throne in the National Eisteddfod. 'There are still about 500 people in Wales who can use the *cynghanedd*,' he says. 'It's the most difficult of the traditional 24-beat metres[1] with its complex alliteration, but it's more popular than it was twenty five years ago, especially with people like me.'

The idea that this is also Wales's most political festival is hotly disputed by some of the participants, and in the next breath they'll confirm that it is. Is it political because it provides a platform for the Welsh Language Society and other radicals? Or because political plays are performed here, such as one that attacked the Falklands War?[2] No, it's political mainly because only one language is allowed here, and that's Welsh.

'*Bore da* – good day.' – '*Sut mae?* How are you?' That's not too difficult to learn. And in due course you'll realize that Merched are ladies and Dynion are gentlemen. But the classic Eisteddfod greeting is already a bit more complicated: '*Y ma am yr wythnos?* – Are you also here for a week?' And if you want to learn more, you'll have to go to the '*Pabell y Dysgwyr* – the tent of learners'. If you continue their one-week intensive course at home, you might even win a prize at the next Eisteddfod as 'Welsh Language Learner of the Year'. At the Eisteddfod in Llangefni one Welsh MP from England was wearing a special

1 There is a society and a magazine devoted to classic Welsh verse, 'Barddas' (founded 1967), and they guard the rules laid down for 24-metre verse at the Carmarthen Eisteddfod of 1450.

2 250 British soldiers were killed in the Falklands War, of whom 36 were Welsh Guards – a relatively large proportion of the total, as indeed were the casualties among the Scots Guards and the Gurkhas.

badge: 'Beginner, please speak slowly!' Despite all the centuries of anglicization, this small nation still clings fiercely to its own language and culture, and nowhere is this more evident or more impressive than at an Eisteddfod. A man from Cardiff courageously whispered to me in English that the Welsh spoke English all b....y year long, and this was the week when it was Welsh only. 'It peps us up for the rest of the year,' he said. The pep also comes from the harpists and the singers, folkdancing, choirs, and even Welsh rock-operas. But above all, it comes from poetry reading. And where else in the world will you win a chair for your poems?

'Chairing the bard' is the highest honour a poet can attain in Wales. According to Iolo's bardic fictions, the original chair was part of the Round Table, over which Arthur presided as 'chairman'. It's a myth or metaphor perpetuated by such poetic placenames as *Cadair Arthur* – Arthur's Chair.[1] There are many places in Wales that invite you to sit and poetize, like *Cader Idris* – the Seat of Idris, a legendary giant and bard. This mountain in Snowdonia is the holy seat of poetry for the Welsh, and anyone who spends a night on its summit will wake up a poet – or a madman. The tale vividly illustrates the risks of mountain-climbing, and of poetry, and it also tells us something about the nature of bardic chairs. George Borrow found a bardic throne in the wilderness. He was visiting the house of the 17th-century poet Huw Morris in the Ceiriog Valley, and to satisfy his professional as well as his touristic curiosity, he wanted first of all to see the bard's famous chair. He was told that it was outside. The 'Nightingale of Ceiriog' had sat upon a lonely rock by the river, his back against the slate.[2] George Borrow took off his hat, sat down, and began to recite, 'though the rain was pouring down'. Nature, then, is the seat of poetry, and its chairs are mighty hard.

How and where you sit also denotes your rank. At the table of the 10th-century King Hywel Dda, a chair was specially reserved for the *pencerdd*, the chief poet. Bards had prestige, and their art was important. Not only did they have to provide verses for all occasions – weddings, funerals, war and peace – but they were also entertainers, chroniclers, and genealogists. And so Hywel Dda's exemplary code of law gave the Royal Bards eighth place in the royal household. They were each worth 126 cows, which was a small fortune in those days; and anyone who insulted them was fined 6 cows. Nowadays, when your ox and your ass are all equal in the eyes of the law, only a symbol remains of Hywel's bardic refinements: the chair. A chair instead of a rank, and social prestige instead of a position at court.

An award-winning *awdl*[3] – an ode in strict metre – can bring the poet an elaborate

---

1   This was the name Giraldus Cambrensis gave to the valley between the two main peaks of the Brecon Beacons.

2   The theme of the bard and bardic chair in Nature also applies to a rocky seat at Cynfal Falls near Ffestiniog: Hugh Lloyd's Pulpit, where a bard of that name is said to have recited his verses during the 17th century.

3   The prize for the best poem in free verse, pryddest, is a stylized silver crown.

bardic chair of solid oak, not only at the National but also at the regional Eisteddfodau, and indeed there are some Welshmen who have so many chairs that there's no room left for anyone to sit down. Carellio Morgan from Dyfed for example: with over 100 Eisteddfod victories to his credit, he is undisputed Lord of the Chairs, and his prizes have furnished the houses of his friends as well as many a chapel. In the Welsh Folk Museum at *St Fagans*, where the Gorsedd regalia are kept, there are some of the finest bardic chairs on show. The most exotic of them all was donated by the Welsh community in Shanghai. The Reverend William Thomas achieved unusual Eisteddfod glory in the 19th century – he is the only poet in Britain to have a parish named after him: Islwyn in Gwent. Today it's the constituency of the Labour leader Neil Kinnock.

Poetry's Grand National is a lot more than a poetry competition, though. Before it became the national anthem, *'Hen Wlad Fy Nhadau'* first rang out at an Eisteddfod, and the national party Plaid Cymru was founded at the Eisteddfod of 1925. Here poets have been discovered, singing careers have begun, plays by Saunders Lewis and many others have had their premières. With prizes, scholarships and commissions, this Welsh institution has created a unique platform for Welsh artists and the Welsh language. It's a talent competition, a fair, Open University, picnic area and bazaar all rolled into one. And it's also a fine place for the protesters, with a little demonstration in front of the Welsh Office pavilion being almost de rigueur. One Minister for Wales, Nicholas Edwards, announced phlegmatically that he'd been a lot more impressed by the singers than by 'the rather nasty demonstrators'. No doubt the demonstrators were rather more impressed by the singers than they were by the Minister.

'Tafran Tomato Jiws' – a pint at last? You can get anything in the marquee bar except alcohol. That is part of the Eisteddfod's tradition of temperance. It's equally traditional that in the evening the pubs all around are full to bursting. And never more so than on the Friday. This is the day when patriotism and nostalgia rise to a crescendo, as Welsh exiles from all over the world celebrate their return to the land of their fathers. There are some 80 Welsh societies overseas, and they have their own journal, *'Yr Enfys'*, The Rainbow. It's not all maudlin stuff however. At one famous Eisteddfod in Llangefni, the Reverend R. S. Thomas (picture, page 21), the grand old man of Welsh literature, launched an attack on the bitter and humiliating experience of being an emigrant in one's own country. He railed against the dominance of the English language, and against the cowardice and apathy of his fellow-countrymen. He called for national independence. The *Taffia* (the Welsh establishment) and their English guests were shocked. This was hardly the festive speech they had expected – especially bearing in mind the fact that the Welsh Office was contributing about one sixth of the total cost of the Eisteddfod. And now there are many Welsh people who fear that even this, the last bastion of Welshness, will one day become anglicized: bilingual first, and then defunct. And so they insist all the more stubbornly on the 'Welsh only' rule that has been in force since 1937. As a result, some predominantly English-speaking communities have cut their grants. 'Keep your money!' cry the

die-hards, 'and hold your own festival in English!' But it is a real dilemma, for by excluding the English language, they also exclude the majority of the Welsh population. Thus the Eisteddfod moves round the country like a brave ship of Welsh in an endless sea of English, parading folklore to strangers, giving light to the enlightened, and ever searching for converts that will bolster its identity. It's a paradox: the fewer people speak Welsh, the more important – and the more extensive – the festival becomes; and the more the minority identify with it, the more they and it become isolated from the majority. In the 19th century it was the Eisteddfod that did most to awaken Welsh national consciousness. Today it battles to keep that consciousness alive – the living voice of the old Wales, and yet little more than the cultural self-assertion of a would-be nation.

Sometimes the most unusual items are to be found outside the official programme. One evening during that same Eisteddfod at Llangefni, hundreds of young Welshmen sat on the floor of a barn listening to the folk group *Ar Log*. Then onto the improvised stage stepped Dafydd Iwan, the Welsh Bob Dylan, to perform his now legendary satirical song about 'Carlo Windsor', the fake Prince of Wales; then he sang about the death of the freedom fighter Llewelyn the Last, 700 years ago, and made it seem as if it all happened yesterday. Such occasions create a timeless, shared consciousness, and for a while in the barn at Llangefni, as fists waved in the air and hundreds of voices joined in the song, it was as if one soul had taken possession of the building.

In recent years there have been a few violent incidents, with English people's holiday homes being set on fire, but for the most part the Welsh make their protests peacefully. The explosion of voices at an Eisteddfod is infinitely preferable to the explosion of bombs that almost daily shatter the peace of Northern Ireland. And the songs and poetry of the Welsh bards may yet have more potency than the violence of the Irish bombers.

Non-Conformism: From Religious to National Awakening

Every national Eisteddfod traditionally ends on Sunday with hymn-singing, just like a church service. And in a sense, that's what the whole week has been – the Welsh soul soaring through word and song in a kind of secular chapel. The image is not inappropriate, for until more recent times, if one thing has shaped the Welsh way of life more than the Eisteddfod, it is the chapel. So dominant was its influence on work and leisure, culture and politics, society and the individual, that people even talked of the 'chapel society'.

Bethlehem is to be found in Dyfed, and Bethania in Gwynedd. There are also places named Hermon and Cesarea in Wales, not just in the Holy Land. But what strikes the tourist most is the vast number of chapels that remain as monuments to the great awakening of a tiny nation (plates 32–45). It is not their age, splendour, style, size or any other particular feature that distinguishes them, but quite simply their ubiquity. They are in every village, seem sometimes to be in every street, they are out in the country, and they are even to be found where there are no pubs, no phone booths, no houses. At first sight they look harsh and forbidding. 'And yet, that is the most beautiful place where I have ever been. It is the place where I began to think, it was there I fell in love for the first time, there I felt the dread of damnation and the joy of forgiveness ... that old grey chapel. It was void of all architectural and pictorial beauty, but through a window opposite our bench I could see the rain driven by gusts of wind across the mountain-slopes ... paradise to me is exactly like the old chapel at *Llanuwchllyn*.' These words echo down from another age, the end of the 19th century, from a village near Lake Bala where the pedagogue Sir Owen M. Edwards spent his childhood.

Such memories permeate many a Welsh biography. They recall chapel not merely as a place of religious worship, but as a way of life. The English always prayed in stately churches, but the Welsh gathered in these little stone buildings. Why the difference?

Everyone knows that in Great Britain the Reformation came about, not because of some valiant theologian, but because of a king who wanted a divorce. When Henry VIII declared himself supreme head of the Church of England in 1534, other doctrines besides Protestantism were also diverging from the Roman path. The Dissenters founded so many free churches that Voltaire remarked that the English had a hundred religions but only one sauce. Here, like everywhere else, the sects were initially suppressed, and it was for this reason that prior to the 1689 Act of Religious Toleration some 2,000 Welsh Quakers emigrated to Pennsylvania. After that date, the secret meeting-places of the non-conformists were legalized, so that barns and houses could be turned into chapels. The first Independent chapel, 'the Jerusalem of Wales', was built in 1639 in *Llanfaches*, Monmouthshire. Ten years later there followed the first Baptist chapel, in *Ilston* on the Gower Peninsula, and in 1742 the Methodists built their first chapel in *Groes Wen*, near Caerphilly. Of all the sects, it was the Methodists who brought about the great revival, the reawakening of religion in the 18th century. Itinerant priests shook the communities with their fervour and their visions of hell and salvation, hymn-writers filled their tortured souls with hope and unaccustomed emotions, and peripatetic teachers saw to it that even in the poorest, most isolated places the faithful could learn how to read and write. Without this religious education, whose foundation stone was Bishop Morgan's Welsh translation of the Bible (1588), the unparalleled surge of Methodism could never have come about. This was religion of a special, Welsh kind,[1] with its own hymns which are still sung even today. One of the great leaders of the movement was Howell Harris, the Welsh equivalent of John Wesley (see page 157). It was the 'ecstatic musical religion' (J. C. Powys) that distinguished Welsh Methodism from the sterner Puritanism of the English and the Scots, who never took to the diverse cultural approach of the Welsh chapels.

---

1   Although the Welsh Methodists worked together with the English leaders of the movement, John Wesley and George Whitefield, in 1743 they formed their own Calvinist movement, which today is known as the Presbyterian Church of Wales.

'Dissent is no religion for a gentleman,' said King Charles II. In England the upper and upper-middle classes generally belonged to the state church. This social split into 'Church people' and 'Chapel people', like that between Public School and State School, Conservative Party and Liberal, later Labour, has always been more apparent in England than in Wales. Of course, in the early 19th century the often stormy mass movement of and conversion to Methodism was partly motivated by the social struggle between Non-Conformist peasants and aristocratic landowners, but the really decisive factor was something else: church services were held in English; chapel services were in Welsh. For too long the London Parliament and the Welsh aristocracy had ignored the needs of the country, and the Church itself was conservative, pro-English, and like the aristocracy, too remote from the people. From about 1700 till 1870 every Bishop of Wales was an Englishman, and often they did not even reside in their own diocese. Just as in the 12th century Giraldus Cambrensis had fought all his life against the supremacy of Canterbury and for the establishment of a Welsh archbishopric,[1] so too, 700 years later, the Church of England remained a symbol of foreign rule. The general aim of all Dissenters to separate Church and State took on a specifically nationalist note in Wales: to separate from England. And thus it was that the religious revival of the 18th century led to a movement of national protest. Even though the Methodists originally regarded any interference with divine Providence as a sin, and refrained from all political action, ultimately Pietism and patriotism spoke the same language, and that was Welsh. Countryfolk and workers all sang the same Welsh hymns, while religious and political non conformists lived together under the same roof. But although they became increasingly radical, they were never out-and-out revolutionaries. The integration of the two movements was the great social achievement of the chapel in Wales, and it goes hand in hand with the cultural achievement of preserving the Welsh language.

The dynamism of the chapel lasted well into the 20th century, even if its religious message was to fade. And despite the fact that there are areas, like the anglicized coastal region of Pembrokeshire, where the language is no longer understood, the fascination still remains: 'The fervid singing, the praying and the preaching, in a language the more moving for being incomprehensible, affected me powerfully, and when the orator broke into the hwyl or afflatus, with which all Welsh sermons should terminate, it sounded to me like the veritable voice of God,' wrote the painter Augustus John, recalling his childhood in Tenby. But as Wales became increasingly modernized and anglicized, the chapel increasingly came to symbolize a backward step, the relic of an old and inflexible code: 'The Temple and the Sabbath / Be ever my estate' proclaimed Ceiriog's famous hymn 'Jerusalem', and that was the chapel watch-word throughout the 19th century, engraved on every heart and hearth in Wales.

1 It was not until 1920 that Wales had its first Archbishop. The separation of church and state took place in Wales in 1919, and since then the Church in Wales, unlike the Church of England, has no longer been subject to the English Parliament.

What of today? 'If 25 people come to service, that's a good congregation.' How often have I heard that in the valleys of South Wales, which had once been the proud stronghold of the chapel society. Those days are long gone. I talked to Mrs Lillian Rose Pryse-Griffiths from Swansea (plate 34), a character who might have stepped straight out of Dylan Thomas's Milk Wood. With vacuum cleaner in hand, and a fund of stories in mind, she is forever dusting and polishing the largest, quietest, most desolate house in *Morriston*. Its portal is flanked by eight gigantic columns with Corinthian capitals, and through it the crowds used to come flocking into the House of God, the 'Tabernacle', which was the biggest and most expensive chapel in Wales when it was built in 1872. This was the 'Great Cathedral of Welsh Non-Conformity', with its gigantic interior full of dark brown benches surrounding the pulpit like waves lapping round an island, and its thunderous echo for the preacher – space transmuted into rhetoric – swelling up and up into the gallery, swirling round the cast-iron pillars, rich with biblical allusions, with hwyl ... You can imagine this place, packed solid from front to rear, Sunday after Sunday, with the copper smelters of Morriston and their rich, throaty, coppery voices, the rattling and rustling, hymning and hushing, and that typical chapel smell, stone tiles reeking of soap, the benches of wax, and the Sunday suits and dresses of camphor. It was a living, breathing, singing, speaking place then. And now it's empty and still, watched over only by Mrs Lillian Rose Pryse-Griffiths and her duster. 'There used to be 3,000 people here of a Sunday,' she says. 'And now you're lucky if there's a hundred.' But at least she can show me one remnant of former glory. Proudly she points to the highlight of all her days as caretaker of the Tabernacle: 'Here, row 47. That's where the Prince of Wales sat.'

O Tabernacle Chapel, abandoned – Jerusalem Chapel, closed – Salem Chapel, forgotten – Tabor, Seion and Siloa, silent, sold, or left to eternal decay – once they were all houses of hope, strongholds of faith, palaces of song. Now they're empty and disused, nearing their end. And what will that end be? Bingo hall, garage, studio, holiday centre, or headquarters of the Red Cross. No more hymns here, no requiem but memories.

Chapels: The Architecture of Enthusiasm

After the faithful come the gravediggers. The rise and fall of chapel culture is itself a piece of architectural history. It is only recently that people have begun to take note of this great heritage (plates 32–45). Until then, the chapels had all been taken for granted – there were so many of them, and there was nothing there to catch the eye, for they're all over Wales, and they all look alike. At first I barely noticed them either. In fact, I thought they were boring – the shabby relics of a golden age. No, the chapels were not sights for seeing. Of course they had always been national emblems, like rugby and choirs, but who would ever have thought of designating them 'national architecture'?

To non-Welsh eyes, the chapels seem dull and uninteresting, even off-putting. They can't compete with the varied and attractive churches of English villages, as warm and welcoming as a cosy hearth, with coloured windows, ancient stone, carved figures that tell stories. Chapels by comparison are monosyllabic. What they have to say is biblical, not architectural. If religion is based on The Word, never have God's houses been so parsimonious with their language.

Chapels are purely functional architecture: assembly rooms for preachers and their congregation. They arose out of poverty and need. The first Dissenters, in constant fear of persecution, met secretly in farmhouses and stables. One of the very few completely preserved 'barn-chapels' of earlier times is to be found in *Maesyronen* (plates 32, 33), tucked away in the cornfields on the hills overlooking the Wye Valley near Glasbury. It's a room 50 feet long and 23 feet wide, with open beams, originally a barn adjoining a little farmhouse. Maesyronen Chapel was built in 1697, just a few years after the Act of Toleration. The floor, once bare clay, is covered with flagstones, and the pulpit against the long wall is slightly raised, surrounded by a semi-circle of benches, some of them without arms. Originally the farmers used to shear their sheep on them. One Sunday morning I heard a handful of worshippers singing and praying here, just as their ancestors had done nearly 300 years before. This was shortly after Margaret Thatcher had been re-elected, and the lay preacher urged the flock to include in their prayers 'even those for whom we may not have voted'.

Maesyronen Chapel is the oldest Non-Conformist chapel still in use in Wales, and it is an impressive example of the simple piety of those early Dissenters. From these primitive beginnings, and from the functional tradition of indigenous houses and barns, there developed a sort of naive, Spartan architecture. Its basic form was the rectangular box with pointed roof and gabled walls. Its plainness, inside and out, stood in deliberate contrast to the Neo-Gothic decor of Anglican churches. The Puritan character of the chapel was conveyed by a few basic features: the façade, with a symmetrical arrangement of door and windows, and a stone plaque with Old Testament names and the date of construction; the pulpit, usually opposite the entrance, and the gallery running round three sides – a sort of folk theatre for the sermon, which was the most important part of the service. In

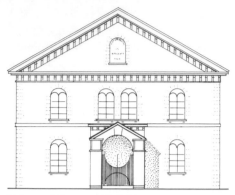

Tabernacl, Pontypridd, 1861

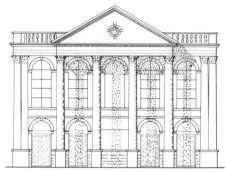

Mount Pleasant, Swansea, 1875

Tabor, Maesycwmer, 1876

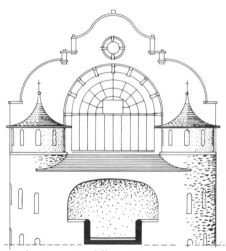

Heol y Crwys, Cardiff, 1899

the first comprehensive study of this form of architecture, Anthony Jones writes that the simplicity of these early chapels became 'eloquent' in the hands of those who assembled the parts.

Since the needs of the community were simple, and initially they lacked funds anyway, their architectural aspirations were also simple. This is why most of the chapels, at least till the middle of the 19th century, were designed not by professional architects, but by members of the community and local craftsmen, sometimes using illustrated catalogues. 'It was folk-architecture, by and for the people.' Indeed the label of amateurishness has stuck to the chapels ever since. Sometimes the master builder would be the pastor himself. The most famous of these 'preacher-designers' was the Reverend William Jones, originally a carpenter, to whom over 200 chapels have been attributed, including Jerusalem (1881) in *Ton Pentre*, known as 'the Methodist Cathedral of the Rhondda'. But by then professional architects had long since been employed, and a chapel boom without parallel had begun.

In the first half of the 19th century, a new chapel was built every fortnight. While the number of new Anglican churches increased by only 25%, the chapels raced ahead by more than 600%. The Non-Conformists had replaced the Church of England as the most powerful religious movement in Wales. In *Pontypool*, for instance, there were two Anglican churches and twenty-two chapels. They were the great refuge for the poor during the misery of the Industrial Revolution. With the growing number of believers, there was also growing rivalry between sects. Baptists, Congregationalists, Methodists, Independents, Wesleyans and Presbyterians – they were all fishing for souls, and they did not only fish with words. The chapels began to extend their rhetoric to their façades, and often, when money was short, it was limited to the façade. This led to satirical verses such as the following: 'The Trellwyn Methodists have built a church, / The front looks like an abbey, / But thinking they can fool the Lord / They've built the back part shabby.' This was the time when Puritanism was entering its phase of pomp and circumstance. They adorned the 'poor' architecture of those pioneering days with pilasters, columns, porticos, fancy gables, ledges and balustrades. 'Mad Façadism' is the name which the Welsh architect and author John B. Hilling gives to this most obtrusive feature of post-1850 chapels, whose exterior often resembled that of banks, and whose interior was like Victorian concert halls. The façades reflect all phases of architectural history, from Neo-Romanesque to Neo-Gothic, culminating in the extraordinarily eccentric Capel Heol y Crwys in *Cardiff* (1899; illustration opposite). With this Art Nouveau centrepiece of Methodist fervour, the great age of what John Betjeman called the 'Architecture of Enthusiasm' reaches its manneristic climax.[1]

Castles, Bridges and Portmeirion

Today there are still around 5,000 chapels in Wales – more than in England and Scotland put together. It would be a disaster if just a selected few were to be preserved at the expense of the great mass, which are less attractive perhaps, but no less typical. Whatever

1   An example of the late Neo-Romanesque style is Capel Salem (1899) in Senghennydd, and of Neo-Classicism, Crane Street Baptist (1846) in Pontypool. Some of the best chapel interiors of the 19th century are to be found in Haverfordwest (Tabernacle), Brecon (The Plough), and Merthyr Tydfil (Bethel). Two of the most beautiful 18th-century chapels have been reconstructed for the Open Air Museum at St Fagans: Capel Pen-rhiw (1770) and Capel Newydd (1771). The most isolated chapel in Wales must be Capel Soar (1828) at the end of the Llyn Brianne, with a Sunday School under the same roof.

they may look like, and wherever they may be, they are part of a great Welsh pattern, and they have their special place in the street or square or village. They are not mere 'amateur architecture', or the 'grim heritage' or the 'blot on the landscape' that modern prejudices suggest they are; the Welsh chapel is the unmistakable and irreplaceable home of Welsh faith. Their aesthetic rehabilitation owes a great deal to the efforts of an English artist in the 1930's, John Piper, who photographed, sketched and painted them, and saw their shapes and colours as an integral part of the landscape. They may not have given rise to a uniform style, to any great architects, or to any school of architecture, but if anything can claim to be the national architecture of Wales, then it is the chapels.

And yet there are other much older, much more impressive edifices in Wales, and the most impressive of these are the castles. They, too, are all over the land, and even when they are in ruins, they remain vastly more imposing than the finest chapel. For the Welsh, so a Welshman told me, the castles are as commonplace as traffic lights. They stand on lonely cliffs, in the centre of towns big and small, in forests and on riverbanks, and there is no country in Europe that has as many castles per square mile as Wales. Altogether there are more than 400. The most spectacular of these military strongholds were built by an English King, Edward I, with a master-builder who came from Savoy. Originally, then, they were foreign bodies, architecturally and politically, while today they are Wales's trump cards in the game of catch-the-tourist. It must be added that even the great industrial architecture of Wales – the bridges, viaducts, and workers' estates – were designed, not by the Welsh, but by the Scot, Thomas Telford or the Englishman, Robert Stephenson.[1]

At the end of the 12th century, Giraldus Cambrensis wrote that the Welsh had no towns. This changed with the invasion by Edward I. A successful invasion requires successful methods of settling, and so around his fortresses the King built well-defended towns in which only English citizens had the right to reside and trade. Thus most of the 80 or so towns and markets of medieval Wales were of foreign, Anglo-Norman origin. What we see today is the result of centuries of assimilation. And yet it is all unmistakably Welsh, and emphatically not Anglo-Welsh. 'The actual towns and villages in Wales, with their prevailing slate roofs, their ugly chapels, their austere, unpicturesque and melancholy architecture, have nothing of that old-world warmth, and glow, and atmospheric welcome that such places have in England,' wrote John Cowper Powys, the Englishman who chose to be Welsh, in his 'Obstinate Cymric'.

Poverty and labour were the two great builders in Wales. The buildings tend to be smaller and simpler than in England. The picture is one of huts rather than palaces. The

---

1 Only about two dozen original Welsh castles are still in existence, including the ruins of Castell Dolwyddelan, Dolbadarn (plate 97), Dinas Bran, Dinefwr, and Castell-y-Bere at the foot of Cader Idris – the headquarters of Llywelyn the Great, and one of the most splendid of all the indigenous fortresses. A classic Celtic refuge in a romantic setting is Carreg Cennen.

Samuel & Nathaniel Buck: Caerphilly Castle, 1740

farmhouses vary from one region to another, from cottages to long-houses in which man and beast all lived together under one roof. But the great country houses which were central to social and cultural life in England are almost completely absent from the Welsh scene. This was due largely to the fact that, as we saw, after union in 1536, the Welsh aristocracy went to seek its political fame and fortune in London. The new Tudor class built no palaces in Wales. Lord Pembroke, who built Wilton House in Wiltshire, came from South Wales, as did the Earl of Worcester, who left *Raglan Castle* in favour of Badminton House. Hatfield House and Burghley House also belonged to Welshmen. And when the aristocrats went to England, the architects and artists went with them. Only with the Industrial Revolution did the balance shift again, for then the English entrepreneurs came to Wales, and a new aristocracy of coal and steel barons and industrial magnates established their estates – built, of course, by English architects such as William Burges and Thomas Hopper. Did the Welsh have no architects of their own?

Even the two greatest Welsh architects are claimed by the English, though probably with some justification: Inigo Jones is said to have been born in *Llanrwst*, but there is no documentary evidence; there is, however, proof that he was baptized in London. And John Nash, whose talents were first unfolded in Wales, made his career in England as the great Regency architect. As for the eccentric master of modern British architecture, Sir Clough Williams-Ellis, *Portmeirion*, his Italian village in Cardigan Bay, is the Mediterranean opposite of Welsh architecture (plate 79) – 'a sort of Celtic exoticism' (J. B. Hilling). Born in England, he moved to North Wales as a child, and found himself in what seemed to him a strange and barren land, where there was no architecture and scarcely any building. This he set out to change. Yet there is a clear link between his Portmeirion and another Welsh tradition: that of the aesthetic theory of the picturesque. This was born in Wales during the 18th century, and was to have a more lasting effect on the English landscape than any single architect could ever have had.

Pioneers of the Picturesque: Artists and Tourists on the Move

In August 1771 a strange procession wound its way through North Wales: a painter and his patron, accompanied by three friends, nine servants, and thirteen horses. Sir Watkin Williams Wynn of Wynnstay had come to see the sights of his homeland. Since the camera had not yet been invented, he took an artist with him, and as he was a man of some taste as well as being one of the richest landowners in Wales, he engaged the services of an English artist who had made his name as a topographer for the Crown: Paul Sandby. For two weeks Sir Watkin's art caravan wandered from ruin to ruin, through Harlech, Caernarfon, Conwy, Llanrwst and Holywell – a Grand Tour which is still the classic route today. When the wars that followed the French Revolution made it difficult to go to the Continent, people discovered Wales and Scotland as a substitute for Switzerland and the Rhine, and even before then the Welsh naturalist and archaeologist Thomas Pennant, an expert on Europe, had set out in Sir Watkin's footsteps and written a detailed description of landscape, architecture, customs, trade, flora and fauna. 'The best traveller I ever read,' was Dr Johnson's verdict. Pennant also took a painter with him – a man who was his lifelong servant: Moses Griffith.[1] His topographical views helped to popularize the sights of Wales, as did Paul Sandby's drawings, which were published as aquatints in 1776 under the somewhat ponderous title: 'Views in North Wales, being part of a tour through that fertile and romantick country'.

'Fertile and romantick' were not the epithets that all of his contemporaries would have used. Until the middle of the 18th century, the bad roads, primitive living conditions and plentiful highwaymen would have made a trip through Wales more of a nightmare than a dream. This may explain why, after a two-month tour with his friend Hester Lynch Thrale in 1774, Dr Johnson provocatively announced that Wales 'offered nothing to the speculation of the traveller'. Why undergo all the stresses and strains when all there was to see was the barren barbarism of Nature? Those at least were the feelings of a visitor to Snowdonia in 1742: 'the Fag End of Creation ... the very Rubbish of Noah's Flood.' Not all Englishmen saw a trip to Wales as a foretaste of purgatory, and Daniel Defoe was one of the first to take a more positive view, but even he, when he toured the Principality in 1722, had found the mountains 'barbaric', and the country 'looking so full of horror' that more than once he felt tempted to go straight home. Defoe, like his contemporaries looked at Wales through the eyes of the rationalist, for whom all things wild and ungoverned were alien, in landscape as in life. For them beauty was only that which was cultivated and useful. It was an attitude that was not to change until the Age of Romanticism. Rousseau's 'Nouvelle Héloïse' (1761) taught people to cherish emotion as a force of Nature, and to see

---

1   Like Pennant, Griffith is buried in Whitford churchyard, in North Wales. Most of his 700 surviving sketches, watercolours and engravings are in the Welsh National Library in Aberystwyth and the National Museum in Cardiff.

Nature as the source of endless emotion. With this new feeling for Nature there arose a new love of mountains, and while Europe discovered its Alps, the English discovered Snowdonia. Even before the poet Thomas Gray visited the Scottish Highlands, he wrote his ode 'The Bard' (1757), in which the poet is seen as the voice of Nature and freedom, and the Welsh mountains as the last bard's refuge from Edward I's invaders. With its concern for matters poetic and political, Nature and nation, this poem heralded the way for early Romanticism and the Celtic revival. Here as elsewhere, the newly awakened feelings for the homeland were only a step away from the national consciousness that gives birth to nationalism. And the patriots laced up their hiking boots, and by the end of the 19th century there were not only nationalist states everywhere, but also nationalist tourists.

The fact that Thomas Gray's poem became so popular, and his landscape of the soul was seen not as a literary image but as a specific part of Wales – at least in those days – was due above all to painters. For his portrait of the Bard, Paul Sandby chose Snowdon as the background. John Martin used Harlech Castle (1817; illustration, page 431). But at this time the Welsh motif became 'Ossianized': the Cymric bard Taliesin was replaced by the Gaelic Ossian, and Thomas Gray was pushed out by James Macpherson. It is thanks to the latter's literary fiction that the Scots won the battle of Celtic ideals, and their Highlands

Thomas Jones: The Bard, 1774

rather than Welsh Snowdonia became the vital spring of European Ossianism. That was why Felix Mendelssohn-Bartholdy composed a Hebrides Overture rather than a Snowdon Symphony, and Goethe's Werther quoted the fake Ossian instead of the genuine Taliesin, whose medieval 'Mabinogion' is the classic epic of Welsh myth. Even the Welsh artist Thomas Jones painted his major work 'The Bard' in the spirit of Ossian, though his choice of background was Stonehenge. This painting (now in the National Museum in Cardiff) was painted in the year Goethe wrote 'Werther', 1774; it is one of Wales's contributions to the history of European melancholy.

But Wales has its own brighter, more picturesque side. Before the word 'picturesque' became tourism's catchphrase, it was a key term in late 18th-century aesthetic theory. It was an Englishman who made it into a concept, but he was influenced above all by what he saw in Wales: 'Observations on the River Wye, and Several Parts of South Wales … relative chiefly to Picturesque Beauty' – this was the Reverend William Gilpin's first book (1782), which was followed by further volumes, all illustrated with his own etchings. Gilpin described real landscapes as if they were paintings, and he recommended that artists use specific picturesque motifs, such as the ruins of old castles and abbeys, and shepherds with their flocks. In three essays of 1776 Gilpin developed his theory. In opposition to the strict rules of Rationalism he set the romantic categories of 'roughness and irregularity'. Ambiguity, provocation, distortion – all these were elements of the picturesque to be used as guidelines for composition. This was why Gilpin – and after him, generations of artists and photographers – preferred to go to the wilder regions: Wales, the Lake District, the Scottish Highlands. Thus the pioneer of the picturesque unwittingly became a trend-setter for tourism, and his 'Picturesque Journeys' not only started a fashion, but also set new standards for travel books, which now became vehicles for aesthetic education.

Wales is the original Land of the Picturesque. The Reverend Gilpin was not the only contributor to the cause, however. In 1794 the Welsh landscape gardener Sir Uvedale Price, from *Aberystwyth*, published his scarcely less influential 'Essay on the Picturesque'. He was one of a circle of cultured landowners that gathered around Thomas Johnes, who had moved to the wild valley of Ystwyth in 1783 in order to 'practise' the picturesque. *Hafod House*, with its landscaped park, is one of the finest and most popular examples of this style in Wales (illustration, page 279). It is no coincidence that the cult of the picturesque, with its purely aesthetic view of the world, arose precisely at the time when the Industrial Revolution was beginning and was making its presence felt with such brutal force in Nature and in society. This was a romantic, aristocratic counter-attack – an aesthetic theory that ended in the clichés of today's travel prospectuses and package tours. And now these places of the picturesque are among the few remaining refuges from the world of exhaust fumes.

The Romantics themselves were great travellers, but for them the aesthetic term had already become pejorative. Coleridge, for instance, referred disparagingly to Sir Walter Scott as 'a picturesque tourist', and contemporary satirists did not spare even the originators of the fashion. The Englishman Thomas Rowlandson caricatured Gilpin (and himself) in 1799 as the artist on horseback, sketchbook and easel under the arm, riding through Wales in the pouring rain (page 2). This picture of discomfort and sheer misery may serve to remind us that the real trail-blazers for Welsh tourism were not the romantic artists, but Thomas Telford's road-builders.

Picturesque Landscape and No Welshmen to Paint It?

Is there such a thing as Welsh art? Or is Wales simply the embodiment of the picturesque, an inexhaustible model for English artists without any Welsh palette to add its own characteristic art to the history of British painting? There is always the danger, when enquiring into national character and such offshoots as national art, that one will be trapped into making absurd generalizations, but all the same the art historian Nikolaus Pevsner wrote a whole book about the Englishness of English art, and his observations seem to me to be so convincing, so fair, and so delightful that I should like to try and emulate him with at least a paragraph on the Welshness of Welsh art. 'None of the other nations of Europe,' Pevsner writes, 'has so abject an inferiority complex about its own aesthetic capabilities as England.' Is this not even truer of Wales? Or is it simply not possible for a country which for centuries has been politically and economically dependent on London to go its own way artistically?

In 1792 William Turner went on the first of his five trips to Wales, which brought forth hundreds of sketches and 96 watercolours in preparation for his series of engravings 'Picturesque Views in England and Wales' (1825–38). But he did not go there solely as the ideal tourist following the path of Gilpin and his aesthetics. Turner knew Paul Sandby's etchings, as well as those of the brothers Samuel and Nathaniel Buck, who in 1740 had been the first to make a systematic, topographical study of Welsh castles, churches and towns.[1] The greatest influence of all was that of Richard Wilson, the father of British landscape painting (picture, page 338). If the majority of Welsh artists are still unknown today, that cannot be said of Richard Wilson. 'He was one of those appointed to show the world what exists in nature but which was not known till his time,' said John Constable. The light and the atmosphere of his native North Wales, and the naturalistic details of the wild mountains and their rugged fortresses – Richard Wilson was the first to unveil these glories as masterpieces of art. Half a century before Wordsworth and the new romantic love of Nature, Wilson's pictures of Snowdon and Cader Idris were pioneering achievements of Welsh art (illustration, pages 339 and 357). At the same time, he tamed the savagery of Nature in the classical style of Claude Lorrain and Poussin. He transformed

1   One of the earliest topographical artists in Wales was the Englishman Francis Place (1699), and one of the last was the Frenchman Henry Gastineau, whose 200 or more sketches served as a model for the popular collection of etchings entitled 'Wales Illustrated' (1830).

Wales into another Campagna, a British Arcadia. The joys of country life, and the harmony of his pictures, were of course a beautiful invention, a social myth. Eighteenth-century Wales was poorer and more backward than most of England, and Wilson was painting through patrician eyes.

Not only Wilson's art but also his life story has typical Welsh features. At the age of 15 he went to London to study painting, and after that he went to Rome – the first in a long line of Welsh artists to seek fame and fortune far from home.[1] In Wales there were few patrons, and also the artists were cut off from the mainstream of European art movements. In those days the British aristocracy preferred continental painters, and if they did look closer to home, it was English and not Welsh painters they chose – or at best, Welsh painters who were resident in London. Such geographical and economic disadvantages could hardly lead to any great upsurge in Welsh art. And even Richard Wilson, after his initial success in Rome and London, was to die in 1782 impoverished and practically forgotten back in his native Wales. For a long time that first breakthrough by Welsh art was also to remain its last. Thus it was that Turner and the 19th-century English watercolourists did far more for the picture of Wales than any indigenous artist. John Sell Cotman, John Crome, Thomas Girtin, David Cox, Samuel Palmer, Thomas Rowlandson, and many others travelled through Wales with brush or pencil in hand.[2] Wilson himself had led the way by informing the world that everything a landscape painter could desire was to be found in North Wales. Next to the Lake District and the Scottish Highlands, there is no other region of the British Isles that has been so thoroughly and so vividly portrayed by so many artists as Wales, its natural as well as its industrial landscapes.

It was not by chance that Turner chose a Welsh theme for the picture he submitted for his election to the Royal Academy in 1802: 'Dolbadarn Castle'. With its castle, mountain lake, rocks and waterfall, this painting epitomizes the landscape and all its pictorial possibilities, and it shows just how vital a role Wales played in Turner's artistic development. With such a wide variety of landscapes within so small an area, Turner developed his own style of sketching – a spontaneous, up-to-the-minute language of watercolour. He combines man and Nature, climate and living-conditions, history and genre into an artistic unity that goes far beyond the topographical and the picturesque concepts of the landscape in the 18th century. Andrew Wilton calls these pictures a 'dramatic vision of Wales', and reckons them to be among the most 'intense of all romantic landscapes'. In the last years of his life, Turner wrote to an artist friend: 'I do not think that you could have hit upon a more desirable spot for your pencil and hope that you may feel – just what I felt in the days of my youth when I was in search of Richard Wilson's birthplace.'

Not until the beginning of the 20th century did a Welsh artist once more take the world

1   They include the Neo-Classical sculptor John Gibson from Conwy: he was a pupil of Canova, and spent much of his life in Rome, where he died in 1866. English patrons were especially drawn to his classical technique of colouring marble statues.

2   A Swiss artist also toured and painted the Welsh mountains in 1777: Samuel Hieronymus Grimm (1733–94).

J. M. W. Turner: Conwy Castle, 1802

by storm: Augustus John, enfant terrible of the London salons (illustration, page 235). For half a century he was *the* portrait artist of British society. Thirty-eight of his pictures were exhibited at the legendary, avant-garde Armory Show of 1913 in New York. Shortly before, he and his fellow-countryman James Dickson Innes, together with the Australian Derwent Lees, had rented a cottage in *Nant-ddu* in Snowdonia, and had painted *Arenig Fawr* over and over again, 'in search of the magical moment' – a Welsh contribution to Post Impressionism. But apart from his subjects, what was specifically Welsh about Augustus John's painting? The rhetoric of his lines, the vivid colours? Or was that not due more to the heritage of 'Les Fauves', to a 'Zeitgeist' rather than to national character? The paintings by his sister Gwen John are also influenced more by her personal development than by her origins. She was born in Pembrokeshire, went to the Academy in London, and died in France in 1939: the typical career of a Welsh artist. Gwen John was a great painter, with an intensity of expression that often far exceeded that of her always more successful brother. For European art history, Gwen John remains a powerful force as yet barely noticed (illustration, page 235).

After her, only one Welsh painter has made any real impression on modern British art: Ceri Richards (illustration, pages 214–5). Celtic and Surrealistic forms combine with motifs from the Welsh landscape. But he, too, spent most of his life away from Wales, teaching at the Academy in London, where he died in 1971. With few exceptions, the Welsh have always been purists in matters of fine art. In the 20th century it has once again been English artists that have made the most significant contributions to the history of

Welsh art: the sculptor and typographer Eric Gill, who founded an art commune in *Capel-y-ffin* during the 1920's (illustration, page 196); his pupil David Jones, whose themes from Arthur and Mabinogion made him the most Welsh of all English artists; John Piper, who found landscape and chapel themes in Wales, as well as a wife (illustration, page 238); and above all, Graham Sutherland: 'From the first moment I set foot in Wales I was obsessed.' From this first visit in 1934 onwards, Pembrokeshire, with its magical light and the strange shapes of its landscape, was one of his greatest inspirations, and it was here that he 'began to learn to paint' (illustration, page 237). How elemental this encounter was can be gauged from the Sutherland Gallery in *Picton Castle*. Today, the only internationally known artist from Wales is Barry Flanagan from Prestatyn.

For European emigrants, Wales provided more than mere subject-matter. The Pole Josef Herman found refuge in the mining village of *Ystradgynlais*,[1] and Heinz Koppel, a Jew from Berlin, became a teacher in *Merthyr Tydfil* – he was a late Expressionist whose work influenced a whole generation of Welsh painters. Two postwar English artists who have lived for many years in Wales prove yet again that the country has lost none of its fascination since the Age of Romanticism: Jack Crabtree, chronicler of a dying mining industry (plate 31), and David Nash, who found ideal conditions here for his Land Art (plate 45). Australia's most famous painter Sir Sidney Nolan also spends several months of the year on his Jacobean estate in Hay-on-Wye in the Welsh Marshes.

The old but ever-present combination of Nature, art and life have lured not only artists but also hippies, drop-outs and other non-conformists to the green and pleasant land. One of their prophets was John Seymour, who demonstrated self-sufficiency on a farm near Cardigan; another was the Austrian economist Leopold Kohr, who taught in Aberystwyth, not far from the Centre for Alternative Technology, and persistently advocated Welsh independence. And the creative 'alternative' potential is supplemented by large numbers of men and women skilled in the arts and crafts – many of them also having come across the border from England.

'Wales is a land of ochres and umbers, only occasionally going mad in a riot of colour,' says Kyffin Williams, who paints in Anglesey. With his portraits and landscapes, depicting the harshness of the farmer's struggle for existence in Snowdonia, Williams is one of the few genuinely Welsh artists still at work in Wales. 'My Welsh inheritance must always remain a strong force in my work, for it is in Wales that I can paint with the greatest freedom,' he writes in his autobiography. 'I have worked in Holland, France and Austria, in Italy and in Greece, but in none of these lovely countries have I found the mood that touches the seam of melancholy that is within most Welshmen, a melancholy that derives from the dark hills, the heavy clouds and the enveloping sea mists.'

1 Josef Herman, son of a Jewish shoemaker from Warsaw, fled in 1938 and spent eleven years in this village north-east of Swansea. A constant theme of his sombre paintings is miners returning from work: 'This image of the miners on the bridge against that glowing sky mystified me for years with its mixture of sadness and grandeur, and it became the source of my work for years to come.'

Yr iaith: A Language of Their Own – A State of Their Own?

On February 17 1984 the London *Times* informed its readers that the fire brigade of Clwyd had acquired a computer. For in spite of people spelling and carefully enunciating the sounds of Welsh placenames, there had been constant difficulty over locating the actual site of fires. The new computer was not cheap, but 'at least it will stop the land of their fathers burning down before they can find it'.

Since Shakespeare's popular figure of fun Fluellen, the tongue-twisting names of Welshmen have always been the butt of English humour. 'Taffy was a Welshman.' Taffy was not in himself a tongue-twister, but he did have a funny way of speaking, and to the English, Taffy's language was not a thing of beauty. 'The names of some of these hills seemed as barbarous to us who spoke no Welsh, as these hills themselves,' wrote Daniel Defoe during his journey through North Wales. Much later, when the charms of the country were no longer a secret, the poet Gerard Manley Hopkins considered that the rhythm of the landscape was echoed by the rhythm of the language. The sounds and magic of those Cymric words fascinated J. R. R. Tolkien all his life, after his very first visit to Wales in 1904 as a 12-year-old. 'I heard a call coming out of the west. It struck at me in the names on coal trucks; and drawing nearer it flickered past on station signs, a flash of strange spelling and a hint of a language old and yet alive. It pierced my linguistic heart' and of his own accord Tolkien set himself the task of learning Welsh, 'the Senior British Language'. The Elvish language of his fantasies echoes the sounds of Welsh, just as the Misty Mountains and the Iron Mountains reflect the Welsh landscape.

How old is *yr hen iaith*, the ancient language? Together with Breton and Cornish it is the Brythonic branch of Celtic, very different from the Goidelic branch, which constitutes Scottish and Irish Gaelic and Manx from the Isle of Man. Linguists trace the beginnings of Welsh as an independent language back to the 6th century. Writings of the time attributed to Taliesin and Aneirin are amongst the most ancient products of Cymric culture. That, say the proud Welsh, was a culture we had centuries before the first English sentences were pronounced on the British Isles. Here a tiny nation on the fringes of European civilization created its own literary cosmos: from the 'Mabinogion', the medieval epic of Celtic myth, to Bishop Morgan's Welsh translation of the Bible, and from Hywel Dda's code of laws, in classic 10th-century prose, to the 14th-century poems of Dafydd ap Gwilym. According to Gwynfor Evans, the history of Wales is the history of its language, and that is 'the one great tradition that Wales possesses'.

Since they lost their land to the English, the Welsh have defended their language with mighty fervour. As we have already seen, it was the anchor of their identity and the symbol of their national aspirations, and has remained so even now, when ever fewer people speak or understand it. Henry VIII had decreed in the 1536 Act of Union: 'That his said Country or Dominion of Wales shall be, stand and continue for ever from henceforth incorporated, united and annexed to and with this his Realm of England.' With the introduction of the English county system in Wales, the Lords Marcher lost their feudal privileges. The Welsh now had the right to send representatives to Parliament in London, but this was no compensation for the loss of independence. Did the constitutional union of the two countries really put Wales on a social and legal par with England? How this 'equality' worked out in practice can be seen from Section 17 of the Act of Union: For all court sessions, administration and official acts, English was henceforth to be the one language, 'and also that from henceforth no person or persons that use the Welsh speech or language shall have or enjoy any manner office or fees within this realm of England, Wales or other the King's Dominion upon pain of forfeiting the same offices or fees, unless he or they use and exercise the English speech or tongue.' Equality meant that the English were more equal than the Welsh. The price of assimilation was the sacrifice of Welsh culture. To get on in Henry VIII's kingdom, you had to speak English, and so what had begun as the willing anglicization of the Welsh aristocracy under Henry VII now became the official policy and educational goal for centuries to come. In 1855 the English poet and schools inspector Matthew Arnold declared that a government must always strive to make its regions as homogeneous as possible. 'Sooner or later the difference of language between Wales and England will probably be effaced ... an event which is socially and politically desirable.' And from the point of view of British power politics, desirable is certainly what it seemed to be.

So it was that the Welsh became a nation of two languages. English was the language of laws, offices, government, the Empire, power, management, promotion, success, progress and prosperity. Welsh was for the family, for peasants and tenants, miners and steel-workers – but it was also the language of chapel and the Eisteddfod, of poets and singers. In 1847 an English government commission decided that the Welsh language was a great disadvantage for Wales, and a hindrance to moral development and economic progress: 'The Welsh element is never found at the top of the social scale ... his language keeps him under the hatches.' The education policy of the Victorians set out to change all that. And yet in 1849 Queen Victoria herself wrote to Lord Landsdowne that in Wales Welsh should be taught as well as English. But this astonishingly far-sighted declaration of sympathy, engendered by the Queen's love of things wild and natural (paralleled by her enthusiasm for the Highlands and for Gaelic), had no political consequences. The Education Act of 1870 made the English school system compulsory in Wales. What Edward's castles and Henry VIII's laws had failed to achieve was now to be forced through by the teachers. A symbol of this draconian system for the good (i.e. the Englishness) of the Welsh was the 'Welsh Not'. Anyone who spoke Welsh in school had a piece of wood hung round his neck on a leather strap, the 'cribban'; and anyone else caught speaking the mother tongue would then have to take it over. Whoever had it at the end of the day was given a good thrashing. Irish children had Gaelic beaten out of them in similar fashion in the 19th century. In Richard Llewellyn's 'How Green Was My Valley' there is a harrowing school scene describing the implementation of the Education Act on the little daughter of a miner:

'About her neck a piece of new cord, and from the cord, a board that hung to her shins and cut her as she walked. Chalked on the board, in the fist of Mr Elijah Jonas-Sessions, "I must not speak Welsh in school".'

The fact that the ancient language, *yr hen iaith* has survived all these centuries of suppression is little short of a miracle. Proudly Sir Owen M. Edwards, a Welsh scholar and educationalist at the turn of the century, reported that he never passed the 'Welsh Not' on to any of his fellow pupils: 'I talked one language, my teacher talked another – and I learned nothing.' If it hadn't been for Sunday School in Welsh, he would have remained illiterate. And indeed Sunday School, the peripatetic schools of Griffith Jones, Bishop Morgan's translation of the Bible, and the chapels all played a vital role in the preservation of the Welsh language. In no other Celtic land did religion and language intertwine as they did in Wales. And that was why, according to Gwynfor Evans, Welsh resisted the fate of Gaelic, Cornish and Breton. The struggle has gone on for centuries. When Dr Johnson sat at Mr Myddleton's table in Gwaenynog in 1774, what did they talk about? 'After dinner, the talk was of preserving the Welsh language. I offered them a scheme: I recommended the republication of David ap Rhee's Welsh Grammar.' Earlier, in 1751, a group of Welshmen had founded the 'Honourable Society of Cymmrodorion' in London, with the aim of saving and translating old Welsh manuscripts, and fostering native customs and language. This included reviving the Eisteddfod as a national institution. The Celtic revival of the 18th century was a literary and antiquarian movement – which found a lively echo in English Romanticism – and it took place among people who were still predominantly Welsh-speaking. The Celtic revival of today has a similar intellectual background, but its basis is much narrower, and its aims much more political.

One evening I got to know an American in a hotel in Beaumaris. 'My parents left Wales in 1913,' he told me, 'and this is my first trip here.' Then he began to speak Welsh – fluently, though with a strong Milwaukee accent. 'There you are!' cried my host in triumph. 'They even speak Welsh in America!' The picture is false, for *yr iaith* is in decline. Yet the Welsh manage to make the retreat sound remarkably like an advance.

Every census in Wales records the decline. In 1851 over 90% of the population still spoke Welsh; in 1951 it was down to 29%, and in 1981 it was a mere 19% – just 500,000 out of 2.8 million. There are many reasons: text books, newspapers, films, radio, TV, advertisements – for a long time these were all in English. That is the everyday side of anglicization. And now more than ever there are economic reasons. High unemployment drives young Welsh people into the towns, and especially to England. At the same time thousands of English people leave the industrial centres to look for holiday or retirement homes in Wales. 'No jobs, no people – no people, no language': that is Wales's predicament. 'The Welsh Office subsidizes our language,' I was told by a trade unionist, 'but if we can't find work in Wales, we can't speak Welsh!' But at least in the meantime there are state-run courses in Welsh for the unemployed.

Wherever you go, you will see posters with the slogan: 'Don't forget your Welsh'. But

Fighting tolls and social injustice: the Rebecca Riots, 1829–44

it's not a language campaign. It's an advertisement for a product that's far better known to the Welsh than their own language – Welsh Bitter (plate 55). This patriotic-sounding advertising campaign is by no means a matter of chance. Since the 1960's the spiritual descendants of Llywelyn and Owain Glyndwr have waged a whole series of astonishingly successful campaigns: they kept destroying and painting over English street and place names until at last the authorities allowed them to be bilingual; they refused to pay their taxes and bills until the official forms were also bilingual; and they kept sabotaging TV stations until, in 1982, they finally got their own Welsh-speaking 4th Channel. 'To restore the Welsh language in Wales is nothing less than a revolution. Only revolutionary methods will succeed.' These were the fighting words of the author Saunders Lewis (picture, page 21), taken up by the militant defenders of Welsh culture, who knew that their principles would lead them into conflict with the law. But in a memorable radio broadcast in 1962, *'Tynged yr Iaith'* (The Fate of the Language), Saunders Lewis had prophesied that by the end of this century Welsh would have died out if there was not a radical change in the linguistic situation. This Cassandra-like cry from so respected a figure of Welsh literature led to the founding one year later of *Cymdeithas yr Iaith Gymraeg*, the Society for the Welsh Language. Pulling no academic punches, this group soon developed into the most effective protest movement since the Rebecca Riots.[1] We have already looked at its emblem – the tongue of the Red Dragon. Its methods are a combination of action and discussion, of targeted law-breaking and tireless campaigning within the law. And its modes of civil disobedience certainly bore fruit, ensuring that the Welsh Language Act was really put into practice. This Act, passed in 1967, guaranteed 'equal validity' to the Welsh language for the first time since 1536. Even if it does not mean a de facto bilingualism in all public life, the fact is that now every Welsh person can enter his or her name in Welsh in the birth register, can fill in his or her tax form in Welsh, and can claim his or her pension in Welsh. But for all this, the struggle continues. A wine dealer in Cardiff named Paul Morgan was shocked to receive the threat of a fine from Brussels. Was his wine adulterated? No, but he had dared to label some bottles of white wine exclusively in Welsh, with the romantic name 'Calon Lan' (Pure Heart), and for all the innocence of his pure-heartedness, the European Community does not recognize Welsh as one of its official languages. A target for the future, perhaps.

When in 1969 – the very year of the investiture of Prince Charles – the language guerrillas were painting over street signs, and furious drivers were unaware that Swansea is called Abertawe, the Hennessy duo sang on behalf of many of their compatriots: 'Now they're trying to alter all our signposts / And make us live in streets we cannot say / I don't mind the Pakistanis or the Eyties / But I wish the bloody Welsh would go away.'

The most important and the most controversial battleground is education. The possibilities of bilingual training from kindergarten through to university have never been so good in Wales as they are today. In the great rural counties of Dyfed and Gwynedd, the Cymrian heartland, Welsh is now the first language and English the first foreign language. It is compulsory in all primary schools and in the first five years of secondary school, whereas in the rest of Wales it is compulsory only in the first year at secondary school. The majority of bilingual schools are in the south and the north-east. For the champions of the language, this is not enough, and for the rest it's too much. I met many English-speaking Welsh people and English immigrants who were quite happy to send their children for Welsh lessons, but they would have preferred them to learn a language that they could use abroad. ('Even in Welsh Patagonia they've long since learned to speak Spanish!') And now, in fear of an 'English Not', there is even a new Language Freedom Movement, whose goal is to campaign against compulsory Welsh, and against professional discrimination concerning non-Welsh speakers (how the wheel turns)! In the Welsh heartlands it seems only right and proper that those in senior administrative posts should speak Welsh, but the opponents of bilingualism conjure up visions of a new two-tiered society: a Welsh-speaking elite lording it over the majority of monolingual Anglo-Welsh. Personally, I see

---

1   The Rebecca Riots: This name (based on Exodus 24, 60: 'Let thy seed possess the gate of those which hate them') was given to the riots when impoverished Welsh peasants attacked customs barriers and other social injustices in 1839–44.

a greater danger: namely, of a new generation of semi-educated people who are masters of neither language. In the 1950's, the educational standard in Wales was higher than anywhere else in Britain. Today some 14% of school-leavers have no qualifications whatever (compared to 8% in England). This alarming drop in standards has been attributed by some experts to the fact that many teachers and parents consider learning Welsh to be a top priority in education.

The Welsh Language Society has in fact drastically increased its demands. In the 1982 manifesto they said that bilingualism was only an intermediate stage, and their real aim was not equality but 'full status' for Welsh, i.e. it is to become the official language of the country. Other languages, including English, will be tolerated only as official additions. The achievement of this aim requires a proper sociolinguistic policy influencing tourism, industry, and the housing market. 'Planning status for the language' is the watchword, which means in short that if the language is to be saved, society must be changed. But the militant class struggle of the linguistic left has proved too radical even for some of the early apostles, and compared to its heyday, when the Welsh Language Society boasted some 3,000 members, by the mid eighties this had dwindled to about 1,000.

The problem is a real one, however. Barely one Welsh person in five is still able to speak Welsh, and they are a minority over whom the epithet 'disappearing' hangs like a death sentence. Compare Wales with other Celtic lands: there are six Welsh speakers for every Gaelic-speaking Scot.

But as always with endangered minority groups, the threat of extinction produces its own dynamism. For such a small nation, they are astonishingly creative. Poets, singers, artists, craftsmen abound, and as the language fades, the literature blossoms: there are some 300 new books published in Welsh every year, and over 30 regional monthly magazines have a total circulation of a good 70,000. *Yr Academi Gymraig*, the Welsh writers' association founded in 1959, has also had an English section since 1968 – a forum for authors in both languages. 'Despite our speech we are not English,' they insist, and even though many Welsh authors write only in English, like R. S. Thomas (page 416), they remain indefatigably Welsh. And indeed Anglo-Welsh literature is bound to be stamped with the background, historical consciousness and political convictions of its authors, not to mention the music and rhythms of their language. It first came to the fore in the 1930's, when a new generation had no hesitation in publishing their work in English, in the hope of reaching a wider audience – 'to be, like some valley cheese, local but prized everywhere' (W. H. Auden). In those days, the English regarded such work as Welsh, and the Welsh regarded it as English. But the Anglo-Welsh concept is neither a hybrid nor a cop-out – it reflects the true nature of a bilingual country with two literatures. Its authors are far from being representatives of insidious British integration, and their Welsh-speaking colleagues are not to be seen merely as separatists: both political and literary creeds permeate both camps.

But for all this fecundity, books are comparatively powerless in the battle for Cymru

1 THE PRINCE OF WALES
  a Investiture in Caernarfon Castle, 1969
  b With the Princess of Wales visiting Caernarfon, 1981, on investiture stools

2 NEWPORT On the River Usk

3 NEWPORT Transporter Bridge, 1902–06

4   MARGAM PARK   Orangery, 1786–90, by Anthony Keck

5   CARDIFF   Queen's Chambers, Queen Street, *c.*1870

6   CARDIFF   City Hall, 1901–05

7   CARDIFF   City Hall, Marble Hall with Heroes of Wales, 1916

8 CARDIFF   Docks, Pierhead Building, 1896: Bute coat-of-arms ('Through Water and Fire')

9   CARDIFF   Castle, restored by William Burges, 1865–90

10 CARDIFF   Castle, Banqueting Hall by W. Burges, 1877

11–12 CARDIFF Castle, corbel figures in Library

13 CARDIFF Entrance to restaurant, Westgate Street   14 CARDIFF Castle, Animal Wall, 19th century

15 LAUGHARNE Dylan Thomas, *c.*1950

16 LAUGHARNE The Shed, Dylan's workroom

17 LAUGHARNE The Boat House, Dylan's house on the Taf

18 LAUGHARNE Dylan's grave in St Martin's cemetery

19 BARRY The Knap, beach near Cardiff ▷

20   PENTRE IFAN   Neolithic dolmen

21   BRYN CELLI DDU   Megalithic burial chamber on Anglesey, 2000–1500 BC

22   Caerleon   Roman amphitheatre, *c.*80 AD

23   Din Lligwy   Celtic hut settlement, 3–4th century AD

24 RHONDDA   Children of the Valleys

25 ABERFAN   Graves of children killed in the 1966 disaster

26   MERTHYR TYDFIL   Robert and Lucy Thomas Fountain, 1907

Cymraeg, Welsh-speaking Wales. The Language Society points to English and American TV series as the worst threat, even more damaging than the 'Welsh Not' used to be for schoolchildren. Without access to the media, they say, the language is doomed to die. A government commission in 1974 actually concluded that the three English channels then existing in Wales should be supplemented by a fourth in Welsh, which would be an 'investment' in domestic, cultural and social harmony in the UK. But London's reaction was the usual blend of cynicism and 'keep smiling'. One MP declared that there were more deaf people in Great Britain than Welsh speakers in Wales; what was being done for them? Once more there were demonstrations: three Welsh university professors paralyzed a TV transmitter in Dyfed; the principal of the Theological College in Swansea, Pennar Davies, went to court to defend his protest against 'English language imperialism'. And when, at the climax of the campaign, the president of Plaid Cymru, Gwynfor Evans, threatened to go on hunger strike, the Thatcher government finally gave way and approved the fourth channel in Welsh. Gwynfor Evans announced euphorically that this victory would ensure a future for the language. But 'Telly Welly', alas, attracts only about 70,000 viewers even at peak periods. Sianel 4 Cymru (S4C) has been in existence since 1982, and it is the most expensive minority channel in the world. But to redress the balance, there have also been some internationally successful films in Welsh, with English subtitles – notably, Stephen Bayley's 'Coming Up Roses' (1986), the story of an unemployed projectionist in the valleys.

'We speak Welsh when we're in love, and English when we're counting,' said a friend, not without self-mockery. To outsiders – and not only the English – the language battle often seems bizarre and irrational, a sort of romantic obsession. 'The Welsh-speaking Welsh, the "Cymry Cymraeg", form an inner people within the nation,' writes the Anglo-Welsh author Jan Morris. And even if the struggle does have some sectarian features, this is not a matter of Celtic freemasonry; it is a political phenomenon. The language is the nation – or at least that's what it was. And now the nation's identity has been submerged, fragmented, diversified, and the question has to be asked: Who are we? In his book 'The Welsh Extremist', N. Thomas, a lecturer in English at Aberystwyth, calls the struggle a 'communal neurosis' – it's a sort of national schizophrenia. And this strange emotional ambivalence shows itself in the lives of many prominent people. 'A student career of fairly passionate nationalism gives way to a careful public career, but on retirement the passionate nationalist again emerges.' For centuries the Welsh national identity was marked, not by their own political institutions, but by their language and their literature, and during the last two centuries also by their religion. Thomas, however, writes: 'You cannot be a cultural nationalist only. The language is itself an indicator of what is happening to us, and very often when we speak of defending the language we are in

◁ 27 MONMOUTH Monnow Bridge, 13th century

fact, through the language, defending other aspects of our life, and ultimately our own right to have some control over the future.'

Welsh is one of 35 minority languages in Europe, statistically more popular than Rhaeto-Romanic, which is spoken by about 30,000 Swiss, and less popular than Euskarian, which is still spoken by about a quarter of the Basque population. Bretons, Catalans, Sardinians – not all of them demand national sovereignty on the basis of their different culture, and indeed many of these people would be satisfied with greater regional autonomy. Some have achieved it already, like the Basques, but still fight on despite their partial independence and their regional parliament. Others, though, including the Scots and the Welsh, see themselves not as a mere region but as a nation. Scotland was not united with England until 1603, when James VI of Scotland became James I of England, and it was only in 1707 that its parliament was merged with that of the United Kingdom. Even today, statistically it is treated as an entity, whereas Wales is generally incorporated into England. Since the death of the last Welsh prince in 1282, Wales has remained subjected. It is therefore all the more extraordinary that after all these centuries, despite the dominance of its mighty neighbour, the 'province' has maintained its cultural identity to such a degree that the latter can still be invoked as a legitimation for national aspirations. It is a nation caught on the wheel of its own history, or, as Saunders Lewis has put it:

> Condemned in this world to endure the pain of Sisyphus
> To push from age to age through a thousand years
> A stone nation to the summit of the hill of Freedom ...

But I do not think Taffy is truly a Sisyphus. If the national question is blown up to such proportions, the man in the street will become invisible. Throughout its long history, the problem has solidified into a kind of national monument: for some it is an ancient pedestal without a statue, and for others a statue looking for a base.

Saunders Lewis was not only a patriotic poet. He was also co-founder and president of the Welsh National Party (picture, page 21). Plaid Cymru was founded in 1925 under somewhat inauspicious circumstances. At that time the unemployed were interested only in a solution to their social problems, and not in a nationalistic message or a political programme calling for Wales to return to the good old days of agriculture and cooperatives. Furthermore, in Welsh eyes there was a certain reactionary tinge to the party: Saunders Lewis and initially several other leading figures were Catholics. Plaid Cymru found itself up against a Protestant, Liberal electorate, tightly organized unions, and an up-and-coming Labour Party. Not surprisingly, its electoral debut was a disaster: 609 votes. Its pacifist policy of neutrality during the Nazi era did little to increase its popularity. Not until 1966 did the first Plaid Cymru MP take his seat in the House of Commons: Gwynfor Evans, a long-standing symbol of Welsh nationalism (page 270 and picture, page 21). For years Plaid Cymru had the image of a party whose main concern was Welsh language and culture. Its voters came largely from the rural, Welsh-speaking areas of the north, and scarcely any were from the anglicized, industrialized south. But even under the charismatic leadership of Gwynfor Evans, the Party never achieved more than 11% of the vote (1974); in the same year, the Scottish Nationalists – thanks to North Sea oil – polled 30%.

1974 was also the year in which the 27-year-old Dafydd Elis Thomas of Plaid Cymru entered Parliament as its youngest MP. His grandfather was a slater, his father a Presbyterian minister – the classic Welsh background. In Westminster, as a lone fighter for lost causes, Dafydd Elis Thomas needed all the diplomacy he could muster. In Wales he would speak of 'national' interests, which in London suddenly became 'regional' (rather like the BBC's Solomonic definition of Wales as a 'national region'). It is because of such compromises that the poet R. S. Thomas (picture, page 21) dismissed Plaid Cymru as 'a milk and water movement'. Little wonder, then, that this National Party, which had over 30,000 members in the early 1970's, has now dwindled to around 10,000. Dafydd Elis Thomas has told me that many young Welsh people now prefer to work for the peace movement or other alternative causes, rather than Plaid Cymru. At the National Eisteddfod in 1983 he declared: 'I can see a real danger that at the end of the 20th century, some of us will be more concerned in maintaining a fossilized version of the Welsh language on the back of British state money, than in creating the necessary social change to ensure that we can control our own economy, society and state.' Dafydd Ellis Thomas, who is on the extreme left, so-called red wing of the party, became its president in 1984. His aim: a new blend of nationalism and socialism: 'The Labour Party in Wales never had a national programme, and the national party never had a social one. We want to bring them both together. Our aim is a democratic, socialist state of Wales.' This mixture of Marx and Merlin attracted only 132,000 votes, which constituted 8% of the electorate and won just two out of 38 Welsh seats in the House of Commons.

The decline of Plaid Cymru appears to be unstoppable, and has been so ever since a referendum on St David's Day 1979, in which 80% of Welsh people voted against having a parliament of their own in Cardiff. It was a democratic vote, but the question has to be asked, what exactly did it mean? The majority of Welsh people were not rejecting the idea of Welsh autonomy in itself, for that was not the issue; what they objected to was a form of partial autonomy which seemed to them superfluous, inadequate, and, in the end, pointless. As a blueprint for 'devolution', it did admittedly provide for a Welsh Assembly, but this would have had no fiscal or legislative powers; its authority would have covered social, health and educational administration (apart from universities) and nothing else. Industry, the environment, transport, housing, foreign policy, defence, trade, justice, finance – all this would have remained in the hands of Westminster. *This* was the 'self-government' that the Welsh rejected. No doubt they were also influenced by fear of increased bureaucracy, greater costs, and perhaps also of a Celtic, Welsh-speaking elite. 'Power for Wales' is something they would like, but not a Cymric-Socialist Republic. They do not regard themselves as merely a part of England, but nor do they see themselves as a 'British colony fighting for its independence', to quote the Plaid Cymru MP Dafydd Williams.

What, then, do the Welsh want? Like everything else in their spiritual lives, the Welsh political soul is full of ambivalence. John Cowper Powys has captured the essence of their nationalism: 'Welsh patriotism is like air, like water, like an invisible musical sound. It is something that refuses to assume an incarnate shape, but something at the same time upon which no shocks, no tyrannies, no indulgent underminings, seem to have the smallest effect!' They prefer to be known as patriots rather than nationalists, and fortunately they are more inclined to fanatical views than fanatical actions. Who would want Wales to turn into another Northern Ireland? They have made their language battle into one of faith, but not a religious crusade; their cultural struggle has never turned into civil war. At the same time, it would be wrong to underestimate the significance of their battles. As Gwynfor Evans has said: 'We are Welsh ... not British.' They are not prepared to disappear in the British melting-pot, and they will not.

After a century of national and cultural renaissance, and a period of remarkable political success, the referendum of 1979 marked a dramatic downturn. Many commentators saw it as an overwhelming endorsement of union with England, and a further blow to the concept of a Welsh identity, Wales was seen to be 'lapsing into a mere metaphysical construct adapted for intellectual recreation' (Kenneth O. Morgan). But I have a feeling this is more a matter of English wishful thinking than Welsh reality. Of course, Wales cannot live on its myths, or on its romantic, 19th-century visions of a national state, or on socialist Utopias built round Celtic fireplaces. But there is still room for a Welsh Wales. The people are too dynamic to hide away in England's backyard, and too extrovert to be fossilized in their Cymric stone circles. Jan Morris unfolds a vision of a Welsh republic with Machynlleth as its capital, the little market town in Powys where Owain Glyndwr held a crown council in 1400: it would be a nuclear-free, neutral, demilitarized, ecological State for young idealists. A Welsh Utopia.

Yr iaith: a language of their own – a state of their own? Against the cultural and ethnic arguments of the Welsh, as with the Scots, there stands the geographical logic of the English: *one* island, *one* state. For this pragmatic reason, the reunification of Ireland, despite its massive complexity, would seem more likely in the long term than the independence of Wales. And that is even assuming that the Welsh wanted their independence.

South Wales

Offa's Dyke: A Hike Along the Border

In the 1990's barriers are coming down all over Europe. It is a fact to be celebrated. In 1966 the Welsh and the English celebrated together the disappearance of an age-old gap between them. Where the Wye flows into the Severn, and the Severn flows into the Bristol Channel, the elegant curves of the *Severn Bridge* now stretch across the water, linking England and Wales as they had never been linked before. Opened by Queen Elizabeth II, it is one of the longest suspension bridges in the world, with a central span of over 3,000 feet. But there are some who wonder whether it was meant to be, for this bridge of the century had not even lasted a quarter of a century before metal fatigue and the sheer volume of traffic brought it close to a state of collapse. Now there is to be a second bridge across the Severn. Plans were also afoot for a dam to produce hydroelectricity. The barrage was to be over nine miles long, would stretch from Weston-super-Mare to Cardiff, and when it was finished, by the end of the millennium, it would be the biggest tidal power station in the world. But will it ever be built? Ecologists say it would destroy the ecological balance of the Severn Estuary, and certainly the plovers, herons and other rare wading birds would lose their nesting grounds for ever. Their claims, however, seem to carry less weight than those of the economists, and if they are saved, it will be for reasons of costing rather than nesting.

In the 19th century, when technology was almost a creed, hymns would have been sung to such miracles as the suspension bridge. Even today, the poets are inspired, though Harri Webb's 'Ode to the Severn Bridge' (1969) is rather more political than ecumenical: 'Two lands at last connected / Across the waters wide / And all the tolls collected / Upon the English side.' Welcome to Wales – but pay in England. Still, it's a happier solution than greeted Daniel Defoe in 1722, when he reached a 'little dirty village called Aust' on the bank of the Severn, wanted to cross over into Wales, and saw nothing but 'an ugly, dangerous, and very inconvenient ferry'. As the currents were notorious and the weather was bad, he turned straight back and chose the land route via Gloucester.

The Severn, Wye, Usk and Dee – the chief rivers of Wales open up their broad valleys to the invaders. But the mountains are also there: to the South, the Black Mountains, which rise up like a long, dark wall as you approach them from the Golden Valley of Hereford; to the North, Snowdonia, the great barrier. It was a fluid frontier. Already long before the Norman Conquest, King Offa of Mercia had a protective wall built against the plunderings and the territorial ambitions of the Welsh. *Offa's Dyke* (c.784) was not a continually defended frontier like Hadrian's Wall in northern England, but rather a line of demarcation. It was an earthwork 60 feet broad, up to 15 feet high, with a ditch about 12 feet deep on the Welsh side. At one time any Welshman caught with any weapon on the east side of the dyke would have his right hand cut off. And the Welsh gave an equally friendly welcome to any Englishman caught on their side. The wall ran for 170 miles from the Wye estuary in the South to that of the Dee in the North, passing over moors and marshes, dales and vales, highlands and lowlands. East of the wall, all the placenames are English, and west they are nearly all Welsh. But today this age-old political boundary is a favourite walk, though the Dyke itself has in the meantime crumbled, less from the attentions of enemy invaders than from erosion and rabbits. But there are still some well-preserved sections, for instance north of Montgomery, or near *Knighton*, whose Welsh name is Tref-y-Clawdd – Town on the Dyke. Even today, old Welsh people often say they are 'going across Clawdd Offa' when they mean they are going to England. And the hiker setting off along Offa's long distance path will as often as not fortify himself with a drop of 'King Offa' – apple brandy.

The first castle built by the Norman conquerors on the Welsh side of Offa's Dyke was *Chepstow Castle* (colour plate 41). Grey and rugged, hewn from the very limestone on which it stands, as if it were growing out of the rocks, it towers over the west bank of the Wye. Because of its strategic importance it had to be built entirely of stone instead of wood. It was begun in 1067 by William FitzOsbern, one of William the Conqueror's main followers. On the narrowest section of the castle mound stands the 'Great Tower', similar to the rectangular keeps of Normandy. Late into the 13th century Chepstow Castle was continually being renovated and extended, until finally there were four courtyards, divided by walls, with a whole array of splendid domestic buildings. In 1403, twenty men and sixty archers withstood an attack from the rebel Owain Glyndwyr. In the Civil War, Sir Nicholas Keynes, abandoned by his treacherous men, fought on alone. When Cromwell finally captured it, he made the castle into a garrison instead of razing it to the ground. Later it became a state and military prison.

Nestling in the shadow of the castle and the great loop of the Wye lies the little market town of Chepstow (colour plates 38, 60). In the 19th century it boasted some 75 pubs, when the harbour, trade, and the ship-building industry were all flourishing. There are still a few houses preserved from this time and earlier; they can be seen on the way from the medieval town gate to the Wye. And over the Wye the Scottish engineer John Rennie – who built London Bridge – constructed, in 1816, a five-arch cast-iron bridge, one of the first of its kind. In 1852, Brunel built a tubular bridge there as well.

William FitzOsbern, as Earl of Hereford, was one of the three great Lords Marcher, whom William the Conqueror appointed to secure the borderlands, or Marches. The other two, the Earls of Shrewsbury and Chester, had the status of counts palatine, with their own armies and jurisdiction. Chester and Shrewsbury had been the two great legionary camps of the Romans, and so were already important strategic centres on the Welsh border. The Norman overlords ruled their subjects like little kings, and in time their number and influence increased. For the English King they provided welcome defence of the borders, but at the same time they were a more or less constant threat. Henry II finally clipped their wings in matters of land ownership, but it was not until the reign of Henry

VIII that their juridical powers were removed and the last of them, the Duke of Buckingham, was executed. From then on it was the Council of the Welsh Marches that put into practice the dictates of central government. It was also Henry VIII who declared the River Usk from Crickhowell to its estuary to be the Welsh border. The region between Usk and Wye – formerly Monmouthshire – remained English until the boundary changes of 1974. Only then did it return to Wales under its original name of Gwent.

Tintern Abbey: A Mecca for Romantic Pilgrims

If you travel north from Chepstow, you will come to the biggest racecourse in Wales, and on the edge of this stand the ruins of *Piercefield House*. Once it was a cultural centre, designed in Neo-Classical style by the English architect Sir John Soane in 1785, inhabited until 1923, used for target practice by the American army in the Second World War and virtually shot to pieces. The Chepstow Racecourse Company plan to build a hotel here and put an end to this scandalous, not to say vandalous tale which is all the more incomprehensible in a country so lacking in truly historic architecture. Piercefield Park, where the horses now race, was once the strolling ground for Coleridge, William Gilpin, and Thomas Gray. For the poets, painters and gentlemen of leisure that toured Wales in the late 18th century were enamoured of the Wye Valley. 'The chief grace and ornament of my journey was the river Wye,' said Thomas Gray, who in August 1770 had himself rowed downriver from Ross to Chepstow. 'Its banks are a succession of nameless wonders.' That same summer found the Reverend William Gilpin wandering through the Wye Valley, and he wrote a book about it which became a best-seller and made the Wye tour into the epitome of the picturesque journey (see p. 38). The early romantics had had to blaze their own trails through the dense forests and up to the heights, but today we can follow the well-worn paths to classic vantage points. *Symonds Yat*, north east of Monmouth, or the 365 steps up to *Wyndcliff*, the limestone rocks south of Tintern Abbey. And the Wye curves its silver coils through the green hills of the border country, in a perfect display of the picturesque landscape, before finally disappearing in the hazy colours of the distance.

'O sylvan Wye! thou wanderer thro' the woods, / How often has my spirit turned to thee!' It is indeed one of those landscapes that inspires the literary wanderer to blend the pleasures of the eyes with those of the memory. The 28-year-old William Wordsworth wrote his famous 'Lines Composed a Few Miles above Tintern Abbey' in July 1798, when he and his sister Dorothy went up the Wye Valley from Chepstow to Goodrich Castle. He had already visited this 'pastoral landscape' five years earlier, wondering at the 'steep and lofty cliffs, / Which on a wild secluded scene impress / Thoughts of more deep seclusion; and connect / The landscape with the quiet of the sky.' This reunion with the Wye becomes a reunion with his own, not too distant youth and its 'dizzy raptures'; the pure experience of Nature leads to reflection on human nature and its developments, to a lyrical experience of the self, and to an exemplary, romantic *weltanschauung*. Thus the Wye becomes the river of memory, and the imagination senses 'something far more deeply interfused':

A motion and a spirit that impels
All thinking things, all objects of all thought,
And rolls through all things. Therefore am I still
A lover of the meadows, and the woods,
And mountains; and of all that we behold
From this green earth; of all the mighty world

Of eye and ear, both what they half create,
And what perceive; well pleased to recognize
In Nature and the language of the sense,
The anchor of my purest thoughts, the nurse,
The guide, the guardian of my heart, and soul
Of all my moral being.

What this 'worshipper of Nature' wrote some 200 years ago on the banks of the Wye, in certain knowledge that 'all which we behold / Is full of blessings', may sound to our modern, less romantic ears like News from Nowhere. And yet not only is the landscape still there – so, too, down in the valley, older even than these romantic longings and still potently symbolizing them, lie the ruins of *Tintern Abbey* (colour plate 64).

The Wye Valley was still wild and remote, far from the eyes of wanderers, when the Norman monks founded their monastery here. This was in 1131, just three years after Waverley Abbey, the first Cistercian abbey in England. This order of monks, which originated in 1098 in the forest of Cîteaux, believed in a strict monastic life devoted to the liturgy and to physical labour. The isolated, inhospitable conditions were ideal for their purposes. Altogether they founded 15 monasteries in Wales, of which the best known are Margam, Neath, Cwmhir and Strata Florida. But the most splendid of them all was Tintern Abbey: pure, radiant Gothic. The Abbey Church (1270–1301) had a six-arch nave with clerestory, a three-arch transept, and a four-arch chancel. These dimensions, carefully worked out, create an unconscious effect of rhythmic harmony throughout the edifice, epitomized by the lofty, elegant archways. Even after hundreds of years the exquisite quality of the stonemasonry is evident from the capitals and columns, as well as the almost perfectly preserved tracery of the west window. Although it is a ruin, Tintern Abbey, through the balance of its proportions and the beauty of its carvings, remains a magnificent piece of architecture. Between the cloister and the north side of the church, nothing remains except the foundations. The north wing of the monastery contained, among other things, the kitchen and refectory, while the west wing housed the lay brothers' cells. There was a separate building for the sick and the old.

Tintern Abbey was so remote that it was largely spared from plunderings and frontier wars. But generally the Cistercian monasteries in Wales were regarded by the English as breeding-grounds for nationalism. And so in 1536 the abbey on the Wye fell victim to Henry VIII's Reformation. The church silver was confiscated, the bells melted down, and the lead ripped off the roofs. Tintern Abbey fell into ruin. But since there were no villages nearby that could use the abbey as a quarry – as frequently happened elsewhere – the ruins remained relatively well preserved. In time they attained a kind of aesthetic holiness which once more made it the destination of pilgrims, though now their pilgrimage was a

J. M. W. Turner:
Tintern Abbey, 1794

picturesque rather than a religious one. When the originator of these picturesque journeys, the Reverend William Gilpin, stood before the ruins in 1770, he actually thought that, in accordance with his own rules for judging the beauty of a view, this model of the picturesque still left room for improvement: 'Though the parts are beautiful, the whole is ill-shaped ... A number of gable ends hurt the eye with their regularity ... A mallet judiciously used (but who durst use it?) might be of service in fracturing some of them, particularly those of the cross-aisles, which are not only disagreeable in themselves, but confound the perspective.' Fortunately, Tintern Abbey was spared such cosmetic surgery, though William Gilpin's followers did not spare it their attentions. They came in boatloads from Ross-on-Wye, used the services of one of the many self-appointed guides, and are to be seen in contemporary etchings clambering over the ruins, sometimes with burning torches in the moonlight, hunting for the picturesque. Even in those days, the amateur archaeologist Sir Richard Colt-Hoare – Turner's patron – was expressing concern over the conservation of the Abbey and other beauty spots.

Turner first visited Tintern Abbey as a seventeen-year-old in 1792. He returned twice more, and each time sketched and painted this most romantic of settings. His pictures, reproduced as etchings, attracted more and more visitors and artists. 'And such an Abbey! The lightest Gothic – trellised with ivy and rising from a wilderness of orchards – and set like a gem amongst the folding of woody hills,' wrote Samuel Palmer, who painted several watercolours of the Abbey in 1835. Carl Gustav Carus, Saxon court physician and painter, a friend of Goethe and of Caspar David Friedrich, also wondered at it during his tour of Wales in 1844: 'This vision in the fading twilight seemed magical and most inward-reaching – so moving as almost to make one weep! I had never before experienced anything so complete in itself in this way, so utterly poetic! ... That so much noble architecture was preserved as to give the effect of a real whole, but that upon this might, through the even mightier force of Nature given its full freedom, an even higher authority had been stamped – this alone explained why the effect was so significant! – Once more I had to think of Friedrich! – here was that which he had so often striven for in his paintings, given in complete and most lofty truth to Nature! ... And how typical that here, too, one was forced to acknowledge that *genuine and true* reality was ultimately even loftier and even mightier than anything the fantasy ever can or does produce!'

The fashion of the picturesque has long since faded, the walls have been cleared of their ivy, and the Abbey now belongs to the nation. We no longer see the ruins that the romantics saw, but we still travel the same routes, and we still gaze at places like Tintern Abbey with the same insatiable thirst for a lost and beautiful world.

Monmouth: Princely Moments

Upriver, where the Monnow merges with the Wye, lies *Monmouth*. Here everything is still within reach of the pedestrian, for the old town has scarcely altered its basic lay-out since the middle of the 15th century. Priory Street, built in 1837, is the only major extension to the network of streets in the last 500 years. For centuries, though, this was a major junction on the highway from London to South Wales, and even today, Monmouth is an intersection for many main roads, though the traffic has been diverted round the outskirts. This is a border town where two cultures meet, but it is a very long time since anything but English was spoken here. It has all the atmosphere of a rural market town, but its houses have an urban elegance about them. A county town until 1939, it is a medieval relic on the fringes of the modern world, a province impregnated with world history. A king was born here, as was a maker of luxury cars; an admiral came to visit the town, and in recent times it has boasted the very first Magic Lantern Theatre in Britain.

The bridge over the river, the castle on the hill – the old pattern is still to be seen today.

Harry Monmouth, Henry V, by an unidentified painter, early 15th century

William FitzOsbern's Norman castle survives only in ruins, but the bridge over the Monnow still stands in all its splendour, along with its 13th-century gatehouse (plate 27). Monnow Bridge is the only surviving medieval bridge-house in Britain, and indeed there are very few left in Europe. It was part of the town's fortifications, built to protect one of the most vulnerable spots. It looks rather like a squashed archway with a sloping tiled roof. A portcullis could be lowered from the area above the arch, and attackers could be greeted with boiling tar or other such niceties. Whoever controlled the frontier stronghold on the Wye controlled access to South Wales. Next to the bridge, and made of the same sandstone, is a little church, built in 1180 and dedicated to St Thomas Becket, though even he could do nothing to stop the sinful Neo-Norman restorations of 1832. Like an inverted funnel Monnow Street leads uphill from the bridge to the town centre: broad and roomy down below, where the markets were always held, but increasingly narrow as it climbs upwards to where St Stephen's Gate used to stand. It's a perfectly normal street, with its old houses, shops and pubs, and all the usual small-town bustle – but then suddenly it broadens out into an unexpected square that echoes with a sort of distant heroism: Agincourt Square. And here our little town takes on a new and unforeseen greatness. A cue for the entrance of Harry Monmouth.

Agincourt, October 25, 1415. The Hundred Years' War, England versus France. The French have a far bigger army, but the English have an elite force: the Welsh archers.

Against a cavalry attack they have developed a new weapon: the longbow. The hail of arrows cuts through the French chainmail like razors through paper. These Welsh mercenaries are fighting for a king who is their fellow-countryman: Harry Monmouth, Henry V. Two years after his victory at Agincourt, Normandy is his, and not much later, the French crown. But just as Germany's princes are debating whether to offer him the imperial crown too, Henry V dies, just 34 years old. A national hero, darling of the people, who wages war and dreams of peace – that is the king Shakespeare portrays: Harry Monmouth and his mentor Falstaff, who no doubt would have won the battle single-handed, if only he had lived to pretend to fight it. And then there is Captain Fluellen, the most famous Welsh mercenary in the history of world literature. His name is a parody of Llywelyn – a private English joke of Shakespeare's day, mocking the ethnic aspirations of their neighbours. Thanks to Fluellen, we know what the Welsh bowmen wore on their heads at Agincourt: knitted caps from Monmouth, decorated with leeks. Or did they? These 'Monmouth caps' were a slight anachronism on Shakespeare's part, for they did not appear till the middle of the 16th century. They continued to be produced in Monmouth, however, during the following century as well, a major industry in the town, and even today veterans of the Welch Regiment still wear a leek in their hats on St David's Day.

The victor of Agincourt was born in Monmouth Castle in 1387 – probably in the Great Tower. His father, Henry Bolingbroke, Henry IV, was the first member of the House of Lancaster to mount the throne. During the Civil War, Monmouth Castle was razed to the ground. The noble house that stands on the castle hill next to the ruins, Great Castle House, was a gift from the third Marquis of Worcester to his daughter-in-law. It was built in 1673 in Palladian style, with a simple, symmetrical façade decorated on the inside with ornate wooden panelling and stucco ornamentation. Shire Hall, in Agincourt Square, built in 1724 by an unknown architect, also has the classic proportions of the Neo-Palladian style: the arches of the open entrance hall, the narrow, round-arched double windows, the elegant Ionic pilasters – these all make the house a true masterpiece of early Georgian architecture. Until the Second World War, the courts met here, and it is thanks to the judges who resided in the town that Monmouth acquired its many rich Victorian and Georgian houses.

Great moments: from his pedestal on the façade of Shire Hall, Henry V gazes over the old market-place at another of the town's famous sons: Charles Stewart Rolls (bronze statue by Goscombe John, 1911). Rolls is to Royce what fish is to chips – an inseparable partnership. In 1896, when he was 19, he sat at the wheel of the first car, which drove through Monmouth having taken three days to get from Cambridge – for the speed limit then was the speed of a walking man. When his father, who was an MP in London, had guests to stay at his Welsh country estate (and these included George V and Queen Mary), young Mr Rolls would drive them through the Wye Valley in a Panhard. He also went racing and ballooning. In 1903 he met his lifelong partner, Henry Royce. Royce owned an electrical appliances firm, and had just designed his first car. Rolls wanted to put it into production: 'I wanted to be able to recommend and sell the best cars in the world.' And that was how Rolls Royce was born. The legendary Silver Ghost six-cylinder car of 1906 was the first in the line of luxurious Anglo-Welsh productions. But for Charles Stewart Rolls, the story ended just four years later: on June 2 1910, he was the first to fly non-stop across the English Channel and back, but not long afterwards he was killed in a flying accident, thus becoming the first victim of British aviation.

His mother, Lady Llangattock, had a different sort of passion: not cars and not planes, but Lord Nelson. At the Rolls family home The Hendre, outside the gates of Monmouth, she collected anything and everything to do with the hero of Trafalgar: pictures, books and relics, his sword and his Bible, Lady Hamilton's harp, Nelson's letters and logbook, pieces of the *Victory*'s sail, plates, cups and glasses commemorating his battles, his death-scene in Staffordshire china. This historical and patriotic collection, second only to that of the National Maritime Museum in Greenwich, was presented by Lady Llangattock to her

Charles Stewart Rolls in the basket of his balloon 'Midget', around 1900

hometown, and it is still to be seen today in Monmouth Museum – which was built in 1834 in Neo-Classical style as an indoor market. The oak plank on which Nelson died during the Battle of Trafalgar, was made into an amazing number of snuff-boxes, and his hair grew with equally amazing fecundity after his death, thereby allowing an ever-increasing number of genuine Nelson locks to appear on the souvenir market. Their price was an accurate gauge of the Admiral's popularity: at the beginning of this century, a lock cost £125, whereas a lock of Napoleon's hair was a mere £20, and the poor old Duke of Wellington could command no more than 30 shillings. Everything that Nelson used was collected – as indeed were many things he had not used. Even his glass eye managed to multiply itself as it went the rounds. But what, you may ask, did Lady Llangattock's hero-worship actually have to do with Monmouth?

One Sunday in July 1802, the Admiral made an excursion on the Wye – a picturesque journey in picturesque company: his mistress Emma Hamilton, and her husband, 35 years older than her, the former ambassador Sir William Hamilton. They were on their way to the latter's estate in Pembrokeshire. The boat had set out from Ross, and when it put in at the Wye Bridge in Monmouth, a military band was playing Handel's 'See, See the Conquering Hero Comes'. The hero of Abukir had one arm and one eye, with a boyish figure, and face and body badly scarred. He wore a blue coat with gold epaulettes and decorations. It was on the return journey three weeks later that Nelson stopped at the Beaufort Arms (where Wordsworth also spent a night). The following morning they all took a coach ride up to *Kymin Hill*. There the 'first gentlemen of Monmouth' had erected the crenellated Round House, where they would meet every week for dinner and to admire the view. Nelson also enjoyed the panorama of the Wye Valley, but was even more taken with the Naval Temple. This Neo-Classical building had been erected beneath oaks and beeches by the citizens of Monmouth in 1800, with round plaques commemorating Nelson and 15 other famous admirals, as well as a panoramic painting of the Battle of the Nile (now destroyed). 'The only monument of the kind to be erected to the English Navy in the whole range of the Kingdom,' enthused Lord Nelson, and then suggested that they should return to Monmouth on foot as the weather was so fine. In the Beaufort Arms the illustrious honorary citizen was served a banquet which included roast venison, toasts were drunk to the King and against the French, Lady Hamilton sang 'Rule Britannia', and then the whole company adjourned to have tea in the garden. Wonderful days in Monmouth, just three years before Trafalgar. And so began the Nelson connection which, thanks to Lady Llangattock, has remained a feature of Monmouth to this day.

Another of Monmouth's features is an inconspicuous little house in Church Street. In a town of just 7,000 inhabitants, it is perhaps rather surprising to find a Magic Lantern Theatre, for not even London can boast such a thing. It's a sort of 19th century cinema, with pictures that predate the film projector, the TV and the video. A private collector with some 15,000 glass pictures opened the theatre in 1983, and it is the only one in Britain. He and his wife welcome patrons in Victorian dress, just as the projectionists did in those olden days. The building itself is the music-hall of 1928, the restoration of which saved a splendid cultural relic from falling into ruin. The illusion itself is perfect: this is precisely how it must have been when 19th century showmen projected their 'dissolving views' – miniature pictures on glass which thanks to a sophisticated technique of superimposition actually give the impression of coming to life. Volcanoes erupt, ships are wrecked, you follow expeditions, catastrophes, curiosities, biblical stories, the circus, the railway – this was a vivid optical theatre for the educated classes, enabling them to absorb and process all the scientific, colonial and touristic conquests of the world that had been captured on glass and made available by the magic of the 'laterna magica'. It was the beginning of the age of reproduction, when everything could be recorded and distributed through the wizardry of projection. For us, who take the TV and video for granted, the magic may now seem almost primitive, but anyone who sits in Monmouth's old music-hall will, I guarantee, fall completely under the spell of this, one of the most enjoyable chapters in the history of visual aesthetics.[1]

King Arthur: Another Never-Ending Story

One may leave Monmouth without going to see 'Geoffrey's Window', but not without sparing a thought for Geoffrey himself. Monmouth's most famous son had nothing to do with its most famous window, for the former Benedictine monastery in Priory Street (now a youth hostel) was not built till 350 years after his death (1154). Who was Geoffrey of Monmouth? Everyone has heard of King Lear[2] and his favourite daughter Cordelia, and of King Arthur and his magician Merlin. Their fame is due in the first place, not to Shakespeare or to Malory, but to Geoffrey. He was a chronicler, a poet, and archdeacon of Llandaff Cathedral, a Welshman who wrote in Latin and had more influence on the history of English literature than any one of his contemporaries. In his 12-volume 'Historia Regum Britanniae' (completed in Oxford c.1135), Geoffrey worked out a genealogical tree for his countrymen, much as Homer had done for the Greeks, and Virgil for the Romans. The ancestral line goes back to Brutus, the mythical great-grandson of Aeneas, and it culminates in King Arthur. Even in those early days, King Arthur was already a national symbol and a vehicle for separatist politics. Geoffrey's 'Historia' was not history, but political myth-making, and although it purported to be a chronicle, it was really the very first Arthurian romance, a Welsh contribution to the European history of ideas.

No hero of the western world has survived the centuries so unscathed as Geoffrey's King Arthur. In books, films, comics and paintings, musicals and ballet, the legend of King Arthur is as alive today as it ever was. In 1982 the choreographer John Neumeier had Merlin, Lancelot and Guinevere dancing across the stage in Hamburg to music by Henze and Sibelius, in a ballet of profound psychological implications. In 1981 John Boorman directed a Hollywood spectacular called 'Excalibur' as a positive orgy of blood and

1   The Magic Lantern Theatre has now sadly closed.
2   Geoffrey's 'Leir' is an early Brythonic king whose name is derived from Llyr, the Celtic god of the sea.

passion. In the same year Tankred Dorst adapted his mythical, Utopian novel 'Merlin or The Waste Land' as an eight-hour stageplay: 'The great world-tale of man's fears, dreams and hopes in the blind horror of the universe.' Arthur and Merlin stand as modern cult figures in an age devoid of its own myths, ersatz knights for a society that has lost its ideals, a world of wonders entering the twilight, all clothed in Celtic mystery. The public clamours for fantasy, and a whole line of Arthurian novels has succeeded T. H. White's 'The Once and Future King' (1958). Not since the courtly Pre-Raphaelites has there been such an Arthur cult. A wave of popular historical and archaeological literature has swept the market. A survey published in 1983 under the title 'The Return of King Arthur' lists more than 500 Arthurian books published in English alone since 1800.[1] One of the most recent asks, in mock despair, 'Will the Real Arthur Please Stand Up?' It's a pertinent request, for who *was* this Arthur? Did he ever exist?

Geoffrey of Monmouth wrote the first Arthurian romance. He did not, however, invent his hero, he simply made him what he is. His history of the Kings of Britain became the principal source of all the later Arthurian writings, but Geoffrey himself had sources, even if they were only sparse. The most important was Nennius's 'Historia Britonum'. Nennius was another Welsh monk, probably from Bangor, and in his chronicle, dating from around 800, there is the first known mention of an 'Artorius', some 300 years after his death, which was assumed to have followed the Battle of Camlan in 539. Nennius calls him the 'dux bellorum', the leader of the British army which defeated the Saxon invaders in 518 at the Battle of Badon Hill. The historical background is as follows: When the Romans left Britain at the beginning of the 5th century, Angles, Saxons and Picts all rushed in to fill the power vacuum. The Britons, now influenced by Roman culture and Irish missionary monks, fought bitterly to defend their way of life and their new faith against the heathen hordes. It was an age that needed heroes and created heroes. One of them emerged from all this turmoil with a charisma that outshone all the rest – a military commander and idol of the people: but was he 'Artorius'? Could he have been the same as Riothamus, the Britannic 'High King', as suggested recently by the historian Geoffrey Ashe?[2] Or was he a synthetic hero, symbolizing the heroic age and the corporate will to survive? Was he simply the archetypal early Christian knight, guardian of the Holy Grail? Certainly this is what King Arthur has become, but he remains an unknown quantity, a myth that became more and more real as the historical figure faded further and further into the past. Thus he lives on, whether he lived or not.

If there is a gap in history, the best way to fill it is with fiction. After all, whatever is in

---

1 It is worth mentioning Robert Bresson's film 'Lancelot du Lac', and 'Monty Python and the Holy Grail'. There is also an 'International Arthurian Society'.

2 In: 'The Discovery of King Arthur' (London, 1985). According to some researchers and theorists, the Arthurian legends stem from the Bronze Age and not the post-Roman, Christian Middle Ages (John Darrah: *Paganism and the Arthurian Romances*, New York, 1981).

writing must be true. And so minstrels from the court of Henry II spread Geoffrey's 'Historia' round the Continent. Chrétien de Troyes in France and Hartmann von Aue in Germany took up the theme, and created the great courtly epics that made the Celtic Arthur into the ideal knight of medieval Europe. What has come down to us is the topography of a never-ending story. The first authors came from Wales, but in the meantime all the Celts, from Scotland to Brittany, claim Arthur for themselves. His legendary tracks have provided the route for many a tour, and only the Devil has had more places named after him in Britain. His court was located in Camelot, but where was Camelot? In Wales, says Geoffrey of Monmouth, in Caerleon. In England, says Sir Thomas Malory, in Winchester. Malory wrote his 'Morte Darthur' c.1470, during the Wars of the Roses. Others placed Camelot elsewhere – Tintagel, for example, or Cadbury Castle. But Arthur's real country is the land of myth, and the more theories there are, the greater the fascination. Where was his last battle, where his grave? Popular belief in England is that the last battle was in Cornwall, but that he died and was buried in Glastonbury, Somerset. The Welsh tradition is equally definite (or indefinite): the battle against his treacherous nephew Mordred was fought at *Bwlch-y-Saethau* in Snowdonia, the pass of arrows. On the bank of the *Llyn Llydaw* at the foot of Snowdon a black bark was waiting, with three beautiful women who rowed the dying king out into the night to the Isle of Avalon. The faithful Merlin sank the crown jewels in *Llyn Cwmglas*, a fishless mountain lake above Llanberis Pass, and they were never seen again. Nor was the sword Excalibur, which Sir Bedivere threw into *Llyn Ogwen*, where an arm reached up from the depths and caught it. And King Arthur himself remained likewise wrapped in the mists of Avalon, which in Wales, it must be said, are particularly dense.

The Isle of Avalon remains a kind of national dream, a patriotic myth of liberty, and for the Welsh it was always associated with ideas of a Celtic second coming, and triumph over the Anglo-Saxons. When in 1485 after the Battle of Bosworth the Welsh Tudors came to power, the legendary hope seemed to have been fulfilled. Henry VII at once engaged the services of King Arthur for purposes of propaganda, but now as a symbol of integration, uniting the British kingdom. From then on Arthur's chances of spearheading separatist movements were severely curtailed, but for nationalist historians he still remained 'the Welsh-speaking hero who was not a Welshman'. For Gwynfor Evans this was Geoffrey of Monmouth's greatest achievement for his fellow countrymen: 'He reinforced their sense of a separate identity.'

Caerleon: From Roman Camp to Rocket Base

Geoffrey was a genius of local history. He transformed the ruins of a Roman camp into royal palaces with golden roofs, and a Welsh province into a second Rome: *Caerleon*, where Arthur was crowned and held his court. Some 700 years after Geoffrey's death, Lord Tennyson, in 1856, followed in his poetic footsteps. He stayed in the Hanbury Arms, a 16th-century inn, near the remains of the medieval docks: 'The Usk murmurs by the window and I sit like King Arthur at Caerleon.' And over a century later, the Usk still splashes beneath the window, and I sit like Lord Tennyson in the selfsame pub. But no-one here is bothered about Arthur or his followers; the talk is only of salmon and trout and other equally illustrious inhabitants of the Usk.

Time flows on like the Usk itself, but Tennyson's 'Idylls of the King' are happily still with us, even if they are not quite the best-seller that they were in 1859,[1] when the British flocked to read about this Celtic-knight-cum-Victorian-gentleman, and his court-cum-symbol of the British Empire. When the Poet Laureate visited Caerleon, his imagination was fired by a large, overgrown hill on the outskirts. It was called 'King Arthur's Round Table'. When archaeologists investigated this mound in 1926, what they discovered was almost as sensational as if they had found the Round Table itself, for it contained a Roman amphitheatre that was built around AD 80, at the same time as the Colosseum in Rome (plate 22). It is the only amphitheatre in Britain to have been excavated intact. The elliptical shape (180 by 135 feet) had eight vaulted entrances with earthwork walls, reinforced with masonry, some 30 feet high; these were sloping and once supported wooden stands. Here gladiators fought with bears and wolves, which were still to be found in Wales in those days: a bit of light entertainment to brighten the military routine. There was room for about 6,000 spectators – the whole garrison of Isca Silurum. The Usk[2] gave its name to the legionary camp beside the river of the defeated Silurians, while the Latin Castra Legionis in turn gave rise to Caerleon. Julius Frontinus, a Roman governor, founded Isca c.AD 75 as a base for the Second Augustan Legion. Caerleon in the south and Chester (Deva) in the north were the headquarters of the Romans, and were meant to secure access to Wales.

From the amphitheatre I walked across to the rugby pitch, once the parade ground for the legionaries. Next to it, neatly demarcated by the grass, are the foundations of the Roman barracks, which have been only partly excavated. Like all legionary camps, Isca was shaped like a playing card – a rectangle with rounded corners (1,600 by 1,350 feet), with four symmetrical gates, a main road running from west to east, and several parallel roads. Thus the groundplan of their settlements disseminated Roman principles to the furthest provinces: discipline, order, functionalism. The first rampart was made of earth, 10 feet high, with palisades and ditches; around AD 120 it was replaced by a stone wall twice as high. The via principalis, 25 feet wide, had a road-metal surface four layers thick, and gutters on the sides. This was road-building at its best. The road led into the heart of the camp, around which were grouped all the most important buildings: baths, drill hall,

---

1   In the first week alone, 10,000 copies were sold; by 1889 the cycle of the 12 Arthurian Romances was complete. Apart from Malory's 'Morte Darthur', the sources included the 'Mabinogion', which places Arthur's court in Cornwall. Tintagel, which both Tennyson and John Steinbeck visited during their research, proved to be the most popular target for Arthur-orientated tourists.

2   Usk, in Cymric 'Wysg', which means water – similar to the Gaelic word for whisky (uisge beatha, the 'water of life').

Caerleon: mask of Tragedy, with Phrygian cap,
2nd or 3rd century AD, in the Legionary Museum

hospital, store, workshops, granary (with enough supplies for two years). Behind lay the barracks for nine cohorts (infantry) and the cavalry: narrow blocks some 250 feet long, each one containing a century. A cohort consisted of six centuries, each of 100 men, who slept in twelve dormitories with separate chambers for weapons and uniforms. The barracks, built of stone some time after the second century AD, had blue-green windows and red pantiles. The rooms themselves were without heating. This, then, was where the legionnaires from the sunny south were made to live. They wore sandals, woollen tunics, and when necessary a chainmail coat and a bronze helmet. And they put up with this for a yearly salary of 300 denarii, while the captains were paid 5,000 and also froze.

Isca was not a frontline camp, but an administrative and supply base for a network of smaller camps. At the end of the 3rd century it was cleared, and Cardiff took over as the Roman headquarters in South Wales. Today most of Isca lies under the houses and gardens of Caerleon, and the former garrison has become a dormitory for nearby Newport. The streets do not follow the groundplan of the camp, but the walls of many of the houses still contain the old Roman blocks of sandstone. Other remnants, excavated since the middle of the 19th century, are to be seen in the Legionary Museum, which was once visited by Tennyson. The little Neo-Classical museum-cum-temple displays everyday items of camp life: oil lamps, nail-cleaners, tools, ornaments, gravestones and monuments, dental instruments, and a bronze finger from an emperor's statue. The more valuable finds made their way to the National Museum in Cardiff, but Caerleon is still the only place in Britain where one can see a Roman legionary bath.

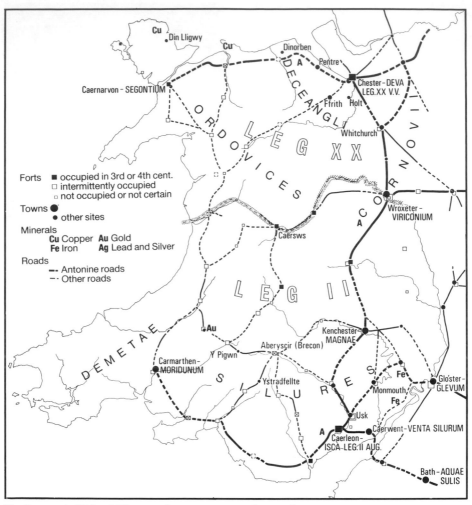

The Romans in Wales: Military roads, camps, towns and mineral resources

It took thirty years for the mighty imperial power of Rome to subjugate the little province of Wales. The Emperor Claudius sent four legions across the Channel in AD 46, but their advance through Wales was held up by a chain of hill fortresses[1] – more than anywhere else in Britain. The Celtic prince who organized the resistance of the Silurians in

---

1 In 1960 it was proved that there had been nearly 600 prehistoric hill forts in Wales. One of the biggest, Y Garn Goch in the Tywi Valley, at times had up to 4,000 inhabitants.

the south and the Ordovicians in the north-west was the first national hero of Wales: Caradog, son of Cynfelyn, Shakespeare's Cymbeline. In AD 78, Wales was conquered, and three dozen camps controlled the country, none of them more than a day's march (about 19 miles) away from the next. Without an efficient road system, this would not have been possible. At the peak of their occupation of Wales, the Romans had more than 30,000 men stationed there. Supplies must have been a major logistical problem. In Caerleon, for example, there was even grain from the Mediterranean.

Why did the Romans go to so much trouble and expense? Certainly not just for sheep-rearing. It was, of course, strategically necessary to secure the western side of England, but the real reason for the conquest was mineral resources. The spoils of victory, according to Tacitus, were 'gold, silver and other metals': gold from Dolaucothi, silver from Flintshire, copper from Anglesey and Llanymynech. The Romans stayed in Wales for 300 years, and when they finally pulled out in AD 383, they left behind a well organized country. Since the Emperor Caracalla's edict of AD 212, its people had been Roman citizens, with the same rights and duties as all other nations in the Roman Empire. Even if generally the artistic standards tended to lag behind those of the English province,[1] a far more important factor for the development of the country was the road network of over 750 miles, which bound the different areas together; these also provided the basis for the railways of the 19th century as well as many of our modern holiday routes. The Romans also contributed to the Welsh language, with a good thousand or so words that have been derived from Latin: *llyfr* comes from *liber* (book), *pont* from *pons* (bridge), *eglwys* from *ecclesia* (church); *corff* is related to *corpus* (body), *pyscodyn* to *piscis* (fish), *mur* to *murus* (wall) and *ffenestr* to *fenestra* (window); all this can be learnt at *ysgol*, which is not unlike the Latin *schola* (school). The Welsh did indeed learn a great deal from the Romans, and at least one Welsh patriot has been inspired to compare the benefits of those early colonial days with those of the more recent past: in his book 'Land of My Fathers' Gwynfor Evans has no doubt that the Imperium Romanum 'contributed more to our life than it took out: the British Empire took much more out than it put in'.

It might be said that with the end of the Roman occupation began the history of Welsh independence. There was even another national symbol, historically more tangible than King Arthur – a man who towered over these transitional years, and rejoiced in the name of Macsen Wledig, or Magnus Maximus. He was a Roman general, and in AD 383 he was proclaimed Emperor by a group of discontented legionnaires in Britain. Five years later, when he marched on Rome, his ambition led to his own death, but also to the withdrawal of the last occupying forces in Wales. As Eliseg's Pillar shows in *Valle Crucis*, the Princes of Powys and various other aristocratic Welsh families traced their lineage back to Macsen Wledig. Unfortunately, he left behind him a land whose sovereignty was under threat right

---

1   For instance, the mosaics of the Roman villa in Llantwit Major (2nd to 4th century) in South Glamorgan are much inferior to those in Lullingstone (Kent) or Fishbourne (Sussex).

from the start. What happened to Wales was what happens to so many colonies when they become independent. The end of Pax Romana meant the beginning of a ceaseless struggle for survival. A weak, Celtic-Christian province, still far from national unity, found itself suddenly under attack from five different heathen nations: the Jutes, the Angles, the Saxons, the Picts, and the Scots. Around the year AD 400, from the region that is now Scotland, there came a Breton warrior, Pictish by birth: Cunedda. Under his successors the Kingdom of Gwynedd became a leading power in the land. In the centuries that followed the withdrawal of the Romans, Wales came under the influence of Ireland, Cornwall, Scotland and Brittany, but not of England. Thus the Cymry developed their own Welsh culture, back to back, as it were, with their mighty Anglo-Saxon neighbours. And then in Caerleon and elsewhere, the Normans arrived, built their fortresses, and began a new Anglo-Welsh tradition. What started as an imposition then became a commonplace, but even today it remains in conflict with the old Cymric heart of the country.

If you want to reflect on the many changes that have taken place during Wales's history, there is no more melancholy setting for your thoughts than *Caerwent*. It was a warm summer's day when I wandered along the massive Roman walls, which reach up to sixteen feet in height. Children were throwing balls against the bulwarks, cows were grazing on the ramparts, and sheep were being sheared where once there had been a forum and a temple. An idyllic pastoral scene, perhaps, but built on ruins. Caerwent, Venta Silurum, was the only non-military Roman town in Wales, built at more or less the same time as the neighbouring military camp of Isca Silurum, Caerleon. After their conquest of the Silurians c. AD 75, the Romans forced them to move from their old hill fortress of *Llanmelin* to Caerwent, a mile to the south, and to adopt the new, Roman way of life. Thus began the Pax Romana, imposing here – as it did everywhere else – an urban culture on a community of shepherds and farmers. A rectangular network of roads split the 40 acres of land into 20 compartments (insulae), each containing three or four houses. Caerwent – from which is derived the county name of Gwent – probably had about 2,000 inhabitants and some 100 houses, many of them with mosaic floors and hypocaust heating, as has been revealed by excavation of an insula to the west of the forum (Pound Lane). The various finds are to be seen in the museum in Newport. But much of the settlement remains buried, as in Caerleon, beneath gardens and fields. The present main street follows the via principalis from what used to be the east gate to the west. The Roman road, however, was nearly 70 feet broad – three times the size of the modern one.

In recent times, Caerwent has been in the news for political rather than archaeological reasons. It became one of the biggest American rocket bases in Europe, and as such was the target for protest marches and peace demonstrations. During the Second World War British scientists worked here on the development of chemical weapons, while today RAF Caerwent is said to be the central European depot of poison gas for the American army. Pax Americana.

The Duke of York (George VI) tests the Newport Transporter Bridge, 1925

Newport: The Super Tramp and the Lords of Tredegar

A ferry that's afraid of water is in the wrong business. And a bridge you can't walk across can hardly be called a bridge. But when you get both combined, and their eccentricities are a matter of principle, what you end up with is an aerial ferry. The matchless joy of crossing a river in this unique manner is supplied by the Transporter Bridge in *Newport* (colour plate 29; plate 3). And that was the only reason why I stopped here.

On spidery legs the bridge stalks across the Usk, supported by four iron, lattice-work pillars each 250 feet high, visible from far away as they tower above the roofs of Newport. Resting between these pillars is an iron grille some 650 feet long, and running along this on sixty wheels is an electric trolley. Suspended from its steel cables hangs the platform itself, and this carries you slowly but surely from one bank to the other, at a safe height above the choppy brown waters of the Usk. Only Blondin's tightrope walk across the Niagara could compare for aesthetic quality. Why was this eccentric contraption built in the first place? At the turn of the century, the city fathers wanted better access to the industrial zone on the east bank of the Usk, and so they needed a new bridge to the docks. This, however, should not hinder shipping, and should also be able to resist the strong

The Chartists attack the Westgate Inn in Newport, 1839

tides, so that it needed to be very high. The best solution offered was that of the French engineer F. Arnodin. He had built the first aerial ferry in Portugalete, near Bilbao (1893), as well as the now defunct transporter bridge in the port of Marseilles. It was a popular type of bridge at that time – one of those symbols of progress denoting that there is no such thing as an unbridgeable gap. Newport Transporter Bridge (1902–06) is one of the last surviving specimens,[1] and even today it still combines the functional aesthetics of masterly engineering with the quaint charm of a working toy. The ferryman sits in his sky-blue cabin, roofed like a pagoda, and surveys the world like a river god.

When something becomes an industrial monument, that is usually a bad sign for the industry concerned. The Transporter Bridge is itself a reminder of better times, when the port at the mouth of the Usk was the major centre for the export of coal and iron from South Wales – even ahead of Cardiff. The measure of the boom can be gauged from the increase in population, from 1135 in 1801 to 67,000 in 1901. Today the population has virtually doubled again. In its heyday, in the middle of the 19th century, Newport exported nearly seven million tons of coal a year; now this has dwindled to a mere 300,000. But the town has not yet had to close down all its steelworks, and Newport is still one of Britain's biggest harbours for imports. New industries, particularly electronics, have revived the hopes and fortunes of the town. Its motto is *'Terra Marique'* – By Land, By Sea

---

1 Altogether there are just 16 transporter bridges left in the world; these include the Teeside Transporter Bridge in Middlesbrough (1911).

Augustus John: W. H. Davies, 1918

– and its heraldic animals, the lion and the dragon, symbolize the political changes that have marked the history of Anglo-Welsh relations.

One of the most dramatic chapters in this history was also a highlight of the early working-class movement in Britain: the Chartist uprising. The weavers of Montgomeryshire and Yorkshire, the cotton-mill workers of Lancashire, the miners of Northern England and Southern Wales – all felt alike that they had lost out in the Industrial Revolution. Together with groups from the middle classes, they fought for social reform and basic political rights. In 1838 they drew up a 'People's Charter' – hence the name Chartists – setting out their demands: universal male suffrage, secret ballots, equal electoral districts, abolition of the census, payment of MPs – for at the time there were property qualifications which ensured that only the rich could enter Parliament – and yearly elections. Today these demands of the Chartists, apart from the last, are all standard democratic practice. But at that time, they led to bloody conflicts. In Wales the movement also had nationalistic undertones, for the Welsh-speaking Chartists saw themselves as fighting factory-owners and bureaucrats who were, for the most part, English. Brilliant orators like Henry Vincent fanned the flames of class war: 'When the time for resistance comes, let your cry be "To your tents, O Israel", and then with one heart, one voice and one blow perish the privileged orders! Death to the aristocracy!' One rainy November night in 1839 about 7,000 South Wales Chartists, mostly miners, marched from the valleys to Newport. Their demonstration ended outside the Westgate Hotel: soldiers fired into the crowd, killing 24 people and injuring countless others, and subsequently there was a political show trial which Michael Foot has called 'the biggest class-war clash of the century'. Queen Victoria bestowed a knighthood on the man who gave the order to fire, and the leaders of the Chartists, the chief of whom was John Frost, former mayor of Newport, were sentenced to death by hanging and quartering for having committed high treason. This draconian sentence was eventually transmuted into lifelong deportation. Not until 1854 did an amnesty permit the exiles to return from Australia. Today John Frost Square in Newport's town centre commemorates the Chartists' uprising, and this – the last real workers' rebellion in British history – is fully documented in Newport's museum. And it was there that, in addition to a splendid collection of British watercolours from the 18th and 19th centuries, I discovered the Super-tramp.

'What is this life if, full of care, / We have no time to stand and stare.' The poet who wrote these lines not only took the time to gaze at the wonders of everyday life, but he also gave himself the freedom to go wherever he pleased. William Henry Davies was his name, and he was a Welsh descendant of the legendary French criminal-poet François Villon. Davies was a tramp-poet, who lived and wrote about life as an outsider long before the beatniks and hippies were even thought of. At the age of 22 he sailed to America on a cattle steamer, and spent five years wandering through the country doing casual labour, before he lost a leg in 1899 trying to jump on board a goods train, whereupon he returned home. Next he limped and begged his way round England on his wooden leg, trying to get enough money to print his first volume of poems, which no-one wanted to publish: 'The Soul's Destroyer' (1905). In these poems he described, quite realistically and without sentiment, his various experiences with hoboes and prostitutes, with Molly, Kitty, Frisco Fatty and Red-nosed Scotty. Then in 1908 his masterpiece was published: 'Autobiography of a Super-Tramp', with an admiring foreword by Shaw. This opened up the salons of Vita Sackville-West, Edith Sitwell, Ottoline Morrell and many other society ladies curious to meet the great drop-out. For London's sophisticated literati Davies, like Dylan Thomas many years later,[1] personified the exotic charm of these Welsh forces of Nature. But Davies was not born to be a social lion. In London he found himself homesick for Wales, but in Wales he found himself disorientated, not least because he hardly spoke a word of Welsh. Even Welsh dogs, he noted bitterly, refused to make friends with someone who only spoke English. And so he settled down within seeing distance of his home, in the Cotswolds, where he died in 1940, a tramp on whom the University of Wales had bestowed an honorary doctorate. In his poem 'Selfish Hearts' W. H. Davies offered the following ironic advice to the rich: 'Weep for the poor / You find in books: / From living poor / Avert your looks.'

Some strange people have come from Newport, Steve Strange, for one, who started out as a punk, and became a millionaire in London, setting trends in the Camden Palais. Yet how can even Strange's glittering discos compare with *Tredegar House* and the exotic

---

1 Dylan Thomas held W. H. Davies in the highest esteem. 'There was inevitability in his slightest verses; unique observation in his tiniest reflections on the natural world. His most famous poems are about birds and clouds and animals, the journeying of the planets and the seasons, the adventure of the coming and going of simple night and day.' (Welsh Poets, 1946)

parties Evan Morgan used to hold there? Lackeys in rococo livery served the guests, boxing kangaroos entertained them, and the guest-list included Chaplin, Caruso, Nancy Cunard of luxury liner fame, artists and writers like Evelyn Waugh, H. G. Wells and Augustus John, and even the artistic mole Anthony Blunt was there when, in the 1930's, Tredegar House enjoyed its golden days. With glamorous feasts and remarkable journeys the fourth Viscount Tredegar squandered the family fortunes of the Morgans. They it was who had founded Newport and owned much of the town and its docks. They were landowners and born businessmen, like Sir Charles Gould, who was quicker than most to recognize the potential of the Industrial Revolution, and whose success in building mines and ironworks, canals and railways, was so great that his grandson Sir Godfrey Charles Morgan in 1908 became one thousand pounds richer every day. The last Morgan of Tredegar died in 1962 in the tax haven and gambler's paradise of Monte Carlo. He had already sold up the family seat and most of its art treasures. 'Only one plate survived all those dinner parties,' said the guide, and pointed sadly to a lone blue treasure.

What remained is nevertheless the most splendid country house in South Wales. Its core goes back to an older Elizabethan manor which Sir William Morgan rebuilt on a grand scale after 1664. No-one knows who the architect was. This was the time of the restoration of the Stuarts, and the whole country was enjoying the new opulence that followed the grim austerity of the Puritans. The simple exterior of Tredegar House is a modest cover for the glories of the state apartments. The façade is symmetrical with projections at the sides, a portal with twisted columns and a split gable – motifs of the Italian baroque – and stone garlands and fruits beneath the first floor windows – another imported motif familiar from the Mauritshuis in the Hague and from the City Hall in Amsterdam. Another Dutch feature – certainly unusual in Wales at the time – is the use of bricks, occasionally combined with limestone. Grouped round an inner courtyard are the state apartments, the service areas and the servants' quarters. (In the 18th century there were about 50 servants.) The Lords of Tredegar lived in exquisite salons, Flemish and French in style, beneath ceilings of gilded stucco and surrounded by ornate wooden panels. It was to be a feast for all the senses, not just the eyes: an elegant closet on the first floor is panelled entirely in cedar, a precious wood prized especially for its fragrance. Beneath the cedars in the garden rest the family pets, Peeps and Friday, two faithful dogs, as well as Sir Briggs, the horse which Captain Godfrey Morgan rode in 1854 in the Crimean War, when he took part in the attack on Balaclava, the legendary Charge of the Light Brigade. The former stables with their brick pilasters (c.1690–1725) today house an aquarium, which is part of Newport's great leisure park: the town took over Tredegar House in 1974 and restored it beautifully, including the baroque railings round the park by William Edney (1714–18). Equally exemplary is the new estate between the country house and the industrial zone: Dyffryn Estate, in the west of Newport, was built in the 1970's, with meandering, one-storey terrace houses, and pedestrianized paths and squares – a model of good social and architectural planning.

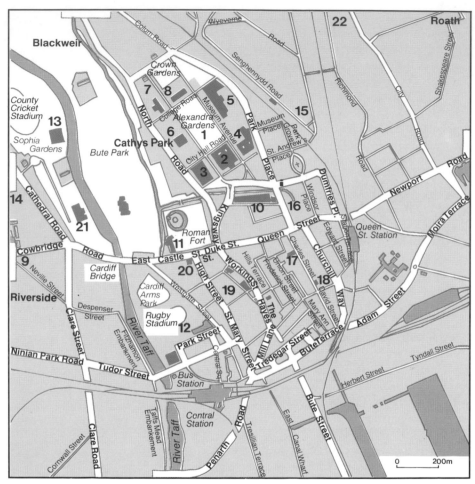

Cardiff. *1 Welsh National War Memorial 2 City Hall 3 Law Courts 4 National Museum of Wales 5 University 6 County Hall 7, 8 Temple of Peace and Health and Welsh Office 9 Chapter Arts Centre 10 Municipal Buildings and City Information Centre 11 Castle 12 Cardiff Arms Park, Stadium 13 National Sports Centre 14 Llandaff Cathedral 15 Sherman Theatre 16 New Theatre 17 St David's Cathedral 18 Welsh Arts Council 19 St John's Church 20 WTB Information Centre 21 Sophia Gardens Pavilion (conference centre) 22 Welsh Regiment Museum*

Cardiff: The Delayed Capital

Was it an honour, a farce, or a mere formality? Whatever it was, everyone agreed that it was high time (if not too late) when in 1955 Queen Elizabeth II declared *Cardiff* to be the capital of Wales (colour plate 40; plates 5–8, 13). The national flag followed in 1959. The

Welsh had to wait until 1985 for their own pound coin; unlike the Scots they are still waiting for their own bank notes. In contrast to colonial independence, the promotion of Cardiff to the status of a capital meant nothing politically. Wales is still governed by London, and Cardiff is merely an administrative centre. Any Swiss canton has more regional autonomy than Wales. Nevertheless, the city on the Taff plays its role as Europe's newest capital with all the aplomb of an ancient nation, even if state receptions still take place on the Thames.

Cardiff is a port, and as such it thinks of itself in cosmopolitan rather than smalltown terms. But its patriotism is often fiercely parochial: 'I'm Cardiff born and I'm Cardiff bred / When I'm gone I'll be Cardiff dead', sing the Hennessys, a popular group whose typical Cardiff accent is harder and throatier than the more melodious tones of their Swansea neighbours. Swansea and every other major town in Wales had laid claim to becoming the capital, and most of them had better historical justification for their claims. In their eyes, Cardiff was a town without a past, a nouveau riche fishing village which made a career for itself in the 19th century as a coal port, and did not even receive a town charter until 1905. But what rival could really claim any sort of capital tradition in the manner of, say, London or Edinburgh? The nearest equivalent would in fact have been an English frontier town – Ludlow, in Shropshire, which until 1689 had been seat of the Council of Wales and the Marches. Indeed for some time the judges in this legal and administrative district, a sort of precursor of the Welsh Office, actually planned to make Ludlow part of Wales and to have it named as capital. Provincial ambitions born out of and nourished by a national dilemma.[1]

'Wild Wales' had neither a political nor a geographical centre. In the middle of the country there were moors, with no trace of any capital. Nature dictated that the centres should develop, so to speak, at the edges: the kings of Gwynedd resided for centuries in Aberffraw, a village in Anglesey; Machynlleth was the seat of Owain Glyndwr's first Welsh parliament; the great national institutions were established in Aberystwyth – though not before time: the University of Wales (1893) and the National Library (1907). The National Museum, however, went to Cardiff. There is no Welsh National Theatre (no doubt partly owing to language problems), but there is an internationally renowned Welsh National Opera, even though it has no permanent home of its own. The Royal National Eisteddfod in its way symbolizes this decentralization as it moves each year between North and South Wales as a peripatetic capital of Welsh culture. So Cardiff became the centre of a decentralized country, favoured above all for its convenience in matters of transport and administration. Welsh nationalism still has no real centre nonetheless. How many people know that No. 51 Cathedral Road is the headquarters of Plaid Cymru? How many people even know where Cathedral Road is? And yet the heart of the nation certainly beats loudest in Cardiff – at *Cardiff Arms Park* in Westgate Street. That is the true centre of the city, and so hallowed is this rugby ground that fathers are said to bring their newborn sons

1 In 1634 Milton's pastoral entertainment 'Comus' was performed at Ludlow Castle, in the presence of the Earl of Bridgewater, Lord President of Wales. It contains the oft quoted line about the Welsh: 'An old, and haughty nation proud in arms'.

here to baptize them in grass made wet with the sweat of the Welsh and the tears of the English. And when it came to putting up a statue in the middle of the new St David's shopping centre, what better choice could there have been than the great scrum-half Gareth Edwards? If only the Welsh could produce a national drink, like Scotch Whisky, to match the glories of their rugby stars, their national identity would be complete. Could Brains Bitter, brewed in Cardiff, really fit the bill?

When I arrived in Cardiff, coming from the valleys of the north, my first impression was of a garden city rather than a capital. Where else do you reach the town centre through four miles of parkland? What the Romans would have called 'rus in urbe' extends from Llandaff Cathedral along the banks of the Taff to Cardiff Castle. Bute Park, a favourite picnic area for Cardiffians in summer, is just part of 2,700 acres of green in this 'City of Parks'. In the most popular of all, Roath Park, there is a large lake with a lighthouse erected as a monument to Robert Scott, who left Cardiff in the 'Terra Nova' on his fatal, last expedition to the Antarctic. Another spacious park contains the city's magnificent Civic Centre. It's in Cathays Park, and is nicknamed 'Welsh Washington', although it must be said that a dome doesn't make a Capitol. Cardiff's White Houses in the green constitute neither a genuine seat of government nor a real urban centre – they seem to claim capital status, but at the same time betray a lack of capital tradition. They look impressive, and yet they have the aura of sterility that surrounds so much purpose-built government architecture. The Cardiff architect John B. Hilling rightly compares the Civic Centre to one of those permanent building exhibitions – 'an unusually fine collection of Neo-Classical buildings of the early 20th century.'

The Civic Centre did not evolve; it was planned. At its heart stands the Welsh National War Memorial (1928), a circular temple with a colonnaded ambulatory. Around this, in Alexander Gardens, are grouped a dozen public buildings, the chief of which is the City Hall (1901–5), with its domed hall and 185-foot-high belltower, whose baroque top is pure wedding cake (plates 6, 7). The gleaming white Portland stone of the façade, with its allegorical figures, the staircase with its columns of Siena marble, and the gallery with its statues of Welsh heroes[1] – all these reflect the richness of Cardiff at the time when it was the biggest coal-exporting port in the world. The City Hall is flanked by the lawcourts and the National Museum. Behind is the main building of the University, and opposite is the neoclassical Glamorgan County Hall (1912). The first section of University College was opened in 1909, but building continued until 1962, with correspondingly disparate results. Classical Philology is one of the University's specialities, which would no doubt appeal to Prince Charles, who is the University's Chancellor. Some 7,000 students are registered here and at the Institute of Science and Technology. Next door is the Temple of Peace, consecrated in 1938 on the eve of the Second World War; this grew from the ideals of

1 These 'Heroes of Wales', erected in 1916, and sculptured by Goscombe John and others, include St David, Hywel Dda, Llywelyn II, Giraldus, Henry VII, and Owain Glyndwr.

Henry Richards of Tregaron, the Welsh apostle of peace, who dreamed of a genuine League of Nations. Opposite, and built in the same year, is the Temple of Health, which is now the headquarters of the Welsh Office.[1] The Welsh were not given a Ministry of their own until 1951 (compared to the Scots, whose Ministry goes back to 1885). The modern annexe of the Welsh Office seems to me to be thoroughly off-putting – bureaucratic architecture built to keep the public out rather than welcome them in. One is therefore relieved to turn to the *National Museum*.

This was founded in 1912, opened in 1927, and is still not finished. Nevertheless, it admirably fulfils its task: 'to teach the world about Wales, and the Welsh people about their own fatherland.' Nowhere could one be more vividly informed about the geology, botany and zoology of the country, and its prehistory and its industry. There is even a faithful reconstruction of part of a coalmine in which one can experience for oneself the methods and the arduousness of the work. In one darkened room is a spectacular, prize acquisition: four monumental tapestry cartoons by Rubens, with themes from Virgil's 'Aeneid', purchased in 1979 at vast expense, but now, alas, deemed to be of questionable authenticity. One should not, however, go to Cardiff to see Rubens or not-Rubens. Despite its magnificent gallery of old masters (Cranach, Bellini, Claude Lorrain, Rembrandt, Gainsborough etc.), what is unique to this museum is its collection of Welsh artists, from Richard Wilson, through Augustus and Gwen John, to Ceri Richards – plus the superb Davies collection. The fact that Cardiff boasts masterpieces by Corot and Daumier, Rodin, Renoir, Monet, Cézanne and others is due to the sisters Gwendoline and Margaret Davies. At the beginning of this century their country house Gregynog Hall (see page 294) housed what was then the biggest collection of French Impressionists and Post-Impressionists in the world, and this is without a doubt one of the highlights of the Welsh National Museum.

But art is not confined to the museum. In a former girls' school in the district of Canton is a most unconventional, multi-faceted art forum known as the *Chapter Arts Centre*, with theatre, cinema, concerts, workshops and art exhibitions. Somewhat less impressive is the new prestige complex of *St David's Hall* (1982), a multi-storey cultural centre linked to a shopping centre, with something different on every floor, but in no way a cultural showcase for things Welsh.

All the same, Cardiff is rich in good architecture. It is a pleasure simply to stroll through the arcades in the town centre – shopping in Victorian style. On both sides of St Mary Street are examples of these partly two-storeyed passages. The façade of Queen Street Arcade (1870) offers a surprising display of Venetian Gothic – a sort of Doge's Palace in Cardiff (plate 5). Non-Conformist in all respects is the Methodist Chapel in Crwys Road, *Heol y Crwys* (1899), a mixture of romantic, medieval fortress and Flemish baroque, and an eccentric late flourish from Welsh chapel-builders (plate 41). Cathedral Road, with its

---

1 The Minister of Wales, who used to be responsible for other matters as well, became Secretary of State for Wales in 1964.

various Neo-Gothic and Neo-Classical façades, is a fascinating gallery of late Victorian terraced housing. This street leads up to Llandaff Cathedral.

For centuries the 'Place on the Taff' was an independent market town. And even now, as part of Cardiff, *Llandaff* still retains its own special character, with an atmosphere of garden city and middle class prosperity. Like all Welsh cathedrals, this one is small compared to English cathedrals, and like St David's it stands in a dip, as if it were trying to hide from the big bad world. St Teilo, the Celtic missionary, is said to have founded a monastery here in the middle of the 6th century. The early Christian church is commemorated only by a high Celtic cross (10th century) in the southern aisle of the chancel. Little is left also of the Norman cathedral, begun in 1120, other than the north and south portals, the noble Romanesque chancel arch with its four zigzag bands, and reminders of the fact that two of Wales's greatest ecclesiastical figures were associated with Llandaff: Geoffrey of Monmouth who was archdeacon here until his death in 1154, and Giraldus Cambrensis who preached the Third Crusade here in 1188, together with Archbishop Baldwin of Canterbury. The nave was extended in early Gothic style, and in 1220 the twin-towered west façade was built with its three large lancet windows; the chapterhouse and Lady Chapel followed soon after, but it was not until the end of the 15th century that the massive north-west Jasper Tudor Tower was added, in Perpendicular style. Wars and storms took their toll, the worst destruction being caused by a German bomb in 1941, but astonishingly this cathedral, next to Coventry the most badly damaged of all British cathedrals, rose again. The chief architect, George Pace, remained scrupulously faithful to the original, but at one point he evidently decided that it was time for a bit of innovation: where previously a screen had separated choir and nave, these are now straddled by a parabolic arch of concrete which bears a cylindrical organ-case. The whole thing is like a space capsule on a launching pad, and towering over it is a monumental figure by the English sculptor Jacob Epstein. His 'Christ in Majesty' combines the asceticism of Romanesque sculpture with the material of the modern technical age: aluminium. But for my taste, the whole construction is a modernistic slap in the face, murder in the cathedral. A much more convincing addition was made in the 19th century by the Pre-Raphaelites. For the high altar, now situated beneath the north-west tower, Rossetti painted a triptych (1856–64) in which he depicted his Pre-Raphaelite artist friends Edward Burne-Jones, William Morris and his wife Jane, and the poet Swinburne as 'Seeds of David'.[1] Rossetti's wife Elizabeth Siddal in her turn acted as Burne-Jones's model for the angels in his porcelain relief 'The Six Days of Creation' in the north aisle. There are also several Pre-Raphaelite windows in the south aisle. And in their billowing red robes, black capes and white ruffs there is almost something Pre-Raphaelite about the choirboys as they race across the Cathedral Close and through the gatehouse of the former Bishop's

---

1 Rossetti also designed the sedilia with the pelican sculptures. John Piper designed the 'Emmaus' window above the High Altar.

28 PONTYPRIDD John Hughes, potter ▷

29   HAY-ON-WYE   Richard Booth, Book King

31   BARRY ISLAND   Jack Crabtree, painter, with his portrait of a miner 'Big Eric' ▷

30   LLANDWROG   Dafydd Iwan, folk and political singer

32 MAESYRONEN CHAPEL United Reformed Church service

33 MAESYRONEN CHAPEL Barn Chapel, *c.*1697

34   Swansea   Lillian Rose Pryse-Griffiths, curator of Tabernacle Chapel (1873) in Morriston

35   Porth   Ebenezer, 1903: Chapel in the Valleys

36 ABERYSTWYTH Unitarian Chapel, c.1812

37 MONMOUTH

38 RHYMNEY Tabernacl, 1871

39 LLANIDLOES Zion, 1878

40 CARDIGAN Tabernacl, 1870

41 CARDIFF Capel Heol y Crwys, 1899

43 MERTHYR TYDFIL Bethesda, 1880

44 BLAENAU FFESTINIOG Chapel garage, 1906

42 CRICCIETH Berea, 1886

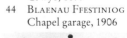

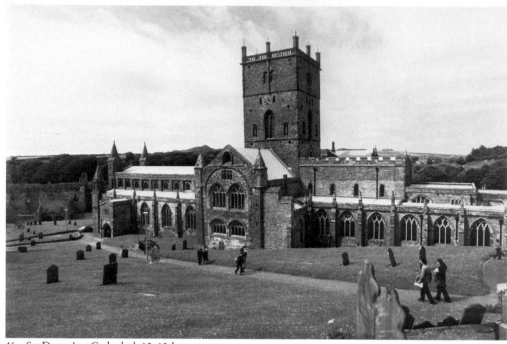

46   St. David's   Cathedral, 12–13th century
◁ 45   Blaenau Ffestiniog   Chapel studio of sculptor David Nash
47   St. Asaph   Cathedral, 14th century

48 St. Govan's Head   St. Govan's Chapel, 11–13th century

50 Tenby   Seaside resort in Carmarthen Bay ▷

49 Corwen   Llangar Church, 14th century

51 LLANGURIG Sheepdog Trials, 'tossing the bar'

52 LLYN TRAWSFYNYDD Restful fishing at the nuclear power station

53   LLANDOVERY   Mid Wales Women's Bowling Association, President's Day tournament

54 ANGLESEY The longest place name in Wales

55 SWANSEA Beer advertisement

56 MACHYNLLETH   Bed & Breakfast

57 BARMOUTH   Take Five

Palace. Llandaff Cathedral Choir School, which dates back to the 9th century, is the only boys' choir school in Wales.

The way back into town leads along the Taff and through *Bute Park*. This was designed in 1777 by the landscape gardener Capability Brown, and is a legacy from the Marquesses of Bute. It was they who laid the foundations of modern Cardiff, for during the 19th century they owned much of the town and of the surrounding valleys. The massive coal deposits had made them into one of the richest families in Britain. They owned mansions in Wales. Scotland and Spain, but they also used their immense wealth to promote art and to develop the town of Cardiff. In 1801 this contained a bare 1,000 inhabitants, whereas by 1901 it had grown to over 164,000, and today has well over a quarter of a million. What began as an obscure little market town on the Taff grew into the largest port and trading centre in Wales. What the first Marquess of Bute began with a canal, his son completed with the docks. The Glamorganshire Canal (which has long since been filled in) was opened in 1794 to transport coal from the valleys to the coast. This was a much faster, cheaper and simpler method than using mules, which had hitherto done all the carrying from the mines around Merthyr Tydfil, along the rough tracks, and down into the valley. The 2nd Marquess of Bute began the construction of large-scale docks in 1839, and from here Welsh coal made its triumphant journey out into the waiting world. Soon afterwards, King Coal made its way out of the valleys on the railways, and Cardiff became the world's biggest port for the export of coal and iron. But all this came to an end in 1939. Newport, Port Talbot and Swansea – bigger ports, with oil refineries and steelworks – took Cardiff's place. Even the neighbouring docks of Penarth and Barry have a bigger turnover than King Coal's former capital. Of *Butetown* and its boom, nothing remains except the name.

If you walk down the seemingly endless Bute Street from the town centre to the port, you will see the reverse side of Bute Park: it's a no-man's-land full of derelict sites or, at best, melancholy estates which have replaced the old slums. 'Tiger Bay', the notorious district which once attained fame as the setting for a film of that name, has gone, but the new Butetown is at least on its way, with a huge project including a controversial wall across the bay. But what still reigns supreme here is the melancholy of idleness, settling like a pall over what used to be. The docks are closed, and an old Norwegian seamen's chapel stands desolate in its corrugated iron frame. At the side of Bute Street, between the rows of terraced houses, the dome of a new mosque shines out like a gold tooth. Butetown might have become the seat of a Welsh National Assembly, for if the referendum of 1979 had resulted in a vote for devolution, the new parliament would have been housed in the splendid, wood-panelled hall of the former Coal Exchange. Built in 1883–86, this and various other Victorian fossils grouped round Mount Stuart Square still display something of the urban flair that marked the turn of the century, when Cardiff was second only to Liverpool as Britain's largest international port. On the crumbling quayside the Pierhead Building still stands in all its glory, erected in 1896 as the headquarters of the Bute Docks

◁ 58 LLANGEFNI   National Eisteddfod, sword-bearer and Mistress of the Robes

Company, and still marking time with its crenellated clocktower. The brick façade contains the Bute coat-of-arms with its motto: *Wrth Ddwr a Thân* – Through Fire and Water, and above these words, the mighty emblems of progress, the steamship and the railway engine (plate 8). And so the symbols of progress nostalgically survive the decline of what they stood for. Where now are the coals of Bute and the ships of Tiger Bay?

Where there's death the vultures will gather, but in really civilized places, museums clear up the carrion. The *Welsh Industrial and Maritime Museum* (1977) found an ideal position for itself in the docks of Butetown. There are diesel motors and model ships and, in a place all of its own, a pioneer of the machine age – a replica of the famous Penydarren Locomotive, which in 1804 honoured the valleys with the first successful railway journey in the world (see page 149).

What are the people of Cardiff really like? You can hardly call them city-dwellers, but nor are they really provincials. Small-town folk with a cosmopolitan spirit, perhaps. Traders, civil servants, descendants of businessmen and longshoremen, with coal-dust, balance-sheets and Brains Bitter in their blood? In the 'Golden Cross', a pub between Butetown and the City, a docker told me a joke: 'A man from Cardiff is due to be hanged, see, and it's pissing with rain. On the way to the gallows, he's chattin' away with the hangman, and the hangman says to him: "It's all right for you, boyo, but I've got to walk all the b . . . . y way back!"'

Victorian Dreams of Chivalry: William Burges and Lord Bute

Peacocks squawk on the battlements, while traffic roars round the walls: this is *Cardiff Castle* (colour plates 33, 40; plates 9–12, 14) right in the heart of the city. It's not really one castle, but three – a Roman camp, a Norman fortress, and a Victorian fairytale palace. Like the Russian dolls that contain dolls that contain dolls, Cardiff Castle reveals one splendour after another, each emerging from the long shadow of history to display its glories. The

Samuel and Nathaniel Buck: Cardiff Castle from the north-west, 1741

William Burges: Design for a Capital, Summer Smoking Room, Cardiff Castle, 1872

Romans came here in AD 76, and gave the place its name: Caer-Dyff, castrum on the Taff. In 1081, Count Robert Fitzhamon, a follower of William the Conqueror, settled himself down on the foundations of this camp, whose high walls were reconstructed in the 19th century. The late 12th-century Norman keep – a classic example of this type of structure – was built on an artificial mound, and it was from here that the conquerors could keep watch over the fertile valley of Glamorgan and the rest of South Wales. When times became more peaceful, the lords of the manor turned their attention to matters of comfort, and in the middle of the 15th century a residence with a great hall was built in the south-west corner of the Roman camp. This was modernized in 1777 by Henry Holland, son-in-law of Capability Brown, and architect to the Prince of Wales, later George IV. But the golden age for Cardiff Castle came with the meeting of two Victorian eccentrics: one the heir to millions, and the other the brilliant heir to art history – and both of them crazy about the Middle Ages. They were Lord Bute and William Burges, the fairytale prince and his magician.

John Patrick Crichton Stuart, 3rd Marquess of Bute, was not only reputed to be the richest man in Britain but was also, in addition to being the owner of Bute Docks, an expert on heraldry and Coptic church history, translator of Turgenev and the Roman breviary, and a critic of contemporary Russian literature, Celtic history, and the works of Richard Wagner. This eminent Victorian, arch-Conservative, Catholic convert, and model for the hero of his friend Benjamin Disraeli's novel 'Lothair' (1870) had a dream: Cardiff Castle was to be the home of the Grail, the apogee of medieval courtly culture. For the fulfilment of this dream, he could not have found a better partner than William Burges: born in London in 1827, son of an engineer, widely travelled, highly cultured, a lifelong bachelor, eccentric and luxury-loving, who declared that he had grown up with a 13th-century faith, and intended to die the same way. Back to the Middle Ages, that was his battlecry, for the present was ugly and banal. Back to handicraft, for industrial products were devoid of style and imagination. William Burges was a Romantic in the machine age, inspired by the novels of Walter Scott, the Gothic of Pugin, and the theories of Carlyle and Ruskin. But he did not build in order to save souls; his object was to entertain himself. He was an aesthete, not a social reformer – a medievalist and a fanatic collector of medieval

William Burges, 1881

weapons and illuminated manuscripts. He made Pre-Raphaelite furniture, and his 'Medieval Court' at the World Exhibition in London in 1862 caused a sensation. Burges designed everything: cathedrals and country houses, dog-collars and door-locks, teapots and chamberpots, bottles and brooches, carafes and carpets and crucifixes, beds and benches, knives and forks … He used all materials, but preferred the most precious: marble with silver inlay, amber, bronze and painted wood were not too grand for a washstand in the guest-room of his house in Kensington.[1] He was master of foreign styles and periods, as of personal fantasy – Byzantine and Pompeian, Renaissance and Islamic, Roman Antique and French Gothic were all employed with equal facility. And so he became guardian of the past, precursor of the Arts and Crafts Movement, high priest of the Victorian Dream, and Lord Bute's architect.

Shortly after his first major commission in 1866, Cork Cathedral, William Burges began work on the west wing of Cardiff Castle. His spectacular design – he extended two towers and built two new ones – reveals his predilection for the dramatic, as well as his sure geometrical touch and his love of allusion. The many towers of medieval Nüremberg, the campaniles in Florence and Siena, the papal palace in Avignon, and the Tower of London are all god-parents to the towers of Cardiff Castle. The allegorical statues of the planets and the signs of the zodiac shine out from the façade of the clocktower (1869), heralding the mass of colours and figures to be found in the interior of the castle. Every tower has its own iconographic pattern, and every room its own theme. The murals and stained glass windows of the octagonal Chaucer Room depict the Canterbury Tales; the Arabian salon, with its cedarwood panelling, marble, and gilt coffered dome, exudes an atmosphere of oriental

1 Burges' Tower House (1875–81) in Melbury Road, London, can still be visited. For the Chief Engineer of Bute Docks, Cardiff, Burges designed the Neo-Gothic McConnochie's House, Park Place (1871–74).

Cardiff Castle, Cupolas in the Arab Room by William Burges, 1880–81

splendour, half harem and half mosque; on consoles at the entrance to the Library, monkeys fight over a book, and between the statues of poets, philosophers and kings, the architect has placed his patron, Lord Bute, dressed in the robes of a Celtic scholar.[1] For the children of the family there were rooms with labyrinthine floors and lettered tiles, while the wood panels contain inlays of all the plants in the country. It is said that there was once a table with a vine growing through it – the Butes were born with silver spoons and grapes in their mouths.

Cardiff Castle is an unending source of joy, eccentric and eclectic, a sophisticated mixture of the oriental and the catholic, the exotic and the religious. It is a triumph of 19th-century romanticism, not so much to be lived in as to be admired – a masterpiece on a truly Wagnerian scale. Its ancestors are perhaps Fonthill Abbey and Xanadu, Beckford's grandiose Neo-Gothic palace and Coleridge's 'stately pleasure dome'. Burges and his helpers went to extremes: walls, ceilings, windows and furniture are all bursting with heraldic colour, as he had imagined medieval interiors to be. Together with Rossetti, Burne-Jones and other Pre-Raphaelites he created the earliest examples of painted Neo-Gothic furniture, and he designed cupboards with quatrefoils, finials, gables and ramparts, as massive as fortresses, each narrating its own story. His ornate fireplaces are like studio theatres, though they warmed as well as entertained. Burges' design was without doubt one of the more esoteric expressions of the Victorian soul. During the 1930's, when the pomp and this literary furniture and this rhetorical ornamentation was no longer in fashion, Evelyn Waugh, the great novelist and – like Bute – a convert, surrounded himself with Burges's work. And the Victoria and Albert Museum in London also collected it avidly. But nowhere is it to be seen to greater effect than in the setting for which it was made.

1   Most of the sculptures, and also the stone animals on the park wall, were designed by Burges and executed by his sculptor Thomas Nicholls.

*William Burges: Cupboard, mahogany
and pine, painted and gilt, 1858*

The Butes continued to live in Cardiff Castle until 1947, but then they moved to their Scottish home, Mount Stuart on the Isle of Bute. Today, when the 6th Marquess visits the old family residence, he always uses the luxurious bedroom of his great-grandfather, and the bath with its 60 different sorts of marble tiles. Now anyone can dine here surrounded by Burges' decorations and sitting beneath the angels that hover from the wooden beams: for just a few hundred pounds, you can hire the banqueting hall and be Lord of the Castle for an evening (plate 10). In the adjoining room, the Scottish painter Harry Holland continued the tradition of Burges's murals with entrancing realism (1982): for the first time, however, it is not the conquering English that take the stage, but Owain Glyndwr's rebels, who captured the town and the castle in 1404. And further Welsh glory is celebrated in the Welsh Regiment Museum, covering 250 years of unbroken Celtic heroism, up to and including the Falklands War, in which the famous regiment suffered heavy and disproportionate losses.

The passion for the past which brought Burges and Lord Bute together had some strange consequences. While the 'King of the Goths' sat at home in London, wearing medieval clothes and planning to turn the interior of St Paul's Cathedral into a Byzantine orgy of coloured marble and mosaics, his Welsh patron was collecting ruined castles and restoring them. Thus Falkland Palace, the Stuarts' hunting lodge in Scotland, was saved from ruin, and whatever was too far gone to be saved would be recreated by Billy Burges, who would make it even better than the original. For example, Castell Coch, in the hills north-west of Cardiff (plate 73), was nothing but a pile of stones lying on its 13th century foundations when Burges was called upon in 1875; by the time Lord Bute moved in (1891) it had become a Welsh Neuschwanstein. 'Mad' King Ludwig II was not the only one to have been inspired by medieval fairytales, for the French architect Viollet-le-Duc had already re-constructed medieval fortresses and towns, such as Carcassonne and Château de Pierrefonds (for Napoleon III). But for sheer erudition and imagination, combined with an unmistakably individual style, William Burges – himself an admirer of the Frenchman – surely stands out on his own, and of all his achievements, the greatest are surely to be found in Wales.

If you go from the Taff Valley to the village of *Tongwynlais*, between the trees on the hill-side you will see the pointed turrets of Castell Coch, the 'Red Castle', so called because of its former red sandstone walls of the earlier castle. Burges enhanced this already romantic set-ting with picturesque architecture that is superficially reminiscent of older models such as Château Chillon on Lake Geneva. On the triangular-shaped foundations of the old castle, Burges built three massive round towers, all slightly different in height and shape, with conical roofs that seem almost to submerge the high chimneys. The walls, ten feet thick at the base, are steep and solid, punctuated with embrasures and narrow Gothic windows; there is a brattice over the castle gate. If a Welsh knight were to come riding out of the 13th century, across the drawbridge and into the cobbled courtyard, he would feel perfectly at home here. But if he then went into the castle itself, he'd get a shock, because he'd find himself in the middle of a Victorian dream, a mass of 19th-century fantasy.

As he did in Cardiff Castle, Burges once more revels in arabesques, myths, exotic figures and, above all, colour. The two-tiered, octagonal drawing-room, orbited by a gallery, is covered with decorations, including even the window niches, and yet it never seems overloaded. The dome arches over the room in a radiant blue, butterflies flutter across the gilded beams, while birds fly through the star-studded vault; the walls display the wonders of the earth: plants and animals, scenes from Aesop's fables, with portraits of the Bute family nestling among the branches. In order that they should not freeze in their painted paradise, Burges provided another huge fireplace, above which sit the Parcae with the thread of Fate: Et in Arcadia ego. Poetry in stone and colour, this in my opinion is the loveliest of all Victorian rooms. It's like stepping into a page from a medieval illuminated manuscript.

As for the military side of this historical fiction, once more Burges was able to do full justice to his patron's fantasy: in a room above the castle gate, Sir Bute could respond in kind to a medieval emergency. He could wind down the drawbridge, lower the portcullis, and pour boiling oil through holes in the floor down upon his enemies. The effect was so terrifying that Burges did not bother to provide any guest-rooms (although there is a large banqueting-hall). Even Lord Bute seldom came to stay in this fantasy world.

This, then, was the architectural entertainment of the 19th century – amusing, sophisticated, popular and elitist at the same time, a Hollywood spectacular for medieval-ists. Lord Bute's summer residence outside the gates of Cardiff was a folly, a millionaire's fancy, a piece of romantic chivalry for those who enjoy building cut-out cardboard castles from do-it-yourself kits. Does it count as restoration? Yes, in more senses than one, for out of the ruins Bute and Burges built an artistic and gloriously artificial refuge, an historical hallucination as far removed from the world of the Middle Ages as it was from that of the coalmines just a few miles to the north.

All that is missing is the fact that it is *not* a ruin, for one can tell at a glance that it lacks

Julius Cæsar Ibbetson: A Group of Welsh Ladies on a Horse by the Ruins of Castell Coch, circa 1792

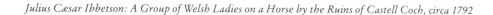

William Burges:
Castell Coch, 1875

historical authenticity. But Lord Bute managed to camouflage the lack of patina by planting a vineyard outside the castle gates, and this survived until the First World War. Thus one could imagine oneself gazing at a castle on the Rhine or on the Loire – at least until one came to taste the Welsh wine. Castell-Coch Riesling actually came on the market, and according to a Punch cartoon, one needed four men for one bottle: one victim, two to hold him down, and a third to force the liquid down his throat. But William Burges never lived to see the entertainment, for he died in 1881, before Castell Coch was completed. Perhaps the most fitting obituary for this short-sighted, plump and lovable man was Lady Bute's description of him: 'Ugly Burges who designs lovely things. Isn't he a duck.'

Saunders Lewis and Other Steam Veterans

You can hear a crunching gurgle, soft and then loud, the ceaseless whispering and hissing of a thousand voices as the sea washes over the pebbles of *Barry* beach. The Knap is the name of the long, grey stretch of shingle ten miles south-west of Cardiff (plate 19). Here anglers and surfers congregate in the cool breeze that comes up from the Bristol Channel. They don't miss the fine sandy beaches of elsewhere, or the fine sandy people for that matter, because those who go to Butlin's Holiday Camp on Barry Island are delighted to be able to afford a holiday at all. Better times are represented only by those who stand on stone pedestals, such as the monument on the quayside to David Davies, a 19th-century entrepreneur and grandfather to the art-collecting sisters of Gregynog Hall. In order to circumvent Lord Bute's dockland monopoly in Cardiff, he built a new railway from his

Rhondda mines, and then in 1884 a new port – Barry. There he installed what was at the time the most modern loading system in the world, and he exported 11 million tons of coal a year, more than is mined in the whole of Wales today. As if to symbolize this decline, the sidings now house the last of Britain's steam engines: Woodhams Barry is the graveyard for these noble veterans.

When British Rail took 'Oliver Cromwell' out of service in 1968, it was the end of an era: 40,000 steam engines had gone for ever. Some ten years earlier the Woodham brothers of Barry had already begun the task of breaking up this national heritage. Now the engines stand there, buffer to buffer, giants rusting by the sea, with birds nesting in their cabs, grass growing from their tenders, and the only whistle from their ruptured boilers that of the wind. Little wonder that tears come to the eyes of all steam fans, and that one has written on the door of a boiler: 'Don't let me die!' It is like an endangered species crying for help. And indeed preservation groups have come riding to the rescue: there are notices on many of these gentle giants, to say 'SOLD' or 'RESERVED'. The London MP Robert Adley, author of four books on railways, bought an engine for his garden. Barry's junkyard became a Mecca for British steam fans. One of them, Philip Davies, a member of the South Gwent Loco Society, hammered a message onto the body of a 1929 Pitchford Hall: 'We bought her for £10,000, and we can sell her to you restored for ten times that much.' Philip took me through this fantastic, open-air mausoleum; he knows all the engines by name – the Stainer 8F, the Churchward, and express stars of the King and Jubilee class. 'Steam is like a brother, everybody likes a piece of the past.' Steam engines are part of childhood dreams, one of the early myths of the industrial age, symbols of technical progress and the national greatness of bygone days. Perhaps British enthusiasts have a particular feeling for these things. For Philip Davies at any rate, this was his only job; he had been working on the restoration of his 'loco' for three years when I met him, and at the age of 28 was living on unemployment benefit.

According to the painter Jack Crabtree, Barry is a workers' town without work. His studio is quite near the loco cemetery and the pleasure gardens – a contrast which he appreciates. Born in England, he has become the chronicler of the dying mining industry in Wales (plate 31). In the 1970's he was commissioned by the National Coal Board to visit some fifty pits in the valleys. With passionate realism, not merely documenting but also participating, 'Jack the paint', as he is known, painted the faces, the technology, and everyday life underground. These are pictures of a disappearing world, a unique record as a tradition approaches its end.

Barry, the town of docks and railways, has a superior neighbour: *Penarth*, once the home of coal and shipping magnates, Cardiff's 'millionaires' corner'. Signs of this past prosperity are still to be seen in the villas around Alexandra Park, the curious four-turreted pier, and the Victorian church of St Augustine (1865), beautifully situated in a hillside graveyard overlooking the town. With its colourful geometrical brick interior, it is typical of the Neo-Gothic style of William Butterfield, the popular church and college architect of the 19th century. There is also a clifftop path south of Penarth pier whose charms are not confined to the landscape, for it was from *Lavernock Point* on May 11 1897 that Guglielmo Marconi sent the first wireless message across to the island of *Flat Holme* in the Severn Estuary. It said: 'Are you ready?'

When Marconi was sending this historic small talk along the Welsh coast, Saunders Lewis was just four years old. He was the son of a Non-Conformist preacher in the Welsh district of Liverpool, was converted to Catholicism, taught Welsh literature at Swansea University, and made a name for himself as a dramatist, story-teller, essayist and political publicist (picture, page 21). In 1925 he was one of the founders of Plaid Cymru, and was indeed its president in the early years. In 1936 he caused a stir reaching far beyond the borders of Wales because of an act of violence. Together with two friends, professors like himself, he set fire to a hangar at the RAF bomber training school of Penyberth in *Penrhos* on the Llyn peninsula. There had been many vain demonstrations and petitions against the establishment of an English military base in this Welsh-speaking heartland, and the attack was more of a gesture than anything else, and caused little material damage. Politically, however, it had far greater repercussions. It was the first time the militant wing of the Welsh Nationalist movement had resorted to violence, and was a precedent for the arson attacks on English holiday homes that marked the 1980's. And it was the first time this century that a Welsh writer had gone to prison for the Welsh cause. In court, Saunders Lewis defended himself with panache: 'What I was teaching the young people of Wales in the halls of the university was not a dead literature, something chiefly of interest to antiquarians, but the living literature of the Welsh people. This literature is therefore able to make demands of me as a man as well as a teacher.' The Welsh jury in Caernarfon acquitted him, but a second jury in London found him guilty, and he was sentenced to nine months imprisonment. 'They yield when faced by Hitler and Mussolini, but they attack the smallest country in the kingdom which they misgovern. This is a cowardly way of showing their strength through violence,' thundered the Welsh lawyer and former Prime Minister David Lloyd George (picture, page 21). 'This is the first government that has tried to put Wales on trial in the Old Bailey ... I should like to be there, and I should like to be forty years younger.' Even if this was only in a letter to his daughter, and was not a public declaration of solidarity, it was a measure of his sense of outrage, and a rekindling of the Welsh nationalism which as British Prime Minister he had been forced to suppress.

In Wormwood Scrubs Saunders Lewis wrote an historical verse drama 'Buchedd Garmon', which is still quoted today at nationalist meetings. Not until 1951 was the former convict allowed to resume his professional duties. Welsh remained the language he fought for and the language in which he wrote most of his work, though recognition was not confined to Wales. One of his theatre plays, 'Gwymerwch chi sigaret?' (Do You Want A Cigarette?) was set in Germany after the war, and in 1962 a radio talk on the fate of the Welsh language caused another stir, and resulted in the foundation of the Welsh Language Society. He never regarded himself as a hero, but he was always the one quoted by the militants: 'careful, considered, public violence is often a necessary weapon for national movements.' When asked whether he advocated bloodshed, he replied: 'So long as it is Welsh blood and not English blood.' He was an extremist and a radical, but he never lost his level-headedness. In his 'Principles of Nationalism' (1926) he made it clear that he saw Welsh problems in a European context. *The Observer* respectfully called him the spirit and conscience of modern nationalism in Wales. He was an institution, with no time for petty squabbles, and increasingly he withdrew from the public eye, remaining silent where once he might have been expected to pronounce judgment. Had he become a renegade, as some activists claim? Had he made his peace with the Establishment, who on his 90th birthday in 1983 conferred an honorary doctorate of the University of Wales on him? The grand old man of Welsh literature spent his last years hidden away in Penarth, saying nothing. Certainly his contemporary Dylan Thomas was a far more popular poet, and as an anglicized Welshman was his country's best-known ambassador abroad. But to the less popular cause of the Welshness of Wales, and to the cultural and political consciousness of the Welsh, no-one in this century has made a greater contribution than Saunders Lewis. One hopes that a place will be found where his work might be properly documented and made accessible to a wider public. Why not in Penarth, where he lived until his death in 1985? A room perhaps in the Turner House. Would not this be a fitting task for the Welsh National Museum?

Saunders Lewis once said that he had come from literature to public life and politics through 'realizing this direct connection between our literature and the traditional life of Welsh society.' In the Amgueddfa Werin Cymru, the national folk art museum in *St Fagans*, all aspects of this life are documented: work and leisure, religion and education, sport and fashion. We see bardic chairs, cooking utensils, harps, ploughs and lovespoons, and indeed the whole history of Welsh everyday life from the 16th to the 19th century. In the spacious open-air museum, there are farmhouses from every region, saved from ruin and faithfully restored with their barns, smithies, tanneries, cockfighting arena and Non-Conformist chapel. It is a rural, not an urban culture, of cottages, not of palaces. But there is also an Elizabethan manor house, the many-gabled St Fagans Castle (*c.*1570). The 3rd Earl of Plymouth donated his family seat and estates in 1946 to the Welsh National Museum on condition that a folk art museum should be built there. His condition has been totally fulfilled.

From St Fagans to *St Donat's*, from a visual demonstration of rural culture to a model and international institution of education, Atlantic College. Here, too, on the rocky coast between Barry and Bridgend, an old castle stands at the heart of things: St Donat's Castle (15/16th century) was restored in the 1930's by the American press tycoon Randolph Hearst, who made it into a luxurious setting for his art collection and his Welsh mistress. For a while, this seaside home was a meeting-place for the international jet set. Then along came a German educationalist, and shook everything up. He was Kurt Hahn, founder of the famous boarding-schools of Salem and Gordonstoun, and in 1962 he set up the first of six United World Colleges here (the others are in Singapore, Swaziland, Italy, Canada and

USA). His aim was to promote international understanding and service to the community. This includes the College's own coastguard operations and, above all, practical social work. Every pupil spends at least four hours a week looking after sick, old or handicapped people in the neighbouring towns and villages. One unit which looks after juvenile delinquents potential and actual has been officially recognized as a rehabilitation centre. This remarkable school, where there are no uniforms or prefects, has some 350 boys and girls from 60 countries, including China and the Soviet Union. The Dutch Crown Prince Willem-Alexander took his school-leaving examinations here. The timetable includes seminars on peace studies and courses in ceramics set up by the celebrated potter Mary White.

South Glamorgan is traditionally an area of learning: working with head and hand, serving God and one's neighbour – these were principles already in operation 1,400 years ago in a village near Atlantic College: *Llantwit Major*, where the Celts had also set up an educational centre. This was where the missionary St Illtud founded a famous monastery school. And among his students there were many saints, including St David and the bard Taliesin. They are legendary figures. But the village is worth a visit for its own sake, as well as for the unique collection of Celtic crosses (9–11th century) in St Illtud Church.

The Valleys of Coal and Tears

He was sitting with his dog outside the Pensioners' Club of *Ton Pentre*, enjoying the first warm, sunny days of spring. Dick Jones wore a tweed cap, and his dog – like so many here in the valleys – was a terrier. Actually, I only stopped to ask him the way, but he said: 'I've got time, I'll go with you some o' the way.' As we wandered down one of those long, seemingly endless streets that wind through the valley like stone snakes, flanked by identical rows of two-storey houses, suddenly he stopped. 'You know what this is?' He showed me some photos of idyllic forest paths, green hills, slopes covered in gorse. 'I took 'em quite recently. Don't it look like your Black Forest, eh?' He laughed. 'A stranger would never guess, but it's only a few miles from here, and it used to be industry there – men, slagheaps, piles of coal! And now? How green is my valley, eh?'

Dick Jones of Ton Pentre raved about an area made famous by Richard Llewellyn's best-selling novel 'How Green Was My Valley' (1939) – an area that became known as the darkest, poorest corner of South Wales – the Valleys (colour plate 26; plate 24). Rhondda, Rhymney, Sirhowy, Ebbw Vale – from all these came the coal that once drove the warships and merchant ships with which Britain built her Empire, a world whose foundations were smoke and iron. In these valleys stood the steelworks that made the cannons for the Napoleonic Wars and the railways through which America opened up her Wild West. And from these valleys came the radical workers' leaders, the famous miners' choirs, the opera singers and the rugby players who fashioned the image of Wales. The only Communist mayoress in Britain, and some of the great socialists who have ruffled so

T. H. Shepherd: Berw Rhondda, 1831

many parliamentary feathers in London, have stemmed from here, including Aneurin Bevan and Neil Kinnock. Just a dozen valleys, but they teem with life, pouring forth a mixture of sweat and tears, Methodism and Marxism, song and silicosis. Industrial magnates here, Chartists there; here coal and iron, there hymns and poems.

The Valleys are the most densely populated region in Wales. A million people live here, more than a third of the total population. By the end of the 19th century the Valleys had become massively industrialized, and yet at the beginning of the 19th century scarcely a soul was to be seen. Isolated farms, a few small villages, barely any streets. One Benjamin Heath Malkin visited Rhondda Fach in 1804, and found it idyllic: 'The stream fertilizes the valley with its pure translucent waters ... The contrast of the meadows, rich and verdant, with mountains the most wild and romantic, surrounding them on every side, is in the highest degree picturesque.' One hundred years later, the dream had turned into a nightmare. In A. J. Cronin's novel 'The Citadel' (1937) Dr Andrew Mason makes a railway journey through the Valleys during the mid 1920's: 'The mountain tops were hidden in a grey waste of sky but their sides, scarred by ore workings, fell black and desolate, blemished by great heaps of slag on which a few dirty sheep wandered in vain hope of pasture. No bush, no blade of vegetation was visible. The trees, seen in the fading light, were gaunt and stunted spectres.' The rural idyll had become an industrial eyesore, but this dramatic change did not happen overnight.

There is documentary evidence that ever since the 17th century at least, the valley farmers had been digging for coal, mainly for their own use. While they were ploughing, they would often stumble upon this 'black gold', for coal is like a huge saucer below Wales, its edges rising to the surface in the north and the south. The seams were not deep, and for a long time only small shafts were needed to cover the requirements of the iron foundries which had been set up from about 1600 onwards on the northern edge of the coalfields. It was not until 1830 that the Valleys began to develop their own export-orientated coal industry. New shafts were sunk, new workers came to the area, and of course they required new housing estates. In 1860 the two main valleys, Rhondda Fawr and Rhondda Fach, contained barely 3,000 people; half a century later there were over 150,000. There alone the amount of coal mined rose from 1.2 to 8.7 million tons between 1870 and 1910. King Coal had arrived, and the expansion of his power was to be without parallel in Wales.

He established his rule from Pontypridd to Tonypandy, from Ton Pentre to Treherbert. The valleys are narrow, and the slopes are steep. The colleries were built in the valleys, and the miners' houses were built above the galleries, and behind their houses towered the mighty slag-heaps. The scaffolding and the settlements followed the valleys upriver, miles

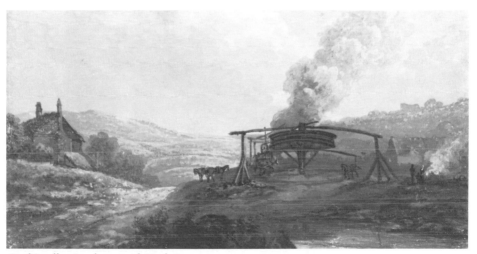

Paul Sandby, Landscape with Coalmine

and miles of terraced houses chiselled into the slopes to form endless streets, the monotony broken only by the chapels (plates 35, 38). They were the only focal points of comfort at the end of the 'long street' and at the end of the long day underground. The chapels were more than just places of prayer – with their Sunday schools and libraries they were centres of education, and with their choirs and amateur theatre groups they were centres of culture too. The chapels were focal points of communal life, and certainly this explains their

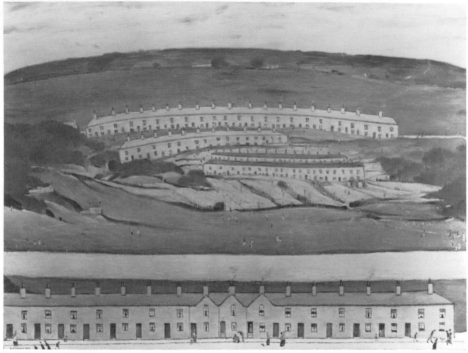

L. S. Lowry: Hillside in Wales, 1962

massive expansion during the late 19th century. In the two Rhondda Valleys alone, more than 150 were built in the years prior to 1914, the biggest being in Ton Pentre: Chapel Jerusalem, famous as the 'Methodist Cathedral of the Rhondda'. Then there were the Miners' Institutes, workers' clubs financed from the miners' meagre wages, but with excellent libraries (whose surviving collections are now in the South Wales Miners' Library in Swansea), lecture-halls, billiard rooms, and places for discussion and entertainment. They were amongst the best adult education centres in Great Britain. The Workmen's Institute in Blaenavon (1894), with its elaborate façade and its 800-seat auditorium, is one of the finest specimens. The religious ethos of the chapels and the educational élan of the Miners' Institutes made the Valleys both culturally and politically citadels of Non-Conformism.

Not until the end of the 1920's were roads built (by unemployed miners) across the mountains and into the neighbouring valleys. This isolation had helped to give each valley its own special character, for each was a world in itself – a village community, with chapel, school and club just round the corner, though at the same time it was a cosmopolitan society, embracing immigrants from many countries. The fact that these were so completely integrated – in contrast to Glasgow or Liverpool, for example – is much to the credit of the Welsh. The hallmark of such a society was unity: one valley where they lived, one industry in which they worked, one class to which they belonged, one attitude of mind which they all shared – and one language, which was Welsh. Despite all the immigrants, Welsh was the language used in the family, in chapel, in the street and at work, and this was so right up until the turn of the century. But even here, anglicization gradually made its inevitable way forwards. Between 1901 and 1911 the number of English-only speakers doubled in the Valleys, while the number of pure Welsh-speakers was halved. Today only two per cent of children in the Rhondda valleys still speak Welsh.

'It's all bingo now, disco or telly,' said my hostess in Sirhowy Valley. No Miners' Institute, no chapel choir, no poetry, no theatre. 'My whole family were down the mines,' she said, 'my father, my five brothers, my husband, they were all miners – but my son isn't. He's a printer.' The change that has taken place over the last few years is almost as radical as that which brought the Industrial Revolution thundering into the peaceful valleys of Glamorgan. King Coal's decline began as dramatically as his meteoric rise. In 1926 there was a month-long general strike, with lockouts and arrests, and for the first time the Welsh miners went on a hunger march to London. One pit closed after another. The Industrial Revolution was turning its children out. Thousands of unemployed men streamed out of the Valleys. In 1920 there had been 265,000 miners working in South Wales, and just 13 years later, the number had halved. At the climax of the Depression a Welsh cabinet secretary wrote in London that the best solution for the Rhonddas would be to build a dam and flood the valleys so that at least they could produce hydroelectricity. Barely less cynical was the advice given by Ramsay MacDonald, the first Labour Prime Minister, to a delegation from the Valleys: '[Solve] your unemployment problem by the removal of these tips.'

Such London answers are not easily forgotten or forgiven in Wales. 'No English party is any use to us,' says Harri Webb, the Poet of the Valleys. 'An independent Welsh Republic could tackle our economic problems far better than any central government in London.' Harri, a former librarian, born in 1920, voted for Plaid Cymru in the election of 1983, but the national party won only two out of 38 Welsh seats, and lagged far behind Labour, the traditional party of the Valleys. But even Labour found its vote dwindling in its old citadel of the Rhondda: from 75% in 1979 to 62% in 1983. Harri Webb lives in *Cwmbach* near Aberdare, in a miners' cottage of 1870: 'two up, two down', all the rooms tiny, and the lavatory outside in the garden. In the old days it was not uncommon for several families to be living in a cottage like this, and for a dozen or more people to be sleeping in a single room. Typhus and cholera struck in epidemics. In his novel 'The Citadel', A. J. Cronin graphically described these terrible conditions, which he had seen for himself as a miners' doctor in Tredegar during the 1920's, in a district which he found strange and hideously 'martyred'.

Of course there were also nicer areas, for instance the model estate which the Marquess of Bute built in 1802 for his iron and steel workers at *Butetown* near *Rhymney*: broad streets and roomy houses, originally planned as the centre of a new town, though this never came to fruition. Butetown has been restored, and is now a conservation area. Another of the earliest workers' estates in Wales, Stack Square and Engine Row in *Blaenavon* (1789–92), is also due to be restored. The houses that nestled in the shadows of the blast furnaces had two floors with two rooms each, a total of 52 to 68 square yards, which was very substantial by the standards of those times. The first, early 19th-century settlements, built without the constraints of speculation and building regulations, blend astonishingly well with the landscape; they used local materials – rust-coloured sandstone, and slate for the roofs; brick was not used till later. But these were the exceptions, and many of the early estates – such as The Triangle in *Pentrebach* near Merthyr Tydfil – have not been demolished. Building land in the narrow valleys was scarce, and demand was high, and so from the middle of the 19th century onwards, terraced houses became the norm. In Rhondda Fawr they merged into a gigantic linear village stretching for ten miles and never more than two thirds of a mile wide: a strange, modern Celtic hill culture. The Scotch Houses (*c*.1865) in *Llwynypia* are a classic example of these terraces: more than 200 houses in parallel lines over the slope, each house with its own little front garden, and a view to the west over the valley – far better than most comparable estates in England at that time. In many places the size and situation of the houses, and also the cast-iron street signs, denoted the social position of their inhabitants: Agents' Row, Engineers' Row, Colliers' Row; the iron and steel workers of *Abernant*, near Aberdare, used to live here in 1850. Their colleagues in Blaenavon, on the Forge Site, lived in A-Row, B-Row, C-Row, for their bosses could not be bothered to endow them with names.

After *c*.1875, when more and more workers were needed, stricter building regulations were brought in for these stereotype dwellings, which now housed increasing numbers of people. Between 1881 and 1911, the population of the Rhonddas almost tripled (from 55,000 to 153,000). Today people try to relieve the monotony of the terraces with bright coloured paint, just to show their individuality and joie de vivre. But living conditions were and still are bad in many places – so bad that a Shelter report of 1980 found 40% of these houses to be uninhabitable. Conditions were regarded as amongst the worst in Britain. The Rhonddas are the second poorest region in Mid Glamorgan, and Mid Glamorgan is the poorest county in Wales and England. Even new estates have brought little relief, and indeed have contributed to the decay of the old valley communities – a decay accelerated by endemic unemployment and the fact that so many young people have understandably gone elsewhere. And yet the true 'Welshies', as they are called in Cardiff, still cling to their valley. 'I've lived in the Mediterranean and the near East,' says Harri Webb, 'and I've seen a good deal of the world, but nowhere was as beautiful as here in Wales.' He points towards Cynon Valley, which he calls 'a stream of songs' – but what we see there are the five giant chimneys of *Aberaman's* Phurnacite factory, empty where once they belched smoke all over the landscape. 'They make smokeless oil for English central heating, and they leave the muck with us here in Wales.' This was the biggest factory of its kind in Europe, and was also 'Britain's dirtiest factory' (*The Observer*) – totally antiquated and, perhaps mercifully, closed in 1990.

In the boom year of 1913, there were 620 pits in South Wales, employing 233,000 miners (about the same number employed today by the coal industry throughout the British Isles). By 1991 all that was left was 3 pits with 1,900 miners.[1] The song of the pits has become a threnody. Welsh hard coal, regarded as the very best in the golden age of steam locomotives and steamships, was supplanted first by oil, and then by cheaper coal from other parts of Britain and abroad. By the 1980's the South Wales pits were the most uneconomic in Britain. And so when the unemployed protesters called on Prince Charles in 1981, during his visit to Swansea, to save the mines and close the Palace, it was a vain appeal. Not even he could save King Coal. 'Farewell to the Rhondda,' sang the Hennessys of Cardiff, linking the old Depression to the new with the same refrain: 'The mines they are closin' / The Valleys are all down / There's no work in the Rhondda, boys / We'll be in London soon.' But the protesters did not lose their spirit. During the Miners' Strike of 1984, the Welsh Valleys burned with the old militancy and community spirit, and when elsewhere resistance was crumbling, Welsh solidarity stood firm, for it was in the Valleys that the economic situation was at its most disastrous. Rather eat grass than return to work, swore the men of *Maerdy* ('Little Moscow'), who had always been the first to join the workers' fight and the last to abandon it. Maerdy was the last pit in the Rhonddas. 'Why on earth do they think we're fighting to defend stinking jobs in the pitch black? There are no lavatories or lunch-breaks, no lights or scenery,' said a miner in Ogmore Valley. 'We're fighting because our community and our culture depends on it.' But Maerdy Colliery closed on December 20 1990.

Even before this hopeless strike, the mass redundancies had made many neutral observers fear that a sociological timebomb was ticking away in the Valleys, an explosive mixture of unemployment and nationalism. But Irish-style political fanaticism is alien to the Welsh nature: instead of revolting, they resign themselves to the inevitable. They had been through worse calamities – hunger, disease, the mining disaster of *Senghenydd* in 1913, when an explosion killed 439 men, and the tragedy of *Aberfan*.

So dark is my valley. Aberfan, the vale of tears. There is no more desolate spot in the Valleys than the hill cemetery of Aberfan (plate 25). In two long and identical rows of graves, just like their terraced houses, they buried their dead children: Corwyn, David, Evan, Gwyneth, Kevin, Myrtle, Tydfil Jane – 116 children between seven and ten years old. They died on October 21 1966, at 9.15 a.m., when after several days of rain, a mass of mine waste slid down from a coal tip, thundered down Merthyr Hill, and buried Pant Glas

---

1   In 1947, when the coalmines were nationalized, there were still about 200 pits in South Wales. In 1913 the mines of South Wales produced 57 millions tons of coal, one fifth of total production in Britain. In 1990 the total was just over 3 million – far less than in 1850.

School and eighteen houses. In the sludge and slurry they found the bodies of 144 men, women and children, the latter still sitting on their benches, or holding hands in the playground. 'In memory of Richard who loved light, freedom and animals' says the gravestone of one ten-year-old. There are quotations from the Bible, striving to ward off despair, and statues of angels as big as the children themselves. Today the tragic heap has been planted with birch trees and broom, and the disaster fund paid for a Community Centre with swimming bath, squash courts and bar. The black cross with 144 names stands on the lawn.

'The Valleys of Wales have suffered many tragedies,' said a spokesman for the miners, 'but never anything like this tragedy of Aberfan.' Aberfan today, and where else tomorrow? Like a bolt of lightning this catastrophe brought home to the Welsh what appalling dangers and pollution the mining industry had delivered to their country. And only now did the authorities in London stir from their lethargy. They began 'Operation Eyesore'. The National Coal Board gave millions of pounds to regenerate the countryside. So, too, did the Welsh Development Agency. Slagheaps up to 600 feet high, that had accumulated since the 19th century, were now dismantled, landscaped, planted. The great cones were flattened to make room for playgrounds, parks were laid out in Aberdare and Abercarn, forests that had been felled for charcoal and pit-props were replanted. The industrial wasteland was turned into an area for recreation. In Rhymney River, once as black as soot, people could once more fish for trout. When 'Tiger Tom' Tom Jones, the pop-star from Treforest, sang of the 'green, green grass of home,' the words no longer sounded ironic.

'This was not the Valley I had known,' says Huw Morgan, the hero of Richard Llewellyn's sequel 'Green, Green My Valley Now' (1975), on returning home from his exile in Patagonia. 'From other brains another valley had been born ... cleaner, happier, greener, than any since the time of my grandfather.' Cleaner? Yes, indeed, for industry had died. Greener? Yes, because the grass had grown over the old wounds. Happier? Who can say? By 1984 most of the Rhondda pits had closed down, throwing hundreds out of work. 77-year-old Annie Powell said: 'I ought really to be pleased that the valley isn't black any more. But the fact that it's green again isn't enough. We gave everything for the coal, but when I see our young people going away to find work somewhere else, I ask myself: What did the coal give us?' Annie Powell was Great Britain's only communist mayoress. When she was young, the Rhonddas were black, there were still 54 pits, and these fed 170,000 in the two valleys, after a fashion. Today the Rhonddas have less than half that number of inhabitants.

Since 1934 the Valleys have been designated 'Assisted Areas'. But effective assistance came later or too late. In 1978 they were a declared special development area, which is a euphemism for a depressed or deprived area. Tax concessions and other inducements for investment helped to clear the way for new industries, as a result of which the Valleys now produce furniture, clothes, books and so on. But for miners, the pits and the blast furnaces represented not only a job but also a way of life. Many of them look down on the new light industries. Who wants to make biscuits after fighting the earth? 'No dignity in that!' they say.

Meanwhile, the dying coal and steel industries have brought a different type of person here – the tourist. 'Visit the Valleys!' exhorts the Welsh Tourist Board, and that's been the cry ever since the end of the seventies. So along come the trippers, photographing rusting machines as if they were the ruins of Carthage, workers estates as if they were igloos or wigwams. It's the Third World in Wales, a working-class peepshow. Holidays in Depression land? But even if there is something almost grotesque about it, the fact is that tourism has become the only growth industry in the Valleys. And to be fair, the Tourist Board does its best to ensure that the ruins do not merely constitute a matter for morbid sightseeing – it also explains the historical background, initiates conservation and restoration, and finances museum projects: in short, it helps to prevent the Valleys from sinking into the eternal sleep of dormitory towns. Yet the conversion from industrial landscape to leisure centre, beneficial though it may be, is still not enough to save the Valleys.

On the day when I met the old man in Ton Pentre, I walked all the way along the seemingly endless street of Rhondda Fawr. Treorchy, Treherbert, chapels, Chinese take-aways, fish and chips, on and on, until suddenly, when I least expected it, the houses came to an end. The mountains of *Blaenrhondda* rise steeply on both sides of the valley, and the road climbs up the bare slopes, between the gorse and a few trees and the threadbare grass. There was something you couldn't see, and yet you could smell it, still permeating the air and the grass. Coal. The Rhondda lay below, that heroic, stoic Rhondda, with its endless road that had enabled the men of yesterday to move away during the great Depression of the thirties across the moors to Hirwaun.

Eccentrics in Pontypridd: Mr Zadek and Dr Price

Like a faded rainbow the old bridge curves across the Taff, right in the middle of *Pontypridd*. This single high arch, a perfect crescent, has a span of 160 feet. When it was built, in 1755, it was a technical miracle, and for many years the bridge of Pontypridd remained the biggest single-arched stone bridge in Europe. In order to reduce its dead weight and to offer as small a target as possible to the racing winds of the Taff valley, the spandrels on either side have three large cylindrical openings. It is a masterpiece of simplicity and elegance, its effectiveness spoilt only, alas, by the fact that a roadbridge has been built directly alongside it. The architect was an amateur, one William Edwards, a farmer and Methodist preacher who had taught himself stonemasonry. He and his sons designed many bridges, that of Pontypridd having been commissioned by a local

P. C. Canot: The Great Bridge over the Taff at Pontypridd, 1775

mine-owner. And this bridge was one of the first signs of the Industrial Revolution in rural South Wales.

Pontypridd is situated at the confluence of the Taff and the Rhondda, and this situation made it an ideal junction for the transport of coal from the Valleys to the docks of Cardiff and Barry. In the boom years, black railway trains rumbled in endless succession through Pontypridd – 250 of them a day. It was here, in this industrial heartland, that the Welsh national anthem was born. A weaver from Pontypridd, Evan James, wrote the words in 1856 after walking along the bank of the Rhondda, and his son James composed the tune: *'Hen Wlad Fy Nhadau'* – Land of My Fathers. It is a panegyric on the homeland, its poets and patriots who died for the freedom of their country, and it ends with the plea: 'O bydded i'r heniaith barhau' – O may the old language live on. *'Glanrhondda'*, as it was originally called, was sung at many Eisteddfodau, until eventually it became the national anthem. Poet and composer, father and son, have a monument in Ynysangharad Park, at the entrance to Pontypridd – a pair of allegorical statues of poetry and music (by Sir Goscombe John, 1930).

When I went home, I took with me a sheep from Pontrypidd. Branded on its back was a message: 'Keep Wales tidy – throw your litter in England.' The ceramic gems are churned out by one John Hughes. 'England is O.K. – if you like foreigners' (plate 28). The

Dr William Price, 1822

house of 'Ponty's' potty potter glows with the national colours of green and red. The entrance is flanked by two more-than-lifesize papier-maché rugby stars, and inside, the shelves are full of 'uglies' – ceramic caricatures of politicians, pop singers, footballers and rugby players. Some fans have whole teams created by John Hughes. He is without doubt the number one producer of national clichés.

The theatre director Peter Zadek began his career in Pontypridd. A Jewish emigré from Berlin, he had to come to deepest Wales for his first practical experience of the theatre. In Pontypridd and later in Swansea Zadek directed a new play every week, running a repertory whose range stretched from Shakespeare to Noël Coward. This was where he learned those things that later were to make him famous: classics with a commercial touch, and commercial plays with a classic touch. But the Welsh were always more interested in music and opera: 'Generally we had half-empty houses,' says Zadek. He remembers 'the miners in Pontypridd, with their lamps on their heads, going past the theatre morning and evening on their way to and from the pits, and they never even looked at our posters. To my amazement they weren't the slightest bit interested in Cocteau! On the other hand, for all their church morality, they *were* keen on bedroom farces, with girls in pink nighties slipping out of bed and hiding in the bathroom or behind a screen. And also, unlike me, they were very keen on politics.'

Peter Zadek has long since been forgotten in Pontypridd, but Dr Price hasn't. He was a 19th-century show-off who has gone down in Welsh folklore as a figure of fun. The suburb of *Glyntaf* still contains the two round Druid towers he built in 1838 as a gate-house for his projected eight-storey Druid palace. Dr William Price, doctor and eccentric, believed himself to be a descendant of the Druids, and at Pontypridd's Rocking Stone he held ceremonies which the chapel Puritans considered to be Satanic. Even his home-made costume hardly corresponded to the normal Victorian idea of sartorial decorum: white cloak, green trousers, scarlet waistcoat, and on his head a fox fur, with legs and tail dangling. This is how he stands in bronze in his hometown of Llantrisant, with a bushy beard, a crescent moon in his hand, and both arms outstretched like the Christ of Rio. It was not just Dr Price's druidism that upset people. He was also a free thinker and an advocate of free love, an avid defender of the countryside, who gave early warning of the consequences of industrialization, a supporter of the working classes, who took part in the 1839 Chartist uprising in Newport, and a very unusual doctor. He considered the wearing of socks to be unhealthy, prescribed a vegetarian diet instead of pills, and refused to treat patients unless they promised to give up smoking. He also attracted nationwide attention as a pioneer of cremation. On January 13, 1884, a Sunday, to the horror of his neighbours, he went to a hill near Llantrisant, and there used an oildrum to burn the body of his son Iesu Grist (Welsh for Jesus Christ). The village policeman was sent for, tipped up the coffin, and out rolled the body of the boy. Only his immediate arrest prevented the good doctor from himself being cremated by the outraged mob. At court in Cardiff he vehemently defended the right for people to be cremated instead of buried. It was this trial, in which he won his case, that led to the legalization of cremation in Britain. Dr Price returned in triumph to Llantrisant, where he lived happily ever after with his young housekeeper Gwenllian, became a father again at 90, and when at last his strength began to ebb away, he lay down on a couch, asked for a glass of champagne, and died. His own cremation in 1893 was attended by thousands of sightseers, and afterwards the pubs of Llantrisant ran dry.

Labour Country: In Search of Lost Jobs

Black valley, green valley, *Sirhowy Valley* (colour plate 23). Between Blackwood and Tredegar, somewhere beyond the pithead of Markham Colliery, I had crossed the river and wandered into the woods. I found myself among fir-trees and larches, and you would have thought there had never been any industry here at all. Then suddenly, in the midst of this idyllic country, I stumbled across rusting metal, an overgrown shaft, foundations ... of what, and from when? For industrial archaeologists, the Valleys are an endless hiding-place for buried treasure. The clues are still to be found, but gradually they are disappearing.

'Industrial Heritage Tourism' is the offspring of those longstanding partners, history and business. It's a form of recycling: when you can no longer make a profit out of something, turn it into art. 'Industrial Discovery Weekends' invite you to travel in a miner's cage back into the age of coal. 'Industrial Trails' are laid just as Nature trails are laid elsewhere. And if there are no signposts, there are literary directions to help you, as in *Gilfach Goch*, south-west of the Rhonddas. This valley, between whaleback humps, was the model for Richard Llewellyn's 'How Green Was My Valley', which became the archetype of all Welsh mining valleys and their history. And yet the reality surpasses even the fiction. On the eastern edge of the area lies one of the most impressive examples of industrial archaeology and of tourist development aid: 'Big Pit' in *Blaenavon*, opened in 1860, closed in 1980, and re-opened three years later as a mining museum. It is a living museum, as authentic as a museum could ever be: the visitor, complete with helmet and lamp, enters the mine in one of the old cages, not without some trepidation, with an ex-miner as guide. You bend double as you go through low-roofed galleries, you see the stables of the pit-ponies, the empty pithead baths and lockers, and you sense the continued presence of generations of miners, their jokes, their silences, their sweat, their dirt, their cameraderie ... all gone now, but not forgotten. For this reason alone, a museum like 'Big Pit' is not something to be taken for granted. For many the pithead is a symbol of a painful past, but the pain is something ambivalent: the sufferings of the miners were painful, but so too is the closing of the mines. In the last eighteen years, nine out of ten have gone.

'People are proud of the Valleys as the workshop of the world,' says Harri Webb, 'but they don't want the old pitheads to stand there as picturesque showpieces to be gawped at like the windmills in Holland.' Presumably, though, they don't mind people gawping at miners' lamps. From the ceiling of the Whistle Inn, once a miners' Pub in *Blaenavon*, hang dozens of lamps from different mines and times. But Masie and Charlie have very few customers now. Tourists seldom find the way from the 'Big Pit' to the 'Big Pub', and the men themselves have long since stopped coming. Blaenavon is one of the most depopulated places in the Valleys. Today there are barely 6,000 people here, compared with nearly 20,000 in the 19th century – and 350 before 1789.

It was in the year of the French Revolution that the Industrial Revolution called on the little village of Blaenavon. Three businessmen from England, experienced in the fields of banking, iron, and canal-building, leased land from Lord Abergavenny and built three blast furnaces in Blaenavon – prototypes of the new technology of iron production in Wales. Just a few years before, in Ironbridge, Abraham Darby's method of coke smelting (instead of charcoal) and Boulton and Watt's steam engines had revolutionized the iron industry. Now the English entrepreneurs were looking to expand, and Blaenavon and its surroundings offered ideal conditions: ore, coal, and limestone – everything they needed for the production of iron. Technology and capital came from England, while the raw materials and labour came from Wales – and that was to be the pattern for years to come.

137

R. C. Hoare: Blaenavon Ironworks, 1799

The blast furnaces of Blaenavon were built on a slope, so that they could be charged with raw materials from above; the molten iron flowed down into the foundries. Functionally and aesthetically, these blast furnaces are amongst the earliest and most beautiful examples of Georgian industrial architecture in Wales. Restoration work is also being done on the houses in the adjacent Stack Square (1792), which, with Forge Row (1804) in *Cwmafon*, is one of the few Welsh workers' estates to have survived from the first phase of the Industrial Revolution. In order that the children of these iron-workers should receive a good English education, the sisters of the iron magnate Samuel Hopkins founded an Anglican school in Blaenavon in 1816. The iron masters also left their mark on the neighbouring church of St Peter's (1805) in the shape of a cast iron font. Before the last of the blast furnaces put out its fires in 1938, Blaenavon made industrial history once again: in Forge Site a young engineer named Sidney Thomas developed a new process of steel production in 1878 – a patent which was purchased by the Scot Andrew Carnegie, and which made him his fortune overseas.

Blaenavon, Merthyr Tydfil, Swansea and Pontypool – these were the early, and as yet unrecognized cradles of the Industrial Revolution, after Manchester, Sheffield and Coalbrookdale. For far too long the Welsh contribution to the British Empire has stood in the shadows of what the English regard as their own success story.

Who built the first American iron rolling mill? An emigrant from the Valleys, one David Morgan from *Pontypool*, who constructed the mill in Sharon, Pennsylvania, in 1871. And where were the wrought iron railings made for the government building in Williamsburg,

Virginia? In Pontypool, 1720. Benjamin Franklin himself visited Blaenavon's neighbouring town in the Llwyd Valley in order to study the new technology and to learn how sheet iron could be rolled instead of hammered flat – the secret of canning. In Pontypool around 1730 the first British iron rolling mill began commercial production of tinplate, which until then had been a German monopoly. The man who achieved this breakthrough was Major John Hanbury, descendant of a London banker and industrialist who in 1577 had acquired a few small foundry and mining rights. Today Park House, formerly the Hanburys' family home, houses a school, while the stables (1830) have been converted into the Valley Inheritance Museum. It documents the rise of the Hanburys, which coincided with the rise of Pontypool. In 1962 the last tinplate factory closed down, and by 1985 unemployment had risen to 17%. It's now about half that. One by-product of the iron industry became a speciality for antique collectors: Pontypool Japan Ware, trays, beakers and other household utensils made of tinplate, brightly coloured and polished, manufactured here between 1730 and 1830.[1]

Torfaen, the valley between Pontypool and Blaenavon, is the most easterly of the coal valleys. Like a pointing finger the valleys descend from the plateau, along the edge of which runs the road from Abergavenny to Hirwaun. In the early 19th century this 'Heads of the Valleys Road' offered an industrial panorama without equal: to the north, the green heights of the Brecon Beacons; to the south, the 'black Alps' of the coal region; and in between the biggest iron-producing area in the world. The mines were in the valleys, and the blast furnaces stood at the head of the valleys; thus coal and iron lived side by side. Even back in the 16th century, the iron-masters of Sussex had transferred their melting furnaces to this region of Wales, for here they found all they needed in abundance: iron ore, limestone, forests for charcoal, and rivers for energy. At the end of the 18th century, they were followed by the big English industrialists. In 1730, there were only four blast furnaces in South Wales, but a century later there were more than a hundred just at the head of the valley. And then during the second half of the 19th century, steel replaced iron, and the industrialists moved southwards to the coast, establishing the new steel industry between Port Talbot and Newport. The 'Heads of the Valleys' wasted away. The highway of the Industrial Revolution turned into the Via Dolorosa of depression, and at the crossroads of Welsh history, one road led to triumph while the other led to disaster. Ebbw Vale, Tredegar, Rhymney, Merthyr Tydfil – all these were stopping-places on the iron road.

Ebbw Vale: the valley is broad here, and the slopes are not as steep as in the Rhonddas. There is plenty of room for men and machines. Row upon row of houses make their way up the hills, but down below in the valley there are huge patches of rust, as if some giant hand had poured weed-killer everywhere. Once the most modern steelworks in Europe stood here, built in 1938, swiftly made obsolete, and finally laid to rest at the end of the

---

1 For chapel specialists, Pontypool's Baptist Chapel in Crane Street (1846) is generally regarded as the best example of Greek Revival in Wales.

1970's. The unemployment rate here has been as high as 25%. All that remained from this vast industrial complex was one rolling mill. In 1829 the rails for the Manchester and Liverpool railways were cast in Ebbw Vale, and the romance of those old steam engines, and the less romantic General Strike of 1926, are among the memories of Dick Watson from Cwm. Once a pitman, then a fish-and-chip man, Dick began to paint at the age of 63. 'I'm a steam-age man,' he says. 'My pictures show a bygone age. I paint what we used to see when we went out, once a year, on our Sunday School outing.' It never rains in his pictures, and all the women have the beautiful eyes of his sister Lily Spinetti. He's a Welsh naive painter, and his work is displayed in Cwm Post Office.

In the next valley, on the edge of *Tredegar* and fenced off by the industrial archaeologists, lie the ruins of the Sirhowy Ironworks (1779), one of the first coke-fired furnaces in the country. Now there are horses grazing on its rubble and slagheaps. But in the centre of Tredegar, the Iron Age has left its victory column: a monumental clocktower of cast iron (1858). Up above, Greenwich Time, and down below, the triumphs of Wellington. The Victorians had an impressive way of combining the useful and the patriotic, and what better way to show how heroism may stand the test of time than a monumental clocktower? And a lot of celebrated people have read the time from the Iron Duke's column: the writer and social critic A. J. Cronin, who lived here from 1921 till 1924 as a pit doctor; the soprano Margaret Price and the socialist Aneurin Bevan, both born in Tredegar; the former Labour leader Michael Foot, whose constituency and second home was here; and his successor Neil Kinnock, also born here (picture, page 21). Could Tredegar be the secret headquarters of the Labour Party?

On the road from Ebbw Vale to Tredegar, on a hill overlooking the town, are four unhewn rocks, a monument in the old Celtic style to Aneurin Bevan. At the age of 13, Nye Bevan became a miner, like his father. At home they spoke Welsh, went to chapel, and went to the Eisteddfod – the Non-Conformist background of a typical valley family. In the radical South Wales miners' union, Bevan gathered his first political experiences, and in 1929 he was elected MP. Later, under Attlee's premiership, he served as Minister of Health and Minister of Employment, and he played a substantial role in the nationalization of the coal and steel industries. He is remembered most warmly, though, for his reformist zeal and for his part in establishing the National Health Service. He died in 1960, and then the non-Welsh Michael Foot took over his constituency, wrote Aneurin Bevan's official biography, became Leader of the Opposition, won the biggest ever Labour majority in Wales during the 1983 election (70%), but never managed to make the final move into Downing Street. And so he had to rest content with No. 10 Morgam Street in Tredegar, opposite the Workmen's Hall. Here he got to know a young worker, red-haired, a rugby player who became his private secretary, and ended up as the youngest ever Labour leader in 1983: Neil Kinnock. Kinnock grew up in a terraced house on the outskirts of Tredegar (No. 24 Vale Terrace), with a view of Ty Trist, a colliery that has since been demolished; his father was a miner and then an iron worker in Ebbw Vale – 'absolutely genuine working class', as Michael Foot said of his successor and political protégé. Neil Kinnock entered the Labour Party at the age of 15, after hearing one of Nye Bevan's rip-roaring speeches. Kinnock himself showed his own Welsh gift of the gab, though not always to the approval of his fellow-countymen: 'He talks better than he thinks,' was the verdict of his old colleague Dafydd Iwan, folksinger and nationalist (see page 408), though *The Times* called him an heir to Nye Bevan and Lloyd George.

This is Labour Country, the traditional heartland of Welsh workers an their party. If we add the name of James Keir Hardie, we have a political line that stretches from Ebbw Vale to Merthyr Tydfil and reaches far back into the history of iron and coal. 'Red Rhondda' was what they used to call the valley of black diamonds. It was not only in Maerdy that the radicals earned their towns' nickname of 'Little Moscow', for some of them had actually studied at the Lenin School of Moscow. During the Spanish Civil War, 116 Welsh miners fought in the international brigades – more volunteers than from all the English mines put together.[1] 'The antifascist barricades reach from Tonypandy to Madrid,' they declared. The fact that the South Wales miners constituted the biggest single group of workers in the international brigades would not have been possible without the influence of their union. The first communist to be elected President of the South Wales Miners' Federation, in 1936, was the legendary workers' leader from the Valleys, Arthur Horner. But the Welsh part in the fight for Spanish democracy was not only a matter of class-conscious Marxism or cadre training; this solidarity was more deeply rooted, in the democratic tradition of their own community. A symbol of this political culture was William Abraham, known as Mabon. He was born in 1843, a miner's son and himself sent underground at the age of nine; he was a choir-leader at 14, a Sunday schoolteacher at 16, then a lay preacher, Eisteddfod organizer, and in 1885 the first Welsh miner to take his seat in Westminster. 'What I am today, whatever that may be, I owe to the Sunday School, Band of Hope and to the Eisteddfod.' In 1898 William Abraham became founding president of the first Welsh Miners' Federation. The necessity for workers' interests to be represented against the mine-owners is evident from the 'sliding scale system' that operated in those days: wages varied according to the rise and fall in the price of coal. Nothing was fixed. Only after the Rhondda miners' uprising of 1910, which was bloodily suppressed by army troops, did the Minimal Wage Act come into force two years later. Mining in the Valleys had long been a matter of exploitation – quick profits for the few, and a pittance for the pitmen.

One of the darkest chapters in the history of the coal valleys and of early capitalism is that of child labour. In 1840, six-year-old Susan Reece reported: 'I have been below six or eight months and I don't like it much. I come here at six in the morning and leave at six at night. When my lamp goes out or I am hungry I go home. I haven't been hurt yet.' Her job was to open and close the ventilator in the Plymouth mine near Merthyr Tydfil. 'Carters'

---

1 One member of the Rhondda Brigade in the Spanish Civil War was the poet and workers' leader Lewis Jones, who wrote two novels in the 1930's about the life of South Welsh miners ('Cwmardy', 'We Live').

was the name given to the boys who, with chains round their waists, pulled trucks of coal through the galleries that were too low for the pit ponies. James Davis, aged 8, reported that he earned ten pennies a week, which his father took from him, and John Saville, aged 7, said that he was always in the dark and only saw daylight on Sundays. These are the recorded statements of children who worked in the Welsh mines during the early 19th century. It was not unusual for these children to be so young that their fathers had to carry them on their backs when they climbed down the shafts, and to pull them up again in the coal-baskets. In those days, wages were low and variable, and so if any member of the family could bring in a little more money, it was welcome, and indeed often essential for their survival. How else is one to explain the exploitation of children in mines and factories? When a commission of inquiry first published the facts, Victorian society was shocked. And yet even then, Lord Shaftesbury was only able to get his 1842 mining act passed through Parliament against fierce opposition. This forbade children under the age of ten to work underground. For those days, such a law represented major progress.

A trip through the Valleys is a trip through political and industrial history, and if you want to see romantic Wales, you must go elsewhere. But the roots of modern Wales lie in these valleys, for it was from here that the Welsh made their contribution to the history of European workers' movements, and it was a spectacular chapter, even if today it is largely forgotten. Literature played its part, too, as Dylan Thomas noted in a broadcast he made in 1946: 'Out of the mining valleys of South Wales, there were poets who were beginning to write in a spirit of passionate anger against the inequality of social conditions. They wrote, not of the truths and beauties of the natural world, but of the lies and ugliness of the unnatural system of society under which they worked – or, more often during the nineteen-twenties and thirties, under which they were not allowed to work. They spoke, in ragged and angry rhythms, of the Wales *they* knew: the coal-tips, the dole-queues, the

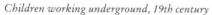

Children working underground, 19th century

Master John Davies, 1911

stubborn bankrupt villages, the children scrutting for coal on the slag-heaps, the colliers' shabby allotments, the cheap-jack cinema, the whippet races, the disused quarries, the still pit-wheels, the gaunt tin-roofed chapels in the soot ...'

Was there no way out of the Valleys except downwards into the earth or outwards through emigration? 'You can box your way out. You can play your way out. And you can sing your way out,' an old pitman once told Wynford Vaughan-Thomas. Those were the classic escape routes. For instance, there was little Jimmy Wilde, the 'Tylorstown Terror' or 'Mighty Atom', flyweight champion of the world from 1916 till 1923, 7½ stone of dynamite. Or Tommy Farr of Tonypandy, the legendary heavyweight who gave Joe Louis the fight of his life at Madison Square Garden in 1937. In those days the Valleys were a cradle for boxing and wrestling champions. In *Pant Cemetery*,[1] the huge hillside graveyard of *Merthyr Tydfil*, where the cholera victims of this iron town lie buried, I also found the grave of Johnny Owen, bantamweight champion of Europe. 'He fought the good fight with all his might' is the epitaph written beside his colour photo on the grave. To look at him, you'd scarcely imagine that he was a boxing champion; he's more like one

1 Also worth visiting is the Victorian Cefn Golau Cemetery (colour plate 10) on the B4256, and on the moors nearby is the abandoned cemetery of the steelworkers of Tredegar.

of those mining children of yesteryear. But he has his thin arms held aloft, and is smiling as he celebrates another victory. Alas, he fought one fight too many, and died in 1980 at the age of 24, as a result of the injuries he received in the ring in his last fight. The way out of the Valleys was a hard one for Johnny Owen.[1]

Merthyr Tydfil: The Iron Town

If you leave Tredegar and go along the 'Heads of the Valleys Road' to Merthyr Tydfil, the first thing you will see is the black hills of Trecatti, where the 'sunshine colliers' work, extracting coal from the open-cast mines (colour plate 24). But it is iron and not coal that has made *Merthyr Tydfil* famous. In the middle of the 19th century the town had 60,000 inhabitants, and was the biggest in Wales – bigger than Cardiff, Swansea and Newport put together. It was the iron and steel capital of the world. The cannons that defeated Napoleon, and the weapons and railways that acquired the Empire, came from the blast furnaces of the Crawshays and the Guests. In 1854 George Borrow could see in the distance 'a glowing mountain' in the night, and another time he noted that all the hills round the town had 'a scorched and blackened look'. After breakfast he went to see 'the great wonder of the place', Cyfarthfa ironworks, and then the blast furnaces of Dowlais which looked like 'Satan's Palace': 'There it stands: a house of reddish brick with a slate roof – four horrid black towers behind, two of them belching forth smoke and flame from their tops – holes like pigeonholes here and there – two immense white chimneys standing by themselves ... I stood staring at the diabolic structure with my mouth open.'

Now this technological devilry has disappeared like a ghost. Only the house of reddish brick is still standing, though now its roof is of corrugated iron. In its isolation it seems all the more impressive, this powerhouse of Dowlais, with its round arched windows, pilasters, and iron-columned portico – a masterpiece of Georgian industrial architecture (1811). Round it is empty space, apart from a chocolate factory. 'There's just a few hundred work here now,' says a Merthyr man, 'and before there used to be over a thousand. It's a dead end, finished altogether. You see that white tip?' He points upwards at the old symbol of the town, the slagheaps from Dowlais's blast furnaces: 'They've been taking those slagheaps away for eight years now, and they're still here!' There's a sort of stubborn pride in the grim heritage. And where are the ironworks of Cyfarthfa, which once filled the valley with their smoke and noise and bustle? Near the Hoover washing-machine factory, on the edge of overgrown mounds, I find the ruins of the old

---

1 Worthy of at least a footnote is the Nurmi of the Rhonddas: Griffith Morgan, known as Guto Nyth Brân. He was an 18th-century shepherd with even more stamina than his sheepdog, and died in 1737 after a legendary run from Newport to Bedwas Church (12 miles in 53 minutes). His grave is in the hillside cemetery of St Gwynno in Llanwonno, Clydach Valley. Every year since 1958, on New Year's Eve, a 6,000 metre race is held in Mountain Ash, in Guto's memory.

J. C. Ibbetson: Working Iron at Merthyr Tydfil

blast furnaces, built on the rocky slope, brickwork, barrel vaulting with side wings … one can imagine how gigantic they were. Water drips everywhere now, and no iron glows. There's a cool, musty stillness in this mausoleum of Cyfarthfa, which in 1800 had been Britain's biggest iron foundry. In that year Richard Crawshay, the Iron King of Merthyr Tydfil, had taken Admiral Nelson through the works and shown him, among other things, a flourishing arms industry. Now it's just another dead end.

In addition to Cyfarthfa (1765) and Dowlais (1759) there are two other foundries in Merthyr, Plymouth (1763) and Penydarren (1784). The owners all came from England. At the height of the iron boom in the middle of the 19th century, they employed altogether more than 15,000 workers. The end came as inevitably here as it did in the Rhonddas, and the Cyfarthfa Ironworks closed in 1910, while the steelworks of Dowlais struggled on till 1936. The legacy was thousands of unemployed, a town built up and then demolished by the iron industry, a ruined landscape, and as always a set of politicians who could do nothing. The situation was so desperate that a parliamentary commission set up in 1939 recommended that Merthy Tydfil be abandoned and its people resettled on the coast or in the Valley of the Usk. Port Talbot or Newport, they thought, was where the steel industry would have its future. Saunders Lewis wrote a poem entitled 'The Deluge 1939', which

Penry Williams: Cyfarthfa Works Furnaces, 1825

Thomas Horner: The Rolling Mills at Dowlais, 1825

begins: 'The tramway climbs from Merthyr to Dowlais, / Slime of a snail on a heap of slag: / Here once was Wales, and now / Derelict cinemas and rain on the barren tips.' 80,000 people once lived in Merthyr Tydfil in the 1920's, and now there are just 45,000. The young people went away, the old people stayed; but now the young people stay as well, for their chances are no better anywhere else. It seemed in those grim days as if a whole town had been put on the scrapheap of history, but the iron town has an iron spirit. Light industry came here, and small firms set up business, with the result that Merthyr Tydfil is now once more the biggest service and retail centre in the 'Heads of the Valleys'. Nevertheless, it's hard to dent an unemployment rate that has reached 20%, and about 60% among young people. 'I was born in the crater of this town / below a ring of tips and heaps / … dreaming of an empire of smoke,' wrote the young poet Mike Jenkins, inspired by the plight of a friend who had just been made redundant from the steelworks. 'Gloom is the uniform I wear …' Anyone who wanted to preserve industrial monuments here was regarded, until recently, as a crank or a reactionary. Whatever recalled the times of depression and repression was ruthlessly destroyed. Nowhere is the destructive tendency of the Valleys more frighteningly evident than in Merthyr Tydfil.

The Dowlais Ironworks with its 18 blast furnaces was one of the first and biggest of its kind in the world, and it was also the first in Britain to produce Bessemer steel. Now nothing remains of it except the powerhouse. And the ironworks of Cyfarthfa have disappeared too, apart from a few fragments. The Sleeper Mill, which produced the iron sleepers that still bear the weight of Indian and Chinese trains – demolished in 1983. The Victorian indoor market, the old centre of Dowlais – demolished in 1971. The Triangle, an extraordinary workers' estate of 1840 – demolished in 1977. Dowlais House, home of the Guest[1] dynasty of industrialists – demolished in 1973. And Dowlais stables (1820), the Georgian stables for the Guests' pit ponies, are falling into ruin. 'Who cares about the stables?' asks Mike Jenkins, teacher, poet and left-wing nationalist, 'how did the workers live?' He considers the conservation of industrial sites to be nothing but nostalgia. Even Cyfarthfa Castle, family home of the Crawshays, the Iron King of Merthyr Tydfil, was threatened with demolition a few years ago because local politicians considered this 1825 castle to be an insult to the workers. 'We have a socialist town council,' explains David Francis, librarian and chairman of the Merthyr Tydfil Heritage Trust. 'Everything that was redolent of capitalism was automatically bad and had to be pulled down.' Since 1979 he has been trying to save whatever is still there to be saved. 'Unfortunately, a lot has gone, but there's still enough left to make it worth while.' Merthyr Tydfil has not lost all its history, and a long overdue policy of conservation could still reveal what this town once was – the

1 Commissioned by Lady Charlotte Guest, Charles Barry, architect of the Houses of Parliament, designed a school in Dowlais (1855), now demolished, and a Neo-Classical library (1863), both for the iron and steel workers. Thanks to its high educational standard, Dowlais in those days was dubbed the 'Prussia of Wales'. With her English translation of the 'Mabinogion' (1838–49), Lady Guest made this classic Welsh epic of the Middle Ages available to a worldwide readership (see page 264).

birthplace of the Industrial Revolution in Wales, the classic early iron town, just as later the Rhondda became the classic seat of coal. Merthyr Tydfil could still become the Welsh equivalent to the Ironbridge Gorge Museum in England, and could easily surpass this if only the effort were made.

In the end the Labour Government did at last set things moving. The ironworkers' estate of Cyfarthfa Row (1840) in Georgetown was restored, and the inner city district of Thomastown was declared a conservation area: this was where the middle classes lived, in the late Georgian and early Victorian houses on Upper Thomas and Church Street. A somewhat romanticized view of how workers lived at the end of the 19th century is offered by some neatly restored cottages, but closer to the truth are the reminiscences of Jack Jones: 'The big industrialists of the time left us without water, and without a hospital to patch us up after we'd broken our bones, burnt ourselves or worn ourselves out serving them. Not even a hall where we could meet or hold any sort of function. Nothing you could have called sanitation, and I could go on and on. Those that people often call "our great benefactors" just took what was worth taking from the filthy lucre – they had the lucre, and we had the filth. All the same, we did have the Cyfarthfa Brass Band ... And Joseph Parry, in his mining gear and with an empty stomach, after twelve hours working his fingers to the bone for a wage of five pence, sang about "The Kingdoms of the Earth".'

When Joseph Parry was born in Merthyr Tydfil in 1841, average life expectancy there was 18 years and 2 months. When he was nine, a cholera epidemic claimed 1,500 people in three days. At ten he became a miner, and at twelve he was working in Cyfarthfa Ironworks. When he was 13, he and his parents emigrated to Pennsylvania. There in his spare time he began to compose, and submitted his songs to the National Eisteddfod, where they were greeted with such enthusiasm that a collection was made to bring him back and pay for him to study at the Royal Academy of Music in London. He did come back, and in 1872 took the first chair of music at the new University of Wales in Aberystwyth, later becoming professor of music at Cardiff University. He composed operas, oratorios, and more than 700 songs and hymns. Many of these are still sung today in chapels, at Eisteddfodau, and at the Cymanfa Ganu, the Easter Song Festival of the Valleys. Thus the foundry worker Joseph Parry became a national and indeed an international figure. But 'Y Doctor Mawr', the great doctor, wanted only to be known as the 'Bachgen bach of Ferthyr', a little boy from Merthyr. The house where he was born can still be seen today, in a little terrace, the restored remains of a workers' estate dating from the early 19th century. It's No. 4 Chapel Row, one of those 'great little houses' which are more typical of Wales than any castles or cathedrals.

When the young Joseph Parry stepped out of his cottage, he would already be standing on the works premises. Outside the front door, he would see the barges that carried iron and coal along the Glamorganshire Canal to Cardiff. Today, though, he would have a renovated view over the Taff Valley, for industry has gone, and the archaeologists have arrived. They have excavated part of the canal as part of what is planned as an open-air

The world's first locomotive: the Penydarren loco by Richard Trevithick, 1804

industrial museum. The original Glamorganshire Canal had 49 locks, which, over a stretch of 21 miles, overcame a height difference of 500 feet. Built in 1792–94, it was a technical showpiece which was of equal economic importance to the development of the Valleys and of the port of Cardiff. By 1865 it, too, had fallen victim to competition from the railways, and so it had to be filled in. Among its gravediggers was one who had assisted at its birth: Samuel Homfray, a Merthyr Tydfil iron-master of vision and with a competitive instinct. He supported the canal, but quicker than most people he switched allegiance to the railways. He reasoned that a steam engine on rails could carry a great deal more than a barge pulled by horses. At the time, this sounded so airy-fairy that Iron King Richard Crawshay bet him 500 guineas that he was wrong. Now Homfray had just lured away from his competitors in Coalbrookdale, England, an engineer who was to build high-pressure steam engines for him in his Penydarren ironworks: Richard Trevithick, a Cornishman. On February 21 1804 the unbelievable took place. Puffing along the track came a bizarre machine with a gigantic flywheel, cylindrical boiler, and hissing funnel, pulling five trucks containing ten tons of iron ore and 70 passengers. Despite the fact that its maximum speed was five miles an hour, the train needed four hours and five minutes to cover the ten miles from Penydarren to Abercynon, because there were trees and rocks that had to cleared on the way. Crawshay had lost his bet, and Trevithick had made his name as the inventor of the steam engine, 25 years before Stephenson built his 'Rocket'. Thus the age of railways began in a remote Welsh valley, though the laurels went, as so often they do, to those who huff and puff the most – towns like Manchester and Nuremburg – while little Merthyr Tydfil is forgotten. Richard Trevithick, too, is forgotten. He lies somewhere in an unmarked grave in a paupers' cemetery in Kent, after a life of adventure in South America. As for his legendary Penydarren engine, there is only a reconstruction of it in Cardiff's industrial museum. The testing-ground in the Taff Valley, the Pennydarren tram road, is now a footpath.[1] So the Industrial Revolution abandons the sites of its former triumphs to the umemployed, the tourists and the hikers. A revolution that ran out of steam.

A virtuoso product of Merthyr's Iron Age is to be found near the town centre. Erected in 1907 in honour of an industrialist and his wife, it is the Robert and Lucy Thomas Fountain, which is not a fountain at all, but a large canopy of cast iron, with filigree as delicate as Brussels lace (plate 26). No less elaborate is the late Victorian town hall of brick and terracotta (1896). G. B. Shaw, visiting Merthyr Tydfil on behalf of the Fabian Society, criticized it quite vehemently though, to my mind, unjustly. On the stairs is an Art Nouveau window commemorating Queen Victoria's Diamond Jubilee (1897); she looks down on the bust of her upstart subject, the workers' leader Keir Hardie. Merthyr Tydfil was the first British constituency to send a Labour MP to Parliament: James Keir Hardie, elected in 1900. A Scot representing Wales in London, socialism and royalism hobnobbing together in the same townhall – for foreigners it must be hard to understand how the United Kingdom can unite such disparate elements. Back in 'Red Clydeside' the former miner Keir Hardie had fought for home rule, and under his leadership the Labour Party, of which he was co-founder, continued to identify itself with the national aspirations and institutions of Wales. But when the workers' party then became increasingly middle class and British, many Welshmen thought it was time to form their own national party. Plaid Cymru, however, did not fulfil their hopes, and in what may turn out to be its death throes, the national party is now striving to follow a socialist line in keeping with Keir Hardie's tradition.

The fact that since it was founded in 1900 the Labour Party has always had a stronghold in Merthyr Tydfil is no coincidence. Nowhere else in Wales were the industrial workers so militant and so well organized as they were here, for they were painfully aware right from the start of the yawning gulf between wealth and poverty. The first Welsh workers' newspaper appeared in 1814 in Merthyr, naturally in Welsh ('Y Gweithiwr', The Worker), and the workers' movement had its first martyrs in the iron town. The unions had just achieved legal recognition, but still had no right to strike, when in June 1831 there was an uprising in Merthyr Tydfil, which was brutally suppressed by the police and the army. There were over 20 dead – more than were killed in the 1819 revolt of the Manchester weavers, which attained lasting fame as the 'Peterloo massacre'. The 'Merthyr Rising' remained, like so much else in Welsh history, a local affair, a mere footnote to 'real' history, which means English history. Such helplessness entails even greater heroism, such as that of Richard Lewis, known as Dic Penderyn, one of the many demonstrators of Merthyr Tydfil. Suddenly he became a national symbol. His fellow defendants were deported to Australia, but he was condemned to death. At the gallows in Cardiff, in August 1831, the 23-year-old miner shouted just one word: 'Injustice!' Not long after, a ritual act of revenge was performed in Hirwaun: a calf was slaughtered, and a flag dipped

1   It goes past Quakers' Yard Viaduct (1841), the only remaining one of four viaducts built in Wales by I. K. Brunel.

in its blood. And thus the first red flag was waved in the Taff Valley. More strikes, lock-outs, hunger and demonstrations followed, but the revolution was to happen elsewhere. The hero of Merthyr Tydfil, however, entered into folklore. There is a rock opera called 'Dic Penderyn', and a Welsh pop group named 'Penderyn', and a monumental plaque near the townhall. It calls him a martyr of the Welsh working class. Thus Socialist legend joins Christian legend, for the name Merthyr Tydfil is derived from the martyred Princess Tudful, who lived and died in the 5th century.

A few years before his workers went out into the streets to demonstrate for their rights, William Crawshay had taken up residence at a new home on the northern outskirts of the town, in a castle on a hill: *Cyfarthfa Castle*, completed in 1825. This was his way of telling the people who was the Iron King of Merthyr Tydfil. He wanted to look down on them, and he wanted to have them looking up at him – that way, there could be no mis-understandings. Hovels down below, palace up above; industrial squalor and cholera in the valley, clean air and a fine view on the hill. Pig iron for the workers, and Neo-Gothic for the masters. And so those workers got to know the meaning of architecture, and their descendants now have a target for sight-seeing. Cyfarthfa Castle was a deliberate anachronism, a romantic digression from the Industrial Revolution, now at its peak; from the iron rolling mill of progress it was a flight back to medieval aestheticism, a crenellated, turreted refuge from the filth and the misery of the blast furnaces. The Crawshays sought a noble detachment, though they were no aristocrats. They were the nouveaux riches, iron-makers, but like so many parvenus anxious to acquire some sort of historical image. Did not a castle signify noble stock? Robert Lugar's architecture reflects the needs but somehow also the deficiencies of his patron. It is richly solid, but unnaturally stiff.

From Crawshay's hillside castle you can see the gigantic *Cefn Coed Viaduct* high above the Taff Valley, a masterpiece of Victorian engineering (1866). It bore the railway that ran from Merthyr to Brecon – at Crawshay's insistence making a wide sweep round his estate. Today the castle is part school and part museum. What used to be the salons now contain part of the Crawshays' art collection, their iron, the tools of their workers, and the family silver with coat of arms. Plough and bulldog on a pile of cannonballs – that is the heraldic biography of Richard Crawshay, a farmer's son from Yorkshire, who founded an iron empire in Wales (ploughshares into cannons) and called it Cyfarthfa, place of the barking dogs. In 1792 the painter Julius Caesar Ibbetson, a guest of the Crawshays, painted this dramatic scene of early industrialization, and a local artist named Penry Williams owed his career to the Crawshays' patronage. He studied under Fuseli in London, and lived as a successful landscape painter for nearly sixty years in Rome, where he died in 1885. His early watercolours are still to be seen in their place of origin: castle, industry and landscape are all depicted with topographical accuracy, precise and yet pleasing.[1] There is also a

1 Hans Koppel, a German Late Expressionist painter and Jewish emigrant from Berlin, also lived in Merthyr Tydfil from 1941 onwards. As director of the Merthyr Tydfil Arts Centre, he influenced a whole generation of Welsh artists.

portrait of a Victorian gentleman with patrician beard, leaning casually against a hedge: Robert Thompson Crawshay, the last of Merthyr Tydfil's Iron Kings. Unions? A patriarch of his ilk had nothing to do with workers. He preferred to close the works down in 1874. And when years of lockouts still failed to get him what he wanted, he finally died in 1879. It was the end of an industrial dynasty. Round his coffin they wound chains from Cyfarthfa – a fitting gesture for this man of iron.

I drove out of Merthyr Tydfil to visit Robert Crawshay's grave in *Vaynor*. It's a lonely, wildly overgrown cemetery high above the Valley of Taf Fechan. Looking down over the deep gorge, you get a feeling of profound peace. There are no steam hammers here, no workers' demonstrations, no town of barking dogs. In 1870 Robert Crawshay had had a small church built; below the window of the church tower are traces of rust – iron columns from Cyfarthfa. A massive stone slab covers his grave: Robert Thompson Crawshay 1817–1879, GOD FORGIVE ME. The hunting grounds of the Iron King reached beyond Vaynor to the woods round *Pontsticill* Reservoir. Here, at Brecon Mountain Railway Station, the valleys of coal and iron fade away like a ghostly vision in the steam of the narrow-gauge railway.

Brecon Beacons: Where Adelina Sang and Sarah Acted

Beacons are fires lit on hills, an integral part of medieval communications. 'Brecon' is a corruption of Brycheiniog, the land of Brychein, the legendary 5th-century British king who divided his kingdom between 12 sons and 24 daughters without any quarrelling. This land really exists, and it is as beautiful as the legend: green, full of forests, waterfalls, caves and hills, the highest of which are the Brecon Beacons. In the absence of Brychein's sons and daughters, a National Park has been established here in order to keep paradise just as it was. Although this task involves considerably fewer county councils than the King had children, there is rather more trouble in the park than there was in Brychein's day, but more of this anon.

You leave the coal valleys, cross the iron road, and on the other side you find yourself in the bosom of Nature, far from industry, and already almost in Wild Wales itself. The 'Heads of the Valleys Road' and its extension to Ystradgynlais is more or less the southern border of the National Park. The other borders are formed by hills: to the east, the Black Mountains, where semi-wild ponies graze on the moors; to the west, again a Black Mountain, from the sides of which spring the Usk and the Tawe; and to the north, Mynydd Epynt, where Her Majesty's soldiers use tanks to shoot the moorhens. The *Brecon Beacons National Park* was begun in 1957, the last of eleven such national parks in Britain. Of the three in Wales, it is the least known: not so wild and dramatic as Snowdonia, and not so spectacular as the rocky coasts of Pembrokeshire. It has a serene, pastoral beauty, with gentle hills, thickly forested valleys in the south, but also barren moorland like Fforest Fawr, whose Arctic tundra vegetation is a relic of the last ice age.

In the whole Brecon Beacons area, some 520 square miles, there are 30,000 inhabitants, most of them concerned with agriculture and forestry. National Parks in Britain are not parks in the usual sense, nor are they owned by the nation, as they are, say, in America. They are areas of national importance, but under the control of regional authorities. They are financed two-thirds by the State and one-third by the region. Representatives from the regions form the National Park Authority, an administrative body with advisory functions, but without any real executive powers. They have local planning authority, and the right to object to industrial projects, but they cannot control the forestation of wasteland. And this is precisely what causes the occasional conflict in Brecon Beacons National Park. Instead of native oak or other deciduous trees, North American conifers tend to be planted here because they grow much more quickly and so are more profitable. And in order that planting and felling can be done economically, the former is generally done en masse, creating dark clumps which hide the gentle contours of the hills. But the problem is more than one of aesthetics. In Nature the aesthetic very often has ecological significance, and a change in the landscape also means a change in its character and in its ecological balance. The sharp reduction in deciduous forest here – by about half in the Black Mountains alone during the last 30 years – is a development that must cause some alarm. Equally alarming is the slow but sure disappearance of the moors – every year a good 12,000 acres are lost in Britain's national parks through forestation, cultivation and grazing. Food and timber production attract more public subsidies than nature conservation. However, in the last few years, thanks largely to the efforts of the conservationists, Brecon Beacons National Park has switched to a more differentiated programme of forestation, and so far the planners have managed to resist the pressures of heavy industry in favour of small firms whose activities fit in more closely with local needs. One must also mention the first-class information centres run by the park authorities. The most popular of these, the Brecon Beacons Mountain Centre in Libanus, also happens to be situated in one of the most beautiful landscapes of the park – *Mynydd Illtyd Common*, south-west of Brecon.

One warm June day I wandered over this wide and gently undulating hill country. There were lumps of wool hanging on the gorse, and the whitethorn was in flower. I walked up a long ridge, the *Twyn y Gaer*. The panorama was breathtaking: stretching as far as the eye could see was a great patchwork of fields and moors and forests, in every shade of brown and green, with the clouds playing games of light and shadow over them all. The Devil could have led me up a higher mountain to offer me all the riches of the world, but he'd have been hard pressed to surpass the beauty of that view of Twyn y Gaer. Once, though, such vantage-points served not to feast the eyes of happy wanderers like me, but to provide the sites for hill forts, refuges for man and beast. The *Pen-y-Crug* north-west of Brecon was one such fortress in the Iron Age, with no less than five earthwork walls and trenches for defence. The *Brecon Beacons* themselves are twin peaks, the higher of which, Pen-y-Fan, is not even 3,000 feet high – a none too ambitious mountain, which is all the more popular with hikers for its modesty. Even the hardest Devonian Old

Red Sandstone cannot withstand so many tramping feet indefinitely, and the most direct (and therefore favourite) of the nine paths to the top – that of the Storey Arms – is the most threatened with erosion. The park wardens also fear that in many areas pony trekking could become an even bigger problem. Mind you, there is not only erosion from tourism; there's also tourism thanks to erosion. Limestone caves are one of the attractions on the southern borders of the park. 'Caving country' is near Llangattock, south of Crickhowell, where more than 12 miles of '*Ogof Agen Allwedd*' (keyhole caves) have so far been explored. The caves of *Dan-yr-Ogof* in the upper Tawe Valley are said to be 'Britain's Largest and Longest Showcaves'. They were inhabited in the Bronze Age, and today are effectively illuminated and concreted, their attractions being supplemented with a dinosaur park.

Not far from the caves, where Tawe Valley stretches out as majestically as the highland glens of Scotland, lies *Craig-y-nos*, the rock of the night. Here, at the turn of the century, lives the Queen of Song, Adelina Patti. Her father was a Sicilian tenor, her mother a Roman soprano, and Adelina was born while they were visiting Madrid in 1843, but grew up in New York. Her career took her from Covent Garden on to the opera houses of Paris, Milan, Vienna, Berlin, even as far as Moscow. The effortless beauty of her voice entranced all who heard it. She sang for the Kaiser, the Tsar and the Queen. On a guest appearance in St Petersburg six generals carried her in a seat of flowers, accompanied by a brass band, to her hotel suite. She was a superstar, and the highest paid soprano of her day. For one performance of 'La Traviata' in Boston she was paid 5,000 gold dollars. The upper-class yearning for beauty found its apogee in opera, and Patti, with her fairytale rise to riches and even a title (Marquise), was such stuff as dreams are made on. It was not enough for a prima donna to have a voice, she also had to have mystique and romance, and Patti had all these things in abundance. After her first marriage to Napoleon III's equerry, she married an Austrian tenor and in 1878 moved with him to Wales.

To Wales? It was one of her admirers, Lord Swansea, who succeeded in luring her from the social whirl to a remote Welsh valley. He showed her the lonely valleys of Fforest Fawr, the serene beauty of the Brecon Beacons, and a Neo-Gothic manor-house built by Thomas H. Wyatt: Craig-y-Nos (1843, coincidentally the year of her birth). And so Wales became the great love of her life. With her third husband, too, a Swedish masseur and baron, Adelina returned to her 'Rock of the Night'. In Craig-y-Nos she could recover from her hectic tours and love affairs, finding peace and renewed strength. Her daily routine included walking for hours in the pure mountain air. In 1890, she had a little opera house built there, a miniature Theatre Royal, Drury Lane, with Corinthian columns, stucco decor, and a curtain showing her in her favourite role as Semiramis. For the poor of the region she gave free concerts, and the poor came in droves. She would hold court in Craig-y-Nos, and it was here that she sang 'Last Rose of Summer' to her ageing friend Bertie, who was still Prince of Wales; here she received the director of the Grand Opera in Paris, who wanted her to make a guest appearance. Only when he had left did she signal her acceptance by hoisting the flag on the castle tower. She would talk in four different

Adelina Patti,
about 1875

languages to her parrots, and her husbands would fish for trout in the Tawe. At the little station in *Penwyllt*, the Queen of Song had her own waiting-room, and whenever she returned in her special train from world tours, it was like Queen Victoria arriving in Balmoral for her Scottish holiday – the people would form a guard of honour, crying 'Mrs Patti for ever!' She died in 1919 at Craig-y-Nos, but was buried at the Père Lachaise in Paris. Today her Welsh home is a geriatric hospital, and now beneath the stucco ceilings where Patti once held her glamorous court and her soprano voice rang out so light and pure, old people lie in silence. Craig-y-Nos is indeed the Rock of the Night. And Tawe Valley, where she used to go walking, is now a country park. In her private theatre, a real gem of Victorian stage architecture, her admirers meet every June for a little opera festival. 'Adelina for ever'.

Patti married her third husband in *Brecon*, and it was here, a century earlier, that the great tragedienne Sarah Siddons was born – 'the beau ideal of acting' (Lord Byron). She entered the world in 1755, at the 'Shoulder of Mutton', an inn in the High Street. Her parents were strolling players, belonging to the Brecon Company who used to tour the border towns. From an early age, Sarah acted with them, until she was discovered by David Garrick and went to London's Drury Lane. She seldom returned to Wales. After all, where could such a heroine act in Wales? There was no theatre life in the towns, and no national theatre, and she had no desire to go back to the little provincial stages. And so Sarah Siddons, like many of her compatriots, stayed in London, where she became the most famous actress of her time, and had seven children too. Her monument is in Westminster Abbey, but you can also honour her in the house where she was born – by having a drink there, for it is now the pub 'Sarah Siddons'. The inn-sign reproduces the portrait Gainsborough painted in 1785 ('Damn it, Madam, there is no end to your nose').

Brecon lies at the foot of the Brecon Beacons, whose bare peaks seem to be ubiquitous, changing constantly according to the time of day and year. You can get the best view with an iron in your hand – from Cradoc Golf Club, north-west of the town. The settlement goes back to Norman times, but the tale that impressed me most was that of the Brecon people's courage during the Civil War. They actually demolished their own castle and town walls in order not to become a target – a successful example of effective unilateral disarmament in the 17th century. The ruins of the castle now provide a picturesque setting for the Bishop and for a hotel. The Church of St John has been a cathedral since 1933. Benedictines from Battle in Sussex, site of the Battle of Hastings, had come west with the Norman invaders, and in 1093 they founded a monastery in Brecon. Of this, all that remained – with a good deal of restoration and alteration – was the Priory Church of St John – small but solid, with a thick crossing tower, 'half church of God, half castle 'gainst the Welsh'. The chancel ends in a Benedictine-style rectangle (1201–08), dominated by a lancet window which points upwards, like the five fingers of a hand – exemplary early English Gothic. One must also mention the Norman font (1130), a sculptured tomb by the English Neo-Classicist Flaxman (1812) in the nave, and a monk named Dr Hugh Price. To him generations of Welsh students owe their Oxford English, for he founded Jesus College in 1571, intended originally only for his fellow-countrymen. The 'Taffia' still meet in the Dafydd ap Gwilym Society in Oxford (1886).

As cathedral, market, garrison and former county town, Brecon has remained surprisingly small, with its 7,000 inhabitants. It's a relaxed, rural town with Georgian houses and Victorian shop fronts. The museum has moved into what used to be Shire Hall, built by Thomas H. Wyatt in 1843 in Greek Revival style – a Paestum temple in a Welsh province. On the far side of the old bridge over the Usk (1563), which has been desecrated by a modern upper section, lies the suburb of *Llanfaes*, containing Christ College, with its Gothic chapel (1240) and its Neo-Gothic Public School, founded in 1853. If you want to, you can drift back as far as Pontypool on the Brecon and Abergavenny Canal (1801), or stroll along the towpath beside the old industrial waterway, between alders and drawbridges.

Trefecca: Sing, My Soul, for God is a Welshman

In the green hills north-east of Brecon lies a weird and wonderful place. At first sight, *Trefecca College* (1752–72) looks like the house of some eccentric millionaire, and in a certain sense it was: pink in colour, with curious corner towers, Neo-Gothic ogival windows. But this early Welsh variant of Strawberry Hill was not the country estate of an aristocrat headcase; it was the headquarters of an 18th-century sect. On the roof, a weathercock hovers between Heaven and Hell, an angel blows the trumpet to resurrect all who can speak Welsh: '*Cyfodwch feirw, a denwch i'r farn*' – Rise up, you dead, for the Last Judgment. This is Trefecca's Angel of the Lord. Here Howell Harris lived, with his 'family'. Trefecca was the Wittenberg of the Welsh Methodist leader, though it was a place where ideas were not just formed, they were put into practice.

Howell Harris was the son of a carpenter. He spoke the Welsh of the farmers and shepherds, understood their problems, and so won their ears and their hearts, first as a teacher, then as a preacher. The official church suspected people like him and Wesley of sectarianism. He was refused ordination, but this only strengthened his sense of vocation. The only authority he needed was that of the Bible, and if he was forbidden to preach in church, he would preach in the open air. He travelled astonishing distances, especially if one considers the conditions of those times: between 1738 (when he was 24) and 1743, he rode some 30,000 miles round the country, driven on by his mission in life. Sometimes he fell asleep on the way and dropped from his horse out of sheer fatigue. But when he began to preach, his passion fired him with new energy, and he would often go on for up to three

Howell Harris (?): Trefecca College, 1751–73

hours non-stop, even in the pouring rain. The farmers came from miles around to attend his open-air meetings. It was not unusual for him to have a congregation of up to 2,000. He was said to describe Hell as if he had been there himself. He was a firebrand who has since been matched by none save Christmas Evans, the one-eyed Baptist preacher from Llandysul (picture, page 21). Howell Harris was known as *'Utgorn y Diwygiad'* – the Trumpet of the Awakening. But this was not enough for him. Like all religious reformers, he wanted not only to revive people's faith, but also to make new men and women out of them and create a new society. In Selina, Countess of Huntingdon, he found the ideal patroness – interested in new ideas, pious, rich, and a widow. She knew Horace Walpole, supported the Methodist Movement in England, and also gave her support to the Wesley of Wales.[1]

Perhaps Howell Harris wanted his Gothic Revival building in Trefeca to show that the revival of the Methodists was part of the new spirit of the age, an aesthetic reflection of the new soul – elegance and ecstasy to replace the plain and joyless ethos of Puritanism. For many people still had unhappy memories of Cromwell's rigid Puritan rule. No-one knows who designed Trefecca College – perhaps it was Harris himself. Gradually his community moved in. The place was completely self-sufficient, providing its own food, wool, clothes, shoes and books. There were 60 different professions practised in Trefecca, which was half monastery and half a sort of crafts co-operative. Howell Harris did, of course, know the Moravian Brethren in Fulneck, Yorkshire. *'Y Teulu'*, his 'family', shared everything as the early Christian communities had done, and there was no such thing as private property. Indeed Trefecca was a precursor of Robert Owen's Co-operative movement. 'Howell Harris's house is one of the most elegant places which I have seen in Wales,' wrote John Wesley in his diary after a visit to Trefecca, 'and the gardens, orchards, fish-ponds and the mount adjoining make the place a little paradise.' The day in Paradise began at 4 a.m. and ended at 10 p.m. In between there was hard work in the fields or workshops, interrupted three times by prayer and a sermon. Howell Harris died in 1773, and is buried in the hillside church of *Talgarth*, where he often preached. His 'family', which contained up to 350 people, lived on for another fifty years. Then Trefecca became a Methodist seminary. Lady Huntingdon had long before that already converted a neighbouring farmhouse into an academy for Methodist preachers. The Neo-Classical oak panelling of her guest-room in Trefecca College is one of the few remaining sections of the original interior. Painted right in the centre of the star-shaped stucco ceiling, the eye of God once gazed down upon Lady Huntingdon herself. Now the College is a lay training centre for the Presbyterian Church of Wales. And what have they done? Deaf to the spirits of the founder and his 'family', they have set right next to this Neo-Gothic extravaganza a new building of quite stunning plainness. Only the Victorians managed to surpass them in tastelessness, by tearing down

---

1 One of Lady Huntingdon's friends was Handel. This devout lady is said to have persuaded him to go and hear the famous Methodist Daniel Rowlands preach in Llangeitho, near Tregaron. Rowlands' ecstatic 'Gogoniant' (Gloria), repeated by a congregation one thousand strong, may have inspired Handel to write his Hallelujah Chorus – a story that has no evidence but is both plausible and typically Welsh.

one wing to make room for a memorial chapel to Howell Harris. Exhibited in the sacristy are some of his open-air pulpits and some of the books printed by the press of Trefecca. Their hymnbooks and religious tracts did a great deal to help the spread of the new piety. But people would not have been able to read these books if it had not been for another great preacher: the Reverend Griffith Jones.

This simple country parson succeeded where professional educational reformers seldom do – he set up a workable school system. For Wales at that time, this meant conquering illiteracy. To his consternation, Jones had discovered that his faithful flock could not even read the Bible. In 1730 he founded the 'Circulating Schools' in *Llanddowror*, a village close to Carmarthen. Teachers whom he had trained himself, and whom he paid out of the donations he himself had collected, were sent out all over the country with the single task of teaching people to read and write. The only textbook was the Bible. Griffith Jones's peripatetic teachers, who included the young Howell Harris, gave lessons to the farmers after they had finished their day's work. By adapting to the workers' routine, the schools made sure of success. And they gave their lessons in the language of the people, not in English. If anyone criticized Griffith Jones for this, he would invoke the wrath of God: whoever tried to destroy the Welsh language would be violating God's will, for when the Tower of Babel had been built, was it not God who had put a multitude of languages into the world? The Reverend Jones was a powerful preacher, whose one aim was to save the souls of his people. The fact that he also saved the Welsh language was, however, one of his greatest achievements. Between 1737 and his death in 1761, his circulating schools taught no less than 158,237 pupils. News of this feat even went as far afield as Russia, where the Empress Catherine II sent for a detailed report on the schools run by the Welsh parson.

Educational reform, religious revival, a new national consciousness – all these things were interconnected, and made Non-Conformism and the Welsh language into a political force to be reckoned with. But perhaps the root of all this was something much simpler. Perhaps what really made the Methodists so successful in Wales was the fact that everyone could sing his heart out during their services. Griffith Jones sent his teachers, and Howell Harris preached about the new Jerusalem, but the songs and the hymns that people sang on their way to Paradise were given to them by William Williams, called Pantycelyn (picture, page 21). William Williams was a farmer from near *Llandovery*. It was the custom in rural Wales not to use first or second names, but for instance to name a farmer after his farm. Hence Pantycelyn. Having been converted by Howell Harris, Pantycelyn travelled the land as a wandering preacher, and published some 90 books and pamphlets, with more than 800 hymns. If Harris was the Trumpet of the Awakening, William Williams was its singer, giving melody to the soul of Methodism. 'Guide me, O Thou Great Jehovah,' sang the congregation out in the Welsh fields, and they still sing it today in the churches of Wales and England. Many of his hymns became folksongs for the Welsh. 'I gaze across the distant hills, / Thy coming to espy; / Beloved, haste, the day grows late, / The sun sinks down the sky.' Even in English one can sense the simple but deep inner feeling, and the lyrical sweetness of these songs. This is the music of the soul. Pantycelyn, the mystic peasant, combined Nature and love of God in these direct, personal expressions of emotion, and Saunders Lewis is undoubtedly right to call him the first romantic poet in Wales, 'the great discoverer of the unconscious, the stronghold of the passions.' 'Search, my soul, to your heart's corners / search the long paths thoroughly, / and search all the secret chambers / that within its limits be.' Pantycelyn's monument stands in the gallery of the 'Heroes of Wales', in Cardiff City Hall (plate 7). He is one of a long line of Welsh peasant poets, whose tradition extends right up into the present. But now their platform is no longer the chapel or the field, it is the literature tent of the Eisteddfod.

'My soul listen / to the voice of purest peace.' And so from Trefecca I went into the Black Mountains, to a landscape of purest peace.

In the Black Mountains: The Treasure of Partrishow

Hedgerows and hearts are singing; this is the road to *Partrishow*. At Crickhowell's thirteen-arch bridge over the Usk (plate 103), I turn off into the Black Mountains, past the broad shoulders of the Sugar Loaf, and into the valley of the Grwyne Fawr, which gently eases its way out of the mountains. The river is small, but the valley is broad and luxuriantly green. Just a few farms, pastures, whitethorn hedgerows, marigold-yellow fields, and then blue slopes full of bell-flowers leading to open moorland with a brown and green patchwork of moss and ferns. These are the colours of the road to Partrishow. Why bother to go all the way when the route itself is so beautiful? Well, in Partrishow there's an old church which I simply have to see.

Now the road narrows, climbs up the steep slope, and almost turns into a kind of mountain pass. Then we're in a little gorge with a stream – Nant Mair, the stream of Mary – and a spring. Someone has stuck some fresh wild flowers in a yoghurt tub, and someone else has carved 'Thanks' on a hazel branch – votive offerings at the spring of St Issui, who lived and was killed here in the wilderness. In the early Middle Ages, this became a little route for pilgrims, first to a hermitage beside the holy stream, and then, up above on the slope, to the church of St Ishow.

From here there's a wide view of the valley, and a sense of total isolation. Outside the entrance to the church, there's an age-old yew which has two other trees growing out of it – a mountain ash and a holm oak. The church is tiny, made out of rubble stone, late 14th century. Built on to the western end is a chapel with an altar over the tomb of St Issui. All that remains from pre-Norman times is the baptismal font (c.1055). The treasure of Partrishow is the choir screen, separating nave from choir: the rood screen and gallery are of wood, and the main beam is profusely decorated with three ornamental bands covered in waterleaf and vines that intertwine in a mass of luxuriant foliage. It's a frieze of life, a celebration of existence. And at each end of the beam there is a dragon swallowing the vine – the eternal

1 CORRIS   House below slate quarry in North Wales ▷

6 Nanteos   The park

7 Bodnant Garden   Waterlily pond with the 18th-century Pin factory

8   LLANDEILO   Hill town on Towy

9   GWIDYR FOREST

10   Cefn Golau Cemetery near Tredegar

11   Farm on Anglesey

12   MACHYNLLETH   Main street with clock-tower (1873)

13   SWANSEA   Victorian terraced houses

14　Merthyr Tydfil　Victorian fountain

15　Berriew　Two peacocks in yew

16 MACHYNLLETH Early Victorian façades in Maengwyn Street

17 ADFA Methodist cemetery, 18–19th century

18 PORTH DINLLAEN Sailing idyll on Llyn Peninsula ▷

19 LLANGADOG Evening in Towy Valley

20 TENBY Harbour with ruined castle and Georgian houses

21 MENAI BRIDGE   Telford's suspension bridge (1819–26) with Snowdonia

22 BARMOUTH   Beach in Cardigan Bay

23 SIRHOWY VALLEY Markham Colliery

24 MERTHYR TYDFIL Pendarren workers' estate, open-cast coalmine

25   Pontcysyllte   Telford's aqueduct (1795–1805) for the Llangollen Canal

26   Tylerstown and Stanley Town   Miners' settlements in Rhondda ▷

27   BRITON FERRY   Golf course in industrial zone near Swansea

28   MILFORD HAVEN   Oil refineries in Pembrokeshire Coast National Park

29 NEWPORT Transporter Bridge (1902–06) across Usk

30 LLYN Figurehead

33 CARDIFF CASTLE Interior by William Burges, 1867 ff.

31 ADFA Methodist gravestone 1902

32 PORTMEIRION Shakespeare in Italian village

34 ANGLESEY Remembering the stagecoach

35 GREGYNOG HALL Sculpture in the park

36　MONTGOMERY CANAL　Dog Days

7　ABERYSTWYTH　Two old dragons

38　CHEPSTOW　Victorian fountain

39 KIDWELLY CASTLE   Norman coastal fort, 13–14th century

40 CARDIFF CASTLE   Victorian town castle, William Burges 1865–90

41   CHEPSTOW CASTLE   Norman border fortress on Wye, 11–13th century

43   CONWY CASTLE   Built by Edward I (1283–87), and Telford's Suspension Bridge (1822–26) ▷

42   POWIS CASTLE   Norman border fortress (13–16th century) with terraced garden (17th century)

44–51　Y DDRAIG GOCH　Little collection of Welsh dragons

CYMRU
AM BYTH

FAIRBOURNE RAILWAY LIMITED

PELDROED

Y DRENEWYDD '83

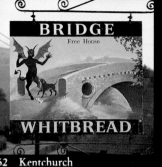

52 Kentchurch

56 Shelton

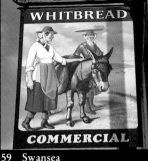

59 Swansea

53 Llanthony

57 Chepstow

54 Cardiff

55 Tredegar

58 Rhymney

60 Llangollen

61–2 ROYAL NATIONAL EISTEDDFOD   Gorsedd ceremonies in the stone circle at Llangefni
63   PONTYPRIDD   Merlin with goat and leek, outside pub, 19th century ▷

struggle between good and evil. These are carvings from an age when decoration was not a crime but narrated never-ending stories, concealed or revealed symbols, and could set the Devil in amongst the heavenly juices (plate 61). The beam bears the weight of the gallery. This sounds heavy and cumbersome, but it is not – the impression here is almost of weightlessness. The balustrade of the gallery is pure geometry, late Perpendicular, tracery-like filigree that seems almost porous, hovering between nave and choir, between space and time, between time and eternity. 'My soul listen / to the voice of purest peace.'

Modest in scale, rich in detail, beautiful in execution, this screen fulfils its function of marking off two spaces and yet not separating them. It joins priest and congregation together without blurring the distinction between them, and at the same time it creates additional space for the singers. The screen covers the whole width of the choir, which adds breadth and majesty to the single nave. It was made c.1500, of Irish oak. Unlike most such screens of the time, it was never painted. No-one knows whether the masterly hand that crafted it was Welsh or Flemish, and indeed very few people even knew that it was there at all, for who would expect such a treasure in so tiny a church, so remote from all habitation? Certainly the iconoclasts of the Reformation, Cromwell's soldiers, and all the other vandals left it alone. Undisturbed, Death gazes down from the west wall, with his scythe, spade and hourglass, a memento mori opposite the celebration of life, in a fresco of faded red and ochre, earthcolours easily applied by the wandering artists who struck immortality in Partrishow.

Among the ancient graves in the little churchyard there is a bright, slender stone. It bears a relief showing palette and brushes, and on the palette is a picture of a farm and animals, such as one often sees in these valleys. Here lies Joan Barnes, who died in 1977, a painter from the Black Mountains (plate 60). Who she was, what she painted, whether she was or will become famous, I do not know. But what is being hung in the Louvre when one can have a grave in Partrishow?

Llanthony, Capel-y-Ffin: Recluses and Drop-Outs

The paths through the Black Mountains are like Celtic knots, twisted, endless, timeless. If you walk from Partrishow over the crest towards the east, you'll come to the next valley on the river Honddu. This is the valley of recluses and drop-outs, monks and artists, legends, dreams and ruins. Giraldus Cambrensis visited *Llanthony Priory* in 1188, and describes the deep Vale of Ewyas, 'encircled on all sides by lofty mountains, but only an arrowshot broad.' There stood the abbey church of St John the Baptist. Like all good topographers and reporters – he accompanied the Archbishop of Canterbury on his campaign for the Third Crusade – Giraldus also informs his readers about the weather: 'owing to the mountainous situation, rains are frequent, the winds boisterous and the clouds in winter almost continual. But generally, the climate is temperate and healthy, the air, though heavy, mild and soothing, and diseases only rare.' Once the Vale of Ewyas was

◁ 64 Tintern Abbey Cistercian Abbey in Wye Valley, 1270–87

covered with dense forest – wild country, and a valley of isolation. Here is the spot to build a hut and live far from the world and close to God. A saint, a knight, monks, poets, artists: they all came, gave to the valley something of their lives and their dreams, and took from it something of its seclusion. And the magic lived on.

St David gave the place its name: Llanddewi Nant Honddu David's church on the River Honddu – the immortal, unpronounceable poetry of Welsh place-names, which the English therefore made into Llanthony. Places like this were made for legends. The Norman knight William de Laci, it is said, came to this lonely valley when he was out hunting, and decided at once to renounce the hurly-burly of the world. He was followed, confusingly, by William de Lacy, the mighty Earl of Hereford, who became a hermit, and founded the monastery of Llanthony. Is it a romantic tale of a man's true calling, or a piece of Norman Realpolitik? After all, monasteries in the border country served not just for prayer and contemplation – they were also solid means of colonization. The thick towers of Llanthony Priory were no doubt built as a defence less against the Devil than against the rebellious Welsh. Nevertheless, in 1103 King Henry I sent the Queen's chaplain Ernisius to tempt the drop-out back. So perhaps William really was the equivalent of the man who today slips out to buy the paper and is never seen again – abandoning family and friends, running away to make a fresh start, wherever it may be. In William's case, it must have been contagious, for Ernisius, too, followed the call of the wild and did not return whence he came. Together, in the valley of Ewyas, they built the first Augustine abbey in Wales. So much did those early monks value their seclusion that they did not even clear the woods around them 'lest they be tempted to recede from their hermitical mode of life'. But in 1136 they founded another monastery, Llanthony Secunda, near Gloucester. Had they been driven away by marauders, or were they simply tired of singing only to the wolves? Whatever the reason, the English house soon became richer, mightier and more attractive than the Welsh. On his visit in 1188, Giraldus Cambrensis complains rather bitterly that his would have remained a place 'truly fitted for contemplation, a happy and delightful spot, fully competent, from its first establishment to supply all its own wants, had not the extravagance of English luxury, the pride of a sumptuous table, the increasing growth of intemperance and ingratitude added to the negligence of its patrons and prelates, reduced it from freedom to servility'. Social and religious criticism, with undertones of nationalism. For Gerald the Welshman was an ecclesiastical politician, and he fought for an independent church in Wales (see page 240). The monastery church of Llanthony, whose ruins can still be seen today, was still under construction in Gerald's time – begun in 1175, and completed around 1230, Romanesque on the threshold of early Gothic, Norman round arches next to Early English lancet windows. But after Henry VIII's dissolution of the monasteries, the Valley of Ewyas returned once more to the peace and quiet of its ruins. Cows then grazed in the gardens of the monks, and ivy spread itself over the arcades.

At the end of the 18th century, there was renewed interest in Gothic and in national antiquities, and Llanthony was then rediscovered. And once again it was an English gentleman who sought refuge in Wales, an Oxford graduate escaping from the big city to the wild woods, a knight of the Order of the Blue Flower: the poet Walter Savage Landor. As Byron fought for the freedom of Greece, so Landor fought in Spain against Napoleon. And now, like Wordsworth in the Lake District, Landor came to the Honddu Valley seeking to live and write in harmony with Nature. He was not one for the romanticism of ruins. Instead, he restored part of the ruined building, got married in Llanthony Priory in 1811, and with his wife moved into the former residence of the abbot. And then the poet followed the fortunate instincts of all good Englishmen when they take possession of some land – he planted trees. But he planted so many that the farmers round about protested bitterly, for where they had always been permitted to graze their sheep, the English landlord now decided to restore the forests of old. In the end, he had nothing but trouble, and so shortly before he went bankrupt, in October 1813, he finally gave up. Eventually he found his Arcadia not in Wales, but in Italy. Disappointed though he was, Landor never forgot his Llanthony and its 'ungenial clime': 'I loved thee by the streams of yore, / By distant streams I love thee more.'

The river foaming over the rocks, the mountains almost swept away by the squalls, sunbeams breaking through the rain, and behind a veil of effervescent light, the pale silhouette of Llanthony Abbey: this is how William Turner painted in 1834 the scene he saw and felt, and his vision is so elemental that one can almost hear the silence of its seclusion. This watercolour marks the height of Turner's romantic Welsh landscape-painting. Today it's to be found in a museum in Indianapolis, USA. Once it belonged to Turner's friend and patron, John Ruskin, who considered it to be 'the most perfect piece of painting of running water in existence'. Painters like Turner were the forerunners of the mass tourism which, since the romantic age, has spared not even the remote Valley of Ewyas. In April 1870, the Reverend Francis Kilvert hiked with a friend from Clyro to Llanthony Priory (and returned the same evening – a round trip of some 25 miles). The day was cold and clear, and in high spirits the two men approached the Abbey: 'What was our horror on entering the enclosure to see two tourists with staves and shoulder belts all complete postured among the ruins in an attitude of admiration, one of them of course discoursing learnedly to his gaping companion and pointing out objects of interest with his stick. If there is one thing more hateful than another it is being told what to admire and having objects pointed out to one with a stick.' And the Victorian parson – who, let it be remembered, was himself out on a sight-seeing tour – applies the coup de grace: 'Of all noxious animals too the most noxious is a tourist. And of all tourists the most vulgar, illbred, offensive and loathsome is the British tourist.'

It is, therefore, with a slight feeling of superiority that I, a German tourist, reach Llanthony Priory some 100 years later, prudently carrying my Kilvert in my pocket. And there his fellow-countrymen and mine sit picnicking in the ruins. None of us are pointing our sticks at the timbers. We're too busy pointing our telescopic lenses. And nobody is holding a lecture either; instead we're holding our bag of chips in one hand and our glass of

Eric Gill: Self Portrait, 1927

beer in the other. Where once the abbot and then the poet lodged, now the Abbey Hotel will lodge anyone (colour plate 56). From the ceilar bar in the monastery I obtain a portion of genuine Caerphilly cheese, sit on the stump of a column in the side aisle, and dip into the Reverend Kilvert's Diary, surrounded by Landor's lofty beech and chestnut trees. All this is the stuff of dreams. Landor himself had a successor, though not in Llanthony but four miles upriver. In November 1869 the Anglican priest Joseph Leycester Lyne, known as Father Ignatius, retired with a novice to Capel-y-Ffin, in order to serve the Lord in seclusion. He did this in his own way, as a self-proclaimed 'Evangelist Monk of the British Church'. In order to renew monastic life, he founded in 1870 a Benedictine monastery of a far more joyful kind, even permitting pious women to join the Order. The official Victorian church denied him their financial support and their blessing. 'Llanthony Tertia' was the name Father Ignatius gave to his abbey in Honddu Valley. A fool in Paradise? His earnest good nature made a deep impression on all who met him, including the Reverend Francis Kilvert: 'A monk, he says, must either be a philosopher or a "holy fool". He also allows that monastic life has a strong tendency to drive people mad.' Father Ignatius died in 1908. Initially, Benedictines from Caldey Island took over the incomplete monastery, but then it stood empty.

When monasteries fall, along come the artists. One rainy August day in 1924, a strange band approached the buildings of *Capel-y-Ffin*: three families with their children, cats, dogs, chickens, ducks and geese, and out in front of them all, the English sculptor and eccentric, Eric Gill. The hard core of his artists' guild, which he had started up in Ditchling, accompanied him from Sussex to this Welsh wilderness, 'that dark and almost uninhabited and uninhabitable place'. Eric Gill, a Catholic convert, had bought Father Ignatius's monastery, together with several acres of land. Here he and his followers planted what they needed, baked their own bread, brewed their own beer, and made their own butter and cheese. Everything else had to be fetched by pony and trap from Abergavenny, 15 miles away, along an unpaved country road which even today is still dangerously narrow. 'Postman on horseback once a day. Doctor on horseback from Hay once a week. Any complaints?' Yes, there was cause for complaint: the Father Ignatius pilgrims, who came in their inquisitive hordes. 'You can't imagine their impudence. They would walk in without asking and you would find them wandering in and out of your bedrooms. And when you asked them what they were doing, they would say: "Can we see a monk?"' Some of them probably thought Eric Gill himself was the Abbot. 'He looked like Tolstoy in his overalls and coat, a sort of half-farmer, half-monk,' reported his German friend, the diplomat, publisher and writer Count Harry Kessler, who visited this artists' commune in Capel-y-Ffin. 'They have no-one to serve them,' observed Kessler in astonishment, 'make everything themselves, cook their food on an open fire ... and are perfectly happy and contented.' Before breakfast, they went to mass, and during breaks between work they met to pray or sing psalms. It was a mixture of Beuron and Bloomsbury, the 'Nazarenes' and the Arts and Crafts Movement, workshop and worship. It was a gesture of life renewal after the First World War an attempt to set up a Utopian 'News from Nowhere' in this remote Welsh valley.

It was in Capel-y-Ffin that Eric Gill designed the typeface named after him: Gill Sans-Serif. In the coal-cellar of the monastery he created his black marble 'Descent from the Cross', now in King's School, Canterbury. Despite such well-known works as the relief for the League of Nations Palace in Geneva, or the Stations of the Cross in Westminster Abbey, Gill was always overshadowed by the avant-garde. Some of his best works date from between 1924 and 1928, when he was in Capel-y-Ffin; beautifully carved inscriptions with exquisite lettering, woodcuts for the bibliophile editions of the Golden Cockerel Press, classic examples of the art of illustration. His most famous colleague was the painter and poet David Jones. Born in a London suburb, and resident for many years in Harrow, right up until his death in 1974, he was the most Welsh of all English artists. Capel-y-Ffin was a turning-point in his life. It provided the landscape for his Arthur illustrations and also the Mabinogion themes of his last years. In the refectory of the monastery, and in need of restoration, is a crucifixion fresco by David Jones, and in the simple chapel is a painted tabernacle, which Gill designed as well as inscribing the wooden beam. All his life Eric Gill was against the distinction between pure and applied art, and many of his theoretical writings were based on his practical experiences in Wales. He wrote essays on 'Work and Responsibility', 'Aesthetic Pleasure', 'Property, Ownership and Holy Poverty'. 'Look after goodness and truth, and beauty will look after herself,' he would say. Classical ideals, cloistered aesthetics practised in the seclusion of the Welsh mountains.

The problems of the simple life, however, proved to be even greater here than elsewhere.

John Piper: Derelict Cottage, Llanthony, c.1940–41

After four years, the experiment came to an end. The artists' colony broke up, and in 1928 Eric Gill moved to the less rigorous Chiltern Hills. But again and again he would return to the Welsh monastery, where his daughter Betty lived with her family. There he also wrote his autobiography, which appeared in 1940, the year he died. He recalled the period of 'my spiritual puberty', the years in Capel-y-Ffin, which were perhaps the happiest of his life: 'And we bathed, naked all together in the mountain pools and under the waterfalls. And we had heavenly picnics by the Nant-y-buch in little sunny secluded paradises, or climbed the green mountains and smelt the smell of a world untouched by men of business.' But even then, he wrote, their 'evil influence' could be felt everywhere: 'The population of the valley was but a quarter of what it had been fifty years before. There were twenty ruined cottages between Capel-y-Ffin and Llanthony four miles lower down the valley. The young men had gone to the mines and were wandering unemployed in the Rhondda ... We were living in a dying land – unspoiled but dying. It is still the same paradise and it is possible that it will long remain so. For by the mercy of geographical accident all the valleys are cul-de-sacs. Let the industrial-capitalist disease do its worst – the Black

Mountains of Brecon will remain untouched and their green valleys lead nowhere.' Half a century later we know just how threatened these last Arcadias are. There are indeed green valleys that lead nowhere. But the acid rain is falling all over them.

The former monastery in the hills above Honddu Valley still belongs to relatives of Eric Gill.[1] 'My work is my leisure, my leisure is my work', it says at the entrance. Down below on the path there are seven old yew-trees standing solemnly round a little, whitewashed chapel (1760): Capel-y-Ffin, the chapel at the end, frontier chapel ... On the other side of the hill lies England. But ahead of us is the last highlight of this long trip through Ewyas Valley: *Hay Bluff* (colour plate 2). The journey is worth it for the view alone, a pastoral panorama second to none: on the plateau all around are sheep and wild ponies, and in the distance the Malvern Hills, the heights of Radnor Forest, the Brecon Beacons and the Black Mountains, while down below in the valley is the winding silver Wye.

Hay-on-Wye: The Kingdom of Books

Richard Booth is probably the best known Welsh eccentric of our time. but he's an Englishman. He lives in the border town of *Hay-on-Wye* (plate 29). The town is in Wales, and the station is in England. On April 1, 1977 Mr Booth proclaimed the 'independent state of Haye'. And on that fine April Fool's Day, he also announced that his kingdom had its own national anthem, he distributed national sausages, informed the world that Hay was leaving the European Community, gave out national passports and also the very first edible currency in the world, banknotes made of rice-paper. It was one small step for Richard Booth, and a big day for Hay-on-Wye. 'I put it on the map,' he said. But it wasn't the April Fool's Day joking that did this, for Mr Booth is no fool. He's a businessman. Though one might say that in some respects, the two things go together, since Mr Booth is crazy about books, and putting his obsession and his business together under one hat, he came up with the biggest second-hand bookshop in the world.

Hay is the independent town of books: there are books in the old cinema, in the old fire station, in an old butcher's shop, in the Victorian alms-houses, books here, books there, books everywhere. In Hay there are more books per head of the population than in any other town in the world. Hay has just 1,200 inhabitants and 32 bookshops. Richard Booth himself is reckoned to have some 2 million books, and some 10 miles of bookshelves. In Hay there are more bookshops than chapels and pubs – and you can't say that about many places in Wales. A pub in Lion Street proudly announces: 'More book-buyers have drunk in this pub than in any other bar in the world.' For bookaholics, Hay is Paradise, though some may be seized by a sense of panic. Where do you start, and how can you stop? I only intended to spend an hour there, finished up by browsing for a whole day, and could easily

1   Some of the rooms in the monastery are let out on a self-catering basis (near a farm with pony trekking). Eric Gill also recommends hikers to sample the route from Rhiw Wen, below Lord Hereford's Knob, to Capel-y-Ffin: 'That surely is one of the loveliest and also one of the grandest things in this world.'

have stayed for a whole week. No author likes to have his books sold off cheaply, but the prospect of one day landing in Richard's kingdom, department 'Travel Books', fills me with a strange excitement.

Booth transformed Hay into Boothtown, Booktown. He collects books for book-collectors, not for readers. How did this bibliomania begin? Was little Richard deprived of books in his childhood. 'I was born in Plymouth in 1938. My father was an officer; traditional military, landowning family. Public school at Rugby, one year at Oxford, undistinguished career. Then I started with antiques and second-hand books. Then I got it into my head to have a bookshop for every subject, where you could find everything. One hundred bookshops in one town. That wasn't so easy, but we're getting there!' Richard Booth looks more like a lumberjack than a bookworm. He moved to Hay in 1961, and since then he's sold about one million books a year. He was followed by other antiquarians, craftsmen, boutique-owners, and inevitably hordes of tourists. Now the second-hand-books-cinema has been taken over by the mail-order millionaire Leon Morelli, Booth's arch rival. But everybody profits from the Book King, and it is thanks to him that this little town has enjoyed the first economic boom in its history. 'A town where the bookshops are bigger than the supermarkets is simply an attraction in itself,' he says. 'Through me, about 150 new jobs were created here in Hay.' Amongst the people who work here are people looking to get on, people looking to get away, and at one time there was an opera singer from London, and a professor of philosophy from Berkeley. Booth regards himself as a pioneer of the second-hand trade: 'We're the most successful small town in Wales with an alternative economy.'

In spring 1981, the King of Hay offered 100 tons of books as fuel: £1.50 a box. Hardly the action of a book-lover, Mr Booth. 'Maybe books are a monument to the craziness of people,' he replies. 'The more learned they get, the more stupidly they behave – that's the only thing you learn from books. In 25 years of higher education whose aim is to solve problems, all I've seen is 25 years of rural degeneration.' He mentions one example. 'In the old days, a town like Hay used to have 15 bakers. Now we all eat the same mass-produced bread. If we would only eat home-made things instead of these inferior mass products, we'd soon have our 15 jobs back again.' Back to the culture of the Renaissance, demands Richard, and let's give support to the small town, small firm economy, instead of making them into colonies for heavy industry. Supermarkets, he says, destroy thousands of jobs. Apart from supermarkets, what are his pet hates? Academics, bureaucrats, tourists, brochures, Margaret Thatcher, and the whole of the 20th century. Recently he's been waging a campaign for local milk and eggs and for rural forms of transport. 'Away with all this petrol-driven stuff, and let's get back to the horse and cart!' Does anyone think such ideas are impractical? 'I've created 150 jobs in the book-trade, and I can do the same with horses!' If 'big government' is the basic problem, would an independent Wales be the solution? 'No, no,' says King Richard, 'I'm for an independent Hay! We can solve our problems better than university professors and bureaucrats. In Wales there are thousands of highly paid civil servants who do nothing but destroy jobs.' There can only be one solution: Booth for Parliament! And so this Welshman-by-choice has founded a party of his own, the Rural Revival Party, and he actually stood for parliament in 1983. With 278 votes he didn't quite get the majority he needed for a place in Westminster.

But Booth fights on, as a member of the local council, for his rural revival. There can be few Englishmen with a greater commitment to the Welsh way of life. 'It's deeper country,' he says. And he is certainly the brightest green among Welsh Greens – a feudal anarchist, complete with castle. Well, a sort of castle. He owns the burned-out manor house (1660) in the centre of the town, near the Norman ruins, and he plans to restore it in a manner befitting his kingly status. And one day he will also – to the delight of all his fellow bibliomaniacs, realize an old project: to build a labyrinth of books.

If you only have an hour or two to spare, then, don't go to Hay. It's irresistible, and inescapable, and once you're there, you'll be trapped. But if by chance you've come to Wales without a certain book, Hay is the place you're sure to find it, and find it you must, for no-one should come to this part of Wales without this book. 'Kilvert's Diary' is the title, and it's the diary of a Victorian country parson. We are now deep into Kilvert country, and for the next stage of our journey, Francis Kilvert is an indispensable companion.

Ten Miles for a Kiss: The Curate of Clyro

The Wye flows gently and serenely past Hay and on through the valley. No-one who follows it could possibly want to hurry. The route to Clyro takes you across pastures green that make you want to linger. But on the morning of Friday, February 11 1870, Francis Kilvert was in unusual haste. The frost was so piercing that it froze his beard to his coat. He had left his musical box in Hay, to be repaired by watchmaker Bevan, had bought four Valentine cards at Herthen's, and ordered some cheese from Hadley's. Now he was hurrying across the meadows and up and down the hills of Clyro, in order to get back to the vicarage in good time. He had lived here for five years now, but even this morning he was still struck by the beauty of the landscape: 'The morning spread upon the mountains, beautiful Clyro rising from the valley and stretching away northward dotted with white houses and shining with gleams of green on hills and dingle sides, a tender blue haze over the village and woods in the valley and Clyro Court a dim grey.'

In Clyro Court, the manor house just outside the village, lived the Baskervilles, who owned the whole district. Here Arthur Conan Doyle is said to have written 'The Hound of the Baskervilles', while staying as a guest. But his tale has far more in common with the sinister atmosphere of Dartmoor than with the sweet delight of the Wye Valley. No, this is Kilvert country. Francis Kilvert lived in Ashbrook House, opposite the Baskerville Arms, in those days called Swan Inn. It's a stately vicarage made of fieldstone, with a large, Neo-Gothic staircase window in Regency style. 'Kilvert lived on the first floor, over-looking the street,' a villager informs me. Everyone here knows Kilvert. It's as if he

Sarah von Niekerk:
The Curate of Clyro.
Woodcut from a new
edition of Kilvert's
Diary, 1983

were still their curate. Yet he only lived in Clyro for seven years, from 1865 till 1872, an obscure country parson from Wiltshire, who couldn't even find a publisher for his sentimental verses. And what's special about Clyro? It's just a tiny village with some 400 inhabitants, a few whitewashed cottages, and nothing at all for the sight-seer. But this unassuming Welsh village has become so beloved of so many people that they all feel that they, too, must have lived there long ago. For Kilvert describes it all in minute detail: the village, the people, the lord of the manor, the farmers and their work, their poverty, their little festivals, how they lived and how they died. He tells how a child was baptized in Clyro Church on Septuagesima Sunday 1870, when it was so cold that the ice had to be broken in the baptismal font. Kilvert went to every house, but as well as opening the village doors for us, he opens his own soul, or at least its entrance-hall. We share the work of the young curate, his walks through the country, his love of port, and 'those beautiful Welsh eyes'. Reverend Kilvert had a weakness for beautiful women and little girls ('ten miles for a kiss'), and his vain courtship of Daisy Thomas is a sad little Victorian love story.

Francis Kilvert kept his diary for the last ten years of his short life. Only three of his 22 diaries have survived, the others having been burnt by a prudish female relative. But 'Kilvert's Diary' was not published until 1938–40, and it was only in the 1960's that suddenly it became an amazing success: filmed as a TV series, dramatized for the National Theatre, published in special editions, and reprinted time and again in paperback. This success is not just a 'middlebrow' phenomenon, reflecting middle-class longings for idyllic

19th-century country life. Kilvert stands in the great tradition of British diarists that began with Pepys, and his book also belongs to another typically British genre, the portrait of village life. Like the letters of the 18th-century country parson Gilbert White of Selborne, Kilvert's descriptions are both a topography of the rural landscape and a social document of life in the country. The curate of Clyro had the gift of capturing all the minutiae of this life, and his lucid style and lyrical nature have made this book into a minor classic.

From the vicarage in Clyro, Francis Kilvert would walk diagonally across the street, past two cottages, along an avenue of shady yew trees, and through the cemetery to the church. St Michael's, with its rectangular, crenellated tower, is a typical Victorian village church, accurately reflecting the gentleness of the place and its people. There is a memorial plaque to Kilvert ('thou good and faithful servant'), and in the sacristy, near a collection of religious engravings that he loved, there is an old photograph of him, with full beard and book. After lunch he used to spend half an hour or so in the cemetery, and he especially liked to sit on a Catholic grave near the choir door – that of Thomas Bridgwater. *'Requiescat in pace'* – he found these Catholic inscriptions much more comforting than the colder stones of the Puritans and Protestants. Here he would linger for a while in the midday stillness. A few crows would be cawing in the village, and sometimes a spider would scurry over the grave 'with most indecent haste'. Then he would get up and walk away. 'An intense feeling and perception of the extraordinary beauty of the place grew upon me in the silence as I passed through the still sunny churchyard and saw the mountains through the trees rising over the school, and looked back at the church and the churchyard through the green arches of the wych elms.' That is how it was in summer 1871, and that is how it was when he died. And that is how it still is today.

Francis Kilvert lies buried a few miles away on the other side of the border, in Hereford-shire, in the village cemetery of *Bredwardine* on the Wye, where he was vicar till his death in 1877. But his posthumous congregation still makes its pilgrimage (thank heavens, only in small groups) through Kilvert country, with his diary as its guide.[1] They go to the old mill of *Rhosgoch*, to the 'poor humble dear little white-washed church' of *Colva* (13th century), to the half-timbered inn at *Rhydspence* (16th century), where the drovers of Tregaron would stop off on their way to the cattle markets in the Midlands. And in autumn they will see the valleys of the Arrow and the Glasnant, 'which seemed to come out of a fairy land of blue val-ley depths and distances and tufted woods of green and gold and crimson and russet brown'.

Port Talbot: Where the Steel Industry and Richard Burton Went Bathing

Tearing ourselves way from Kilvert Country on the Wye, we return to the coast – from rural fairyland to the industrial realities of South Wales. Even in the densely populated

---

1   See also '24 Walks in the Kilvert Country', published by the Kilvert Society, 27 Baker's Oak, Lincoln Hill, Ross-on-Wye, Herefordshire.

industrial belt, you can still find the odd oasis of countryside, and places where industry, Nature and art have all left their mark. *Margam*, for example, a few miles from Swansea: the ruins of a medieval monastery and a Victorian manor house stand in a park with red deer grazing, while in the background the steelworks of Port Talbot pour forth their clouds of smoke. Margam Country Park, by contrast, contains a hill fort from the Iron Age, from where hang-gliders sail over the plain, and there's also a collection of Roman and Celtic stone masonry, and a modern sculpture park. 'Margam for Sport, Margam for Fun, Margam for the Arts'.

It all began with a religious foundation. In the forested hills on the edge of the broad dunes of Margam Burrows, Robert of Gloucester, an illegitimate son of King Henry I, founded a Cistercian Abbey in 1147, the year of his death. All that now remains of Margam Abbey is the ruined chapterhouse (13th century) and part of the church with its Norman arcades. In the 19th century this was given two belltowers, like campaniles, and a western window by William Morris. In the side aisle are the magnificent alabaster tombs of the Mansels, who took over the monastery after the Reformation. In the middle of the 18th century an English branch of the family inherited the estate – the Talbots of Lacock, in Wiltshire. They soon realized what was missing from Margam Park. It was not enough merely to have a residence for the lords of the manor. You could only live in style if you also had a house for your plants. Hampton Court, Blenheim Palace, Chatsworth, all the great English houses and estates were rivalling one another with their orangeries. Hothouses combined a love of oranges with the delights of a country walk during which one could keep one's feet dry even when it was raining. And the finest British example of a hothouse for a cold climate is Margam Orangery, designed in 1787 by Anthony Keck for Thomas Mansel Talbot (plate 4). The grandiose Georgian style evokes the royal associations of Baroque orangeries. Despite the length – 330 feet – and symmetry of the façade, it is never monotonous, for architecturally it is divided up by high, round-arched windows and alternating smooth and rusticated masonry. The classical training of the architect, who lived in Rome for several years, is reflected by the triglyphs, the cornices with their urns, and the Palladian motif of the Venetian windows in the two corner pavilions. The orangery is only 30 feet wide, and so the light coming through the high windows can reach the whole of the interior, which was warmed by heating in the floor. Talbot's orange and lemon trees flourished here, flanked by his collection of antiquities in the corner pavilions. In 1802, Nelson admired this place and, as gentlemen tourists did in those days, gave the gardener a handsome tip of no less than three shillings. Today Margam Orangery is the setting for concerts, exhibitions, conferences and weddings – and so the hothouse remains highly productive.

Young Christopher Talbot may well have felt that his plants had better accommodation that he had himself, in the old manor house of the Mansels. Scarcely had he taken over his inheritance when he had his ancestor's home pulled down, and built a new one in its place. With its towers, gables, oriels, battlements and pinnacles, Margam Park (1830) is typical

The Cross of Cynfelyn, 10th century

Tudor Neo-Gothic, a romantic country house, designed in the picturesque style of the day by Thomas Hopper, whose handiwork we shall also admire in Penrhyn Castle. Here, then, lived Christopher Rice Mansel Talbot, the greatest landower in Glamorgan, enthusiastic rider, huntsman, art collector, and sailor, whose luxury yacht 'Lynx' was the first ship to pass through the Suez Canal (1869). He also had a remarkable record in Westminster: for 59 years in succession he was Glamorgan's MP; it is said that only once in all this time did he speak in Parliament, and that was when he asked someone to close the window because he was sitting in a draught. He was a classic backbencher, and perhaps a prototype of the 'enjoying classes'. Christopher Talbot was a Victorian entrepreneur, and one of the early promoters of the Welsh economy. He helped to finance the first railway through South Wales, as well as the extension of the old port in Aberavon, which was renamed Port Talbot in his honour. Christopher Talbot's wealth was transcended only by his frugal style of living. He wore no jewels, had no secretary, worked at night, breakasted at 1 p.m., and lived till he was 87. Among his relatives were two pioneers of photography: Henry Fox Talbot, his cousin from Lacock Abbey, and John Dillwyn Llewelyn, his son-in-law from Swansea, the first well-known photographer in Wales.[1] The scene and subject of their early experiments with the camera was Margam Park.

The end of this house came when in 1941 the family had all the furniture and the art collection auctioned by Christie's. All that remained, as so often happens, was an empty shell, uninhabited, soon falling into neglect, and ultimately almost burnt to the ground. Now, at great cost, the county council is restoring it, after acquiring the estate and developing it into a model leisure park. This includes an annual theatre and music festival, and a maze of hedges built like castle walls ('to a-maze the visitor'). But Margam's showpiece is its museum of stones. In this Lapidarium near the church are Roman and early Christian inscribed tablets, and some of the most important Celtic crosses in the country, including the elaborate wheel cross of Cynfelyn (c.900). A contemporary counter-part to this early stonemasonry is the sculpture park, which was opened in 1983. Apart from Carrbridge in Scotland and Bretton Hall in Yorkshire, this is the biggest open-air exhibition of modern British sculpture in Britain, with works by Henry Moore, Barbara Hepworth, Anthony Caro, David Nash, and many Welsh artists. On the crest of the hill, above the luxuriant rhododendrons, hovers a sun wreathed in wooden rays, a work by Jake Kempsell. It typifies the way Nature and sculpture provocatively intertwine here in this classical park, whose landscape takes on yet another plastic, disturbing dimension through the cooling towers and blast furnaces of Port Talbot.[2]

The gigantic industrial complex along the M4 between Bridgend and Port Talbot represents miles of Welsh despair. Once the name of Port Talbot stood for a Victorian entrepreneur and the prosperity of a harbour town. Now it is a synonym for the decline and fall of the Welsh steel industry. When in 1951 the British Steel Corporation opened what was then Europe's most modern steelworks, it seemed as if there could be another upturn. Thirty years later, more than half of the 12,000 workers had been made redundant. Bad planning and rationalization also led to mass dismissals in Shotton (North Wales) and to the closure of Llanelli steelworks. It was the worst industrial collapse since the end of the war. At the start of the century there were 35 steelworks in Wales, and today there are just two: Llanwern, near Newport, and Port Talbot. Who knows what the future holds for these, now that the steel industry has been privatised? Port Talbot is the sick man of

1 J. D. Llewelyn started taking photographs in 1839, with rock formations and family picnics on the beach at Caswell Bay (Gower). Queen Victoria liked and collected his photographs. Llewelyn was a founding member of what later became the Royal Photographic Society (1853), and died in 1882 in Penllergaer near Swansea. His photographs are displayed in the museum there, and also in the National Museum in Cardiff.

2 Two worthwhile excursions from Margam: north along a 10-mile footpath to the Afan Argoed Country Park, a reforested coalmining area; and south along the B4283, the Roman Via Julia Maritima, to the seaside resort of Porthcawl with its royal golf course, past the town of Kenfig that was buried under sand dunes in the Middle Ages.

Swansea Bay. But in old Aberavon, just a mile north-west of the port, there is a huge lido which can at least offer cheap seaside entertainment to those both in and out of work.

Less obvious, but also less depressing, than the ruins of the coal and steel industries are the new 'sunrise industries' – computer and electronics firms, and a wide variety of small enterprises through which Wales is slowly beginning to break its economic dependence on the traditional heavy industries. The newcomers are thriving particularly along the M4 between Newport and Bridgend. Favourable conditions for investment, tax concessions, the general reluctance of Welsh workers to go on strike – these are factors that are especially attractive to foreign companies. And so the Japanese, for instance, manufacture nearly all their television sets for the European market in Bridgend. American firms alone now employ more Welsh people than the Welsh coal and steel industries put together. When the politicians in Westminster boast of the success of their aid programme, however, they tend to keep quiet about its reverse side: in times of recession, the first firms to close are those whose parent companies are abroad; furthermore, they rarely employ Welsh engineers, researchers, planners or advertising executives – these remain at headquarters, and so Welsh specialists tend to go abroad to find suitable jobs.

One of the birthplaces of Welsh industry is *Aberdulais*, a village near Neath. This is the meeting-place of two rivers and two canals: the Neath Canal (1795) and the Tennant Canal (1824). A beautifully curved towpath bridge leads across the Tennant Canal, and this in turn crosses the River Neath by way of a ten-arched aqueduct, beside which is a former railway bridge. 'Venice in the rain' is what local people call their little village of waterways. At the beginning of the 19th century Aberdulais, with its waterfall and its ruined copper-smelting plants, was a picturesque theme of industrial romanticism, visited and painted by William Turner and other artists. The industrial archaeologists of the National Trust have now reconstructed the origins of the Welsh copper industry, which began in 1584 with a German, Ulrich Frosse. He was a specialist in copper-smelting, and had worked in the mines in Cornwall before coming here – a technological expert and export of the 16th century. In the densely forested river valley near Aberdulais, all the necessary sources of energy for firing the smelting furnaces were present in abundance: water, wood, and coal. From Aberdulais the copper industry expanded downriver to Neath and Swansea – It was a 'Sabbath in Hell', for George Borrow, when he came to Neath during his 1854 tour of Wales. 'Somewhat to the south rose immense stacks of chimneys surrounded by grimy diabolical-looking buildings, in the neighbourhood of which were huge heaps of cinders and black rubbish. From the chimneys, notwithstanding it was Sunday, smoke was proceeding in volumes, choking the atmosphere all around. From this pandemonium, at the distance of about a quarter of a mile to the south-west, upon a green meadow, stood, looking darkly grey, a ruin of vast size with window holes, towers, spires, and arches.'

What George Borrow saw in the coppery smoke had once been one of the most beautiful Cistercian monasteries in Wales: *Neath Abbey*. Around 1130, Norman monks had settled on the west bank of the Neath, at the mouth of which lay the Roman camp of Nidum.

Neath Abbey was a victim not just of the Reformation, like the neighbouring Cistercian monastery of Margam, but also of the Industrial Revolution. Copper-smelting furnaces and smithies pushed their way right into the abbey ruins in the course of the 18th century, and what was left is not worth seeing.[1]

One thing that I did want to see, though, was where the actor Richard Burton came from. He was the twelfth of thirteen children, son of a Welsh miner. The house where he was born is near the viaduct of *Pontrhydyfen*, a village near Neath. He went to school in neighbouring Port Talbot, where Sir Geoffrey Howe also grew up (one year Burton's junior). After taking elocution lessons in order to overcome his Welsh accent, Burton made his London debut as a 19-year-old in Emlyn Williams's comedy 'The Druid's Rest'. It was to his English teacher, Philip Burton, that Richard owed his acting name, for he was born Richard Jenkins. From the Old Vic, where he made his reputation as a Shakespearian actor, the man with the Celtic charm and the aura of romantic melancholy made his way to Hollywood. In the film of Dylan Thomas's 'Under Milk Wood', Burton played the narrator, and his sonorous tones helped to make this an unforgettable homage to the Welsh people, of whom he was perhaps the most popular of all personifications. He loved his own wild image – a degenerate genius, risen from the Welsh gutter, a drinker, a lady-killer. When he died of a stroke at the age of 58, he went into British mythology, just as Dylan Thomas had done, as the archetypal, self-destructive Celt. He had a villa in Céligny, on Lake Geneva, called 'Pays de Galles', and there he was buried in 1984, to the sounds of 'Sospan Fach', the anthem of Welsh rugby.

Swansea: City of Arts, Valley of Copper

Of all the industrial towns in South Wales, *Swansea* has the most beautiful setting and the most exotic food. This is where people eat seaweed. I've tasted it, and it's good. Laver bread is what they call this protein-rich speciality, made from seaweed collected from the coast of Gower, cooked in oatmeal, eaten with bacon or ham. Once it was a dish for the people, and now it's a delicacy.

Even in the 19th century, the English poet Walter Savage Landor claimed that Swansea Bay was more beautiful than the Bay of Naples. The rivalry has continued, for in recent years the pollution of Swansea Bay reached Neapolitan proportions.

The Welsh name for this place on the mouth of the Tawe is Abertawe. This is certainly more accurate than the name Swansea, which is derived from Sweyne, the Viking who is said to have founded a settlement here before the arrival of the Normans. When Cardiff

---

1 Far more interesting is the upper Vale of Neath with its waterfalls, e.g. near Pont Nedd Fechan. In 1870 the Neath Abbey Iron Forge was turned into a textile factory, and one of its spinning machines can be seen in Swansea's industrial museum, still in good working order.

*Evan Walters: A Welsh Miner,
c.1926–30*

was still a fishing village, around 1700, Swansea was the biggest coal-exporting port in Wales. And yet it was the newcomer on the Taff that gained capital status, and this still annoys the folk on the Tawe. The rivalry is similar to that between Edinburgh and Glasgow. But whereas Edinburgh, the older city, even if it was outstripped economically by Glasgow, still maintained its political precedence, Swansea finished up by losing both. And so many people here feel closer to London than to Cardiff, which psychologically seems a lot further away than just 45 miles. In Swansea, it is traditional to vote Labour; Cardiff is Conservative (apart from Cardiff South-East, which produced the former Labour Prime Minister James Callaghan). The people of Cardiff are regarded as being more distant and reserved than the warm-hearted folk of Swansea. Dylan Thomas was the embodiment of the Swansea heart and soul. 'Ugly, lovely town,' he called it, 'crawling, sprawling, slummed, unplanned, jerry-villa'd, and smug-suburbed by the side of a long and splendid curving shore ...' He spent his childhood in this town, which for him had as many layers as an onion, and in which anyone and everyone could 'move you to tears'. With its glorious situation between mountains and sea, one can almost forget that Swansea lies at the centre of a vast industrial conurbation that stretches from Port Talbot in the east to Llanelli in the west (colour plate 27). Over half a million people live here, though only

Samuel & Nathaniel Buck: Swansea, c.1750

200,000 of them are in the city itself. What a mixture it is: the hills and beaches of Gower confronting the blast furnaces and oil refineries across the bay. An ugly, lovely town indeed.

Swansea is an old town, but the old town is no longer there. It was almost completely destroyed by German bombs in the blitz of 1941. Since then, the centre has been rebuilt, none too impressively, round the ruins of a medieval castle (*c.*1330). All that is left of the old town – single-storey houses and little workshops – can be found between the Victorian Grand Theatre and the Guildhall, on the south-west edge of the city (colour plate 13). In Dillwyn Street there is still the antique shop where Dylan Thomas loved to browse, 'Ralph the Books'. The city hall, with a tower that can be seen from miles around, was built between the wars (1929–34), symbolizing the prosperity of the port at a time when else-where in the country, industry was already in decline. Behind the severe, Neo-Classical façade of Portland stone, wooden panels and gilt, coffered ceilings display all the splendour of municipal wealth. The highlight is the 'British Empire Panels' in Brangwyn Hall. These monumental pictures were painted by Sir Frank Brangwyn, one of the most famous artists of his day, and were commissioned for the House of Lords (1925–32), only to be rejected. The city fathers of Swansea were delighted to have such metropolitan magnificence in their

new city hall. They leapt in before Cardiff, and sealed their bid with an offer to fit the great hall to the dimensions of this mighty cycle of 18 paintings. Brangwyn's stated theme was the British Empire in all its wealth and majesty. In a jungle of exotic plants and animals, people of all races go peacefully about their business: Pax Britannica, the Commonwealth as Paradise. Here the Empire parades itself in all its glory. What today seems like a naive apotheosis of British colonialism was Brangwyn's homage to his second home. (He was born in 1867 in Bruges, Belgium, and lived in Ditchling, Sussex, from 1918 until his death in 1956.) It was also the expression of an aesthetic credo, in the tradition of the Nabis – the world as ornament and colour. It is the last echo of 19th-century orientalism. Brangwyn learnt his brilliant, decorative style in the workshop of William Morris, for whom he copied Flemish tapestries. Later he designed posters, church windows, decorations for billiard rooms and luxury liners, and mural decorations for the London Stock Exchange and the Rockefeller Center in New York. The city fathers of Swansea can be proud of their Brangwyn Hall, and as the setting for the yearly music festival, it must certainly be one of the most unusual concert halls in Europe.

Not far from the city hall, along the coastal road to Mumbles, there is the University, founded in 1920. The 4,000 or so students come not only to sail in Swansea Bay, but also, and above all, because of the outstanding Science Faculty. Few universities have a more beautiful setting than Swansea: Singleton Park, once the country estate of the industrialist Lord Swansea (1826). One of his descendants, the copper manufacturer Richard Glynn Vivian, founded the municipal art gallery (1905) named after him in Alexandra Road, opposite the College of Art, and he also donated his fine collection of paintings and porcelain. The latter is particularly rare, for porcelain was only manufactured in Swansea over a very short period (1814–24). Amongst the Welsh painters represented in this museum are two local artists who deserve particular mention: Ceri Richards and Evan Walters. The latter was Post-Impressionist, and used vivid colours to paint the miners and market-women of his hometown, always with a sympathetic eye to their problems and their weaknesses. When he died in 1951, he left some 50 works to the Glynn Vivian Art Gallery, including his portrait of a 'Cockle Woman', a popular figure at Swansea Market. Ceri Richards, the most famous Welsh artist of the 20th century, has a room of his own. In 1936, he took part in the international Surrealist exhibition in London, and after the war he taught at the Royal College of Art. He was a many-sided artist, and his work includes paintings, book illustrations, stage sets, and church windows for the cathedrals of Derby and Liverpool. His rich and colourful pictures are full of abstract forms drawn from myth and Nature and influenced by Cubism. He was inspired by the local landscape of Gower and the waterfalls of the Teifi, as well as by industry (his father worked in a tin factory). His most important lithographs are those based on poems by Dylan Thomas. The Glynn Vivian Art Gallery is deeply committed to contemporary art, and in this respect has stolen a clear march on the National Museum in Cardiff, which has tended somewhat to neglect this field.

The mustiness of learning, and the quaint charm of Victorian museums – this is the overriding impression exuded by the Royal Institution (1835), a museum of art and natural history of which Dylan Thomas once said that it was itself a museum-piece. The same might be said of its neighbour, a former warehouse (1898), with cast-iron archways, now housing Swansea's newest and most popular attraction, the Maritime and Industrial Museum. Here, with machines, models and illustrations, we can follow the development of the town and the port, including the building of the Swansea Canal (1794–98) and the docks (mid 19th century) which soon outstripped even Bristol. Now, where ships once anchored before picking up their cargoes of coal and minerals, crowds of sailing boats bob up and down. All round this new yachting harbour in the south docks – the north docks were filled in after the war – there is to be a whole new complex of holiday homes, hotels, offices and businesses. The industrial museum and the neighbouring leisure centre are part of the large-scale revitalization of the dock area, as is the re-opening of the Little Theatre, where the young Dylan Thomas himself once trod the boards. There is a bronze statue of him by John Doubleday (1984) with a verse from 'Fern Hill'; some of the locals, however, call this statue 'Portrait of the Artist as Someone Else'. The Georgian terrace houses in Cumbrian Place (1812) have also been restored, and not far from there is one of the few examples of Neo-Classical architecture in Swansea: the former Town Hall and Law Courts (1825–48), which is now a school. The symbol of the old docks, and Swansea's most unusual industrial monument, was demolished in 1984: Weaver's Flour Mill, the first multi-storey reinforced concrete building in Britain, designed in 1897 by two French engineers. The reconstruction of the dock area, with its new sea park, is part of a comprehensive programme of redevelopment, called the 'Lower Swansea Valley Project'. This is an exemplary effort by the town to free itself from the debris and the poison of its industrial heritage before it's too late.

In the 19th century the Lower Swansea Valley was the biggest copper-processing area in the world. Along a narrow strip of land, just four miles long, between what is now the M4 and the mouth of the Tawe, there were no less than 150 metal-processing works in 1890. Half a century later, this area of 1,200 acres has become the biggest industrial wasteland in the whole of Britain. The history of 'Copperopolis' began in 1717, with the first copperworks in *Landore*. The industrialist Robert Morris built the workers' estate of *Morriston* in 1768, and the Cornishman John Vivian set up a whole series of smelting-furnaces in *Hafod* in 1810. This marked the beginning of large-scale industrialization in the valley. By the middle of the 19th century, more than half of all British copperworks were to be found in Lower Swansea Valley. The Vivians, after whom several streets in Hafod have been named, owned the biggest copperworks in the world at that time (they were also the last to close, in 1982). Lead, cobalt and nickel, silver and gold, zinc and tin were also processed here. When Cardiff became the most important coal-exporting port in Wales, Swansea was the international centre for metals. One can also say that it was the biggest devil's workshop in the country. In order to extract one ton of copper, you needed 13 tons of ore and 18 tons of coal. The slag-heaps piled up in the valley, and the sulphur hung over the town. Trees couldn't survive in 'Copperopolis', and the cattle had to be driven out of the meadows. 'Abandon Hope All Ye Who Enter Here'· with Dante's immortal cry of despair, Murray's 1877 guide to Wales warned the traveller about the nature of Lower Swansea Valley.

A local rhyme of 1890 did full justice to the reputation of Swansea at that time: 'It came to pass in days of yore / The Devil chanced upon Landore / Quoth he: "By all this fume and stink / I can't be far from home, I think".' In 1868 an engineer from Lenthe, near Hannover, built a steelworks in Landore, which soon became one of the four biggest in the world. His name was Wilhelm Siemens. When, at the end of the 19th century, copper production moved to America, Swansea concentrated on smelting other metals, especially tinplate.[1] In 1913 there were 106 rolling mills in and around Swansea; in 1955 there was just one.

---

1   The tsarist rolling mills in Moscow were built in 1905 on the Welsh model, and with the help of advisers from Swansea.

Ceri Richards: Tinplate workers, c.1942

The dying industry left behind a dying valley. By the end of the 1960's, Lower Swansea Valley was like a ghost town: crumbling factories, deserted railway lines, abandoned canals. The Tawe was a sewer, the valley a vast dump of toxic waste: black with tin, orange with copper, grey with steel. But in the midst of all this desolation, the University of Swansea came riding to the rescue. Its report, published in 1967, was a pioneering work, and made its authors into leading authorities on questions of environmental pollution. A vain attempt was made to get private industry to help with the great clean-up, and when this failed, the town itself set about acquiring land, removing slag-heaps, and planting trees. The ground was so contaminated that of thirty types of tree used, only four were able to flourish: pine, birch, alder and Japanese larch. The slag-heap of White Rock – 330,000 tons of it from a single copperworks, tipped onto the slopes of Kilvey Hill between 1737 and 1928 – was used for the foundations of the M4 and on the site of a new morganite works. Where once the biggest slag-heap in Wales had formed the man-made mountain of Hafod, there arose a new school.

When I went through the Lower Swansea Valley, the last of these heaps had only just been removed, at a cost approaching two million pounds – it was that of the Mannesmann steelworks in Landore. The day was appropriately grey, and the wasted valley was still a depressing sight. It was a valley where scarcely a single tree was more than twenty years old, and the great cleaning-up process itself had left a huge gap. Instead of a forest of chimney-stacks, there were now just two or three machine shops, left as a reminder of the copper industry for a planned open-air museum. The laboratory where Wilhelm Siemens had worked on the Siemens-Martin, or open-hearth, process of steel production has also been demolished. And like a ruined castle on the hill overlooking Morriston,[1] one could see the remains of the seven-storey tenement-house that John Morris built for his workers in 1760, above the smog of the industrial valley. The process of redevelopment has cost hundreds of millions of pounds, and yet it was not until 1966 that London agreed to subsidize the project. It is worth bearing in mind that 92% of Swansea's tax revenue flows into the coffers of Westminster, and the town keeps only 8%. But now, gradually, the valley is taking on a new shape, the plans are impressive, and what has been achieved so far promises much for the future. Not for nothing was the Lower Swansea Valley Project – Wales's contribution to European Conservation Year, 1980 – held up by the European Council as a shining example of how environmental pollution can be successfully countered by local initiative. By the end of this century, Swansea's Copper Valley will have been transformed into a green lung. The gigantic design includes a chain of five parks, reaching from the mouth of the Tawe as far as the motorway – a single recreation area with yachting harbour, riverside walks, sportsfields, and picnic places. The new zone for light

---

1   The Tabernacl Chapel, 1873 (see page 30 and plate 34), is home to one of the most famous of all Welsh choirs, the Morriston Orpheus Choir.

John 'Warwick' Smith: The Forest Works for smelting copper, Llansamlet, Lower Swansea Valley, 1792

industry will also be laid out as a park, round an artificial lake, with trees and fields in between the workshops. What does not fit into the framework of this 'Enterprise Park', such as the American Alcoa Aluminium Works or Europe's largest nickel refinery in Clydach, will remain on the outskirts. Alas, however, despite all the successful new industries, male unemployment in the region remains a good 15%.

Ugly, lovely town. The best place for a picnic is still not Tawe Valley, but *Mumbles*, at the southernmost point of Swansea Bay, where the Victorians used to bathe, and mutter: 'Mumbles is a funny place, / A church without a steeple, / Houses built of old ships wrecked, / And most peculiar people.' One of these most peculiar people lies buried in All Saints Church at *Oystermouth*, in the centre of Mumbles: Thomas Bowdler, who died in 1825. His life's work was to censor, or 'bowdlerize' the works of Shakespeare. But Mumbles is associated with another name, which is somewhat less puritanical.

Dylan Thomas: Poet Under Milk Wood

Let us begin in the Mermaid. Welsh Bitter, please. And let's get the old story off our chests: Dylan Thomas, the drunken poet, who as a young reporter in Swansea[1] boasted that he got drunk four times a week, and who remained true to his image right to the end in 1953, in New York: 'I've had 18 straight whiskies, I think that's the record.'

Poor Dylan. Now we're standing in your pub, which used to be the Mermaid and is now called Dylan's Tavern, and there you are, hanging on the wall, reduced at last to silence, your Woodbine in the corner of your mouth, chainsmoker with curly locks, bulbous nose, and thick lips (plate 15). On the photos you look just as your friends remember you – like an unmade bed. And outside, bluer than it ever was in your day, is Swansea Bay. Your town, your bay, two-tongued with its Welsh and its English, sandy beaches and steelworks, coal valleys and countryside. Mumbles, looking out to sea. But the railway has gone – opened in 1807, running on horsepower, then on steam, then on electricity, and finally not running at all. How often you used to go in those red double-deckers along the shore to Oystermouth and Mumbles Head. Well, one day the railway buffs will reopen that picturebook stretch of line, and no doubt the carriages will be called Willy Nilly and Polly Garter, and children will spit at gulls to bring themselves luck.

Dylan's Swansea wallows in nostalgia, washed in childhood memories as few other places have ever been. It's a town on seven hills, which means you have to be a 'mountaineer' to live in Swansea. I climb up a steep tongue-twister of a street: Cwmdonkin Drive. This district is called Uplands. Tiny houses, tiny front gardens, middle-class smell of fish and roast potatoes. This is the 'smug-suburbed' place where Dylan Marlais Thomas was born in 1914: No. 5 Cwmdonkin Drive. The parents still spoke Welsh at home, but Dylan didn't. His father, an English teacher, gave him lessons to make him lose his Welsh accent. But all the same, he was proud to be Welsh. His Celtic first name of Dylan comes from the 'Mabinogion', in which the golden-haired son of the wizard king Math is called Dylan Eil Ton, son of the sea-surge.[2] This English-Welsh duality permeated his whole existence. Like his Irish model James Joyce, Dylan's creative source was the sounds and images of the Celtic tradition. From very early on he was influenced by the *cynghanedd*, the hymnic, alliterative speech of the bards and preachers: 'The great rhythms had

---

1   With the 'South Wales Daily Post', now the 'Evening Post', which began in Swansea in 1845 as the first daily newspaper in Wales.

2   His second name is equally Celtic and poetic: Marlais, after the bardic name of his uncle William Thomas, a radical Non-Conformist preacher and poet. 'Marlais the Clown / with puckered lips / tasting the air' – this is how Johannes Bobrowski begins his poem 'Dylan Thomas'.

rolled over me from the Welsh pulpits' every Sunday in Paraclete Congregational Church in *Newton* (Mumbles). The world spoke to him in the sound of those words: 'the shape and shade and size and noise of the words as they hummed, strummed, gigged and galloped along.' It is not surprising that he called 'Under Milk Wood' a play for voices.

Today the house where Dylan Thomas was born is rented out (for a considerable fee) to holidaymakers by Frank Jones, a sheep-breeder. 'There's a housekeeper, just as there was in Dylan's time, and you can actually sleep in his bedroom.' From the bay window on the first floor, you can look out over the town and the bay. Just round the corner lies Dylan's Paradise Lost, Cwmdonkin Park, 'a world within the world of the sea town ... full of terrors and treasures'. The little cast-iron fountain, the hunchback on the bench, first kisses, and first poems. Combining the poetic and the practical, the council have erected a memorial here, on the site of the old bandstand, as a tribute to the poet and as shelter against the rain. What is one to do with a poet's immortal lines? They are not to be buried in books, but are to be written on walls, and etched into stones along the path, as they are here in Cwmdonkin Park: 'Oh as I was young and easy in the mercy of his means / time held me green and dying / though I sang in my chains like the sea.' These closing lines from 'Fern Hill' stand on the memorial plaque in Westminster Abbey's Poets' Corner, where on St David's Day 1982 the English officially honoured the Welsh poet just some 30 years after his death. 'Now as I was young and easy under the apple boughs': Fern Hill was a magnet to the young Dylan, a real place of enchantment up in the hills south of Carmarthen (near Llangain). It was the name of the farm belonging to his aunt, Ann Jones, where he used to spend his school holidays. He loved the house with its pointed Neo-Gothic windows and its dark tales of the past. Did there not once live here a hangman who hanged himself? 'There was nowhere like that farmyard in all the slapdash county, nowhere so poor and grand and dirty as that square of mud and rubbish and bad wood and falling stone.' Years later, Fern Hill re-emerged from the compost heap of memory, to fashion itself into one of the most beautiful of all poems.

'The ball I threw while playing in the park / Has not yet reached the ground.' To the magical world of childhood, wrote W. H. Auden, Dylan Thomas devoted all his genius. It was a childhood spent in Swansea, but again and again he would leave the town for the Gower Peninsula with its sandy beaches and its raging cliffs. 'Taking my devils for an airing,' he used to call it. And he would go to *Rhosili*, 'to camp on a bit of rock that wobbles in the wind'. Today the hang-gliders plunge from the slopes, while the surfers fall off their boards. 'We sank to the ground, the rubbery, gull-limed grass, the sheep-pilled stones, the pieces of bones and feathers, and crouched at the extreme end of the Peninsula.' And standing on Worm's Head: 'It could be in the middle of the sea. You could think the Worm was moving, wouldn't you? Guide it to Ireland, Ray. We'll see W. B. Yeats and you can kiss the Blarney. We'll have a fight in Belfast.'

Those were the days in Gower and the dreams dreamt on the gull-swept cliffs. At the age of 16 he left school[1] to become a poet. At the age of 20, he published his first volume of poems and left home. What was next for the 'Rimbaud of Cwmdonkin Drive'? London, of course, to seek his fame and fortune. Wales was too provincial for him. He wrote to a lady-friend: 'It's impossible for me to tell you how much I want to get out of it all, out of narrowness and dirtiness, out of the eternal ugliness of the Welsh people and all that belongs to them.' In London's avant-garde society, he successfully played the role of the provincial Bohemian ('we all have to sing for our supper') – but Chelsea, he found, was no substitute for Swansea. 'Capital punishment' was the name he gave to London. He drank his beer in the 'Six Bells', was a regular customer in the 'Fitzroy', but had left his heart in the pubs in Glamorgan. And so he went back to Wales, doing a pub-crawl through Mumbles – from the 'Marine' to the 'Three Lamps' to the 'Mermaid'. Most places in the area will tell you 'Dylan Thomas drank here', and it's nearly always true. But that he was always drunk – that's a myth. Of course he enjoyed fostering that image of himself, and he used to have two classic answers when he was asked why he drank so much: 'Because it's different every time', and 'Because they expect it of me'. People expected it because he was a Welshman. There you're either a drunkard or a teetotaller, but nothing in between. The fact is that Dylan Thomas could take his drink better than most, never drank when he was writing (at most, the odd cider), and wrote marvellous things about drinking, e.g. on Welsh Bitter: 'I like the taste of beer, its live, white lather, its brass-bright depths, the sudden world through the wet-brown walls of the glass, the tilted rush to the lips and the slow swallowing down to the lapping belly, the salt on the tongue, the foam at the corners. "Same again, miss".'

But once more he would be drawn back to London. He wrote scathingly about the unrecognisably anglicized Welsh: 'They set up, in grey, whining London, a little mock Wales of their own, an exile government of dispossessed intellectuals dispossessed not of their country but of their intellects.' But it was London that had the publishers, the patrons, the public and the BBC. In the 'Fitzroy' he got to know his fellow-countryman Augustus John,[2] and posed for the famous, very idealized portrait of himself: 'provided with a bottle of beer he sat very patiently' (colour plate inside front cover). It was also thanks to Augustus John that he met Caitlin, an Irish dancer. They were married in 1937. There followed months of cruel poverty in London, and in the spring of 1938 they moved to Wales. There at last Dylan Thomas found his place, and the place found its poet: *Laugharne*, 'the strangest town in Wales'. It had 400 inhabitants, two churches, and seven pubs, a nest of eccentrics, 'where some people start to retire before they start to work', and

---

1 Mount Pleasant Grammar School, a little schoolhouse built of masonry rubble (1853) was rescued from demolition in 1984 by a conservation order.

2 In his memoirs Augustus John, godfather to his son Llewelyn, calls Dylan Thomas a 'typical Welsh puritan and Non-Conformist gone wrong' ('Chiaroscuro', 1952).

others sought refuge from the police, or even 'from their wives'; 'and there are those, too, who still do not know, and will never know, why they are here at all: you can see them, any day of the week, slowly, dopily, wandering up and down the streets like Welsh opium-eaters, half asleep in a heavy bewildered daze.' And some simply hung around here, like himself, 'got off the bus, and forgot to get on again'. It was in this 'timeless, beautiful, barmy (both spellings) town' that Dylan Thomas wrote 'Under Milk Wood', that 'timeless, beautiful, barmy' play for voices.

Today Laugharne has 1,300 inhabitants, five pubs, and a legendary dead hero. But apart from the 'Rose and Crown', which is now known as 'Dylan's Diner', and a few antiques, everything is much as it used to be. The people take as little notice of the tourists as they used to take of the poet. The gulls look down from the roofs, and the tittle-tattle doesn't change: 'That woman over there,' says the landlord of the 'Corporation Arms', 'is worth two million. Been married three times before, but she can't get rid of the fourth one.' Material for Milk Wood. 'If your grandfather wasn't born here, you're nothing. Dylan Thomas came from Swansea. He was always a stranger here.' But of course his photo hangs on the wall. I walk along the shore, now known as 'Dylan's Walk', past the ruins of the Norman castle, 'brown as owls', to the whitewashed, slate-roofed house above the bay

J. M. W. Turner: Laugharne Castle, c.1831–32

where Dylan lived with Caitlin and their three children[1] (plate 17). 'The Boat House' is now a museum, well organized as the poet's life never was. The window frames are red inside and blue outside, in their original colour. Down below in the kitchen, now a tea-room, his mother's crutches still lean in the corner, and in the living-room his dark and throaty voice resounds from the radio – 'that old port wine of a voice'. It's all authentic, and rather ghostly. I step on to the balcony, and it's like standing on the deck of a boat out in the mouth of the Taf. It's such a romantic view across the bay, with the flashing sandbanks of St. John's Hill, the cry of the cormorants, the shrilling and shrieking of the gulls – you can easily forget the suffering, the chronic debts, the long lonely winters spent shivering in Wales.

'Under and round him go / Flounders, gulls, on their cold, dying trails.' When he wanted to work, he withdrew to the tiny blue hut up above the house, 'this water and tree room on the cliff' (plate 16). It contained a red-legged table, a few chairs, an iron stove, photos of Walt Whitman, D. H. Lawrence and Thomas Hardy pinned to the wooden wall, a few faded prints of nudes, Renoir, Modigliani's 'Peasant Boy'. Paper lies screwed up on the floor, and on the table between the facsimile manuscripts are two empty beer bottles ('because they expect it of me'). In this shed he wrote 'Under Milk Wood', various short stories, and some of his most beautiful poems. One of them, 'Do not go gentle into that good night' was recited at Richard Burton's funeral. Dylan Thomas wrote slowly ('I write at the speed of two lines an hour'), and often made more than 30 versions of a poem before deciding on a final one. His telescopic metaphors, and the tonal and musical associations of his verse makes it virtually untranslatable. Dylan Thomas did not want to be one of those Welsh authors who give the impression 'that their writing in English is only a condescension to the influence and ubiquity of a tyrannous foreign tongue'. Had there not already been Welshmen who wrote 'from time to time, exceedingly good poetry in English'? 'I should like to think that that is because they were, and are, good poets rather than good Welshmen.' No, he was never the man to be a mouthpiece for a 'Welsh only' movement. Throughout his life he wrote only in English, but it was not the Oxford English of a T. S. Eliot. Against the refined and sophisticated King's English of Bloomsbury, Dylan Thomas flung his boisterous, tumbling welter of imagery, English words fired by the Celtic spirit.

In Laugharne, then, he remained a stranger, even though he boasted that he could 'call several of the inhabitants, and a few of the herons, by their Christian names'. Some of the older folk still remember him. Alan Davies, for example, who owns the general store in Market Street: 'He used to fetch *The Times* every day, and his cigarettes, and his bull's eyes – you know, the black and white striped peppermints.' This store rather than Westminster

---

1   At first he lived in Gosport Street, then moved to 'Sea View', and from 1949 until his death in the 'Boat House', which his patroness Margaret Taylor had put at his disposal. Her husband, the Oxford historian A. J. P. Taylor, in his memoirs of 1983 did not have a good word to say about Dylan Thomas: 'Men pressed money upon him and women their bodies. Dylan took both with open contempt. His greatest pleasure was to humiliate people.'

Abbey is Dylan Thomas's real Poet's Corner. Alan Davies has out-of-print editions and gramophone records that have long disappeared from the scene; his visitors' book has the signatures of Dylan Thomas fans from as far afield as Tasmania. From Alan's shop, the poet would go a few houses on to where his parents lived, in 'The Pelican', and every morning he would do *The Times* crossword with them. After that, it was time for 'Brown's Hotel'. Tony Watts pours me a beer. 'I get sick of it,' he says, 'everybody asks about him, especially the Americans: "Oh, did he always get drunk here?"' But with a little persuasion the landlord of Laugharne's famous pub produces a well-worn bag: photos of the poet, old bills on which he had scribbled verses. Tony Watts has been offered £1,000 for the cast-iron table by the window where Dylan always sat, but he will never part with it. So this is where you sat, Dylan Thomas, pubbing away at midday and again in the evening, betting on the horses, drinking your bitter and your thin, cold tea. Here you sat, in the midst of the town's gossip, and they told you all their silly, strange and tree-tall stories about Organ-Morgan, and Dai Bread the Baker, and Mrs Ogmore-Pritchard in her 'crinoline nightgown, under virtuous polar sheets', and Polly Garter who loved a man named Harry, six foot tall and sweet as cherry ... and you changed Laugharne into 'Llareggub', the real and unreal, recognizable and incomparable town 'Under Milk Wood'.

You don't need to be an English specialist or a Sherlock Holmes to find out that Laugharne also has a little town hall[1] with a bell tower (1745), a house called 'Bay View' and a 'Rose Cottage'. Coronation Street goes straight through the middle of Laugharne, 'Sailor's Arms' is clearly Brown's Hotel, and Milk Wood grows on St John's Hill, which Dylan Thomas could see from his shed overlooking the bay. The sketch that he drew of Llareggub is a mirror image of Laugharne. Little wonder, though, that the people of Laugharne prefer not to see themselves in this imaginary nest of oddities. For everyone else, of course, Llareggub has become synonymous with Wales, which is synonymous with oddities. Dylan Thomas himself denied that there was any similarity at all: he had merely written a play about a day in the life of a small town 'in a never never Wales'. Bloomsday in Laugharne. The province as microcosm. 'We are not wholly bad or good / Who live our lives under Milk Wood,' says the Reverend Eli Jenkins. This joyous, warm-hearted message from Wales became a world-wide success: first as a radio play, then as a book, on stage, on film, as a jazz suite (Stan Tracey, 1965), and even as an opera (Walter Steffens, 1973). There is a general store in Mumbles that proudly calls itself 'Milkwood Arcade', and every two years the little town buzzes as the 'Llaregub Players', an amateur company from Laugharne, perform 'Under Milk Wood'. But Dylan Thomas never lived to see any of this success.

---

1   The Norman town charter dates from 1307, and the community is proud of its long tradition: the mayor wears an official chain of gilded shells.

According to Caitlin's memoirs ('A Warring Absence', 1986), their marriage was one long love-hate relationship, culminating in sheer hell: 'our lives were raw, red, bleeding meat'. The years in Laugharne were overshadowed by jealousy, quarrels and endless debts. While Dylan was creating Llareggub, he was also writing film scripts, radio programmes, and begging letters to friends and publishers. In order to make some quick money, he went on lecture tours to America, and as his 'London reputation for roaring behaviour' (W. H. Auden) preceded him, he read to full houses, and also did his best to live up to his image of a 'wild Welsh wizard'. He shocked and amused, was charming and drunk, a story-teller and a lady-killer. In short, he played the role of Dylan Thomas. At the same time, he made fun of the dollar-crazy 'nightingales' from Europe, the travelling salesmen of poetry who came to the New World. In planes and night-trains he rushed from one university to another, to clubs, cocktail parties and women's associations. 'I'm just a voice on wheels,' he said. But thus did his reputation grow. Years later a young American pop-singer, Robert Allen Zimmermann, named himself after his idol, the great Welsh poet. He became known as Bob Dylan.

In October 1953, Dylan Thomas set out on his fourth and last American tour. He wanted to discuss an opera project with Stravinsky: the rediscovery of Earth after a nuclear catastrophe. But the discussion never took place. After a fatal mixture of medicine and alcohol, he died of a brain haemorrhage in a New York hospital. He was 39. They buried him in Laugharne, one cold November day, in the hillside cemetery of St Martin, beneath a simple white cross of wood (plate 18). When he was a boy, his grandfather told him what to look out for when it came to choosing a final resting-place: 'There's no sense in lying dead at Llanstephan,' he said. 'The ground is comfy in Llangadoch; you can twitch your legs without putting them in the sea.' Fortunately, you can do the same in Laugharne.

From Gower to Carmarthen: Cliffs, Pubs, and Merlin

Tony Cottle owns a little printing works in Mumbles. It didn't take long for him to cotton on to the fact that Dylan Thomas had a worldwide fan club who would want to follow (and drink) in the footsteps of its hero. He therefore devised a very exclusive form of literary tourism: he drives his guests in a Bentley to Milk Wood – 'discovering Dylan Thomas in style', as he calls it. Others with less style, or less money, walk with sack on back and poetry in mind from Swansea to Laugharne, from Brown's Hotel to Worm's Head. 'Dylan Thomas country' is as distinct as the Wessex of Thomas Hardy and the Lake District of the Romantics. And for me the most beautiful part of this literary landscape is the *Gower Peninsula*.

West of Swansea, right next door to the densely populated, highly industrialized coastal strip of Glamorgan, this astoundingly lovely piece of Nature has survived untouched and unpolluted. Gower is the pearl of the Bristol Channel. Generations of miners and steelworkers have come here to relax, and in the early 1950's it was the very first place in Britain to be officially designated an 'Area of Outstanding Natural Beauty' by the

Countryside Commission (there are now more than 30 of these in Wales). It has never had a railway. 'No, no! No rail here!' That was the decision of the 19th-century MP, C. R. M. Talbot, Lord of Margam Park, and it has never been rescinded. 'We can come and enjoy the country; the rail would destroy it all.' What about cars? There are a few roads, but the true beauty of Gower is only accessible to the wanderer – the wild and lonely southern coast with its sheer limestone cliffs and its gentle hinterland, grass and broom-covered hills 'whose heads touch heaven', prehistoric dolmens, and tiny villages with little Norman churches.[1] The clifftop path from *Port Eynon* to *Worm's Head* is incomparable, five miles of sheer magic leading to the stone snake, the promontory where the schoolboy Dylan Thomas once cried: 'Why don't we live here always? Always and always. Build a bloody house and live like bloody kings,' before adding laconically, 'It's too wild for a townee.'[2]

Below and to the west of Port Eynon is one of the most famous prehistoric caves in Britain, *Goat's Hole*. Here in 1823 Dean Buckland found the 'Red Lady of Paviland', a Palaeolithic skeleton whose bones had been reddened by ferric oxide. A radio-carbon test, however, showed the lady to be a young Cro-Magnon man, who had been buried in this cave around 16,000 BC. He now lies at peace in the Natural History Museum in Oxford. *Arthur's Stone*, a Neolithic dolmen (*c.*2500 BC) near the ridge of *Cefn Bryn*, is believed to be the communal grave of Gower's first farmers. Typical of Gower are the rocky splendours of *Caswell Bay* and *Three Cliffs Bay*, or the endless sands of *Rhosili Bay*: 'the wildest, bleakest and barrenest I know – four or five miles of yellow coldness going away into the distance of the sea' (Dylan Thomas). Gower was where the Victorians went bathing: *Langland Bay*, with its green beach-huts, where the Crawshays, the 'Iron Kings' of Merthyr Tydfil, had their Neo-Gothic summer residence, and where Alfred Sisley painted his last pictures of the summer of 1897. But Gower is also the marshes of the north, where the sandbanks of *Llanrhidian* hump their backs in the mouth of the Loughor. Generations of women from *Penclawdd* used to come here at ebb-tide with their donkeys and carts to look for cockles, good healthy food for the workers in the rolling mills of Llanelli and Swansea. Today the cockle-women are part of Gower's folklore, for there are now very few who go to collect the dwindling stocks of this delicacy.

North of Gower is the mythical birthplace of the mythical Celtic magician Merlin: *Carmarthen*. Moridunum was what the Romans called the camp they built at the strategically commanding end of the long estuary of the Towy. The Normans, too, secured the bridgehead to the westward road by building a fortress. In the shadow of this grew the new English town, next to the older Welsh settlement, each with its own municipal rights. It was not until Henry VIII that they were forced to unite – a reform that had favourable

---

1 Mainly 13th century, e.g. in Cheriton, Ilston, Llangennydd, Oxwich and Llanmadog.

2 Gower was also the home of Dylan Thomas's frequent correspondent and close friend, the writer Vernon Watkins. ('Ode to Swansea' and many other works.)

consequences for all concerned. The Royal Charter of 1546 made Carmarthen the only town in Wales with the privilege of opening its inns all day long on market-days, regardless of all licensing laws. After that, nearly every day in Carmarthen was market-day, and the town rapidly acquired the reputation of being the most inebriated in Wales. In its heyday it had over 150 pubs. I haven't counted how many there are today, but take it from me, there are still plenty.[1] The history of the town was correspondingly turbulent. Drunkenness and corruption reached a peak in the election of 1802. The London banker Sir William Paxton, who had a country estate in Carmarthen, was after the parliamentary seat. In one of the most generous election campaigns in Welsh history, this Whig candidate gave away no less than 25,275 gallons of beer, 11,068 bottles of whisky, 8,879 bottles of port, 460 bottles of sherry, 11,070 breakfasts, and 36,901 dinners. After two weeks of high living, Sir William had as good as lost the election, because everyone was convinced that he must be bankrupt. In order to prove to these ungrateful people that he was not, he later built a tower to the east of Carmarthen: *Paxton's Tower* (1805–10), a folly and a vantage-point. Ostensibly, however, it was put up as a monument commemorating Nelson's victory and death at Trafalgar. Whatever it is, Nelson's Tower or Paxton's Folly, it is a notable piece of Neo-Gothic frivolity,[2] with a hexagonal central tower, surrounded by three lower round towers with high ogival entrances and no other purpose than to afford a view. It is a splendid architectural frame to encompass a superb panorama of the Towy Valley.

As the county town of Dyfed, Carmarthen is the administrative centre of south-west Wales, just as it was in Norman times. It's a rural capital with cattle markets, dairies, and just 14,000 inhabitants. If you look at the ruined castle in the beautiful bend of the river, you can hardly imagine that in the Middle Ages this peaceful spot was a flourishing wool centre and trading port, and in the 18th century was actually the biggest town in Wales. From this golden age there remain the Neo-Classical town hall (1767) and several Georgian houses in King Street and Quay Street. Some of them are believed to have been designed by John Nash, who sought refuge here from his London creditors in 1784, and opened an architect's office. Nash, whose mother was Welsh, designed or altered some two dozen buildings in Wales before he returned to London in 1796. There he made a great career for himself as town-planner and architect, popularizing the Regency style, but his genius first showed itself in Wales. The finest example is the country estate at Hafod, though like the prisons he designed for Carmarthen and Cardigan, this has now disappeared.[3]

---

1 Even after the 1982 'Sunday Closing' referendum, Carmarthen remained the only town in Britain whose pub-opening times approximated to those on the Continent: 11 a.m. – 11 p.m.

2 Designed by the London architect Samuel Pepys Cockerell, who in 1803 built the first English house in Hindu style: the country house of Sezincote.

3 John Nash houses still standing in Wales: Ffynone near Cardigan (1793), Whitson Court near Newport (1795) with a lodge in picturesque cottage style.

In the parish church of St Peter (14–16th century) lies the body of Sir Rhys ap Thomas, thanks to whose support in the Battle of Bosworth Henry VII won the throne of England. Also buried there is Sir Richard Steele. He was the editor and co-author with Addison of the *Tatler* (1709–11), the first of the great moral periodicals of the 18th century, and later started the *Spectator* and the *Guardian*, before spending the last years of his life in his wife's country house near Carmarthen.

Going much further back into time, and linked inseparably with the name of the town, is the 'Llyfr Ddu Caerfyrddin', the Black Book of Carmarthen. This is the oldest book in the Welsh language, written in 1105 in the Augustinian monastery of St John, and it contains poetic dialogues on historical, mythological, theological and literary subjects. The original manuscript is one of the treasures of the Natural Library in Aberystwyth, but a facsimile can be seen in the municipal library. The Augustinian monastery is commemorated only by the name Priory Street. Not far from there, at the eastern end of the town, there once stood the most famous tree in the country: Merlin's Oak. Carmarthen's Welsh name is Caerfyrddin, the town of Myrddin, or Merlin.

In recent years, fantasy has enjoyed an astonishing renaissance, and at its head stands the mighty figure of Merlin.[1] Were this not so, we might have left the Celtic wizard sleeping peacefully in his whitethorn, but according to the Swiss mythologist Sergius Golowin, he 'symbolically incorporates a basic attitude towards Nature and life which in a time of spiritual stultification and ecological jeopardy can serve as an example to us all.' Merlin, the guru of the Greens, the great alternative hero? He was a bard and shaman living between prehistory and history, between history and myth, a central yet mysteriously peripheral figure of Arthurian legend. He is said to have raised and counselled Arthur, given him his Round Table, and forged his sword. In the dark century after the departure of the Romans, he was the éminence grise of British history, and in the Middle Ages became a kind of national symbol (colour plate 63). After a battle in 575 he is said to have lost his reason and to have fled into the forests, where he declaimed his poems and his prophecies to the wild animals. He was a Celtic Orpheus, but without any Celtic tradition, for Merlin was a literary creation, brought into the world by Geoffrey of Monmouth. In the hexameters of his 'Vita Merlini' (1148), Geoffrey tells that Merlin was the son of a Breton princess and an incubus. He was an enigmatic, Janus-faced figure. Geoffrey reproduces some traditional prophecies, and invents new ones of his own, and these prophecies had great influence, which stretched even as far as Italy. How seriously the Celtic magician was taken in the Middle Ages can be gauged from the fact that at the Council of Trent in 1574 the 'Vita' was put on the list of forbidden books. 'Amongst these old romances it would be difficult to find one more wondrous and strange than that of the wizard Merlin,' wrote Friedrich Schlegel, whose wife Dorothea wrote a German

---

1   There are Merlin novels by T. H. White, Mary Stewart, Tankred Dorst and others, and a Merlin film by Walt Disney.

*Edward Coley
Burne-Jones:
The Beguiling
of Merlin, 1874*

translation (1804) of Robert de Boron's verse romance about Merlin (1190). For the Romantics, Merlin symbolized mystic harmony with Nature, erotic enchantment, and poetic imagination. In modern Arthurian literature, the warrior king tends to be more of a background figure, while Merlin becomes the focal point, representing as he does an inner, spiritual force. The trend was set by J. C. Powys, with his novel 'Porius' (1951).

'Merlin the Ancient, in shining tomb, / Where as a youth I talked to him,' claimed Goethe, who often used to bid goodbye to visitors with the words: 'Let me, old Merlin, go back to my stones and plants.' Merlin is said to lie buried in the forest of Paimpont in Brittany – or is he on Merlin's Hill near Carmarthen? Such a magician could be under any whitethorn bush. There is a glass cabinet in Carmarthen's Civic Hall, where the town keeps a piece of the ancient oak, almost like a piece of the Cross. Despite every effort to save the tree, and despite Merlin's prophecy, it finally went the way of all living things, and now they must wait (though it must be said, with increasing confidence) for the fulfilment of that prophecy: 'When Merlin's Tree shall tumble down, / Then shall fall Carmarthen Town.'

The Path That Doesn't Go To Brawdy: When Is A National Park Not A National Park?

Those in the know simply call it 'The Path'. It goes along the coast from Carmarthen Bay to Cardigan Bay, 170 miles of cliffs, bays and beaches, seagulls and seaweed. It's the *Pembrokeshire Coast Path*, one of twelve long-distance paths that have been opened up in Britain. This was the first in Wales, opened in 1970. There are hikers who only need a week to go from one end to the other, but that, I fear, will always be beyond me, and I know plenty of others in the same situation, even though they come back year after year to try again. For this path keeps going off at a tangent, and so it's really infinitely long as well as being infinitely varied. Who can resist the temptation to go and look at *Barafundle Bay* or the other little bathing resorts? How can anyone refrain from stretching out on *St Ann's Head* to watch the divers and the razorbills and the tankers from Milford Haven? And if you should come to *Marloes Sands*, that wild and lonely stretch of coast with its three 'chimneys' – the vertical folds in the Silurian cliffs – you can say goodbye to the rest of the day. You may go sailing from Tenby to Solva, surfing in Whitesand Bay, or strolling over the long beach of *Newgale*. 'The Path' is not just for walkers. On the rockfaces of *St Govan's Head* I have seen men with ropes and pitons, doing their Alpine training high above the seething breakers. But the winds will blow many of us away from the cliffs, to seek the stillness of the fields, where the lark's song replaces the gull's shriek, and you can follow the path as it sinks down into the hollow between the hedges and cosily wander your way.

Pembrokeshire Coast Path, like the rest of the countryside, varies with the seasons. In spring the cliffs are covered with wild hyacinths, sea anemones, and every kind of meadow flower. In summer the hills are yellow-carpeted with gorse. In autumn the clouds weigh down on the landscape like heavy rucksacks. But until deepest mid-winter, this coast is still lit by a light of extraordinary clarity. For a painter such as Graham Sutherland, Pembrokeshire was a revelation. This is the coast of artists and saints, Celtic missionaries and Norman conquerors. It is on this coast that St David, the patron saint of Wales, has his cathedral, and Henry VII, the first Welshman to mount the English throne, was born in Pembroke Castle. This coast has seen one invasion fail – that of the French at Fishguard – and another enjoy a successful dress rehearsal – the allied landing in Normandy: in 1943 Churchill, Eisenhower and Field-Marshal Montgomery met at Wiseman's Bridge Inn in order to watch the D-Day manoeuvres. Nearly 100,000 men stormed the beach between *Pendine* and *Saundersfoot*.

'The Path' begins at *Amroth*, and ends on the northern coast at *St Dogmael's*, named after a 5th-century saint, patron of crippled children. 'The Path' is also the connecting thread that binds together the Pembrokeshire Coast National Park, opened in 1952. This national park, more densely populated than any other in Britain, is also the richest coast in Britain for seabirds. When they need a bird warden on the island of *Skokholm*, west of Milford Haven – one lighthouse-keeper, 10,000 rabbits – there are dozens of applications from managers, students, pensioners, all anxious to get away from the pressures of civilization. Nevertheless the strangest birds in this national park are the armed forces.

With unerring instinct they have made their nests where the landscape is at its most beautiful and therefore most urgently in need of defence. What can a humble wanderer do but bow his head in deference to these defenders of the realm? On a still summer's day I went to *St Govan's Chapel*, a tiny building nestling in the rocks (plate 48). There a legendary 6th-century monk found refuge from the pirates and served God from his home in the cliffs.[1] There are seventy steep steps from the cliff edge down to the chapel (11–13th century), which is made from the same grey limestone as the rocks all round it, where the hermit originally had his cell – a strange setting for this Celtic piety. But today the saint's chapel lies in the tank-training grounds of *Castlemartin*, one of the biggest NATO firing ranges in Europe. When I wanted to continue my journey along the clifftops from St Govan's to Linney Head, my way was barred by red flags. 'Red flags will be flying if there is firing.' And today was a firing day. Lots of days are firing days. And no doubt there are thousands of disgruntled explorers like me who have missed the most majestic rock formations of the whole coast: Stack Rocks, Devil's Punch Bowl, and the Green Bridge of Wales. Castlemartin military base comprises some 6,000 acres of national park land: 'some of the finest coastal scenery in the country' and 'some of the best agricultural land in Wales', say the park authorities. But they also say there's a good side to all this: in this military no-go area, plants and animals can develop 'relatively undisturbed' by tourists and

---

1   St Govan is linked with the Irish abbot St Gobhan as well as with Arthur's nephew Sir Gawain, who is said to be buried here.

other such environmental hazards. On page 128 of the Pembrokeshire Coast National Park Plan 1977–82, it actually states: 'The Castlemartin range is of national importance for nature conservation.' No doubt the flora and fauna give daily thanks to the tanks that run over them, for protecting them against me and my ilk.

In this classic conflict of interests between national defence and preservation and use of the countryside, 'The Path' makes a diplomatic detour round Castlemartin. The military were there before us, say the wardens, and that is certainly true. Back in the Ice Age there were hill camps here, and today there are the remains of coastal defences from Norman to Victorian times to add to the charms of the journey. But future ruins will not be quite so romantic, as one glimpse of Castlemartin barracks will tell you. The National Park is also defended by military bases at Penally, Manorbier, Angle and Brawdy. Brawdy, an RAF and US rocket base east of St David's, was a frequent target for protest marches after Dyfed was declared a nuclear-free zone in 1981. But even the combined forces of Britain and America and the national park authorities have been powerless to repel the invasion of the caravan brigade. Lydstep Haven, near Tenby, has turned a whole bay into a gigantic caravan site. Perhaps this is a substitute for the heavy industry so noticeably missing from the National Park – apart, that is, from the oil refineries in Milford Haven. In Saundersfoot, now a popular bathing resort, one of the last coal-pits in Pembrokeshire closed as long ago as 1930.

If you know how to read the cliffs, for instance at *St Ann's Head*, you can go right back into prehistory. The oldest rocks on this coast are Pre-Cambrian, at least 4,000 million years old; the youngest are Carboniferous and were formed just 250 million years ago. The coastal plateau, about 200 feet high, dates back some two million years to when the sea-level dropped. When it rose again after the last Ice Age, relatively recently, about 15,000 years ago, many of the river valleys were flooded.[1] In estuaries such as Milford Haven, the tides now penetrate deep inland.

The tides of history have also helped to shape this coastline. After the departure of the Romans in the 5th century, there began the Age of Saints. Celtic monks like St David and his friend St Teilo made Dyfed into a centre for the conversion of Britain to Christianity. At that time there were many princes fighting for power in Wales. Little kingdoms rose and fell, the Vikings plundered the coastal regions (leaving behind such placenames as Skokholm and Gateholm), and not until the 9th century was Wales almost completely united by Rhodri Mawr, Roderick the Great. The work of unification was then completed by his grandson Hywel Dda, Hywel the Good. In 930 he summoned representatives from the three great principalities of Gwynedd, Powys and Deheubarth[2] to a

---

1   By low ebb-tide along the coast of Amroth, you can sometimes see the petrified stumps of a forest that was drowned thousands of years ago.

2   The area of Deheubarth was approximately that of modern Dyfed. This old name for West Wales was used for the combined counties of Carmarthenshire, Pembrokeshire and Cardiganshire in the regional reforms of 1974.

legislative assembly in Hen Dŷ ar Dâf, the White House on the Taf, now called *Whitland* (west of Carmarthen). It was a sort of parliament, the first in Wales, and it produced the 'Code of Hywel Dda'. He was the first to create a unified legal system out of the different laws and customs of his country, his basic principle being to protect the weak. Far more enlightened than was normal at that time, he even protected the rights of women. If they separated from their husbands, they were to get half the property – though only after seven years of marriage. Grounds for divorce included adultery and bad breath. Building and fire regulations, privileges for bards – these were all covered by Hywel Dda's code, but the most successful of his laws concerned inheritance. If a Welshman died, his land had to be divided in equal shares among all his issue – unlike the law in England whereby everything went to the eldest. Known as 'gavelkind', this system lasted until Henry VII changed it. Certainly it was fairer to the individual, but it also weakened the community through the constant dividing. Hywel Dda united Wales by law, and thus involuntarily hindered the unity of the kingdom. Herein lies one of the causes – or perhaps the tragic consequence – of Celtic particularism.

In 1093 Earl Roger de Montgomery conquered South Wales for King William II, but only in Pembroke Castle was he able to stand firm. Henry I sent a second army of Norman invaders, and in 1107 settled Flemish weavers in the vicinity of *Haverfordwest*, in order to hold the Welsh in check. When he died in 1135, an independent Welsh kingdom of Deheubarth was once again proclaimed. Until the 13th century, Dyfed remained for the most part divided: the southern coastal region under Norman rule, and the rest in the hands of the Welsh. From Newgale on the north-west coast to Carmarthen in the south-east an invisible barrier had been drawn through the land: that of language. North of this line people spoke Welsh, and south of it, English. You can still see the division by way of the placenames. Since that time, this part of Pembrokeshire has always been known as 'Little England beyond Wales'. Augustus John recalled that even at the beginning of this century the language and culture borderline was so distinct that it ran straight through the middle of Haverfordwest: 'where, on a market day, one may hear English spoken on one side of the High Street and Welsh on the other, with a mixture of both in the middle.'

Pembrokeshire: Where Graham Sutherland Learned to Paint

Tenby, sweetly constructed Tenby, tucked cosily away in two neat coves in Carmarthen Bay, blessed by Nature, unspoilt by human hand, magically, coolly, Celtically Mediterranean, warm and cheerful even when the sun refuses to shine, glowing, seductive Tenby. You were loved eternally by the great painter Augustus John, who was born in Tenby, found fame and fortune in London, saw the wide world, and found nothing to compare with his first love: 'You may travel the world over but you will find nothing more beautiful; it is so restful, so colourful and so unspoilt.'

William Daniell: Tenby Pier, Castle Hill, 1814

I stayed in one of those little Victorian boarding-houses on the northern beach, with a view across the gently curving bay to the port and the picturesque, pastel-shaded groups of houses on the peninsula (colour plate 20; plate 50). Only Prince Albert has a better view, gazing stonily out from the top of Castle Hill, from where he can also see the second bay with the long southern beach. There's a fine Norman castle (in ruins, of course), and an even finer town wall, rebuilt in the 15th century with a town gate that has five holes in it. Augustus John compared it to a piece of cheese gnawed by giant rats. In the Middle Ages Tenby was an important trading port linking Bristol, Ireland and France. The Tudor Merchant's House (15th century) dates from this time, as does the neighbouring Plantagenet House – both of which have been restored by the National Trust. The importance of the town is confirmed by its parish church of St Mary's (13–15th century), which in its day was the biggest in Wales. In it is a memorial to the mathematician Robert Recorde, born in Tenby in 1510, and famous for inventing the equals sign. Coal exports and herring fishing were the two things Defoe noted when he visited 'Tenbigh' in 1700. He found it 'the most agreeable town on all the sea coast of South Wales, except Pembroke'. There were, however, no more fishing boats in the harbour when I saw it – only yachts and pleasure boats. But there is a touching reminder of the fishermen and their piety: St Julian's Chapel, the old 'Fishermen's Church' right next to the port.

The Welsh name for Tenby is Dinbych-y-pysgod, Little Fort of Fishes. It owes its popularity as a bathing resort largely to the banker Sir William Paxton (see page 226), who lived here at the beginning of the 19th century. Since the Welsh climate is not always conducive to sea-bathing, Sir William built a public baths in Castle Square, with a quotation from Euripides over the entrance: 'The sea washes all men's sufferings away'. And it's true. In Tenby I finally rid myself of my bronchitis. Dating from Paxton's time are the houses on Castle Hill, whose noble Georgian façades and almost Mediterranean colours give such an incomparable glow to the harbour. This is where people stayed during the Regency period, when Tenby became fashionable – the Summer Queen of 'Little England beyond Wales'.

If the sea's not too rough, you can take a trip to *Caldey Island* and buy perfume while you look at monks. There is in fact a direct connection between the two. The traditional industry of monasteries elsewhere may be to produce Chartreuse or Benedictine to please the palate, but the Trappists of Caldey are famous for their olfactory delights. Since 1953 they have used their island to cultivate lavender and broom for the making of exquisite perfumes 'hand-made, hand bottled and packed' under the expert supervision of the perfumer Father Deseri. Vanity of vanities; all is vanity. One generation passeth away, and another generation cometh. At least let them all smell nice while they're doing it. Celtic missionaries were the first to settle on the island in the 6th century. The ruined abbey, however, was built by the Benedictines when they came in 1127, defying storms and plunderers, and standing firm until the Dissolution in 1538. The oldest part of their church of St Illtud, the choir, was plastered with large grey pebbles from the beach; there is also a stone inscribed in the ancient ogham script (6th century). It was not until the beginning of the 20th century that monks returned to the island and built a new monastery, which was taken over by the Trappists in 1929. Today there are only a dozen or so monks living there – may St Perfume preserve them.

'Religion and art are my life ... You are only free when you have left everything behind. Leave everyone and let yourself be left. Only then will you be without fear.' The woman who wrote these words was left with nothing but her cat Edgar Quinet, and a poor basement flat in Paris. She died in 1939. Her grave is unknown. She was Gwen John, one of the greatest women artists of the century. She painted her first pictures on Tenby beach. Here she spent her childhood, together with brother Augustus, who was two years younger than her, born in 1878 at No. 50 Rope Walk Field (now part of the Belgrave Hotel). 'The beaches, caves, sand dunes and burrows in the neighbourhood provided ideal play-grounds,' wrote Augustus, who shared his first studio with his sister in Tenby. Their father was a lawyer, and he sent them both to the Slade School in London to study art. Then Gwen John went her own way.

She moved to Paris, studied under Whistler, earned her living as a model, sitting among others for Rodin, whose mistress she was for ten years. She was converted to Catholicism, knew Rilke in Meudon, and never stopped painting: interiors, still life, portraits of women

Gwen John: Self Portrait, c.1900   *Augustus John: Self Portrait, c.1920*

and children, modest in scale, simple and strict in form, delicate in colour. She had no success, but never gave up – a painter with the fervour of a mystic, who went every day to Mass and even there continued to draw, a quiet, shy woman who was as easily overlooked as her quiet but beautiful pictures. 'Few on meeting this retiring person in black, with her tiny hands and feet, a soft, almost inaudible voice, and delicate Pembrokeshire accent, could have guessed that here was the greatest woman artist of her age.' This moving epitaph for Gwen was written by her brother Augustus, the successful painter, the spoilt darling of the salons, and the direct opposite of his sister, larger than life and twice as loud.

At the age of 23 Augustus John was already an academy professor in Liverpool. At 29 he had had six sons by two different women with whom he lived in a ménage à trois. After living with gypsies in France and on Dartmoor, he made a name for himself in London Society, which always welcomed a dash of 'Wild Wales' as embodied by the Johns, the Thomases, and the Burtons. 'He looked so exactly like a statue I've seen of Zeus,' wrote John Cowper Powys, who sat for him (illustration, page 309). With his brilliant colours and draughtsmanship, and an unerring instinct for bringing out the true personality, Augustus John reigned supreme for half a century as the greatest portrait-painter in the land. He painted Shaw, Lloyd George, Churchill, King Faisal, and on a visit to Berlin in 1925 Gustave Stresemann ('that square cranium housed a cultured mind, informed with the old German idealism'). In Tenby's museum there are just two relatively small portraits by Augustus John. The museums of Cardiff and London offer a great deal more of his work – landscapes, pictures of gypsies, children and beautiful women. But one can also detect changes in quality. While Gwen John's pictures[1] became increasingly simple and intense, her brother's grew more pompous and yet more trivial. His formats were bigger, his colours more strident, his subject-matter more popular, his appearances more spectacular. And thus it is that in most dictionaries of art, you will find a lengthy entry under the name of Augustus John, while his sister is relegated to a little paragraph at the end. At their old school in Tenby there are two trees in their honour: Gwen's is a birch, and Augustus's – what else? – an oak.

The landscape of their hometown, and indeed of Wales itself, played no real part in the work of the two Johns, but there were two English painters who, after William Turner, did more than anyone to put Pembrokeshire on the map of modern art: John Piper and, especially, Graham Sutherland. 'It was in this country that I began to learn painting,' confessed Sutherland, many years after his first visit to Pembrokeshire in 1934. Until 1945 he came to Wales every year, and resumed these visits between 1967 and his death in 1980 – often returning several times a year.[2] What was it that fascinated this Londoner and brought him back again and again to so remote a corner of the country? 'The quality of light here is magical and transforming – as indeed it is in all this country. Watching from the gloom as the sun's rays strike the further bank, one has the sensation of the after-tranquility of an explosion of light. Or as if one had looked into the sun and had turned suddenly away. Herons gather. They fly majestically towards the sea. Most moving is the sound of snipe which flicker in their lightning dash down the inlet to and from the sea.' The extraordinary clarity of the light gives things an increased plasticity, a disturbing and almost surreal presence. It was at *Sandy Haven*, west of Milford Haven, that Sutherland first experienced the 'exultant strangeness' of this coast. 'The left bank as we see it is all dark – an impenetrable damp green gloom of woods which run down to the edge of low brackish moss-covered cliffs – it is all dark, save where the mossy lanes (two each side) which dive down to the opening, admit the sun, hinged, as it were, to the top of the trees, from where its rays, precipitating new colours, turn the red cliffs of the right-hand bank to tones of fire. Do you remember the rocks in Blake's "Newton" drawing? The form and scale of the rocks here, and the minutiae on them, are very similar. The whole setting is one of exuberance – of darkness and light – of decay and life. Rarely have I been so conscious of the contrasting of these elements in so small a compass.' His experience of the red sandstone cliffs of Sandy Haven inspired his 'Estuary with Rocks' (1937–8) and other such pictures. It was a revelation and a challenge much as Mont Sainte Victoire had been for Cézanne. On these Welsh coasts of light he discovered a pictorial language of his own,

---

1 Cardiff's national museum has by far the biggest collection of her work: paintings, sketchbooks, and over 1,000 drawings.
2 Sutherland's Welsh bases were: Lleithyr Farm between St David's and Whitesands; the Cambrian Hotel and The Ship in Solva; the Lord Nelson Hotel in Milford Haven; Picton Castle, east of Haverfordwest. During the war, he worked as 'Official War Artist' in Swansea, Cardiff, and the steelworks at Merthyr Tydfil.

Graham Sutherland: Welsh Landscape with Roads, 1936

parallel to Nature, and sought to give to the landscape the independence of movement that had hitherto characterized only figures or the objects of a still life. He did not sit down at his easel in front of the landscape, but wandered around with a little sketchbook in his hand, a beachcomber in rubber boots and tweed jacket, with bag over shoulder and walking stick in hand, prodding between the seaweed and the driftwood in search of hidden treasure. Eroded rocks, tree-roots, the bleached skull of a horse, the skeleton of a boat in the mud, strange branches, rusty chains – what Sutherland found between Sandy Haven and St David's Head is what anyone can find even today. But he isolated all these details from their natural surroundings, and in his drawings and paintings associated them with all the emotions and aggressions that he found both in them and in himself. He drew on the infinite variety of forms that he saw in the countryside, and out of them created a vision of Pembrokeshire that is almost a coded, surreal topography. He never had the feeling 'that my imagination was in conflict with the real, but that reality was a dispersed and disintegrated form of the imagination.' Ribs of sand at ebb-tide, with herons flying above them; gorse, whose branches lie like snakes along the cliffs; and over and over again, paths that make curious arabesques across the countryside. In his picture 'Road at Porthclais with Setting Sun' (1975), Sutherland gives an almost hallucinatory intensity to the theme of endless paths: a golden sun against a black sky, darkness with an excess of light.

One of his favourite haunts in later life was *Eastern Cleddau*, near Picton Castle, with its steep embankment and the trees twisted into strange shapes by the ebb and flow. From these things Sutherland derived his characteristic structures of movement and balance, for instance in 'Form over River' (1971–2) in the Tate Gallery. The most comprehensive collection of his work is not in London, but fittingly in *Picton Castle* itself. He and the owner had been friends for many years, and in 1976 he donated a large number of his Welsh paintings to the Graham Sutherland Gallery, his motives being both cultural and political: 'because I think it is high time that there should be some move towards decentralization; also because I believe that work done in a certain area is seen best in that area.' The collection now consists of some 300 paintings, drawings and prints by Sutherland. The majority are on exhibition in the former stables of Picton Castle, which also boasts (but does not display to the public) a small, though exquisite private collection of French Impressionists. The owner, R. Hanning Phillips, is a descendant of the Norman knight William de Picton, who built the castle *c*.1190. It took on its present shape by way of extensions built in the 18th and 19th centuries. There is a magnificent view from the hill and the gardens across Eastern Cleddau and the different branches of the Estuary – Sutherland's favourite hunting-grounds.

The English painter John Piper also came to Pembrokeshire for the first time in the 1930's. In 1963 he bought two abandoned cottages, with no phone or electricity, on the slopes of Garn Fawr, *Strumble Head*, near Fishguard. From here he set forth, as he had done in North Wales, to paint and draw the landscapes, waterfalls, chapels and prehistoric monuments, with a topographical fervour scarcely matched by any of his contemporaries. 'Almost an honorary Welshman,' his Welsh colleague Kyffin Williams called him. 'Trying to see what hasn't been seen before.' It is a principle well worth following, and it rarely leads to disappointment.

From Pembroke Castle to the Throne of England

'Manorbier is the most pleasant spot in Wales.' That was Giraldus Cambrensis's enthusiastic opinion of his birthplace. *Manorbier Castle* is the romantic castle par excellence, its ivy-covered walls standing in majestic isolation overlooking the sea and a little bay nestling between the hills west of Tenby. Thanks to its amazingly durable light-grey Carboniferous limestone – a local building material – this medieval castle (12–14th century) remains well preserved, even as a ruin. Within the walls of the courtyard, where once there had been living quarters, now there are only flowers. In some of the towers and dungeons, waxwork figures made by Madame Tussaud's contribute to an atmosphere of medieval chivalry. There is also the seated figure of a monk, writing, a candle beside him,

◁ *John Piper: Welsh Dolmens near Login, Pembrokeshire, 1979*

the stone floor covered with straw. This is Giraldus Cambrensis, the great champion of independence for the Welsh church.

Giraldus Cambrensis, also called Gerald de Barri, was born in Manorbier Castle in 1146. His father William was a Norman baron, his mother Angharad, a Welsh princess. 'When I see injustice in either race, I hate it.' His dual origins made Gerald into an incorruptible observer of both nations and their characteristics. But the ideal mediator was also a clever exploiter of his dual nationality. He studied at the Sorbonne, at 28 became archdeacon of Brecon, and at 31 was already elected Bishop of St David's. But despite the approval of the Pope himself, England's King and the Archbishop vetoed the election, which seemed to them to endanger their influence in Wales. In 1184, Gerald took part in Henry II's Irish campaign, as Prince John's secretary and court chaplain. Four years later, as a loyal son of the church, he accompanied Archbishop Baldwin of Canterbury through Wales, and preached alongside him on behalf of the Third Crusade. The fact that this publicity campaign also helped to strengthen the authority of the Church of England over the Welsh bishops was scarcely unknown to Gerald. The result of this six-week journey was two books, written in Latin, to which Giraldus Cambrensis owes his undying fame: 'Itinerarium Cambriae' (1191) and 'Descriptio Cambriae' (1193), travel book, diary, topography and history of his homeland, and one of the few authentic sources of information about life in Wales at the end of the 12th century. In this work the author is as vehement about the faults of his countrymen as he is enthusiastic about their virtues: 'The Welsh go to extremes in all matters. You may never find anyone worse than a bad Welshman, but you will certainly never find anyone better than a good one.' His attention to detail even extends to dental care: 'Both sexes exceed any other nation in attention of their teeth.'

Throughout the years, Gerald never gave up his dream of becoming Bishop of St David's. Three times he travelled to Rome to present his case to the Pope. But Innocent III, much as he liked the Welsh scholar, continued to give his support to English interests. Again and again Gerald was offered other sees, also in Ireland, but he rejected them all. He only wanted one: St David's, and it should be the Welsh Archbishopric, independent of Canterbury. This, however, would have undermined the very foundations of English authority in Wales, and so Gerald was bound to fail. He died in Lincoln, probably in 1223. Geralt Gymro, Gerald the Welshman, became a symbol for his fellow-countrymen. His ecclesiastical struggle against Canterbury was 'Welsh nationalism in religious dress' (Gwynfor Evans). This life-long fight was linked to the nonconformism of the Celtic church in Wales, which had not joined the Roman church in England until 768, half a century after Ireland and Cornwall. Along with its own religious rites, the church also defended the Welsh way of life, and so Gerald's nonconformism was equated with a political stand. 'The English are striving for power, the Welsh for freedom; the English are fighting for material gain, the Welsh to avoid a disaster; the English soldiers are hired mercenaries, the Welsh

59 MACHYNLLETH   Centre for Alternative Technology, working group ▷

60 PARTRISHOW Grave of Joan Barnes, 1977

61 PARTRISHOW St Ishow, choir screen, *c.*1500

62 STRATA FLORIDA Norman West Doorway of Cistercian Abbey, 1184–1235

63 GREGYNOG HALL Half-timbering painted on concrete, *c.*1870

64 TRELYDAN HALL Country house, 16–17th century

65   PLAS NEWYDD   The house of the Ladies of Llangollen, 17–19th century

67   ABERYSTWYTH   View from Constitution Hill with mountain railway (1896) ▷

66   LLANIDLOES   Covered market, c.1600

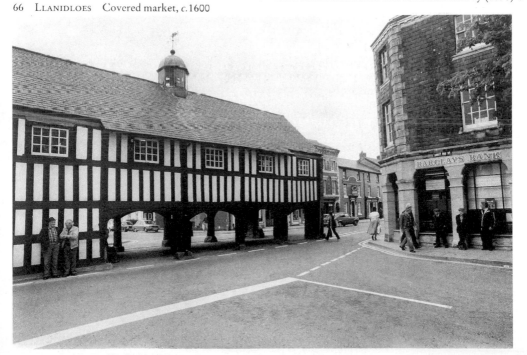

69   LAKE VYRNWY   Water tower, *c.*1890

71 CAREW CASTLE 13–15th century

72 CAERPHILLY CASTLE 13th century

73   CASTELL COCH   1875–91, by William Burges

74   PEMBROKE CASTLE   13th century, birthplace of Henry VII

75 PLAS NEWYDD   Dining-room with wall-painting by Whistler, 1936–37

76 CHIRK CASTLE   Long Gallery, 1678

77 POWIS CASTLE   Lord Powis in castle grounds

78 NANTEOS   Music-room, *c.*1740

79 PORTMEIRION Sir Clough Williams-Ellis's Italian village at foot of Snowdon

are defending their homeland.' Such words, fashioned by a rhetorically sophisticated preacher, instilled national consciousness into generations of Welshmen. If Gerald had not always felt a moral duty towards the Norman part of his origins, he might easily have become the revolutionary leader of his people. Gerald ends his 'Descriptio Cambriae' with the famous story of the old man of *Pencader*: Henry II, on a punitive expedition to West Wales in 1163, asks an aged follower from Pencader how it is all going to end. The old man replies that Wales might be overrun and laid to waste, as so often before, but it will never be completely subjugated. 'Nor do I think, that any other nation than this of Wales or any other language shall in the Day of Judgement answer for this corner of the earth.'

Manorbier Castle always remained on the fringe of the action. But one of the main centres of power in Welsh history lies just a few miles to the west: *Pembroke Castle*, residence of the Norman earls of Pembroke (plate 74). It was from here that Richard Strongbow set forth in 1170 to conquer Ireland. In the chain of Norman castles along the coast, Pembroke was the strongest link. Its situation was made for a fortress: a gently sloping ridge, with water on three sides – Pembroke River to the north, dammed to form a huge millpond; a branch of the Milford Haven to the west; and a tidal branch to the south. The only side accessible by land, where the road runs to Carmarthen, was once sealed off by the eastern gate. The walls of the town have long since crumbled, but one can still see from the remains of the castle why it was well nigh impregnable. There is a mighty gatehouse with three portcullises, an outer wall (13th century), an inner that is almost completely ruined, and in the middle a massive Norman keep (c.1210), four storeys and over 60 feet high, with walls 18 feet thick at the base, made from the same limestone as the rest of the fortress, standing alone with nothing left but its stone helmet. It is a dark, hollow shell emblematic of the power that once was. During the Civil War it took Cromwell seven weeks to conquer this castle by siege in 1648.

This bastion of the Royalists has also been the birthplace of a King, Henry VII (illustration, page 21), though the road from Pembroke to the throne of England was a long one. When matters of war and peace could be settled by means of marriage, Henry V, the victor of Agincourt, married Catherine of Valois, daughter of the defeated French King Charles VI (1415). After Henry's death she secretly married the Welsh knight Owain Tudor from Anglesey. It was he who paved the way for the Tudor dynasty in England (see page 390). His son Edmund married the Countess of Richmond, Margaret Beaufort, from the House of Lancaster. This was during the Wars of the Roses, and Edmund Tudor brought his fifteen-year-old bride to the safety of Pembroke Castle. There, in 1457, shortly after Edmund's death, she gave birth to a son: Henry Tudor. The young Earl of Richmond spent his early years under the protection of Pembroke Castle's thick walls – a Welsh childhood, complete with harp, tournaments and hunting. Suddenly in 1471, he became Lancaster's claimant to the throne; but the Yorkist Richard III seized the crown, and Henry fled to France. There he remained for fourteen years in exile. Then on August 7

1485, he landed with 2,000 French mercenaries in Milford Haven,[1] took Pembroke Castle, and under the banner of the Red Dragon pushed east. By uniting the symbol of the Welsh leaders Cadwaladr and Merlin with the red rose of Lancaster, he cleverly linked family ambition to national aspirations. On August 22, 1485 he defeated Richard III at the Battle of Bosworth Field, and the Welsh celebrated his triumph over the House of York as if Wales had beaten England. Wearing a green and white jerkin (the colours of Wales), the 28-year-old was crowned king in Westminster Abbey. He was never to return to Wales, but since then, the Welsh have remained firm royalists. Even in the Civil War they were, with a few exceptions, on the cavalier side, and today the Prince of Wales is still benefiting from this loyalty.

By his marriage to Elizabeth of York, Edward IV's eldest daughter, Henry VII united the white and the red rose of the two warring families in the double rose of the Tudors. In the 24 years of his reign he brought peace, a degree of prosperity, and a blossoming culture to the country. Many Welshmen went to his court and gained honours and high positions in England. Henry was a broad-minded man and a patron of the arts; he employed French and Italian artists as well as Welsh bards and harpists, celebrated St David's Day in London, named his eldest son Arthur, and fostered Welsh traditions wherever and whenever he could. English historians tend to play down his Welshness, while Welsh nationalists consider it to have been more of an affectation: 'He is the characteristic modern Welshman, confining his Welshness to sentimentality and personal gain,' says Gwynfor Evans, who regards the Battle of Bosworth Field as the most catastrophic defeat in Welsh history. 'Although they had none of the substance of national freedom the Welsh were satisfied with symbols.' For this historian and Plaid Cymru MP, Henry VII's coronation was a 'tragic mistake' by the Welsh, whose great illusion then as now was 'to aim at government by a Welshman in London instead of a Welsh government in Wales'. Henry VII died in Richmond in 1509. He lies buried beneath the fan vaulting of the chapel named after him, in Westminster Abbey. His son Henry VIII removed even the last vestiges of Welsh independence by means of the 1536 union. It is perhaps fittingly ironic that Pembroke, birthplace of the first Welsh King of England, should have become the constituency of an English Conservative Minister for Wales, Nicholas Edwards.

From the battlements of the Norman castle you can see the giant tower of a coal-fired power station, the derricks of *Pembroke Docks*, and in the distance the oil refineries of *Milford Haven* (colour plate 28). Here, where the sea reaches deep inland like some huge octopus, industry has established its solid base, surrounded by a National Park and accompanied by the complaints of the environmentalists. Milford Haven is a gift donated by the last ice age: a drowned valley over 12 miles long, 'one of the greatest and best inlets of water in Britain' (Defoe). Henry II started out from here in 1172 to conquer Ireland, and in 1407 a French fleet landed here to support Owain Glyndwr against Henry IV. In

1 Mill Bay, 1 mile south of Dale, is traditionally believed to have been Henry Tudor's landing-place.

the Second World War, RAF bombers took off from here to fight the battle of the Atlantic. But the town of Milford Haven itself is only 200 years old. Quakers from Massachusetts, refugees from the American War of Independence, settled here in 1793 and started a flourishing whaling industry. It was a model estate, with a chessboard groundplan, and three long, parallel streets on the slopes overlooking the bay: Hamilton Terrace, Charles Street, and Robert Street. Hamilton Terrace is named after the man on whose land Milford Haven was built: Sir William Hamilton, British ambassador to the court of Naples, and best known as the long-suffering husband of the beautiful Lady Emma. It was for her sake that Nelson underwent the stresses and strains of a journey to Wales in 1802. His visit to Milford Haven was also, however, used in the publicity campaign for the new port, to attract industry: could not the British Admiralty have some of its warships built here? And Lady Hamilton's lover himself was impressed: Milford Haven, he said, was the most beautiful natural harbour, apart from Trincomalee in Ceylon, that he had ever seen. With such promotion, the Welsh whaling port awoke from its dreams and became a royal shipyard[1] and the second biggest oil port in Europe. In Hamilton Terrace there are only a few houses between 'Lord Nelson', a hotel, and 'Lady Nelson', a ladies' fashion shop. The parish church of St Katharine (1801–08) does its own little bit of Nelson-worship, and amongst its relics is a piece of mast from *L'Orient*, blown up at the Battle of the Nile.

The British fear of invasion, fed by the French Revolution, resulted in Milford Haven being one of the best guarded ports in Britain: in the middle of the 19th century, its entrance was guarded by no less than 14 forts and Martello towers, named 'Palmerston's Follies' after the Prime Minister of the day. Today the gun batteries of *Dale Point* are a Field Studies Centre. Dale itself, an idyllic sailing harbour, is said to be the sunniest place in Wales, with a daily average 6.4 hours' sunshine from June to August. The yachtsmen love it, but they must share the waters with oil tankers. Before the oil crisis of 1973, Milford Haven was extended to take supertankers, and it became the second biggest oil-refining port in Europe, after Rotterdam. The fishermen were left empty-handed, for water pollution proved disastrous to their industry. The oil boom, however, was short-lived. Recession, North Sea oil, the distance of the port from the major industrial centres – all this contributed to the decline of Milford Haven, and today there is an unemployment rate of around 17%.

St David's: Water, Leeks, and National Consciousness

How must the pilgrims have felt in those days, as they approached *Dewisland* on foot or on horseback, coming nearer and nearer to St David's on the westernmost edge of Wales?

1   It was founded at the beginning of the 19th century as a ship-building town, in competition with Pembroke Dock. There the keels were laid down of the biggest and fastest wooden armoured vessels ever built for the British fleet: 'Lord Clyde' (1864) and 'Lord Warden' (1865).

Before them an almost treeless, wind-swept plateau. Scarcely a hedge, but only earthworks and stone walls through which the wind was howling. Fields full of stones, some piled into pyramids, 'as if the solid rock foundation of the earth had thrown up these spears to transfix and hold the scanty earth of the fields upon it' (Graham Sutherland). *'Angulus remotissimus; terra saxosa, sterilis et infecunda'* wrote Giraldus Cambrensis of Dewisland, St David's peninsula, and that is how it is even today: remote, far from the nearest railway station, wild and desolate, a Welsh Land's End. Where the rocky terraces plunge down into the sea, that is *St David's Head*. *'Octopitarum Promontorium'*, the foothills of the eight perils, was what Ptolemy called this cape, whose rocks were to prove fatal to many a Roman ship. And yet those rocks jutting out beyond the coast bear such innocent names as Bishops and Clerks. Three thousand years ago, the people protected themselves against sea-faring marauders by building *Warrior's Dyke*, a double stone wall near St David's Head. The peasants of the Iron Age also built walls to divide off their fields, and the ruins of these can still be seen below the slate hill of *Carn Llidi*. Dewisland: from this bare isolated corner of the country came the patron saint of Wales, Dewi Sant.

A national saint does not come into the world with a whimper. Dewi Sant, it is said, was born during a hurricane on the cliffs south of St David's. Since a storm in these parts is nothing unusual, Nature also offered a second sign: at his birth, a spring gushed forth from between the feet of his mother Non. And I can vouch for the fact that there is indeed a spring in a meadow not far from the ruins of St Non's Chapel. It may be difficult to distinguish between myth and reality in St David's life, but there is no doubting the effect it had: in West Wales alone, more than 50 churches bear his name. He was one of the pioneers of Christianity in the 6th century, the 'Age of Saints'. He travelled tirelessly round the country on Roman roads from which the Celtic missionaries were the first to profit. The force of his personality is illustrated by a legendary incident in *Llanddewi Brefi*: while he was preaching there, the earth rose under his feet, so that he was standing on a hill above the crowd – Celtic eloquence moving mountains.[1] Because of his ascetic way of life, he was called Dewi Ddyfrwr, David the Water-Drinker. The Swiss mystic saint Nicholas von Flüe was also called 'Aquaticus', and his modern disciple Joseph Beuys has prophesied: 'In 300 years people will be able to live on a glass of water'. That will be when our existence is no longer dominated by materialistic ideas and the consumer mentality. Perhaps the wheel will indeed turn full circle, and the future will bring us back to the past. It must be said, however, that St David did not live on water alone; he also ate leeks. He was a vegetarian. And it is in his honour that the Welsh made the leek their national emblem (while lamb is the national delicacy). It was under the sign of the leek that the Welsh bowmen fired their arrows at the Battle of Crécy. At the Tudor court the Welsh Guards presented their monarch with a leek on St David's Day, and even today they wear

---

1 In the village church of Llanddewi Brefi on this very hill, lies the Idnert Stone (8th century), the gravestone of a murdered bishop, on which is to be seen the first written mention of St David.

a leek in their lapels during their London Parade on that day. And as the Welsh name for daffodil is Cenhinen Pedr, Peter's Leek, the flower is also a national emblem for the Welsh. But what was it that made David the Water Drinker into the patron saint of Wales?

The decisive factor was not his diet or his faith. The reason was political. St David is more than a saint. Giraldus Cambrensis, who was twice elected Bishop of St David's, and was twice rejected by the Archbishop of Canterbury and the King of England for the sake of Anglo-Saxon superiority, wrote: 'The Bishopric of St David's became, as it were, a symbol of the independence of Wales ... and that is why David himself was exalted into a Patron Saint of Wales.' Thus the legend of the saint combined with the struggle of the church to build a national myth. By 1120 Pope Calixtus II had already canonized the Celtic missionary and accepted two pilgrimages to St David's as being the equivalent of one to Rome.[1] Today the Welsh saint, much like the Irish St Patrick, arouses the patriotic feelings of his people. March 1, the day of his death (the year is uncertain, but may well have been 588), became a national feast day for Welshmen all over the world. On St David's Day everyone wears leeks and daffodils, from Llanddewi to London, from Pwllheli to Patagonia. One cannot, in all honesty, say that people only drink water and sing nothing but hymns. But could there have been a more appropriate day to begin a boycott of the water-rates (imposed by the English) than St David's Day 1982? This is the day when national aspirations spring to life, and nationalist campaigns open in his name. Even the failed referendum on devolution took place on St David's Day, March 1, 1979.

It's not often that the visitor to a cathedral town has to ask: Where's the cathedral? You can see the towers of Canterbury, Ely, or Lincoln from miles away, proudly stretching up towards the Heaven they would have us enter, but St David's Cathedral is different. It ducks down in a valley hollow, like a bird in its nest (plate 46). Almost a mile away from the sea, sheltered from the storms and the gaze of marauding pirates, in the Alun Valley, known poetically as Vallis Rosina – Valley of the Roses – in Glyn Rhosyn, that is where St David founded his monastery in the 6th century. Only when you step through the massive gatehouse (13th century) on the edge of the town, and enter the unwalled Cathedral Close, will you see St David's Cathedral standing before you in all its splendour, dominated by its stocky crossing tower, and surrounded by a field full of old gravestones. The present Cathedral is the fourth to have been built here. It's made of honey-coloured oolite and grey-green Cambrian sandstone from cliffs of nearby Caerfai Bay. Begun c.1180, this is the last large-scale Norman church to have been built in Britain. The exterior is as simple as the interior is magnificent: the nave has three aisles with Norman arcades, triforium and clerestory covered with ornamentation in the Decorated Style (14th century). The nave is closed off by a choir screen in the same High Gothic style and decorated with sculptures. In the crossing are the Bishop's throne (c.1500) and the choir stalls (c.1470), filigree

---

1 Out of more than 500 missionaries and martyrs from the 'Age of the Saints' that are listed among Celtic saints, very few were canonized by the Roman Catholic Church.

decorations and misericords with burlesque scenes from everyday life. The highlight is a beautifully carved ceiling of Irish oak, late 15th century, spreading like an exquisite lace canopy over the interior. Since the middle of the 13th century the Cathedral has continually expanded eastwards, from the choir, through the presbytery and ambulatory, to the Lady Chapel. Edmund Tudor lies buried before the High Altar; he was the founding father of the Tudor dynasty, and it was his grandson Henry VIII who had him brought here. Opposite him is the shrine of St David, the centrepiece of the Cathedral and the destination of all Welsh pilgrims. But the shrine is empty. The relics of the saint, if indeed they are his, rest in a little oak casket in a niche of the chapel of the Holy Trinity.

This was one of the great pilgrimages of the Middle Ages. Even William the Conqueror came as a pilgrim to St David's in 1081. He took off his helmet to pray, and then moved on to conquer Ireland. St David's grew rich on the gifts of the pilgrims, and then grew poor after the Reformation and Civil War; it was rescued from ruin in the 19th century, when the London architect Sir George Gilbert Scott set about restoring it. But the floor is still slightly sloping, and the pillars in the northern aisle seem to tilt outwards: these were the consequences of an earthquake and the insecurity of the foundations so near to the river.

Opposite the western façade, on the other side of the idyllic Alun brook, lie the ruins of the Bishop's Palace (13–14th century): elegant arcades, a doorway with chequered patterns made of different coloured stones – all in striking contrast to the simple exterior of the Cathedral and the bleak landscape round about. But for all the importance this see once had, the City of St David's remains as modest as a city can be, with just 1,500 inhabitants – the smallest cathedral city in Wales, not to mention England. There are a few cottages clustered round an old market cross, and a few narrow lanes with souvenir shops. 'Nowadays it lives largely upon its past reputation,' wrote Giraldus Cambrensis, and nothing much has changed. But seven centuries later, St David's is part of an independent Welsh bishopric, and for this reason perhaps the saint sleeps just a little more peacefully in his oak casket.

Invasion of Fishguard, and John Seymour's Alternative World

If you look down on *Fishguard* from the hills across the bay, it seems more like a film set than a town: the tiny port, with its sailing boats, brightly coloured houses on the hill, and the deep blue sea. And as a matter of fact, 'Moby Dick' was filmed here, and so was 'Under Milk Wood', with Richard Burton and Elizabeth Taylor. But Fishguard's first claim to fame is as the scene of an old British nightmare: invasion.

On February 22 1797, some 1,400 Frenchmen landed at Carreg Wastad Point, north-west of Fishguard. They came in the wake of the French Revolution, but they landed on the wrong coast. If they'd gone to Ireland, they would have been welcomed with open arms by patriots like Wolfe Tone, but the Welsh were already anglicized, and all they wanted was to be left in peace. The 'Black Legion' looked in vain for the Welsh guerrillas who in 1407, under the leadership of Owain Glyndwr, had congregated in their

Richard Tongue: Pentre Ifan, 1830

thousands to greet the French auxiliaries in Milford Haven. Times, unfortunately for them, had changed. The 1797 expedition came to an humiliating end. Armed with pitchforks and wearing traditional costume, the bold ladies of Fishguard, under the dauntless command of Jemima Nicholas, a shoemaker's wife, prepared to fight the enemy. When the French saw in the distance the scarlet tunics and tall black hats, they thought they were being met by the King's Infantry, and promptly surrendered without a fight. As the last invasion of British soil, the Fishguard campaign has duly gone down in history. Relics of this amazing battle are to be seen in the Royal Oak. From Fishguard, you can take the ferry to Ireland, but who wants to do so when all around there are clifftop paths and the distant green magic of Preseli Hills?

Rising up like a giant mushroom, the dolmen of *Pentre Ifan* stands on the slopes overlooking Newport Bay: it's a Neolithic burial chamber with a massive capstone (plate 20). *Mynydd Preseli* moor is one of the most fertile archaeological sites in Wales for prehistorians. Megalithic graves, menhirs and hill forts all bear witness to thousands of years of habitation, as well as travel between Wales, Ireland, Scotland and England. A sensational discovery was made in 1922, when it was proved by a geologist that the stones of Stonehenge originated in Wales, from the peak of Carn Meini on the eastern slopes of the Preseli Hills. Only here, and nowhere else in the British Isles, in this tiny area of barely one square mile, can one find in close proximity the volcanic ash, rhyolite, and greenish-blue, coarse-grained bluestones that make up the inner ring of Stonehenge. How did the Bronze Age megalith-builders transport the eighty or so stones, each weighing up to five tons, across more than 200 miles between the Preseli Hills and Salisbury Plain? Perhaps on sledges and rollers to Milford Haven, from there on rafts across the Bristol

Channel, up the River Avon, and finally on sledges and rollers again to Stonehenge. If this is what happened – and it is plausible – it must have been the largest-scale and most expensive piece of road haulage in prehistory. But more recent geological research suggests that during the last Ice Age the bluestones might have been carried eastwards by the ice, and deposited somewhere on Salisbury Plain, where they were found by the builders. Or could it be that our old friend Merlin used his magic powers to shift these great stones? In the Middle Ages, thanks to Geoffrey of Monmouth, Merlin was always regarded as the mythical builder of Stonehenge. As for Mynydd Presili, the source of the bluestones, that is one of the main scenes of the 'Mabinogion'.

'Mabinogi' means a story for or about children. The plural 'mabinogion' doesn't actually exist in Welsh, and this translation error by Lady Charlotte Guest (1838) forms the basis of the title of this epic of Celtic myth, which is a classic of medieval European literature. The current vogue for fantasy has aroused new interest in these tales, and a free rendering by the American Evangeline Walton has brought them to a wider audience. The mixture of poetry and action, psychoanalysis and folklore has even made 'The Mabinogi' into a stage success, as produced by the Cardiff theatre company 'Moving Being' from 1981 onwards. Branwen, the 'White-Bosomed', Lludd and Llefelys reflect the earliest creative impulses of the Celtic world. Since the 6th century, generations of bards had handed these tales down by word of mouth, but it was not until the middle of the 11th century that an unknown author first wrote them down.[1] He came from Dyfed, 'the land of magic and enchantment', as the Celtic kingdom of Deheubarth is called in the 'Mabinogion'. Gwynn ap Nudd, King of the Welsh Underworld, King Arthur,[2] a benevolent giant, and Madawg, an ally of King Henry II's – all these figures, both historical and mythical, meet here on the threshold between reality and another world. Out of these Celtic myths emerges the buried past of Europe, at its most beautiful in the clear, dark tones of Taliesin:

> I was with the Lord of the World in the topmost sphere,
> with Lucifer in the depth of Hell.
> I bore the standard under Alexander.
> I know the names of the stones from the North to the South.
> I have been through the galaxies
> to the throne of the Almighty.
> I am a wonder, whose origin none knows of.
> I was in Asia with Noah in his ark.
> I watched Sodom and Gomorrah as they burnt.

1 The earliest complete version of all eleven texts of the 'Mabinogion' is to be found in the 'Red Book of Hergest' (1375–1400, Library of Jesus College, Oxford); an earlier, but incomplete version is in the 'White Book of Rhydderch' (1300–25, National Library, Aberystwyth).
2 King Arthur's appearance as a folk hero in the story of Culhwch and Olwen is regarded as the earliest description of him in a Welsh text. All continental Arthurian tales go back to Welsh sources (see page 79).

In a great sweep of poetry, the Celtic bard sings of the mysteries of life, and its sources ancient and Christian. He is the poetic voice of an early, mythical self-awareness:

I have been dead. I have been alive. (...)
I am Taliesin.[1]

Taliesin means Radiant Brow, and he was called the Prince of Song. Was he Lleon of Lochlin's bard? Or the court poet of Urien, a North British prince of the 6th century? Or did he never exist, but is just a personification like Homer? Today the 'Llyfr Taliesin' (14th century), the collection of poems attributed to him, is believed in fact to be by different authors writing at different times. The mythologist Robert Graves considers the Taliesin story in the 'Mabinogion' to be a key to all Celtic culture. Just like the magician Merlin, Taliesin knows what was and what is to be:

Then will the Brython
    Be as prisoners
By strangers swayed
    From Saxony.

This famous prophecy of Taliesin's was used by George Borrow both as title and theme of his book on Wales: 'Their Lord they shall praise, / Their language they shall keep, / Their land they shall lose / Except Wild Wales.'

The mythical land of the 'Mabinogion', the other world of Dyfed, has played host to many who have grown tired of the 'real' world. It is the still ocean of dreams, and the wet and fertile Paradise of the Greens. 'The self-supporter is consciously withdrawing from industrial, high technological society because he thinks it is ugly, boring, polluting and dangerous. ... We are mad on making land produce much food with a small input of power and chemicals (it is the small input that seems so important to us); we are keen to build small-scale, humane, rural industries, where the workers all have a share and can feel proud of what they are producing; we are keen to *reduce* our needs to the simple and essential.' This was the manifesto of an Englishman in Wales, John Seymour. His book 'Self Sufficiency' (1973) became a cult work for Anglo-Saxon Greens, and his autobiographical accounts of his experiences 'The Fat of the Land' and 'I'm a Stranger Here Myself' became best-sellers both in Britain and abroad. From their farm in Suffolk, the author and his wife Sally moved to Wales in 1965, and bought a small farm with 70 acres of land on the edge of the Preseli Hills. Here they made their own butter, cheese, bread and beer, kept a cow and pigs, farmed organically, and for manure used a portable lavatory over a ditch – the so-called Wardha-latrine, said to be an invention of Mahatma Gandhi's. 'We must 'de-school' society very urgently, otherwise we shall have a whole nation of clerks and

1 Legend has it that the bard's grave is the prehistoric dolmen Bedd Taliesin near Tre-Taliesin, north-east of Aberystwyth.

scientists and people on the dole and we shall starve to death,' wrote John Seymour. Instead there must be an alternative economy of the land: 'For good professional family farms, in every area of the British Isles in which wheat can reasonably be grown, to grow the wheat for their locality, for this to be ground in the village mill (preferably a mill driven by a non-polluting and non-extractive form of power such as wind or water) and baked in the village bakehouse – that is just the right distance along the road to specialization.' John's farm, Fachongle Isaf, was a happy, hospitable place, always open to 'drop-ins' and self-sufficiency fans. Helping one's neighbour was a thing that could be taken for granted here, and in such a place social welfare, old-age pensions and all the other trappings of the State would be quite unnecessary. John Seymour's valley was a model world, with the farmer at the hub of a new society – or at least that is how John Seymour saw it. The idea was as attractive as it was naive. The flight from civilization to green self-sufficiency was the breeding ground of a great illusion: 'If the rest of the world blew itself up tomorrow we could go on living quite happily here and hardly notice the difference.' Perhaps he really believed it.

When I wanted to visit him in 1981, his Welsh experiment had just ended, and he had moved to Ireland. His daughter Jane and her husband, the wood-carver Philip Layton, had taken over the farm. Fachongle Isaf, a single-storey, 17th-century farmhouse of rubblestone, slate-roofed, is just like many other farmhouses in the area. Cats, chickens and children happily share the chaos of the yard. 'Give me the men with the dirty boots, any time: they are the ones who feed us all, in the last resort.' It reads well. But who wore the dirty boots? Philip Layton explains a thing or two about his famous father-in-law: 'It was his wife who did all the work. John just wrote about it!' Sally Seymour divorced her husband, and now lives in a nearby cottage, working as a potter and children's book illustrator. The attempt to make Fachongle Isaf into a model alternative culture and economy failed, and yet the back-to-the-land movement that John Seymour initiated found many followers, especially in Dyfed: land communes with windmills, self-sufficiency, artists and craftsmen earning their living as potters, turners, weavers, a riding-school, people growing fruit, restoring antiques. From the Centre for Alternative Technology in Machynlleth, all kinds of fertile ideas are promulgated. John Seymour may have come to a rude awakening, but at least some parts of his dream have lived on.

From the Preseli Hills into the Valley of the Teifi. A few miles upriver from Cardigan, in the village of *Llechryd*, I met Bernard Thomas, the King of Coracle. A coracle is like a giant shopping basket, and with the aid of a single-bladed paddle can be used as a fishing-boat. And when you've finished fishing, you can stick it on your back like a snail shell and carry it home. Coracles existed even before Roman times, and the shape has remained more or less the same since then: an oval basket, three feet wide, five to six feet long, weighing between 18 and 27 pounds, according to the size and weight of the owner. Bernard Thomas of Llechryd is the only remaining coracle-builder; he makes the frame out of willow, the edges from hazel, and the seat of ash. He covers the willow basket with tarred canvas (in the old days, it used to be animal skins), and his nutshell of a boat is

George Delamotte: Fisherman with Coracle,
c.1818

then strong enough to carry a sheep, or even a cow. In order to demonstrate how this tiny Welsh boat contributed to the prehistory of British naval prowess, Bernard Thomas rowed a coracle across the English Channel a few years ago in thirteen and a half hours. Normally, though, this light and mobile vessel is used for catching salmon and trout. Two fishermen stretch a net out between their coracles, and row upstream, generally after dark. Anglers object strongly to this age-old method, and Bernard Thomas complains that the number of licences granted is dwindling all the time. In 1860 there were 600 coracles on the Teifi, and a short while ago there were no more than 24. It is a dying trade. Once coracle fishing was common throughout Britain, but now it is allowed on only three Welsh rivers: the Tawe, the Taff and the Teifi. There are just 120 licences for net-fishing in Wales, compared to 22,000 for rod-fishing. The fight of the coracle-fishers has long since become a fight for a national tradition. Once more a piece of their Celtic heritage is under threat, mainly from rich English angling clubs, who buy up whole stretches of the Teifi. 'What's the use of a licence,' growls Bernard Thomas, 'if you can't even get to your river? The rivers should be free!' It seems all too likely that soon the coracle-fishers will be confined to Carmarthen's coat-of-arms, to picture postcards, and the yearly coracle regatta of *Cilgerran*, which brings in the tourists every August.

On a rock high above the Teifi gorge lies *Cilgerran Castle*. Like the village itself, this is built of grey-green rubble masonry. The view from this Norman ruin across the river valley was regarded by such painters as Richard Wilson and William Turner as the highlight of the picturesque journey. Teifi Valley is the home of the Welsh wool industry. Cardigans, however, do not owe their name to the town at the mouth of the Teifi. The originator was the 7th Earl of Cardigan, who led the legendary attack on Balaclava in the Crimean War. *Cardigan* itself boasts a six-arched bridge (1726), a Neo-Gothic town hall (1859), and an old warehouse on the harbour with arts and crafts studios. The people of Cardigan are regarded as the Scots of Wales – a reputation enshrined in many a corny joke. For instance, an Englishman wants to buy some land from a Cardi for about £1,000: 'Come back tomorrow,' says the Cardi, 'and bring your wheelbarrow.'

'The Path', that long-distance trek from Pembrokeshire, ends at St Dogmael's , but it's worth going on beyond Cardigan to have a look at the coast, particularly around *Llangranog*. Edward Elgar spent a holiday here in 1902, and he enjoyed wandering along the cliffs overlooking the rocky island of Ynys Lochtyn. On one of his walks, he heard some Welsh people singing down on the beach, and it was their song that inspired one of his most popular compositions: Introduction and Allegro for Strings. 'On the cliff, between blue sea and blue sky, thinking out my theme, there came up to me the sound of singing ...'

Mid Wales

One of my most enjoyable weeks in Wales was spent in the village of *Cefn Coch*. It isn't even on the map, though it's somewhere west of Welshpool: 136 inhabitants, one pub, and that's all there is. No turbulent history, no famous sons, no picturesque cottages. No sights, and not even any ruins. A place without qualities – if it weren't for Mike and Rusty, a patient farmer and his good-natured horse who taught me to ride. And that was a brand new experience for me – seeing the landscape from up above the hedges, sensing the grass beneath our feet and the wind in our faces, trotting past clear streams and farmyards with their dozing cats. The peace of the fields and the green of the hills, endless depth and stillness.

Cefn Coch is in the least known region of Wales. Between the popular beaches of the south and the spectacular mountains of the north, it's regarded mainly as passing-through country, but I take a different view. There are magnificent stretches of lonely moorland, gentle landscapes and little market towns of infinite charm. '*Powys Paradwys Cymru*', the Paradise of Wales, is the message on the Powys coat-of-arms. But according to an old saying, 'the Devil lives in the middle of Wales' – presumably because for centuries it was cut off from the Bristol Channel and the Irish Sea by impassable mountains. Now its main claim to fame is as a huge centre of administration, formed in 1974 from the old counties of Montgomeryshire, Radnorshire and a large chunk of Breconshire, and renamed Powys after the medieval principality. It also incorporates Ceredigion in the north of Dyfed, and Meirionnydd, the southern tip of Gwynedd. Mid Wales comprises about 40% of the total land surface of Wales, and just 7% of its population. Here you will find the most isolated houses in a country of isolated spots. And so, of course, it is a favourite haunt of romantics and robbers, monks and the military. On the moor of Mynydd Epynt the British Army has a firing range. Not far from there, Twm Sion Catti, the Welsh Robin Hood, used to get up to his rich-robbing tricks. And in places like Cwmhir and Strata Florida, the Cistercians set up their refuges.

'The Green Desert' is what Harri Webb called Mid Wales. In the 19th century some 100,000 people left this green wilderness in order to find work in the coal valleys and England's industrial cities. Forgotten valleys, abandoned farms, ghost villages – that was the price of the glorious isolation. Thus Radnorshire became the most sparsely populated county in Britain, apart from the Scottish Highlands – an impoverished country famous only for its sheep. In these 'Mountains of Mutton', there are three sheep for every human being. And despite the efforts of the Development Board for Rural Wales, emigration is still a major problem in the region. Apart from the Laura Ashley textile factory in Carno, there is virtually no industry worth mentioning. Sheep and cattle have always been the main source of employment, and the old cattle trails used to lead from collecting points on the coast of Cardigan, across the Cambrian Mountains, and into the markets in the Midlands. The reverse route from England saw the invading armies traditionally marching alongside the rivers and into Mid Wales: from Shrewsbury across the Welsh Bridge and through the Severn Valley, from Ludlow along the 'Road of the Castles' to Montgomery, from Hereford through the Wye Valley to Builth Wells. Today the rivers flow quietly eastwards, thick with salmon and legends. The gold of Dolaucothi was famous, and silver and lead were also found in the mountains of central Wales, but the most precious commodity of all was its clean air and its silences. For these the Victorians would leave their polluted, noisy towns, and come to Wild Wales to relax in the valleys of Irfon and Ithon.

Gwynfor Evans: The Nationalist in the Vale of Tywi

I followed the Roman Via Julia, now the A40, from Carmarthen to Llandovery. The broad Vale of Tywi opens up the centre of the land: 'Ever charming, ever new, / When will the landskip tire the view!' Thus did John Dyer, parson and poet, enthuse in 1726 about *Grongar Hill*, embodiment of the Welsh Hills. His enthusiasm lives on, for in 1982 his poem was reissued with lithographs by John Piper (Stourton Press, London). The model hill town lies a few miles east of Grongar Hill: *Llandeilo*, named after the Celtic saint Teilo (colour plate 8). Pastel-coloured houses line the street, which curves elegantly up the slope from the Tywi Bridge to the church. The cemetery is surrounded by homes, the quick and the dead dwelling together in peace. The little town on the hill is watched over by massive beech trees that belong to the grounds of *Dinefwr Castle*, once the palace of the Princes of Deheubarth. The royal ruins of their home, *Castell Carreg Cennen*, are still to be seen on a precipitous limestone rock high above the Cennen. It is said to have been built by one of King Arthur's knights, Sir Urien, but today it belongs to Bernard Llewellyn, a sheep-breeder. The hills around Llandeilo are the very heartland of Wales. This was one of the main bastions against the Norman invasion – a tradition carried on by one of the main bastions against English rule: the personification of Welsh Nationalism, Gwynfor Evans (picture, page 21). He made headlines in 1980 when he threatened to starve himself to death, and thereby forced the British government to set up the first Welsh-speaking TV Channel.

Talar Wen, 'White Furrow', is a house on a slope with a broad view over the Vale of Tywi one mile outside the little town of *Llangadog* (colour plate 19). Here Gwynfor Evans ushered me into a room full of books. 'When we came here over 30 years ago, everybody still spoke Welsh. In the meantime, a lot of English people have moved in. They form foreign enclaves, and interfere with traditional cultural life. Today the school is half Welsh, half English. That's happening all over the country, and we can't stop it. More Welsh-speaking schools and kindergartens, that's what we're fighting for most of all now.' It doesn't take long for Gwynfor Evans to get onto the subject most dear to him: 'When a nation loses its language, it no longer has anything to say at all.' He himself first had to learn the language of his fathers as a foreign language, because in his parents' house in Barry where he was born in 1912, the son of an ironmonger, only English was spoken. His own seven children were brought up to be Welsh. 'The first time I spoke English with one of my daughters was in 1968, in a London prison, where Meinir had been put because of her activities for the Welsh Language Society. When I visited her, I was not allowed to speak Welsh to her.' Gwynfor Evans studied in Aberystwyth and Oxford, where he joined the Dafydd ap Gwilym Society. 'When I was studying Welsh history and literature, I realized that we are a nation in our own right. Then I travelled through our glorious country, got to know the Welsh and their traditions, and knew that these were things that had to be preserved. The only way to do that was to have a parliament of our own, a government of our own. A democratic, Socialist State of Wales.' Socialism with a Welsh face – is this just an illusion, just a Utopia?

Ever since his student days, Gwynfor Evans has been a member of Plaid Cymru, and in 1945 he was made President, a post he occupied for 36 years. In 1966 he became the first Nationalist to enter Parliament since 1906 – that is, when the Welsh Liberals were still in favour of Home Rule. Until 1979, 'Evergreen Evans' remained Plaid Cymru MP in Westminster, 'a nationalist legend in his own lifetime' (*The Guardian*). He regards his parliamentary seat and the Welsh TV Channel as his greatest political successes. But at a time when the Welsh minority were becoming increasingly radical, this lawyer and lay preacher always insisted on moderation: 'Even the winning of national freedom cannot justify the destruction of an innocent life.' He condemned the recent campaign in which arsonists set fire to the second homes of English people in Wales: 'That's against our principle of non-violence.' But even when the referendum on devolution went against him, he did not waver in his beliefs: 'We're not free. We have no self-determination. Every decision on Wales is made by London, not by us. We want national freedom in the framework of a British Confederation. Within a merger of that sort, there'd be many institutions that would hold us together.' He does not, then, seek total separation from England, but partial autonomy, and political control over their own economy. If they had that, Wales would be better off today: 'Luxemburg also has a big steel industry, but nothing like as many unemployed as we have.' Unemployment in Wales has always been considerably worse than in England, although the gap has recently narrowed.

Small countries are capable of big achievements, 'if they have a vision. But we're still afraid to be ourselves.' This is why he considers it to be essential 'to create a national consciousness in Wales, to educate people in nationhood'. He made a major contribution to this in 1971 with his voluminous history 'Land of My Fathers'. The original title of the book was *'Aros Mae'*, It Survives. It concludes, proudly 'We were here before Great Britain ... We shall be here after her too.' In this history of a nation's survival, Gwynfor Evans accuses the English 'Colonial Power' of carrying out both in Wales and in Ireland a policy of 'cultural genocide'. He describes it as 'tragic' that the often heroic struggles of the workers for social justice were not linked to a national programme. But of course such a programme would have been alien to the Labour Party's ideals, since it would have constituted a throwback to nationalist thinking. 'The biggest obstacle on the way to Welsh self-government is the Labour Party,' says Gwynfor Evans. And in the election of 1983 he felt this all the more keenly, when he was beaten by the Labour candidate for Carmarthen – this in a constituency where 63% of the inhabitants still speak Welsh, and where in 1979 Plaid Cymru polled a record one-third of all votes. With Gwynfor Evans' defeat, the era of the National Party was at an end.

That evening in the hotel, we were discussing Welsh independence. 'Nonsense!' said the landlord, 'that would cost us a lot more money and then we'd all have to learn Welsh!' On the other hand, there are some English people who can speak better Welsh than most Welsh people. An outstanding example of a patriotic immigrant was Lady Llanover. She lived near Abergavenny in the 19th century, having come from a family that moved from Lincolnshire to Monmouthshire, into what is now Gwent. Lady Llanover was a champion of Welsh language and customs, collected Welsh manuscripts, tales and legends, gave support to the Eisteddfod, and just as Iolo Goch 'rediscovered' (i.e. invented) the Gorsedd ceremonies, she drew on English fashions and a romantic imagination to create national costumes which had never existed in these forms. She also played a considerable part in the popularization of the *Myfanwy*, the tall black-felt women's hat (stovepipe) that now seems traditionally Welsh. Her husband was the MP Sir Benjamin Hall, to whom 'Big Ben' owes it nickname, for he was in charge of buildings when the clocktower of Westminster Palace was erected. They both gave support to the College of Llandovery when this Welsh-speaking public school was founded in 1848 in the little market town on the Tywi.[1] Apart from the school, *Llandovery* can boast a ruined Norman castle which now witnesses fierce battles between lady bowlers in cloche hats and purple cravats (plate 53), while on Fridays it plays host to cattle trucks called 'Fiery Fred' and 'Enemy', as the drovers gather for the market.

The last major upheaval in Llandovery took place in the 16th century. Twm Sion Catti entered the ironmonger's shop, picked out a large pot, held it up against the light, and declared that it had a hole in it. When the ironmonger protested, Twm told him to see for

1   In the school chapel there is a Crucifixion by Graham Sutherland.

272

Cambrian Costumes, designed by Lady Llanover, nineteenth century

himself, and pulled the pot down over the shopkeeper's eyes. 'Now, my friend, I presume you can see that the pot has a hole in it, because how else could you have got your head inside?' cried Twm, grabbed what he could, and raced away. Welsh people were still laughing about Twm's pranks centuries later. He was a thief and a bard, wrote poems about his own crimes, and was also a quick-change artist who could sell a cow to the same farmer he'd stolen it from the day before. He was a Welsh Robin Hood, as popular with the poor whom he helped, as with the rich whom he entertained with his songs and his tricks – a rogue who finished up as justice of the peace and mayor. Twm Sion Catti's hideout lay in the secluded valleys between Llandovery and the *Llyn Brianne Reservoir* (plate 98). And not far from there, on the road to Lampeter, the hills contained something to gladden the heart of thief and judge alike: gold.

One of the reasons why the Romans, after they had landed in England, were so determined to conquer Wales was certainly the goldmines of *Dolaucothi*. Between AD 75 and 140 they maintained a camp in *Pumsaint*, whose foundations now lie underneath the present village on the A482. In the vicinity, archaeologists found tools, ornaments, and traces of a complex gold-panning system of aqueducts and reservoirs nearly 6 miles long. Specialists consider Dolaucothi to be one of the most important, and technically most advanced Roman goldmines in Europe. The Greek geographer Strabo included the gold of Pumsaint among the most substantial British exports, along with wheat, cattle, silver, iron and hunting-dogs. In 1938, Roman Deep Ltd ended their final attempt (at least for the time being) to reactivate the old mines. Today the land is under the protection of the National

273

Trust and the University of Cardiff. From the barred and bolted mines comes the faint sound of pumping, the golden heart of Wales beating deep inside the mountain.

Llywelyn the Last: A Dream Dies in Cilmeri

In the 18th century, anyone with name and rank and a minor ailment would travel, like Smollett's Humphry Clinker, to Bath – to be cured and, especially, to be noticed. But if you did not regard your heart or stomach trouble as first and foremost a social event, you would withdraw to more discreet watering-places on the Irfon and the Ithon. Thanks to their situation and their strange-sounding names, they were considered slightly eccentric, but soon enjoyed a growing reputation even if they never became truly fashionable spas. They were *Llangammarch Wells, Llanwrtyd Wells*, and *Llandrindod Wells*, and those who stayed there long enough would eventually leave, if not with improved health, at least with improved pronunciation. Their waters were as varied as their clients. The iron and sulphur springs of Llanwrtyd Wells were frequented mainly by Welsh Non-Conformists. The Anglican and more fashionable folk from the English Midlands preferred the luxury hotels of Llandrindod Wells, with their magnesium and salt-water springs and the larger golf course. The barium spring of Llangammarch Wells was honoured by visits from Kaiser Wilhelm and Prime Minister Lloyd George. But *Builth Wells* was the place for the workers, who tried to treat their silicosis with the sulphur springs. Keeping an admirable distance both from Kaisers and from miners, and not having any particularly urgent disease to contend with, I opted to test the waters of Llandrindod Wells.

'Let England boast Bath's crowded springs / Llandrindod happier Cambria sings.' This was the rhyme which, as long ago as 1748, was used in the 'Gentleman's Magazine' to advertise the waters that had cured so many farmers and shepherds of old. The middle of the 19th century saw the heyday of the spas, which ended in a splash of Edwardian elegance when war began in 1914. Draped in feathered hats and expressions of acute suffering, visitors would stroll from the Glen Usk Hotel or the Metropole to the Pump Room in the park, 'to take the waters in style'. From one of the three old china taps, so deceptively arousing expectations of a frothing pint, I had a glass filled with magnesium spring water. Fortunately, you can also get tea here. With various restorations and Victorian festival weeks, Llandrindod is trying to make a comeback as a spa. But what was once part of the health cure ritual – entertainment, dances, love affairs – now seems more appropriate on a Mediterranean cruise than in a small town in Mid Wales. The former Pump House Hotel now houses the administrative departments of the new county town. What remains of those great days is a redbrick oasis in the green hills of Powys, Victorian spa architecture with copper turrets, half-timbered gables, and cast-iron railings.

The painter Thomas Jones was born in Llandrindod Wells in 1742. The hustle and bustle around the springs is vividly described in his childhood memories: 'The number of the

Infirm, the Rich, the Gay, the Idle and Dissolute, like at most fashionable watering places, was so great, that it became an intolerable Nuisance to the Neighbourhood.' The Jones family moved to *Pencerrig*, to a little country house north of Builth Wells. Again and again Thomas Jones painted Pencerrig, an isolated spot nestling in the wide hills, between endless hedgerows, and below heavy, dark clouds. In Birmingham Museum there is one of these small-scale oil sketches, whose freshness and vividness anticipates Constable. Thomas Jones was one of the early 'plein air' painters, a pupil of Richard Wilson's in London, and like Wilson he lived for many years in Italy, mainly in Naples. Later he inherited his father's estate, and ended his days as chief magistrate in Radnorshire. Today Pencerrig is a hotel.

Some towns have such enchanting surroundings that one simply accepts their own lack of enchantment. Builth Wells is one such place. If it were not for the yearly Royal Welsh Show – a popular agricultural fair – the little town on the Wye would have long since been forgotten. But nearby is something truly unforgettable: *Cilmeri*. It's a village on the A483, west of Builth Wells, a granite monument, and a national myth. 'Sad the day, the sun drowning / Sad the army at Cilmeri / Sad the heather on black slopes / Sadder the heartbreak of a nation.' This was the elegy I heard Dafydd Iwan sing, the threnody and protest song of a Welsh radical 700 years after the death of Llywelyn at Cilmeri. Not one portrait, seal or even description of him has survived, but his statue stands in the gallery of 'Heroes of Wales' in Cardiff's City Hall (plate 7). It is thanks to him that Llywelyn (or Llewellyn) has become the most Welsh of all Welsh names, a national emblem almost. One of Dylan Thomas's sons was named after him, as is one of the highest mountains in Snowdonia, the Carnedd Llywelyn. In his honour the best-selling author Richard Lloyd adopted the pseudonym Richard Llewellyn.

Who was this man whose name still echoes down through the centuries?

Llywelyn ap Gruffydd was the first and the last Welsh Prince of Wales to be recognized by the English crown. Since him, no Welsh patriot has ever been able to accept any English prince as Prince of Wales. Even in 1969, on the eve of Prince Charles's investiture, a group of Welsh people gathered at Llywelyn's monument in Cilmeri with banners that proclaimed: 'Here died our last Prince'. But if we look beyond the legend of the national hero, we shall find a man who was, above all, an exponent of power politics. He ruthlessly suppressed his brothers' claims to the throne, unscrupulously reinforced his position by taking hostages and pillaging the smaller princedoms, and skilfully exploited the weaknesses of his English neighbours. This was how, by the treaty of Montgomery in 1267, he achieved official recognition as Prince of Wales from King Henry III, for he bought the title for the then enormous sum of £20,000. If you add three noughts to that figure, you might get something approximating to today's values. When the King died in 1272, Llywelyn refused to give money or allegiance to his son Edward I, and so four years later, Edward took arms against this insubordinate Welshman and defeated him. Llywelyn duly paid the necessary tribute in London, but in 1282 he once more rose up in rebellion against England. Yet again, Edward I's army marched into Wales, the biggest since the Roman

invasion. Llywelyn went westwards, to the region around Builth Wells. And there, on the Irfon Bridge near Cilmeri, on December 12 1282, he met an ignominious death. Whether it happened by chance or through treachery, unarmed or in battle, no-one really knows. But his head was cut off and, to the sound of horns and trumpets, carried through the streets of London on a spear and crowned with ivy – a cynical allusion to Merlin's prophecy that a Welsh Prince would one day be crowned in London. It is said that monks buried Llywelyn's body in *Cwmhir Abbey*, but no trace of his grave has ever been found.

And so ended the dream of Welsh independence. Is that what Llywelyn was really after? Even Welsh historians ask this heretical question. Llywelyn himself never contested the authority of the English King. He wanted to make his country into a sovereign part of the English feudal state, though with its own rights and its own language: 'According to every just principle we should enjoy our Welsh laws and customs like the other nations of the king's empire, and in our own language.' This was how Llwelyn outlined his aims in a letter to King Edward I after the latter's coronation in 1272. Such partial autonomy is not far removed from the 'Britannic Confederation' sought by Gwynfor Evans and his National Party 700 years later. But today the nearest the prince's people come to taking up arms is playing darts in Cilmeri's pub, the Prince Llewellyn.

Wagner in Wales: Holy Grail and Heart-Break

Over the moor to Aberystwyth. I left the Wye Valley near Rhayader and drove through *Elan Valley*. There are wild waters here for romantics and canoeists, and forests with circling falcons, and then suddenly you come up against a wall of stone and water, a seething, foaming curtain which turns out to be the 130 feet high dam of *Caban Coch*. It's the first of four massive barrages in the Elan Valley, and provides the water for Birmingham – over 520 million gallons of it a day. When King Edward VII opened these dams in 1904, 18 farms, a school, and a church had disappeared beneath the waters. And down below Birmingham's tapwater lies the house to which young Shelley took his 16-year-old bride in 1812 – Harriet Westbrook, an inn-keeper's daughter. They lived there for several months, in Nantgwlyllt, 'silent, solitary, old'. In these isolated Cambrian Mountains, the romantic poet wanted to establish a circle of friends around him, but a restless spirit and a lack of money drove him away.

Hundreds of years before Shelley, monks used to come to these lonely moors north of Tregaron. In the fertile Teifi Valley, in the shelter of the hills, they built their abbey: *Strata Florida*, Valley of the Flowers (1184–1235). Perhaps the name derives from the white cotton grass that grows in the Cors Goch Glan Teifi (the red moor on the Teifi), which is now a Nature conservation area. Cistercians from Whitland Abbey came and settled in

◁ *The head of Llywelyn the Last is carried through London in triumph*

Strata Florida. They built paths and bridges, and introduced sheep-rearing and wool-weaving. Of all the Cistercian monasteries in Mid Wales – Strata Marcella, Cwmhir, Cymer – Strata Florida was the richest and most influential, the 'Westminster of Wales'. The church was bigger than St David's Cathedral: a three-aisled nave with three chapels in each arm of the transept, (with some floor tiles still intact). Lord Rhys ap Gruffydd, a Welsh prince and not a Norman baron, was patron of the abbey, and thus it was that Ystrad Fflur – as the natives called it – became a religious, political and cultural centre for the Welsh during the Middle Ages, until the Dissolution of the Monasteries under Henry VIII. When the last monk left the valley in 1539, the once magnificent abbey fell to ruin, and all that remained was a single, though unique portal – that of the western façade (plate 62). It is as if the builders had wanted to lash down the column shafts that curve round into the great arch, in order to protect them against the wild west wind, for encompassing the archivolts are thirteen bands of stone. These bands each end in a sort of knot, like a snail's shell, a Celtic ornament that is not to be found in any other British Cistercian abbey. In fact this was an order that insisted on simplicity and spurned ornamentation. Even now, though, one cannot fail to be impressed by this great gateway of Ystrad Fflur, as one gazes through it at the green hills and the heavens beyond.

In the abbey graveyard stands an age-old yew tree with burst trunk. Dafydd ap Gwilym is said to lie buried here, a 14th-century poet, and the most important of all the Welsh bards. He was a contemporary of Chaucer's, and connoisseurs of Celtic literature regard him as the latter's equal. Dafydd ap Gwilym sang not of battles and war, but of love and Nature. More even than the French troubadours, he was inspired by women – the women of Cardiganshire, his home: Morfudd's snow-white neck, and the dark locks of Dyddgu. 'So I fall in love, I do, / Every day, with one or two, / Get no closer, any day, / Than an arrow's length away.' No lover and no poet has ever confessed so openly to have failed so often to attain his goal. Bolted doors, interruptions, unco-operative husbands, watchdogs, cloudbursts – there was always something to spoil the fun. But Dafydd kept trying, even in church. He cursed the mists that led him off the track instead of into Morfudd's arms, and he called on the wind to be his messenger of love: 'O wind, go to Uwch Aeron ... / If there is a way, find her / And moan the sound of my sigh.' Ah, but how much more magical are these verses of the Welsh Ovid in their original language: *'Digrif fu, fun, un ennyd / Dwyn dan un bedwlwyn ein byd. / Cydlwynach, difyrrach fu, / Coed olochwyd, cydlechu ...'* Dafydd ap Gwilym was a master of the *'cynghanedd'*, a form of verse in which internal rhymes and alliterations link up like Celtic ornaments into chains of imagery and cascading sounds. Dylan Thomas, although he wrote in English, also drew upon this Welsh source of verbal music. The tradition of this great Welsh bard is continued less by the Dafydd ap Gwilym Society, founded in Oxford in 1866, than by a poetry contest: the Eisteddfod of *Pontrhydfendigaid*, which takes place every May in the village next to Strata Florida. A local patron has donated the valuable prizes, and it is one of the most famous of all regional Eisteddfodau.

Between a ruined monastery and the Devil's Bridge there was once a Welsh paradise: *Hafod House*. An 18th-century land-owner, Thomas Johnes, had had long discussions with his cousin Richard Payne Knight and their friend Uvedale Price, developing the theory of the picturesque (see page 36), and here in the wilderness Thomas Johnes put their theory into practice. In 1786 he commissioned the Bath architect Thomas Baldwin to build a Neo-Gothic country house here in the remote Ystwyth Valley, and later the house was extended by John Nash. His pupil Anthony Salvin added a campanile and a pagoda to this bizarre construction in 1853. 'Beautiful but fantastic' was George Borrow's comment when he saw it a year later. The octagonal library in Moorish style, with its copper-covered dome, is said to have inspired Samuel Coleridge to write the poem 'Kubla Khan' ('In Xanadu did Kubla Khan / A stately pleasure dome decree ...') Like Turner, Coleridge was one of a cirle of illustrious visitors who made Hafod House into a Welsh meeting-place for romantics. The owner himself, a collector and translator of medieval manuscripts, a passionate landscape gardener, and also an MP, was a pioneer of agriculture. By using a steel plough and a system of crop rotation, he improved productivity of the soil, planted millions of trees, built cottages for his tenants, designed a park with grottos, bridges and monuments, and laid out concealed gardens with fantastic plants. 'He made the wilderness smile,' was the comment of one of the contemporaries. The remnants of this smile are still visible today, but Hafod House alas is no more, for it was demolished

J. M. W. Turner: Hafod House, c.1811

in 1959. On the terrace where Coleridge and Turner once sat, you will now find parked caravans: from the picturesque to the grotesque. But why did it come to this? What drove Thomas Johnes out of his paradise was a cruel blow of fate: the death of his only daughter, Marianne. She died in 1827, at the age of 27. Francis Chantrey, then a young and unknown sculptor, created her monument: the parents at the bedside of their dying daughter – a deeply moving scene that encapsulates every parent's secret terror. This lifesize marble group once stood in Hafod's little church, and was certainly one of the finest achievements of Neo-Classical monumental sculpture, but a fire in the church left nothing but fragments.

A few miles further north, we come to a strange bridge and a waterfall. *Devil's Bridge* is the name of the spot. There are in fact three bridges, one on top of the other, and all of them spanning the racing Afon Mynach, or Monk's Stream. The lowest bridge dates back to the Middle Ages, presumably built by monks from Strata Florida, but attributed by legend to Old Nick himself; above it is a stone bridge (1753), and above this a steel bridge (1901). Before the waterfalls of Mynach and Rheidol were hidden behind a devilishly narrow revolving door, so that they could become a source of income, this had been a romantic gorge. Today in the high season, it is packed solid with tourist buses, just like Betws-y-Coed, the famous beauty spot in Snowdonia. Under the circumstances the Devil can keep it, *pace* George Barrow: 'Have no more sight-seeing that day, for you have seen enough'. No, the best bit about Devil's Bridge as far as I am concerned is the narrow-gauge railway that takes you away to Aberystwyth. Can British Rail boast any more romantic stretch than these twelve miles by steam train through the vale of Rheidol?

Just before Aberystwyth comes *Nanteos*. The 'Grove of Nightingales' (colour plate 6) is a dreamy park with a Palladian country house (1739), fine Georgian stables and several ghosts. Richard Wagner may be one of them. Edwina Coalgate, owner of Nanteos, confirms the tale told by all the guidebooks: 'Wagner worked on his *'Parsifal'* here.' And she shows me exactly where: in the elegant music-room on the first floor (plate 78). The Wagner legend is part of another, older tradition – the story of the Grail. According to Thomas Malory's Arthurian romance, Joseph of Arimathaea took the Holy Grail, the cup used by Christ during the Last Supper, from the Holy Land to Glastonbury Abbey. From there the healing cup made its way to the monks of Strata Florida, and after the Reformation came into the possession of the Powells of Nanteos. There is therefore logic in the legend that Wagner actually saw the symbol of his opera in Nanteos. Was he not in London in 1855? And is it not possible that there he met George Paul Powell – a friend of Swinburne's and of Oscar Wilde's – who may have invited the great composer back to his country estate so that he might see the Grail for himself? Make no mistake, the legendary *'cwpan'* exists, and today the 'Nanteos Cup' belongs to Fiona Mirylees, the last Powell heiress. She sold the family home of Nanteos in 1983, but she took the Holy Grail with her. It now resides in a bank safe in Herefordshire – an ancient cup of olive wood, with a diameter of four inches.

Aberystwyth: University by the Sea

With no less than three bays, the sea comes courting *Aberystwyth*. So beautifully is the town situated on Cardigan Bay that Nature has even supplied three hills to allow appropriate viewing: Pen Dinas, an Iron Age hill fort; Penglais Hill, with the National Library and the University; and Constitution Hill, in the north of the town. The latter is blessed with a leg-saving Victorian cable-railway (1896; plate 68) whose cabins are step-like in shape, and carry us in comfort up to the panorama at the top.

Poised between North and South Wales, urban, maritime, University town and seaside resort, Aberystwyth has the best of most worlds. It is also the Welshest of all Welsh towns (colour plate 37; plates 36, 67, 68). It has the Welsh National Library, the first Welsh university, and in 1969 it played host to the newly invested Prince of Wales when he took a one-month crash course in Welsh. It was in a street of Aberystwyth that the protest movement of the Welsh Language Society took its first steps in 1963, and its headquarters remain here, in a basement office at the end of the Promenade. One member was caught cycling with his girl-friend perched on the back; he was summoned, and duly ignored the summons on the grounds that it was in English. This apparent trifle led to a nationwide campaign which ended some years later in official recognition that all official forms and placenames should be written in both languages. The fact that Aberystwyth is on a higher spiritual plane than most comparable towns will strike the stranger most forcibly when he tries to catch a train on a Sunday. There are none. But on the Promenade you can hear the Côr-y-Castell singing Welsh hymns. This Promenade stretches over a mile, and has a ruined Norman castle, benches held up by cast-iron snakes, a line of stately houses and hotels that have seen better days, and the remains of a spidery-legged pier of 1865 on which once upon a time you could stroll 260 yards out to sea.

Diagonally opposite the pier stands the building that began Aberystwyth's rise from fishing village on the Ystwyth to seaside resort. The building was originally called Castle House, and it was a Neo-Gothic villa built by John Nash in 1790 for Uvedale Price, one of the founding fathers of the picturesque. When the railways came to Aberystwyth in 1864, the entrepreneur Thomas Savin bought the villa on the Promenade, and had it extended by John Seddon into a pompous grand hotel; then he offered special rates to anyone who bought a return ticket in London, thus anticipating the modern package tour. But Savin's Grand Hotel went bust even before it was finished, and in 1872 he had to sell it. This turned out to be a good thing, because in that same year a group of Welsh patriots founded the first Welsh university, and a hotel seemed just the place to house it. Once again Seddon was employed to reconstruct and extend – hence the somewhat amorphous appearance of this Neo-Tudor palace, whose Victorian splendours were not enhanced by a disastrous fire in 1885. The rear façade is particularly striking, with its round stairwell tower and the porte-cochère, a projecting, triangular portal beneath whose porch the hotel guests could get in and out of their coaches untouched by Welsh rain (plate 68). And so the hotel became a seaside University. In the 1880's it was joined by the colleges of Cardiff and Bangor, and not until 1893 did it earn the right, as University of Wales,[1] to confer academic titles of its own. This was an act of national sovereignty, for until then any Welshman who wanted to get a university degree had to study in England or Scotland.

Since those times, the main section of the Old College has moved to Penglais Hill east of the town. There a modern campus houses most of the 3,000 students, some 40% of whom come from Wales. The best known faculties are those of art, geography, and Welsh literature and history. Celtic traditions go hand in hand with current affairs, and professors such as Leopold Kohr (see page 283f.), Alwyn D. Rees and Ned Thomas have ensured that this University promotes and fosters a new and productive national consciousness. But nothing has made a greater contribution to this consciousness than the neighbouring National Library of Wales.

Started in 1907, opened in 1937 – it took a long time for the Welsh to get their own National Library, as it did with all their other national institutions. Cardiff, which at the time was a long way off becoming a capital city, also applied for the privilege of housing the library, but had to make do with the National Museum, begun in the same year. Two things were in Aberystwyth's favour: it lay in the centre of Welsh-speaking Wales, and it already had the basis of an excellent library in the 25,000 volumes of the private collection donated by Sir John Williams, one of Queen Victoria's personal physicians. Today the National Library has some three million books, four million archives, 300,000 photographs,[2] 22,000 paintings and prints. As one of the five British National Libraries (alongside London, Edinburgh, Oxford and Cambridge), its stock grows by about 80,000 books a year thanks to the Copyright Law, by which a copy of every new book must be deposited with each of these libraries. But Penglais Hill is not just the nation's bookstore; it's part of Wales' own cultural identity. Here are the repositories of the Welsh language, manuscripts such as the book of Taliesin (13th century), the laws of King Hywel Dda (10th century), and the Black Book of Carmarthen (12–13th century). As well as special collections on Euclid and on papyrology, there is the most comprehensive collection of Breton books and manuscripts that you will find anywhere – an act of solidarity with a Celtic sister nation that has no national library of its own. All I wish is that the National Library in Aberystwyth could have a suitable room in which to exhibit its marvellous collection of prints by Welsh and English artists. In deference to the treasures stored here, one has to forgive the uninspired, impersonal architecture (by Sidney Kyffin Greenslade, 1911). It was all financed by 'the pennies of the people', donations from Welsh miners, who allowed a shilling to be deducted from their wages. Their motto: 'All knowledge is a privilege'.

---

1 Today the University of Wales also incorporates Swansea College, the Welsh School of Medicine, the Institute of Science and Technology in Cardiff, and the Anglican St David's College in Lampeter.
2 These include over 3,000 photographs by John Thomas. No-one provided a finer record of everyday life in Wales during the second half of the 19th century.

Leopold Kohr: Little is Great

Aberystwyth has 12,000 inhabitants and Leopold Kohr. Since 1974 this adopted Welsh-man has lived in this little town in this little country, in a little house in a little street – all in accordance with his theory about true greatness. The basic theory is that whenever things go wrong, it's because they're too big. This applies to the dinosaurs, the European Community, the Soviet Union, and America, all of which have collapsed or will collapse in due course. So he argues in his book 'The Breakdown of Nations', which many regard as the most important contribution to political philosophy in recent years. Long before the Club of Rome, Leopold Kohr described the limits of possible growth, and opposed central governments with too much power. He wants less of the State, and more of politics on a human scale, and was campaigning for this long before 'Small is beautiful' became the catchphrase of the day.

Leopold Kohr was born in 1909 in Oberndorf, near Salzburg, and in 1938 fled from Nazism to America, where he taught economics at Puerto Rico University for 20 years. How did Aberystwyth become the home of an Austrian professor with an American passport? Celtic manuscripts in the National Library seem an unlikely inducement. 'What I like about Aberystwyth,' he says, 'are the short distances. I can get to my baker, my office, my bank, my butcher quite easily on foot, without a car. And if I want to go and worship, I can choose between three chapels. And if I want to go and drink, I've got several pubs just round the corner.' In Aberystwyth the old gentleman is a familiar figure – jogger, scholar, story-teller, and gentle anarchist. He greeted me at his home in Baker Street, with a vacuum cleaner in his hand. 'The Celts are very similar to the Austrians, in character, temperament, and unfortunately also in untidiness. After all, they come from the region of Hallein. The Austrians are the Welsh that stayed at home.' It was not, however, Celtic nostalgia that drew Leopold Kohr to Wales, but a Utopian political experiment.

When his famous work 'The Breakdown of Nations' first appeared in 1957, he was still in Puerto Rico, and there he received a letter from Wales. The writer said that he himself was attempting to put into practice the very things Leopold Kohr had written about, and he invited Kohr to come to Wales. The writer of the letter was none other than Gwynfor Evans, who at that time was still an unknown, provincial politician. In Kohr's book he had found a theoretical basis for his campaign for an independent Wales: namely, that behind all forms of social misery lay a single cause – size. Only in small states could true democracy prevail, because citizens there could have direct influence on the apparatus of government, and only there could culture and the individual be free to develop in their own way. In 1936, Leopold Kohr had been a journalist during the Spanish Civil War and had visited the separatist provinces of Catalonia and Aragon. This had aroused his interest in the problems of national minorities. When in 1967 the 6,000 inhabitants of Anguilla declared their island to be the smallest republic in the world, he played an active part in the colony's revolt against the British. A country like Wales was therefore bound to attract him. And indeed as early as 1957, he spoke at a Plaid Cymru seminar in Merthyr Tydfil: 'The reason I love the Welsh is because they are so few ... I would advocate a Welsh state even if all the Welsh were English.' Ten years later, Gwnfor Evans arranged a visiting professorship for him in economics at Swansea University. He gave lectures on 'The Overdeveloped Nations', and on the greater viability of smaller communities. He argued that the administrative power of a central government decreased as distance increased. London could not give Wales what Wales wanted, and this proportionate incapacity led to the independence movements of the more distant regions. Here, then, was a nationalist enthusing about small states, but this same visiting professor was also an expert on problems of an international customs union.

There can be no doubt that Kohr's identification with Wales had a strong romantic element, but it was still based on realistic, economic considerations, as he proved in 1971 with his book 'Is Wales Viable?' His answer to this question was that unlike Denmark or Switzerland, Wales was rich in raw materials, but it was suffering from the effects of a 'typical colonial economy'; there was a one-sided development of heavy industry with a neglected hinterland, impoverished by emigration ('the law of peripheral neglect'). Kohr's thesis was violently opposed, but never disproved: Wales 'is both large and rich enough, once she becomes master of her own resources, to produce for herself the bulk of what she requires.' He argues in favour of 'a British Common Market', with a politically independent Wales forming an economic community with England. In such an association of British states, everything that was worth preserving, including the monarchy, would remain, but the British Prime Minister's power would end at the Severn. Kohr's study bears the dedication: 'To Gwynfor Evans in admiration'. Gwynfor Evans and his National Party owe more to the Austrian economist than people realize – not least, for international publicity.

From 1973 till 1977, Kohr was Professor of Political Science at Aberystwyth University, and after that he travelled all round the world as the guru of 'Cymru Fach', Little Wales. And he informs the world that the alternative to red is not black or green, but small. He also argues, however, that problems are not solved by smallness, they are only made smaller, so that man with his small stature is then better able to master them. A Socratic mind, a Celtic raconteur – that's how I remember him in his home in Baker Street, Aberystwyth, far from the coffeehouses of his native Austria, advocate of a little nation. He adopted Wales, and Wales adopted him, this American citizen with a second home in Austria and a burial plot waiting for him in Hellbrunn.

Owain Glyndwr: The Short-Lived Glory of Machynlleth

North of Aberystwyth lie the sandbanks and shingle of *Borth* and the marshes of *Cors Fochno*. This is where the Dyfi flows into the sea, and at flood tide the estuary forms a massive lake, five miles long and two miles wide. Since 1968 the 5000 acres of the Dyfi estuary, with their rich plant and animal life, have been an official nature reserve, as well as the subject of ecological research by UNESCO. But if nature reigns supreme downstream, it is history that dominates upstream, for there lies the town of Machynlleth, for ever associated with the name Owain Glyndwr.

Machynlleth consists of two streets and a pronunciation problem. The point at which the two streets intersect is most impressively blocked off by a Neo-Gothic clocktower (colour plate 12). It was erected in 1874 to celebrate the coming of age of Lord Castlereagh, eldest son of the Marquess of Londonderry. The Victorians' mania for monuments meant that anything was game for commemoration. I arrived in Machynlleth on a Wednesday, market-day. In Maengwyn Street (colour plate 16) the traders, farmers and craftsmen had put up their stalls, and you could get anything from fresh vegetables to cheap Bibles, second-hand clothes to CND pamphlets. But even on a market-day, this little hill town retains its solid air of respectability: the houses are mainly Victorian, and in Brickfield Street there are a few weavers' cottages (1826) that recall the heyday of the wool industry. In the mid 19th century Machynlleth and its surroundings boasted no less than 12 flannel and 5 yarn factories. Edward III brought seventy clothworkers and their families from Flanders and established them in Montgomeryshire in 1331. Rolls of cloth and other wares were then transported from Machynlleth by 'merlins' to Shrewsbury – merlins being a name for Welsh ponies. It was in this little market town on the edge of Powys that the first Welsh parliament was convened in 1404, and it was here that Owain Glyndwr was crowned King. He was the last hero of the last major Welsh rebellion.

In Shakespeare's 'Henry IV', the 'irregular and wild Glendower' is a bitter opponent of the King, but he is only a secondary character in a play virtually dominated by Falstaff. Even at his birth, he tells Hotspur, the earth shook: 'I tell you once again that at my birth / The front of heaven was full of fiery shapes, / The goats ran from the mountains, and the herds / Were strangely clamorous to the frighted fields. / These signs have marked me extraordinary.' Owain was descended from the Princes of Powys and Deheubarth. The place of his birth (*c.*1354) is marked only by a mound – *Sycharth Castle* in the borderlands near Oswestry. Owain's second name of Glyndwr was taken from one of his favourite domains – *Glyndyfrdwy*, a village on the Dee near Llangollen. This son of a Welsh prince enjoyed the best education available in his day, which naturally included learning English. For seven years he studied law in London, and he also served in the English army, thereby absorbing all the strategems of his later enemies. Initially he was a loyal subject of Richard II, which made the Welsh rebellion even more unexpected for the latter's successor Henry IV. The cause had nothing to do with the overthrow of Richard, but – as is so often the case – was something quite banal: Owain's English neighbour had appropriated a piece of land which the Welshman claimed was his. His claim was rejected by the courts, and so Owain Glyndwr took justice and his sword into his own hands.

With 4,000 followers he attacked the town of Ruthin in summer 1400. A local dispute thus developed into a national uprising. The long-suppressed resentment at English dominance had simply been waiting for a spark, and in Owain it found the leader to ignite it. He realized that this was the right moment, since a rebellion in the north of England was already engaging the attentions of the new King. And had not the court poet Iolo Goch prophesied that he would one day seize the crown of Wales? On September 16, 1400 Owain Glyndwr had himself proclaimed Prince of Wales in Glyndyfrdwy, and to this very day patriots like Gwynfor Evans celebrate September 16 as Glyndwr's Day.

'Owain, the rivers of Wales are numberless / And every river a battle, and every battle a song' (Harri Webb). Now even the English had to accept that this was a popular uprising. Henry IV fought back. Parliament sharpened the laws: no Welshman was allowed to bear arms, take public office, or try an Englishman before a Welsh court. Bards were banned, assemblies forbidden, and the Welsh were made into second-class citizens in their own country. These draconian measures were not lifted until Henry VII came to the throne. But still Owain Glyndwr marched from victory to victory: Criccieth, Harlech, Cardiff, Aberystwyth, one castle after another fell into his hands. In the summer of 1404 the first Welsh parliament was convened in Machynlleth – though not in Parliament House, near the Owain Glyndwr Institute, which is now a museum. This low building of rubble masonry and with a slate roof was not built until after the great event it commemorates, though undoubtedly it owes its preservation to that same parliament, and is now one of the few surviving late medieval town halls in Wales. Owain Glyndwr sent ambassadors to France and Spain, and Wales acted with a sovereignty it never had either before or since. On 14 July 1404 Glyndwr, having been crowned King in Machynlleth, formed an alliance with Charles VI of France. The wax seal of this treaty shows a man enthroned under a baldachin, with a sceptre in his right hand, bareheaded, bearded. Perhaps this is 'Owynus, Dei Gracia, princeps Walliae' himself. Otherwise, there is no known portrait of him. What did he really want for his country? On March 31, 1406 he wrote to Benedict XIII, the antipope in Avignon, 'that our chapels shall be free'. He demanded the independence of the Welsh church from Canterbury, and two universities, one for the north and one for the south. At least one of his demands was met, when the University of Wales was founded, but it took quite a while – till 1872 in fact.

It was a strange and ultimately futile campaign. In August 1405 a French auxiliary force of 2,600 men landed at Milford Haven; six months later they were sailing home again. Owain Glyndwr advanced almost as far as Worcester, but there he encountered the English army, hesitated, then withdrew again to Wales. And now the tide turned. He lost territory, lost his castles, and fled into the mountains of Snowdonia[1], having long lost hope of victory. From now on, he was a man on the run, defeated but not destroyed, powerless but still free. The rest of the story is unknown. He may have died in the Golden Valley in Herefordshire, and he may be buried in Monnington-on-Wye. But no-one really knows. What *is* known is that by 1417 he was dead. It was, however, an end that was not an end,

---

1   There is an isolated cave in the rocks of Moel Hebog, where Owain Glyndwr is said to have taken refuge from his pursuers. It is called 'Ogof Owain Glyndwyr'.

for historic defeat turned into national myth, and thus Owain Glyndwr became immortal, a symbol like King Arthur. The bards wrote no elegies on his death, for they awaited his return: 'Oh! I know Owain will return / Like a flood after ebb / like a rainbow after rain / like dawn after night / By God! I know he'll come! / ... to lead us to the dawn of a Free Wales.' These lines were written by a 20th-century bard, the political singer Dafydd Iwan.

In countless songs, ballads and inn-signs the name of Owain Glyndwr lives on, as what John Cowper Powys, English poet and Welshman by choice, regards as a cult figure in which 'the deep-suppressed hero – worship of this race of mythologists finds its apotheosis.' Powys himself contributed to this cult with his massive historical novel 'Owen Glendower' (1940), whose main thesis is that the Welsh fashioned political defeats into a 'mythology of escape'. Thus the defeated Glendower became a moral victor, prince of a world outside the world, 'Prince of Annwn'. In this escape mythology, already inherent in the geography and climate of the country, Powys detects 'the secret of the land', a vital element of the national character: 'Other races love and hate, conquer and are conquered. This race avoids and evades, pursues and is pursued. Its soul is forever making a double flight. It flies into a circuitous Inward. It retreats into a circuitous Outward.' The Welsh flight is also a projection of his own flight to Wales, and it is not by chance that Powys lived for many years in Corwen (see page 309), one of the headquarters of his hero. The living spirit of the great rebel of 1400 is vividly captured in Harri Webb's poem 'Owain Glyndwr' (1977):

> The centuries have passed but the battle's not done,
> And the cause that he died for has yet to be won,
> With his memory to stir us, his deeds to inflame,
> We will conquer our freedom in Owain's great name,
> Strike hard at the traitors and cleanse all the land
> With the keen sword of vengeance we take from his hand.
> Our country is calling, we strive for her sake,
> Sleep soundly, Prince Owain, your sons are awake!

But that Owain's sons should really awake, and that extremists should actually take up the keen sword of vengeance, so lightly invoked, was probably not quite what the patriotic singer had envisaged. However, at the beginning of the 1980's, dozens of English second homes in Wales went up in flames, and the group of arsonists concerned dubbed themselves 'Meibion Glyndwr', the Sons of Glyndwr. This was the guerrilla instinct inherited from Owain, a pathetic echo, and not the fulfilment of a national dream.

CAT and MADRYN: Anti-Nuclear Fox and Alternative Energy

The 'Village of the Future' lies in an abandoned slate quarry north of Machynlleth (plate 59). A Cretan type windmill glows red on the slope, and aerogenerators rotate with flashing wings: this is CAT, the 'Centre for Alternative Technology', known to its friends as 'The Quarry'. When the owner offered the land to anyone who could do something

*Wales declares itself the first
nuclear-free country in Europe:
cartoon by Wren, 1983*

useful with it, various young engineers and social workers came forward. Their message was short and to the point: alternative technology, they said, was the means whereby the Earth could be saved from ecological catastrophe. This was in 1974, in the early stages of energy crisis, when the public at large was only just becoming aware of the dangers of environmental pollution. Today the centre is a tourist attraction, and is Britain's most successful experimental site for environment-friendly technology. What is developed here concerns us all: the search for new sources of energy, research into health foods, cheap and effective methods of self-help that could be of vital importance to third world countries, such as the drought-stricken regions of Africa.

This village is not joined to any public supply network. It produces its own electricity, through water turbines, windmills and solar panels. It must, however, be admitted that the Welsh sun by nature tends not to be the most abundant source of energy. The houses – a dozen of them – are equipped with various modes of heat insulation and recycling. Cooking, for example, is done with methane gas from a biological lavatory. Food comes from the biogarden. You might think that the rubbish tips from a slate quarry would not be the ideal place to grow food, and so it's all the more impressive to see how these alternative farmers increase the fertility of poor soil without using any chemicals, and ward off pests simply with the aid of weeds. There are, of course, limitations, and these have to be accepted: 'If the chickens lay fewer eggs in winter, then we just eat fewer eggs.' The workshops demonstrate the efficiency of small enterprises. Here you can see how to make bricks with simple moulds, how to turn a barrel into a rotor for water pumps, and how to make a bicycle into a 5-watt windmill. 'Simple design and fun to make.' And you can learn a hundred and one new ideas during the week-end and summer courses they hold here, as well as in the centre's specialist bookshop. For many people spending their holidays in the Machynlleth region, a trip to the 'Quarry' is the first encounter with alternative forms of energy and economy, and they go away with a new or at least heightened awareness of the environment and methods of saving it.

Practical demonstrations and public education had not been among the original aims of the 'Quarry' people, but now these are seen as an integral part of their work, and their acceptance of this role is much to be admired. Not many of us would like to go about our daily business under the gaze of up to a thousand visitors a day. As a non-profit-making organization devoted to improving the environment, the centre finances all its research itself, from donations, entrance tickets, and the sale of books and its own products. Howell Harris and Eric Gill would no doubt have approved. When I visited this ecological haven, there were 30 people at work, of whom only three were Welsh; the rest were English. They are not professional drop-outs, or amateur drop-outs for that matter, but architects, biologists, teachers, engineers and gardeners, as well as some students and some unemployed people. Most of them stay for about four years. They all work for the same (low) salary, vary in age from 20 to 60, and regard themselves as a co-operative rather than a commune – a group of enthusiasts and friends of the Earth, in the tradition of William Morris and John Seymour. This abandoned slate quarry in Wales is setting a simple and immensely impressive example of how man can live in harmony with Nature and its resources, and in peace with himself and his surroundings.

But even here, peace can come under threat. For many a long year the lords and masters that reside in Westminster have known about the special qualities of Wales. And in their great wisdom they asked: would not this remote, thinly populated mountain region be the ideal spot for nuclear waste? And so they fixed on a site between Machynlleth and Dolgellau as a possible subterranean dump. 'When the geologists came to do their test drilling, we blocked the roads with tractors. The farmers were even ready to set the woods on fire.' The man who told me this was not, as you might have expected, a young hothead; he was Her Majesty's Inspector of Schools in Wales, now retired, Mr Geraint Bowen. He lives with his wife and two daughters and one harp up above Tal-y-Llyn, a magnificent mountain lake on the edge of Snowdonia National Park. He is a bard, member of the Welsh Academy of Writers, honoured with the Eisteddfod throne and the title of 'Archdruid of Wales'. This in no way inhibits him from playing a leading role in the anti-nuclear movement known as MADRYN. The word is Welsh, and means Sly Fox, and it's also an acronym for '*Mudiad Amddiffyn Dulas Rhag Ysbwriel Niwclear*', Defence Movement Against Atomic Waste in Dulas Valley.

It was Geraint Bowen who, in 1982, wrote a proclamation for Gwynfor Evans to declaim in Mold to the effect that Wales was declaring itself to be the first nuclear-free country in Europe. This so-called Clwyd Declaration was then telexed to Prince Charles. It was also sent to Reagan and Brezhnev, with the plea that they should follow the Welsh example. As in centuries gone by, when the Welsh were fighting wars for their freedom, beacons were lit on many Welsh hills on that February night in 1982. They announced to neighbouring England that Wales had declared its own anti-nuclear independence. '*Cymru Ddi-Niwclear*' stood on signs erected at the borders. It was not merely a symbolic act of defiance. The powers of the regional councils are such that they can make plenty of trouble for central government. The response from London was, however, predictable: on such matters the Welsh had no jurisdiction, even if they put it to the vote. 'So much for English democracy,' commented the Welsh poet and parson R. S. Thomas.

It is a paradox: many English people would like to make the whole of Wales into a nature reserve; and at the same time, they want to steal in and put their nuclear waste and their rockets here, as far away as possible from their own cities. It is, I think, no coincidence that key figures in the anti-nuclear movement of British women actually come from the Welsh valleys. It was these 'Women for Life on Earth' who began the Greenham Common protest in 1981 in an attempt to blockade the US rocket base there.

Robert Owen: The Utopian Socialist from Newtown

'Take a trip through the Dulas Valley,' advised Geraint Bowen, 'and then you'll see what I mean.' And from the ridge overlooking Afon Dulas I saw one of the most beautiful and charming, melancholy and desolate landscapes in the whole of Mid Wales. The road from Machynlleth across the hills to Llanidloes is a narrow, a prehistoric route later used also by the Romans. It crosses the shoulder of *Plynlimon*, a moor with five peaks, none higher than 2500 feet, but high enough for you to see half of Wales if the day is clear enough. Only don't build up too many hopes, because the Plynlimon is famous for its mists. Here Wales is as wild as it always used to be. Polecats and martens still live in these parts, and buzzards circle above the bare hills. Everywhere you can hear the dripping and dropping, rushing and rustling of water. One source is the Severn, another the Wye, and the reservoirs on the edges of the moors replenish their supplies with effortless ease.

The dam of *Llyn Clywedog* is nearly six and a half miles long, and the road runs above it, and through deserted mining country. From the 17th century onwards, lead was the mineral extracted here, until at the end of the 19th century prices on the world market made the Welsh mines unprofitable. And so *Dylife*, once a flourishing community with a church and several chapels, turned into a ghost village. Just one building remained – the pub. The mines of Van, which once employed over 500 people, were abandoned around the turn of the century. The centre of the Welsh lead-mining industry lay near *Pont-rhyd-y-groes* in the Ystwyth Valley. There were more than 90 pits in northern Ceredigion alone. Silver and zinc were also mined. Queen Elizabeth I brought German experts from Saxony to Wales, and later miners came from Cornwall. Near *Ponterwyd*, at the foot of the Plynlimon, the old bucket wheels and galleries of the Llywernog Silver-Lead Mine have been restored to make an open-air museum with a small exhibition that includes photographs of 19th-century miners looking like adventurers in helmets and clogs: the Silver Rush in the wild west of wild Wales.

The boom was short-lived. At the end of the 19th century, hundreds abandoned their bare shacks in the mountains. All that remained were the sheep, together with the oldest industry in the country – wool. *Llanidloes* also owed its golden days to the weavers of the early 19th century. Six flannel factories and some 800 hand-looms used to grace this little town on the eastern slopes of the Plynlimon. For me, Llanidloes is the most charming and most beautiful little town in Mid Wales (plates 39, 66). It was planned as a 'New Town' during the Middle Ages, was given market rights by Edward I in 1280, and had broad, straight roads. In the centre of the crossroads stand the wooden arcades of the indoor market, and here the old men of Llanidloes sit and gaze and gossip, sheltered from the rain, the sun and their wives. Little has changed since 1600, when the market was built – a long, half-timbered edifice with roof turrets and an open ground floor. This was the setting for markets, court sessions, and for Wesley preaching both heaven and hell. It's the focal point of the town – all eyes are drawn to it, all cars must circle it, and every day it sets the rhythm of life in Llanidloes. When the old men go home in the evening, there is nothing left to see, and nothing left to talk about. Until tomorrow, that is.

It's a little town full of big eyes. When I was photographing the wood and iron decorations on the front of Edward Hamer's Victorian butcher's shop, his neighbour waved to me from the shoe shop. 'Just imagine,' said Mrs Rees, 'our Labour Party actually wanted to take down that beautiful royal coat-of-arms over Mr Hamer's shop door!' Then Mrs Rees announced with satisfaction: 'You're the second person this week who's taken photographs of our street.' Had I been to see St Idloes? I hadn't. But I did. The church of the town's Celtic patron saint has a dragon beam with winged angels, dating from 1542. At around the same time – and this is St Idloes' real claim to fame – the Early Gothic archways from the neighbouring Cistercian abbey of Cwmhir, which had just been dissolved, were brought here and reconstructed: Early English in its purest form (c.1200–30).

Two things alone link Llanidloes to London, Tokyo, Hamburg, New York and Sydney: one is the telephone, and the other is Laura Ashley. 'Queen Cotton' had a branch in Llanidloes, as she had in some 130 towns elsewhere in the world. Her rustic, romantic fabrics with their flowery patterns and ruches have become so much a trademark of the English Country Look that their originator has almost disappeared behind her name: Laura Ashley was, along with Mary Quant – designer of the miniskirt – the most successful fashion designer ever to come out of Wales. Born in 1925 in Merthyr Tydfil, the iron town, she designed her blossomed dreams for all who longed to get out of the industrial cities and breathe in the pure country air; at least her fabrics could foster the illusion. Her preference for natural, traditional patterns reflects people's desire for a natural, healthy way of life, much as her Victorian predecessor Kate Greenaway had done with her ever-popular country idylls. Laura Ashley's worldwide success was based on a universal projection of the English mentality, 'where home is where the heart sees a country cottage with roses round the door' (*The Times*). This poetic, nostalgic fashion typifies what Sir Roy Strong, guardian of British good taste, describes as the new British Biedermeier. The designer herself saw the Laura Ashley woman as one who raised a family and enjoyed domestic life. 'I like to think that I create calm.' She herself found this calm in the little village of *Carno*, north of Llanidloes, which became the Welsh headquarters of the LA empire in 1963. And

Robert Owen, 1851

it was there that Laura Ashley was buried in 1985, leaving her widower, Sir Bernard, as one of the 50 richest men in Britain.

'Flannel' is a Welsh word. It's derived from *'gwlan'*, which in turn comes from the Latin *'lana'* (wool). The historic centre of the Welsh flannel and wool industry was *Newtown*. Today it seems almost inconceivable that this little town on the Severn was once known as 'the Leeds of Wales', but in the early 19th century there were 1,200 looms rattling away in the houses of Newtown. When the situation of the weavers became increasingly desperate, the Welsh Chartists met here for the first time (1838) to discuss their demands (see page 89). In the northern part of the town, Penygloddfa, you can still find signs of the old weaving district, with large warehouses and terraced brick houses dating from 1830. One of these is now a textile museum, with all the rooms set up just as they used to be: living quarters down below, loom up above – workplace and family all housed under one roof.

Cartwright's invention of the power loom in 1785 put an end to the cottage industry, and the consequence in Wales was widespread poverty and unemployment. It was Northern England and the Midlands that prospered, with burgeoning wool and textile industries. In the middle of the 19th century, Newtown was also subjected to fierce competition from the great cotton mills of Yorkshire and Lancashire. Nevertheless, in 1859 the entrepreneurial Pryce Jones opened the first mail-order firm in the world, dispatching Welsh flannel from Newtown: 'The Royal Welsh Warehouse', still standing, at Newtown Station.

Today, however, the Welsh textile industry is concentrated in the Teifi Valley, around Llandyssul. Newtown did not recover from the decline of its traditional industry until 1960, when it was declared a special development area, in order to arrest the continual fall in population. Today the town produces golf clubs and equipment for offices and aircraft. But its chief claim to fame is not its weavers. Robert Owen is the name for ever associated with Newtown. He was born here in 1771, and died here in 1858, and in between he proved himself to be the greatest social reformer and Utopian socialist of the 19th century.

Robert Owen grew up at the beginning of the Industrial Revolution, and so was among the first to feel its effects. The house where he was born, near the Victorian clocktower, is now a bank. He was the son of a saddler, but left his hometown at the tender age of ten, became a cloth merchant in Manchester, then rose to be manager of a cotton mill, and by the age of 23 was co-owner of the New Lanark Mills in Scotland. But for all his success as a businessman, his concern was not only the making of profits but also the welfare of his workers. He was, however, much more than a philanthropist. He was the prophet of a happy society. He believed that with the right means, people could gradually be taught to free themselves of all poverty, crime and punishment. He regarded competition as the root of all evil – competition between individuals as well as between nations. Even before Marx he was preaching that man is a product of his environment. 'Surround him with evil circumstance or conditions, and his thoughts and conduct must become evil,' he wrote in his autobiography. But if living and working conditions were improved, then man would become good and happy. New Lanark was Robert Owen's first step towards Utopia. He offered his workers spacious, cheap and hygienic homes, free medical attention, kinder-gartens (the first in Britain), and also fought to outlaw child labour. He gave support to the unemployed, and shortened working hours. But even on the road to an ideal society, he was not prepared to lose control over efficiency. Next to every workplace hung 'The Silent Monitor', a pendulum with four different-coloured sides. The colour facing the worker showed him the standard of his achievements the previous day: black meant bad, blue was average, yellow was good, and white was excellent. These grades were entered in a book, and it is said that they duly led to the desired effect. A specimen of this apparatus is to be seen in the little Robert Owen Museum in Newtown. However, the Old World turned out to be too set in its ways, and Robert Owen went to America. 'New Harmony' was the name he gave to the model estate that he set up in 1825 in Indiana. It was to be a haven of peace and human solidarity, but his society of equals disintegrated through egotism, vested interests, and class consciousness. Two years later, he abandoned his experiment and, close to ruin, returned home. There, in the meantime, his co-operative movement had spread, with shops and production all controlled by the workers themselves. In 1830 there were already over 300 co-operatives, and the term 'Co-op' became a household word. Robert Owen gave passionate support to the union movement, which for the first time merged into a unified organization in 1833. His 'New Harmony', however, remained one of the great Utopian attempts of modern times. On a visit to his hometown, where he was to reorganize the school system, Robert Owen died in 1858. His grave lies near the ruins of St Mary's, Newtown's old parish church on the Severn, and is surrounded by magnificent Art Nouveau railings made in 1902. On it stands Robert Owen's final message to posterity: 'It is the one great and universal interest of the human race to be cordially united and to aid each other to the full extent of their capacities.'

In Newtown's northern suburb of *Llanllwchaiarn* is a simple brick church, built in 1815, with some unusually beautiful, Victorian stained-glass windows, including two made by William Morris & Co (*c*.1870): St Stephen and St Peter, the latter based on a design by the painter Ford Madox Brown. It is amazing to find brilliant, Pre-Raphaelite windows tucked away in Welsh village churches: Burne-Jones designed a radiant east window, for St Michael in *Forden*, which was made in 1873 by his friend William Morris's company. In it, the Adoration is framed by archangels Michael and Gabriel, and crowned by three angels playing instruments; and the whole composition is shot through with the Pre-Raphaelite triad of red, blue and green.

It's the unexpected that makes these trips exciting. You take a sideroad, and suddenly come across a church window that encapsulates a whole aesthetic brotherhood; or you come to a house, and find that it set the tone for the whole country. That was the tale of *Gregynog Hall*. It's a country house five miles north of Newtown – half timbered, many-gabled, symmetrical, and typically Elizabethan ... or is it? Only when you come close do you realize that it's actually made of concrete, and the timbers are painted on (plate 63; colour plate 35). But the real surprise is that this is not one of those nostalgic deceptions of our own time; it is in fact a Victorian experiment with a modern building material, and it dates from as long ago as 1860. The architect was probably the owner himself, Henry Hanbury Tracy, who had concrete cottages built all round his estate – concrete from floor to ceiling – as well as the village school in *Tregynon*. Gregynog Hall was one of the very first concrete buildings in Britain, and as such certainly merits a footnote in the history of architecture, but it was also an institution in itself, as a Welsh arts centre. In the 1930's its guests included Edward Elgar, Adrian Boult and Benjamin Britten, and between 1923 and 1939 the Gregynog Press, one of the great hand presses in the Arts and Crafts tradition, produced many a delight for the bibliophile; and from here came the Monets, Renoir's 'La Parisienne', and many of the other French Impressionist paintings now hanging in Cardiff's National Museum. This rural artistic miracle was wrought by two sisters, Gwendoline and Margaret Davies. They bought Gregynog Hall in 1920, having inherited a fortune from their grandfather, the coal and railway magnate of Barry, and they invested it in the two best possible ways: art and welfare. The ladies of Gregynog were the first connoisseurs in Britain to collect and exhibit Cézanne: their Daumier collection can still compare with that of the Louvre; and before they died, both spinsters, these art-loving sisters donated their collection to the National Museum, and their country estate to the University of Wales. Some masterpieces have remained in Gregynog: Rodin's bust of Mahler, and pictures by Richard Wilson, Augustus John and others, and the spirit of the Davies sisters lives on through the many concerts, poetry readings, seminars and conferences organized here by the University. Even the tradition of the famous Welsh handpress is continued through the books printed by the Gwasg Gregynog, set up in 1975. So the concrete hall still has a living heart.

Praise Be to Montgomery and to All Small Towns

I wonder why it is that at home I like large towns, and in Wales I like them small. It may perhaps be because in Wales there *are* no large towns – not even Cardiff. My native German towns often seem like cultural backwaters, musty and dull, whereas Welsh towns are so much more enjoyable. Maybe they are less provincial, maybe the neighbours are less nosy, less intolerant. Or maybe my small German towns are too obsessed with cleanliness, riddled with pedestrian zones, shopping precincts, anonymous glass buildings, and the desire to be like a big town. Or maybe it's simply because the grass is always greener Under Milk Wood.

Montgomery lies there, perfectly at peace, like an abandoned bowl on the bowling green. Up above, on the hill, stands the inevitable castle. On one of the gentler slopes are the church and cemetery. In between, and with middle-class centrality, you will find the town hall and the market-place (plate 94). Go uphill again, and you'll come to a few more streets and houses and a lot of greenery – trees, lawns, gardens. That's it. That's Montgomery. Market town, hill town, border town – but 'town', or even 'small town' sounds too big for Montgomery. It used to be the county town of Montgomeryshire, but now it's just a little nest for 1,000 lucky people. The markets are finished, the frontier fortress is in ruins, and the only large-scale item left is the view from the hill. But the panorama you enjoy today offered alarming prospects in the past: columns of smoke on the plains, mighty armies – Roman, Norman, Welsh – decade after decade, century after century. Montgomery is situated just a mile from Offa's Dyke, nicely placed strategically above the Severn Valley, on the invaders' route from Shrewsbury to Mid Wales. It was a base for the first Earl of Shrewsbury, Roger de Montgomery, from whom it took its name. Early in the 13th century, Henry III gave it a castle, which was razed to the ground in 1649. Only very little remains of the medieval town walls. When Edward I conquered Wales, it lost its importance as a frontier town, and the new castles were built on the coast, particularly in the north. The medieval street-plan has remained virtually unaltered, with Broad Street forming the main axis. In the 18th century most of the old houses were given new Georgian façades, and the market-place received its town hall (1748). If this were a country of street cafés, Broad Street would be my Welsh Piazza. Brick houses, plastered in pastel shades, two or three-storeyed, with eaves of different heights, everything expressive of the joyful spontaneity that reigned before building regulations brought in standardization.

The meaning of 'structural change' in a town like Montgomery is graphically illustrated by a list of professions compiled in 1840: at that time there were 5 bakers, 3 butchers, 8 grocers, 4 maltsters, 2 seedsmen, 2 smiths, 4 drapers, 2 tailors, 3 shoemakers, 3 carpenters, 2 plumbers, 3 saddlers, 3 coopers, 2 stonemasons, 1 bricklayer, 1 coppersmith, 1 timber merchant, 1 currier, 1 tanner, 1 watchmaker, 1 bookseller, and 1 scrivener. And so in 1840 there were over 50 craftsmen and businessmen in Montgomery; today there are just a

Moses Griffith: Montgomery, 1776

dozen or so. The parson has managed to keep his job – though even that is something that can no longer be taken for granted. St Nicholas, built at the same time as the castle in the early 13th century, has a magnificent Elizabethan monument (1600) to Sir Richard Herbert and his wife, who owned the whole of Montgomery in those days. Behind their elaborate figures their eight children kneel under archways. One of them became famous as a 'parson poet': George Herbert, born in Montgomery in 1593, educated in London and Cambridge, a friend of John Donne, he became a country parson in Wiltshire, where he died in 1633. He was one of the greatest early English poets, passionate about religion and Nature. His collection of religious poems 'The Temple' gave comfort to King Charles I while he waited in prison to be taken to the scaffold.

And so Montgomery lies there in its perfect peace, far from the busy roads and major events of the big, bad world. Nineteenth century railways and canals took no notice of Montgomery, and carried their business to *Welshpool*, ten miles further north. This is a market town of 7,000 people, busy, bright, more brick than timber, English in appearance, English in sound; it is, after all, only three miles from the border. The climax of the week here comes right at the start: Monday. That's the day of the cattle market, the biggest in Wales. If you miss that, all that's left for you – apart from a trip to the pub – is the church or the museum. I didn't fancy either, but I did want to go on a boat – for what is the point of a canal if you can't go boating on it? The long red 'Llinnos' carried me gently away from the town – the 'Llinnos' being a barge which has given up transporting coal and other such commodities, and instead encourages idlers like me (colour plate 36; plate 80). These 'narrow boats' used to be drawn by horses, and were of standard size for all British canals, to fit the narrow-gauge locks that were designed by the engineer and canal-builder James

Brindley around 1770: 70 feet long, 7 feet wide. And so we went chugging through the valley, within touching distance of the canal bank, past fields and creepers, the smell of hay in the nostrils, musty odours, a coot clicking away somewhere. A dragon-fly hovered motionless over the reeds. The *Montgomery Canal*, which is a branch of the Shropshire Union Canal of 1794 (plate 82), used to cover the 35 miles to Newtown. It was no longer profitable in 1944 and was partly drained, partly filled in, until 1969, when restorations began. A stroll along the towpath is a pleasure in itself, and so is a slow chug in the 'Llinnos'.

Now I must tell you about Mrs Iona Trevor-Jones. Without Mrs Iona Trevor-Jones, the Prince of Wales's investiture in July 1969 would have been without its most important feature: daffodils. Daffodils are the national flower of the Welsh, but where can you find daffodils in July? In such cases, the Commonwealth is a better bet than a greenhouse. And so this Welsh flower artist had daffodils flown in for her Prince from Africa. Iona Trevor-Jones is in fact Britain's top TV floral artist, and for many years she has gone all over the world lecturing on the art of flower arranging. She has two great talents, she says: flowers and talking. I can vouch for her being a great hostess, and I reckon her two great talents are cooking ... and talking. I'd swap an investiture any day for a dinner at Mrs Trevor-Jones's – superb food, accompanied by harp music and Welsh dancing. It all takes place at *Trelydan Hall* near Welshpool, the most beautiful, half-timbered country house in Wales, restored by none other than John and Iona Trevor-Jones (plate 64). Generations have added on to this picturesque example of Montgomeryshire's black and white architecture, from the 16th right through to the 19th century. It's a geometrician's paradise, with a façade full of circles, semicircles, squares, rhombuses and rectangles: it's kinetic architecture, a fine example of op art created long before Vasarely even thought of it.

Powis Castle: All About Earls and Sheep

In his 'Book of Snobs', the Duke of Bedford mentions, among those of his fellow peers who did not dress quite as they should, the late Duke of Norfolk. He used, apparently, to wander round the gardens of Arundel Castle in the most appalling, worn-out suits, and visitors would sometimes take pity on him and offer him something to eat. He would always accept the offer. I was reminded of this tale when I first saw the Earl of Powis, in the carpark at the foot of his castle: he was wearing a battered old jacket, tattered hat, and looked for all the world like a pensioner who'd scraped together enough for a trip to Powis Castle and was now hunting for his coach party (plate 77). I was about to offer him my assistance when a fellow visitor whispered: 'That's the Earl of Powis. Must be terrible for him to have all these strangers wandering round his castle.'

It's not without good cause that *Powis Castle* is the most popular National Trust house in Wales (colour plate 42). It towers heavenwards with its ramparts and tall, round chimneys, and its massive walls glow dull red, made from the same red sandstone as the rocks on which they stand: this is '*Y Castell Coch*', the Red Castle above the Severn Valley. The heart of this ancient frontier fort near Welshpool consists of two semi-cylindrical western towers (*c*.1300), and it was not until the end of the 16th century that some Elizabethan comfort arrived to soften the defences. The prison became a wine cellar, and one of the watchtowers was made into a bathroom; but more important still was the Long Gallery, with its oak floor and plaster work ceiling (1593). Here people could walk even when the weather was bad, admiring the pictures, sculptures and Mortlake tapestries. In the Oak Drawing Room, also decorated with plaster work, there is Gainsborough's portrait of the First Earl of Powis and Bellotto's View of Verona. The State Bedroom (*c*.1668) holds the apotheosis of royal bed culture: an alcove with gilded balustrade, half altar, half theatre box, the only surviving bed stage of its kind in Britain – a touch of Versailles here in Wales. Whether King Charles II actually spent the night here, as suggested by the initials CR, or this majestic chamber was simply installed for him without ever being occupied, we do not know. Many of the superb pictures, tapestries, items of furniture and Indian treasures came from the collection of Lord Clive, the driving-force behind British rule in India, whose son married into the Powis family. In this castle, with its legacy of a lost Empire and its history of a fast fading family, the Sixth Earl of Powis a bachelor, lived alone, attended only by a butler and a cook, until his death in 1988. Of some 100 rooms in this castle, half were for his private use. 'Why do you need so many rooms?' I asked him. 'Nowhere else to put the furniture,' he replied.

In front of the castle are propped-up yew trees, looking like characters from a bad dream. The terraced gardens go down the steep rock face in four stages to the landscaped park below, laid out by Capability Brown. With their arches and balustrades, urns and sculptures, Powis terraces are reminiscent of the hanging gardens of Italian Renaissance villas. This architectural jewel, which also boasts an orangery, was designed by the Welsh architect William Winde at the end of the 17th century. The lawns down in the valley used to include a Flemish water garden, in the middle of which was the baroque lead statue of 'Fame and Pegasus' by Andrew Carpenter, which now greets visitors in the forecourt of the castle. The view from here reaches far across the Severn Valley to Long Mountain, which separates Wales from England.

But such country seats and feudal heritages are not typical of modern Wales. Apart from its industrial edges, this is a country whose culture is predominantly rural. The Eisteddfod provides an exemplary link with courtly and literary traditions, but the happiest expression of this culture is the *Sheepdog Trial*, a truly traditional festival for farmers and shepherds. If you are travelling through Mid Wales in the summer, you must not under any circumstances miss this treat. One hot August day I was lucky enough to see the Sheepdog Trial in *Llangurig* (plates 51, 104). This is a day for the hill farmers and their dogs. The men climbed out of their dust-covered Land Rovers, in wellingtons and tweed caps, wind- and weather-beaten, their black and white border collies always at their heels.

This is the occasion when they make a sporting contest out of what they do all the year round as work. The course was laid out on a broad, grass-covered slope. It was rather like an obstacle course, with several wooden gates that had narrow openings, and a little pen at the end. There the shepherd stands, giving instructions to his dog with short or long whistles and terse commands like 'come by' (go left), 'away' (go right), 'stand', 'stop' etc. It's fascinating to watch the dog ducking, stalking, waiting, circling the little flock. Every moment produces a countermovement as intelligence battles against instinct, subtlety against obstinacy. This pastoral ballet has all the grace of a 'Swan Lake'. The 'top dog' is not necessarily the one that gets the flock into the pen the fastest. Other marks are given, as in ice-skating, for such items as precision and smoothness of movement. It's not surprising that a good sheepdog can cost around a thousand pounds. The first Sheepdog Trials took place in Bala in 1873 – an essentially Welsh country sport which has became increasingly popular in England, Scotland and Ireland, particularly since its introduction to the TV schedules in the programme 'One Man and His Dog'. There is even an international championship in September, and the Welsh National Championships are in August.

It would be unfair if only the dogs and the owners took the prizes, and so there are awards for the best sheep as well. The breeders proudly present their Kerry Hill, Welsh Mountain, or Speckled Face specimens. But Llangurig's Sheepdog Trials are not just for sheep and dogs either. Over on another part of the field you'll find plenty of other activities. Just like the Scots at their Highland Games, the Welsh toss tree-trunks (tossing the bar, they call it), and instead of rocks they hurl sacks of hay over a fence with a pitchfork (bale tossing). Amongst these rural tests of strength is one that entails sawing a section off a tree trunk as fast as possible, and speed and dexterity are the qualities needed for the sheep-shearing competition. There's a dog-show, a dog-race, a dressage event, and a Glamorous Granny contest – something for everybody, in other words. In the exhibition tent there are prizes for the fattest onions, the longest cucumbers, the fanciest cakes, and the juciest grass. And the beer flows, and we lounge on bales of straw in the sun, and the trophies shine out from a trailer. Llangurig's big day.

North Wales

For centuries the swampy highlands of the Plynlimon Hills separated North and South Wales. Even today communications between East and West are better than those between North and South. The Vale of Conwy lies like a moat in front of the great bulwark of the Carnedd Mountains, which for so long acted as a natural barricade against the invading English, and behind them, hidden in mists and myths, lies Snowdonia, the heartland of the North. This is where the Cymry held on longest to their freedom and their language, and it was here that England's King Edward I built his mightiest castles. From here the Welsh House of Tudor ascended to the English throne, and it is here that the heir to the throne is proclaimed Prince of Wales. The National Party, Plaid Cymru, was founded in the North, and not in Cardiff. It was Lord Lyttelton, writer and politician from Worcestershire, who in the middle of the 18th century wrote an account of his travels and called North Wales one of the greatest natural phenomena of the British Isles; since that moment, even the remotest corners of the country have been opened up for discovery. As in the Scottish Highlands, patriotic history and picturesque landscape, myth and art have combined into a romantic vision of Wales. And yet the most popular tourist attraction of all is not a castle, not a museum, not even a 'Great Little Train'; it's the 'Sun Centre' in Rhyl, complete with heated surfing pool.

When the Aqueducts Dance on the Dee

All through the year, *Llangollen* lies on the Dee and is bored. But once a year the town floods its banks with people from all over the world, and then it hustles and bustles and races and rustles, sings along with the Dee at the top of its voice, grabs the surrounding hills by the hand and goes hopping through the vale until even Telford's aqueduct is dancing the quadrille. This, you see, is the International Eisteddfod of Llangollen, the Bayreuth of folk music and of folk, the Welsh festival of the Musical United Nations. Soloists like Menuhin and Rostropovich, Margaret Price and Geraint Evans have appeared here, and choirs from Kapstadt and the Carpathians, dancers from China and from Africa, the Vienna Boys' Choir, and so on. But above all, this Eisteddfod is a Mecca for amateur

J. M. W. Turner: Llangollen, c.1828–36

singers and dancers. It began in 1947 with 40 choirs from 14 different countries, and today there are more than 120 choirs and dance groups from more than 30 countries. The number of applicants is twice as great, and the town could easily hold two festivals a year. A good 130,000 visitors come to Llangollen in this one festival week – an amazing feat of organization by a community of just 3,000. The fact that the world comes to stay in this little Welsh town goes back to a tale that has a legendary quality about it. In spring 1945, just after the war ended, a young man named Harold Tudor was cycling along a country road, and heard a milk boy singing hymns. He thought to himself: 'Couldn't we get the whole world together in Wales to sing?' A musician from Llangollen, Gwynn Williams, took up the idea, and so this music festival came into being as an expression of international understanding. In summer 1953, Dylan Thomas enthusiastically recorded his own impressions: 'The town sang and danced, as though it were right and proper as the rainbow or the rare sun to celebrate the old bright turning earth and its bullied people. Are you surprised that people still can dance and sing in a world on its head? The only surprising thing about miracles, however small, is that they sometimes happen.'

But long before the Eisteddfod, Llangollen was a much visited and much praised town. In this valley, said the writer Ida Hahn-Hahn in 1846, 'English culture [had] gained just enough control over Welsh wildness to allow both to appear in the best possible light' (a classic cliché: here the barbarism of Wales, and there the sophistication of England). John

Julius Caesar Ibbetson: Llangollen and Dinas Brân, 1794

Francis Jukes: Pontcysyllte Aqueduct, 1808

Samuel Lane: Thomas Telford and his aqueduct at Pontcysyllte, c.1822

Ruskin also enjoyed the temperate beauty of the untamed landscape ('entirely lovely in its gentle wildness'), and his friend Turner painted it: an open, densely forested river valley, a man on the bank fishing for trout, the ruins of Castell Dinas Bran on the hill, and in the background the medieval bridge over the Dee and the silhouetted town – the whole thing a subtle study in paint of a romantic experience of Nature. At around the same time, in the summer of 1828, Pückler, a German prince, also came to the vale of Llangollen, 'a region which in my judgment far transcends all the beauties of the Rhineland'. This seasoned traveller also took care to inform his sweetheart in Muskau about the delights of a Welsh breakfast: in the Hand Hotel he was served on white damask 'steaming coffee, fresh guinea fowl eggs, dark yellow mountain butter, thick cream, toast, muffins, and finally two freshly caught trout with delicate red spots'. Think about that next time your host plonks a continental breakfast in front of you.

John Sell Cotman: Chirk Aqueduct, 1806–07

Along the northern slopes of the Dee Valley runs the *Llangollen Canal*, opened in 1804 as a branch of the Shropshire Union Canal, linking Chester and Shrewsbury, the Dee and the Severn, for the transportation of limestone, slate, coal and wool. There's no more romantic way of getting to know the vale of Llangollen than wandering along the towpath, or drifting along the canal in a houseboat. The little canal museum documents the everyday life of the bargees. Like other gypsies, these 'water gypsies' used to paint their floating homes in bright colours, as they did their cupboards, mugs and plates. The most spectacular section of the Llangollen Canal lies east of the town – the aqueduct of *Pontcysyllte* (colour plate 25). Almost 1,000 feet long, resting on nineteen slender arches, it carries the canal at a dizzy height over the Dee Valley – 'a piece of work that would have done credit to the Romans' (Pückler). This watery road in the sky was constructed by Thomas Telford between 1795 and 1805. His idea of setting a cast-iron channel, more than nine feet wide, on a series of stone pillars was quite new at the time, and is one of the great engineering feats of the age. Walter Scott regarded it as the finest work of art that he had ever seen. A trip across Pontcysyllte Aqueduct is to canal-lovers what a flight in a hot air balloon is to aviators. At about the same time, just a few miles further south, Telford also designed the *Chirk Aqueduct* (1796–1801), which carries the Shropshire Union Canal on ten stone arches high over the Afon Ceiriog (plate 81). The geometrical rhythm of the arches, the very essence of the aqueduct, were captured in a watercolour by John Sell Cotman (1806–07) which bears striking testimony to the fascination that such pioneering works of the Industrial Revolution exercised on the romantic artists of the day. After 1848, Telford's aqueduct was overshadowed by a Great Western Railway viaduct, which potently symbolized the manner in which the railways supplanted canals as a mode of transportation. But even the well-loved Great Western Railway, whose colours of cream and chocolate still adorn Llangollen Station (1862), has long since had to close many of its old lines (though one of its most romantic stretches, through the Dee Valley to Corwen, is being restored by railway fans, complete with steam engines).

North of Llangollen in one of the side valleys before the mountainous wilderness of *Horseshoe Pass* begins, the Cistercians built a monastery in 1201: *Valle Crucis*, the very last abbey that they were to construct in Wales. It was the perfect example of architecture in seclusion. Today it is right next door to a camp site. Dozens of caravans have totally ruined the ruins. Let us therefore hasten back to Llangollen, and its ladies.

The Ladies of Llangollen

Some people thought they were scandal-mongering bluestockings, and others regarded them as two eccentric, lesbian society ladies of the provinces. They were daughters of Rousseau and the romantics, a mixture of George Sand and Barbara Cartland – two strange, clever and emancipated women. The great figures of their day came and had tea with them, from Wordsworth to the Duke of Wellington. Pückler, an Anglophile and a

The Ladies of Llangollen, 1828

philanderer, respectfully called them 'the most famous virgins in Europe'. They were not particularly beautiful, and they were not even rich, but they lived their lives with so much freedom and love that even their critics admired them. They were Eleanor Butler and Sarah Ponsonby, but they were known to the world simply as 'The Ladies of Llangollen'.

They didn't actually come from Llangollen at all and had never planned to go there.

These two most famous of Welsh ladies in fact came from Ireland. Their story begins with a romantic friendship and a romantic flight. No, they were not seduced by some laughing cavalier, but escaped on horseback, wearing men's clothes – two young ladies from good families with good prospects for good marriages. Drop-outs, in 1778. The first attempt at escape failed, but the second succeeded. With their servant Mary Carryl they came to Wales, which Lady Eleanor described as the most beautiful country in the world, entering this observation in her diary after her first sight of Llangollen. Not that they actually knew much of the world, but they did know the latest publications, such as Thomas Gray's ode 'The Bard' and Gilpin's 'Picturesque Journeys'. Wales in those days, like Ossian's Highlands, was synonymous with elemental Nature, a spiritual landscape of new emotions. It was the great age of European sensibility, and Sarah and Eleanor shared the romantic longings of Goethe's Werther, Richardson's Clarissa, and Rousseau's Héloise. They wanted their lives to be natural and simple, and their friendship to be deep and pure. In their rebellion against the conventions of their families, and in their retreat from society to a cottage in the country, they were following both the spirit of the age and their own personal inclinations. Their period of Storm and Stress came to a peaceful end on the banks of the River Dee. Instead of going on to England, as they had originally intended, they stayed in Llangollen, having discovered, like so many drop-outs even today, that life was cheaper in Wales. They rented a cottage on the edge of town, and called it Plas Newydd, New Court (plate 65).

The odd couple: Sarah Ponsonby, Protestant, the practical partner who looked after the household affairs; Lady Eleanor Butler, Catholic, raised in a French convent, who did most of the talking and took all the decisions; Sarah was the gentler one, and Eleanor the more active and dominant; she was, after all, 16 years older than Sarah. With their short, powdered hair (the Titus look), riding clothes and Directoire top-hats they looked more male than female, more French than Irish/Welsh, and definitely very eccentric. They planted fruit and vegetables for their own use, kept four cows, bred roses in a much-admired garden, and struggled along for years on a tiny allowance, in fact being chronically short of money all their lives. Their daily routine was planned to the minute: up at eight, breakfast at nine, gardening from half past nine, then correspondence, language learning, painting or walking; dinner at three, and then from half past three till nine they would read to each other: Tasso, Petrarch, and especially and repeatedly, Rousseau; after supper they would read again, or play backgammon until one o' clock. 'Heavenly evening. Reading. Writing,' Eleanor wrote in her diary in April 1785. 'A day of such exquisite such enjoyed retirement. So still. So silent.' Was it really so still and silent, though, in their miniature convent? Llangollen in those days lay right on the main road from London to Holyhead, the ferry port to Ireland. A good 30 coaches a day used to stop there. And soon word went around that two unusual ladies were living in Llangollen – strangely sociable recluses, intelligent and somewhat eccentric. The literati and the aristocracy came to have a look: the Duke of Gloucester, the Russian Ambassador, the French educationalist

Madame de Genlis, Sarah Siddons, Edmund Burke, Wedgwood, Walter Scott, Southey, Sheridan – and so the hermitage turned into a salon.

Evidently they could talk about everything with everyone. What, for instance, were Lady Eleanor's interests when she was 67? According to her diary for 1806, she was keen on fossils, ghosts, Egyptology, Russian dances, scandals at the French court, underground passages, Pompeii, and minting money – a bizarre 'Gothic taste' which constantly took her visitors by surprise. The house of the Ladies of Llangollen is itself a perfect illustration of their picturesque fantasy: it is so full (and so dark) with oak carvings that it is like walking through a gigantic display case. 'Oak carving mania' Sarah called it. A wood carving was always the most welcome of presents – 'the regular passport'. And they were proud of their elaborately decorated entrance, the top of which was supported by two early 17th-century bedposts. Wellington contributed a pair of lions. Plas Newydd is a cottage ornamented in Neo-Gothic style, with ogival windows and Sheraton furniture. It was not till Victorian times that the façade was given its Elizabethan timberwork.

For half a century they lived together in this house, with their faithful servant Mary, nicknamed Molly the Boxer, and their two tame crows, a dog named Chance, and Tatters and Mrs Silk, their cats. The Ladies became a Welsh institution. They were visited, just like the waterfalls and the ruined castles, as part of the picturesque journey. If they had just been blue stockings or suffragettes, or gossip-mongers spreading their tales between England and Ireland, or mere 'name droppers and name collectors' as De Quincey rather viciously dubbed them after his visit, their fame would surely have died with them. No, there was more to them than that. Here were two women living together quite openly and harmoniously, which for Puritan minds was, and often still is, slightly shocking. They were surrounded by an aura of poetry with just a hint of perversion. This was a female community without any feminist ideology, a combination of country life and lesbianism – an irresistible mixture, and an endless source of tittle-tattle. On 2 December 1785, Eleanor wrote in her diary: 'My Sally, My Tender, My Sweet Love lay beside me holding and supporting My Head till one o' clock.' Her biographer Elizabeth Mavor believes that this refers to a migraine rather than to the pleasures of lesbianism. Eleanor Butler and Sarah Ponsonby shared their large, four-poster bed just as naturally as they shared everything else. In all the books, the front page bears the initials E.B. and the back page S.P. They signed all their letters together, thousands of them, with gold borders and delicate handwriting. Even when they were old, they learned Italian and Spanish together. 'Sisters in love, a love allowed to climb / Ev'n on this earth, above the reach of time,' wrote William Wordsworth in 1824, in the garden of Plas Newydd, where he took tea with the two old ladies on the banks of the Dee in the Vale of Friendship.

When Lady Eleanor died in 1829 at the age of 90, all the shops in Llangollen closed. 'My Sally, My Sweet Love' followed her two years later into the cold earth of St Collen. Even in their own lifetimes, just like Nelson, the two ladies were famous enough for souvenirs of them to be made in Llangollen. A china service made in Swansea shows them both on horseback. A retired general made their house into a museum back in 1876. The little road that leads to it is called Butler Hill, and a pub in Llangollen bears the name Ponsonby Arms. In the garden of Plas Newydd, the yew hedges lean on supports for all the world like fossilized visitors from a bygone age. In 'The Second Sex', Simone de Beauvoir wrote: 'The union of Sarah Ponsonby with her beloved lasted untroubled for some 50 years. They had apparently learned how to create for themselves a peaceful Eden on the edge of the world.'

To Corwen and John Cowper Powys

A man crosses the Berwyn Mountains. He is tall, gaunt, almost archaic-looking, with his silver hair and hawklike nose. It is autumn, and the moors are glowing. A light mist hangs over the hills. The man is in no hurry, is quite familiar with his route, lets his hand trail through the wet ferns, stops occasionally to touch the moss, lift up a stone, or stroke a rock. He is seeking solitude, but the solitude is densely peopled. There are so many voices

Augustus John:
John Cowper Powys, 1957

– the voices of the stones, the grass, the insects, the birds, voices from below the earth, from the water, the clouds, the distant planets, from history and from worlds beyond time. Everything speaks to him. From the beginning the voices have been speaking to him, though never so clamorously as here on the moors of Berwyn. When the mist lifts, he goes back to Corwen. He spends the rest of the day on his couch, reading, writing, with his hero Porius in the cottage on the hill overlooking the town: Cae Coed No. 7. Have I got it right, Mr Powys?

The newsagent in *Corwen* market still remembers the man in the thick coat who often walked that way. 'He used to love going to the Berwyns, whatever the weather – the old man of the mountains.' My guess is that most people have never heard of John Cowper Powys, any more than they've heard of Corwen. It's a little town on the Dee, nestling between river and mountains, with a lot of fresh air, not too much of a breeze, and a lot of beautiful countryside, though no more than elsewhere in this beautiful region. If Dylan Thomas had lived here, no doubt we would have talked about the pubs and the characters, and perhaps we would have visited a shed with a desk in it. But Corwen is not Laugharne, and Wolf Solent is not Willy-Nilly, and there is no Milk Wood growing in the Berwyns. Dylan Thomas died at the age of 39. Powys did not write his first novel till he was 57. Dylan Thomas was a waterfall, or a firework; Powys was a river with no banks, or lava glowing beneath the ashes. The one was the great entertainer, and the other an esoteric loner. The one was filmed, the other forgotten. His name is not even mentioned in the guide to Corwen. I went to the district office to ask about him. 'Powys? Never heard of him.' And yet this is where he lived after his most important work had been published: 'Wolf Solent' (1929) – described by Hermann Hesse as 'a cumbersome chunk of genius'. For twenty years this author lived in Corwen, where he was visited by Henry Miller: 'He is one of the few persons I shall always revere, whom I shall feel forever indebted to.' Authors as disparate as Elias Canetti, Simone de Beauvoir, and Peter Handke admired his work. Much praised, little read – the most unknown genius of the 20th century. Who was J.C.P.?

The family itself was already a phenomenon. The legendary fecundity of Protestant parsonages reached new heights with the Powys clan. Seven of the eleven children distinguished themselves in the arts. The three brothers, John Cowper, Theodore and Llewelyn alone wrote more than 60 books between them – the most celebrated of English literary families, next to the Brontës, whose father was also a parson. John Cowper was the eldest, born in Derbyshire in 1872. He was a boarder at Sherborne, suffered the usual boarding-school traumas, read history at Cambridge – with moderate success – became a teacher in Sussex, then a kind of literary one-man travelling circus, lecturing especially in America, where he was on the road for years, talking, philosophizing, story-telling; he stayed for a while in New York State. All this can be found in his masterpiece, the 1934 Autobiography, which alas finishes precisely at the point that concerns us most: his move to Wales.

John Cowper Powys was an Englishman who was obsessed with the idea of being Welsh. Not just Welsh, but 'aboriginal' Welsh. And yet for at least 400 years the family had been English. His father, however, did think he was descended from a Cymric king, but such claims could scarcely be taken for gospel, even coming from a parson. For his eldest son, Wales meant a great deal more than a tenuous link with ancient royalty: it was a symbol of the poetic life, of untamed thought, of prehistoric origins, a mythical home, ultima Thule: 'I have Wales, Wales, *Wales*, to take refuge in.' It was a battle cry, an invocation, a vortex. All spiritual roads led to Wales. Simultaneously it was Powys's obsession and his therapy, fiction and reality all bound together in a single creative principle. From his earliest days he dreamed of being Welsh, and of playing the part of a Magician, as he says in his autobiography: 'only the Magician wish lent itself, and that not altogether, to an enjoyment, half-mystical and half-sensual, of this bewildering Universe.' As a student teacher in Sussex he was already struggling to learn Welsh, but he soon gave up. Then all the more passionately he devoted himself to studying Welsh history and Celtic myths, elements of his own individual mythology. 'When the old Druidic spirit, the spirit of Taliesin of the many incarnations took possession of me, I could become inanimate objects, I could feel myself into the lonely identity of a pier-post, of a tree-stump, of a monolith in a stone-circle; and when I did this I *looked* like this post, this stump, this stone.' And so like a reincarnated Merlin, he left the New World and came to Wales, more Welsh than any Welshman. A mythical homecoming.

For years, Powys had been corresponding from America with the writer James Hanley, who had sent him many photos of his village near Corwen: 'It was the sight of Welsh hedges that had finally got him.' With his lifelong American companion Phyllis Playter, he moved at last to Corwen in 1935, into the Vale of Edeyrnion. In the same year, by a neat coincidence, his book 'The Art of Happiness' appeared, extolling the power of the imagination, intensity of emotion, and the transfiguration of sensory experience. From his cottage on the slopes of the Berwyns, he could look down over the Dee Valley, and northwards to Caer Drewyn, a prehistoric hill fort. On a lintel in the parish church, he discovered a carved sword: 'Glyndwr's Sword', and the local name for the hill of Pen-y-Pigyn is 'Glyndwr's Seat' – another reminder that the great rebel had his headquarters here in Corwen for a while. 'I live within Owen Glendower's patrimony,' Powys observed with pleasure, and proceeded to write his novel 'Owen Glendower' (see page 287). Everything around him was permeated with history and myth, and voices came from everywhere: 'Bards and Gods and Demons and Druids have all left indelible impressions on the landscape of my new home,' he wrote, and it was as if he were now reliving the ancient tales of the 'Mabinogion'. 'Here in Corwen I am constantly aware of the presence of creatures as pre-historic as the rocks and streams.' This fiction was as real to him as reality, and from it he developed a whole philosophy of Welshness – his own and that of his chosen people. 'We Aboriginal Welsh People are the proudest people in the world. We are also the humblest.' This 'proud humility' is their trademark, as is their 'harmless, patient, unfathomable, evasive soul'. The evasiveness was another keynote – part of his own singular and complex psyche, his strategic flight (into himself, and to

Corwen), his Protean love of change, but also part of that special Welshness which always eluded him and therefore fascinated him all the more. He was 'obstinately Welsh', and that was what he called the book that grew out of this elective affinity: 'Obstinate Cymric' (1947) – essays that are full of dazzling insights and strange theses. Brazenly he linked Celtic nationalism to vague Communist and internationalist ideas. Politics and social problems were not of any real interest to him. He was, rather, a kind of historical masochist, for 'characteristically he delighted in identifying himself with a conquered race', as his biographer H. P. Collins explained. This was part of his 'race-illusion'. At an Eisteddfod in Corwen[1] the 'Old Earth-Man' was crowned bard, as if one last piece of evidence were needed to prove that he really was a Welshman.

'Old John-Cow-Pow', as he liked to sign his letters, was still writing into his ninetieth year: 'Porius' – a novel set in medieval Wales, much influenced by the atmosphere of the Berwyns – and fantasies and tales of dark obsessions. His later writing is full of weaknesses, signs perhaps of senility – and yet, what a feat. He was a chain smoker, and because of stomach ulcers lived for decades on a strict diet: milk and bread, oranges, and four raw eggs a day. Every day he would read a few pages from 'The Iliad', and wander out to the Dee and into the Berwyns. There he felt closer to the 'whole fluctuating mystery of the obscure relation between man and nature', and there he 'learned secrets of humility . . . simply by walking over these moorlands.' But eventually Corwen became too 'noisy and popular' for him, and so in 1955 he moved again, to the slate-quarrying town of Blaenau Ffestiniog. One condition was essential in his new cottage: 'I *must* have a flushing lavatory.' Eight years later, he was dead: the last bard, a great story-teller, a magician, a jester, a sage; a man who had collected neuroses assiduously and then learned triumphantly to live with them and in them and through them.

One of J. C. Powys's favourite walks was to a little church south-west of Corwen (plate 49). It stands in the fields above the River Dee, sleepily nestling in the grass amongst the graves, scarcely visible from the road – as isolated as if it had been long since forgotten by its people and even by God Himself. This church without a village is called *Llangar Church*, or in full Llangarw-gwyn, Church of the White Stag. It is dedicated to All Saints, and was erected in the 14th century on the very spot where legend tells that a white stag appeared to the faithful. It is a simple building with a single nave and a roof turret; the interior contains the remains of some rather stilted wall paintings: opposite the entrance is the figure of Death, ochre coloured, with pick and shovel, hourglass and arrow, oversized for such a tiny space. In a window bay, the fragile skeleton of a bat. Gravestones are all round the church, crumbling, broken, half sunk into the earth. The stones follow the dead. Many of the tombs have flat slabs over them, 'so that the children can play on 'em,' says an old man. You can even picnic on these dead men's tables. A scythe nearby flashes in the sun.

---

1   The first Eisteddfod of 'modern' times to admit a large audience took place in May 1789, in the Owain Glyndwr Hotel in Corwen.

Chirk Castle: When Decoration was not a Crime

'There's night and day, brother, both sweet things; sun, moon, and stars, brother, all sweet things; there's likewise the wind on the heath. Life is very sweet, brother; who would wish to die'? These sentences come from George Borrow's autobiographical novel 'Lavengro'. 'Wild Wales', was not his only book, nor was writing his only occupation; he was an amateur philologist and a Victorian adventurer, he sold bibles in Spain, was a friend of the gypsies, and could speak their language as well as forty others. As a 16-year-old sales assistant in Norwich he learned Welsh. In summer 1854, when he was 51 years old, he travelled through Wales. 'Travelled' makes it sound too comfortable. He wandered through Wales. On some days, he covered 30 miles. South of Llangollen, where the River Ceiriog comes shining down from the slopes of the Berwyns, in the village of *Glyn-Ceiriog* there is a monument to George Borrow, who loved this valley.

'My cry is for my city': thus sang the creator of the hymn 'Jerusalem', the Methodist hit of the 19th century – and he, too, has a monument in this quarry village: John Hughes, farmer, poet, station-master, named Ceiriog after the vale where in 1832 he first came into the world. And since God-fearing people are usually loyal subjects as well, the nation owes to Ceiriog the very secular hymn 'God Bless the Prince of Wales'.

Up on a broad ridge overlooking the Vale of Ceiriog lies *Chirk Castle*. Lady Myddelton's stud horses graze peacefully in the meadows, and sheep lie at their ease in the great park. When George Borrow once stood admiring the old oak trees, his ever practical servant John remarked: 'They would make fine chests for the dead, sir.' With its thick round towers, this borderland castle crouches down as if to offer as small a target as possible to any attackers. In the gardens one can still see remains of Offa's Dyke, and in the distance are the shimmering plains of Shropshire. Until the defeat of Llewelyn the Last, this was a Welsh stronghold – Castell-y-Waun, the Castle in the Meadows. Edward I turned it into a powerful Norman frontier fort, though it was not completed until 1310. The groundplan is rectangular, built round a large inner courtyard. For a while Chirk Castle belonged to Robert Dudley, Elizabeth I's favourite, and then in 1595 it was acquired by a merchant adventurer and banker, Sir Thomas Myddelton, who later became Lord Mayor of London. It was he who introduced the wolf into the family crest. Next to the Wynns of Wynnstay,[1] the Myddeltons were for centuries the richest and most influential family in the borderlands. The castle remained in their possession until 1978, when inflation, taxes, and the astronomical cost of maintenance forced them to sell it for £192,500. It was acquired and restored by the State, but is administered by the National Trust, and the Myddeltons still have a residence of their own in the east wing, which was rebuilt by Pugin in Neo-Gothic style in 1845–47.

---

1 The country house of Wynnstay, near Ruabon, is now a school, and it has a landscaped garden by Capability Brown (1777). In Ruabon parish church are the tombs of the Wynn family by the Neo-Classical sculptors Nollekens and Rysbrack.

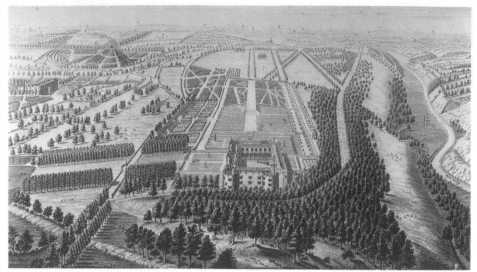

Badeslade: Chirk Castle, 1735

The exterior is that of a medieval fortress, but inside there is all the elegance of the cultured court: staircase and salons in the style of Robert Adam (1762–73), with delicate stucco decor and Chippendale mirrors, state rooms with magnificent coffered ceilings, Mortlake tapestries with scenes from Ovid's 'Metamorphoses' (1672), family portraits by the Scot Allan Ramsay and the Swede Michael Dahl, while the southern wing still has the timbered walls of Tudor times and the four-poster bed in which Charles I slept. Charles II presented the family with a superb ebony cabinet, inlaid with ivory and mother-of-pearl, and also decorated with biblical scenes which are probably the work of a Flemish craftsman. It stands in the Long Gallery of 1678, which is oak-panelled, 100 feet long, 33 feet wide, temperate in its decor, perfect in its proportions (plate 76). In front of the east wing stand rows of hedges cut into figures, looking like enchanted guardsmen. The regimentation of the garden was matched by that of the domestic staff: 'No noise no strife nor swear at all / But all be decent in the hall' is the motto written over the mantelpiece in the servants' quarters. Bad behaviour was punished by deprivation of beer: first offence, one day; second offence, three days; and a third offence meant a summons before the master. Between 1911 and 1946 Chirk Castle was rented by Lord Howard de Walden, who devoted it to the arts, supporting or entertaining, among others, Kipling, Chesterton, Thomas Beecham and Eric Gill; he commissioned the latter to design the war memorial in *Chirk*, had Welsh translations made of Hofmannsthal and Ibsen, and used to go hunting with bow and arrow in the company of Augustus John. The latter one day confronted his host – who loved the Middle Ages – wearing a complete suit of armour. One can just

*Chirk Castle: ornaments on the park gates,
by the Davies Brothers, 1711–21*

imagine the effect, particularly as his Lordship was sitting in the salon at the time, reading the morning paper.

One of Chirk Castle's treasures is to be found in the gardens: wrought-iron gates, as fine as filigree, with acanthus leaves and flowering branches, eagles' heads, spirals, urns, gilded masks, the whole thing crowned with oak leaves and singing birds, and in the middle the Myddeltons' coat of arms with the symbol of their baronetcy, the blood-red hand of Ulster. Hence the many Hand hotels in the region. This magnificent gate (1711–21) was originally in the forecourt of the castle, and is the work of Robert Davies, the greatest Welsh metal-worker of the 18th century (plates 88, 91). Unjustly he has always been overshadowed by his English contemporary Robert Bakewell of Derby. Together with his brother John, Robert Davies worked in their father's smithy Croes Foel near Bersham, an early centre of the iron industry south of Wrexham. Most of their commissions came from land-owners and parsons in the north-east of Wales and beyond the border, especially in Cheshire and Shropshire. My enthusiasm aroused by Chirk Gate, I at once went on to the splendid gates at *Leeswood Hall* (plate 89) near Mold. The Black Gates and the White Gates (1726) – representing hell and heaven – accurately reflect the wealth and taste of the lead-mine owner Sir George Wynne, whose lifestyle was described by Dr Johnson's Welsh friend Hester Lynch Thrale as 'madly magnificent'. The White Gates are 100 feet long, their bars rigidly vertical, echoing the Perpendicular Style, and wrapped in arabesques: function and ornament all in one. The park gates of Chirk and Leeswood and the Golden Gates of *Eaton Hall* near Chester, seat of the Duke of Westminster, are highlights of

315

baroque metal-work.[1] Robert Davies's model, and perhaps even his teacher, was the Frenchman Jean Tijou, a Huguenot who fled to London, and whose principal works include the gates at Hampton Court and Cholmondeley Hall (1695). The arrival of Capability Brown and cast iron put paid to the art of the Davies Brothers, for in the new landscaped gardens there were to be no more fences or gates to obstruct the view, and as for the new technology of cast iron, it had other functions to perform.

But I wanted to see at least one of the Davieses' church gates, and so to find the most elegant of them all, I went to *Wrexham*, the heart of the North Wales coal-mining region. Behind a wrought-iron cemetery gate of 1720 lies a church which thoroughly deserves its magnificent entrance: St Giles (1472–1520). Its western tower, almost 150 feet high, is like a cathedral, with its pinnacles and figured façade, and it was always regarded as one of the 'Seven Wonders of Wales': 'Pistyll Rhaeadr and Wrexham steeple, / Snowdon's mountain without its people, / Overton yew trees, St Winifred's Wells, / Llangollen bridge and Gresford Bells.' Thus sang the people of the 18th century, significantly locating all seven 'Wonders' in the North, from the waterfall in the Berwyns to the 21 old yews in *Overton* cemetery. But let us return to Wrexham. In St Giles' churchyard lies the body of Elihu Yale, who gave his name and his patronage to Yale University in Connecticut, on the campus of which there is a replica of Wrexham's church steeple (1920's). He was born in America in 1648, the son of a Welsh émigré, was brought up in England, and rose to be governor of the East India Company in Madras; he became immensely rich – not altogether legitimately – retired, returned to London, and turned to philanthropy partly from conviction and partly because of his bad conscience. His last years brought him a country estate in Wales, a grave in Wrexham, and an epitaph that sums it all up:

> Born in America, in Europe bred,
> In Africa travell'd, and in Asia wed,
> Where long he liv'd and thriv'd, in London dead,
> Much good, some ill he did, so hope all's even,
> And that his soul thro' mercy's gone to Heaven . . .

Erddig Park: The Manor House of Servants

It's unusual for a visitor to have to enter a manor house through the servants' entrance, but in *Erddig Park* that is the way things are done (plate 90). Like one of a long line of servants, you go in through the back door, past the joiner's, the blacksmith's and the butcher's, across the courtyard – where the dungheap used to be – past coach-house and stables, laundry and bakery, into the kitchen and from there, last of all, into the drawing-rooms of those who

---

1 The most important works (partly undocumented) of the Davies brothers include the park gates in Erddig, near Wrexham, Newnham Paddox (Warwickshire), and Aldenham Park, near Bridgnorth (Shropshire), as well as church gates in Wrexham (also rood screens), Ruthin and Oswestry.

lived upstairs in Erddig. *How* they lived is already clear from the route we have taken. All this work and all this staff was necessary to keep such a place going: cook and kitchen-maid, laundress and seamstress, gardener, handiman, housekeeper and steward, coachman and stable lad, gamekeeper, forest warden and shepherd, nurse, nanny and governess, butler and footmen. And yet Erddig Park, with just 50 rooms, was not even one of the larger or more glamorous manor houses in the land. Built in 1684 for the High Sheriff of Denbighshire, who shortly afterwards went bankrupt (one of his most hard-hearted creditors was his neighbour Elihu Yale), Erddig Park came into the possession of John Meller, an early Georgian playboy, who set about establishing a London way of life behind the simple Palladian façade. Mr Meller, a lifelong bachelor, had some 30 servants. One of his coachboys was black, which was not unusual at the time. What was unusual, however, was the fact that his master had a portrait made of him, complete with horn and splendid uniform. Sixty years later, the owners added a dedication to this painting, which is still hanging in the servants' quarters: 'Of the conditions of this Negre, / Our information is but me'gre, / However here, he was a dweller, / And blew the horn for Master Meller.'

The history of these country houses is usually that of their architecture and their families. The servants' wing is normally the first to be demolished, and their furniture the first to be sold off when the time comes for economies. Manor houses always had servants, but the servants never had a history. They came and went, though some never went, spending all their lives in the same house, and yet they remained anonymous, less well known even than their master's furniture, which they polished and which we now admire. In the endless portrait galleries of all these manor houses, how often have you seen the portrait of a servant? Well yes, in hunting pictures or group portraits you may see one holding his master's horse, or opening the carriage door, or doing what servants are supposed to do – namely, staying in the background, in pictures as in life. It was not even unusual for the Great Ones to have their horses or their dogs portrayed – by top artists at that. But servants? Never. Except in Erddig Park. Here they not only step out of the background, they even take up the whole picture, and are presented as people with faces, names, and histories. Thomas Rogers, for example, pictured in 1830 at his workbench; he started out in Erddig as a lad looking after the pigs, rose to be carpenter, and served the family for 73 years until at the age of 90 he finally retired, and died four years later. Or there is the maid Ruth Jones, 71 years in service: 'She from our treasures swept the dust, / And kept them from the moth and rust.'

Erddig Park was the first stately home to direct public attention to its servants. Credit for this must go, not to the Labour Party, but to the National Trust and in particular their Merlin Waterson. It was they who, over a four-year period, restored the house, out-buildings and magnificent garden, thereby rescuing a piece of social history from oblivion – an exemplary achievement by any standards. But none of this would have been possible without the Yorkes, who lived in Erddig from the 18th century onwards. They com-missioned more portraits of their servants than of their own family, and they also wrote reports and poems about them, recording their deeds in letters and diaries over generations. The staff never had a separate wing of their own – they lived with the Yorkes under the same roof. Even if a servant misbehaved and had to be sacked, nevertheless his portrait remained in place. Erddig is the House of Servants. And perhaps if it weren't for the servants, we would not take any notice of the masters, for the Yorkes were land-owners, but not aristocrats, reasonably wealthy, but quite happy simply to look after their estate and preserve it for their heirs; a family without ambition, without any great statesmen, soldiers, artists. What they were good at was writing occasional poems. For instance, Philip Yorke wrote a 48-verse eulogy of a maid named Sarah Davies (known as 'Lalla'). And his son, also Philip – all the male Yorkes were called either Philip or Simon – wrote the epitaph for his former nurse Lucy Jones, who had served the family for 40 years.

The tradition of staff portraits in Erddig began with the Philip Yorke who in 1780 had himself painted by Gainsborough for 31 pounds and 10 shillings, in a three-quarter length portrait. He was an MP, armorist and, according to his neighbour Nimrod, the famous huntsman-author, the worst horseman ever to sit in a saddle. He himself said that he had never taken part in a foxhunt or even shot a hare. This lovable man decided to have portraits made of his servants, though not, it must be admitted, by Gainsborough, but by an all-round artist from Denbigh named John Walters. He painted them without fuss or frills: William the smith, Jack the game-warden, Edward Prince the jointer, axe on shoulder, full-length and all carrying the tools of their trade. These are simply, honest pictures, not meant as universal showpieces, but full of respect for the individuality of their subjects. The portrait gallery of servants was not intended either to display their uniforms, as is evident from the verse accompanying a daguerrotype of the coachman Edward Humphreys (1852): 'No outward ornament was he / To Equipage or Livery.' Jane Ebbrell sits eternally there, old and worn, 'spider-brusher to the master', painted in 1793 after 70 years as a maid in Erddig: 'And by the virtues of her mop / To all uncleanness, put a stop.'

Portraits and verses – these certainly put the servants of Erddig a step ahead of their peers. But were they better off in any other ways? Better accommodation, perhaps, or better wages? They may have been well painted, but they were miserably remunerated. Their wages, especially those of the women, lay below the average pay in other stately homes. Even in 1910, a maidservant in Erddig received a yearly salary of just £12. On the other hand, when it came to pensions and medical care, the Yorkes were generous. And the rooms they gave their servants were thoroughly adequate, and certainly better than the dark, damp cellars that staff usually had to put up with in the manor houses of the day – those ideal breeding-grounds for tuberculosis. What, then, did the Yorkes expect from their maids in return for £12 a year? What, for instance, did Bessie Gittins do on a day in 1910? Well, in the morning, just after six o'clock, she had to make tea for the older servants, for she was the youngest. At half-past six they would all meet in the servants' room to sort out the post. Before breakfast at eight, all the shutters had to be opened, the 40 oil lamps collected and filled, the fireplaces cleaned and prepared for new fires. The rest of the morning, apart from a tea-break at eleven, was spent cleaning and tidying. After lunch, at twelve, there was sewing, darning and patching. There was always something to do. Tea was at four, and then it was time to start preparing the dinner. 'Waste Not – Want Not' Bessie Gittins would see written on the vaulted arch in the kitchen. And while the family dined, she would get their beds ready, and fill the hot water bottles and light the oil lamps. The staff ate at nine. And if, between ten and eleven o' clock, Bessie did not crawl into her bed below the rafters, she might perhaps have played a round of whist with Alice from the laundry and John Jones, the smart footman, in the servants' room under the servants' gallery.

Upstairs, Downstairs ... but the servants' portraits in Erddig are in no way meant to embody a class division, or even to hint at one. After all, did not the maid Matilda Boulter, known as Tillie, sometimes play duets with the master, she on the violin and he on the cello? What the National Trust shows in Erddig as a perhaps almost too harmonious unity between family and staff would certainly have been unusual to say the least in the stately homes of the 18th and 19th centuries. The Upstairs, Downstairs hierarchy was pretty inflexible. All the same, we must not delude ourselves entirely: these portraits still represent a degree of Upstairs authority. This artistic tribute to old servants was a subtle way of instructing the new ones: Look, said the portraits, you must be as loyal and true as we have been, and then you and everyone else will be happy in Erddig.

The invention of the camera brought a few changes to this Welsh household. At least once, every generation of Yorkes would collect their staff on the front steps or before the sun-dial to have a group photograph taken. Several would still be there after 50 years. And so a record was kept of continuity and of community. When in 1824, Simon Yorke came of age, the party guests all had their photo taken, and then so did the servants. But don't be misled by the vast number of the latter: most of them had been employed just for this one occasion. This was no longer the age of the large domestic staff – and alas it was not only the social structure that changed. Erddig itself began to crumble, and threatened to collapse. The coalmines of nearby Bersham Colliery, which since the 18th century had provided the Yorkes with much of their income, had sunk their shafts right under the house. The last of the Yorkes – another Philip, who incidentally was a vegetarian – could not raise the funds to save the family home, and in 1973 he gave it to the National Trust. And so now Erddig belongs entirely to its servants.

The Prime Minister's Axes: Gladstone in Hawarden

When Queen Victoria first summoned him to be Prime Minister in 1868, Gladstone was busy felling trees in *Hawarden*. 'My mission is to pacify Ireland,' he said, on receiving the dispatch, and at once resumed work. This, at any rate, is how the story goes, and this is how the natives think of him, the Grand Old Man of Victorian times.

There is nothing Welsh about this village outside the gates of Chester. Hawarden might just as well be part of England, and on and off during the border wars, it was. You can see this from the ruined Norman castle in the park. Anglo-Welsh weddings added another dimension. In 1839, Catherine Glynne, heiress to Hawarden Castle, said 'I do' in the village church to a merchant's son from Liverpool. His name was William Ewart Gladstone. At 23 he took his seat in the House of Commons, became Prime Minister four times, and a father twice as often. All eight children grew up in Hawarden Castle, and today his grandson Sir Ewart William lives there. The house itself (1752) is private, but in 1874, after his first period of office, the Prime Minister opened the gardens to the public, and they flocked there in their thousands to see 'People's William' felling trees and to take a shaving with them as a souvenir. How can a politician achieve such popularity? As Chancellor of the Exchequer, Gladstone had lowered taxes – always a popular move. But people liked him for much deeper reasons. He fought ceaselessly for the political and social rights of the under-priviledged, among whom he included the working-classes and the Irish. Home Rule for Ireland was a goal that eluded him right to the end, but he did succeed in bringing about parliamentary reform, extending suffrage to agricultural workers and to miners. The Welsh were especially fond of Gladstone: he had a Welsh wife, he was a Liberal, and in 1873 he attended the National Eisteddfod in Mold – though here, unfortunately, he committed a dreadful faux pas: he called the Welsh language 'a venerable relic of the past', for which Gwynfor Evans has never forgiven him. Some took more offence at a law that his cabinet put through in 1881, banning Sunday drinking in Welsh pubs. This 'Sunday Closing Act' caused much tearing of Welsh hair, but it also made constitutional history, for it was the first legislative sign of Welsh independence. And indeed it was thanks to Gladstone and the Liberals that Wales finally obtained its own University, National Library and National Museum.

Hawarden was Gladstone's 'Temple of Peace'. He always came back here from the tumult of Westminster, recharged the batteries, and set forth again refreshed and reinvigorated. Here he wrote his letters and his speeches, translated classical authors, and welcomed eminent Victorians such as Ruskin and Tennyson. Here he was pater familias, country gentleman, and happy. Nowhere happier than in Hawarden Castle, he lived here for nearly fifty years. Every day before breakfast, he and his wife went to church. The Bible was his guiding light. In an age when faith in the superiority of the British nation was akin to the dogma of papal infallibility, and when Victorian imperialism was celebrating bloody triumphs in the colonies, Gladstone continued to act (and ultimately failed) as a Christian statesman. He was one of the very few such statesmen in history. His policies were moulded according to ethical principles and not national interests, and this was borne home to me in Hawarden, when I saw his library and his church. In the year of his final retirement, 1894, the G.O.M. presented his people with a gift of national importance: St Deiniol's Library. He started it up, financed it, and provided 30,000 books from his own private collection, particularly from the spheres of theology and history, and today this

80 MONTGOMERY CANAL Exploring industrial archaeology ▷

81 CHIRK   Telford's aqueduct (1796–1801) with railway viaduct (1846–48)

82 SHROPSHIRE UNION CANAL   Near Chirk

83   FAIRBOURNE RAILWAY 'Great Little Train' at the mouth of the Mawddach

84   TALYLLYN RAILWAY Polished narrow-gauge veteran

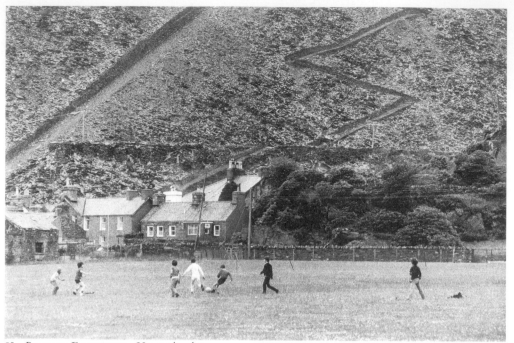

85 Blaenau Ffestiniog   Houses by slate quarry

86 Abergynolwyn   Slate fencing   87 Blaenau Ffestiniog   Town in the slate mountains ▷

89 LEESWOOD HALL   The White Gates, by John and Robert Davies 1726
◁ 88 CHIRK CASTLE   Wrought-iron gates by the Davies brothers 1711–21
90 ERDDIG HALL   Park Gates by John and Robert Davies 1721

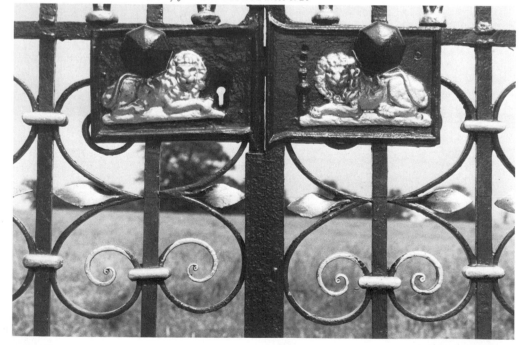

92 LLANDUDNO   Victorian hotel
◁ 91 CHIRK CASTLE   1711–21
93 LLANYSTUMDWY   Where Lloyd George grew up

94   MONTGOMERY   Broad Street with Town Hall, 1748

95   NARBERTH   Ronald Edwards cutting his hedge

96 Llanberis Pass

97 Dolbadarn Castle   Llywelyn the Great's fortress on Llyn Peris, 13th century

98   Llyn Brianne Reservoir

99   Criccieth   Lloyd George's home in Cardigan Bay

100   Betws-y-Coed   Pedestrian suspension bridge over Conwy, 1930

101   Llanrwst   Conwy Bridge, 1636

102 BARMOUTH   Railway bridge over Mawddach, 1867

103 CRICKHOWELL   Bridge over Usk, 17th century

104 LLANGURIG   Spectators at Sheepdog Trials ▷

library and its 120,000 books is a true reflection of the spirit of a great Victorian and the time he lived in. For anyone wanting to study Gladstone's century (as well as the legacy of letters, speeches and writings, some of which have never been published), St Deiniol's Library in Hawarden is as rich a source as the British Library in London. You will also find his spare beds and a most unusual collection for any library: two dozen axes, with which Gladstone used to do his sparetime chopping.

The Squire of Hawarden died when he was nearly 90. The nation gave him a tomb in Westminster Abbey, while the family honoured him in the village church with a magnificent Pre-Raphaelite stained-glass window by Edward Burne-Jones, an Adoration of the Kings. This was the artist's last completed work, for he died in the same year as Gladstone, 1898. Not only this western window, with its dark, glowing blues and greens and two smaller flanking windows of allegorical figures, but also the eastern window, a Crucifixion, and a side window in the choir are by Burne-Jones, and were made by the firm of William Morris & Co (1907–08); they were all donated by members of the Gladstone family and are another of those glorious Victorian surprises to be found in a Welsh village church. Equally in the spirit of the age is the marble monument by Sir William Richmond (1906), one of Gladstone's portrait painters. It shows the statesman and his wife lying next to each other in the boat of life, with the four patron saints of Britain in the niches of the sarcophagus, together with the figures who had most influenced Gladstone: David, Homer, Aristotle and Dante, each illustrated in the bronze reliefs too. There is also a monumental statue of Gladstone in front of the library (by John Hughes, 1925), which seems quite out of keeping in the village setting. It was originally intended for Dublin, but the city fathers rejected it. Shortly after the civil war, Irish Republicans had no place for an English statesman.

Why it's Bad Luck to be Welsh: Wilson in Mold

The attention and devotion afforded to the English Gladstone in Wales was something never enjoyed by the Welsh Richard Wilson in his own country. All that you'll find in the little market-town of *Mold* is his grave and a rather inferior memorial window in the church. There *is* a memorial in Mold to Daniel Owen, a local master tailor who wrote novels that not even every Welshman can read (only those with a good knowledge of Welsh). But Richard Wilson, whose paintings can be enjoyed by anyone regardless of language or nationality in the museums of Cardiff and London, Melbourne and Munich, is rewarded by his nation – whose greatest painter he undoubtedly was – by the backward version of Dylan Thomas's Llareggub. The Welsh, you see, are a literary nation, and a musical nation, but not a visual nation. Poets, choirmasters, coal barons and rugby players all have their monuments in Wales, but a painter? No, Richard Wilson had the bad luck to be Welsh.

We do not even know the exact date of his birth: 1713 or 1714 is the nearest we can get. His father was a parson in *Penegoes* near Machynlleth – a few houses, church and parsonage long since rebuilt, and a childhood spent on the remote green fringes of Snowdonia. At an early

Anton Raphael Mengs:
Richard Wilson, 1752

age he was already learning to take in the light of this pure mountain scenery, this special atmosphere that permeates all his pictures. In order to study painting, which at the time meant above all portrait painting, he went to London in 1729. But the turning point came when he went to Italy in 1750: there he truly discovered landscape, Antiquity, and the grandeur of Claude. It was in Rome that Richard Wilson found his own style and his circle of buyers – English gentlemen making the Grand Tour; he painted the classic elements of that tour, souvenirs of the very finest quality: landscapes to satisfy the eternal Latin longings of lords sitting in cold English houses. Even after he returned to London, Wilson was still able to live off these southern motifs seven years on. In 1744 he had already painted Caernarfon Castle, topographically vague, a ruin, a moral and melancholy comment on transience and the passing away of power. This is Wilson's first Welsh study, as far as we know, and it is at the same time an early example of the romance of ruins, the style of the picturesque. After his Italian intermezzo, Wilson now focuses again on the mountains of his childhood. But which mountains are they? The Cambrian wilderness or the gentle hills of the Campagna? With his painting 'The Lake of Nemi or Speculum Dianae with Dolbadarn

Castle' (c.1764) Wilson shows that art can move mountains. What we see is not the Italian Lake of Nemi but Llyn Peris with Snowdon in the background – Ovid's nymphs before a ruined Welsh castle, and Wales as Arcadia. Wilson depicts his homeland in the best, the Italian light, no longer England's barbaric hinterland, but a classic realm, civilized by artistic composition, framed with Claude's trees, and with an historical and literary aura all its own. It is no coincidence that Thomas Gray had published 'The Bard' shortly before, a Welsh subject in the form of a Pindaric Ode. Even Wilson's most famous Welsh paintings, 'Snowdon from Llyn Nantlle' and 'Cader Idris, Llyn-y-Cau' (both 1765) transform the wild mountain country into classic harmony and clarity: no storm, no mists, no rough and jagged edges. If the painter had been asked to create a prospectus, he could not have come up with any more attractive pictures than these. Indeed the first tourist has already come on the scene, led safely and comfortably to Cader Idris by pony and guide. There he stands on the bare mountain, a tiny figure like Caspar David Friedrich's monk by the sea, but 50 years earlier; he has a telescope in his hand, for even the immeasurable can be grasped and calculated. This tourist is not frozen in cosmic isolation like his German successor, dwarfed by a sea of mist; no, this man is enjoying the fine view, a true romantic even before the European soul entered into its emotional crisis. But he will not be able to enjoy this undisturbed view of Nature for much longer. At the foot of Cader Idris and Snowdon, groups of hikers and climbers are gathering in order to conquer these picturesque peaks. Once again it is no coincidence that two of Richard Wilson's most important patrons were amongst the first

Richard Wilson: Llyn-y-Cau, Cader Idris, c.1765

dedicated tourists of Wales: Lord Lyttelton and Sir Watkin Williams Wynn (see page 36).

Wilson discovered Wales for the British public, and landscape painting for British art – these were undoubtedly his two major accomplishments. A country long underprized was at last revalued, and an inferior genre was at last liberated from its purely topographical purposes. Wilson achieved this in the classical style of continental painters, which initially aroused Ruskin's hostility ('corrupted by the study of the Poussins') but subsequently his unstinting praise. He credits Richard Wilson with the beginning in England of 'the history of sincere landscape art, founded on a meditative love of Nature'. But what is this contemplative love based on? Wilson's temperament? The character of the landscape? The influence of both is undeniable and inseparable, but there was also something else that was vital: we can never see Nature pure and simple in life, let alone in art. Our own personal experience of it is rooted in our history, culture, society, and in changing moods, conventions and fashions. It is no different with Wilson and his landscapes. What speaks through them is not just the seeing heart or the feeling eye, but also, looking over the artist's shoulder, the person who has commissioned the picture, the patron whose estate is being painted, or the educated public whose approval is to be sought. The hand that makes the picture is guided not only by the landscape itself but also by the social perspective. The contemplation reflects the leisurely life of the so-called landed class, and an idealized harmony that makes the class hierarchy seem as God-given and natural as Creation itself. Nature in Wilson's art bears the signs of a 'pre-stabilized social harmony' (Leibniz) – pastorale without poverty. In the catalogue for the exhibition in London (1982), David H. Solkin offers a penetrating analysis of this 'landscape of reaction': he sees Wilson's Wales as 'a type of gentleman's utopia, as a place for virtuous retirement, where the man of culture can contemplate the lessons of an heroic past', and where land-owners and agricultural workers, rich and poor, can take equal pleasure in the joys of the countryside – which of course is pure fiction if one considers the living conditions of agricultural workers during the 18th century, especially in a Wales that was then so economically backward.

As co-founder of the Royal Academy in London in 1768, Richard Wilson was at the peak of his career. His downfall came swiftly and mysteriously. Suddenly there were no more commissions, and he began to drink; he had to paint on wood taken from old coaches, because in the end he could not even afford to buy canvas. In Italy he found his style, in London he found success and then disillusionment, and to die he returned to Wales. His cousin in *Colomendy Hall* near Mold took him in, and there he lived for a year, indelibly marked by gout and old age, embittered, and forgotten. In 1782 he died. Not until the emergence of Constable and Turner was his true value restored, and it was they who completed what he had begun. Colomendy Hall is now an institute for environmental research. Near it, on the road to Ruthin there stands the Three Loggerheads Inn. Wilson is believed to have painted the inn sign for the price of a few pints. That is a common enough story, but the sign is not quite so common: it consists of two men's heads, with the inscription 'We three Loggerheads'. It is not a mistake. You or I are the third.

'Peace, Wild Wooddove': Holywell, St Asaph

It may be that *Holywell* was once the Welsh equivalent of Lourdes, but that must have been hundreds of years ago. When I visited this little industrial town on the mouth of the Dee, the main attraction was reckoned to be the military museum in the limestone cave, and not the holy spring to which the town owes its name and its fame. The spring has, of course, long since dried up, having been diverted in the 19th century to make way for a mine; what bubbles there now is water straight from a reservoir. This does not bother the faithful, and as for the unbelievers, they have plenty to admire in the architecture and the legend.

An attempted rape, subsequent death, and miraculous resurrection – this is the tale of St Winefred, who lived and died in the 7th century. When this pious virgin repulsed the unwanted attentions of Prince Caradoc, he cut off her head. Her uncle, St Beuno, patron saint of North Wales, rejoined head and body and thus brought her back to life. She then became a nun. But on the spot where her head had fallen, a spring appeared which could perform miracles of healing. The waters of Holywell must however already have had healing powers, since the Romans used to come here to rid themselves of the effects of the climate, rheumatism and gout. But now it became a Christian spa, and along came the crippled and the blind, beggars and kings. Among the VIP's was Henry V, who came here in 1416, after his victory at Agincourt. Around 1490, Margaret Beaufort, mother of Henry VII, built the present pilgrims' chapel, a real gem of a building, in Perpendicular Style with a Gothic fan vault, in the crypt over the spring. One of the figured capitals shows a pilgrim on the back of another, and indeed even today sick people are sometimes carried through the water, just as they were in the Middle Ages. 'The bath is completely and indecently open: a woman bathed while we all looked on,' Dr Johnson observed indignantly in 1774. At least present-day regulations ensure that the sexes bathe separately: 'Men 8–9, Ladies 9–10'. After the Reformation, St Winefred's Well became a focal point of resistance to Protestantism. The Catholic Stuart King James II made a point of visiting Holywell, and it was run by the Jesuits until the 1930's.

On 8 October 1874, a young theology student tested the waters: 'The spring in place leading back the thoughts by its spring in time to its spring in eternity.' Word play, metaphors and metaphysics – it's a typical (though unusually simple) example of the writing of Gerard Manley Hopkins. Here is another, written six years after his visit to Holywell and taken from his unfinished verse tragedy 'St Winefred's Well':

> How to keep – is there any any, is there none such, nowhere
>   known some, bow or brooch or braid or brace,
>   lace, latch or catch or key to keep
> Back beauty, keep it, beauty, beauty, beauty, ... from vanishing
>   away?

Since John Keats, no poet had written so elegiacally, so ecstatically about beauty, and until

Dylan Thomas no poet ever used the English language so 'Welshly'. Hopkins entangles his readers in these cascades of sound, and these Celtic images and rhythms. The latter he called 'sprung rhythm' – a lyrical flood of almost pre-Expressionist Expressionism, verses that spring breathlessly through their cadences of alliteration, assonance and dissonance. They reflect the poet's conviction 'that the poetical language of an age shd. be the current language heightened, to any degree heightened and unlike itself, but not (I mean normally: passing freaks and graces are another thing) an obsolete one'. For me, Holywell was Hopkins, since it was here that I discovered a great poet. It was by no means a matter of chance that he came here, and Wales was by no means a single episode in this English poet's life. It was here that he was ordained, learnt the Celtic tongue, and became familiar with its wealth of rhythms, sounds, and poetry. He came originally from Essex, son of a businessman, and at the age of 22 was converted to Catholicism; in 1874 he entered the Jesuit College of *St Beuno's*, west of Holywell. During one of his very first outings into the hills of Clwyd, overlooking the College, he felt 'an instress and charm of Wales', and he continues, with almost missionary zeal: 'Indeed in coming here I began to feel a desire to do something for the conversion of Wales ...' In St Beuno's he wrote a long religious poem about the wreck of the 'Deutschland' (winter 1875) – 'O Deutschland, double a desperate name!' And he wrote poems in which a precise observation of Nature reflects an almost ecstatic experience of God, for instance 'Hurrahing in Harvest':

> Summer ends now, barbarous in beauty, the stocks rise
>   Around; up above, what wind-walks! what lovely behaviour
>   Of silk-sack clouds! has wilder, wilful-wavier
> Meal-drift moulded ever and melted across skies?

Hopkins wrote to a friend that this sonnet 'was the outcome of half an hour of extreme enthusiasm as I walked home alone one day from fishing in the *Elwy*.' Before he left St Beuno's in 1877, after ordination, to become a parish priest in England, and later Professor of Greek in Dublin, Hopkins wrote once more in praise of Elwy Valley: 'Lovely the woods, waters, meadows, combes, vales, / All the air things wear that build this world of Wales.'

On a hill overlooking the banks of the Elwy stands *St Asaph*, the smallest cathedral city in Britain apart from St David's. The cathedral is only just over 165 feet high – little more, in fact, than a large village church (plate 47). Nevertheless, its importance is beyond question, for this was where the first Welsh translator of the Bible worked, and it was a bastion of the Celtic church in its struggle against Anglo-Roman supremacy. The first Archbishop of Wales, A. G. Edwards, was enthroned in St Asaph in 1920. The church was founded *c*.560 by St Mungo, who as Bishop Kentigern (the patron saint of Glasgow) was driven out of Scotland. He appointed as his successor to the abbotship a monk named Asaph, which means Boy of God. The monastery flourished for centuries, the cathedral grew, was destroyed by the Normans, rebuilt, and then destroyed again. The bulk of what remains today was constructed in the late 14th century, and is very Welsh in its simplicity. Sir George Gilbert Scott generally preserved this style when he restored the cathedral in 1869–75 and reconstructed the choir in Gothic style. It is here that the most important of St Asaph's bishops lies buried: William Morgan. He was the first to translate the complete Bible into Welsh (1588), and we shall meet him again later. For the moment, suffice it to say that his grave is here, and in front of the church stands a monument to him that also commemorates his fellow scholar, the judge William Salusbury, who had translated the New Testament into Welsh in 1567. His plea for the mother tongue is as direct as any by Luther: 'Unless you wish to be worse than animals, insist on getting learning in your own language – and unless you wish to abandon utterly the faith of Christ, insist on getting the Holy Scriptures in your own tongue.' The cathedral museum in the crypt accommodates these early Welsh translations of the Bible and many prayerbooks – strongholds of national consciousness. It also houses a fine example of scholarly eccentricity: the Welsh-Greek-Hebrew dictionary by the self-taught Richard Robert Jones. Dic Aberdaron, as he called himself, was a carpenter's son from *Aberdaron*, on the Llyn Peninsula, a tramp and a linguistic genius. He is buried in the cemetery of the parish church in St Asaph.

From the crossing-tower of the cathedral, one can see far across the *Vale of Clwyd*. It is a green and fertile valley which made Defoe think that he was 'in England again all of a sudden'. Clwyd, which is the same as Clyde, actually means entrance or gate. Since the local government reforms of 1974, this has been the name for the old counties of Denbighshire and Flintshire. For a long time the River Clwyd formed the boundary between England and Wales, until Edward I took control of the valley by building fortresses at Rhuddlan, Denbigh and Ruthin – key positions on the road to the North. Now, after so many hundreds of years of bloody battles, the Vale of Clwyd seems like a haven of peace. As I stood on the tower at St Asaph, I couldn't help thinking of some lines by Hopkins – the beginning of his poem 'Peace':

> When will you ever, Peace, wild wooddove, shy wings shut,
> Your round me roaming end, and under be my boughs?
> When, when, Peace, will you, Peace?

Conwy Castle: How to Conquer Your Neighbour

It was a bright, clear morning in June when I came to *Conwy Bay*. There were gulls waddling through the mud, and sailing boats were gliding through the wide mouth of the river and out to sea. On the shore lay a little town with bright-coloured houses, and nearby, towering massively upwards and presenting to the world the solid stone face of history, stood Conwy Castle (colour plate 43). In front of it flowed the river, and behind it rose the green forested hills – the mountains of Snowdonia. A more picturesque panorama would be hard to imagine. It has been captured by Turner, Cotman, Girtin, and countless millions of cameras, this romantic setting for an historical drama entitled 'Edward I Conquers Wales.'

They came from the east, from Chester. They had taken the Vale of Clwyd, and now they had come to the Conwy – first the soldiers of King John, and then those of his son, Henry III. They had destroyed Deganwy Castle, the old Welsh fortress on the eastern bank of the river, but they had never got beyond the Conwy. It was Henry III's son Edward I who succeeded in building his own fortress on the western, Welsh side of the river. Conwy Castle was built in the amazingly short time of four and a half years: begun in March 1283 and finished in autumn 1287, one of the greatest achievements of military architecture in the Middle Ages. Edward I had brought some 1,500 workers from England and France to create this bridgehead, and they included the best stonemasons of the time. In charge was a Savoyard, James of St George, previously chief architect to the Counts of Savoy. As Master of the King's Works in Wales, this brilliant fortress-builder also designed the castles of Caernarfon and Harlech for Edward, both begun in the same year as Conwy: the three great Welsh castles. As we still have the records of payments made to the workers, we know the names of joiners such as Henry of Oxford and Laurence of Canterbury, and we also know the cost of the castle and the town walls (begun at the same time) – £13,690, the equivalent today of about £11 million. The walls of Conwy Castle are made from the hard Silurian stone of the rock on which it stands, and from brownish yellow rhyolite; the red sandstone around the windows and forming the roof arches comes from Chester. There are eight huge, almost identical drum-towers, four facing north and four south; in order to soften the massive severity of these towers, the battlements are made to taper. It is astonishing to think – and almost inconceivable, since one is now so used to the naked masonry – that originally the whole castle was whitewashed. Conwy Castle was meant to be beautiful as well as functional, not just a garrison but also a royal residence, and a shining symbol of English power and glory. The Great Hall is almost

Samuel & Nathaniel Buck: Conwy Castle, 1742

Conwy Castle, plan
 1 Castle Gate   12 Bakehouse Tower
 2 N-W Tower   13 Prison Tower
 3 Kitchen Tower   14 S-W Tower
 4 Kitchens   15 Great Hall
 5 Stockhouse Tower
 6 Well
 7 Site of Drawbridge
 8 Granary (?)
 9 Chapel Tower
10 State Presence Chamber
11 King's Tower

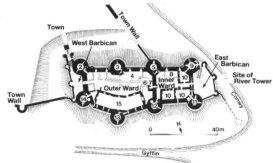

130 feet long, and was once the most magnificent room in the castle. The walls of the Prison Tower are thirteen feet thick – a place from which there was no escape. The King's Tower housed the King's bedrooms, and his state chambers were in the adjacent southern wing of the inner court. This small, eastern court was protected on the one side by the river and on the other by the larger court of the garrison. Here, in the winter of 1294, the Welsh mounted an unsuccessful siege against Edward. And again in 1646, as a royalist castle, it withstood the assault of Cromwell's troops for four months.

Conwy Castle was one of a chain of fortresses that Edward I built along the coast of North Wales – the stone fist clenched round Snowdonia. The castles, from Flint to Aberystwyth, lay on rivers or on the sea, an essential strategy in view of the insecurity of land routes. Flint was the first, begun in 1277, and Beaumaris the last, begun in 1295. There were 17 castles altogether – a huge exercise in military logistics. Yet castles alone would not have sufficed to break Welsh resistance. While the masons were still hammering away in Conwy, Edward I's Statute of Rhuddlan (1284) were already forming the legal basis whereby Wales was to be for ever bound to England. As a 'Principality' it was made subject to the jurisdiction of the English crown, and was divided into counties, in accordance with English administrative practice (apart from the territory of the Lords Marcher). Soldiers can conquer a country and laws can gag its people, but it can only be occupied and retained if the conquerors settle there. And so England's King put the principle into practice and settled the western bank. Conwy and Conwy Castle were planned and built right from the start as a unit. The castle protected the town, and the town looked after the castle; the steward of the castle was also mayor of the town. Settlers were attracted by the offer of favourable conditions for trade, building and leasing. In Edward's time, there were 100 families in Conwy, and only the English were allowed to live within the town walls, or to run a business or trade. The Welsh had to live outside the gates, and could only be farmers or shepherds. Every nook and cranny of the castle was a little piece of England, complete with English language, customs, songs and curses. And this applied to all the castles and all their adjacent towns, so that the Englishness would mix in with Welshness, spread itself, and ultimately make all the Welsh into good English

Paul Sandby: Conwy Castle, c.1766

citizens. Not until 200 years later, after the coronation of Henry Tudor in 1485, did the Welsh acquire civil and residential rights within the town walls. The fact that all these towns are still in existence today says a great deal for Edward's far-sightedness if not for his sense of democracy.

In earlier times, Conwy Castle served to repulse; today it attracts. Such an historic power house is what people love to see. Very few, however, bother to walk along the town walls, and yet these are the really unique feature of Conwy. Harlech and Caernarfon can boast equally impressive castles, but a medieval town wall of such uniformity and so well preserved is to be found nowhere else in the British Isles. The wall is ¾ mile long, and about 5½ feet thick, contains 4 town gates, 21 towers, and 12 latrines that bulge out of the wall like swallows' nests. Anyone strolling along these ramparts will have the best of two worlds: a view over the bay in one direction, and a view into the backyards and kitchen sinks in the other. What else is there to see? On the quayside there's the 'smallest house in Britain', in Castle Street the oldest surviving half-timbered house in the town,

Aberconwy House (15th century), and in the High Street, an Elizabethan palace of 1580 with elaborate, Renaissance stucco decor: Plas Mawr, now the Royal Cambrian Academy of Art. As is evident from the pictures exhibited, this represents the conservative, regional remnants of a now defunct National Academy of Art founded in Cardiff by Welsh artists (1881). It was from a house near Conwy that the Neo-Classical sculptor John Gibson came, once almost as famous in Europe as his teacher in Rome, Canova. A bust of Gibson stands in the parish church of St Mary's, which was built on the site of the old Cistercian abbey of Aberconwy. In 1186 the monks became the first settlers on the western bank of the river. But they could never find the peace and quiet they needed for their prayers and their fishing.

Three bridges lead to Conwy. One is a brilliant design by Telford, the second a technical curiosity, and the third a tragedy. The first is the wrought-iron suspension bridge that Thomas Telford designed in 1822, its piers being miniature copies of Conwy's towers – an almost light-hearted approach to the forbidding fortress, and an elegant link between medieval military architecture and the art of 19th-century engineering. Next in line to cross the river was the railway. Robert Stephenson's Tubular Bridge (1847) swallows the trains up in two rectangular tubes of sheet iron, and at either end of the bridge is a crenellated tower.[1] Camouflage it may be, but it serves its purpose, for the historical showpiece – the view of the castle itself – remains undisturbed. Not until modern times, with the advent of

1 Both Conwy bridges are miniature editions of Telford's and Stephenson's Menai bridges, which were built at the same time (see page 385): they were successful means of testing materials and new methods of construction.

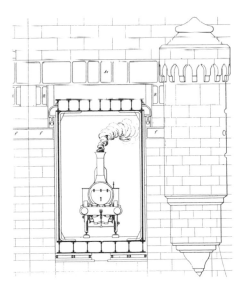

Conwy: Tubular Bridge 1847–48

the Great God Motor Car, have the bridge builders succeeded in ruining the townscape. The roadbridge of 1958 abruptly cuts off the castle from the river, sandwiches Telford's masterpiece, and instead of taking the traffic round the old town centre, discharges it right into the middle. Believe it or not, there was even a fourth bridge projected for the North Wales 'Expressway', a sort of motorway extension of the A55 from Liverpool. But after years of campaigning by the environmentalists, the plan was shelved in favour of a tunnel. Originally, the town council even wanted to demolish Telford's bridge, but protests led to a local referendum in 1965. The result of this must for ever cast doubts on the artistic validity of such democratic processes, for the majority voted in favour of demolition. Fortunately in this hour of crisis, as in so many other hours of other crises, the National Trust came to the rescue.

Fairy Glen and Swallow Falls: We're Off to Betws-y-Coed

On *Llandudno* beach I met Alice and the White Rabbit. Alice was made of papier-mâché and was sitting with the hatter in the garden of Gogarth Abbey Hotel. In summer 1864 she did actually play here: Alice Liddell, 12 years old, was one of the daughters of the Dean of Christ Church, Oxford. They were spending their holidays in their summerhouse Pen Morfa. Here Lewis Carroll visited his little Muse, and in the evenings read excerpts from 'Alice in Wonderland' to her, the family, and their guests. Amongst the latter was the Victorian literary critic Matthew Arnold, who was inspired by his summer holiday in Llandudno to write an essay on Celtic literature. He had unbounded enthusiasm for all that he found here, with the profusion of cultures Celtic, Roman, Saxon, Druid and medieval, and all the forts, dolmens and monasteries, together with the glorious sea and mountains. In those days the peninsula town north of Conwy was never short of illustrious visitors: Napoleon III, Bismarck, Disraeli, Gladstone – and later Churchill, too – all strolled along Llandudno beach, and if they were very lucky, they might have heard Adelina Patti singing 'La Traviata' in the pier pavilion, reducing even the seagulls to tears. Queen Elizabeth of Rumania spent five weeks in the Marine Hotel, and on departing remarked that Wales was a heavenly 'haven of peace', a compliment that Llandudno incorporated into its town coat-of-arms: 'Havdd, Hafan, Hedd'.

The bay is wide and gently curved, and there is a broad promenade with a phalanx of hotels that follow the curve of the bay in a profusion of Victorian cupolas and oriels, culminating in the onion tower on the pier-head. Llandudno is understandably hailed by many as the 'Naples of the North' (plate 92). 'But I doubt,' said my friend Dafydd, 'whether anyone has called Naples the Llandudno of the South.' Until the middle of the 19th century, it was a fishing village with some copper mining on *Great Orme*. And the railway came, and that meant tourism, hotels and shops. Building was strictly regulated, but was always on a generous scale, and the result was a garden town on the sea, a model

Victorian resort for the upper middle class that came from Liverpool and the industrial cities of the Midlands. Even now the promenade is generally free of those amusement arcades, fish and chip shops and so on, that have so disfigured Rhyl and other town-cum-fairgrounds. Llandudno once aspired to becoming another Brighton, but 'Prinny's' successors all missed their chance to embellish their Principality with a Royal Pavilion of pleasure and culture – they preferred to have their seaside affairs in the Bahamas. Today, Llandudno is in danger of becoming a bit too matronly, and unless something is done soon, she may well turn into the Old Mother Riley of Costa Geriatrica.

Let us leave Llandudno and go to Betws-y-Coed. The *Vale of Conwy*, once a line of defence for the princes of Gwynedd, has long since turned into the romantic road par excellence, skirting the edges of Snowdonia. It's an open, densely wooded valley, full of meadows, cows and sheep. Through the Vale of Conwy came Celts and Romans, Edward's soldiers, Glyndwr's rebels, artists, travellers, and in 1846 a German countess named Ida Hahn-Hahn: '... fantasy comes with the river out of the mountains, and goes with it to the sea.' High above the valley, at the turn of the century, the Lords of Aberconwy laid out a terraced garden which blooms in great steps up and down the hill: *Bodnant Garden* (colour plate 7), a triumph of landscaping when one considers the bareness of the Carneddau. Further upriver, the peacocks of *Gwydir* make shrill publicity for the family home of the Wynns. Their graves, with 17th-century brasses, lie in the Gwydir Chapel in *Llanrwst* Church, together with a sarcophagus believed to be that of Llewelyn the Great.

The Gwydir Chapel (1633) is attributed to Inigo Jones, as is the neighbouring bridge over the Conwy (1636; plate 101). The latter has three beautifully proportioned arches (43–61–43 feet), slender, hexagonal piers, and a low parapet. Its stonework reaches elegantly across the river with a lightness of touch that in fact marked the first break with the traditional, heavy style of medieval Welsh bridges. It is undoubtedly the work of a master, though whether it is really by Inigo Jones must remain a matter for conjecture. The English Palladio is said by the Welsh to have come from Llanrwst, but all that is known from official records is that he was baptized in London, and that his father was a draper in Denbighshire. Quite a few Welsh buildings have been attributed to him, including Plas Têg, near Mold (1610) and Ruperra Castle, north-east of Cardiff (1626, now a ruin), but the only one known for sure to have been designed by him is the simple, symmetrical gatehouse of *Cors-y-Gedol* near Barmouth (1630), whose owner was a friend of the great architect. In those days, Britain was still half immersed in Gothic, and it was Inigo Jones who brought the Renaissance out of Italy and into the British Isles. In all honesty, the 'Welsh Connection' is of minor significance.

Whether or not Inigo Jones built Pont Fawr, whoever wanted to cross the river to Conwy was obliged to use the great bridge of Llanrwst – until 1826, when Telford's Suspension Bridge shortened the journey. The Conwy is full of salmon, and Wales is full of rivers, but if I love anything more than Welsh salmon and Welsh rivers, it's Welsh

Moses Griffith: Llanrwst Bridge, 1776

bridges. For instance, there's a miniature Golden Gate Bridge that leads from a rape field to *Betws-y-Coed* (plate 100): it's an iron suspension bridge for pedestrians (1930), and is as dainty and bouncy and shiny as a bridge can be. On the edge of the town is Telford's Waterloo Bridge, built in 1815 (the year of the battle); the cast-iron spandrels contain the four national emblems of the United Kingdom: England's rose, Scotland's thistle, Ireland's clover, and the Welsh leek. Telford's bridges also grace the road the Holyhead, the link between London and Dublin and one of the great technical achievements of the time.

It was the art of the engineers and the road-builders that first opened up North Wales to the world; but it was the painters who made the world interested. David Cox from Birmingham was one of them. Between 1844 and 1856 he travelled nearly every summer to the Vale of Conwy, to a village with the pious name of Betws-y-Coed, the Sanctuary in the Wood, which he made his very own open-air studio. He painted *Swallow Falls* and other waterfalls in the area, the ruins of *Pandy Mill*, the old bridge *Pont-y-Pair*, and in 1847 for the landlord of the Royal Oak, where he stayed, he painted an inn sign: King Charles II in the branches of the Boscobel oak, that popular escape story of the Civil War that seeded a whole forest of Royal Oaks throughout the kingdom. The inn sign from Betws-y-Coed now forms part of the Cox collection in the Birmingham Art Gallery, as does his painting 'A Welsh Funeral' (1848): this was the burial of his landlord's daughter, shortly before sunset, in accordance with the customs of rural Wales in those days. 'Farmer Cox', as

Turner called him, had no success at all during his life, and died in 1859, an unknown painter of everyday life, of all the shades of wind and weather, an English Impressionist *avant la lettre*. Betws-y-Coed became more famous than David Cox, although it was David Cox who made it famous. The landlord of the Royal Oak built a new and bigger hotel, and the Sanctuary in the Wood became a popular beauty-spot, especially for honeymooners. Victorian tourists came in their hordes, complete with their fishing-rods, walking-sticks and easels, and they swarmed through *Fairy Glen* and around Swallow Falls. A beech wood near the waterfall became known as Artists' Wood, because it was painted so many times – the best known version being perhaps James Dickson Innes's 'The Waterfall' (1910) in the Tate Gallery. Eventually the owner, Lord Ancaster, realized that one Swallow did make a very good summer, and proceeded to charge for entry. For my taste, Betws-y-Coed is a little overrated. It is most certainly overcrowded. Maybe it should be left alone for a while, and then rediscovered.

Tŷ Mawr: How the Bible Saved a Language

People love seeing sights. Anything spectacular will draw the crowds, and given the choice between a ruined castle and a dead bishop, they'll go for the castle every time. And so what chance does a Welsh Bible have against a Welsh waterfall? In high season, Swallow Falls attracts some 4,000 visitors a day; *Tŷ Mawr* gets barely 2,000 visitors a year. And yet this is the birthplace of one of the great figures of Welsh history: Bishop William Morgan, translator of the Bible. Let us, however, be thankful for the absence of the hordes, for thus the secluded house at the edge of the Gwybrnant Valley is able to enjoy the same peace and quiet that it enjoyed some 400 years ago. There are sheep and horses grazing in the valley, and the surrounding hills are covered with thick forests. Tŷ Mawr, The Big House, is a rubblestone cottage, unplastered, single-storey, slate-roofed – a typical Caernarfonshire farmhouse, such as dotted the landscape after about 1560. But William Morgan was born in Tŷ Mawr in 1545 (the date over the door, 1541, is wrong), and the house where he was born bore the same name and stood on this same spot. The interior is narrow, stone-tiled, with a fireplace that has a black oak beam, and there's an old chair in which, of course, he never sat. Not much for sightseers, but you can still sense something of the man's presence. His origins were simple, and he ended in poverty. When William Morgan, farmer's son, died in 1604, venerated as Bishop of St Asaph, the room in which he died contained a bed, a cupboard, a pot, two candles, some books, and a pair of glasses – barely enough to cover the cost of his funeral. He was an unusually abstemious church dignitary, but this is not the reason why he is remembered in Wales today. Bishop Morgan translated the Bible into Welsh, and if that sounds like nothing special by today's standards, for the time it was a stupendous feat. And the fact that Welsh is still spoken today may not seem so special, but without Bishop Morgan's Bible, it would have been unthinkable.

The background, briefly, was as follows: King Henry VIII had suppressed the Welsh language in order to reinforce the union of the two countries. His daughter Elizabeth I recognized the fact that the policy of anglicisation was not only alienating the aristocracy and the people, but must also lead to the loss of old religious ties – which was contrary both to the faith and to the moral code of the State. What benefit could the Welsh have from the beautiful English 'Book of Common Prayer' (1558) if it could not be understood 'by the greatest number of her majesty's most loving and obedient subjects inhabiting the country of Wales'? So said the preamble to a law of 1563, by which the Queen demanded a Welsh Bible and prayerbook, in order that her Welsh subjects should not remain in ignorance even greater than at the time of the popery. A Welsh theologian in Cambridge, William Morgan, preacher at St John's College, heard the summons and set to work. The Welsh translation which he finished 25 years later was not the first – William Salusbury's version had appeared in 1567 – but it was the only complete one and, far more importantly, it was written in a language whose power and beauty were an inspiration to all who read it. What Luther's Bible gave to the Germans, namely a uniform written language, William Morgan's gave to the Welsh: it was the Word of God in the language of the people, a solid foundation for that language as well as for their faith, accessible to peasant as to nobleman, authoritative to worshipper as to scholar, and exemplary to the man in the pub as to the man in the pulpit. The difficulties William Morgan faced, not least because his mother tongue had no true equivalent of many of the phrases used in the Bible, is made clear by his Dedication to Queen Elizabeth I: 'The words requisite for a Welsh exposition of the mysteries treated of in Holy Scriptures had either disappeared utterly, wiped out as by the waters of Lethe, or had been lying buried, so to speak, under the ashes of disuse.' He reiterated his fundamental conviction: 'Religion, if it is not taught in the mother tongue, will lie hidden and unknown.' What G. M. Trevelyan said about the importance to the English of the King James Version of the Bible (1611) – which, let it be remembered, was the work of nearly fifty translators – is even more applicable to the Welsh and their Bible: 'The effect of the continual domestic study of the book upon the national character, imagination and intelligence for nearly three centuries to come, was greater than that of any literary movement in our annals, or any religious movement since the coming of Augustine.'

William Morgan's Bible was published in 1588, with an initial print-run of 1,000 copies. Of this first edition, only 19 copies remain. In Tŷ Mawr, the National Trust memorial to the great translator, there is not one to be seen, whereas the Bodleian is sitting on no less than five. During the investiture of Prince Charles as Prince of Wales in 1969, a Morgan Bible lay open on the altar – the first edition from St Asaph Cathedral Library. This was no mere symbol, for Morgan's version is still used today, with very few revisions, in Welsh services. 'Last Sunday,' said Wyn Jones, curator of Tŷ Mawr, 'there were just twelve people in our chapel.' In Wales as elsewhere the churches are getting emptier and emptier, and at the same time the number of Welsh speakers is also declining. 'A Book saved the culture of this bookish people,' wrote J. C. Powys. But alas, Bishop Morgan's Bible is no longer integral to the nation. Welsh could live on as a language without faith, but it cannot live only through faith in the language.

Champagne Time: Pückler Conquers Snowdon

Day by day Mr Briggs's opinion of me went down. I'd been in Pen-y-Gwryd for almost a week, and still I hadn't conquered *Snowdon* (colour plate 5). 'I haven't even seen the peak yet,' I complained, pointing to the mist. But you don't spend the night or nights in Mr Briggs's hotel just in order to mooch around the foot of the mountain. Pen-y-Gwryd – known to regular customers as P.Y.G. – is the legendary hotel for mountaineers at the entrance to Llanberis Pass. The P.Y.G. was Sir Edmund Hillary's training camp before he conquered Everest, and indeed all British Himalayan expeditions used Snowdonia for their training. In the bar I saw a climbing rope used by the famous Abraham brothers in 1899, and a piece of rock in a glass case, a souvenir from Mount Everest. You have to go. 'Been up Snowdon, / A nice ascent. / William Boden, / Burton-on-Trent' stands in the visitor's book. 'Set off in the wet, arrive in the dry,' advised Mr Briggs.

And so the following morning I did as I was told. I'd chosen the longest and easiest of the four classic Snowdon routes, the *Llanberis Track*. A notice on the way gives the latest weather report: 'Occasional sun, heavy showers, thunder, possible hailstorms. Ground conditions: wet in places. Visibility: good, bad if misty.' The route is stony but not particularly steep. There are ferns and gorse, but later just rocks and a little grass. Sheep poke around between the rocks, and the rocks look rather like sheep. And then the first curtain of mist drops down the mountain, suddenly and silently. The stillness seems infinite. But in the summer, a hiker won't be alone for long. Causing a small-scale landslide, a runner comes pounding towards me – he's training for the international Snowdon Mountain Race in July. The record for this yearly, 9 mile run to the peak and back is about 66 minutes. The runners have my admiration, but not my emulation.

I could have taken the *Watkin Path*, which is a more romantic route to the summit and was named after Sir Edward Watkin, a railway pioneer of the 19th century. He dreamed of opening a railway line from Manchester to Paris, and actually began building a Channel tunnel; he was the first to undertake such a project, and had progressed for almost a mile on both sides of the Channel when Parliament called a halt. When Watkin was 70, he conquered Snowdon. He began by buying land at the foot of the mountain, where he built himself a chalet in *Nant Gwynant*, between two idyllic lakes. It was this same Nant Gwynant that William Wordsworth once visited, taking a holiday from his beloved Lake District, and he was enchanted by *Llyn Dinas*, one of these two mountain lakes nestling amid rocks and forests. It was, he said, 'the only Welsh lake which has any pretensions to compare with our own.' Sir Edward Watkin could hear the rustling falls of the *Cwm Llan* from his chalet, and since he wanted to get to Snowdon direct from his house, and also wanted to give others the chance to do the same, he had a path made. This was what one might call a peak period for Victorian mountaineering. The Watkin Path was opened in 1892 by his friend Gladstone, and the rock where the 83-year-old Prime Minister made his speech, on the subject of justice for Wales, is called *Gladstone Rock*.

If you can't make it to the top of Wales' highest mountain (and England's, too, for that matter) along one of the four paths, you can get there sitting down. 'Opened 1896 and still puffing' is the slogan of the *Snowdon Mountain Railway*, and indeed the little grass-green steam engine goes puffing up the bare, north-west flank of the mountain, for safety reasons pushing rather than pulling the carriage along the Victorian pony path from Llanberis. When it was opened, on Easter Monday 1896, Locomotive No. 1, 'Ladas', overturned and went down the hill. The driver was able to jump clear, and the carriage stayed where it was, but one passenger panicked and jumped to his death. Since then, there has never been another No. 1 engine, and there has never been another accident. The Snowdon Mountain Railway is Britain's one and only rack-and-pinion railway, and is a flourishing concern. Some 150,000 people a year go chugging up to the summit, though twice as many brave the climb on foot. And these are more feet than even the best mountain can cope with.

For many years now the environmentalists have been warning against the dangers of erosion and this mass assault. The path I took is wide enough for a procession, and it is used all the year round, even when the weather is bad. A few years ago it needed major restoration, as did all the other main routes. As long ago as 1854, George Borrow set out from Llanberis with his wife Henrietta and a guide to climb to the peak, and he too noted that there were hikers, single and in groups, as far as the eye could see. He must also have felt the truth of the Welsh proverb: 'It is easy to say yonder is Snowdon, but not so easy to ascend it.' But at last the effort was rewarded, and 'there we stood enjoying a scene inexpressibly grand ...' At and on the peak of his enthusiasm, Borrow liked to declaim poetry, and in keeping with the temperature, he chose a virtuoso piece on Snowdon, consisting only of vowels, apart from the one, frosty-sounding consonant 'r':

O Ri y'Ryri yw'r oera, – o'r ar,
Ar oror wir arwa;
O'r awyr a yr Eira,
O'i ryw roi rew a'r ia.

Welsh word-music at its best, and Borrow's own English translation lags far behind:

A hill most chill is Snowdon's hill,
And wintry is his brow;
From Snowdon's hill the breezes chill
Can freeze the very snow.

After revelling in the view and the recitation, Borrow treated himself to a beer, and his wife to a cup of coffee, in a refreshment booth which he calls 'a rude cabin' and which today has been replaced by a rude restaurant that is even more depressing in the mountain mists. 'In good weather,' gushes the waiter, 'you can see Ireland from here.' But both Ireland and tea seem improbably slow to reveal themselves. I retreat into the past.

On 12 July 1844, having come all the way from Saxony, the physician and painter Carl Gustav Carus stood on Snowdon: 'Of course, no sign of any view!' There was not much joy to be had from the refreshment booth then either: 'The man was making a strange brown drink which he sold as coffee, and he was also offering some grey oatmeal bread.' Finally, the descent, according to Carus, was certainly a mere trifle for 'Alpenjäger'. 'But if one is not used to such things, this sort of climb can always be regarded as good practice for the muscles, as a kind of training which, if it ends happily, must be of benefit to the elasticity of the organism!'

The first recorded conquest of Snowdon took place in 1639, beneath an overcast sky: Thomas Johnson, a botanist, found 'our British Alps veiled in cloud'. But the real study of Snowdon, and its extraordinary popularity among geologists, painters, poets and tourists, did not begin until late in the 18th century, inspired initially by Thomas Pennant's 'Journey to Snowdon' (1781). With great precision this Welsh scholar describes the continual changes in the weather and scenery, and the fascinating atmosphere surrounding the peak: 'A vast mist enveloped the whole circuit of the mountain. The prospect down was horrible. It gave an idea of numbers of abysses, concealed by a thick smoke, furiously circulating around us. Very often a gust of wind formed an opening in the clouds, which gave a fine and distinct vista of lake and valley. Sometimes they opened only in one place; at others, in many at once, exhibiting a most strange and perplexing sight of water, fields, rocks, or chasms, in fifty different places. They then closed at once, and left us involved in darkness.'

Pennant's off-putting experiences on the way down already gave Pückler a few nasty surprises on the way up: 'It became blacker and blacker, and I had scarcely been climbing for half an hour, ahead of my pony, which the guide was leading on its bridle, when a dark cloak was enveloping mountains, valleys and us, and torrents of rain came pouring down on us, against which my umbrella soon gave me no protection.' This was in July 1828. The storm became increasingly violent, and the guide suggested that they should go back. Pückler, however, had no intention of giving up. He defends his folly with a single, delightfully silly statement of intent: to drink to his 'good Lucie' on the summit of Snowdon. Lucie was his wife who had sensibly stayed at home. In most other respects, this Prussian prince behaved just like a normal tourist: 'I scratched my name next to thousands of others on a big stone, and then picked up the cow horn which my host had given me to drink from, and I ordered my guide to uncork the champagne ... Three times I then emptied my animal beaker, and truly thirsty and exhausted as I had good cause to be, I have never in my life enjoyed champagne as much as that.' Then with a feeling of elation, he went down into a valley.

On my own way back, I started wondering just what it was that was so special about Snowdon. Why does it bully us into this masochistic admiration, which survives even the rain and the non-existent view? You'd have thought that with all the overcrowding, it would have lost its appeal by now, but it hasn't. What gave it its appeal in the first place? Is it famous because so many famous people have climbed it, so many artists have painted it so superbly, Baedeker has kept on describing it? Certainly the size of its reputation has nothing to do with the size of the mountain: at a modest 3,560 feet, it would barely poke its head above the foothills of the Alps. But of course the average-sized man is a giant among dwarfs, and in Wales Snowdon has no competition. Experienced mountaineers, however, also know that Snowdon, for all its comparative modesty as regards height, can be exceedingly temperamental in other ways. And it certainly seems higher than it is. 'Snowdon Hill is a monstrous height,' wrote Daniel Defoe, with a shudder. The impression is based on an optical illusion: deep valleys, bare slopes, no trees by which to make comparisons – these factors enhance the sensation of loftiness, together with a strange, almost mystic light and, above all else, a feeling that overcomes us even today, once we have left the beaten track: 'Grandeur and desolation' was William Wordsworth's description of that feeling. In his autobiographical poem 'The Prelude' (1798–1805), he recollects in tranquillity that a sunrise on Snowdon was the high point of the mystic, poetic experience of Nature. It is, in fact, an adventure of the imagination, for Wordsworth never reached the summit of Snowdon. But the popularity of Snowdon during the romantic period was not confined to poets and artists, and was also due to purely worldly factors: during the Napoleonic Wars, it was difficult for Britons to travel abroad, and Snowdonia was a good substitute for the Alps.

It has to be admitted that Snowdon is only eighty feet higher than Carnedd Llewelyn, but Snowdon is the mountain everyone has heard of, and for the Welsh it is the mountain of mountains. The passes of Llanberis, Nant Gwynant and Llyn Cwellyn enhance its glorious isolation, and if it is not mysteriously veiled in mists or clouds, it emerges all the more majestically out of these hollows, with its pyramid-shaped peak, borne on five rocky ridges like buttresses. This is what a mountain should look like, and the clarity of the form, the rugged surroundings, and the wild magic of its ever-changing appearance are what have made this mountain endlessly fascinating to painters of all eras. They have portrayed it from all angles, in all weathers, in all lights, and at all times of day and night: 'Snowdon from Llyn Nantlle' (Richard Wilson, c.1765), 'Snowdon from Llanberis Lake' (Thomas Rowlandson, 1797), 'Snowdon from Llyn Dinas' (John Sell Cotman, c.1809), 'Snowdon from Capel Curig' (John Varley, 1836), 'Snowdon from Llanfrothen' (Stanley Spencer, c.1937). These are the classic, 'picturesque' views which have since determined the way the photographers and the tourists see the mountain. Where the B4418 now passes along the western side of Llyn Nantlle, Thomas Pennant went walking in 1781, and recognized a view that was already famous at that time: 'It is from this spot Mr Wilson has favoured us with a view, as magnificent as it is faithful. Few are sensible of this; for few

Richard Wilson: Snowdon from Llyn Nantlle, c.1765

visit the spot.' But what the artists painted is more than just a topographical landmark, and Snowdon is more than just a mountain. It is a myth, and a national symbol.

The Welsh name for the summit is *Yr Wyddfa*, the Great Tomb. Rhita Fawr is said to have been buried under the Cairn – Rhita the Giant, who wove his robe from the beards of slain kings. And the legendary battle between the white and red dragons (see page 11) took place on the slopes of Snowdon. To complete this mythical picture there is, of course, King Arthur, who died in the Pass of Arrows, *Bwlch-y-Saethau*, the ridge below Yr Wyddfa – though this is not the only Arthurian link with Snowdonia. Myth and history, patriotism and poetry, bards and mountaineers have always been associated with the highland peaks. In his ode 'The Bard' (1757), Thomas Gray describes how the last Welsh bard flees from Edward I's invading army, and hurls himself from the top of Snowdon. Edward the Bard-Killer: in historical terms, this is clear defamation of character, but as a poetic symbol, it signifies the Celtic Revival. With this dramatic death, Gray endowed the local mountain with the majesty of Antiquity, and the bard became the classic tragic hero: his death is on a par with that of Empedocles, who plunged into Etna.

Like the walls of some great fortress, the mountains of Snowdonia stand massively round their centre – a view so terrifying to Defoe that it moved him to classical comparisons: 'Even Hannibal himself would have found it impossible to have marched his army over Snowdon ...' When the Romans invaded, and then the Normans, and in the days of Owain Glyndwr, this was the final refuge, the heartland, and here the last king reigned. Here the Cymric heart beat most strongly, and here the language put up the longest resistance. And so the fame of Snowdon spread, a mythical symbol of survival, a prehistoric emblem of endurance, the Welsh Parnassus, mountain of mountains.

Romantic Eryri: The National Park with the Nuclear Power Station

If someone says *Yr Wyddfa* rather than *Snowdon*, that doesn't necessarily make him a Welshman. But if, rather than the gentle sound of *Snowdonia*, someone prefers the whirring of *'Eryri'* – a word that evokes great rocks, romantic longings, aeolian harps and the cry of eagles – then you can be sure he's Cymric through and through. The name of Snowdon is said to have been bestowed on the mountain by English sailors, who saw the snowcapped mountains as they said along the coast, and dubbed them 'Snowdunes'. Snowdonia was already the collective name for all the mountains in the region as long ago as the 13th century. Eryri is the original, Celtic name for the three main ranges – Snowdon, Glyder and Carnedd. The popular poetic translation is 'Seat of Eagles', from the Celtic 'eryr', eagle; but the more likely one is 'Highland', from the Latin 'oriri', to arise. Llywelyn the Great ignored the older, Welsh term and in 1230 gave himself the title Lord of Snowdon. It is a title which (like that of Constable of Caernarfon Castle) always retained royal connections, and was bestowed on Anthony Armstrong-Jones when he married Princess Margaret.

Snowdonia is a mixture of fire and water, volcano and glacier, and an everlasting battle between the volcanic rock and the forces of erosion. Dolerite, lava and tuff bear witness to eruptions that took place some 600 million years ago. The summit of Snowdon consists of tuff covered with boulders; the summit of *Carnedd Llewelyn*, bearing the name of a national hero, is of dolerite, solid, primitive rock; the wild and eerie summits of *Glyder Fawr* and its neighbour *Glyder Fach* are of lava, grey rocks and stones swept by an uncanny-sounding wind. Beneath the Glyders and the three peaks of the Tryfan, the Ice Age left behind 'hanging valleys': hollowed-out edges of overhanging crags. It was only about 10,000 years ago that the last glaciers melted into the basin-like valleys of Snowdonia. What remained was the ice-age landscape of the *corries* and *cwms*: pools of rock, and the typical U-shaped valleys, not V-shaped like most river valleys, but rolled flat by the departing glaciers. That is how *Nant Gwynant* was formed, a romantically overgrown, almost idyllic version of an ice-age valley, and also its elemental opposite, *Nant Ffrancon*. Together with Llanberis Pass, the latter is the wildest of all Snowdonia's wild valleys: stripped bare by the primeval force of the ice, the top consists of rock worn

Thomas Girtin: The Cayne Waterfall at Beddgelert, 18??

smooth, and the bottom of nothing but loose stones. The entrance to this ice-age theatre is grandiose: a rocky step nearly 230 feet high down below *Llyn Ogwen*, the lake in which Arthur's sword Excalibur sank for ever. The geologist Adam Sedgwick came here in 1831, searching for fossils, in the company of his friend Charles Darwin. They found a perfect ice-age valley south-west of Nant Ffrancon: 'We spent many hours in *Cwm Idwal*, examining all the rocks with extreme care . . . but neither of us saw a trace of the wonderful glacial phenomena all around us,' Darwin recalled later, after a second visit to the valley of *Llyn Idwal* in 1842, this time taking due note of the forms of this glacial landscape: 'These phenomena are so conspicuous that a house burnt down by fire did not tell its story more plainly than did this valley.' Since then, Cwm Idwal has been the sacred valley for all ice-age researchers – a nature reserve administered by the National Trust, a vast, open-air natural museum in which one can even find a form of alpine flora that has long since died out everywhere else. It is a last living link to the Ice Age.

The mountaineers also have a high regard for the craggy rocks of Eryri. There are over 1,500 recognized climbing routes in the National Park, with new ones added every year. And every year there are at least a dozen fatal accidents on and around Snowdon. Cemetery Gates, Cenotaph Corner, The Skull: these ominous names mark the most dangerous of the routes. One of the most popular, though most difficult climbs (apart from the Devil's north face) is the 'Cloggy', the *Clogwyn Du'r Arddu*, The Black Cliff of the Black Height. If during high season one of the 'rock tigers' gets stuck on these vertical, overhanging rockfaces, the route below is soon jammed as tight as Piccadilly Circus in the rush hour.

The light of Snowdonia is iridescent, other-worldly. For some it can become an obsession. David Woodford, for one, is an English painter who elected in 1971 to live in the valley of Nant Ffrancon. From his studio, a former chapel in Ty'n-y-Maes, he sets out on excursions into the mountains in order to watch the unfolding display: 'The greatest sensation is light'. And the changing colours and texture of the rock, and the way the same prehistoric landscape can constantly take on new appearances – these moments of light are David Woodford's constant motif. Anyone who thinks of these mountains as mist and rain, does not know Snowdonia. It is a landscape of light, particulary in its darkest months, when the winter days are short and ice-clear. The only other place where I have seen anything similar is the Hebrides – four seasons can pass in a single hour, or these can be days on end of depressing gloom, suddenly broken by an epiphany of light. In Snowdonia too it has a crystalline sharpness, an intensity due to the maritime climate, the volcanic rock, and the latitude. Another English painter to rent a cottage in the valley of Nant Ffrancon was John Piper in 1949. Here he painted his first landscapes: 'For the first time I saw the bones and the structure and the "lie" of mountains, living with them and climbing them as I was, lying on them in the sun and getting soaked with rain in their cloud cover

David Woodford:
Tryfan, 1976

James Dickson Innes:
Arenig, 1913

and enclosed in their improbable, private rock world in fog.' John Piper's watercolours and pen-and-ink drawings (together with his very precise notes on the weather) stand solidly in the tradition of British landscape painting. But by the beginning of the 1960's, he had had enough of the rain, and moved his holiday home to the coast of South Wales. One step back again in time, at the beginning of this century, another young painter had moved in the opposite direction, from the industrial town of Llanelli, in South Wales, to the remoteness of Snowdonia: he was James Dickson Innes. His mountain was the *Arenig Fawr*, not even 2,800 feet high, surrounded by moorland, treeless and, at first sight, charmless – a bare and massive, melancholy mountain, which he painted again and again, from every angle and in all weathers, on small wooden panels in glowing azures and purples, his mountain of desires, his Mont Saint-Victoire. Innes's 'long rambles over the moors in search of the magical moment' were described by his friend Augustus John, with whom he shared a cottage in *Nant-ddu* in 1911 and 1912, at the foot of the mountains, which 'he loved with religious fervour'. An Australian painter, Derwent Lees, also joined in this Welsh Bohemia for a while, and Augustus John wrote that Lees thought Innes was never happier than when painting in this region, 'perceived by him as the reflection of some miraculous promised land'. James Dickson Innes died of consumption at the age of 27. But even before him, there had been a traveller who was more impressed by Arenig Fawr than by any other mountain in Wales. George Borrow discussed it one day with a local man: 'I asked him if anybody lived upon it. "No," said he, "too cold for man." "Fox?" said I. "No! too cold for fox." "Crow?" said I. "No, too cold for crow, crow would be starved upon it."'

That is Eryri. Most people know it by its more consumer-friendly name of *Snowdonia National Park*. For me this evokes pictures of lions running around in carpet slippers.

But a park it is, with carparks, picnic areas, nature trails, restaurants, well-maintained footpaths, well-marked climbing routes, information centres, adventure playgrounds ... the complete open-air leisure centre. Here the wilderness is perfectly administered. Many parts of North Wales have changed more in the last fifty years than they had done for centuries. In the most remote valleys, reservoirs and roads have been constructed, conifers planted where none had ever grown before, and caravan sites laid out. And there are nuclear power stations. When Snowdonia National Park was set up in 1951, it was already almost too late. 'Far from lasting forever, it may not last for a generation. Far from being consecrated for national enjoyment, it is likely to be devastated for private profit. Far from remaining a national pleasure, it may become a national disgrace (...) the Park is in grave danger.' This shocking prognosis was delivered by Amory Levins in 1971, and was reproduced in an outstanding Eryri picturebook by Friends of the Earth. There is, alas, no reason to believe that this warning was an exaggeration, or that it is no longer valid.

With an area of 850 square miles, the Snowdonia National Park is the second largest in Britain. It embraces not only the most popular northern region around Snowdon, the Glyders and Carneddau, but also extends to the south as far as Dolgellau and Aberdyfi. About 75% of the park is under private ownership, some 13% comes under the Forestry Commission, 8% belongs to the National Trust, and 4% to the State. Within the bounds of the park there are some 25,000 inhabitants. Their main business is tourism, followed by agriculture and forestry. About eleven million people a year visit the park, which has three proclaimed goals: conservation of Nature, the welfare of visitors, and the welfare of the inhabitants. It therefore faces the institutional impossibility of serving three masters, and is therefore constrained to find plausible compromises for all its built-in conflicts. The local people want work, and if necessary industry; the visitors, who come from the towns and industrial zones, want Nature pure and unadulterated. And Nature wants to be left alone.

Let us begin with those who live in and from the National Park: 25,000 people, reduced from 31,000 at the end of the war. Even in Snowdonia the population dwindled as the young left for the cities and the old folk stayed behind. Often the vacant cottages have become holiday homes for outsiders – up to 30% in some areas. The result: the disintegration of rural culture in one of its Welsh heartlands. The two traditional industries of slate and hill farming have radically declined, and rationalization has cost the jobs of about half of Snowdonia's hill farmers. The soil is poor. Snowdonia is 'sheepscape' – 25 sheep per person, so they say. But the sheep-breeders have been subsidized for years, even more than the farmers down in the valleys, where again the industry is in decline. It is ironic in the extreme that while half the world starves, these food-producers can barely scrape a living, and in order to do so, must turn to other activities. There may be Welsh Black in the meadow, but in another field you'll find caravans. Keeping tourists instead of keeping cattle. At least half the hill farmers rent out rooms or fields for campers and caravans. 'Some of these caravan sites completely ruin the countryside,' complain the

No nukes: cartoon from Ynni, 1982
(PWR: pressurized water reactor)

officials, 'but we can't close them down.' Snowdonia's economy depends on tourism, and there is no way round that fact. Everyone fears the consequences of uncontrolled growth: 'Too much public pressure damaging the landscape – too many people in too small a space, always at the same beauty spots.' Snowdonia is the tour operators' trump card, but if the card is thrown away, what are you left with?

Similarly, forestry in Snowdonia is outside the jurisdiction of the National Park's administration; their function is purely advisory. Critics complain that the Forestry's Commission's afforestation policy is too aggressive. Trees are driving away sheep – and that means driving away the hill farmers, too – and furthermore these trees are mostly alien to the landscape: up to 97% are conifers – American Douglas firs, Corsican pines, Japanese larch. Native hardwood trees, oak or beech, are virtually excluded, because 'they grow too slowly, and so there's no money in them,' explains a member of the Forestry Commission in *Coed y Brenin*, King's Forest, north of Dolgellau. 'Our main aim is to produce wood. It's a business. We don't just plant in order to make the landscape beautiful.' In Coed y Brenin itself, for instance, there are 91 acres of oak forest, which produce four tons of timber a year; but there are 8,980 acres of spruce, which produce more than three times as much timber per acre as the oak. The result of this simple economic fact is row upon row upon row of pines and spruces – conveyor belt plantations which are an eyesore. For Welsh poets such as Gwenallt Jones, these new forests symbolize the loss of the homeland. In his poem 'Rhydcymerau' he recalls his birthplace, his grandparents' farm:

> And by this time there's nothing there but trees.
> Impertinent roots suck dry the old soil:
> Trees where neighbourhood was,
> And a forest that once was farmland.
> Where was verse-writing and scripture is the South's bastardized English.
> The fox barks where once cried lambs and children . . .

The romantic setting of Eryri is deceptive, for the National Park of Snowdonia is not a park, and does not belong to the nation. This 'Seat of Eagles' is a gigantic reservoir for the energy industry. Let us take the A470 from Dolgellau to Ffestiniog. It runs through a magnificent plateau of meadows, moorland, and in the distance, the mountains. This is a wide, fast road, for according to the Minister, the tourist wants to see as much as possible as fast as possible; straighten the bends in the old country roads, get rid of the old dry stone walls at the sides, and let the driver put his foot down. I've already reached *Trawsfynydd*. In this village there's a lifesize monument to a shepherd-poet with the bardic name of Hedd Wyn, Beautiful Peace. Beautiful Peace fell in Flanders in 1917. For his poem 'The Hero' he was posthumously awarded an Eisteddfod prize, the Black Chair of Birkenhead.

Beautiful Peace. Down by the lake a fisherman sits (plate 52). 'Trout?' you ask. 'Yes,' he says, 'you get really big ones here.' The trout obviously thrive on the waters round *Trawsfynydd Nuclear Power Station*. Built in 1959–64, it was the first inland nuclear power station in Britain, designed by Sir Basil Spence, who also built Coventry Cathedral. The Welsh employed a top British architect to dump this monstrosity right in the middle of their National Park of Snowdonia. At the headquarters of the park authorities in *Penrhyndeudraeth*, just a few miles away, the shock waves have long since subsided. 'We could do nothing about it,' they say, 'though we would oppose a second power station.' How effective would their opposition be? 'Well, if they decide to set up an industrial complex in the National Park, and the Minister says it's in the national interest, we're help-less.' There will be a pause now, while the nation decides how much it truly wants nuclear power. But no pause in vigilance: there are still, officially, plans for Trawsfynydd II.

The administration is always helpless when 'the national interest' is invoked. The expression is of course a euphemism for British (as opposed to Welsh) interests and, above all, for Big Money. Test drilling has shown that the Snowdonia National Park is probably the richest area in Britain for mineral resources. Gold, copper, lead, zinc, manganese – they're all especially concentrated in what's known as the *Harlech Dome*, 300 square miles of age-old volcanic rock. And there is indeed a mining tradition in Snowdonia – there were more than a dozen lead and zinc mines north of Betws-y-Coed until 1914, and copper was mined in Nantlle Valley. Even the slopes of Snowdon itself still show traces left behind by miners and prospectors. The magic eye of Snowdon, the deep blue *Glaslyn* below the summit, owes its blueness not to Merlin the Magician, but to the salt from copper ore, which was mined on the shores of the lake from the mid 18th century until the beginning of the 20th. The miners used to carry the ore on their shoulders down the steep, zig-zag path to the sleighs below. Their *'Miners' Track'* is now one of the popular routes to the summit. And so in historical terms it is hardly surprising that at the beginning of the 1970's the Rio Tinto Zinc Corporation started looking around Snowdonia. But the Golden Calf of Snowdonia had grown into a Holy Cow, and drilling is not allowed in the National Park. So the Rio Tinto Zinc Corporation turned its attention to the Mawddach Estuary,

John Sell Cotman: Road to Capel Curig, 1807

one of the most beautiful of all Welsh landscapes, with a view to open cast copper-mining. There was a massive protest from the environmentalists. But this was not enough to stop the project. Nor were the regulations governing the National Park – for there are none. No, what stopped the project in the end was the sordid fact that it would not have been profitable enough. Meanwhile, other companies have brought up land in Snowdonia, in the hope that one day it will be worth their while to get at those minerals. 'If the world market price for copper and lead should go up again,' says Mrs Kirby, 'mining around the Mawddach could become very lucrative indeed. It would pollute and devastate Snowdonia.'

Esmé Kirby is one of those who are all in favour of the National Park, and consider the measures taken to protect it as totally inadequate. She is English by birth, but has been breeding sheep on her little farm near *Capel Curig* for over forty years. 'Farmers,' she says, 'are the salt of the earth.' Her former husband Thomas Firbank wrote a best-seller in 1940, called 'I Bought a Mountain', an autobiographical tale about life on a farm in Snowdonia. Esmé Kirby is the valiant president of the Snowdon National Park Society, of which she was co-founder in 1968. This private initiative has attracted some 1,600 members, of whom

Paul Sandby: Dolbadarn Castle and Llanberis Lake, 1764

only about 200 are Welsh, the rest being English. Like the National Park authorities themselves, the society has no control over planning, and can only act in an advisory capacity. But Mrs Kirby's club is not just for ramblers. They have protested against the monotonous conifer plantations, the plan to straighten the road through the Pass of Llanberis, and a road extension through the Pass of Aberglaslyn. 'The Department of Transport,' she says, 'has done more damage than anybody else in the National Park.' They also resisted the gigantic industrial complex at the foot of Snowdon, though of course their protests were in vain. In 1984, after a ten-year period of construction, Europe's largest hydroelectric power station was opened on the shores of *Llyn Peris*. It was built on the site of Dinorwic Slate Quarry, which had already shown back in the 19th century how industry held the reins in Snowdonia, despite the protests of a few idealists like William Morris.

Step by step the terraces of the old quarry climb the slopes of *Elidir*. And the slag heaps go steeply down to Llyn Peris – all the waste from millions of tons of slate, as if someone had wanted to fill the whole lake in. Over on the other shore, on a projecting crag, lie the ruins of *Dolbadarn Castle*, a Welsh fortress at the entrance to the legendary Pass of Llanberis (plates 96, 97). This is the chronology of a beauty spot: 1255, Llywelyn the Last keeps his brother Owain prisoner in the tower for more than twenty years. 1762, Richard Wilson paints castle and lake like a piece of classic Italy. 1798–99, Turner comes – twice – and paints Dolbadarn Castle as the apotheosis of his Welsh experience: this work gains him entry to the Royal Academy. 1832, Princess Victoria visits the romantic mountain lake, and is 'exceedingly struck with the scenery'; the result is inevitably a Royal Victoria Hotel, and Llanberis becomes the focal point for Snowdon tourists. There are still a few signs that this holiday resort was founded as an industrial new town during the 19th century. Once 3,000 people earned their living here in the slate quarries of Dinorwic. From about 1890 onwards Dinorwic meant slate, until in 1969 the last of the workers had gone, and the quarry became the North Wales Quarrying Museum. Its director, Dafydd Roberts, is a slate expert and a nationalist: 'It's easy enough to be an environmentalist when you've got a fat bank balance, like most of the retired, middle-class English people here in Wales.' For the younger generation of Welsh people like him, the National Park of Snowdonia has no taboos when it's a matter of finding jobs for local people. This is why the neighbouring hydroelectric power station at Dinorwic presents no problems as far as he is concerned. And after all, where is it? The fact is that the mountain has actually swallowed it up.

Deep inside Elidir are six giant turbine generators that pump the water up to *Marchlyn*

Cornelius Varley: The Pass of Llanberis, 1805

J. M. W. Turner: Llanberis Lake and Snowdon, c.1833

Mawr Reservoir through tunnels five and a half miles long from Llyn Peris, 1,729 feet below, and back again – a maximum of 88,000 gallons of water per second, which is enough to produce up to 1,880 megawatts. This would be enough to supply the whole of Wales, but in fact the generators are the safety net for the whole of the U.K. Full generation capacity can be achieved within ten seconds, and electricity sent anywhere if there is a sudden shortage. Not for nothing is Elidir now known as Power Mountain. In order for all this water to be converted into electricity, and for such quantities of energy to be stored, the mountain itself has been reconstructed as a power station: the 'pumped storage power station' in the interior of Elidir is taller than a sixteen-storey sky-scraper. And in order to hollow out the mountain's inside, over three million tons of slate had to be removed. The myth-makers of old could never have dreamt up such a colossus of power. It took ten years to build, and cost £450m, and is the pride of British technology in Wales.

All this, then, is Snowdonia – Dinorwic and Dolbadarn, ruined castle, mountain lake, wild gorges, slate quarries, narrow-gauge railways, and Snowdon towering over every-thing. Mythical Wales, modern Wales, everything thrown together in the melting pot of the National Park that is not a national park. In the Pass of Llanberis the rain pours down, and electricity pours out of Elidir. The power of Eryri is primal and inexhaustible, for these mountains are Ordovician, and have for millions of years withstood the onslaught of the elements of fire and flood, the Ice Ages, the ceaseless rain. They will doubtless survive the tramping feet of the tourists and the dragging feet of the bureaucrats. Those who live here know the score. 'These people know the mountains, but do not ascend them. They gnaw at them for small pay, and die early, silted up.' In his essay 'The Mountains', R. S. Thomas describes Snowdonia, these sources of tribulation and romantic yearnings: 'It is to this that men return, in thoughts, in reality, seeking for something unnameable, a lost Eden, a lost childhood; for fulfilment, for escape, for refuge, for conquest of themselves, for peace, for adventure. The list is endless. The hills have all this to give and more.'

My Grey Town: Blaenau Ffestiniog

A thin slab of slate stands on two boxes, and on the slab stands a very fat man in a bowler hat, evidently delighted that he can so convincingly put the weight of his authority behind the claim: 'Welsh slate – best in the world'. This publicity photo from the turn of the century was one of the first things I saw when I came to *Blaenau Ffestiniog* (plates 85, 87) from Betws-y-Coed, just 25 miles away in the National Park of Snowdonia. The landscape changes as gratingly as a pencil slipping over a slate. And that *is* Blaenau Ffestiniog – a scratchy scrape in the countryside, the echo of a million little slates.

Nothing in this world can be as grey as a grey day in Blaenau. The road winds down from the heights as if it were reluctant to enter this valley. To the left and the right are the towering slag heaps from the slate quarries, great terraced piles that join forces with the scarred and pitted rockfaces and the surrounding mountains to form one gigantic pit. At the bottom of this pit lies Blaenau Ffestiniog, the slate town. One long main street, behind which are the terraced houses of the workers: one storey, made of rough stone or granite, with slate roofs, slate front steps, slate numbers, slate nameplates. Behind each house is a tiny garden with flowers, a shed, a few vegetables. There's a sheep in one. They are houses with wet roofs and damp interiors, and the clouds lie like a permanent lid over the Blaenau basin. It rains twice as much here as it does nearby on the coast. 'We're the sink of Wales,' say the locals. If you want to go to Blaenau Ffestiniog, choose a grey day (which won't be difficult), for then the town in the grey mountains is in its true element – it luxuriates in grey, all shades from the lightest to the darkest, not to forget grey-green and grey-blue and the special fragmented, dripping grey of the rocks, and the equally special invisible grey of the slate dust, and dull grey and glossy grey and silver grey and silk grey, and the grey of poverty and despair, of labour and silicosis, of shadows and memories, of prehistory, of mists and mice and lead and steel and fields and puddles and the Welsh Sunday and the Welsh chapel and grey eminences and grey Puritans ... If Gershwin had been to Blaenau Ffestiniog, he would have written a Rhapsody in Grey.

Blaenau is built on slate and is surrounded by slate. Slate is its origin, its wealth, and its whole history. But not its future. Before Blaenau Ffestiniog became synonymous with

Samuel Palmer:
At Ffestiniog, 1835

Welsh slate, there was only *Ffestiniog* – a village three miles further south, famous for the beauty of its surroundings. Samuel Palmer painted watercolours here, and back in 1756 Lord Lyttelton was enthusiastic about his visit: 'With the woman one loves, with the friend of one's heart and a study of books, one might pass an age in this vale and think it a day.' About a hundred years later the wandering George Borrow sang the wild war songs of the bard Rhys Goch, follower of Owain Glyndwr and born in Ffestiniog. Borrow did not know that just a few miles away the Age of Slate had begun. But a long time ago the local people had already discovered the uses of this stone. Samuel Holland, a businessman and mining speculator from Liverpool, began large-scale slate quarrying in 1818 on land belonging to the Oakley family, and the success of the Oakley Slate Quarries brought more entrepreneurs to Blaenau Ffestiniog. They were all English, as was the case almost throughout the slate industry of North Wales, and the coal and iron industries of the South. In 1849 a banker's son from Warwick discovered a vein of slate on the site of what is now Llechwedd Slate Caverns, where previously nobody had done anything except hunt moorhens, and the size and quality of Merioneth Old Vein made it internationally famous. Soon there were endless slate trains rumbling down the hillsides with over a hundred trucks, accelerating with the weight of their loads, and then roaring through the Vale of Ffestiniog down to the coast and the port of *Porthmadog*. From there in 1873, 52 million pieces of slate were shipped all over the world. Welsh slate from the Oakley Quarries went into the roofs of Cologne Cathedral, the Peace Palace at the Hague, the AEG factory in Berlin, and houses as far away as Australia and New Zealand. In my own home town of Hamburg there are many houses that were built after the great fire of 1842 with roofs made from Blaenau Ffestiniog slate. At the turn of the century, when the Welsh slate industry was at its peak, the Blaenau quarries alone were producing some 140,000 tons a year. The output was impressive, but what was the cost in human terms?

Gloddfa Ganol is one of the abandoned Oakley Quarries, but was reopened in 1974 as a slate museum. The tunnels, some almost two miles long, burrow deep into the *Moelwyn Mountains* on twenty-eight different levels – galleries that run altogether for more than forty miles, a veritable labyrinth of passages and chambers that have hollowed these mountains into a honeycomb. The slate was quarried in a series of parallel chambers with walls and props in between, securing the roof. The so-called rockmen worked inside these chambers – one is said to be as big as St Paul's Cathedral – hanging on the rockface with a chain round their legs to hold them while they fixed explosives in the stone. Until 1947, the only light they had was candles, which they attached to the rock with a lump of clay. They had to pay for the candles themselves. They worked under appalling conditions: legs were torn off by the chains, some men were crushed by falling rock, and others died of typhus ('Ffestiniog fever'). But more than anything else they feared the silent, lingering death they breathed in day after day – the fine slate dust that accumulated in their lungs and gave them silicosis. 'If a Victorian quarryman lived to be 40,' said Bryan, our guide, 'he'd reached a ripe old age. I wouldn't have wanted to work here – not for all the tea in China.' During the twenties and thirties the Welsh slate quarriers had the highest incidence of tuberculosis in Great Britain.

When the rockmen had finished their blasting, the rubbishers brought out the slate and the slag, and then the splitters and dressers went into action. The former split the blocks of slate, and the latter broke them up into standard sizes. The work has long since been taken over by machines, but in Gloddfa Ganol or the slate museum at Llanberis there are demonstrations of how it used to be done: the splitter sits cross-legged on a low stool, the block propped up by his knee, and with a miner's hammer and chisel he chips off very thin slices. Out of a good quality piece two inches thick, an expert could conjure up to sixteen slates. There were standard sizes for these, all given aristocratic names, from 'Empress' (26″ × 16″) through 'Duchess' and 'Countess' down to 'Lady' (16″ × 8″). This was the work of the dresser, who could then make ribald remarks about the females he was dressing.

Like the Rhondda miners, the Blaenau slate quarries constituted a special breed of highly qualified workers, Non-Conformists, and radical Liberals. For their *'te bach'*, tea break, they would congregate in a dead section of the tunnel, the '*caban*': this was more than just a canteen; it was an underground club, where the men would talk about God or the union, sing songs and make up extempore poems. Each '*caban*' would organize its own Eisteddfod. As in the Valleys, this was a chapel society. In 1880, Blaenau had 11,300 inhabitants, 18 slate quarries, and 26 chapels. 'Y Chwarelwr' (The Quarryman) was the title of the first Welsh-speaking film, which was made in 1935 in the Llechwedd Slate Caverns of Blaenau Ffestiniog. Today you can take a special cabin railway down into Deep Mine, another of the dead tunnels kept open for tourists. At the end of the 19th century there were some 4,000 quarrymen working in this one town – a quarter of all those employed in North Wales's slate industry. Today there are just two quarries left, both open-cast, with 150 workers. The population has halved, and the unemployment rate is around 18%. Lying there surrounded by the slag of its past, this grey slate town has no future. But it won't give up.

Once upon a time, there were two sisters, Ffestiniog and Blaenau. The first was a child of rivers and woods, spoilt by Nature and enchanting everyone with her beauty. Blaenau came into the world with nothing but slate, a scarface with a heart of stone and blessed only with a pair of strong arms. She was left to do all the dirty work in the mountains, while her sister stayed young and beautiful down in the valley. The years went by. Blaenau grew ever greyer and weaker. In the beginning people had secretly hoped that beneath the face of slate there might be a heart of gold, but it was Dolgellau that had the gold. And in the end, no-one wanted Blaenau any more. For a while she lived on the remains of her work, piled up all around her, and those who had been to visit her beautiful sister Ffestiniog came to have a look at the ugly sister. With a mixture of curiosity and sympathy they peeped, and then hurried away.

In the days when wishes used to come true, perhaps a fairy god-mother might have touched Blaenau with her magic wand, transformed her into a beauty like her sister, and then married her off to a handsome prince. It never happened, but in all honesty it can be said that a lot of princes did come to Blaenau – intellectuals, poets and artists with the independence of mind not to be put off by an ugly face. Indeed they may well have been strangely attracted by the plainness and the poverty. How else can one explain the fact that Arthur Koestler, John Cowper Powys, A. S. Neill, and David Nash all came to live in Blaenau Ffestiniog?

Shortly after the beginning of the Second World War, when the Crown Jewels and various masterpieces were brought from London for safekeeping in one of Blaenau's quarries[1], the educationalist A. S. Neill also arrived here, bringing with him his model school, Summerhill. He stayed here till 1945: 'the longest years of my life. It rained and

---

1   Valuable items from the British Museum and about 1,000 paintings from the National Gallery were stored in the slate chambers of Manod until 1945. The tunnels are to serve as emergency government headquarters in the event of a nuclear war.

rained,' he recalls in his autobiography. 'All around us were Welsh-speaking people; some of the aged knew no English. I had returned to the atmosphere of my native Scottish village.[1] Chapels and hymns were everywhere, with their accompanying hypocrisy.' For this pioneer of anti-authoritarian education, the years in Blaenau were 'a misery to me'; this was partly due to the death of his wife, but there were other painful factors, too: 'the pubs closed at 9 pm as against 10.30 pm in England … I had also returned to the joys of the Scottish Sabbath. One dared not dig the garden on a Sunday.' In short, 'Wales was Hell for me.' There was only one thing the Scottish A. S. Neill liked about the Welsh: 'I discovered a deep resentment against England and its war laws.'

After 1945, Arthur Koestler lived for many years in a farmhouse near Blaenau Ffestiniog (Bwlch Iccyn). And there is another literary address which the town itself has almost completely forgotten: Waterloo Terrace, *Manod*. Here, John Cowper Powys, that great English lover of Wales spent the last eight years of his life. Because of his abhorrence of public life, he had left the little town of Corwen in 1955 (see page 312), and come to Blaenau, '*the most difficult place to reach* within 50 miles! Once there I shall become an *absolute Hermit …*' But of course even here they found him, the journalists, scholars, and portrait painters. From Japan came a professor, from London came Augustus John, and from Cardiff an honorary doctorate. Tucked away in his quarryman's cottage, buried in slate like some venerable fossil, almost 90 years old, 'old brother John' went on writing: on Homer, on the Mountains of the Moon, but nothing about Blaenau Ffestiniog, unless one counts the beginning of his fantasy tale 'Topsy Turvy' (1959), which is set on the first floor of his house. (But the town *is* immortalized in Alexander Cordell's popular slate epic 'This Sweet and Bitter Earth'.) In Blaenau as in Corwen it is now as if Powys had never been there. He has vanished from the town without a trace. And that is how he would have wanted it. Otherwise, he would surely have had himself buried here, in Welsh earth rather than in English waters. But he shunned public death as much as he had shunned public life, and so, mythical and mystical to the end, he had his ashes scattered on the sea, off the coast of Dorset, which was the setting for his novel 'Weymouth Sands'. Here not even the most literary-minded of tourists can get to him.

But of course there are better reasons for coming to Blaenau than just to survive a war or to die in peace. You can live cheaply here, and you can concentrate on your work. Indeed, there is little else for you to concentrate on, which is good for the creative mind. Where there isn't much to do, you can get a lot done. In an old water-mill on the outskirts of the town, I made the acquaintance of Falcon D. Hildred: architect, designer, industrial archaeologist, and inveterate carrier of sketchbook and pencil. 'Here in Blaenau we're kept out of the National Park of Snowdonia, because we're not beautiful enough. All right, we're the ugly bit of industry – so let's be an industrial park!' In Pant-yr-Ynn Mill, which has been his studio and home since 1969, Falcon D. Hildred has made a fine beginning.

1   A. S. Neill was born in 1883, the son of a village teacher in Kingsmuir, Forfar.

Under the name of 'Worktown', this Englishman has set up an exhibition of utensils, machines, tools, photographs, depicting the history of the British industrial town, beginning with Blaenau, and also his own drawings: 'Blaenau Ffestiniog is a well-preserved 19th-century industrial town, very old-fashioned and very poor. We shouldn't make the same mistake here as they made in the Valleys, where they've got rid of nearly every trace of industry. Fortunately, Blaenau hasn't got enough money to tear things down and replace them with hideous bungalows.'

The grey 'worktown' in the green doesn't only attract industrial archaeologists. For over a decade the English potter Adrian Childs has lived in this 'wet, work-a-day town', producing superb household ceramics – earthenware in the rural tradition. A few streets away from him lives David Nash. He finds his materials in Nature, and his studio is the landscape, for David Nash is quite literally a land-artist, and one of Britain's finest.

I met him in Capel Rhiw, a Victorian Methodist chapel (plate 45) that squats like a toad at the foot of giant slag heaps. 'I bought the chapel for £200,' he says. 'In those days people would rather have demolished it than let an artist have it.' All the same, this is certainly a much more apposite continuation of the Non-Conformist tradition than the garages I saw in two other chapels (plate 44). David Nash was born in London in 1945, and moved to Blaenau in 1967. He had always come here in the school holidays to visit his grandfather. 'I never liked the place. It's ugly. But I knew I could survive here.' As a young artist with no commissions and no patrons, he kept the wolf from the door by making souvenirs out of slate, but since those early days he has stopped using slate altogether. His favourite material is wood. Whole tree trunks, beams, blocks and branches, and wooden sculptures fill the large interior of his chapel. He has converted the sacristy, and there he lives with his wife, the sculptress Claire Langdown, and their two sons. Beds, tables and shelves are all home-made. 'I want to live and work in a simple way. I want life and work to reflect the balance and continuity of Nature. By identifying myself with the time and energy of the tree and with its mortality, I feel myself drawn more deeply into the joys and sorrows of Nature.'

David Nash is a 'woodman', in the tradition of the Romanian sculptor Brancusi, with his emphasis on simplicity, and he's avant-garde, yet faithful to the tradition of the peasant wood-carver. Influenced by Jakob Böhme's creed of the energies of nature, Nash tries to combine mystic and minimal art: he uses cheap materials to create elemental signs, and his art emerges from the rhythms and forms of Nature. Initially he regarded trees as the raw material for sculpture to be created in the studio; but now Nash does his work increasingly outside in the country, using the structural and growth laws of the tree itself. Water, smoke and snow are also his materials, and he has worked in the sculpture parks of Yorkshire and Holland, and in the forests of Cumbria and Japan. There is a field near Maentwrog, south of Blaenau, where you can see one of David Nash's living sculptures: 'Fletched-Over Ash Tree', a circle of ashes planted in 1977, which he has arched over into a dome, and intends to bend into shape again three times, at ten-year intervals, after which he will leave them alone. 'A silver structure in winter, a green canopy space in summer, a volcano of growing energy.'

Davis Nash is an Englishman who lives in Wales, regards himself as a British artist, and is having his children taught Welsh. 'I love this land, I like the people, but at a distance.' For him the grey town is like a bare canvas, challenging his creativity. He has had two vital experiences in Blaenau Ffestiniog: 'the raw reality of Nature, rain and wind, and the raw reality of society, work, and unemployment. Both make me aware of what elementary survival means.'

Lord Penrhyn's Businesses: Slate for the Roofs of the World

Behind every house a coalmine, and in the front garden a flock of sheep: that's the cliché view of Wales. The importance of the slate industry has been generally underestimated. It was only when I travelled through North Wales that I realized just how ubiquitous this stone is, and not just in Blaenau Ffestiniog. They have roofed their houses with slate, walled their meadows with slate, and buried their dead beneath slate. The tiles on the floors of Boston Airport are made from the same green Penrhyn slate as the memorial plaque to Dylan Thomas in Poets' Corner in Westminster Abbey. In the corridors of King Abdul Aziz University in Jeddah, Saudi Arabia, you can sit on benches made from Corris slate, pleasantly cool, though not so pleasantly hard. The Prince of Wales may have had a similar experience, since the stool made specially for his investiture was, naturally, made from Welsh slate, though the impression may have been softened by the addition of a cushion (plate 1b). This stool represented an ingenious mixture of national pride and respect for royalty: the English Prince had to sit as Welshly as possible — bolt upright and uncomfortable, in a posture of unconscious resistance. The choice of Welsh slate gave this act of state an unmistakable prehistoric dimension, a moment almost of fossilization, for the Prince was sitting on volcanic ash and mud that had sedimented some 600 million years ago and then, through massive pressure, had been compressed into mountains. The geologist Adam Sedgwick was the first to investigate these sediments, and in 1852 he coined the term 'Cambrian System', after the Roman name for Wales.[1] The girdle of Cambrian slate stretches from the slopes of the Carneddau, through the Glyder and Elidir Mountains, across the north-west side of the Snowdon massif, as far as Nantlle – a colossal seam, mostly accessible to open-cast quarrying, and at its richest in Penrhyn and Dinorwic. The shafts and tunnels in Blaenau Ffestiniog were necessary, however, because Ordovician slate lay awkwardly in diagonal seams. If you add the area around *Corris*,

1   The Silurian and Ordovician geological formations are also derived from the original Welsh inhabitants – or their Roman names – i.e. the pre-Celtic tribes of the Silures and the Ordovices.

where slate fences stand like rows of beautiful (though disappearing) sculptures, the great North Welsh slate basin lies between Machynlleth and Bangor (colour plate 1; plate 86).

The houses in Segontium, the Roman camp near Caernarfon, were roofed with slate. And from the 16th century onwards slate was quarried commercially, though never systematically. It was only when more and more people needed roofs over their heads (the population in England and Wales tripled between 1801 and 1881) that the great industrial towns began to expand, with row upon row of terraced houses requiring unlimited supplies of slate. It was a cheap, weather-resistant material. And when people in the United Kingdom sat snugly under the Welsh slate roofs, warming themselves by the Welsh coal fire, people in the colonies decided they too would like Welsh slate roofs over their heads. In 1882, the total production of slate in Great Britain amounted to almost 505,000 tons; 93% of this came from North Wales. At the peak of the slate industry, in 1898, some 16,700 workers produced over 490,000 tons, and Welsh slate was roofing the world.

The two biggest slate quarries at that time belonged to two English families, who also owned large sections of North Wales: they were the Pennants of Penrhyn and the Assheton-Smiths of Dinorwic. When the workers of Dinorwic began to chisel out the giant steps in the slopes of Elidir (1809) – terraces almost 2,000 feet high, and each gallery

Kenneth Rowntree: School at Upper Corris, with Cader Idris beyond, 1948

Alfred Sumners: The Slate Quarry at Penrhyn, 1852

with its own name, like Virginia, Abyssinia, Jubilee – Lord Penrhyn's quarrymen were already knocking a giant hole in the other side of the mountain, forming an amazing amphitheatre of slate: *Penrhyn* Quarry. There I was, fresh from the nature trail of Snowdonia National Park, and suddenly, at the end of the ice-age valley of Nant Ffrancon, I was confronted by the mighty slag heaps deposited by the industrial age. Richard Pennant could hardly have imagined such dimensions, but he was the one who started it all off: he was an English entrepreneur, MP for Liverpool, opposed to the abolition of slavery because his fortune was derived from the sugar plantations in Jamaica. In Wales this highly efficient man found mountains which God had certainly not put there merely for the purpose of climbing. And so in 1782 he set about quarrying them. By 1792 he was Baron Penrhyn, employed 150 workers, and exported more than 12,000 tons of slate a year. Ten years later, he had doubled his work force, laid down the first narrow-gauge, horse-drawn railway in Wales (1801), running through Ogwen Valley and down to the coast (the railway was finally closed in 1962), built *Port Penrhyn* near Bangor, erecting a slate factory on the quayside, and – as might have been expected – opened up the West Indies as a slate market. Lord Penrhyn died in 1808, leaving behind a flourishing family business and a widow who gave each of her horses a pension of £45 a year. Lady Penrhyn's quarrymen

Slate Factory in Bangor, c.1910

earned 17 shillings a month, i.e. a quarter of what the horses had. Nevertheless, the slate baron did at least build houses for his workers, and by comparison with the depressing rows of terraced houses to be found in English industrial towns, Llandegai could truly be called a model estate. The graves of the Penrhyns lie in the village church, surmounted by a lifesize marble quarryman.

The workers' estate of Llandegai stands at the entrance to the grounds of *Penrhyn Castle*. Just like the industrial barons of the South, the slate kings wanted to emulate the landed gentry. In fact the country house which the first Lord Penrhyn had built in Neo-Gothic style by Samuel Wyatt (*c.1782*) was a comparatively modest affair, but his successor, George Hay Dawkins Pennant, stuck a mighty castle in the middle of the landscape, as if to ward off assaults from rebellious Welsh quarrymen (who actually developed a most effective siege weapon: the unions). The five-storey Neo-Norman keep of Penrhyn is a copy of the one in Castle Hedingham, in Essex. This mock-medieval romanticism reflected the longing of the nouveaux riches to endow themselves with all those trappings of origin and style for which they so envied the Establishment. For this purpose, George Pennant engaged an architect in 1827 who had made a name for himself through his work for King George IV at Carlton House and Windsor Castle: Thomas Hopper. He was a brilliant eclectic, who built a Tudor Gothic country house for the Talbots in Margam (see page 204), and for the Pennants in the North pulled out all the Neo-Norman stops as if Penrhyn Castle were to take its place among Edward I's chain of fortresses: massive walls, crenellated towers, and a groundplan that is picturesquely irregular. The outer walls are bare and solid, while the interiors combine the monumental with the ornamental in almost nightmarish splendour. A long, low, crypt-like passage leads to the lofty Great Hall – a dramatic change of dimension, typical of Hopper's theatrical Norman style. The most spectacular coup de theatre is the staircase, whose stone masks, round arches and decorations are more redolent of some eastern potentate than a slate baron. This rise in social status cost some £50,000 – a huge sum in those days. Hopper also designed the Norman-style furniture (c.1830) – solid oak, to fit in with the oak columns in the drawing room, with their zig-zag and rhomboid decorations; there are even Norman-style bedside cabinets. Another material that had to be used, of course, was the family's very own slate, and so there is a slate billiard table in the library, a slate fireplace in the dining-room, and a slate four-poster bed that weighs no less than four tons. This was too much even for Victorian tastes, and when Her Majesty Queen Victoria herself visited the house in 1859, she refused to spend the night in this slate coffin.

Whether you like it or not, Thomas Hopper's Penrhyn Castle is an outstanding example of the Norman Revival.[1] But just when it was completed, in 1840, the owner died. And so it passed to his elder daughter 'Slate' (the younger daughter was nicknamed 'Sugar'). Her husband, Colonel Edward Douglas Pennant, brought the family empire to its peak: in 1862 there were almost 3,000 workers in the Penrhyn Quarries, producing some 128,000 tons – more than a quarter of the total production in Wales. When 'the arch magnate Colonel Slater' (Charles Dickens) died in 1886, he left behind the biggest slate quarry in the world, a gigantic amphitheatre in the rock, over 1,100 feet deep. But for every ton of slate, there are nine tons of slag, and so the slag heaps grew to horrendous proportions: about six square miles of rubbish. These are gradually being whittled away for use in road-building.

The town at the feet of these slag heaps is called *Bethesda*. Originally this was the name of the chapel that the Independents built in 1820 on Telford's road to Holyhead. The village of the quarries grew up round the chapel, as did the Welsh Nazareth, Carmel, Cesarea, and other settlements with biblical names, for during the 19th century the religious revival was at its height, a fact not unconnected with the growth of the slate and coal industries. It was in Bethesda, this strange world of slate, choirs and depression, that in 1937 an English woman-artist took up residence – initially quite out of place, soon

---

1 Hopper built the first important example of British Neo-Romanesque in Ireland: Gosford Castle, Co. Armagh (1819).

Penrhyn Castle: the Great Hall, lithograph by Hawkins, c.1850

Penrhyn Castle: the Library

greatly loved, and in the end admired both in and beyond Bethesda. Her name was Mary Elizabeth Thompson. You won't find her name in the art history books, for her brush never contributed to the evolution of modern dots and dashes. She simply went into the quarries and drew what she saw and felt there: rock formations, work, men, Welsh everyday life. With patience, precision and passion she opened up a whole new world with her drawings. The Penrhyn Quarry, where she began, possessed for her 'a secret beauty and majesty, uncommunicable'. She was fascinated by geological structures ('happy in the company of rock'), and also by the rockmen themselves, their work and their life in the stone. 'Ifor Morgan, splitting a block of slate' – thanks to her drawing, we know what he looked like, how he spent his life, and that he once existed and was real. 'Wil Harri, slate splitter' – he, too, was one of thousands, but unlike Constantin Meunier, the artist who had so inspired her, Mary Thompson was interested in the individual rather than the archetype. She went to all the Welsh slate quarries, as well as to some granite quarries, and for seventeen years she drew what she saw, a tiny little woman with congenital curvature of the spine. Nearly all her pictures, this topographical record of Welsh quarrying, are now in the National Museum in Cardiff, and with each passing generation their value grows, for the time will come when they will be all that remains of an extinct form of life.

In 1955 Mary Thompson wrote sadly: 'There is a different spirit in the slate quarries today. The wrong type of men are going in who only care for the wage packet and nothing

M. E. Thompson: Ifor Morgan, splitting a block of slate, 1947

for the work.' She gave up her work in the quarries, and left Bethesda.[1] 'Tradition once lost will never return. It was a great tradition.' Shortly before that date, the Pennants had sold their business and handed over their country estate to the National Trust. At the turn of the century the Welsh slate industry had employed almost 14,000 people, and now there are barely 500. With diamond-tipped stone-cutters one man can now do the work of five, but the high costs of transportation and the development of cheap substitutes have hastened the decline of this once flourishing industry. Nevertheless, Dafydd Roberts, director of the slate museum in Llanberis, believes that there will be a renaissance: 'Some of the quarries could be reopened. There's a continual need for good quality slate for roof tiles, floors, fireplaces and snooker tables.' Today the main export from the Penrhyn Quarries is slate dust for use in the manufacture of paint, cosmetics, and the enamel protective layer for oil pipelines. Clocks, chessmen, souvenirs, and an endless amount of kitsch can be made out of slate. It can also be used for art, which brings us to Jonah Jones in *Porthmadog*. His memorial plaques show just how expressive slate can be in the hands of a master. What canvas is to the painter, slate is to Jonah Jones. He is a calligrapher,

---

1 The Welsh painter Peter Prendergast has lived in Bethseda since 1970. He paints and draws the industrial structures in and around Bethseda, as well as the Penrhyn Quarries in a style derived from Expressionism.

sculptor, watercolourist and author, and he works in a 19th-century slate workshop in Porthmadog, the port to which the old slate trains used to come from Blaenau Ffestiniog.

The end of the slate boom marked the beginning of the *Great Little Trains* (plates 83, 84). Narrow-gauge railways are the prettiest of all the industry's by-products. These rolling fossils from the Age of Slate and the Age of Steam have miraculously survived, thanks to the nostalgia of the steam enthusiasts. Once these trains carried millions of tons of slate, and now they carry about a million tourists a year. For these people, the narrow-gauge railway is a true symbol of this little country. Who can resist the green engine of Talyllyn, the red engine of Llanberis Lake, the blue engine of Bala, all the bright colours, the gleaming brass pistons and rods, shining like the faces of the men who polish them as if they were diamonds? Who could fail to fall in love with the tiny train of Fairbourne, or the puffer mounting Snowdon, with trains panting up the hill, whistling in the tunnel, or rattling happily through the Vale of Ffestiniog? And then there are the stops, each one proud of being a mainline station, surrounded by green, and full of fun as the engine lets off steam, or takes on water, while the walls preach the Bible, and everything you need is there – tickets, tea and toilets. Great Little Trains: there are ten of these railways left, and each one has its own character, its unmistakable charm, and its history. On the Llanberis Lake Railway, the doors only open on one side, to make sure that passengers don't fall into the lake. The Welshpool and Llanfair Railway has engines from

Loading Slate in Porthmadog Harbour, 1908

Sierra Leone and a Pullman car from the Ziller Valley Railway (1900). The Ffestiniog Railway is the oldest narrow-gauge passenger line (1863) and also the most successful (around 400,000 passengers a year), while Fairbourne is the narrowest with a gauge of just 15 inches. Connoisseurs can distinguish one line from another with their eyes blissfully closed, judging by the sound and the smell alone.

Great Little Trains: part of their charm is the fact that they carry on steaming out of pure love, and not for commercial gain. All credit to the narrow-gauge enthusiasts, and pride of place to those who fought to preserve the Talyllyn Railway, since it was their campaign that set the example for all the others. When the slate quarry closed in 1947, shortly before the death of its owner, the Preservation Society took it over, restored it themselves, and kept it going at their own expense. Today the Society has around 3,000 members, 12 paid employees and, even more important, over 300 volunteer helpers who spend their weekends or their holidays cleaning the engines, selling tickets, or – to achieve a lifetime's ambition – switching the points. It may well be that the man punching your ticket is a computer specialist from Liverpool who has just taken a few days off in order to play with 'his' railway. Or the engine-driver may be on holiday from his job as a ticket inspector with British Rail. If it were not for these steam freaks from England, some of the railways would have long since run out of steam. 'We have about 800 members,' says Graham Farr, director of the Welsh Highland Light Railway Ltd, 'including architects, truck-drivers, clerks, students, and every profession you can think of. Most of them are English – 15% at most are Welsh.' It's the same story with the other Railway Societies. Graham Farr was in his mid thirties when I met him, a civil servant from Stafford, and totally dedicated. His ambition was to restore seven miles of line from Porthmadog, so that his Russell steam engine could run through the Pass of Aberglaslyn to Beddgelert. But there are other travellers who have long since taken over the old line: the hikers. And they are totally opposed to any railway going through the National Park of Snowdonia. The director of the narrow-gauge railway is left casting a sorrowful eye over the rusting rails in the gorse.

The Menai Bridge: Telford Builds and Schinkel Takes Notes

What the Golden Gate Bridge is to America, the *Menai Suspension Bridge* is to Wales (colour plate 21). It's not quite so big, and not quite so famous, and it leads to *Bangor*, which is not quite San Francisco. But for all that, I think it's one of the most beautiful bridges in the world. Its two piers are Snowdonia's mountains and the island of Anglesey – or at least that's how it looks if you see it from far enough away. In a gale it swings like a giant hammock, and its iron cables hum like the strings of a harp. Since prehistoric times people have stood by the *Menai Strait* waiting for the tide to go out, or for the ferryman to take them across. The Menai Strait runs for over twelve miles, separating Anglesey from the mainland, and every summer it is the scene of a popular regatta. At its narrowest point, the Menai sound is just 600 feet wide, but treacherous currents, strong tides, sandbanks and storms make these waters more dangerous than any river you can think of. The ferry could cross, and sometimes cattle, bellowing in fear as they swam against the currents, but no-one else, until the early 19th century; until Telford.

On our journey through Wales, we have already met Telford quite a few times. We have admired his aqueducts and his bridges and, less strikingly but even more importantly, we have used his Holyhead Turnpike Road, the modern A5, which begins in London at Marble Arch. Before Telford was commissioned by the government to build this (1815–29), the 268 miles to Anglesey were a nightmare for travellers: narrow, insecure, and positively dangerous, with a maximum speed of 7½ miles an hour for coaches. Telford made a proper road out of it, in keeping with the increased comforts of the time as well as the rise in commercial traffic that followed union with Ireland. Even in Snowdonia, the gradient never exceeded 1:20. It was more solid than any Roman road, and was so expensive that it had to be financed by tolls. The Menai Strait represented the last great barrier on the route to Holyhead, and the Menai Bridge was the crowning-point of Telford's road and of his career.

Thomas Telford was the son of a Scottish shepherd. He qualified as a stonemason, taught himself engineering, and already in 1801 he had proposed that the new London Bridge should consist of a single cast-iron arch 660 feet wide – a construction which people considered to be much too daring. Now, in 1819, for the Menai Strait Telford designed a bridge that would hang from two limestone piers on wrought-iron chains 580 feet long. It was suspended 100 feet above the level of the water at high tide, so that ships could pass beneath. This was not the first suspension bridge in the world,[1] but for a long time it remained the longest. Telford had each of the sixteen chains tested over and over and over again before he floated them into position between the pylons on a giant raft and then had them hoisted up. The whole thing was assembled without scaffolding – which with such an enormous span was no mean undertaking, and was certainly not without danger. But on 30 January 1826 the first post-chaise crossed the bridge, followed by cheering crowds. In his autobiography, Telford notes with satisfaction that his bridge became 'an object of national curiosity and delight'.

Six months after the opening, in July 1826, the Prussian architect Karl Friedrich Schinkel sat in a coach that crossed his colleague's bridge. 'An admirably bold piece of work,' he said, 'with no shaking as the coach went across.' He noted the exact dimensions and, as he had done before in Conwy, he made a sketch 'in order to capture the colossal scale of the thing'. With such constructions, British architects and engineers had attracted attention

---

1 The oldest surviving iron suspension bridge in Europe is the Union Chain Bridge over the Tweed in Berwick (1820), built by Samuel Brown, a naval officer. His patent iron chain was originally designed for shipping, but Telford was also able to use it for his bridges.

Karl Friedrich Schinkel: Menai Bridge, 1826

from all over Europe, and they were of especial interest to Herr Schinkel as he travelled through England and Wales. He admired Rennie's bridges over the Thames, the London Docks and various ironworks and textile factories, and was impressed by Telford's roads and bridges. This was a journey into the land of the Industrial Revolution, and an invaluable lesson to an industrial architect like Karl Friedrich Schinkel. But to someone seeking the picturesque, and making a Sentimental rather than an Industrial Journey, the Menai Bridge was a disappointment. The Saxon Carl Gustav Carus stood before it in summer 1844 and noted: 'There was a total lack of charm and beauty in this huge work, dominated through and through by the principle of functionality. Uniform and rectilinear, it cuts through the landscape like a black ruler curved on one side, and nearby are the pylons without any decent architectonic or plastic decoration, and the eternal iron bars in their monotonous succession just give you a feeling of the despair a painter must be plunged into if he should try to make a precise drawing of this tedious road of railings ... It is in fact a thoroughly English, dry, pedantic character that usually emerges from such constructions.' Blind to the beauty of the technical form, and to the modernity of this streamlined and functional structure, Carus (who was a romantic painter and a friend of Goethe's) asks in despair: 'What sort of style is art to employ here in order to instil the charm of beauty? Egyptian and Greek styles are totally inappropriate for iron structures, and likewise there can be little place for Gothic ... This remains for ever nothing but a large mathematical symbol!'

The stylistic solutions to such problems were provided by the Victorian gingerbread architecture. Telford, however, was faced with very different problems. Just a few days after the bridge had been opened, a storm set the deck swinging, the carriageway rose and then sank nearly twenty inches, and many of the struts broke. Another storm in 1839 completely destroyed the deck. Such experiences with the powerful winds of the Menai Strait reinforced Telford's conviction that the limit for a suspension bridge was 600 feet.

He was all the more disappointed that towards the end of his life, the commission for the Clifton Suspension Bridge went, not to him, but to a 23-year-old novice: Isambard Kingdom Brunel. The latter's design for a suspension bridge 702 feet long was dismissed by Telford as sheer folly. No doubt he would have refused to set foot on the Severn Bridge, whose overall span is over 3,000 feet. We may perhaps marvel even now at such a construction, but I wonder how many of us know the name of the designer. It seems that only the pioneers are immortalized.

Another pioneer was Robert Stephenson. He built the second Menai Bridge to carry the railway from Chester to Holyhead, and this bridge is another masterpiece of technology: the *Britannia Tubular Bridge* (1846–50). The train would disappear into two rectangular tubes of wrought iron, 100 feet above the water, and re-emerge on the other side – to the delight of the on-looker – like a rabbit out of a hat. It was a monument to the age of the railway that had been inaugurated by Robert's father George. But after a fire in 1970, the bridge had to be demolished, all except the three limestone piers. When it was rebuilt, a second deck for road traffic was built over the railway deck, in order to relieve some of the pressure on Telford's suspension bridge. The Menai bridges were hailed as Welsh wonders of the world, commemorated on plates and cups, pictures and banknotes, while every

George Arnold: Menai Suspension Bridge, 1828

G. Hawkins: Britannia Bridge, 1851

phase of construction was recorded on coloured lithographs. All this can be seen in Bangor Museum. Telford and Stephenson: their bridges stood side by side over the Menai Strait, and their bodies lie side by side in Westminster Abbey.

And so we come to the island of Anglesey. Long before the engineers and businessmen set foot on the island, the pilgrims were here. On a promontory between the two bridges there is a cemetery with a little 15th-century church. This simple, rectangular site goes far back to the time of the Celtic missionaries. It was St Tysilio that founded this prayer-cell around 630, close to the whirling currents of the Menai Strait.

Behind the Hedges of Anglesey: The Island of the Tudors

When I crossed the Menai Bridge back in the summer of 1983 to go to the National Eisteddfod in Llangefni, a strange reception committee had stationed themselves on one of the pylons. High above the waters of the Menai Strait, demonstrators from the Welsh Language Society greeted visitors from the mainland with a banner that said: 'No welcome for newcomers to Anglesey or the Malvinas'. Were the English as unwelcome here as on the 'liberated' Falkland Islands? Was this more than just delayed criticism of the Iron Lady?

There was a much clearer message daubed on cottage walls: 'Welsh homes for Welsh people'. At the end of the 1970's, about 3,000 people a year were moving onto the island, most of them from England. A nationality-conscious minority was afraid of being swamped.

But what is it that makes Anglesey so attractive to holiday-makers and second-home owners? At first sight, I must confess I was disappointed – the island seems flat and uninteresting. 'Oats and Methodism' was George Borrow's description of an area he considered poor, with no scenic charm, though packed with bards. However, you can't always trust even the best of guidebooks or, for that matter, your own first impressions. What George Borrow found interesting on Anglesey in 1854 was of no interest to me, but what I liked, others might well regard as dull. It's all a matter of taste. Anglesey's charms are not spectacular (colour plates 11, 34). It's a green, gently undulating landscape, quietly soothing after the drama of Snowdonia's peaks and valleys. It doesn't force itself on you, doesn't demand to be admired or climbed, but simply rests behind its hills and hedges, stretching itself out, and waiting with all the time in the world. It's easy on the eye. It almost invites you to lie down behind those seductive whitethorn hedges and gaze up at the clouds.

When Charles F. Tunnicliffe, a member of the Royal Academy, was asked why he came to London so infrequently, he replied that he preferred the birds of Anglesey to those of Piccadilly. Until his death in 1979, Tunnicliffe lived for thirty years at *Malltraeth Bay*, in the south west of the island. There the sands, marshes and dunes, and *Newborough Warren* nature reserve offered him everything he needed: birds, peace, and light. It is no coincidence that a bird specialist should have become Anglesey's most famous painter. What Audubon did for the French and the Americans, Tunnicliffe did for the British: he was a master of animal and, especially, bird portraiture. The largest collection of his watercolours and sketches was acquired by the island's administration in 1981 at an auction. The price was £100,000, paid for partly by the yearly compensation from the oil companies for damage to the environment round about the oil port of *Amlwch*. Tunnicliffe's birds are a symbol of what many people seek on this island – freedom and solitude. Anglesey consists of more than a hundred miles of coast, a mild climate favoured by the Irish Sea, bathing beaches like *Rhosneigr* and *Church Bay*, little coves like *Borthwen*, *Hen Borth* and *Cemaes Bay*, and in between, nothing but cliffs and wind. But what cliffs they are! Geologists come to kiss these rocks. Pre-Cambrian, they cry, primal rock a thousand million years old. I can't say that this excites me as much as it does them, but you do get a strange feeling when you see the foundations of the earth laid bare like the rocks at *South Stack* and *Rhoscolyn*, folded – as the geologists so vividly put it – as so many pieces of cloth. As for the impression that the island is flat, there is a scientific explanation: the Menai plateau, which probably goes back to the tertiary period, i.e. about 37 million years, is the worn-down centre of what used to be highlands. The island only emerged in the Ice Age, when the glaciers melted, the sea level rose, and the valley of the Menai Strait sank beneath the water.

'*Môn Mam Cymru*' was the name Giraldus Cambrensis gave to the island – Mother of Wales. The name Anglesey is probably derived from the old Norse word '*öngull*', meaning Fjord, and not from the 'Angles'. Once this was the granary of the country, Europe's richest copper mine, centre of Celtic druidism, seat of the Princes of Gwynned, and island of the Tudors. The ancestors of Henry VIII and Elizabeth I came from the Anglesey village of *Penmynydd*. Of course, they had to come from somewhere, but nevertheless it was a surprise to me that they should have come from behind these whitethorn hedges. The Tudor dynasty lasted for 118 years, beginning with a Welshman and ending with a Scot. The family tree was free from all knots: Owain ap Maredudd ap Tewdwr was born in 1385 in Plâs Penmynydd, and fought alongside Henry V at the Battle of Agincourt. After this successful campaign, the King made his faithful follower head of the Royal Household. At the English court he was known as Owen Tudor, though from his home he had brought with him another name, redolent of his good looks and his nobility: 'The Rose of Mona'. There ensued a famous historical romance. Catherine of Valois, the beautiful daughter of the French King Charles VI, married Henry V, who died shortly after the wedding, whereupon she fell in love with the Rose of Mona. They secretly married, probably in 1429, and the King's widow secretly bore three sons, but this was a liaison dangereuse which displeased King Henry VI. He sent his mother to a convent (where she died), and his stepfather to prison. After escaping twice, he was eventually pardoned, and his son Edmund was made Earl of Richmond. The latter's son was born in Pembroke Castle (see page 257), and on his behalf and that of the House of Lancaster, the old knight from Anglesey rode once more into battle, during the Wars of the Roses. Ironically, the Rose of Mona met his end in this war, beheaded by the Yorkists in 1461 in the marketplace at Hereford. Not until 1485 did the bloody civil war end with the victory and coronation of Henry VII, Owain Tewdwr's grandson. Merlin had prophesied that England would have a King from Anglesey, and the Welsh had long awaited the fulfilment of this prophecy. Achim von Arnim's historical novel 'Owen Tudor' (1821) tells the full story of the founder of the Tudor dynasty – a somewhat delayed fruit of this German romantic's journey to Wales in 1803.

Not many Welsh royalists marked the 500th anniversary of the Tudors' accession to power by making a pilgrimage to the obscure birthplace of their king-maker. The graves of the Tewdwrs lie in the village church, but not that of Owen Tudor; the farmhouse Plas Penmynydd stands a little way outside the village, on the historically correct spot with the historically correct name, but it is not the house in which Owen was born, for it was not built until nearly a century after his birth. It is perhaps a little sad that the authentic birthplace of a legend should have disappeared, but perhaps also it is history's way of getting its own back. The historical victim of the Tudor's accession was Henry's adversary Richard III, who thanks to Shakespeare is regarded as the villain of all villains. Modern research suggests that this is a false picture, based on a Tudor plot to legitimize their claim to the throne.

Druidic scene. Caractacus receives British Warriors. Stone circle, hermitages, megalithic graves, holy oaks and processional avenue all visible in the background

The royal Welsh past is even less in evidence in *Aberffraw*, the little fishing village on the south-west coast of Anglesey where once stood the palace of the Princes of Gwynedd. When the Romans left in the 4th century, the Latin name of the administrative district of Venedotia became the Cymric Gwynedd, and Aberffraw became the capital of the new principality. Here reigned the legendary Cunedda, later Maelgwyn – known as the Island Dragon – then Cadfan, Cadwallon, and Cadwaladr, all names that have vanished in the mists of time. They called themselves 'Brenin Aberffraw', Kings of Aberffraw. This was their capital until the 13th century, and Llywelyn the Great held court here, as did Llywelyn the Last. Their palace may have been made of wood. No-one even knows where it was. The Princes of Anglesey, Mother of Wales, are long since gone, and where they lived there is nothing but hedges and sand dunes. Even the sacred groves have disappeared, along with the priests that worshipped there. 'It is in the oak forests that the Druids have their places of worship,' wrote Pliny, conjuring up visions of bearded men in flowing robes emerging from the shadows of gnarled oak trees, performing their strange rituals amid their strange circles of stone. This, at least, is the popular image of the Druids, doubly distorted by Roman propaganda and romantic folklore, but it's a caricature. According to Celtic historians such as Nora Chadwick, there is no doubt that that the Druids were the most inspiring and civilizing spiritual influence in prehistoric Europe. They were great teachers and priests, and their monopoly on the wonders of knowledge, which they communicated purely by word of mouth, gave them an influence that modern intellectuals can only dream about. But their power also cost them their heads.

According to Tacitus, Anglesey was the centre of the Druids. Even young Gauls from the Continent came to study here. The Druids did not confine themselves to philosophising about the immortality of the soul; they also inspired Welsh resistance to the Romans, and Anglesey was their most remote refuge, with the Menai Strait as their castle moat. Nevertheless, in AD 61, Suetonius Paulinus set out across the strait with his forces, and attacked: 'On the shore the enemy was assembled, one man next to another in a dense line. Among them were women running back and forth, like Furies with flying hair, bearing torches. All around stood the Druids, uttering terrible curses, their hands raised to heaven. This extraordinary sight set the soldiers in such a fright that, as if paralysed, they allowed themselves to be beaten, and only when the army commander reprimanded them, and they also tremblingly encouraged themselves by saying that they should not tremble before a raging crowd of women, did they launch themselves into an attack. They threw down whoever stood in their way, and drove the enemy into the fire of the torches. Afterwards, a garrison was stationed on the conquered island, and the groves dedicated to savage superstition were hewn down …' These are the last days of the Druids as recorded in Tacitus's 'Annals'.

This massacre struck at the very heart of Celtic culture. From then on, the Druids became part of national myth, and a symbol of resistance. Gwynfor Evans even saw them as predecessors of the Christian saints. The tradition of political martyrdom continued with the Druids' successors, the bards. For when Edward I banned them, shutting the door of censorship on their protests, the Norman conquerors may be said to have emulated the brutality of their Roman predecessors. The Welsh, at least, put the suppression of their poets on a par with physical destruction. The cult of the Druids and the myth of the bards duly took on the gloss of Romanticism, and in pictures and poems they were celebrated as fighters for national freedom. The rediscovery of the nation's past, of vital importance to the cultural self-awareness of the Welsh, resulted in the Celtic Revival of the 19th century, which sometimes had rather bizarre consequences. The National Eisteddfod was resurrected, with Iolo Morgannwg's remarkable Gorsedd fiction (see page 22). The folkloric spectacle in the circle of stones may seem like an historical caricature, although the Arch-Druids are certainly not Celtic carnival princes, and a modern Bárd does not relish being confused with a druid.

If ever a landscape could convey a feeling of time gone by, it's that of Anglesey. The dunes of Aberffraw and the dolmens of the Stone Age, standing stones from the Bronze Age, Celtic dwellings, hill forts – nowhere on the Welsh mainland will you find such a concentration of prehistoric remains. Some 5,000 years ago, in the Neolithic Age, the first settlers came to Mona. We do not know what race they were, where they came from, or what language they spoke, but they may well have come from the Mediterranean. They were certainly not Celts. They buried their dead in communal graves made from large stones, and twenty of these megaliths are still to be seen in Anglesey. The finest of them is on the cliffs north-west of Aberffraw, *Barclodiad y Gawres*, where there are drawings scratched into the walls of the main chamber. The most famous, though, is *Bryn Celli Ddu*, Hill of the Dark Chamber, (2,000–1,500 BC), not far from Plas Newydd (plate 21). The burial chamber is reached through a long, dry-stone passage, and the whole thing lies beneath a mound. It is very rare to find these megalithic tombs in such a perfect state of preservation. There are sheep grazing all around. I must confess that after I had seen my second megalith, I felt rather like Dr Johnson when Boswell wanted to show him yet another Scottish stone circle: 'seeing one is quite enough.' But what did interest me was to know how these people used to live.

In 1943, south of Holyhead, the RAF base at *Valley* was extended so that it could become a major transatlantic airbase for the American air force. During excavations, sensational finds were made dating from the Iron Age: the treasure of *Llyn Cerrig Bach*. No less than 144 magnificent artefacts were uncovered, mainly jewellery and weapons, possibly Druid votive offerings. They give us an idea of the extraordinarily high standard of Celtic arts and crafts in those times, and their work can still be admired today in the National Museum in Cardiff.

RAF Valley and the cliffs of Holy Island: for thousands of American bomber crews this was the first sight of Europe – a Welsh idyll before they took off for Hitler's inferno. Anglesey is full of time-leaps, from the Pre-Cambrian to the digital. If you put a coin in the one-armed bandit of history here, it might come up with megaliths or megawatts, since the island embraces all ages and cultures. In *Lligwy* you'll find Stone Age tombs and Celtic dwellings (plate 23); in *Wylfa* there's a nuclear reactor. During the 3rd and 4th centuries AD the Celts lived on this island in round or rectangular houses, whose limestone walls are still standing. Their Lligwy settlement was on the edge of a forest which in those days covered much of the island. There is a fine view of the Bay of Lligwy, even if it now also takes in a caravan site, home of the postmodern nomads of the Computer Age.

We would not be in Wales if, in the midst of this pastoral, prehistoric landscape, there were not some monuments from the Industrial Age as well. How do you explain the ruin of a Cornish engine-house on the slopes of *Parys Mountain*? Why is this mountain, in the north-east of the island, so threadbare, covered in slag heaps, shimmering sulphurously in yellow, orange, red and rusty brown? At the end of the 18th century it was the biggest copper mine in Europe. Almost the whole mountain has been ransacked. The Romans had had two good reasons for coming to Anglesey: copper and corn. Between 1768 and 1798 about 1,500 workers were employed here, and they produced 80,000 tons of copper ore a year. At the peak of this boom, the Parys Mine Company minted its own copper coins, 'Amlwch Pennies', with a bearded Druid's head on the front, and these coins remained valid currency here until 1817. Today they are much coveted collector's items. Between the workers' estate in *Amlwch* and the export harbour, there were some thirty blast furnaces in operation, belching poisonous copper-laden fumes. It was one of the earliest

Julius Caesar Ibbetson: Mining Copper at Parys, 1792

industrial centres, and the damage to the environment was proportionate: 'On the Parys Mountain, there is not even a single moss or lichen to be found,' wrote a visitor in 1798. Today the deepsea port of Amlwch plays host to supertankers which cannot get into Merseyside to discharge their loads. But the main centre for trade and industry is *Holyhead*: 11,000 inhabitants, an aluminium factory, and ferryport to Dublin since the 16th century. Holyhead is a product of the port and the railway, and this is its misfortune, for people only come here in order to go away. Why else should one come to Holyhead? Well, you can wander for over a mile out into the bay on the longest breakwater in the British Isles. Or you can stroll as I did along the cliffs of Holy Island, and get a more dramatic view of the peaceful island of Anglesey. The rocks watched over by the lighthouse on South Stack, the panorama over the Irish Sea, the gentle green undulations of the land reaching as far back as the distant silhouette of Snowdonia – these alone are worth the trip to Holyhead. 'The storms, the sea mists, the wrecks, the wailing sirens, and in summer the peculiar haze that hung over the island, all made Tre-Arddur Bay a very special place.' These are Kyffin Williams' recollections of his childhood on Holy Island. Born in 1918, he is famous for his landscapes and portraits, in which light seems to be refracted in the paint, which he applies with a palette knife. In his autobiography 'Across the Straits', this President of the Royal Cambrian Academy assembles his ancestry – smiths, bards, pirates – to make up a vivid portrait of Anglesey. 'The light was more pearly than that of the mainland, the cottages whiter and more welcoming.' Even when he was teaching art in Highgate, a Welsh 'exile' in London, he never ceased to paint his home country. His room 'became peopled with farmers and sheepdogs, and bounded by stone walls and rocky cliffs'. Wales was his motherland, English his mother tongue – a combination which has carried many Welsh artists beyond ideological frontiers.

Mon Mam Cymru, the Mother of Wales, has approximately 70,000 inhabitants, of whom 60 per cent still speak Welsh and in the 1987 elections 43 per cent voted Plaid Cymru. Unemployment is high. 'Many people try to earn a bit and use the time by learning one of the old crafts, like spinning and weaving,' a local man told me. It must also be mentioned that there are 270,000 sheep on the island, a lot of wool, and still a lot of tourists who haven't bought a Welsh woollen pullover.

Industrialization and urbanization have never got far on Anglesey. In *Beaumaris* the main focus of interest is the castle which, it was once hoped, would start everything off. 'Beau Mareys', Beautiful Marshland, was the euphemistic name the Normans gave their stronghold, in the hope of attracting English settlers once they had resettled the local inhabitants. Beaumaris Castle guards the northern end of the Menai Strait, and Caernarfon the southern. Caernarfon was the administrative centre for North Wales, while Beaumaris was the trade centre until the late Middle Ages. The port, now filled in, used to come right up to the castle walls.

Beaumaris Castle is the last of Edward I's great fortresses on the northern coast of Wales, begun in 1295, under construction until after 1330, never actually completed, and yet even as it stands, a perfect example of medieval fortress architecture. This masterpiece

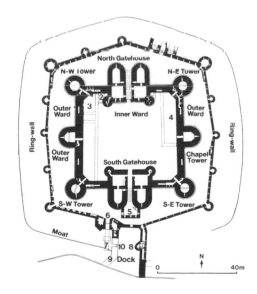

Beaumaris Castle, plan
1 Llanfaes Gate   2 Wells   3 Kitchens (?)
4 Living Quarters   5 Barbican
6 Gate next the Sea   7 Site of Drawbridge
8 Mill   9 Town Wall   10 Sluice

of symmetry and stonemasonry was designed by James of St George, Master of the King's Works in Wales. A square inner courtyard is surrounded by walls almost eighteen feet thick, with two twin-towered gatehouses and massive corner and central towers, the whole thing enclosed in an octagonal outer wall and protected by a broad moat. It is a triumph of concentricity. The beauty of the layout compensates for the unspectacular situation, which unlike many such castles does not dominate the town or the countryside. Perhaps this is why most painters have tended to overlook it. The military history is equally unobtrusive, with no major victories or defeats. Initially, about 3,000 workers were employed on the construction, and the cost to the tax-payer was exactly £14,344 8s. 10d. On the day when I was walking on the castle walls, a school choir from St Asaph was enjoying its big moment, with TV cameras filming them in this historic setting. History itself, however, passed Beaumaris by, just like the lead-grey waters of the Menai Strait. Now there are no more ferries from Lafan Sands, and no-one stops here on their way to Ireland, for the Menai Bridge has made Beaumaris into a mere diversion. Only yachtsmen come here now, though this quiet and beautiful little town, with its very English aura, does all it can to remain attractive. They have even opened up their prison to visitors. A rectangular stone block in the middle of the town, built in 1829, Beaumaris Gaol was regarded as a fine example of the progressive, Victorian penal system. Even children were incarcerated here. 'Anyone who was old enough to commit a crime, was old enough to go to prison,' explains our guide. He also waxes lyrical about the hygiene: 'Running water in every cell. Outside, only the upper classes had such a thing.' Everyone was weighed on arrival, and everyone had to have the same weight when they were discharged. This was regarded as proof that they had been properly looked after. 'No-one ever escaped,' says the guide, and if conditions were that good, I should imagine no-one ever wanted to escape.

North-east of Beaumaris, on the last of the promontories, lie the secluded rocks and fields of *Penmon*. It has a holy well, perhaps dating from the Druids, a Celtic mission cell, a ruined medieval monastery with a little church, a 16th-century dovecote, and is wrapped in the peace that one always hopes to find at the end of all roads and all journeys.

Plas Newydd: An Important Picture and a Patented Leg

Henry Paget is an average-sized, fine-looking gentleman with greying hair, a tweed jacket, and a title. He is the 7th Marquess of Anglesey, born in 1922, and has written a best-selling biography of his distinguished ancestor the 1st Marquess, who was Wellington's cavalry commander at the Battle of Waterloo. He receives me in the Library at *Plas Newydd*, his country seat on Anglesey. He has just finished writing the third volume of his planned five-volume history of the British Cavalry. As well as being a military historian, he is a member of the Conservative Party, and a Wagner fan who loves going to Bayreuth and who himself played the cello when younger. His family owned land in thirteen English counties as well as in Ireland and North Wales – a total of more than 100,000 acres. The considerable wealth of the House of Anglesey was substantially increased by what was found under their land: coal in Staffordshire, copper on Anglesey. The Marquess can trace one branch of his family back to the Tudors of Penmynydd, but despite the Welsh roots, he sees his spiritual and political home as being on the other side of Offa's Dyke: 'People like me are more English than Welsh. Our centre is London, not Cardiff.' But he is quick to add that he also makes an appearance in Cardiff every three weeks.

This has always been the way with anglicized Welsh aristocrats ever since the days of the Tudors. Unlike the Scots, the Welsh upper classes were never – or rarely – nationalistic, but always looked towards London. The court was there, society was there, and so was power. 'If your centre is London, oh, you're damned!' Lord Anglesey can laugh about it, but it can sometimes be a problem: 'You're treated like a foreigner, you're not one of them, if you don't speak their language.' Twenty years ago, his butler used also to be his interpreter, because in those days many people on Anglesey spoke no English. 'That's the split, the great difference: the language.' He doubts whether there will be a true renaissance of the language now: 'If a language can only be kept alive by artificial means, then it's not worth doing.' His standpoint is a radical one, and he is opposed to the vehemence of the campaign, which he thinks could have serious consequences: 'When the market is as limited as it is in Wales, the one who gets the job is probably not the one who's best qualified, but the one who speaks Welsh.' His comment on this fact, and on Plaid Cymru, is simply: 'It's dotty.'

The Marquess of Anglesey is a founder member of the Historic Buildings Council for Wales, which has spent many millions of pounds on conservation since 1953. A lot more money is needed, but no really important building has been lost since then. He has ensured the preservation of his own house by acting in advance of any crisis. For a private person to maintain an estate of this size and keep it attractive to visitors, 'I would have had to become a showman and that's not my style,' he says. And so in 1976 he gave the house and grounds to the National Trust, whose chairman he is in North Wales. He and Lady Anglesey can carry on living there for the rest of their lives, but they are no longer responsible for upkeep.

Plas Newydd still has the atmosphere of a lived-in house, but the time will come when it will be the museum of a 'landed family' which built its first house here at the beginning of the 16th century. The Tudor residence was altered many times, not always to its advantage, but what has remained unaltered and unsurpassed is the situation on the shore of the Menai Strait, with a view of Snowdon and all along the Sound as far as Britannia Bridge. Plas Newydd is set in a landscaped garden designed by Humphry Repton (1799–1804) in the picturesque style. The tall beech trees, oaks and sycamores date back to this time; tulip-trees, ginkgo biloba, azaleas, camellias, rhododendrons and other plants came later, all of them flourishing in a damp climate favoured by the Gulf Stream.

Plas Newydd may have a beautiful setting, but its architecture is a bit of a mess. Better proportioned and stylistically purer than the main house are the Neo-Gothic stables, with their crenellated towers, built in 1797 and now used as a hostel for schools. From 1793 till 1799 James Wyatt was in charge of the second round of alterations, by which the entrance hall and music room became Neo-Gothic, and the other rooms Neo-Classical. The English architect James Wyatt, successful contemporary of the Adam brothers, had as his assistant and interior designer a cabinet-maker from Lichfield named Joseph Potter, and it was he who designed the stables. The music room and the entrance hall, which is two storeys high, both have stucco fan vaulting and are amongst the most beautiful late 18th century interiors still in existence. These were Wyatt's contribution to the Gothic Revival in Wales, although it must be said that they were overshadowed by, and indeed inferior to his later and greater achievements at Fonthill Abbey and Ashridge Park. There were no more major changes to Plas Newydd until the turn of the century, when the 5th Marquess of Anglesey altered the chapel into a little theatre (c.1900), with red plush and potted palms beneath a Neo-Gothic fan vault. 'Toppy' engaged the best companies from London, loved playing the main part himself, and was quite resplendent in pearl and diamond-studded costumes. This was how he had himself portrayed on picture postcards: the Garrick of Plas Newydd. In winter, 'The Mad Marquess' used to have little stoves lit along the forest paths in case he should want to warm himself while out on his walks. His eccentricities might have earned him a whole chapter to himself, but alas he died at the age of 30. His successor, the 6th Marquess of Anglesey, had no time for his cousin's 'Gaiety Theatre', and demolished the whole of the North Wing, including the chapel-cum-theatre. He put a new dining-room on the ground floor, with guest rooms above it, following the principle that 'every bathroom should have a bedroom'. Following that criterion, Plas Newydd was unquestionably the most comfortable country house in Britain. The 6th Marquess also loved the art of illusion, which he put into practice on the walls of the dining-room: a trompe-l'oeil fantasy by Rex Whistler (plate 75).

This is the most popular room in Plas Newydd – colourful, eccentric, and a feast for the eye to match the feast on the table. Outside, you can see the Menai Strait and the mountains of Snowdonia, while inside there is the panorama of a harbour with bay and mountains, a Renaissance town in the southern sun. Whistler painted a Welsh dream, in cheerful contrast to less cheerful realities. Within this magical landscape there are castles in the air and elements of the real thing, all fantastically mixed together as are quotations from other painters, ranging from Claude Lorrain to Pintoricchio. You can discern the Trajan Column in Rome, St Martin's-in-the-Fields in London, the Round Tower of Windsor Castle, an Austrian baroque church, and passing in front of it, a Venetian gondola. The artist has also paid homage to his patron in this picture puzzle. The triumphal arch on the left-hand side of the picture bears an inscription designating the 6th Marquess as founder of the city, and in front of it is a statue of him on horseback. There are trompe-l'oeil pictures on both sides of this central painting, giving the illusion that the room leads off into colonnades, and in these one can see a book and a pair of spectacles belonging to Lady Anglesey, her daughter's dogs, and a cello belonging to her son Henry, our host. Right at the back of these two arcades are portraits of Rex Whistler himself, as a gardener. 'He was marvellous with us children,' Lord Anglesey recalls. 'He showed us how to paint.' There are several of the old, but always entertaining trompe-l'oeil tricks: a glowing cigarette on the steps of the passageway, the damp footprints of Poseidon, coming from the harbour steps straight into the room. The main picture, which is over 56 feet long, is not a fresco but oil on canvas. Other decorations, such as the coffered ceiling and the grisaille trophies over the mantelpiece, are painted directly onto the wall surfaces. The panorama of Plas Newydd, begun in summer 1936 and finished a year later, is Whistler's finest and biggest wall-painting, bigger even than those in Mottisfont Abbey and the restaurant at the Tate Gallery. This is decorative art at its best, trompe-l'oeil as an ironic presentation of conditions restored to what they were and no longer are, drawing-room painting at the end of the feudal era of country houses, on the eve of the Second World War. Rex Whistler fell in 1944, serving as a volunteer member of the Welsh Guards in Normandy. He was 39. In the former billiard room at Plas Newydd, you can see the whole range of his talents: book illustrations, caricatures, stage designs, costumes and textiles.

A few rooms further on, Lord Anglesey has set up a little cavalry museum, arranged round the famous leg of his ancestor Henry William Paget, Wellington's cavalry commander at Waterloo. While he was riding across the battlefield with the victorious

The first Marquess of Anglesey with his patent wooden leg. Contemporary caricature

Duke at the end of the day, a shell shattered his right leg. 'By God, sir, I've lost my leg!' he cried. Wellington lowered his telescope. 'By God, sir, so you have!' And raised the telescope again, to watch the French in flight. His adjutant's leg was amputated that same day, without anaesthetic. In London this brave hussar was rewarded with the title of 1st Marquess of Anglesey, and was given a wooden leg. Patented as the 'Anglesey Leg', it was still in use during the First World War. The Marquess, known as 'One Leg', lived to be 86 years of age, had 18 children and 73 grandchildren. Right on the edge of his estate, patriots erected a column made of Anglesey marble, the island's grey limestone, in commemoration of Waterloo. Since 1861, 'One Leg' has been standing in bronze, in the uniform of the Hussars, right at the top where he can enjoy the view.

The neighbouring village is a landmark to nonsense. Names make places, argued the cobbler of *Llanfairpwll*, who was unhappy that his native village was so insignificant. And so he multiplied insignificance by insignificance, and came out with: *Llanfairpwllgwyngyllgogerychwyrndrobwllllantysiliogogogoch* (plate 54). This is the longest name in Europe, and means St Mary's church in the hollow of the white hazel near a rapid whirlpool and the church of St Tysilio near the red cave. It's a great invention, and a remarkable publicity coup by a 19th century Welsh Till Eulenspiegel. By caricaturing the phonetic and poetic qualities of Cymric placenames, he made an unknown village into a Mecca for tourists. Since he had his brainwave, they have flocked in their thousands to a place where there is absolutely nothing to see except a name. And this is photographed, spelt, reproduced, dispatched worldwide on postcards, sold on elongated railway tickets and foreign language tapes with precise instructions on how to pronounce it, and – since it is a Welsh name – it can even be sung and purchased as a gramophone record. Pure poetry, or Dada sound-painting, Llanfair P.G., as it modestly called by the Post Office, is the perfect parody of tourism. And there's a cherry to this cake: the village's twin town in Holland is Ee.

Caernarfon Castle: Carlo Windsor Becomes Prince of Wales

Caernarfon Castle has all the charm of an old actor playing his favourite role in his favourite play, 'Edward I', over and over again (plate 70). This castle is known even to people who have never been to Wales: 500 million TV viewers all over the world watched the investiture of Prince Charles here in July 1969, and so the castle became the epitome of Welsh history. When Edward I built it, it was a radiant symbol: 'that most magnificent badge of our subjection' (Thomas Pennant). Some Welsh people still think of it in those terms. On that momentus occasion in 1969, the mayor and constable of Caernarfon, J. B. Griffith, declared: '700 years ago they built these castles to keep us down and now they pay one pound a head to look inside them.'

The historical irony goes even further. Caernarfon has an English castle, and was founded as an exclave for English settlers; today it is a Welsh stronghold. In 1983, the election was won, not by any of the British political parties, but by the then Plaid Cymru President Dafydd Wigley, who gained 53% of all votes. In Caernarfon Town Council, all debates are bilingual, and there are facilities for simultaneous translation. Most of the street names are also bilingual, notices on shop doors will say 'ar gau / closed', and there is a Chinese restaurant that calls itself Ty Bwyta. Even as an English administrative capital, Caernarfon has remained an historic centre of Welsh culture, and is now county town of Gwynedd. As a sign of its resolute Welshness, the pubs are still closed on Sundays. There are not many other towns in Wales that have managed to cling to the old, dry Sabbath.

And yet the town once had no less than 85 pubs. This was when the slate industry was at its peak, during the 19th century. On Slate Quay, at the foot of the castle, now a carpark, the ships used to take on their loads of slate. At the end of the promontory, where the Afon Seiont flows into the Menai Strait, stands Edward's fortress, and behind it 'a small but strong town, clean and well built' (Defoe). You couldn't get lost here: there's one main street, parallel to the castle, crossed at right-angles by three streets running from north to south in a chessboard pattern, which was divided up among the English settlers in standard plots measuring 80 by 60 feet. Around 1300, there were 56 families of English settlers

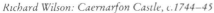

Richard Wilson: Caernarfon Castle, c.1744–45

here, with royal trading prerogatives. It was a much smaller settlement than Beaumaris, for instance, at the other end of the Menai Strait. Close up to the town hall wall is the medieval parish church of St Mary (1307). The West Gate, one of two twin-towered gatehouses, accommodates the Royal Welsh Yacht Club. Most of the houses in the old town date from between the 17th and 19th centuries, and Caernarfon itself has some 10,000 inhabitants who have to entertain half a million visitors a year. 'To Caernarfon, where I thought to have seen a Town and a Castle, or a Castle and a Town; but I saw both to be one, and one to be both,' wrote a traveller named John Taylor in 1652. The history of this town is the history of its castle.

Richard Wilson painted the castle twice, and on both occasions he hid the town behind it. In Turner's watercolour of 1833–34, the castle stands in a dreamlike evening mist, all pale gold and purple. Almost every English romantic artist has painted Caernarfon Castle, fascinated by its noble architecture, and overwhelmed by its situation, its history, and its sheer size. 'An edifice of stupendous majesty and strength,' remarked Dr Johnson, who was generally more given to mockery than to admiration. 'One of the castles of Wales could contain all the castles I have seen in Scotland.' It was built to be a palace as well as a fortress, and this is already evident from the towers and the masonry, which are art-historical quotations. The towers are octagonal and not round, as they are in Edward

J. M. W. Turner: Caernarfon Castle, c.1833

John Boydell: Caernarfon, 1750

I's other castles (apart from Denbigh), with dark strips of sandstone inlaid in the otherwise bright limestone walls. These two stylistic features which give the castle such a striking appearance were copied by the King's architect, James of St George, from the towers and city walls of Constantinople, where the alternating pattern is formed by bands of Roman bricks. This Byzantine model was not a matter of aesthetic choice, but of political calculation. According to Welsh tradition, Constantine the Great was born in the nearby Roman camp of Segontium. Caer Cystennin, Town of Constantine, was the name the Welsh gave to Constantinople, and this was also the old name they gave to Caernarfon, the Town in the Region of the Arfon. The English conqueror wanted this Welsh tradition to be incorporated into the new power structure of his state, pointing to himself as the legitimate ruler, and making Caernarfon the Constantinople of Wales. Hence the symbolism of the architecture – a sort of aesthetic strategy. These imperial aspirations were also symbolized by the sculptures of three Roman eagles at the top of the main tower, the Eagle Tower, which together with its three smaller turrets stands out so strikingly in the silhouette of Caernarfon Castle.

These eagles come from the ruins of *Segontium*, the Roman camp on the edge of the town. Set up in AD 78, it had served as a supply base for north-west Wales, and originally housed a regiment of 1,000 men, not the least of whose tasks was to guard the Roman

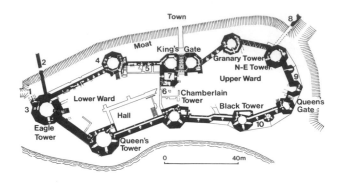

Caernarfon Castle, Plan
1 Watergate (unbuilt)
2 Town Wall
3, 4 Side gate
5 Kitchens
6 Projected drawbridge
7 Prison Tower
8 Town Wall
9 Watch Tower
10 Cistern Tower

copper mines on Anglesey. When the general Magnus Maximus – who plays a mythical role as Macsen Wledig in 'Mabinogion' – proclaimed himself Caesar and led his troops out of Great Britain to march on Rome, Segontium was soon abandoned (c.395). From the time of Edward I, this site – an area of more than five acres – became a useful source of building materials for the inhabitants of Caernarfon. Not until the 19th century was Segontium rediscovered, and it has still not been fully excavated even today. Nevertheless, its museum, next to that of Caerleon, offers the best possible insight into Roman life in Wales.

Now only one of the three Roman eagles is left to keep watch from the Western tower, but Edward's castle remains a magnificent symbol of his conquest, and as for its fortifications, one need only look at the King's Gate to have some idea of their strength. Nowadays the only resistance to the invader is the ticket office, but in earlier times you would have had to overcome one drawbridge, five gates and six portcullises, not to mention the embrasures at the sides and the vividly named 'murder holes' up above. Only once did Welsh rebels succeed in capturing the castle, and that was in 1294, before it was finished. It is said that a garrison of just 28 men withstood two sieges by Owain Glyndwr.

The design (1285) differs from the earlier castle in Harlech and the later one in Beaumaris, in so far as it is not concentric but asymmetrical – rather like a slightly tilted hourglass. Originally the two inner courts were separated by a wall. The governor of North Wales lived in the Eagle Tower, in decagonal rooms behind walls that were almost eighteen feet thick. There was also plenty of room in the other towers for supplies, weapons, clothes, servants, soldiers and everything else that made up the royal household. Queen's Tower actually accommodates a whole regiment today, since it is the museum of the Royal Welch Fusiliers. 'Welch' was the original spelling of this, the oldest infantry regiment in Wales (1689). They won much glory, at the cost of much blood: Alexandria, Waterloo, Gallipoli, Dunkirk, the Boer War, the Boxer Uprising – at all times, they were there, fighting in the front line. Since 1777 the regiment has always gone into the field with a goat. Its horns are gilded, and it takes part in all parades, including St David's Day in

London, when the veterans lay daffodils on the Cenotaph in Whitehall; and of course once it's in the officers' mess, it's allowed to chew a leek. This Welsh goat – who also seems to be Merlin's pet (colour plate 63) – is certainly from the same Celtic stock as the wild Irish billy that is crowned king every year at Killorglin's Puck Fair. And talk of crowning brings us neatly on the investiture of the Prince of Wales.

The very first Prince of Wales was closely connected with Caernarfon, though his investiture wasn't. Shortly after the final conquest of Wales, in the year of the Statute of Rhuddlan (1284), the King of England had a son, thus ensuring the succession, which was vital in such violent times. However, the story of how Edward I presented his first-born to the Welsh as Prince of Wales in Caernarfon Castle is rather more fiction than truth. 'I give you a prince born in Wales who could speak never a word of English,' the King is supposed to have said, followed by the ominous '*eich dyn*' – your man. The story goes that these two Welsh words were later corrupted to '*ich dien*', the motto on the Prince of Wales' coat-of-arms. How such a Prussian-sounding motto could have found its way onto the royal lips is much disputed by historians and armorists on both sides of the Channel. What is not disputed is the fact that '*ich dien*' was the motto of King John of Bohemia,

St David's Day in London: 'Goat Major' Kenneth Barrow leads Billy, regimental mascot of the Royal Welch Fusiliers to the Cenotaph

who wore it on his head together with three ostrich feathers during the Battle of Crecy in 1346. He fought alongside Philip VI of France against the English, and was killed in the battle. The great hero of this event was the sixteen-year-old son of Edward III, the Black Prince. He picked up the headband of the fallen King of Bohemia and put it on his own head; he was thus the first Prince of Wales to use the motto *'ich dien'*.[1] It is the German, meaning, 'I serve', and not the Welsh, that has shaped Prince Charles's view of his position: 'It means just that. It is the basis of one's job: to serve other people.'

Whatever words Edward I may have used in order to present his son to the Welsh as their new Prince, the choice of title was a neat political move – or a nasty one, depending on your point of view. He had conquered Wales, and so as well as taking over the land, he took over the title of a native ruler. From now on, there could be no Welsh pretender to the throne, for Wales was a 'Principality' to be inherited by the legitimate heir to the English throne. It was a classic example of how power can authorize itself. An old right had been destroyed, and a new one took its place. This constitutional injustice inaugurated the long line of Princes of Wales. But when we think of the latest in that line, does anything strike us as unjust? The title is something we take entirely for granted – simply a decoration like the three ostrich feathers. If its provocativeness is to be truly understood, we must remember that the solemn investiture of the first Prince of Wales directly preceded the humiliating end of the last: Prince Llywelyn was killed at Cilmeri, his head cut off and carried triumphantly through London on a spit; shortly afterwards his brother Dafydd III was hung, drawn and quartered at Shrewsbury. This is the real background to the investiture – not the picturesque ruins of Caernarfon Castle.

In fact, the first investiture did not take place in Caernarfon at all. While Edward I was having his fortress built in occupied Wales, he decided that his son's official appointment as Prince of Wales should be made in Lincoln (1301). It is one of the historic ironies that the bearers of the title have rarely formed any relationship at all with their principality. Indeed eight of the twenty so far never even set foot in Wales. George IV, who was Prince of Wales for nearly sixty years, hated the place: 'unattended with any sort of comfort or accommodation', he said, and so whenever he could, he avoided the land route, preferring to make the journey to Ireland entirely by sea, even though he was horribly seasick every time. The title became merely an ornament, generally bestowed in a private ceremony in Westminster Abbey or Windsor Castle. It was a Welsh cabinet minister, Lloyd George, who in 1911 proposed that the future King Edward VIII should be invested at Caernarfon Castle. Nationalistic masochism, or paradoxical national pride? Lloyd George was a Welsh patriot who wanted to make a career for himself in British politics. And he was a politician

---

1 In his will, the Black Prince stipulated that the three ostrich feathers should be worn at his funeral as a sign of peace. However, they were used singly, even by his successors, and not in threes. Not until the Stuarts are the three feathers to be seen inside a crown as an emblem of the Prince of Wales.

who, with this display of Anglo-Welsh unity, sought to obtain a bit of publicity on behalf of the MP for Caernarfon. The MP for Caernarfon being, of course, Lloyd George. The whole thing worked beautifully. The castle looked an absolute picture,[1] and in July 1911 the then governor and Chancellor of the Exchequer, Lloyd George, led the seventeen-year-old Prince Edward to his place in the inner court. Since then Lloyd George (a bronze version) has had a permanent position in the square in front of the castle, where he stands in characteristic oratorical pose. There were just two people opposed to this investiture: the Prince of Wales himself, later Duke of Windsor, who found the whole masquerade absurd, and   the alliance is somewhat remarkable – the radical leader of the Welsh miners, James Keir Hardie, MP for Merthyr Tydfil, and first chairman of the Labour Party: 'Wales is to have an "Investiture" as a reminder that an English king and his robber barons strove for ages to destroy the Welsh people and finally succeeded in robbing them of their lands … and then had the insolence to have his son "invested" in their midst.' Just half a century later, Britain had a Labour Prime Minister who approved of the investiture, and a Prince of Wales who took the whole thing with the best possible grace. By 1969 the ceremony had become an accepted part of the royal repertory, treated as a spectacular media event and smoothly fulfilling its dual purpose of exposing the monarchy in a favourable light, and doing the same for England's Welsh policy. Edward I could never have dreamed of such national glamour and celebration. It did, however, cost two lives.

By the end of the sixties, a nationalist protest movement had become active in Wales. English placenames were painted over, and BBC radio stations and government offices were attacked. With the investiture, Prime Minister Harold Wilson saw an opportunity to counter these separatist tendencies with a display of British unity, knowing full well that ever since Cromwell the Welsh have had a soft spot for royalty. Radical nationalists, however, considered the investiture to be a symbol of foreign rule. The descendants of Owain Glyndwr moved into action: 'Free Wales Army' and 'Movement for the Defence of Wales'. On the evening before the ceremony, two extremists died in an attack on the Prince's train, killed by their own bombs. Since then, the 'Meibion Glyndwr' (Sons of Glendower) and other nationalist groups have commemorated the day (July 1st) by a march through Abergele. The spectacle at Caernarfon, however, went ahead as planned, under the direction of Lord Snowdon. As brother-in-law to the Queen and a world-renowned photographer, he was uniquely qualified to act as master of ceremonies, constable, and TV producer; in keeping with the times, this was 'a big show for a big audience', the leading role being taken by a 21-year-old prince, somewhat gauche, a supersonic pilot, parachutist and frigate captain, and the dream prince of thousands of Lady Di's all over the world (plate 1a). With sword and crown, sceptre and Welsh gold

---

1   The Victorian architect Anthony Salvin began restoring Caernarfon Castle in the mid 19th century, and the work continued until the beginning of the 20th.

ring, on a seat of Welsh slate with a pink cushion, somewhat uncomfortable and anachronistic, the new Prince of Wales sat in Caernarfon Castle on that grey July day in 1969. 'He permitted / himself a small smile, / sipping at it in the mind's / coolness,' wrote R. S. Thomas, 'poet unlaureate' of the Welsh nationalists. And the folksinger Dafydd Iwan paid homage to 'Carlo Windsor' with a satirical song that was a great success within a narrowly confined circle. 'Carlo' is a name Welsh shepherds often give to their dogs. Does Prince Charles deserve these irreverent jokes? Even if his polo is certainly better than his Welsh, he is the first Prince of Wales to have taken the trouble to study the language. He is also the first to have been educated at a normal school, to have cleaned his own shoes, and to have passed a public examination. None of his predecessors have ever gone to the lengths that he has to identify with his principality. He has written many a foreword to books on Wales, stressing the importance of 'Welshness', he is Colonel of the Welsh Guards, an honorary citizen of Carmarthen, and he founded an exemplary organization for the protection of the Welsh environment: the Prince of Wales's Committee. I do not think the Welsh could ever find a better Prince of Wales; at least not outside their own borders.

There was therefore great rejoicing in the Principality when the Prince finally found a Princess. Only a few people still insisted, 700 years later, that Llywelyn was the last legitimate Prince of Wales, and they proceeded to organize a 'Movement to Ignore the Royal Wedding'. On the great day, some 300 of them took the ferry from Holyhead to Dublin, and along with their Celtic friends sang anti-English songs. But when 'Carlo Bach' (little Charles) and 'Di the Shy' went on their obligatory tour of the Principality (plate 1b), the cheers were loud and heartfelt, especially from the Welsh girls lining the streets, crying 'We want Charles, we want Charles!' There were also, it must be said, some stink bombs, a firebomb that was defused in good time, and some cries of 'Go home Charlie, go home English Princess!' No-one knows when Prince Charles will become King Charles III – after all, one of his predecessors had to wait 59 years before becoming Edward VII – but Caernarfon Castle is in no hurry. The next Prince of Wales is in no hurry either to be invested. William Windsor is his name, and the genealogists tell us that he has 39% English and 16% Scottish blood, but not one drop of Welsh.

Pot of Paint and Guitar: Dafydd Iwan Fights for Cymru

Dafydd Iwan was born in 1943, five years before Prince Charles (to whom he dedicated a rude song) and one year before Neil Kinnock, who he says can talk better than he can think. Three men of the same generation, all bound in different ways to the same country: a Welsh protest-singer, a Welsh Labour politician, and a titled and titular Welshman. The singer comes from a Non-Conformist parsonage, the Labour leader from a mining family in the Valleys, and the Prince from Buckingham Palace. It is a pity that these three gentlemen are unlikely ever to sit down at the same table, for they would certainly stage an explosive chat show on the subject of Wales.

A year after the Caernarfon investiture, the three men were, as is to be expected, engaged on very different activities. Prince Charles was launching ships by smashing champagne bottles against them, Neil Kinnock was sitting in Westminster as the youngest Labour MP, and Dafydd Iwan was sitting for the first time in a prison cell. He had committed a particularly reprehensible offence: he had painted out the 'a' on the nameplate of Conway. For this was done before the English spelling was officially changed to the Welsh. The patriots fought to the last (or in this case the first) letter for a Cymric Wales, and Dafydd Iwan, armed with paint and guitar, was in the forefront. Fifteen years later I was sitting in a barn on Anglesey, attending a pop concert. Barns in Wales are traditional stages, for this is, after all, a rural culture. Dafydd Iwan was singing classic protest songs ('I'R Gad' – To Battle), interspersed with tender lovesongs ('My love dwells in Eryri'), and he finished up with a new Maggie Thatcher song, which the BBC refused to transmit: 'For our language and jobs, boys / We will fight now, boys / And we'll get rid of Magi Thatcher / We'll get rid of Magi Thatcher!' In 1990 the Tory Party did the job for him, and I can picture him and his audience responding to the news, with hearts and fists soaring as they did in the barn and as they did at the end of the 1960's. Dafydd Iwan has one of those soft, melodious voices that are typical of the Welsh, and his charismatic presence would make him a powerful force in politics. A few days after the concert, I met him in 'The Harp' in Llandwrog, south of Caernarfon, and asked him about his background.

Dafydd Iwan (plate 30) comes from a village on the edge of the coal fields, Brynamman, north of Swansea. 'At home in the village no-one spoke anything but Welsh. My grandfather was one of the co-founders of Plaid Cymru in 1925. My father was the minister of an Independent church, and a member of Plaid just like my mother. I've always felt myself to be a nationalist.' He studied architecture at Cardiff, where he got to know a miner's son from the Valleys, who was studying politics and economics: Neil Kinnock. 'I know him from what he used to do in College. I think he's a dangerous sort of Welshman, because he uses his origins and rugby and all that just to create an effective image for himself. In fact he's an enemy of the Welsh and their language. In 1979 he was one of the chief opponents of devolution. He led a very nasty campaign against Welsh being used in schools. Neil Kinnock tries to convince people that the answer to Wales's problems can only come about through British parties and London politics. It's not true and it never was true. Because as soon as a Welsh politician gets into power in London, Wales disappears from his list of subjects.' According to Dafydd Iwan, this was the case with Lloyd George, and it will be no different with Neil Kinnock.

His own political route was through the Welsh Language Society and the choir – a very Welsh route. In his village chapel and later in College he sang in the choir. Then he began to write his own political songs – about Owain Glyndwr and past rebels, and modern heroes of protest like Mali, the girl who painted over some 300 English street names. 'I don't think songs can change much, but you can reach people's deepest feelings with them. And when you manage to do that, your songs become part of the movement.' His models are the Chilean protest singer Victor Jara, and also Pete Seeger and Joan Baez. He has written songs against the madness of the arms race, unemployment, and the anglicizing of Welsh children by means of the educational system. He has also written and sung cheerful songs and melancholy songs, children's songs and folksongs. With his versatility, charisma, intelligence and commitment, Dafydd Iwan could have been a British Bob Dylan, but he has chosen to remain a Welsh singer, popular in his own country, recognized at international folk festivals, and in his own way a symbol of Celtic independence. Not through his choice of themes but through the medium he uses, he has restricted his own impact, because he sings only in Welsh. (I have translated the quotations above). This you may find regrettable, pig-headed, provincial, or perhaps heroic. For him it is a matter of policy.

'I only sing in Welsh. That is part of our campaign. We want to show that it's possible to have something that's pure Welsh, and that even today there's still a living and independent Welsh culture.' But he realizes, too, that through this linguistic isolation, the culture must lose some of its political effectiveness, and that remaining in the double ghetto of an ethnic and a cultural minority – at the Eisteddfod as well as with the fourth TV programme – runs the risk of being counter-productive. Preservation of the language at the cost of isolation – that is the insoluble problem of Welsh culture and those who have fought for so long to preserve it. And the dilemma is exacerbated by unemployment: 'We don't have enough jobs for our people in our own country. Our Welshness is suffering more and more under the influence of the English immigrants. We're not racists. But if you're fighting for the survival of a language, for a different way of life, or at least for another way of seeing things, then you have to protect the structure of Welsh society. Basic material conditions can change so drastically in just a short time that the language will disappear altogether. In actual fact you can no longer exclude the possibility that the Welsh nation itself will come to an end.' Gloomy prospects, but countered by songs such as 'We Are Still Here', written in 1983 – a proudly defiant allusion to the year 383 and the exodus of the Romans under Magnus Maximus: 'That was the beginning of an independent Wales. For sixteen centuries we've been speaking Welsh, more or less the same language. That's a long time, but the big thing is that we are still here, despite everything, and we will be here for ever!' Welsh poetry and pathos, love of singing and fighting, obsession with the past and with wounds that can never be allowed to heal – these are the ingredients of Dafydd Iwan's success, and they are also his limitations.

When I met him, he already had more than 25 albums to his credit, with sales of nearly a quarter of a million, which is remarkable for such a small market. When he left College, he started a record company named 'Sain' (Sound), became president of the Welsh Language Society – which is anything but an academy for language and literature – organized their campaigns, and went to prison. Hardly had he been discharged when the powers-that-be at the Eisteddfod pointedly made him a member of the Gorsedd. And so one year after the investiture of the Prince of Wales there followed the investiture of the Prince of Protest Singers, dressed in the green robe of the bard. But singing folksongs in the Old Boys' Club of the 'Taffia' is something he doesn't enjoy. He has been a member of the National Party since he was fifteen, and is now one of its leading figures, but 'Plaid Cymru has never quite achieved the breakthrough to the working class. We've been too much of an elitist, culture party.' What would he like to see instead? 'Wales being taken out of the backwaters of British provincialism, without a complete separation. A democratic state of Wales, with governmental power being decentralized in the communities, according to firm socialist principles.' Twice since 1974 he has stood in parliamentary elections as Plaid Cymru's candidate, in constituencies where he hasn't a chance. His fellow student Neil Kinnock went the other, British way, at the head of the Labour Party.

He still sings in chapel sometimes, and reckons some of his songs could count as hymns. For instance: 'Leave me alone'. But for that to have its proper effect, perhaps he would have to sing it in English.

Pilgrimage to Llyn: The Chequebook Invasion

From Caernarfon there is a road that heads south-west, far out into the Irish Sea to *Llyn*. The words means 'peninsula' (connected with the Irish name Leinster, from where in fact the first settlers came), and centuries ago pilgrims used to travel along the Llyn Peninsula to the fishing village of *Aberdaron*. From there they would take the boat across to *Bardsey Island* – a difficult route, and a dangerous crossing to a place that was barren and bare. There must, then, have been something of great importance to make these pious tourists of the Middle Ages undertake such an arduous journey to the utmost tip of Wales. Great was their faith, but great too was the propaganda. On the heavenly scorecard, three pilgrimages to Bardsey were worth two to St David's and one to Rome. What the distant Hebridean island of Iona was to the Scots, Bardsey was to the Welsh: a refuge for persecuted monks, a mission cell of the Celtic church, and for centuries the burial place of its bishops and its faithful. Thus arose its legendary name: 'Island of the 10,000 saints'. How one could possibly bury so many dead on so tiny an island was a question that bothered Thomas Fuller, the historian, as long ago as 1662, though he did admit that it would be 'more facile to find graves in Bardsey for so many saints, than saints for so many graves'. Gulls and other seabirds wheel ceaselessly overhead, and there are some profane philologists who claim that Bardsey is really 'Birdsey'! 'Am I too late? / Were they too late also, those / first pilgrims? He is such a fast / God, always before us and / leaving as we arrive.' These lines are from the poem 'Pilgrimage' by R. S. Thomas, the great poet of Llyn, and former vicar of Aberdaron.

On the Llyn Peninsula I visited the churches of *Llanfaglan* and *Clynnog Fawr*, little

Moses Griffith:
Bardsey Island and St
Mary's Chapel, 1777

gems on the edge of the pilgrims' route, but close to *Nefyn* I must confess I departed from this route and went down to the coast. And from that moment on, Bardsey had no hope. I was seduced by the bays and beaches of Llyn. Next to Nefyn lies *Morfa Nefyn*, and next to that an even more romantic bay, *Porth Dinllaen* (colour plate 18), and between them both, high on the cliffs, a golf course which compares with the best that Scotland can offer. This coastal panorama, under the clear Llyn light, also fascinated Oskar Kokoschka. The Austrian Expressionist painter fled from the Nazis to England, and when the bombing raids on London became too intense, he came to North Wales in April 1943. He returned to Nefyn in September that year and drew the bay, the fishing boats in the harbour, people bathing, a shark, and the ever-moving sea – moments of colour captured during those carefree weeks.

Llyn has over sixty miles of coast – a smaller version of Cornwall, with some coves that are overcrowded and many that are not. There are also paths that stretch high up across the hills in the south of the peninsula, near *Sarn* for instance, where the Czech émigré potter Oldrich Asenbryl dreams of spring in Prague. In summer *Abersoch Bay* is white with sails and the former fishing village is fairly bursting at the seams. But just a few miles further north, on the cliffs of *Mynydd Cilan*, there is nothing besides the wind and the sheep and a glorious view of the great sandy beach of *Hell's Mouth*. On this huge crescent even the 10,000 saints of Bardsey could have gone bathing and there would still have been plenty of room. The whitewashed houses glow coolly in *Aberdaron Bay*, and you can take tea in the 'Great Kitchen', Y Gegin Fawr (14th century), the pilgrims' last resting-place before they crossed to Bardsey Island. High above the beach stands the church of Aberdaron, encompassed in weathered slate, the sea gnawing at the gravestones.

There is coast wherever you look, and gently undulating fields and pastures. Llyn resembles Anglesey in many ways. But the railway only came as far as Pwllheli, and even though it is only a peninsula, Llyn is more remote than Anglesey. With no copper and no Druids, it was never worth attacking, and so the Norman conquerors and the Anglo-Saxon settlers simply obeyed Dafydd Iwan's 20th-century plea, and left it alone. What would have been the point in Edward I building more castles west of Caernarfon and Criccieth? Even though Llyn may have played some part for prehistoric travellers on their way to the Irish Sea, it lay for centuries in history's shadows, 'Little Wales beyond Wales', perfect only for monks, pilgrims, and pirates. I felt a little bit like Alice falling down the rabbit hole and landing in another world, and of all the places I visited in Wales, this was the one where I would most have liked to buy a little cottage and spend a few relaxing weeks every year. I am not the only one. Twenty per cent of the houses here are weekend or holiday homes. It's the highest percentage anywhere in Wales, including Anglesey and the South of Gwynedd. 'Isn't it nice to live in a summer house?' people used to sing, but at the beginning of the eighties, there was a macabre variation being sung on the streets of Llyn: 'Isn't it nice to burn a summer house?' The newspapers were full of headlines like: 'Another English Holiday Home Set On Fire'. Dozens of these second homes went up in flames, and the damage was reckoned in millions. It was as if the peaceful Welsh had suddenly turned into a nation of arsonists.

Since the 1960's, more and more English people, particularly from the industrial towns like Liverpool, Manchester and Birmingham, have bought cottages in the country, particularly in North Wales. There were and still are plenty of empty houses, largely as a result of the decline in the slate industry and agricultural mechanization. Between 1939 and 1970, over 20,000 Welsh farmers gave up the land. Cottages were therefore cheap and in plentiful supply. '*Ar werth*' was one of the first Welsh expressions I learnt. It means 'For Sale'. Gradually, though, prices rose, and soon the local people could no longer afford places in their own neighbourhood. In some districts there are as many English holiday homes as there are Welsh people looking for accommodation. There are at least 50,000 on the waiting list for council accommodation, and at the same time at least 20,000 second homes. These 'would be a far more socially acceptable luxury if everyone else had a first home', said Dafydd Iwan, who is Plaid Cymru's spokesman on housing. The problem is not one of envy or of xenophobia, but simply one of glaring social discrepancies. The average income in Gwynedd, which actually has the largest number of second homes though not the highest proportion, is almost 40% lower than in Britain. Furthermore, in 1984, 15.4% of all Welsh houses were substandard, compared to 9.6% in England. All this quite apart from the fact that unemployment in Wales has always been substantially higher. But the people had almost resigned themselves to being the country cousins, and what finally set the friendly Welsh dormouse roaring at the visiting English town mouse was, above all, the definitive surrender of their land, their language, and their identity. In many of the villages that had once been pure Welsh, Cymric is no longer spoken at all. In Richard Llewellyn's novel 'Green, Green My Valley Now', the militant architect Lys rails against the invasion: 'The heart of the land is being sold to foreigners, isn't it? For solid profit.' The second conquest, the chequebook invasion, was too much for the nationalists, and so the Red Dragon began quite literally to spit fire. The Abergavenny holiday home of Nicholas Edwards, Welsh Minister at the time, was one of those to go up in flames.

'Come home to a real fire. Buy a cottage in Wales.' Many were surprised at this violent turn of events. After all, there are just as many second homes in Devon, Cornwall, and the Lake District. But there the situation is different: there everyone speaks English, and the newcomers are not driving out a language or a culture – that indefinable 'Welshness' that is so precious to Wales. The majority of the arsonists were never caught. Responsibility for some of the attacks was claimed by dubious fringe groups like the 'Workers' Army of the Welsh Republic' and the 'Cadwyr Cymru' (Guardians of Wales), said to be supported by the IRA and the Basque ETA movement. Plaid Cymru and the Welsh Language Society denounced such radical protests, although it is difficult to ignore the fact that these organizations had stoked up the historical resentment against the English, even if they did not literally apply the matches. Saunders Lewis had already anticipated this battle for the Welshness of Wales when in 1936, on the Llyn Peninsula, he too had lit a flame: his part in the arson attack on the RAF base at Penyberth in *Penrhos*, together with the trial that followed, became legendary in Welsh nationalist circles (see page 123). 'Penyberth' is the name of Dafydd Iwan's house in Waunfawr, and it's also the title of an all-too-inflammatory poem by the valley bard Harri Webb (1977):

> Those flames still burn in hearts that yearn
> To free our ancient land,
> And may that fire proud hearts inspire
> And many a loyal hand
> Ready to do what must be done
> And many a valiant man
> Who'll strike a light in the cause of right
> With three matches and a can.

Even if the cause is right, should one strike a light? 'I'm a nationalist, but I'm against violence,' says Dafydd Roberts. 'Only you can't make an omelette without breaking an egg.' He is a member of Plaid Cymru and of the Welsh Language Society, and is director of the Welsh Slate Museum in Llanberis. Instead of lighting fires, he belives in occupying houses. 'After such protest actions, we clean the house and even pay the owners for any toilet paper we've used.'

'Ours is a country with behavioural disturbances,' says the writer Esmé Kirby, who lives in Snowdonia. She and other English people, some of whom have lived in Wales for many years, are hurt by this anti-English campaign, even though it is not directed against them. John Davies, for instance, a potter from Essex, who lives on the Llyn Peninsula, bought an abandoned farmhouse in *Y Ffor* in the mid 1960's. It's over 200 years old, and is called 'Glyddyn Mawr, Big Roots.' John bought it cheap, and made these roots his very own. But in recent times he has become aware of a new anti-English feeling from some quarters, and regards it as 'very unfair, absolutely ridiculous, it splits the country'. His own case emphasizes both the unfairness and the absurdity: he and his Welsh wife, Anne, collect recordings of historical and contemporary Welsh folk music – a genuine contribution to the preservation and dissemination of native culture. No-one in Llyn questions the fact that John Davies, an internationally renowned potter, and his workshop enrich the rural scene of Llyn, and no-one disputes the many-sided creative contribution that English and other immigrants have made in Wales. Even if they do not speak Welsh, they have also enhanced Welsh culture by reviving traditional crafts such as weaving, pottery, and cheese-making. But the second-homes campaign is not directed against them, or against English pensioners who have retired to Wales. The anger flares when in some villages more than half the houses remain uninhabited between September and Easter, and shops, schools, chapels have to close for lack of custom, and village traditions and social structures disappear along with the language. The argument rages back and forth. One side bemoans the loss of Welshness, and the other asks which is better, a dead village or an English village. A stonemason from Llyn told me that if the English had not come to convert the old cottages into holiday homes, he'd have been out of work ten years ago. Then he asked me if I knew Nant Gwrtheyrn.

One cool May morning, I went in search of this abandoned village somewhere on the coast of Llyn. On the easternmost peak of *Yr Eifl*, the highest mountain on the peninsula, lies *Tre'r Ceiri*, the Town of Giants, the remains of a Celtic hut settlement from the Iron Age. But this was not what I had come to see. I left my car at the foot of the mountain, walked through a pine forest, and there at the bottom of a deep gorge, down by the sea, lay *Nant Gwrtheyrn*. Two rows of houses and a chapel are what made up this little workers' estate of 1870. When the last granite quarry closed on the slopes of Yr Eifl – you can still see the old quay in the neighbouring village of *Trefor* – the last family departed. This was in the early 1950's, but the village did not die. Instead it turned into a Welsh language centre. Over the years a Trust, with a large number of volunteers, has restored the houses, and now once more they are lived in, and people learn Welsh there: local folk, foreigners, beginners, specialists, farmers and academics all come here. It's as remote a spot as you'll find, far from all other centres of culture, and it's a shining example of what can be achieved by self-help. The restoration of the village symbolizes the renaissance of the language itself, and also the amazing resilience of a linguistic minority who refuse to disappear.

On the other side of the peninsula, I visited the writer Alun Jones in the little harbour town of Pwllheli. He writes only in Welsh. This, understandably, doesn't earn him enough to live on, and so he also runs a bookshop in *Pwllheli:* 'Llên Llŷn'. There he sells nothing but Welsh literature – in Welsh. And from this he *can* live. He was born in 1946, and his father worked in the granite quarry. 'Out of my class of twenty, only two stayed in the village. Anyone with any intelligence leaves Wales. Going away gets you better education, and good education has always meant English education. We don't have class differences, only educational snobbery. Wales has produced thousands of teachers, and nearly all of them went to England. And who do most of the hotels and businesses belong to in Wales? The English, not the Welsh.' He feels that his compatriots don't have enough self-confidence or business acumen. 'Money and a career – that's not for them.' This, it must be said, is not always the case. Michael Heseltine is a millionaire, thanks to his property and publishing interests, and no-one could accuse him of not pursuing a career, but Mrs Thatcher's nemesis started off as an auditor in his native Wales. As for Alun Jones, when I met him he had written two novels, each with an initial print-run of 2,000, still awaiting translation into English, but with the prospect of being filmed for Welsh television. His second novel is called 'Pan Ddawr'r Machlud', When Twilight Comes: it's the story of a group of terrorists and their hostages.

If Butlins Holiday Camp were not nearby, and if the harbour were not a yachting centre for Cardigan Bay, you could say that Pwllheli was a quiet seaside resort. And out of season, that's what it is: just 5,000 inhabitants in this, the 'capital' of Llyn. Here in this heartland of Welsh-speaking Wales, in August 1925, six participants in the National Eisteddfod met at the Maesgwyn Temperance Hotel and founded a political party. The necessity for this party was confirmed in the 1929 election by a grand total of 609 votes. It was, of course, Plaid Cymru.

Land of Bitter Love: The Poet R. S. Thomas

At the end of the Llyn Peninsula, in a grey dolerite house hidden behind green hedges, lives the most radical critic of the Welsh and their English way of life: R. S. Thomas (picture, page 21). No-one has written finer, or more bitter verses about his homeland, and no-one embodies more convincingly the struggle of the Welsh for their own identity. His life is shot through with paradox: 'I write English about Welsh affairs, and the Welsh have even less regard for me than most English people. I live in a kind of no-man's-land.' But many young left-wingers in Wales take R. S. Thomas as their model (whereas the far more famous Dylan Thomas is mere Welsh folklore). When I met him, he was 70 years old, and had just taken part in a protest meeting in Pwllheli: 'I made a speech attacking the construction of a new sailing harbour. At most that would bring us another dozen jobs, but hundreds of English people – one more nail in the coffin of the Welsh language.' And with a certain degree of satisfaction, the poet and retired parson describes the reactions of his listeners: 'They threw eggs and stinkbombs at me.'

R. S. Thomas is not perhaps on his way to becoming a national monument, but that won't stop him fighting. He lives with his wife Elsie in a farmhouse owned by the National

Trust. It's a typical 17th-century long-house, where man and beast used to live under the same roof. The main room has a huge open fireplace, and in earlier times the family would sit in the hearth around the fire. In order to get into his study, R. S. Thomas has to bend low. He's a tall, gaunt man ('that resigned look!') who resembles even more closely the verbal portrait that he drew of himself at the age of 59: 'Time running out / now, and the soul unfinished'. A thoughtful man, much friendlier than one would imagine from the severity of his features: 'Keep the lips / firm; too many disappointments / have turned the mouth down / at the corners.'

Ronald Stuart Thomas was born in Cardiff in 1913, son of a sailor, and an angry hybrid: 'What I had to say as an author I would have liked to say in Welsh, but I'm the product of English-speaking parents.' This has clung to him like a birthmark: '... and sucked their speech / in with my mother's / infected milk, so that whatever / I throw up now is still theirs.' He did not learn Welsh until he was 30 – and he married an Englishwoman: 'There are so many of them, you can't get away from them.' The turning-point came when he was rector in an English village just a few miles across the border. 'I had become an exile.' This was the real birth of the Welshman R. S. Thomas, and it was a new calling: to rediscover his home and its language, the lost 'Welshness', and to save that language. With this mission of poetry and patriotism, he stands in the tradition of all those Welsh poets and priests who, ever since the 18th century, have fought against the policy of anglicization through the Church of England. He has done so not only by means of manifestos, but also in his daily practical work as a country parson in remote parishes: *Manafon* in Montgomeryshire, *Eglwysfach* near Machynlleth, and finally *Aberdaron*, the last stage in his long homecoming. But it has been a bitter journey, and now he finds himself 'to be an exile in my own country' – for even in Llyn, the English language is taking over.

It is the typical Welsh combination of poet and priest, but outside the pulpit, R. S. Thomas is not an artist for art's sake. Poetry is for him an attempt to give language a new dimension, so that poetry and life can stand firm against the Puritan inheritance: 'Protestantism – the adroit castrator / Of art; the bitter negation / Of song and dance and the heart's innocent joy' ('The Minister'). In a 1964 lecture on 'Words and the Poet', he named the two things that most inspired his imagination: Wales and Nature. What about God? 'God is that great absence / In our lives, the empty silence / Within, the place where we go / Seeking, not in hope to / Arrive or find.' This experience of God in absence also oppresses the lonely priest in the poem 'In Church': '... testing his faith / On emptiness, nailing his questions / One by one to an untenanted cross.' An empty church and an empty cross are very real metaphors for a modern priest in this land of chapels. Since his very first volume of poetry 'The Stones of the Field' (1946), R. S. Thomas has written about the simple people of his parish, 'the negligible men from the village', the everyday lives of small farmers, sheep-breeders, farmworkers: 'This is pain's landscape. / A savage agriculture is practised / Here ...' This is the reverse side of the sightseer's landscape: the poems tell of toil in the fields, not beauty, of pathos, dirt and rain. He identifies with his countryfolk, but he does not make heroes out of them. Sympathy has sharpened his gaze almost to acerbity, for what he sees hurts him, and he says so with wounding directness: 'There is no present in Wales, / And no future; / There is only the past,' he wrote in 'Welsh Landscape' (1952), concluding savagely: '… And an impotent people, / Sick with inbreeding, / Worrying the carcase of an old song.' Again and again he has attacked his people for this impotence. Wales 'is the botched land'.

At a reading he gave in York, a man in the audience said that he was a Welshman but couldn't speak Welsh. Did this, he asked, mean that he was not Welsh? 'I had to say to him: "Sorry, you're not a Welshman".' Not many Welsh people share this uncompromising attitude, and not many have joined him in his crusade for the language, and so he declares that 'Wales is a dead nation'. Llyn itself used to be 100% Welsh-speaking, but now? 'My neighbours speak English: for business reasons, out of politeness, out of obsequiousness, out of idleness, out of indifference, out of spinelessness. They don't stand up for Welsh affairs!' At the National Eisteddfod in 1983 he was expected to deliver a celebratory speech, but instead he read the riot act: 'Too many of our people create a situation in which a Welsh-speaking Welshman is not only a foreigner in his own country, but is also regarded as something indecent and for the neighbours to mock at.'

R. S. Thomas uses English to convey his implacable Welshness, but at the same time he is conscious of the deep complexity of this paradox: 'We have to face the possibility not, I think, of the disappearance of Welsh, but of its inadequacy as a medium for expressing the complex phantasmagoria of modern life. But if we choose English as that medium, have we the singleness of mind, the strength of will to remain primarily Welshmen?' He wants Welsh independence, but regards the presence of Plaid Cymru MPs in Westminster as a farce, and thought Prince Charles's investiture to be a scandal. He has accepted the Queen's Gold Medal for Poetry, but refuses all invitations to garden parties at Buckingham Palace. 'I reply very coldly,' he says. 'One has to exaggerate and pretend to hate the English, unfortunately.' But the exaggeration does not produce works of hatred, or sympathy, and certainly not self-pity. There is a degree of scorn, and there is bitterness and resignation, but above all there is a kind of rebellious defiance:

> We were a people wasting ourselves
> In fruitless battles for our masters,
> In lands to which we had no claim,
> With men for whom we felt no hatred.
> We were a people, and are so yet.
> When we have finished quarrelling for crumbs
> Under the table, or gnawing the bones
> Of a dead culture, we will arise,
> Armed, but not in the old way.

This is the end of his poem 'Welsh History' (1955), a tragic summing-up, but finishing with a mysterious promise, almost Merlin-like. In his Eisteddfod speech in 1976 in Cardigan, Thomas described the lost land of 'Abercuawg', an imaginary Welsh Eden: 'Wherever Abercuawg may be, there we find trees and fields and flowers and clear, unpolluted streams, where the cuckoos still sing. For that kind of place I am willing to sacrifice, even, perhaps, to die. But what of a place too full of people, with street after street of characterless contemporary houses, each with its garage and television aerial ...?' Abercuawg is a Utopia far back in the past, the village beneath the waters of the reservoir.

So the Angry Old Man of Welsh literature, the pessimistic patriot, stays in the seclusion of Llyn, looking out over the foaming surge of Hell's Mouth. At the end of the sixties he wrote a poem about what was then an emotive issue and a symbol of a terrible loss, and perhaps more than any other of his poems, it sums up R. S. Thomas's view of Wales. The poem is called 'Reservoirs':

> There are places in Wales I don't go:
> Reservoirs that are the subconscious
> Of a people, troubled far down
> With gravestones, chapels, villages even;
> The serenity of their expression
> Revolts me, it is a pose
> For strangers, a watercolour's appeal
> To the mass, instead of the poem's
> Harsher conditions. There are the hills,
> Too; gardens gone under the scum
> Of the forests; and the smashed faces
> Of the farms with the stone trickle
> Of their tears down the hills' side.
> Where can I go, then, from the smell
> Of decay, from the putrefying of a dead
> Nation? I have walked the shore
> For an hour and seen the English
> Scavenging among the remains
> Of our culture, covering the sand
> Like the tide and, with the roughness
> Of the tide, elbowing our language
> Into the grave that we have dug for it.

Lloyd George in Llanystumdwy: How British can a Welshman be?

Llanystumdwy lies a little way inland, on the coastal road from Pwllheli to Criccieth. From this unassuming village on the edge of the Llyn Peninsula came David Lloyd George (picture, page 21). He also insisted on being buried here, beside the river of his child-hood, and not in Westminster Abbey. This was the homecoming of a man who began his political career in Wales as a nationalist, continued it in London as the Liberal leader, led his country to victory in the First World War as Prime Minister, and as a British statesman came to stand as the epitome of Welshness. The 1st Earl of Dwyfor – a title bestowed on him shortly before his death in 1945 – is not buried in the village cemetery, but lies in splendid isolation on the bank of the Dwyfor, the Great Water. It's a politician's grave, with the same sense of showmanship that imbued everything else that he did in his life. But this last piece of rhetoric, his tomb, he left in the hands of his fellow countryman Clough Williams-Ellis, the architect of Portmeirion. There is an oval lawn beneath oak trees, partly enclosed in a wall of weathered stones, and in the centre is a wrought-iron portal, above which there is a gable with an oval opening; you go down four steps to an irregular-shaped rock. The same grey stone on which the old man used to sit beside the river now covers his grave. Life and death, Nature and history meet in a simple but dramatic gesture, a fitting monument to the man himself.

David Lloyd George was born in Manchester in 1863. His father was a teacher and died shortly after his son's birth. The boy grew up in the house of his uncle, a shoemaker and Baptist preacher in Llanystumdwy (plate 93). What did Lloyd George learn there? That godly speech is golden, and drink is from the Devil. He was a Non-Conformist through and through. In 1880 he left the little granite house with the four mullioned windows to become a lawyer in the neighbouring slate port of Porthmadog. There young Lloyd George swiftly gained a reputation as a natural political genius and a terror to the middle classes. In 1888 he founded a newspaper in Pwllheli, where his grandfather was a headmaster: 'Udgorn Rhydidd', The Trumpet of Freedom. He blew his trumpet so hard that it fanfared him two years later into Westminster – a nationalist with a revolutionary social programme, a firebrand orator though none too competent a solicitor, MP for Caernarfon, which he represented for over fifty years. His maiden speech in Parliament was on the explosive subject of reforming the licensing laws. As a Baptist and Liberal in the Gladstone tradition, he knew that the temperance movement had powerful political implications. And as leader of the radical wing of Welsh Liberalism, he also argued passionately against the Boer War and in favour of Home Rule, in both cases opposing what most people regarded as the best interests of Britain. 'I am sure that Wales would be an example to the nations of the world if it were given self-government,' he declared. But in spite of these sentiments, he duly became Prime Minister, and when he was Prime Minister, he never expressed such sentiments again.

Since Gladstone, the Liberals had been by far the strongest party in Wales: in 1868,

Augustus John: David Lloyd George, 1908–15

Cymru Fydd (Wales Future) had won 22 of the 30 Parliamentary seats then allotted to Wales. Plaid Cymru, of course, did not yet exist. A national party in those days would have been superfluous, since the Welsh Liberals represented Welsh interests. They continued to do so until the First World War, and then they were replaced by Labour as the dominant party. Today the Liberals have even less influence than Plaid Cymru. Initially, Lloyd George himself played the role taken over by the Labour party, and he did so with panache. As a member of the Liberal cabinet after 1905, he declared categorically that he intended to break the power of the Conservative upper classes by means of high inheritance and income taxes. His comrade-in-arms in those days was the young Winston Churchill. The English aristocrat and the Welsh warrior of the class war, the 'terrible twins' formed a strange alliance. With his 'People's Budget' of 1909, Lloyd George created a storm in the House of Lords. He proposed it as a wartime budget, the war being against poverty and filth. In a New Year's speech, he promised that 'we are going to drive hunger from the hearth' – a quotation still being used by the 'Bistro Lloyd George' in Conwy. The House of Lords rejected his budget (which created a constitutional crisis, and ultimately led to a reduction in their own powers), but the social reforms that mattered most to him got through: pensions and insurance relating to old age, sickness, disability and unemployment, partly along the lines of Bismarck's social security laws which Lloyd George had

421

studied during a trip to Germany in 1908. And so the Welsh politician laid the foundations for Britain's welfare state. But was he still a Welshman?

'I am only a bit of a Welshman in an office in London,' he confessed in 1915, at the National Eisteddfod in Bangor. This was the truth, although in his perfect Welsh he made it sound like an understatement. He had not, of course, forgotten the language or his own country, and for years he enjoyed the honour of being President of the Eisteddfod, while the Welsh enjoyed the feeling that through him they could share some of the power of London, as they had done in the days of the Tudor King Henry VII. They called him the 'Welsh Wizard', a latterday Merlin, a nickname actually bestowed on him originally by the economist Keynes when Lloyd George attended the Paris Peace Conference in 1919. The Welsh Wizard even succeeded, after a break of many centuries, in getting the Prince of Wales to come to Caernarfon Castle for his investiture. British court theatre in the place of home rule: Lloyd George had gone to Westminster bearing his country's hopes for nationhood, and he returned to Wales with a Prince from the House of Windsor. Not surprisingly, the nationalists were disappointed, but Lloyd George saw it differently. On every St David's Day he reaffirmed his loyalty to the Land of his Fathers, just as he had done in a speech he had made in Cardiff in 1906: 'Let no man despise Wales, her language or her literature. She has survived many storms; she has survived many Empires. Her time will come. When the last black diamond is dug out of the earth of Glamorgan, there will be men then digging gems of pure brilliance from the inexhaustible mines of the literature and language of Wales.' The declaration was one of enthusiasm, but its implications were bitter: Wales was now nothing but a cultural heritage, and no longer a political goal. This had died with the failure of the home rule movement in Parliament, and so all that was left was the Eisteddfod, the Prince of Wales, and speeches on St David's Day. But what speeches they were. The power of his Welsh oratory was unique. He was the tenor of the political stage, master of the whole range of emotion, not merely through rhetorical devices, but also through the magic of his voice. The American photographer A. L. Coburn noted the reactions of the crowd during one of Lloyd George's speeches: 'He had them under his spell, as a conductor holds his orchestra, and he could do what he pleased with them.' In his house in Criccieth, where Coburn photographed him in 1918, he was 'just a quiet, simple country gentleman.' Harold Macmillan, looking back on his own distinguished career, recalled the lecture Lloyd George – one of the 'giants of my generation' – gave him after his well received maiden speech in Parliament: 'You have no idea how to make a speech,' said Lloyd George, 'yours was an essay.' And the advice given to young Macmillan was: 'Never say more than one thing; when you are a minister two things, and when you are a Prime Minister winding up a debate, perhaps three.'

Lloyd George loved strawberries. He was a passionate fruit-grower and gardener, and loved to relax at his country house in Churt, Surrey. Shortly before he retired as Prime Minister in 1922, he had the house built, and gave it a Welsh name, though not – according to Pevsner – very much else: 'a gauche, almost styleless house'. Not until 1944 did Lloyd George return to Wales. One year later, he died in Llanystumdwy, the place where he had spent his childhood. Winston Churchill, his former Minister of War, said of him in Parliament: 'He was the greatest Welshman which that unconquerable race has produced since the age of the Tudors.' As a British statesman, he became the model for all the Anglo-Welsh and for all future aspiring Lloyd Georges in London, including Michael Heseltine and Neil Kinnock. But for the nationalists, his name can still act like a red rag to a bull. 'He probably did more harm than good to Wales,' wrote Gwynfor Evans. 'Lloyd George tightened the hold of Briticism on Wales at the cost of its Welshness.' He and other 'Britishers' plunged the Welsh into conflicts of loyalty, in a sort of 'national schizophrenia'. Many would call this a gross exaggeration. But there can be no denying the split that Lloyd George brought about in the Celtic island next door: it was during his period of office, in 1921, that Ireland was partitioned, and Northern Ireland has been an insoluble problem ever since.

Welsh national consciousness and the feeling of 'being British' were by no means a new combination. They do, of course, constitute the split personality of the Welsh, and especially since the break-up of the Empire and the breakdown of chapel life have contributed substantially to an identity crisis, but according to the Welsh historian Gwyn Williams, the term 'British Empire' was actually coined by a Welshman. He was the mathematician, astronomer and alchemist John Dee, as respected at the court of Rudolf II in Prague as he was by Elizabeth I in London. John Dee expected the Welsh Tudors on England's throne to restore the old Britain. Included in this British Empire was America. He justified the Queen's transatlantic aspirations by way of the fact that the Welsh Prince Madoc had colonized America around 1170 (see page 429). But the origins of the term 'British Empire' are perhaps not quite so tangible as the phenomenon itself, and to this the Welsh certainly made a major contribution. In the 19th century, it had been Welsh coal that had fuelled the ships which controlled the Empire, and it was Lloyd George who led the nation when it was threatened by global war; if the Crown had not already united it, Lloyd George did. The Labour Leader James Keir Hardie was shouted down by his own followers in the Valleys, as they sang 'Rule Britannia'. Welsh national feelings gave way to British patriotism, or 'a wider circle of service', as Lloyd George liked to call it. Do people still think the same way? A Welsh schoolboy told me that during history lessons, if an Englishman's achievements are being discussed, he is always referred to as English; but a Welshman is always described as British.

In the Lloyd George Museum in Llanystumdwy, the life of the great man is fully documented. There are the usual relics – a lock of white hair, walking sticks, tobacco pipes, a cabinet full of silver knick-knacks and honorary citizenships. His sayings are everywhere: concerning the Anglo-Welsh relationship, 'Others have the jam. We have the pots.' Or 'We can conquer unemployment.' Great Britain had 2½ million unemployed when Lloyd George resigned. Not much has changed. Dafydd Iwan sang in 1980:

If you don't have a job, the answer of course
Is to move, says Magi Thatcher,
Hitch up your tent and move over to Kent
Like your fathers, says Magi Thatcher.

My next destination was *Criccieth*, but not because of Lloyd George (plates 42, 99). His house on a hill overlooking the bay is called Brynawelon, if you want to know, but neither that nor the ruined castle was what took me to Criccieth. I was after just one thing: ice cream. Not any old ice cream, but ice cream with a princely Welsh name: Cadwalader's. The original Cadwaladr was a 12th-century collaborator: 'fickle Cadwaladr' Gwynfor Evans calls him, for he made a pact with the Norman King Henry II. Personally, I would make a pact with anyone in order to lay my hands and tongue on Cadwalader's ice cream. Rich, creamy, heavenly vanilla ice cream – they make no other flavour, only vanilla: 'Into it goes: 18 gallons of milk, 34 pounds of sugar, 12 pounds of butter, 3 dozen eggs, 6 lb shan't tell you – and a great deal of love and care.' For fifty years and more the Cadwaladers have been making their legendary ice cream – and even old Mr Lloyd George must have had a taste. 'Others have the jam. We have the ice cream.' That's what he ought to have said.

Portmeirion's Bag of Tricks: Sir Clough's Italian Village

When I left Criccieth, there was a warm evening glow over *Tremadog Bay*. On the other side one could see the dusky blue shadows of the mountains of Snowdonia. 'There is no corner of Europe that I know, which so moves me with the awe and majesty of great things as does this mass of the northern Welsh Mountains, seen from this corner of their silent sea.' It was Hilaire Belloc who wrote these lines, and I felt exactly the same way.

The next morning I awoke in very strange surroundings. Looking out of my window, I could see a campanile, the dome of a Florentine cathedral, here a piazza, there a loggia, palms, cypresses, oleanders and eucalyptus trees. I was in the middle of a Mediterranean fantasy, a man-made paradise, a Welsh dream: in other words, I was in *Portmeirion* (plate 79).

The idea for an Italian village on the Cambrian coast occurred to Clough Williams-Ellis in the trenches during the First World War. He came from an old Welsh family, was born in Northamptonshire in 1883, grew up in Caenarfonshire, studied at Cambridge ('Cambridge in my family was as axiomatic as porridge for breakfast, eaten with salt'), and then went to London as a young architect, mixing with society and picking up his first commissions. He restored historic country houses, built new ones,[1] designed an old people's home, a youth hostel, a dogs' home, churches, restaurants, the post office at Aberdaron, and the summit station for the Snowdon Mountain Railway. All of these were thoroughly useful, but none of them would have earned him a place in the history of architecture. This he achieved through Portmeirion. It was an idée fixe, a folly in the best British tradition, eccentric, exotic, picturesque, a refuge, an attraction, an experiment. It took Clough Williams-Ellis a long time to find the right spot for his fantasy village. In his 'continued island hunting' he was inspired by Crete, Rhodes, Capri and Corfu, and his head whirled with colourful façades, classical colonnades, views of bays and squares, fountains, statues, Greek island villages, Italian hill towns ... they were all there in his mind, waiting for a home, and at last he found it outside his own Welsh front door: a sheltered peninsula in Tremadog Bay, with cliffs and bays and hills. And so in 1925 he bought a Victorian country house on the waterfront, complete with overgrown gardens, and there he began to build the great architectural theatre of Portmeirion.

His set came from all over the place: he collected old houses which had been demolished elsewhere and which he brought back to his 'home for fallen buildings'. At an auction he bought for just £13 the stucco ceiling from the ballroom at Emral Hall, depicting the labours of Hercules, and before this Flintshire country house was finally demolished, he also bought various other sections and put them together in Portmeirion's Jacobean Town Hall. No councillors ever sat in this Herculean hall, but Benjamin Britten gave concerts there. The campanile he constructed in 1928 from the stones of a 12th century castle built by his supposed ancestor, Prince Gruffydd ap Cynan, and knocked down in 1870: 'This 19th-century affront to the 12th is thus piously redressed in the 20th,' states a plaque on the tower. This Italian village also contains surrealistic elements worthy of a Max Ernst collage. What, for instance, are the gilded Siamese temple dancers doing on the Ionic columns of a piazza? Why are the Neo-Gothic colonnades from Bristol's Arnos Court next to a baroque portal from London? It's a veritable masked ball of styles. Long before the German 'happening' artist Wolf Vostell began concreting motor cars at his Happenings, the great Welsh eccentric had done the same thing with an old ship on Portmeirion's quayside. Here everything goes with everything, even if nothing goes with anything. It's all one big 'happy architectural family' full of foundlings. Even the cypresses have been cut out of yew trees – a piece of natural trompe-l'oeil, in keeping with the illusory architecture. Shakespeare looks down from a balcony (colour plate 32). We are the Fools on Clough William-Ellis's open-air stage. 'Half private spleen, half Conservative Utopia, this Welsh Williamsburg offers what the rougher reality of Great Britain – and not only

1 His first important commission in Wales was the reconstruction of the Jacobean manor-house Llangoed Hall (1913–19) near Builth Wells: it was an attempt to revive the country house tradition in modern style, following the example of the contemporary, but more original houses of Lutyens. Llangoed Hall belongs today to Sir Bernard Ashley, and is a luxury hotel.

Great Britain – precludes: the cheerfulness of a more tasteful Disneyland,' writes the architectural historian Wolfgang Pehnt. 'Like a Fool's mirror, Portmeirion's bag of tricks contains an element of truth in all its distortions: the longings that have not been fulfilled by the planners of our century.'

There are many things that have made Sir Clough's potpourri popular, not the least of which is that it defies description. It's a mixture of Port Grimaud and Hollywood, holiday resort and film set. 'The Inn of the Sixth Happiness' and other films have been made here, together with countless advertisements. It's architecture as entertainment, bright, heterogeneous, full of surprises just like life itself, but much more beautiful, more crazy, and amazingly more harmonious. It's a sight for the sore eyes of the people from high-rise blocks and terraced houses, countering the sober functionality of the modern age, not with the underhand tricks of post-modernity, but with the uninhibited high spirits of premodernity – Madhouse rather than Bauhaus. Sir Clough was highly delighted when the American avant-garde architect Frank Lloyd Wright appeared to approve of Portmeirion: 'He took it all without a blink, seeming instantly to see the point of all my wilful pleasantries, the calculated naiveties, eye-traps, forced and faked perspectives, heretical constructions, unorthodox colour mixtures and general architectural levity.' He recalls in his autobiography how the American was particularly taken with the bold changes in levels and perspectives. And indeed a fair proportion of Portmeirion's impact comes from such kaleidoscopic charms. The axis is continually shifting, not just historically but also geographically: one moment you are gazing at mountains, then at the sea, or gardens, or woods. Variety is the spice of Portmeirion. No guest better embodied the spirit of this place than Noel Coward, who most appropriately wrote his famous comedy 'Blithe Spirit' here.

In life as in architecture, Sir Clough Williams-Ellis was a born entertainer, amusing and stimulating – the perfect host in the perfect setting, where he entertained such celebrities as G.B.Shaw, H.G.Wells, Daphne du Maurier, Arthur Koestler, Julian Huxley. 'One finds an intellectual under every stone in the valley,' was what people used to say of Portmeirion. Bertrand Russell observed that it was just like the Place de l'Opéra: one had only to sit down in Portmeirion, and in time everyone would pass by. 'Bertie' was Sir Clough's neighbour, and spent the last fifteen years of his life in Plas Penrhyn, a Regency house near Penrhyndeudraeth,[1] where he wrote 'Common Sense and Nuclear Warfare' (1959) as the culmination of his passionate anti-nuclear campaigning. It was Russell who did the honours when Portmeirion was officially opened. In those days Portmeirion was almost like a club for intellectuals, politicians, and other public figures. The place was tailor-made for these 'peacocks in paradise' and was the apt setting of their last parties before the War. But it was not made exclusively for the elite, for Sir Clough had made plenty of provision for us humble tourists.

1 World-famous as an English philosopher, he was in fact born in a little village near Tintern Abbey, Trelleck (Trelch) in Monmouthshire.

His great dream had to be self-financing, as he was no millionaire, and so tourism was an integral part of his scheme. He also wanted to show that catering for tourism need not ruin a landscape, but indeed could even enhance it. Portmeirion is a school for seeing, an attempt to get a public with little interest in town and country planning to take pleasure in architecture 'by a gay, light-opera sort of approach'. It was a sophisticated highbrow foretaste of the mass tourism that was to find its epitome in the lowbrow holiday camps of Billy Butlin. Yet Sir Clough was no snob. Butlin's Holiday Camp near Pwllheli was used as an army training camp during the war, but after 1945 it was to be restored to its original use. Immediately there were massive protests, particularly by the forerunners of environ mentalists, and the whole project was in danger, but Sir Clough entered the debate on Butlin's side, pleading at the hearing that the camp was already there, and should stay there for 'the greatest happiness of the greatest number'. This he regarded as a fundamental right. He and Billy – later Sir Billy – Butlin won the case. Sir Clough also sat on many committees for the protection of the countryside and the environment, including the one responsible for setting up Snowdonia National Park. He regarded himself as 'part of the local fauna', and a specimen of the dying breed of eccentrics. In his riding breeches, yellow woollen stockings and canary-coloured waistcoat he used to mix with the visitors, litter-picker in hand to clear the path of sweet and ice cream wrappers 'I like figures in my land-scape,' he would say, especially when the fashion was for bright colours, but he didn't mind who came so long as people kept coming, and they did and they do: upwards of 200,000 a year.

Every autumn, Sir Clough used to invite the artist Jonah Jones from neighbouring Porthmadog for a meal and a discussion on whether the summer had been worth recording. If it was, the artist would make a memorial plaque: 'To the Summer of 1959 in Honour of its Splendour', or: '1975 excelled even 1959'. The years were like vintages, and the finest were recorded with inscriptions on Portmeirion's Hercules monument. At 89 the great man was knighted, and when he was 90 he was still climbing up scaffolding every day to consult with his workers. 'He didn't care what we did with the interiors,' Terry MacDermott, the supervisor, told me, 'so long as the façade and the dimensions were right.' At 95, Sir Clough declared that Portmeirion was finished, and then he died. He de-creed that his ashes were to be fired into space in a rocket, and when they returned, they were to be scattered over the peninsula. The RAF proved hopelessly inadequate to this task.

While I was searching for his grave, I stumbled across Portmeirion's dog cemetery. The old lady who had previously owned the peninsula had set it in the midst of the damp and scented jungle of this great park. She was considerably fonder of dog society than human, and there the dogs lie now, beneath pines and yew trees, their empty feeding bowls on their graves. For 'Dear Dog Jim, once a stray' Mrs Adelaide Haigh quoted a verse from the Bible: 8 Romans 19–21. What sort of names did these Welsh dogs have? Of course there was Merlin, and Jezebel, and also a Pepys, and there is one whose plaque of slate bears no name at all, but only the following verse: 'My dear dear dog gone before / To that unknown and silent shore / Shall we not meet as heretofore / Some summer morning.'

Sir Clough himself did not spend all his time in Portmeirion, but lived mostly a few miles inland in *Llanfrothen*, in his family's old country house Plâs Brondanw. There I met Amabel Williams-Ellis, his widow, who at the time was almost 90 herself. A Grand Old Lady, who sat as straight as a candle at her typewriter, writing 'my 42nd or 43rd book, I'm not sure which.' Many of them were children's books or biographies, but then she was working on her memoirs, 'All Stracheys are Cousins'. Her brother was John Strachey, Attlee's Minister of War. The most important thing, she said, was aesthetic education, and then the peace movement. She showed me the garden of Plas Brondanw: avenues of yew trees with classical statues, ponds, wrought-iron gates of rococo elegance, and all through this comparatively small space, the art of perspective – a little gem cut by the master of Portmeirion.

Someone else who had a dream was William Alexander Madocks. He, too, built a little town: *Tremadog*. He was an early 19th-century entrepreneur, and his ambitions concerned practical matters like land reclamation. He wanted to drain the two inlets north of *Morfa Harlech*, the Marsh of Harlech. One can just imagine the howls of protest that would greet such a plan today. But not then. In fact, Parliament granted to this Lincolnshire MP the huge sum of £100,000 as development aid for Wales. He succeeded in dyking a great deal of the Traeth Mawr, and in 1811 completed a stone dam that ran for more than almost a mile through the mouth of the Glaslyn, and is known as The Cob. It was not, however, until after his death in 1828 that the slate trucks began to roll from Blaenau Ffestiniog over the dam to Porthmadog. This port, which bears his name, survived the end of the slate boom as a holiday resort, thus faring much better than the slate town itself in the mountains. Porthmadog also outstripped the place that was meant to be the centre of Madock's industrial empire: Tremadog. There you will find an elongated square flanked by two-storeyed terraces, with the former town-hall (1807) and covered market at one end, at the foot of a cliff. This is the centre of the town that never was.

The parts of his new town that Madocks did build are still standing almost unaltered, and they include two churches at the entrance to the town: one Neo-Gothic for Anglicans, and the other Neo-Classical for Non-Conformists. Capel Peniel (1811), with its Tuscan columned portico and rose window in the gable, may have been inspired by Inigo Jones's design for St Paul's in Covent Garden: a small, austere but radiant place of worship which for me is the most beautiful chapel in the whole of North Wales. In order to enable Tremadog to stand on its own economic feet, Madocks set up a textile factory in 1805, producing military uniforms which he sold to both sides during the Napoleonic Wars. He was a man of many parts, and he had great plans for Tremadog. He named one main road Dublin Street and the other London Street, as he wanted his new settlement to be a stopping-place for stagecoaches on the new Ireland route. Unfortunately, despite his fervent lobbying in Parliament, his project failed by just one vote. It was Telford's Holyhead Road that won the day, and Port Dinllaen on the Llyn Peninsula, which Madocks had favoured as the ferry port, remained a sleepy yachting bay. Madocks was on the verge of bankruptcy. And then, rushing to his aid in a manner scarcely conceivable today, there came a poet, fascinated by the heroism and romance of land reclamation. He was Percy Bysshe Shelley.

It was the year he had been sent down from Oxford, and had married the sixteen year old Harriet. They moved into a cottage (since demolished) on Madock's estate Tan-yr-allt, Under the Wood, in 1812. The rest of this dense oak forest on the promontory overlooking Tremadog is now a nature conservation area. This was how large areas of North Wales used to look, before conifer plantations took the place of the oaks. At Tan-yr-allt, Shelley wrote some of 'Queen Mab', a revolutionary didactic poem about a just society, but he quarrelled with neighbouring farmers because on his walks, he insisted on killing their sick sheep out of sympathy, and when he then started to agitate among the workers at Porthmadog, his house was broken into one evening and some warning shots were fired. The Shelleys got the message, and moved out.[1]

Tremadog Bay: home of eccentrics, poets, entrepreneurs, land reclamation and a dream town that never came true. But before we leave here, let us consider one fascinating thesis: that it was from here that America was discovered. In 1170 with 13 ships and 300 men, Prince Madoc ab Owain Gwynedd left the islands of Ynys Fadog in the mouth of the Glaslyn,[2] in search of a country west of Ireland. He never returned. But in the 17th century tales spread about an Indian tribe with white skin, the Mandans, whose language was similar to Welsh. In 1953 a memorial plaque was erected on the beach at Mobile Bay in Alabama. It reads: 'In memory of Prince Madoc, a Welsh explorer, who landed on the shores of Mobile Bay in 1170 and left behind, with the Indians, the Welsh language.' Historians can neither prove nor disprove the theory that America was discovered by a Welsh Columbus. Perhaps it is all a myth cooked up by Welsh story-tellers and fostered to fuel the colonial rivalry between England and Spain during the Age of Discovery. Sir Walter Raleigh mentions the legend of Madoc in his History of the World, and the romantic poet Robert Southey wrote a poem about him. For many Welsh emigrants to America in the 19th century, the Madoc myth turned into reality. His descendants were miners, farmers, pioneers of the American union movement, and Mormons. Hundreds of Welsh 'saints' followed their Captain, Dan Jones, from the Mormon centre in Merthyr Tydfil to Salt Lake City in Utah. Welsh was the first foreign language into which the Book of Mormon was translated. The American census of 1890 recorded that there were some 100,000 people of Welsh extraction, and in Llanfair Ceiriog there is a memorial plaque to President Thomas Jefferson, whose father was Welsh. If Madoc had not been there before, he was certainly there now.

---

1 There is a memorial plaque in the garden of a house called 'Odstone' which lays claim to Llandrillo-yn-Rhos, near Llandudno, being Madoc's point of departure.

2 Another short-time literary resident of Tremadog was Lawrence of Arabia, who was born in 1888 in a house called 'Woodlands' at the entrance to the town (now a Christian hospice for mountaineers), but moved with his family to Oxford eight years later.

On Harlech's Battlements: The King, the Birds and the Photographer

Bendigeid Bran, the son of Llyr, was 'at Harlech in Ardudwy, at his court, and he sat upon the rock of Harlech looking over the sea, and there Britain's King beheld thirteen white sails, the fleet of Ireland's Mallolwch, who wanted Bran's sister to be his wife – the beautiful Bronwen of the white bosom.' Thus begins the second book of the 'Mabinogi'. After much feasting and terrible fighting, Bran's men finally return to Wales defeated. ' "In Harlech you will be feasting seven years, the birds of Rhiannon singing unto you the while" says the King to them, commanding them however to cut off his head. "And all that time," he reassures them, "the head will be to you as pleasant company as it ever was when on my body." All that he told them came true: the certain song of the birds was so beautiful that all the songs they had ever heard were unpleasant compared thereto, and the birds seemed to them to be at a great distance from them over the sea, yet they appeared distinct as if they were close by.'

This is *Harlech*: the castle, the King on his rock, and birds flying over the sea. The rest is history and tourism. But Harlech looks back a long way, deep into myth and into Cambria. The rock of Harlech is the rock of the old Kings, and it is a king of rocks. 'Harlech Dome' is the name geologists give to the grey Cambrian gritstone that comes from time immemorial to the surface of the Rhinog mountains. Harlech Castle stands on one of their foothills. King Edward came here late to build his castle, and still later, in the Wars of the Roses, there was heard for the first time the legendary march of the 'Men of Harlech': 'Harlech raise your banners, / see the enemy, / inspire the strength / of all the men of Meirion to shout / "Wales for ever".' But after all the myths, battles and songs, all that remains is a ruin on a rock. Time, then, for the painters to move in, the picturesque late vintage of history, a melancholy apotheosis. John Martin painted the last bard with Harlech Castle as the heroic backdrop; Turner pictured it with peasants and poor hovels set against a glorious panorama of the mountains; John Sell Cotman, Henry Gastineau and others painted it, so that Harlech was once more seen in all its magnificence. Today all that remains is preservation and photography: those who come here now are the restorers and the tour guides – the last bastions in the battle against wind and weather, and oblivion, and they, too, are heroes in their own way, patching together that which defies patching, and summing up a history that defies summary, from the Mabinogion up to the present day.

If you follow the inlet of Traeth Bach to its end, leaving Portmeirion behind you on the other side, and you wander south across the long beach of Tremadog bay, over sand and shingle, suddenly in the distance you will see the castle rise up over the broad marsh of Morfa Harlech, between sea and mountains, and the power of this vision will overwhelm

John Martin: The Bard, 1817 ▷

J. M. W. Turner: Harlech Castle, c.1834

you with that same mythical force of its origins. Such moments are what one travels for. Even standing on the peak of Snowdon cannot compare with standing on the walls of Harlech Castle. The bay of Cardigan, the mountains of Caernarfonshire, Criccieth Castle beyond Tremadog Bay, and the long finger of the Llyn Peninsula – all this combines into one of the classic views of Wales. Harlech is a great synthesis of landscape and history, power and beauty. It is a symbol of foreign power, long since become its own myth, still a possession of the English Crown, but a rock carved out of Welsh rock. 'Harlech raise your banners', and on the battlements of the castle you can feel where Welsh patriotism stems from, and you can feel the national pathos of the men of Harlech. 'Wales for ever.' The sea stretches out before you, and Snowdon looms behind you. But the 20th century will not let you get carried too far away. Perhaps you can imagine the ships of the Irish or of the Normans here, but your imagination will have to be pretty strong to obliterate the caravans now anchored in their place. The sea has withdrawn nearly a mile from Harlech Castle. Just like Edward I's other fortresses in North Wales, Harlech was to get its supplies by sea. A solid flight of steps led down from the west side to the harbour, where today there is a railway. And where the birds of Rhiannon once sang above the water, you will now find golf balls whistling round your ears among the dunes of Royal St David's Golf Club.

James of St George, the King's fortress builder, could not have found better foundations than the rock of Harlech. The castle's groundplan is almost square, with a low outer wall, four round towers, and a twin-towered gatehouse, the whole thing topped by four slender stair turrets. It is a fortress of perfect symmetry, almost completely windowless. It was built during Edward's second and last campaign (1283–89), but it was not impregnable. Owain Glyndwr conquered it in 1404, and held court here for nearly five years. When the English recaptured it, Owain's fortunes sank into decline, and he fled into the mountains, his rebellion over. During the Wars of the Roses, in 1460, Margaret of Anjou, wife of the captured King Henry VI, sought refuge in Harlech Castle. For seven years Dafydd ap Ifan ap Einion and his fifty men, supporters of the Red Rose, resisted a siege by the Yorkists, and it is their bravery that is said to have inspired the famous 'Rhyfelgyrch Gwyr Harlech', the March of the Men of Harlech. In 1647 the fall of Harlech Castle, last Welsh bastion of the Royalists, signalled the end of the Civil War. Cromwell's troops were ordered to destroy the castle, but they did not do so, and at least its basic structure remained intact. In 1295 Edward's settlement contained a mere 86 inhabitants, whereas today there are around 1,200. But what used to be the county town of Merionethshire is no more than a village. 'Nothing to see here apart from the Castle,' says the lady in the Tourist Office, with an air of apology. You don't often hear such things, and I find it rather comforting.

At the foot of the crag on which the castle stands, and next to the round Theatr Ardudwy (1972), is Coleg Harlech. This is what they call a 'second chance college', for adult education, started in 1927. When I went there, out of a total of 120 students, only ten spoke Welsh, and of the ten teachers, only one was Welsh-speaking. 'In this situation, you have to be militant,' says Gareth Llwyd Dafydd. I met the 25-year-old student shortly after he'd finished his hunger strike. This had lasted for seventeen days, and was his protest against the appointment of a non-Welsh-speaking administrator for the college. His action was successful: the new man, from Manchester, proceeded to take an intensive course in Welsh. Since 1982 this has now become compulsory for all 'foreign' appointments in

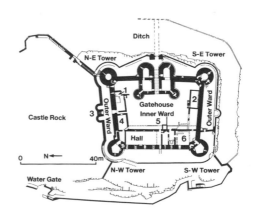

Harlech Castle, plan
1 Wells   2 Granary   3 Side gate
4 Chapel   5 Steps Stairs   6 Kitchen

Harlech. Gareth himself never spoke a word of English until he was 15, and unlike many of his friends, he does not see the battle for Welsh culture in terms of an indirect battle for freedom: 'We do need more power for the individual regions, but we don't need our own parliament in Cardiff. The English exploited Wales in the 19th century, just as they did Ireland, but now it's economically too late for independence.' He's a farmer's son, and when I met him, he hoped to become a teacher in a district where Welsh was still spoken, 'so that they'll carry on speaking Welsh in the future as well'.

At the heart of Coleg Harlech is a 1910 villa named 'Wernfawr', designed by George Walton, a pupil of William Morris, and one of the few examples of the Arts and Crafts Movement in Wales. This house belonged to the English photographer, anarchist, and former Kodak manager George Davison. In summer 1916 he was visited by a young colleague from America who had made a name for himself with scenes and portraits: Alvin Langdon Coburn. A few years earlier, Coburn had moved to England, but now, on his very first visit to Harlech, he knew that Wales was the place for him. He was so enamoured of the landscape that in 1918 he bought some land in Harlech, built a house there ('Cae Besi'), and in 1930 moved permanently out of London to Wales. Like John Cowper Powys, Coburn had found the country of his soul, a land that fitted in perfectly with his introvert nature and mystic way of thinking. At the National Eisteddfod of 1927 Coburn was awarded one of those high honours that mean more to those that receive them than any official citizenship: it was the green habit of the Gorsedd, and the bardic name of Mab-y-Trioedd, Son of the Triads. 'Of this I am very proud, for it seems to bring me close to Wales, my adopted country, which I very greatly love.' In 1919 the photographer had already become a freemason. His move to Wales proved to be the turning-point in his life, a journey into his own interior. He donated his entire collection of photographs to the Royal Photographic Society, and destroyed all his 15,000 negatives. The road to Harlech was a road away from his photographic career, a farewell to fame, and a total withdrawal from the flashlight society he had hitherto frequented. He became a lay preacher, Red Cross auxiliary, and Grand Master of the Freemasons' Lodge. Wales was the ideal country for such a man to take refuge in, and to find sweet oblivion.

But the country was too beautiful for him to renounce photography altogether. 'I sometimes climbed mountains as an excuse to use a camera on clouds, rocks, little lakes nestling in valleys overshadowed by the heights, and prehistoric stone monuments.' The result was a little volume of pictures entitled 'Book of Harlech' (1920). In freemasonry, Coburn discovered the 'art of the inner life', and in Wales he discovered a form of Nature that corresponded to his own mystic view of the world. He was not interested in spectacular shots of landscapes, but in simple things that seemed somehow to encode spiritual experiences: 'The movement of a cloud's shadow across a landscape makes all the difference.' For days on end he would return to the same tree in order to photograph its cracked bark in different lights. In 1916 his photographic abstractions of the 'Vortographs' demonstrated the absolute experimental and intellectual limits of his medium, but now he returned to the laboratory of Nature, using the camera as an instrument of meditation. Behind the ever-changing wonders of the visible world, he could feel some eternal power behind it all: 'We cannot photograph this, but if we can glimpse it with the eyes of the soul, life is changed for us' (An Autobiography, 1966).

For nearly thrity years, Coburn lived in Harlech. At the end of the war he moved to *Rhos-on-Sea*, where he called his house 'Awen', Inspiration. There, after the death of his wife, he turned increasingly to the study of freemasonry, astrology and Zen Buddhism. Few people even knew that he was still alive. He scarcely did any travelling, and now spent the winters in Wales, whereas formerly he had always sought the sun in Madeira. When he was over 80, he was still taking photographs: 'Reflections', the frozen sea near Colwyn Bay, structures of 'simple beauty', reflections of captured movement, of time standing still. 'Towards the end of life when its restlessness is stilled and the soul is drawn inward towards its own centre, there arises a peace which is very satisfying.' Alvin Langdon Coburn died in 1966 in his house of 'Inspiration'. He is buried in the cemetery at Llandrillo-yn-Rhos.

Even in his lifetime, his early work was part of photography's history, but the 'Welsh' Coburn is still waiting for adequate representation. In his chosen home country of Wales, there could be no better place for a Coburn centre than Harlech.

Harry Gastineau: Barmouth, c.1830

Dolgellau: Gold Fever in the Forests of the Mawddach

Since the AA guide to Wales praised the 'quiet charm of *Barmouth*', the little seaside resort south of Harlech has never again been as quiet or as charming as it was in Darwin's day (colour plate 22, plate 57). Charles Darwin loved the place on the Mawddach Estuary, and here he spent several weeks writing about the 'Descent of Man'. Now Barmouth Man sits with labrador and ice cream on the beach, and alternates his gaze between the sea and the 'Daily Mirror'. He will do this on the sand, on a bench, or in his car, according to the state of the weather. And if Barmouth Man should happen to have not only holidays but also children to share his holidays, he will certainly be forced to stop at the 'Las Vegas Amusements', which constitute 'traditional seaside fun for all the family'. If he hasn't already got his tea in the boot of the car, he'll go to 'Davy Jones's Locker' on the front. Once it was called 'Ty Gwyn', White House, and was a meeting-place for supporters of the House of Lancaster. In the evening, Barmouth Man goes to bed early, unless –

Richard Wilson: The Valley of the Mawddach, with Cader Idris beyond, c.1770

Samuel Palmer: The Waterfalls, Pistil Mawddach, 1835–36

exceptionally – he goes to the Dragon Theatre, a chapel converted into an arts centre. Otherwise, the town's hemmed-in position between sea and mountains prevents it from any further unfortunate developments.

Just behind the main street, the road rises steeply to the cliffs of Dinas Oleu, the very first piece of land in Great Britain to have been acquired by the National Trust (1895). This is where the glorious *Panorama Walk* begins, leading you across the heights of Mawddach Valley. If you want to leave Barmouth by boat, you can take the ferry to a promontory, and there between the dunes you can catch the smallest and sweetest of all the Great Little Railways of Wales: the *Fairbourne Railway* (plate 83). The driver towers head and shoulders over his engine. Then you can return on foot over the *Mawddach Estuary*, across a railway bridge which is two-thirds of a mile long, and which is exactly the same as it was in 1867, when the Cambrian Coast line came to Barmouth. It's made entirely of wood (plate 102). Time and the tides gnaw ceaselessly at it, and storms assault its timbers, and the authorities fear that one day it will collapse altogether. I would willingly pay double the meagre toll in order to help it survive. It is the best of all promenades on the

Cambrian coast. The sandbanks shimmer like gold in the broad estuary, and when the ebb-tide comes, the river recedes into the distance, a silver band between the thickly wooded slopes on either side, in stark contrast to the bare hills of Cader Idris in the south. 'A sublime estuary,' said Wordsworth in 1824. And 150 years later, Günter Kunert in his 'English Diary' was of the opinion that 'to be a tree or a rock here would be a happy career'. He compares it to 'a painting from another epoch. No present, or a present that has lasted for eternities and has come to a standstill in this place.' The estuary of the Afon Mawddach is some seven and a half miles long – a drowned valley from the Ice Age, hollowed out by glaciers, and then increasingly filled in by the sea with sand and shingle. An age-old river valley whose beauty seemed to Ruskin so incomparable that he wrote one could only compare the journey from Barmouth to Dolgellau to the journey from Dolgellau to Barmouth.

At the top end of the estuary, in the shadow of Cader Idris, lies *Dolgellau*, a small town of granite and slate houses, grey, solid and imperturbably tedious. Three Roman roads once met here, for reasons that were not only strategic. There was something the Romans could see glinting in the mountain streams that flow down into the Mawddach, and it gave off a reddish shimmer from the quartz. It was gold. But then there was nothing more until 1864, when news came out of Dolgellau that more major finds had been made. By the turn of the century, there were over two dozen mines with more than 500 miners. Between 1891 and 1911 the Clogau St David's Mine produced two tons of gold, which may not sound a lot, but actually constituted over 70% of total British gold production. In the 1920's, however, the mines began to close again. Gold fever in this Welsh California was short-lived, though it did last long enough to start off a tradition: when the future King George V and Princess Mary were married in 1893, they exchanged wedding rings of Welsh gold. And it was also from St David's mine that the gold came for the wedding rings of the Queen Mother, Elizabeth II, and Prince Charles and Lady Diana. It seemed almost a matter of course that when Prince Andrew and Sarah Ferguson got married in 1986, Garrard's the court jewellers once more turned to Welsh gold for the rings. Since it is so rare and so exclusive, gold stamped with the Red Dragon has a particularly high market value. This much sought after metal lies in the sedimentary rock of the Harlech Dome, not in compact veins, as in South Africa for instance, but scattered piecemeal in veins of quartz that might be anywhere in the rock. In order to extract one ounce of gold in Wales, you have to shift thousands of tons of rock. A geological survey suggested that the Clogau Mine might be viable, and so a mining company began making probes in 1984, but otherwise, when the big firms are not interested, it is individuals who come to try their luck, deep in the forests of Coed-y-Brenin, the royal forest in the upper reaches of the Mawddach. 'Some people spend their weekends panning here, prospecting down in the river,' said a miner from Gwynfynydd – once one of the richest of all the mines. 'One day I'll be lucky!' he smiles, echoing the dreams of centuries. But for the moment, rearing sheep in the gold belt of Dolgellau is considerably more lucrative than sifting rock.

'*Cader Idris* is the stoniest, dreariest, most desolate mountain I was ever on,' wrote Francis Kilvert in his diary on June 13 1871. The parson from Clyro had obtained the services of a guide in order to make the ascent from Dolgellau. Old Pugh knew the way, and also knew the right stories. For instance, there was the foolish rambler who was not found until months had gone by: 'It was a skeleton in clothes. The foxes and ravens had eaten him.' This put the parson in exactly the right frame of mind when 'the mists crawled down and wrapped us as if in a shroud blotting out everything. The mists and clouds began to sweep by us in white thin ghostly sheets as if some great dread Presences and Powers were going past and we could only see the skirts of their white garments.' It all reminded the Reverend Kilvert of Moses on Sinai. When, despite the mist and rain, he reached the summit, his guide compensated him for the missing panorama by presenting him with a hard-boiled egg and another story. For three whole months in the summer, the leader of a surveying team camped at the top of Cader Idris. 'And how many clear views do you think he got in that time? "Twelve", I hazarded. "Nine", he said.'

The intrepid parson made the descent along Fox's Path, the shortest route to Dolgellau, having climbed up the Pony Track, which is still the easiest. The most interesting way up the 3,000 feet to the top, however, is said to be that of the road near Minffordd via *Llyn-y-Cau*. This volcanic lake down below the summit of the mountain is the subject of Richard Wilson's famous painting now in the Tate Gallery. He was probably not the first artist to climb Cader Idris, but he was the first to paint it, around 1765 (see page 339). Llyn-y-Cau is the eerie eye of a mysterious mountain. The Welsh regard it as the seat of poetry. Anyone who spends a night on the peak will, it is said, wake up blind the next day, or mad – or a poet. Cader Idris is generally translated as the Throne of Idris, who was a legendary giant, or bard or warrior. There is also an historical figure who may possibly have been the eponymous hero. Idris, Prince of Merioneth during the 7th century. The idea that I like best, though, is that Gwyn an Nadd, Lord of the Celtic underworld, has his home at the top of the mountain. With his dogs he encircles the souls of the recent dead, and then leads them into the world of shades on Cader Idris.

From Bala to Patagonia: Drowned Villages and an Imaginary Country

When the glaciers of Cader Idris melted, they created on its southern side one of the most beautiful mountain lakes in Snowdonia: *Tal-y-Llyn*. On the shore stands a little old church, a few houses, and a lot of glorious seclusion. The lake lies at the end of a valley that stretches as straight as an arrow for ten miles to the coast. On their way to the sea, the glaciers followed a geological trench called the *Bala Fault*, which seems almost to have been sliced with a giant's knife in a north-easterly direction as far as *Bala Lake*. People have often talked and sung of the magic of Welsh lakes, but as we have already seen (page 419) there are other watery places in Wales that were not made by Nature:

> There are places in Wales I don't go:
> Reservoirs that are the subconscious
> Of a people, troubled far down
> With gravestones, chapels, villages even ...

The bitterness of R. S. Thomas's poem was something that I only understood fully when I talked to Gareth, the student at Coleg Harlech whom we have already met, and whose father farms on the hills northwest of Bala (see page 433). 'I only became politically aware when a neighbouring village was cleared and flooded, against the will of its inhabitants, to make way for a new reservoir in this valley.' *Llyn Celyn* is the name of this dam on the edge of the moor in the Arenig Mountains. It became notorious in the 1960's under the name of *Tryweryn Valley:* 'Cofia Tryweryn' – Think of Tryweryn – was the message on many a Welsh wall, when despite nationwide protests the village of Capel Celyn had to be drowned in order for the people of Liverpool to get their drinking water. Dam Wales for England – it's an old running sore for the Welsh. Many were built back in the 19th century, when the industrial towns in the Midlands grew so rapidly, with a concomitant need for more water. It was then that the largest artificial lake in Wales came into being: *Lake Vyrnwy* (1881–90). This reservoir, five miles long, on the eastern slopes of the Berwyns also supplies Liverpool with water, some 350 million gallons of it a day (plate 69). Picturesquely built into the lake is the tower of the water purification plant, reminiscent of Château Chillon on Lake Geneva, and the dense pine forests all around could almost be the Black Forest. These artificial lakes have long since been accepted by the majority as if they were part of Nature; they are tourist attractions and leisure centres. But 'The serenity of their expression / Revolts me, it is a pose / For strangers,' wrote R. S. Thomas. Reservoirs only became an emotive issue again when a large group of Welsh people in the 1960's realized that their linguistic island was being swamped by the English tide, just as their villages had disappeared beneath the man-made lakes.

'The place will drown. We are not the masters of our own house. We are only the poor pricks with a begging bowl,' says a Welsh farmer in Richard Llewellyn's 'Green, Green My Valley Now' (1975). 'Remember Tryweryn' did not mean think of that one village, but think of the whole tragic history, of Cilmeri, the death of Llywelyn, Owain Glyndwr, the diktat of Rhuddlan. 'The Land Remembers' is the title of a book by the Welsh historian Gwyn Williams. 'Remember' is a key word for the concept of Welshness – a signal to roll the centuries back and show the present in the past, and the past in the present. 'Cofia Tryweryin' means don't let them take your language away, because it's your memory, your history, your home. We are the Welsh tap in the English kitchen. The accumulated resentment of the years was sparked off again by a new cause at the beginning of the 1980's. The English were paying lower rates than the Welsh for the water they were taking (or 'stealing', said the nationalists) from Wales. *'Cymru piau 'r dwr'* was a slogan daubed on the wall of the dam in Lake Vyrnwy – 'The water belongs to Wales'. For this cause thousands of Welsh people refused to pay their water rates, a campaign of civil disobedience similar to their refusal to pay their TV licence fee, when they were fighting for a Welsh-speaking channel of their own.

A narrow road leads from Lake Vyrnwy through the lonely forests of Cwm Hirnant to *Llyn Tegid*, or *Bala Lake*, to give it its English name. This is the largest natural lake in Wales, and it has everything: trout, perch, legends, sailing boats, and a narrow gauge railway. All around there are mountains modest enough in height to welcome hikers – the Berwyns to the east, and the twin peaks of the Arans to the south. Bala lies at the northern end of the lake. In the 18th century, this little town produced such useful items as woollen socks, Bibles, and Sunday School. King George III, tormented by rheumatism, used to keep himself warm with socks made in Bala. George Borrow drank the best ale of his whole trip here ('nearly as strong as brandy'), and enjoyed the delights of a Welsh breakfast: 'A noble breakfast it was; such indeed as I might have read of, but had never before seen. There was tea and coffee, a goodly white loaf and butter; there were a couple of eggs and two mutton chops. There was broiled and pickled salmon – there was fried trout – there were also potted trout and potted shrimps. Mercy upon me!' This was in the White Lion in the High Street, and alas is another piece of history long gone.

Bala's main street is lined with trees, and at every corner you will find the shadow of a Methodist. From the Berwyn Bakery to Barclay's Bank there are plaques and statues

E. C. Mountford: Michael D. Jones, c.1865

commemorating the great days of the Non-conformists. Howell Harris preached here, and at the beginning of the century a congregation of some 20,000 believers assembled on the green at the northern end of the town, where the tourist buses park today and a Gorsedd has left behind its circle of stones.

In 1800 a sixteen-year-old girl came barefoot across the mountains to Bala. She was the daughter of a weaver from Llanfihangel-y-Pennant, near Cader Idris, and her name was Mary Jones. She had walked twenty-five miles, carrying all her savings in order to buy a Bible in Bala, because at home they had none. The Reverend Thomas Charles gave her his last copy. Deeply moved by the girl's commitment, he founded the British and Foreign Bible Society. The object of such societies is to ensure that every home in the world possesses a copy of the Bible in the local language. I had often wondered how the Word of God found its way into hotel bedrooms. Now I know that it's all because of Mary Jones's legendary walk to Bala. But the Reverend Thomas Charles's activities were not confined to spreading the gospel solely by way of distributing Bibles; he also contributed to the education of the Welsh by starting up Sunday schools. In those days, this was a sort of elementary school for the children of poor people, but in Wales – unlike England – adults were also instructed, regardless of age, class or level of literacy. The classes were small and always in Welsh. And so Charles of Bala fulfilled the educational needs of farmers and shepherds in even the remotest of regions.

In the middle of the 19th century, a preacher arrived in Bala who wanted more than the awakening of souls. The Reverend Michael D. Jones, author of a Welsh grammar and director of the College of Independents, was one of the driving-forces behind a new nationalist movement. In contrast to some other European countries in the 19th century, this did not lead Wales to the establishment of an independent state, but it did go as far as to bring about a kind of model Welsh state in a distant land. This was a colony in Argentina: Welsh Patagonia. It was Michael D. Jones who founded it. A radical Non-Conformist, he criticized his compatriots for their loss of self-confidence, 'because the Welsh are a conquered people in their own country.' He argued for a strong national party, and a Celtic alliance between the Irish, Scots and Welsh. He was realistic enough to know that Queen Victoria would never permit a free and independent Wales, but he was dreamer enough to conceive of a new Wales elsewhere. There the farmers would own the land themselves, and the workers would run the factories – 'New Harmony', Welsh fashion. In May 1865, forty years after the failure of Robert Owen's Utopia in America, 153 emigrants sailed away from Liverpool in the 'Mimosa', in order to build their Welsh Utopia in Argentina.

Poverty, hunger, disease, and attacks by Indians and bandits took heavy toll of these pioneers in Welsh Patagonia. But ten years after their arrival, the flag of the Red Dragon was still flying over the River Chubut. Wheat was growing in the fields, and sheep were grazing in the meadows. Part of the pampas had indeed become Welsh. They called themselves 'Y Wladfa', The Colony. They had devised their own constitution according to democratic, socialist principles, firmly rooted in Non-Conformism, with universal franchise from 18 onwards, including women – something the British did not adopt until many years later. Laws, text books, official and everyday language – everything was Welsh, and Welsh only. It seemed as if a dream had come true. Only the Argentine government was less than delighted to have this tiny, autonomous state within a state, especially as it was slowly expanding and visibly prospering. But what proved far more effective than any official restriction was the process of natural integration, as gradually local people and immigrants mixed together. All told, only 3,000 Welsh people migrated to the Patagonian plateau in the 19th century, and there were no more after 1912. Today the common language is Spanish. And yet of some 25,000 descendants from these first settlers, there are still several hundred that speak Welsh – enough for them to have their own literary magazine, Welsh chapel services, and a yearly (bilingual) Eisteddfod in October. On the promenade in Puerto Madryn there is a monument to the first migrants with their Bibles. Welsh Patagonia was a romantic offshoot from the golden days of Welsh nationalism in the 19th century. What has remained of this Utopia in the minds of Welsh people today? Very few would share Gwynfor Evans's unquenchable optimism that such a model could be successful even in the Motherland: 'The results there were indicative of what the Welsh could have done had their own country been free.'

I came across Patagonia twice in Wales. Once was at the Maes Manor Hotel in the Valleys, where the menu boasted an adventurous hors d'oeuvre: cauliflower with shrimps in a white wine and garlic sauce. This was Cauliflower Patagonian style, or, in other words, *Corgimwch dull Patagonia*. The name stumbled from my tongue, and the food settled firmly in my stomach. But Corgimwch dull Patagonia was a brave, even romantic, effort. It put me in mind of my other Patagonian encounter: Ffransis Green, at the National Eisteddfod in Anglesey. At that great reunion of exiled Welsh people from all over the world, the old man stepped onto the platform to introduce himself. He was 70, he said, he came from Patagonia, and he was a radio ham. Was this eccentric figure Wales at its most exotic or its most homely? Was Ffransis Green living in the past or the future? It must have taken him most of his seventy years to find a Welsh speaker on his Argentinian wave-length. But a Welshman is always a Cymry, after all, a compatriot, wherever he may be, and those decades of radio exploration were simply another Cymric quest.

Chronology

AD 43 Roman invasion of Britain; only the Celts resist

61 Romans massacre druids on Anglesey

78–84 Subjugation of Wales

383 Romans leave Wales (Magnus Maximus)

432 St Patrick, from Wales (?), brings Christianity to Ireland

after 450 The Anglo-Saxons drive British Celts into Wales, where they mix with the native Cymry

c.518 Battle of Mons Badonicus: British Celts defeat Anglo-Saxons – historical background to Arthurian legend

c.550 Taliesin and Aneirin: earliest Welsh poetry

6th cent. Century of Saints: conversion of Wales

c.588 Death of St David (March 1)

c.613 Ethelfrith of Northumbria defeats Britons at Chester ('the Massacre of the Saints')

768 Welsh-Celtic church accepts authority of Rome (recognizes Easter date)

784 Offa's Dyke: King Offa of Mercia's defence against the Welsh

844–878 Welsh Prince Rhodri Mawr unites Gwynedd, Powys and parts of South Wales; beginning of dominance by Principality of Gwynedd

916–950 Rhodri's grandson Hywel Dda introduces legal code

1067 Beginning of Norman subjugation of Wales; William the Conqueror places Lords Marcher in Hereford, Shrewsbury and Chester

1131 Tintern Abbey founded: First Cistercian monastery in Wales

1136 'Historia Regum Britanniae' by Geoffrey of Monmouth

1176 First documented Eisteddfod in Cardigan

c.1200 Giraldus Cambrensis fights for Welsh Arbishopric independent of Canterbury

1194–1240 Llywelyn I (the Great) rules Wales

1267 Treaty of Montgomery: Llywelyn II (the last) is recognized by Henry III as Prince of Wales

1276–77 First War of Welsh Independence; beginning of Edward I's chain of Norman castles

1282 Second War of Welsh Independence; death of Llywelyn the Last

1284 Statutes of Rhuddlan: Edward I imposes English system of administration on Wales

c.1301 Edward (II) is first English heir to the throne to be given title 'Prince of Wales'

1400–12 Third War of Welsh Independence: Owain Glyndwr's uprising

1404 First Welsh parliament in Machynlleth; French allies land in Milford Haven; Owain Glyndwr has himself crowned King	**1794** 'Essays on the Picturesque' by Uvedale Price
c.1416 Death of Owain Glyndwr	**1797** French troops land in Fishguard: last time Britain invaded
1455–85 Wars of the Roses: war of succession between houses of York (white rose) and Lancaster (red rose), turning into civil war	**1804** Penydarren railroad: Richard Trevithick's steam engine
	1826 Telford's Menai Suspension Bridge
1485 Battle of Bosworth Field: Henry Tudor, Lancastrian pretender to throne, defeats Richard III and becomes King; Welsh Henry VII begins Tudor dynasty in England	**1831** Merthyr Riots: workers' uprising in Merthyr Tydfil
	1839 Bloody suppression of Chartists' demonstration in Newport
1536 Act of Union: Henry VIII finally binds Wales to England; dissolution of the monasteries	**1839–43** Rebecca Riots: impoverished Welsh farmers protest against customs tariffs and other social injustices
1588 'Y Beibl Cymraeg' – Bishop Morgan translates Bible into Welsh	**1858** First National Eisteddfod (in Llangollen)
1639 First Independent chapel in Wales (Llanfaches)	**1865** Welsh colony in Patagonia
1642 Beginning of English Civil War; Wales predominantly royalist	**1881** Sunday Closing Act: no alcohol allowed in Welsh pubs on Sundays
1649 First Baptist chapel in Wales (Ilston)	**1886** Cymru Fydd founded in London: Welsh Liberal Party aiming at Home Rule, supported by Lloyd George
1689 Toleration Act: for Dissenters, i.e. non-Anglican High Church (excluding Catholics and Unitarians)	**1893** University of Wales founded
1731 Griffith Jones starts peripatetic schools	**1898** South Wales Miners' Federation founded: radical Welsh miners' union
1743 Foundation of Welsh Calvinistic Methodist Church; Welsh Methodism reaches peak under Howell Harris	**1900** James Keir Hardie becomes first Labour MP (for Merthyr Tydfil)
1751 Foundation of Cymmrodorion Society in London: renaissance of Welsh language and culture	**1907** Welsh National Library founded in Aberystwyth, and National Museum in Cardiff
1759 Foundation of Dowlais Ironworks	**1920** Wales becomes independent Archbishopric
1785 Thomas Charles introduces Sunday School to Wales	**1925** Foundation of National Party, Plaid Cymru
	1929–34 Depression: mass unemployment, especially in Valleys

1936 Saunders Lewis and others make arson attack on RAF Bomber School in Penyberth/Lyn

1951 Foundation of Welsh Office

1955 Cardiff becomes capital of Wales

1963 Foundation of Welsh Language Society; beginning of campaign for Welsh to have equal status in all areas of public life

1969 Investiture of Crown Prince Charles as Prince of Wales in Caernarfon Castle

1979 Referendum for devolution: 80% of Welsh electorate vote against parliament of their own

1982 S4C: First purely Welsh-speaking TV channel

Bibliography

Ackerman, John: *Welsh Dylan*, Cardiff 1979

Borrow, George: *Wild Wales. Its people, language and scenery*, Glasgow 1980 (1862)

Bromley, Rosemary D. F. and Graham Humphreys: *Dealing with Dereliction. The Redevelopment of the Lower Swansea Valley*, Swansea 1979

Davies, D. Hywel: *The Welsh Nationalist Party 1925–1945: A Call to Nationhood*, Cardiff 1984

Davies, John and Mike Jenkins (eds.): *The Valleys*, Cardiff 1985

Davies, William Henry: *The Autobiography of a Super-Tramp*, London 1950 (1908)

Ellis, Alice Thomas: *Wales, an Anthology*, London 1990

Evans, Gwynfor: *Land of My Fathers. 2000 Years of Welsh History*, Swansea 1974 (1971)

Firbank, Thomas: *I Bought A Mountain*, London 1981 (1940)

Fishlock, Trevor: *Talking of Wales. A Companion to Wales and the Welsh*, London 1976

Fitzgibbon, Constantine: *The Life of Dylan Thomas*, London 1965

Garlick, Raymond and Roland Mathias (eds.): *Anglo-Welsh Poetry 1480–1980*, Ogmore-by-Sea 1983

Gerald of Wales: *The Journey through Wales and The Description of Wales*, Harmondsworth 1978

Gill, Eric: *Autobiography*, London 1940

Haslam, Richard: *The Building of Wales: Powys*, Harmondsworth 1979

Hilling, John B.: *Cardiff and the Valleys*, London 1973

The Historic Architecture of Wales, Cardiff 1976

Wales: South and West, London 1976

Hopkins, K. S. (ed.): *Rhondda Past and Future*, Rhondda 1980

Humphreys, Emyr: *The Taliesin Tradition. A Quest for the Welsh Identity*, London 1983

Jones, Anthony: *Welsh Chapels*, Cardiff 1984

Jones, David J. V.: *The Last Rising: The Newport Insurrection of 1839*, Oxford 1985

Jones, Gwyn (ed.): *The Oxford Book of Welsh Verse in English*, Oxford 1977

Kilvert's Diary 1870–1879, Harmondsworth 1977

Kohr, Leopold: *Is Wales Viable?* 1971

Lavender, Stephen J.: *New Land for Old. The Environmental Renaissance of the Lower Swansea Valley*, Bristol 1981

Llewellyn, Richard: *How Green Was My Valley?* London 1939

Green, Green My Valley Now, London 1975

Lloyd, D. M. and E. M. (eds.): *A Book of Wales*, London 1953

Lovins, Amory and Philip Evans: *Eryri, the Mountain of Longing*, New York 1971

Mabinogion, The, translated by Gwyn and Thomas Jones, London 1978

Mavor, Elizabeth: *The Ladies of Llangollen*, Harmondsworth 1971

Merchant, W. Moelwyn: *R. S. Thomas*, 1979

Millward, Roy and Adrian Robinson: *Landscapes of North Wales*, Newton Abbot 1978

Morris, Jan: *The Matter of Wales. Epic Views of a Small Country*, Oxford 1984

Morton, H. V.: *In Search of Wales*, London 1932

Osmond, John (ed.): *The National Question Again*, Llandysul 1985

Powys, John Cowper: *Obstinate Cymric, Essays 1935–47*, London 1973 (1947)

Rees, D. Morgan: *Industrial Archaeology of Wales*, Newton Abbot 1975

Rossiter, Stuart (ed.): *The Blue Guide to Wales*, London 1969

Rowan, Eric (ed.): *Art in Wales 2000 BC – 1850 AD*, Cardiff 1978
Some Miraculous Promised Land, Mostyn Art Gallery, Llandudno 1982

Shanes, Eric: *Turner's Picturesque Views in England and Wales*, London 1980

Solkin, David H.: *Richard Wilson. The Landscape of Reaction*, London 1982

Stephens, Meic: *The Bright Field*, London 1991

Styles, Showell: *Welsh Walks and Legends*, London 1979

Stephens, Meic (ed.): *The Arts in Wales 1950–75*, Cardiff 1979

Thomas, Dylan: *Collected Poems*, London 1952
Under Milk Wood, London 1977 (1954)

Thomas, R.S.: *What is a Welshman?* Swansea 1974
Selected Poems 1946–68, London 1973
Later Poems, London 1983
Selected Prose, Glamorgan 1984

Thomas, Ned: *The Welsh Extremist*, London 1971

Tolstoy, Nikolai: *The Quest for Merlin*, Hamish Hamilton 1985

Vaughan-Thomas, Wynford: *Wales*, London 1981

Wakefield, Paul and Jan Morris: *Wales. The First Place*, London 1982

Waterson, Merlin: *The Servants' Hall. A 'Downstairs' History of a British Country House*, New York 1980

Webb, Harri: *The Green Desert*, Llandysul 1969

Williams, Gwyn: *The Land Remembers*, London 1977
The Welsh in Their History, London 1982
When Was Wales? Black Raven Press 1985

Williams-Ellis, Clough: *Architect Errant*, Portmeirion 1980

Wilton, Andrew: *Turner in Wales*, Mostyn Art Gallery, Llandudno 1984

Some Practical Hints

The scenery is often misty,
Incessant rain blots out the view,
The roads are narrow, dark and twisty,
And so, some say, are the natives too.

Harri Webb: The Absolute End, 1977

Wales

General Wales covers an area of 8,016 square miles (20,720 square km) and has a population of 2.8 million (5% of the total British population). In the year of the first census, 1801, there were 586,000 people. About two-thirds of the population live in the industrial south east. Wales is divided into eight counties: Gwent; De Morgannwg / South Glamorgan; Canol Morgannwg / Mid Glamorgan; Gorllewin Morgannwg / West Glamorgan; Dyfed; Powys; Clwyd; Gwynedd. The capital since 1955 is Cardiff (Caerdydd). Wales has 38 MP's at Westminster.

Accommodation Everything available from cheap B & B to luxury rooms in castles. I recommend farmhouse accommodation. A useful address is: Wales Farm Holidays, Owain Glyndwr Centre, Machynlleth, Powys SY20 8EE, Ø 0654 703453. Self-catering is also popular: holiday flats range from those in the Victorian manor of Plas Rhianfa on the Menai Strait to dairy huts on the River Conwy in Snowdonia National Park (Glan y Borth Holiday Village, Llanrwst, Gwynedd, Ø 0492 641543). There are interesting rooms in restored historic buildings, cottages, converted barns, etc. (see National Trust, and also Landmark Trust, Shottesbrooke, Maidenhead, Berkshire, Ø 062882 5925). For camping sites and many other addresses, see 'Wales: Where to Stay' (Wales Tourist Board).

Pub sign, Crickhowell

Angling With its rivers, lakes and coastline, Wales is a must for anglers. The best rivers for salmon are the Wye, Severn, Teifi, Dee and Mawddach. For sea-trout (also called sewin), try especially the Dyfi and the Dysynni, and the Rheidol and the Ystwyth. Trout season: March to end September. Best time for salmon: July to October. There are plenty of opportunities for deep-sea fishing.

Arts and Crafts Nowhere in Britain will you find so many craft workers per square mile as in Wales: weavers, potters, wood-carvers, furniture-makers, bookbinders, gold and silversmiths, harp-makers, toy-makers etc. Their interests are represented by the Wales Craft Council (founded 1977), 20 Severn Street, Welshpool, Powys, ⌀ 0938 555313. The Craft Council publishes a useful guide, 'Visit the Crafts in Wales'. Arts and crafts centres: Maes Artro, Craft Village, Llanbedr south of Harlech (daily 10–5.30), and Corris Craft Centre. There are many potters in Wales, some of whom have works in international museums and collections: Walter Keeler, Moorcroft Cottage, Penallt, Gwent, ⌀ 0600 713946; Geoffrey Swindell, 35 Murch Road, Dinas Powis, Cardiff, ⌀ 0222 512746; John Davies, Gwynedd Pottery, Glyddyn Mawr, Y Ffor, Pwllheli, ⌀ 0758 612932; David Frith, Brookhouse Pottery, The Malt House, Denbigh, Clwyd, ⌀ 0745 812805 (pottery courses in summer). The Welsh Arts Council and some museums mount exhibitions of Welsh Studio Pottery, and so does Trefor Glyn Owen in a restored 19th-century farmhouse in the Vale of Ffestiniog: Crochendy Twrog, Maentwrog, Gwynedd, ⌀ 076685 302, daily 10–7. For hundreds of years the most important rural industry has been wool, from the early cottage industries through to the textile factories of the 19th century. You can learn about the history of the Welsh weavers in the Museum of the Woollen Industry in Dre-fach Felindre (see page 467). Courses in weaving are held by Martin and Nina Weatherhead on their farm: Snail Trail Handweavers, Penwenallt Farm, Cilgerran, Dyfed, ⌀ 023974 228. Alan Hemmings has his studio in the old restored church at Cilymaenclwyd: Studio in the Church, near Login, Whitland, Dyfed, ⌀ 0437 563676. Also outstanding are Curlew Weavers, Troedyraur, Rhydlewis, Llandysul, Dyfed, ⌀ 023975 357. Very few of the little 19th-century woollen mills are still in operation. Two that are, and also have a museum and shop: Maesllyn Woollen Mill (see page 468) and Wallis Woollen Mill (see page 470).

Bookshops Oriel, The Friary, Cardiff, ⌀ 0222 395548, is a bookshop and art shop run by the Welsh Arts Council, specializing in Anglo-Welsh literature and books about Wales and the Celts. Llen Llyn, Y Maes, Pwllheli, Gwynedd, ⌀ 0758 612907: books and magazines almost exclusively in Welsh, owned by the writer Alun Jones. Hay-on-Wye: Secondhand Book Paradise, see page 199.

Canals These are part of Wales's rich industrial heritage. The six most important, all built at the peak of the canal boom, around 1790: Swansea, Neath, Glamorganshire, Monmouthshire, Brecon & Abergavenny, and Llangollen. Since the 1960's, many miles have been restored by volunteers as 'Cruising Waterways' (with aid from the National Waterways Restoration and Development Fund). Holiday boats on the Llangollen Canal can be hired from: Anglo-Welsh Waterway Holidays, The Canal Basin, Leicester Road, Market Harborough, Leicestershire, ⌀ 0858 466910; Holidays Afloat Ltd, Talbot Wharf, Market Drayton, Shropshire, ⌀ 0630 2641. On the Monmouthshire Canal: Castle Narrowboats, Church Road Wharf, Gilwern, Gwent, ⌀ 0873 830001. On the Brecon & Abergavenney Canal: Red Line Boats, Goytre Wharf, Llanover, Abergavenny, Gwent, ⌀ 0873 880516.

Choirs If three Welshmen meet, they form a choir. Despite the rapid decline in chapel-going, the popularity of Welsh Male Voice Choirs remains undiminished, and there are still more than 300 of them (see page 16). Visitors are generally welcome to attend rehearsals. The famous Cwmbach Male Voice Choir rehearses Monday and Friday at 7.30 p.m. in the Junior School gymnasium in Aberdare. The best choirs take part in the yearly International Music Eisteddfod in Llangollen. Addresses and information: Welsh Amateur Music Federation, 9 Museum Place, Cardiff, ⌀ 0222 394711.

Pub sign near Ystrad Mynach in the Valleys

Countryside Commission State institution founded in 1968 'for the well-being of countryside, landscape and amenity, and for helping people to understand and enjoy it'. Responsible for planning and consultation for Country Parks and Areas of Outstanding Natural Beauty (over 40 in England and Wales) and long-distance footpaths. The central office is in Cheltenham, and the Welsh office is at 8 Broad Street, Newtown, Powys, ⌀ 0686 626799. Responsible for nature conservation in Great Britain is the Nature Conservancy Council in London, but the Welsh office is at Plas Penrhos, Ffordd Penrhos, Bangor, Gwynedd, ⌀ 0298 370444.

Disabled Generally well catered for. Useful information and addresses supplied by: Holiday Care Service, 2 Old Bank Chambers, Station Road, Horley, Surrey RH6 9HW.

Eating Is there such a thing as Welsh cuisine? 'Not even our *own* food? What are we? A kitchen forgotten? That's the history of a people

forgotten, isn't it? What you eat makes you what you are.' Richard Llewellyn's hero Huw Morgan ('Green, Green My Valley Now', 1975) might have to revise his judgment today. Welsh cooking was always simple, if only because of Welsh poverty, but local produce has its own charms. 'Let anyone who wishes to eat leg of mutton in perfection go to Wales,' enthused George Borrow. Lamb is still a Welsh speciality, its incomparable aroma due to the thyme-rich grasslands. Salmon, trout and other fish dishes are also high on the list. Cawl is the national soup, with plenty of bacon or mutton, leek and other vegetables, like Scottish cockie-leekie. Other typical dishes are Bara brith (juicy currant bread), Welsh Rarebit (cheese on toast, originally Caerphilly and ale), and Bara lawr or laverbread (made from seaweed, often mixed with fine oatmeal, rich in minerals, and a particular speciality in Swansea and Gower). Bobby Freeman has written a history of Welsh cooking: 'First Catch Your Peacock', London 1981. The Wales Tourist Board issues a yearly brochure 'A Taste of Wales', with a selection of pubs and hotels that offer good local dishes. An address for fans of genuine (and rare) farmhouse cheese: Leon and Joan Downey, Llangloffan Farm, Ty Uchaf, Castle Morris, near Haverfordwest.

Great Little Trains   Nowhere else in the world will you find so many narrow-gauge railways in such a confined area as North Wales. Originally used for the slate industry, they have long since become a tourist attraction, offering nostalgic trips back into the steam age. The slate magnate Richard Pennant (see page 377) built the first narrow-gauge horsedrawn railway in 1801 from Bethesda to Port Penrhyn (closed 1962). The Ffestiniog Railway was the first to carry passengers (1865). The decline of the slate industry after World War I meant a similar decline for the railways, some of which closed down, while others turned to carrying passengers. After World War II, Preservation Societies succeeded in restoring and reopening many lines for tourists, and today there are still ten in operation:

Bala Lake Railway: Llanuwchllyn–Bala, 5 miles. Newly laid in 1972, partially replacing the BR Barmouth–Ruabon line which had closed in 1965. First railway line to be officially registered in Welsh: Rheilffordd Llyn Tegid.

Brecon Mountain Railway: Pant–Pontsticill, 2 miles.

Fairbourne Railway: Fairbourne–Barmouth Ferry, 2 miles. Laid to transport building materials for the Mawddach railway bridge of 1867; horsedrawn till 1916; the narrowest gauge in Wales, at 12¼ inches.

Ffestiniog Railway: Porthmadog–Blaenau-Ffestiniog, 13 miles. Most successful, longest and most beautiful of them all. Opened in 1836,

closed in 1946, reopened in 1955. Has most passengers (over 300,000 a year) and oldest narrow gauge steam engine in the world – 'Prince', built in 1863.

Llanberis Lake Railway: Llanberis Padarn Park–Penllyn, 2 miles. Reopened in 1971, to replace horse-drawn railway of slate tycoon Robert Assheton-Smith (1824), which ran from Dinorwic Quarries to Port Dinorwic, and closed in 1961.

Snowdon Mountain Railway: Llanberis–Snowdon summit, 4 miles. Opened in 1896 for tourists, only rack and pinion railway in Great Britain, engines built in Winterthur, Switzerland. Only railway in Great Britain with continental gauge of 800 mm (i.e. 2'8½" compared to usual 1'11½").

Talyllyn Railway: Tywyn–Nant Gwernol, 8 miles. Only railway in unbroken service since 1866. From very beginning transported both slate and people. Talyllyn Railway Preservation Society, formed in early 1950's, set the pattern for similar initiatives elsewhere. Now has over 3,000 members. Terminus Tywyn has Narrow Gauge Railway Museum – biggest in Great Britain.

Vale of Rheidol Railway: Aberystwyth–Devil's Bridge, 11 miles. Opened 1902, mainly to transport lead from vales of Rheidol and Ystwyth. Taken over by BR in 1948, its only narrow gauge line, and only one for which it still uses steam engines.

Welsh Highland Light Railway: Porthmadog–Pen-y-Mount, ⅔ mile. Opened 1923, originally from Dinas Junction through Beddgelert and

Aberglaslyn Pass; closed 1937, first stretch reopened 1980. Eight miles planned.

Welshpool and Llanfair Light Railway: Llanfair Caereinion–Welshpool, 8 miles. Opened 1903, closed 1956, reopened 1963. 'The farmers' line' used to carry mainly cattle, feed, turnips and potatoes.

All these lines have to be inspected by the Department of the Environment. The rail network and plant are mostly maintained by steam freaks, with loving care. The season for these little railways lasts approximately from Easter till the end of September. You can get cheap 'Joint Tourist' tickets. Timetables and information from: Narrow Gauge Railways of Wales, Wharf Station, Tywyn, Gwynedd, ∅ 0654 710472.

Hobby Holidays From restoring narrow gauge railways to survival training in Snowdonia's 'School of Adventure', or goat-keeping holidays. Advice and addresses from the Wales Tourist Board. For study of flora and fauna, geology and ecology, see section under National Parks, and also Field Studies Council, both of whose study centres are excellent, e.g. the Snowdonia National Park Study Centre in a Victorian country house: Plas Tan-y-Bwlch, Maentwrog, Blaenau Ffestiniog, Gwynedd, ∅ 076685 324, and the Danywenallt Study Centre in an old farmhouse in Brecon Beacons National Park: Talybont-on-Usk, Brecon, Powys, ∅ 087487 677; also Dale Fort Field Centre in a Victorian harbour fortress: Dale, Haverfordwest, Dyfed, ∅ 0646 636205. For other holiday activities, see sections on Angling, Arts and Crafts, Industrial Archaeology, Painting, Riding, Sport, and Walking.

Industrial Archaeology Welsh collieries, and iron and copper works made a major contribution to the Industrial Revolution in Great Britain, and the remains of this dark heritage are documented in industrial museums and on 'Industrial Trails' in the South Wales coal valleys, the slate quarries of Snowdonia, and the wool mills of the Teifi Valley. Further information and tours from the Torfaen Museums Service in Pontypool, ∅ 0995 752036. Standard work by D. Morgan Rees: *Industrial Archaeology of Wales* (Newton Abbot, 1975).

Information Wales Tourist Board, Brunel House, 2 Fitzalan Road, Cardiff CF2 1UY, ∅ 0222 499909. North Wales Regional Office, 77 Conway Road, Colwyn Bay, Clwyd, ∅ 0192 531731. Mid Wales Tourism Council, Owain Glyndwr Centre, Machynlleth, Powys, ∅ 0654 26563. South Wales Tourism Council, Pembroke House, Charter Court, Phoenix Way, Enterprise Park, Swansea, Dyfed, ∅ 0792 781212. Cardiff Tourist Information Centre, 8–14 Bridge Street, Cardiff, ∅ 0222 227281.

Language Welsh is an ancient, Celtic branch of Indo-Germanic (see page 43). The Welsh alphabet has 28 letters, but omits the consonants j, k, q, v, x and z. The emphasis generally lies on the penultimate syllable. It is a phonetic language, written as it is spoken. Some confusion is caused by the mutation of initial consonants, which depends on the preceding letter. The alphabet:

a – short or long
b
c – like English k
ch – guttural, like Scottish 'lo<u>ch</u>'

d

dd – th, as in then

e – short or long

f – like English v

ff – like English f

g – as in goat

ng – as in hang

h

i – long e sound

l

ll – a mixture of hl and Scottish ch.

m

n

o – short or long

p

ph – English f

r – rolled, like Scottish r

rh – aspirate and made at back of throat

s – voiceless as in mass

t

th – voiceless as in think

u – in South Wales long, as in tree, in North
    Wales short, as in nip

w – short u as in bull, long u as in root, or
    English w

y – e, as in knee, o as in not, or u as in funny

Some useful words and phrases:

agored – open

ar gau – closed

ar werth – for sale

ar osod – for rent or hire

bore da – good morning

nos da – good evening, goodnight

cyfleusterau – toilets

merched – ladies

dynion, meibion – gentlemen

ia – yes

na – no

dim ysmygu – non-smoker

dim parcio – no parking

diolch – thank you

os gwelwch yn dda – please

sut rydach chi – how are you?

Common elements of Welsh placenames:

aber – estuary

afon – river

bach or fach – small

bedd – grave

bryn – hill

bwlch – pass

caer – fort

cefn – ridge

coch (goch) – red

coed – wood

craig – rock

cwm – valley

dinas – camp or town

dre (tre) – house or town

du – black

dyffryn – valley

eglwys – church

fawr or mawr – big

glan – shore

glas – blue

glyn – vale

gwen (gwyn) – beautiful or white

hafod – summer house

heol – path

hir – long

llan – church or holy place

llwyd – grey

llyn – lake or pool

maes – field

moel or foel – hill or bare mountain

morfa – marsh

mynydd – mountain

nant – stream

Neuadd – estate or hall

newydd – new

pant – cave

porth – portal or port

pen – summit or headland

pistyll – waterfall or spring

pont – bridge

plas – manor house or country house ('place', 'palace')

rhiw – slope or rock face

rhos – swamp or moor

ty – house

uchaf – highest

wenallt – sparsely wooded

y – the (before consonants)

yr – the (before vowels)

ynys – island

ystrad – plain or bottom of valley

ystum – river bend

Language Schools English is spoken everywhere, but renewed interest in Welsh language and culture has resulted in a wide variety of places where Welsh can be studied. Addresses of schools and families – as well as over 30 courses held outside Wales, e.g. in Llundain (London)

Lovespoon, 1856

and Rhydychen (Oxford) – are contained in the brochure 'Come and Learn Welsh', issued by the Welsh Joint Education Committee, Arlbee House, Greyfriars Road, Cardiff, ∅ 0222 561231. During the annual National Eisteddfod you can do a week-long intensive course in the Learners' Tent. On the Llyn Peninsula, a group of enthusiasts have restored an abandoned workers' settlement and made the whole village into a language school: Nant Gwrtheyrn Language Centre, Llithfaen, Pwllheli, Gwynedd, ∅ 075885 334. For information on summer courses in Welsh universities and colleges, contact The Director, National Language Unit, Brook Street, Trefforest, Pontypridd, Mid Glamorgan, ∅ 0443 404440. Further information and addresses: Welsh Language Society, 5 Maes Albert, Aberystwyth.

Lovespoons Popular Welsh souvenirs with attractive history: from 17th to 19th century these richly carved spoons were a token of love – the poor people's engagement ring. Initials were carved in the wood, or motifs like hearts, anchors, balls, chains, crosses, rings, castles, keys or keyholes, and the more ornate they were, the more passionate was the lover. The number of chain-links on a spoon indicated to the beloved the number of children desired. Lovespoons are carved from a single piece of wood (mainly sycamore, but also oak, ash or beech). You can watch these spoons being carved by Allan Hemming (Glynborthyn Woodcrafts, Crugybar, Llanwrda, Dyfed), or by Edwin Williams (121 St Teilo Street, Pontardulais, Swansea, ∅ 0792 882723). A beautiful collection of antique lovespoons is to be seen in Brecknock County Museum in Brecon.

455

Maps   A good overall view is given by the map of Wales in Bartholomew's Grand Touring Series, on a scale of 1:250,000. For hikers, I recommend the Ordnance Survey, Southampton, scale 1:25,000.

Markets   In rural Mid Wales, the cattle markets represent the best way of getting to know how Welsh farmers live, hearing the sounds and seeing the animals: Welsh Mountain Bred and Beulah Speckled sheep, or the ponies at Llanybydder horse market. Each market has its own speciality and its own atmosphere, although not all of them can trace their traditions back to 1263, like the Monday market at Welshpool. It's best to ask local people when the next market will be, but here is a small selection:

Bala – Thursday
Builth Wells – Monday
Cardigan – Saturday
Dolgellau – Friday
Lampeter – every second Tuesday
Llanidloes – every second Friday
Llanybydder – last Thursday in month
Machynlleth – every second Wednesday
Newtown – Tuesday
Rhayader – every second Wednesday
Tregaron – every second Tuesday
Welshpool – Monday

Music   Musical and operatic festivals go on right through the year (see page 463f). Wales has two orchestras, the Welsh Philharmonia and the BBC Welsh Symphony, both based in Cardiff. This is also the base of the Welsh National Opera (founded in 1946), famous for its productions of modern operas as well as the classics. On the vibrant folk, rock and pop scene there are many purely Welsh-singing groups, e.g. 'Ar Log' (To Rent), and Sobin a'r Smachaid. The Welsh love of music is particularly evident in the number of choirs (see section on Choirs). The Celtic harp, Ireland's national symbol, is also to be found in many Welsh homes. The Welsh name for it is 'Telyn', from the Irish 'Teillin' (bee hum). Ancient laws decreed that any property could be confiscated except the sword and the harp. The triple harp that used to be in common use in Europe after about 1700 is now to be found almost exclusively in Wales; a virtuoso performer is Nansi Richards Jones. In the Welsh Folk Museum in St Fagans you can see the art of the 18th- and 19th-century Welsh harpmakers. New harps are less elaborately decorated, and can cost over £2,000. A poem written with strict Welsh metres and sung with contrapuntal harp accompaniment is the *penillion:* harpist and singer follow different melodies, until they unite in harmony at the very end.

National Parks   America had the first, in 1872, and Great Britain did not start till 1951. The basis is a compromise between private ownership and public use of the land, but this is also the source of much conflict. In contrast to American national parks, those in Britain are not national but come under local authorities as they only have the status of nature reserves. They are coordinated and subsidised by the Countryside Commission (see separate section). There are eight English and three Welsh National Parks: *Snowdonia National Park*, 1951, Administration: Penrhyndeudraeth, Gwynedd, ∅ 0766 770274. Private society: Snowdonia National Park Society, Mrs Esmé Kirby, Dyffryn Mymbyr, Capel Curig, ∅ 06904 234. *Pembrokeshire Coast National Park*, 1952, Office: County

Offices, Haverfordwest, Dyfed, ∅ 0437 764591. *Brecon Beacons National Park*, 1957, Office: Glamorgan Street, Brecon, Powys, ∅ 4437. The proposal for a Cambrian Mountains National Park was rejected by the Minister for Wales. In his autobiography, Clough Williams-Ellis quotes the Queen Mother, on the establishment of Snowdonia National Park: 'It's fine your preparing this splendid countryside for the people, but are you doing anything about preparing the people to make proper use of it?' Information centres, guided tours, seminars and publications do their best. See R. Bush, *The National Parks of England and Wales* (Dent). A more critical view is given by Ann and Malcolm MacEwen, *National Parks: Conservation or Cosmetics?* (Allen & Unwin).

National Trust The National Trust was founded in 1895, and its first acquisition was Dinas Oleu Cliff, in Cardigan Bay. Unlike Scotland, Wales has no National Trust of its own, but two regional branches of the English National Trust: North Wales Regional Office, Trinity Square, Llandudno, Gwynedd, ∅ 0492 860123; South Wales Regional Office, King's Head, Llandeilo, Dyfed, ∅ 05582 822800. The aim of the National Trust is to preserve land and buildings of particular beauty or historical interest. Also concerned with the preservation of historic houses and old towns is Cadw (Welsh Historic Monuments) formerly the Historic Buildings Council for Wales, founded in 1953: Brunel House, 2 Fitzalan Road, Cardiff, ∅ 0222 465511. It has a much smaller budget than its equivalents in Scotland and England, which is symptomatic of the traditional lack of appreciation for Welsh architecture.

Newspapers and Magazines Here just a small selection: 'Western Mail', national daily, English-speaking with Welsh columns; 'The Western Telegraph and Cymric Times', weekly, and 'Wales on Sunday' – both national. There is no purely Welsh-speaking daily, but 'Y Cymro', appears weekly. 'Y Faner', founded 1843, was a radical Welsh daily but is now weekly. A rival, 'Golwg', is subsidized by Welsh Arts Council. English-speaking literary magazines: 'Poetry Wales', founded 1964, an important forum for Anglo-Welsh literature; 'Anglo-Welsh Review', 'Planet'. Welsh-speaking literary magazines: 'Y Faner', 'Taliesin'. 'Yr Enfys' is the magazine of the Organization of Welsh Expatriates (Undeb y Cymry ar Wasgar, founded 1948).

Painting It's always a delight to travel through a country and paint it at the same time, in the manner of the classical landscape painters – particularly a country as picturesque as Wales. 'Painting holidays' are becoming increasingly popular. Here are a few addresses of recognized tutors, where you can combine painting and holidays individually or in groups, no matter whether you are a beginner or a Richard Wilson: Summer School of Painting and Drawing, Henllan Mill, Llangynyw, Welshpool, Powys,

Near Beddgelert

∅ 0938 810269. Dovey Studio and Gallery, Aberdovey, Gwynedd, ∅ 065472 265. St David's Painting Holidays, The Anchorage, 22 New Street, St David's, Dyfed, ∅ 0437 720414.

Quoits Variant on the French game of 'boules', played with flat metal rings called quoits. These can weigh between 3 and 14 lb. and are thrown some 18 yards to hit a hob or pin in the middle of a small square. Quoits is known to have been played since about 1880, was very popular in the Rhonddas, but faded out after the war. Its revival since 1978 is due largely to the Reverend Howell Mudd of Ammanford. There are now two leagues in Wales, with 20 clubs in Dyfed and Powys. Each team consists of 12 players, and the season is from May to September. There is even an international between Wales and Scotland.

Railways Wales holds two railway records: it produced the first railway engine in the world, Richard Trevithick's Penydarren locomotive of 1804 (see page 149), and it also has the most narrow gauge railways in Great Britain (see section on Great Little Trains). Wales contains some of British Rail's most beautiful lines, and the bridges, tunnels and viaducts are abiding evidence of the 19th-century mania for railways: 'Heart of Wales' line, 120 miles from Shrewsbury to Swansea, 4 hours, 30 stations, crossing the border at Knighton (town in Wales, station in England); 'Cambrian Coast' line, 70 miles from Aberystwyth to Pwllheli, along Cardigan Bay. There are many different types of excursion tickets, and rail cards for young people, as well as a 'Freedom of Wales' ticket allowing unlimited travel for one week.

Riding Pony Trekking has become one of the most popular pastimes, usually combined with holidays on a farm. There are about 80 approved riding centres listed by the Pony Trekking & Riding Society of Wales, Pengelli Fach, Pontsticill Vaynor, Merthyr Tydfil, Mid Glamorgan CF48 2TU. For beginners and also the disabled, I can recommend: Cefn Coch Pony Trekking Centre, R. M. Oliver, Cefn Coch, Welshpool, Powys, ∅ 09381 810247.

Shops Generally open from 9 a.m. to 5.30 p.m., and till 4 p.m. on Saturdays.

Sightseeing A one-month season ticket for all National Trust and Welsh Office houses and gardens is available from the British Tourist Authority, 12 Regent Street, London SW1Y 4PQ, ∅ 071-730 3400.

Sport Surfing, sailing, skiing, riding, rugby, mountaineering, hang-gliding, golf etc. Here a few hints and addresses – *Golf:* Wales has over 100 golf courses, including some of the most beautiful in Britain, e.g. Royal St David's in Harlech, Porth Dinllaen near Nefyn on the Llyn Peninsula, and Cradoc Golf Club at the foot of the Brecon Beacons. Information: Welsh Golfing Union, 5 Park Place, Cardiff, ∅ 0222 238467. *Hang gliding:* Welsh Hang Gliding Federation, Dan-yr-Ogof, Craig-y-Nos, Abercraf, Powys. *Sailing:* centres at Penarth, The Mumbles, near Swansea, Saundersfoot, Tenby, and Milford Haven, all in South Wales; Abersoch, Pwllheli, Caernarfon, Beaumaris, Holyhead, Conwy and Port Dinorwic in North Wales. Information: Welsh Yachting Association, Plas

How to pronounce the Welsh LL

Menai, Caernarfon, Gwynedd, ✆ 0248 670738. *Surfing:* excellent beaches at Whitesand Bay, Newgale, Freshwater West, and North Neigwl. Information: Welsh Surfing Federation, 71 Fairway, Port Talbot, West Glamorgan SA12 7HW. *Canoeing:* International slalom championships have frequently been held on the Dee and the Tryweryn. Information: Welsh Canoeing Association, Pen-y-Bont, Corwen, Clwyd. *Skiing:* mountains of Snowdonia good for all levels. Information: The Ski Council of Wales, 240 Whitchurch Road, Cardiff, ✆ 0222 619637. *Mountaineering:* All British Himalayan expeditions have trained in Snowdonia. The best training centre, also for other sports, with excellent situation, facilities and staff: Plas y Brenin National Centre for Mountain Activities, Capel Curig, Betws-y-Coed, Gwynedd, ✆ 06904 212 or 363. N.B. Don't underestimate the dangers of Snowdonia: storms, hail, rockfalls, cold, snow, mist, slippery rocks and many other hazards. An informative book is Ron James' *Rock Climbing in Wales. Rugby:* The national sport (see page 19). Season from September to April. Tickets for Cardiff Arms Park are the stuff that dreams are made on.

See also *Angling, Quoits, Riding*

Walking George Borrow said: 'I am fond of the beauties of nature; now it is impossible to see much of the beauties of nature unless you walk.' The King of Welsh paths is 'The Path', 160 miles along the Pembrokeshire coast from Amroth to St Dogmael's (John H. Barrett, *The Pembrokeshire Coast Path*, Countryside Commission). Another of Britain's 12 long-distance footpaths is Offa's Dyke Path, 170 miles along the border between the Wye and the Dee (Frank Noble, *The Offa's Dyke Association Book of Offa's Dyke*). Near the Offa's Dyke Centre in Knighton is the beginning of Glyndwr's Way (*c.*112 miles), which passes through many of the historical sites of Owain Glyndwr's rebellion: Llanidloes, Machynlleth etc., finishing in Welshpool. The long-distance paths are marked by an acorn, and require several days or even weeks. The Nature and Forest Trails are generally just a few miles long, and are marked by a flower. Other walks include cattle trails and abandoned railway lines, e.g. the Merthyr Tramroad through Taff Valley, where the first steam engine in the world made its first journey in 1804 – a must for railway freaks (see Hunter Davies, *A Walk Along the Track*). Interesting industrial trails are the towpaths along the old canals. Many walks of varying difficulty are described in a handy and very useful booklet 'The Wanderer', published by the BTA. A more comprehensive guide is Michael Marriott, *The Footpaths of Britain*, Queen Anne Press.

Essential equipment for mountain hiking: map, compass, strong shoes, warm and waterproof clothing. The weather can be treacherous. 'Join A Walk' is the name of a highly commended summer programme run by the three National Parks: these are group excursions with a qualified guide. No matter where you go, bear in mind the Forestry Commission's advice:

459

'Leave nothing but footprints, take nothing but pictures, kill nothing but time.' Further information: The Ramblers' Association, Welsh Council, Pontwood, Marford, Wrexham, Clwyd, ✆ 0978 855148.

The Weather Wales is unjustly notorious for its rain. In the summer of 1897 Alfred Sisley was complaining about the heat. In my experience, May, June and September are good months for travelling, but July and August are high season for holiday-makers, and everywhere is crowded; October can also be warm and quite settled. If statistics can be believed, the average temperature in summer is 17°C, and in winter 10°C – a maritime climate thanks to the Gulf Stream. In the Welsh uplands, however, the rainfall is three times the national average. The wettest spot in Britain (apart from Sgurr na Ciche in Scotland) is Snowdon, with 200 inches of rain a year. But the dedicated traveller will not allow this to deter him: George Borrow, caught in the rain on his way to Bala, sings the praises of the umbrella: 'Oh, how a man laughs who has a good umbrella when he has the rain at his back, aye and over his head too, and at all times when it rains except when the rain is in his face, when the umbrella is not of much service. Oh, what a good friend to a man is an umbrella in rain time, and likewise at many other times' – for it also offers protection against wild bulls, dogs and highwaymen, at least in the 'Wild Wales' of 1854. Waterproof clothing is advisable, though in Wales it affords only relative security: 'Some people carry a waterproof and get wet, while some do not, and get very wet' (H. R. C. Carr). The Snowdon rule of thumb also applies elsewhere: 'Set off in the wet, arrive in the dry.'

Should you nevertheless get soaked through, comfort yourself with the wise words of the AA Guide: 'If it has been raining heavily for two days or more, think of those happy mortals who fly rod and line in the swollen rivers and lakes and who have been praying for such a fine run. Or see the waterfalls in all their power ...' Or read what Welsh poets have to say about the weather – like Dafydd ap Gwilym, who wrote in the 14th century:

O ho! thou villain mist, o ho!
What plea hast thou to plague me so? ...
Thou smoke from hellish stews uphurl'd
To mock and mortify the world!
Thou spider-web of giant race,
Spun out and spread through airy space!

The finest of rain poems was written in 1908 by Newport's Super-tramp, W. H. Davies (illustration, page 89) – weather report and class consciousness all in one:

I hear leaves drinking rain;
I hear rich leaves on top
Giving the poor beneath
Drop after drop;
'Tis a sweet noise to hear
These green leaves drinking near.

Artists have set a good example of how to cope productively with Welsh weather and its hot and cold baths. Thomas Rowlandson rode heroically through the rain in 1799, paintbrush at the ready (see frontispiece). 'Always we have our changing weather with us, for the wind and the rain, the snow and the frost, are as important to us as the sun and we can love even the sea mist that creeps in from Ireland bringing mystery to our hills,' writes Kyffin Williams from Anglesey. You must love this country *and* its weather – otherwise you had better not go there at all. Dylan Thomas's love of Wales was so great that when

Pub sign, Hay on Wye

Lawrence Durrell suggested they spend a summer together on Corfu, he wrote in 1939: 'I like the grey country. A bucket of Greek sun would drown in one colour the crowds of colour I like trying to mix for myself out of a grey flat insular mud.'

Youth Hostels For information and addresses: Youth Hostels Association (YHA), 8 St Stephen's Hill, St Albans, Herts AL1 2DY, ☎ 0727 55215. Urdd Gobaith Cymru / The Welsh League of Youth, was founded in 1922 by Sir Ifan ab Owen Edwards in Llanuwchllyn, a little village near Lake Bala. Urdd is a mixture of scouts, youth club and sports club. A common bond is the Welsh language, though English is also spoken. Urdd holds its own Welsh language courses, a yearly international youth festival (Urdd National Eisteddfod), and various sports, cultural and leisure activities. Information: Welsh League of Youth, Llanbadarn Road, Aberystwyth, ☎ 0970 623744.

Calendar of Events and Festivals

January   Welsh Trade Fair, Aberystwyth, Dyfed: arts and crafts

March   St David's Day: March 1st

Festival of Choirs, Cardiff

May   St David's Cathedral Bach Festival, St David's, Dyfed: classical and modern music

Aberystwyth Festival, Aberystwyth, Dyfed

Eisteddfod in village of Pontrhydfendigaid near Strata Florida, Dyfed: famous regional Eisteddfod

Man versus Horse Marathon, Llanwrtyd Wells, Powys: 22-mile race, riders v. runners and cyclists: 'Britain's most eccentric race' (*The Times*)

Festival of Literature, Hay on Wye

June   Llandaff Festival of Music, Llandaff Cathedral, Cardiff

Abergavenny Festival, Abergavenny, Gwent

Opera Festival in Craig-y-Nos Castle, country home of Adelina Patti in Powys

Gregynog Festival, Gregynog Hall, Powys: classical music

July   International Music Eisteddfod, Llangollen, Clwyd

Royal Welsh Show, Llanelwedd, Builth Wells, Powys: agricultural show with dressage, sheepdog trials etc.

Fishguard Music Festival, Fishguard, Dyfed

Gower Festival: concerts in village churches around Swansea

Margam Festival: concerts in Orangery at Margam Castle, West Glamorgan, and elsewhere

Gwyl Werin, Dolgellau, Gwynedd: Celtic folk festival

Nationalists' Commemoration March in Abergele, Gwynedd: July 1st

Criccieth Festival, Criccieth, Gwynedd: music and art

August   Royal National Eisteddfod of Wales: alternates yearly between North and South Wales

Festival of Cardiff: summer festival of street theatre, exhibitions, sport and other activities

Vale of Glamorgan Festival, South Glamorgan: concerts in Cowbridge, Llantwit Major, St Donat's Castle etc.

International Folk Festival, Pontardawe near Swansea, West Glamorgan: Celtic folk festival

Welsh National Sheepdog Trials: different venue each year

Menai Strait Regatta, Isle of Anglesey, Gwynedd

Abersoch Regatta, Llyn, Gwynedd

Cilgerran Coracle Regatta, Cilgerran, Dyfed

Brecon Jazz Festival, Brecon

September Glyndwr's Day, when he was proclaimed Prince of Wales, 1400: September 16th

North Wales Music Festival, St Asaph, Clwyd

Victorian Festival, Llandrindod Wells, Powys

October Swansea Festival, Swansea, West Glamorgan: music, theatre and art, with fringe

Snowdonia Mountain Race, Llanberis, Gwynedd: 10-mile race to peak of Snowdon and back

Llanarth Sale of Welsh Cobs and ponies, Llanarth, Dyfed

November Cardiff Festival of Music, Cardiff

December Coracle Regatta from Cenarth to Cardigan (on Boxing Day)

New Year's Eve midnight race in honour of Rhondda runner Guto Nyth Brân, Mountain Ash, Mid Glamorgan

Places to See, Times to See Them

NT = National Trust

If there is one thing more hateful than another it is being told what to admire and having objects pointed out to one with a stick.

Rev Francis Kilvert, 1870

South Wales

Aberdulais Falls (3 miles north-east of Neath, A465): Romantic beauty spot, visited by Turner; birthplace of South Wales iron industry. NT. April–Oct. Mon.–Fri. 9–5, Sat. & Sun. and public holidays 11 6, Nov.–March daily 10–4.

Abergavenny: small town on the Usk, beginning of 'Head of the Valleys Road' (A465). Parish church with 14th-century choir stalls and 13–17th-century monuments.

Vin Sullivan & Son, 4 Frogmore Street: famous fish, game and delicatessen shop, Mo.–Sat. 9–5.

Afan Argoed Country Park (Cynonville, nr. Port Talbot, A4107): Welsh Miners Museum in reforested former mining Afan Valley. April–Oct. daily 10.30 6, Oct.–March Sat. & Sun. 10.30–5.

Blackpool Mill (nr. Canaston Bridge, east of Haverfordwest, A40/A4075): Tidal mill of 1803, picturesquely situated on bank of Eastern Cleddau, with café. Easter–Sept. daily 11–6.

Blaenavon (north of Newport, A4043/A4248): Big Pit Mining Museum, Ø 0495 790311, in disused mine.

Remains of 18th-century ironworks, North St.

Brecon: Brecknock Museum, Captain's Walk, Mon.–Sat. 10–5.

Brecon Beacons National Park Office, Glamorgan St., Ø 0874 4437.

Brecon Beacons Mountain Centre (nr. Libanus, 6 miles south-west of Brecon, A470): Information, Ø 0874 3366, daily 9.30–5, winter 4.30.

Caerleon: Legionary Museum, Ø 0633 421462: finds from Roman camp of Isca, daily 9.30–6.30, winter, Sun. 2–4.

Caerphilly (7 miles north-east of Cardiff, A469): 'This isn't a castle. It's a whole ruined town,' said Lord Tennyson when he caught sight of Caerphilly Castle, one of the most important fortresses in Europe (plate 72). After the destruction of the first Norman castle by Llywelyn II, it was rebuilt by Gilbert de Clare in 1271. It is a high point of medieval military architecture, and next to Windsor Castle the biggest and technically most sophisticated British fortress of its time: a concentric citadel whose core is surrounded by an inner moat which in turn is protected by two artificial lakes, a wall nearly 1000 feet long, and an outer moat. This concentric system of defence was the model for Edward I's great castles in North Wales. It was destroyed by royalists in the 17th century leaving only, in the south-eastern corner, 'The Leaning Tower of Caerphilly'. April–Oct. daily 9.30–6.30, Oct.–April daily 9.30–4, Sun. 2–4.

The famous Caerphilly Cheese (Caws Caerffili) is a creamy, crumbly cheese which was a special favourite of the miners in the Valleys.

What is now sold as Caerphilly Cheese is for the most part mass produced in English factories (see page 196).

Caldicot Castle (5 miles west of Chepstow, off M4): 13th–14th-century Norman castle, now a favourite setting for 'medieval' banquets with Welsh food and harp music.

Capel-y-Fin: see Eating and Drinking, page 479.

Cardiff

Castle: Roman walls, Norman keep, Victorian interior by William Burges, collection of over 2,000 Burges drawings. Welsh Regiment Museum. March, April, Oct. daily 10–5, May–Oct. daily 9.45–6, Nov.–Feb. daily 10–4.
Chapter Arts Centre, Market Road, Canton, ∅ 0222 396666: exhibitions, theatre, cinema, workshops. Open from 10 a.m.
Design Centre Wales, Pearl Assurance House, Greyfriars Road: well-designed utensils and household articles, industrial products, books etc. Mon.–Fri. 9.30–5.30.
Ffotogallery, 31 Charles Street, ∅ 0222 341667. Mon.–Sat. 10–5.
National Museum of Wales, Cathays Park, ∅ 0222 397951: founded 1907, archaeology, art, industry, botany, zoology, geology; large collection of Welsh paintings, from R. Wilson to present day; also French Impressionists, Old Masters and silver. Tues.–Sat. and Bank Holidays 10–5, Sun. 2.30–5.
Oriel, The Priory, ∅ 0222 395548: Gallery and bookshop of Welsh Arts Council, specializes in Welsh literature and art.
St John the Baptist: only medieval church in town centre, c.1453, Perpendicular Tower 1473.
Welsh Arts Council, 12 Museum Place, ∅ 0222 394711: founded 1967, state institution for promotion of Welsh culture.
Welsh Folk Museum, St Fagans (3 miles west of Cardiff), ∅ 0222 569441: folk art and open-air museum, founded 1946; life, work and culture of the Welsh, costume collection, musical instruments, agricultural tools and vehicles; in park of Elizabethan manor, more than 20 reconstructed farmhouses with chapels and workshops. Daily 10–5. Closed Sundays in winter.

Carew (between Tenby and Pembroke, A477): picturesque ruin of castle given by Rhys ap Tewdwr at the end of 11th century to his beautiful daughter, the 'Helen of Wales', on her marriage to Gerald de Windsor. In Tudor times extended to palatial residence (16th century; plate 71).
Carew Cross: Monumental Celtic cross c.1033, one of the finest in Wales, over 13 feet high, with Latin inscription (for King Maredudd, Edwin's son); on top half a swastika, symbol of luck and of the sun; underneath, a braided pattern with no beginning or end.
Carew French Tidal Mill: 16th century, not far from castle, on Carew Estuary.

Castell Coch (Tongwynlais, 5 miles north of Cardiff, A470): 13th-century castle reconstructed by William Burges in Victorian style. End March–end Oct. daily 9.30–6.30, Nov.–March daily 9.30–4, Sun. 2–4.

Chepstow: Norman frontier fort on Wye. End March–end Oct. daily 9.30–6.30, Nov.–March, daily 9.30–4, Sun. 2–4.
St Mary's: Benedictine abbey church (c.1070), only the nave and the fine Early Norman portal are original; the rest is 19th century.
Museum, Bridge Street, ∅ 029 12 5981: town history and 18th–20th century artists in Wye Valley. March–Oct. daily 11–1, 2–5, Sun. 2–5.

Cilgerran Castle (3 miles south of Cardigan, off A478): ruined 13th-century castle on crag in Teifi Valley, painted by Turner and others. NT.

End March–end Oct. Mon.–Sat. 9.30–6.30, Sun. 2–6.30, Nov.–March Mon.–Sat. 9.30–4, Sun. 2–4.

Clytha Castle (nr. Abergavenny): Neo-Gothic folly, 'Sham Castle' built 1790 by a widowed landowner 'to relieve a mind sincerely afflicted by the loss of a most excellent wife.' NT, now administered by Landmark Trust as holiday home. On hill opposite: Clytha Park, Neo-Classical country house of Edward Haycock, 1823–26, good example of Greek Revival (private).

Crickhowell: Small town in Usk Valley on edge of Brecon Beacons National Park. 13-arch bridge over Usk (17th century). Regency Villa Gwernvale, now a hotel, was home of Sir George Everest, Surveyor General of India, after whom the mountain then known as Chomolungma 'Goddess Mother of the World' was renamed.

Crynant (5 miles north of Neath, A4109): Cefn Coed Coal and Steam Centre: restored plant, shows history of coalmining and steam locomotion, especially in Dulais Valley. Daily 10.30–6 summer only.

Dan-yr-Ogof Caves (A4067, north of Abercraf): largest Welsh limestone caves. Easter till Oct., daily from 10 a.m.

Dre-fach Felindre (south-east of Cardigan, A484): Most important wool centre in Wales 1870–1930. Museum of the Welsh Woollen Industry, ∅ 0559 370929: April–Sept. Mon.–Sat. 10–5.

Dyffryn House (south-west of Cardiff): built 1893 as country house of colliery-owner, now a hospital. Large park and garden.

Ewenny Priory (1½ miles south of Bridgend, A48): Benedictine Abbey, founded 1141, Early Norman monastery church, preserved as parish church.

Fishguard: Workshop Wales, Lower Town, ∅ 0348 872261: John Cleal's arts and crafts centre, with studios, exhibitions and shops. April–Sept. daily 10–6, Oct.–March only open 4 days a week.

Grosmont (north-east of Abergavenny, B4347): small town on Monnow in the 'Trilateral' mountains on the border; ruined Norman castle, 11th–13th century.

Haverfordwest: capital of 'Little England', during Middle Ages, centre of a Flemish weaving colony. Birthplace of Gwen John (/ Victoria Place).

Castle Museum and Art Gallery, The Castle, ∅ 0437 763708: in former prison of Norman Castle, changing exhibitions, Mon.–Sat. 10–4.30.

St Mary, High Street: Late Norman church, Early English arcades, capitals with animals and grotesques, carved oak ceiling (early 16th century).

Pembrokeshire Coast National Park, County Offices, Dyfed, ∅ 0437 764591.

Kidwelly Castle (10 miles south of Carmarthen, A484, colour plate 39): Founded after 1106 by Bishop Roger of Salisbury as part of Norman chain of coastal fortifications. Core of castle begun c.1275, gatehouses early 14th century. During siege of 1403, successfully defended by two soldiers and six archers.

Laugharne: Dylan Thomas's Boat House 1949–53. Daily 10–6.

Llanelli (west of Swansea, A484): industrial town, largest British tinplate works. The painter James Dickson Innes was born in Greenfield

Villas, Murray Street, in 1887. The novelist George Meredith lived for some years in New Road.

Parc Howard Art Gallery and Museum, Felinfoel Road, ∅ 05542 773538: local and industrial history, Welsh artists (J. D. Innes, Evan Walters etc.). April–Oct. 10–6, Nov.–March 10–4.

Llanfaches (5 miles west of Caerwent): Oldest Non-Conformist chapel in Wales, 1639.

Llansantffraid (5 miles south-east of Brecon, A40): Village church of St Bride with grave of 'Silurian' Henry Vaughan (1621–95), who lived in area as country doctor and poet. His contemporaries called him the 'Swan of Usk', and he wrote mystic, metaphysical poetry in the style of the hermeticists: 'I saw Eternity the other night, / Like a great Ring of pure and endless light …' In the same churchyard is the grave of Colonel Gwynne Holford, who planted a forest on Buckland Hill in rows corresponding to the battle formation at Waterloo – a natural folly.

Llanthony Abbey, see Eating and Drinking, page 480.

Llantrisant (7 miles north-west of Cardiff, A4119): old hill town in Vale of Glamorgan. Monument to eccentric Dr William Price. Royal Mint, where all British coins are made. Every May, feast of the Society of the Black Hundred, descendants of the archers who under the Black Prince defeated the French at Crecy in 1346.

Llantwit Major (west of Cardiff, B4265/B4270): coastal village with rich Celtic history: mission school of St Illtud (6th century); in St Illtud Parish Church (12th–15th century) important collection of Celtic crosses and inscribed stones (9th–11th century).

Maesllyn Woollen Mill (north-west of Llandyssul between A486 and B4571): built 1881, working museum, Mon.–Sat. 10.30–5.30, Sun. in August only 2–6.

Manorbier Castle (5 miles south-west of Tenby, A4139/B4585): 12th–14th-century castle, birthplace of Giraldus Cambrensis. Easter, 25 May–Sept. daily 11–6.

Margam Country Park (2 miles east of Port Talbot, A48; plate 4): leisure park with orangery (18th century), April–Oct. daily except Mon. 10–7, Nov.–March daily except Mon. and Tues. 10–5.

Margam Abbey Museum (near abbey church): important collection of Celtic crosses and early Christian inscribed stones.

Merthyr Tydfil: Cyfarthfa Castle Museum (⅔ mile north-west of town-centre): in former residence of ironmaster Crawshay, history of iron industry, watercolours by Penry Williams, April–Oct. 10–1, 2–6.30.

Parry's Cottage, 4 Chapel Row: birthplace and museum of the composer Joseph Parry, Mon., Tues., Thurs.

Monmouth: Museum, Priory Street, ∅ 0600 713519: local history, with collection of Nelson and Charles Stewart Rolls memorabilia. Mon.–Sat. 10–1, 2–5, Sun. 2–5.

Castle and Regimental Museum, daily 2–5 summer months only.

Neath Abbey (⅔ mile west of Neath): ruined 13th century monastery, and remains of 18th–19th century copper and iron industries. April–Oct. daily 9.30–6.30, Sun. 2–6.30, Oct.–April daily 9.30–4, Sun. 2–4.

Nevern (east of Newport/Dyfed, B4582): Village church St Brynach with one of the finest

Celtic crosses in Wales (10th century) and some Ogham inscribed stones.

Newport: Museum and Art Gallery, John Frost Square, ∅ 0633 840064: town history, Chartist movement, excellent collection of English watercolours (Cotman, Gilpin, Girtin, Turner, Cox etc.), Mon.–Thurs. 9.30–5, Fri. 9.30–4.30, Sat. 9.30 4.

St Woolos Cathedral, Stow Hill: Norman west portal c.1080; nave 12th century; tower 15th century; choir extension with eastern window and mural by John Piper, 1960–62.

Civic Centre, Godfrey Road: 1937–64, in entrance hall town history on 12 murals by Hans Feibusch, 1961.

Inmos Microelectrics Factory by Richard Rogers, 1982. Hall suspended on steel cables without pillars – high-tech architecture at its best.

Pembroke Castle: 11th century, birthplace of Henry VII. Summer daily 9.30–6, Winter 10–4.

Penarth (south of Cardiff): Turner House, Plymouth Road, ∅ 0222 708870: branch of National museum, changing exhibitions. Tues.–Sat. and Bank Holidays 11–12.45, 2–5, Sun. 2–5.

Penhow Castle (between Newport and Chepstow, A48): Norman frontier fortress (1129), 'Wales's oldest lived-in castle', Easter–Sept. Weds.–Sun. 10–6.

Pentre Ifan Cromlech (Temple Bar, 2½ miles east of Newport/Dyfed): Stone Age, on edge of Preseli Hills.

Picton Castle (4 miles south-east of Haverfordwest, off A40): country home of Philipps family since 12th century (private), with Graham Sutherland gallery: daily except Mon. 10–12.30, 1.30–5.30.

Pontypool (north-east of Newport, A4043): The Valley Inheritance, Park Buildings, ∅ 04955 752043: Industrial museum of Torfaen Valley. Daily 10–5, Sun. 2–5.

Crane Street Baptist Chapel, 1845: Neo-Classical chapel with rich interior.

Raglan Castle (A40/A449), north-east of Newport): begun c.1430, glorious climax of medieval castle-building in Wales. Hexagonal belltower, 'Yellow Tower of Gwent', outside the extensive and once magnificent complex. In 1646 was a royalist centre besieged for 11 weeks by parliamentary troops, and finally conquered and razed. April–Oct. daily 9.30–6.30, Oct.–April daily 9.30 4, Sun. 2–4.

Roch Castle (south-east of St David's, A487): birthplace of Lucy Walters, mistress of Charles II: their illegitimate son James, Duke of Monmouth, was executed in 1685 for high treason.

Skenfrith (north-east of Abergavenny, B4512): picturesque village on Monnow. Ruined Norman castle and borderland church St Bridget's: half place of worship, half refuge; hall church with three naves, begun c.1207, massive tower with wooden top, dovecote, store room and bell cage.

St David's: Albion Gallery of South Wales landscape painter John Rogers.

St Fagans: see Cardiff, Welsh Folk Museum

Swansea: Glynn Vivian Art Gallery and Museum, Alexandra Road, ∅ 0792 655006 or 651738: collection of ceramics, Swansea china, 20th-century British art: Ceri Richards, J. D. Innes, Jack Crabtree, Augustus John etc. Daily 10.30–5.30.

Royal Institution of South Wales Museum, Victoria Road, ∅ 0792 53763: archaeology, geology, zoology, Welsh folk art etc. Mon.–Sat. 10–5.

Tenby: Tudor Merchant's House, Quay Hill: 15th century. NT. Easter–Oct. Mon.–Fri. 11–6, Sun. 2–6. Closed Sat.

Museum, Castle Hill: local history. Easter–Oct. daily 10–6, Oct.–March Mon.–Sat. 10–1, 2–4.

Tintern Abbey (4 miles north-east of Chepstow, A466): Cistercian monastery in Wye Valley. April–Oct. daily 9.30–6.30, Oct.–April 9.30–4, Sun. 2–4.

Tredegar House (south-west of Newport, M4/A48): country house (1672) with park, children's zoo etc. April–Sept. daily except Mon. and Tues. 1.30–5. Weekends only in October.

Trefecca (nr. Talgarth, east of Brecon, B4560): Howell Harris Museum: history of famous 18th century Welsh Methodist preacher. Mon.–Fri. 11–5.

Tretower Court (4 miles north-west of Chrickhowell, A40/A479): late medieval country house, mainly 14–15th century. Hall with open roof trusses.

Tretower Castle: ruins of 12th century Norman castle. Mid-March–mid-Oct. daily 9.30–6.30, Sun. 2–6.30, mid-Oct.–mid-March, daily 9.30–4, Sun. 2–4.

Wallis Woollen Mill (Woodstock, 8 miles north-east of Haverfordwest, B4329): built 1812. Workshop and shop. Mon.–Sat. 10–6.

Wolvesnewton (Llangwm, north-east of Newport, A449/B4235): The Model Farm, late 18th century, cross-shaped, bric-a-brac museum and arts and crafts. Easter–Oct. only 11–6.

Mid Wales

Aberdyfi (west of Machynlleth, A493): fishing resort on Dyfi estuary. Up to 19th century, ship-building and export harbour. Now sailing centre. Footpaths in nature reserve at mouth of river. Song 'The Bells of Aberdyfi' recalls legend of town drowned by sea. Centre for sports and nature study founded by German educationalist Kurt Hahn. Model for some 30 such schools worldwide: Outward Bound Wales, Aberdovey Centre, ∅ 065472 464.

Aberystwyth: Arts Centre Gallery, University College of Wales, Penglais, ∅ 0970 623232: changing exhibitions, theatre and concerts; university ceramics collection, especially 20th century. Mon.–Sat. 10–5.

Ceredigion Museum, Terrace Road: local history in former Edwardian music-hall 'The Coliseum' (1905). Mon.–Sat. 10–5.

National Library of Wales, Penglais, ∅ 0970 3816: special collections Celtic culture and Welsh literature; graphics gallery with early topographical views, Welsh portraits, drawings and watercolours by Thomas Rowlandson, Moses Griffith, John 'Warwick' Smith, John Ingleby etc. Mon.–Sat. 9.30–6.

Welsh Language Society, 5 Maes Albert.

Welsh League of Youth/Urdd Gobaith Cymru, Llanbadarn Road, ∅ 0970 623744.

Castell Carreg Cennen (Trapp, A483, south-east of Llandeilo): 13–14th century castle on crag overlooking Tywi Valley. May–Sept. daily 9.30–7, Sun. 2–7, Oct.–April daily 9.30–5.30, Sun. 2–5.30.

Corris (A487, north of Machynlleth): former slate quarrying village. Corris Railway Museum: history of slate quarry narrow-gauge railway from Aberllefenni to Machynlleth.

Corris Craft Centre, ∅ 065473 343: complex

of craft studios and shops (1982), set up in exemplary fashion by Development Board for Rural Wales.

Dolanog (west of Welshpool, B4382): village in Vyrnwy Valley with Ann Griffiths Memorial Chapel (1903) to popular hymn writer (1776–1805), daughter of a farmer from Dolwar Fach (½ mile north). One can visit the house where she was born, and her importance as a poetess is denoted by a volume in series 'Writers of Wales'.

Dolaucothi Gold Mines (Pumpsaint, south-east of Lampeter, A482): from Roman times. NT. Guided tours June–Sept. daily. Open April–Nov. daily 10–6. Last admission 5.

Gregynog Hall (nr. Tregynon, 5 miles northwest of Newtown, B4389): former country home of arts patrons the Davies sisters, and one of the first Welsh buildings in concrete (c.1860). Now study and conference centre for University of Wales. Bibliophile printing-press Gwasg Gregynog. Park public, but house only by appointment.

Guilsfield (B4392, north of Welshpool): Parish church St Aelhaiarn, 14–15th century, with beautiful interior: Perpendicular coffered ceiling and rood screen, c.1500.

Knighton (A488, south-east of Newtown): Old Primary School, West Street, ∅ 05472 528753: information centre for Offa's Dyke, frontier wall and 167-mile footpath (8th century), some of which – between Knighton and Montgomery – is still well preserved.

Llandrindod Wells: Tom Norton's Collection of Old Cycles and Tricycles, Automobile Palace, Temple Street, Mon.–Sat. 8–6.30.

Llanidloes: Museum of Local History and Industry, Old Market Hall (16th century) Easter–Sept. Mon.–Sat. 11–1, 2–5.

Town Hall, Great Oak Street, Jacobean Style, 1908.

Llanwrtyd Wells: approx. 600 inhabitants – the smallest town in Great Britain.

Llywernog Silver-Lead Mine (Ponterwyd, 10 miles east of Aberystwyth, A44): at foot of Plynlimon, ∅ 0970 85620. March–Aug. daily 10–6, Sept.–Oct. 10–5.

Machynlleth: Centre for Alternative Technology (2 miles north of Machynlleth, A487), ∅ 0654 702400: Village of the Future. Daily 10–5 (last admission). Weekend and summer courses.

The Quarry Shop, Maengwyn Street: CAT shop.

Newtown: Development Board for Rural Wales, Ladywell House, ∅ 0686 626965: founded 1976.

Robert Owen Memorial Museum, The Cross: life and works of 19th century social reformer in his hometown. Mon.–Fri. 9.45–11.45, 2–3.30, Sat 10–11.30.

Textile Museum, Commercial Street, ∅ 26243 in former weavers' houses (c.1830). Tues.–Sat. 2–4.30.

W. H. Smith Museum, Mon.–Sat. 9–5.

Pennant Melangell (south-east of Bala, B4391): remote church at foot of Berwyn Hills, where Irish Princess Monacella founded a convent in late 8th century. An unusual romanesque sarcophagus was made c.1160–70 for this Celtic saint (restored 1958–59).

Pistyll Rhaeadr (between Bala and Oswestry): the fall of falls, at 260 feet the biggest waterfall in Wales, and one of the 'Seven Wonders'.

Powis Castle (1 mile south of Welshpool, A483): Country home of Powis family, 13th–17th century, collections of paintings and furniture, Clive Museum of Indian art, terraced garden (17th century), magnificent park. NT. 20 April–June and Sept.–Oct., Weds.–Sun., July–Aug. daily, castle 12–5, park 11–6.

Stanage Park (north of Presteigne, A4113): picturesque country house and landscaped garden of Humphry Repton, 1807–45 (private).

Strata Florida (Pontrhydfendigaid, B4343, south-east of Aberystwyth): Cistercian abbey, late 12th century. March–Oct. daily 9.30–6.30, Sun. 2–7, Oct.–April daily 9.30–4, Sun. 2–4.

Strata Marcella (3 miles north of Welshpool): sparse remains of former flourishing Cistercian abbey Ystrad Marchell, founded 1172.

Trer-ddol (north of Aberystwyth, A487): Yr Hen Gapel, Chapel museum, religious life in 19th century. April–Sept. Mon.–Sat. 10–5.

Tywyn (A493 west of Machynlleth): Railway Museum, Wharf Station, Ø 0654 710472 (Talyllyn Railway museum). April–Oct. 10–5.

Welshpool: Powysland Museum, Salop Road, nr. St Mary's: local history. Mon., Tues., Thurs, Fr. 11–1, 2–5, Sat. 2–5. Also open Sat. 10–1 and Sun. 10–1, 2–5 Summer months.

Wales Craft Council, 20 Severn Street, Welshpool, Ø 0938 555313.

North Wales

Bangor: university city on Menai Strait, bishopric since 546, oldest in Great Britain. Cathedral: founded by St Deiniol in 6th century, but nothing remains of this structure; the present building is as unassuming as a parish church, 13–15th century, West Tower 1532, beautiful Perpendicular east window; major restorations by Sir Gilbert Scott 1868 ff. – North of Cathedral, Bishop's Garden – unusual biblical garden containing only trees, bushes and flowers that are mentioned in the Bible. 16th-century Bishop's Palace now city hall. – University College of North Wales, founded 1883, building 1910 by H. T. Hare; specialist subjects: marine research, agriculture and forestry, electronics; chair of music held by Welsh composer William Mathias; library with complete collection of Welsh translations of Bible. – Art Gallery and Museum of Welsh Antiquities, Fford Gwynedd, Ø 0248 353368: changing exhibitions of contemporary art; prehistory, North Welsh history and folklore, furniture. Tues.–Sat. 12–4.30. – Theatr Gwynedd, University, Ø 0248 351708: English and Welsh-speaking productions. – Pier of 1896, Victorian curiosity with pagoda-like kiosks.

Barclodiad y Gawres Burial Chamber (Anglesey, north-west of Aberffraw, A4080): c.2000 BC, with prehistoric drawings.

Bardsey Island (5 miles west of Aberdaron, Llyn): Ynys Enlli, Isle of Currents, at western tip of Llyn Peninsula, 440 acres; Celtic mission centre and goal of medieval pilgrims; sparse remains of 13th-century Augustine abbey; small farming and fishing community in 19th century, with its own king until 1926; now rarely inhabited; ornithological station manned by Bardsey Island Trust; ferry from Aberdaron.

Beaumaris (Anglesey): Castle built in water by Edward I, begun 1295, concentric layout. May–Sept. daily 9.30–6.30, Sun. 2–6.30, Oct.–April daily 9.30–4, Sun. 2–4.

Old Gaol, Steeple Lane: Victorian model 19th-century prison. June–Sept. daily 11–6. Courthouse 11.30–5.30.

Castle Street with half-timbered Tudor houses

(Old Bull's Head, 1472), Victoria Terrace, 1835, by Joseph Hansom.

Beddgelert (A4085/A498): popular spot in Snowdonia, at intersection of three valleys, and place of pilgrimage for dog-lovers. Tourist attraction: the most sentimental dog-grave in Wales, and a contribution to national psychology and the history of attracting tourists. The name means 'Grave of Gelert', probably the British St Gelert, who lived here in the 6th century. But more attractive than a dead saint is a dead dog whose legend is brought to life. This was done in the 18th century by the landlord of the 'Royal Goat' – a man with a good knowledge of myth and a good eye to business: he identified Gelert with the faithful dog of Prince Llewelyn the Last, which the Prince killed in anger – a bad mistake. The landlord wrote on the dog's princely grave: '… and passers-by will drop a tear / On faithful Gelert's grave.' The Pass of Aberglaslyn (NT), often painted, was the scene of Julius Caesar Ibbetson's picture 'A Phaeton in a Thunderstorm' (1798).

Blaenau Ffestiniog (A470): Llechwedd Slate Caverns, Ø 076681 830306: museum, visit to caverns on Miners' Underground Tramway, reconstruction of Victorian working conditions. March–Sept. daily 10–5.15. Oct.–Feb. 10–4.15.

Gloddfa Ganol, Ø 076681 830664: slate museum with tour of tunnels and 'Safari Tours' on site of what was once the biggest slate quarry in the world. Easter–Oct. Weekdays 10–5.30. Also Sundays mid-July to August Bank Holiday.

Ffestiniog Pottery, Ø 076681 830601; studio of Adrian Childs, daily 10–5.

Ffestiniog Power Station, Tan-y-Grisiau (A496, south of Blaenau Ffestiniog): hydro-electric power station, Easter–Oct. daily 10–5.

Worktown, Pant-yr-Ynn Mill, Ø 076681 830540: Falcon D. Hildred's collection of drawings and artefacts from 19th-century British industry. Mon.–Sat. 2–6.

Bodelwyddan Castle (nr. Rhyl): early Victorian country house in Vale of Clwyd, designed by Joseph Hansom after 1830, now a branch of National Portrait Gallery with first-class collection of Victorian portraits (G. F. Watts, John Gibson etc.). Easter–Oct. daily except Fri. 10–5. Nov.–Easter Sat.–Tues. 11–5. Closed mid Dec.–mid Jan. Ø 0745 584060.

Bodnant Garden (7 miles south of Llandudno, A470; colour plate 7): one of the finest gardens in Wales, laid out in present form 1875 overlooking Vale of Conwy, with glorious view of Snowdon; approx. 100 acres; many rare plants, magnolia, rhododendron, azalea, camellia, laburnum; Italianate garden temple Pin Mill, 1730, with waterlily pond (colour plate 7); terraced garden like giant green steps down to a bay. Best time to visit: spring and early summer. NT. Mid March–Oct. daily 10–5. Not open to public: Bodnant Hall, c.1790, extended 1875–98, family home of Lord Aberconway, President of Royal Horticultural Society.

Bodrhyddan Hall (north-east of Rhuddlan): Late 17th-century manor house, south façade 1696, rebuilt in Neo-Classical style 1872–3. Still seat of Conwy family, hereditary governors of Rhuddlan Castle. Large collection of weapons. Park public, house only open on special days.

Bryn Bras Castle (Llanrug, 5 miles east of Caernarfon, A4086): Neo-Romanesque c.1830, with rooms by Thomas Hopper, daily except Sat. Easter–mid-July and Sept. 1–5, mid July–Aug. 10.30–5 (self-catering holiday flats in castle itself, Ø 0286 870210).

Caernarfon: Castle built by Edward I, begun 1283. March–Oct. daily 9.30–6.30. Nov.–Feb. daily 9.30–4, Sun. 2–4.

Segontium Roman Fort Museum, ∅ 0286 5625 (on road to Beddgelert, A4085): archaeological branch of National Museum, finds from excavated Roman camp. Daily 9.30–6, Sun. 2–6. Closes 5.30 Oct., March & April. Closes 4 Nov.–March.

Capel Curig (A5/A4086, west of Betws-y-Coed): artists', anglers' and tourists' village in wild Snowdonia, ideal spot for hikers. Visited by Byron, Scott, Queen Victoria, all of whom carved their names on the windows of the Royal Hotel, now National Centre for Mountain Activities, Plas y Brenin (see page 459 under Sport). The first pub here was opened by the English slate magnate Richard Pennant (see page 377). In 1791 he also built the first road through Nant Ffrancon to Capel Curig, which he wanted to open up for excursions. – On edge of village, the chapel by the stream with an old cemetery has associations with Shelley.

Castell-y-Bere (7 miles south of Dolgellau, off B4405 nr. Abergynolwyn): ruins of what was once the most important castle in Wales, begun in 1221 by Llywelyn the Great – last castle to be conquered by the English (1283). Secluded, romantic situation in Dysynni Valley at foot of Cader Idris.

Chirk Castle (⅔ mile west of Chirk, A5/B4500): Edwardian frontier fort, c.1310. NT. April–end Sep. daily except Mon. & Sat., but open Bank Holiday. Oct. Sat. & Sun. only. Castle 12–5, Grounds 10–6.

Conwy: Castle of Edward I, 1283–87. Mid March–mid Oct. daily 9.30–6.30, mid Oct.–mid March daily 9.30–4, Sun. 2–4.

Aberconwy House, Castle St/High St: 14th century townhouse with exhibition of town history. NT. April–Sept. daily except Tues., Oct. only Sat. & Sun. 11–5.

Plas Mawr, High Street: townhouse of Robert Wynne, 1580; seat of Royal Cambrian Academy of Art, changing exhibitions. Daily 10–5.30.

St Mary's Church: 13–15th century, rood screen c.1500. In choir, tombstone of Nicholas Hookes: 41st child of his father, himself father of 27 (died 1637). Grave of brothers and sisters outside church, immortalized by Wordsworth's poem 'We are Seven', though connection not proven. On site of St Mary's there was originally a Cistercian abbey founded by Llywelyn the Great, which the latter entered in 1238, two years before his death.

Criccieth: small seaside resort on edge of Llyn Peninsula with fine view over Tremadog Bay. Original Welsh castle with twin-towered gatehouse built by Llywelyn the Great (c.1220–30), captured 1282 by Edward I and strengthened by him, destroyed 1404 by Owain Glyndwr. Watercolour by Turner c.1835 (British Museum).

Cymer Abbey (2 miles north-west of Dolgellau, A494): ruins of small, late 12th century Cistercian abbey.

Denbigh (A525/A543): Hill town in Vale of Clwyd with fine view from medieval hill fortress built in key strategic position on route to interior of North Wales. Town walls begun after 1282, partly preserved. Edwardian castle built by Earl of Lincoln 1282–1322; headquarters of Harry Percy (Hotspur) in 1399; given by Elizabeth I to her favourite Dudley, Earl of Leicester, 1563; after 11-month siege one of last royalist strongholds in Wales to surrender to Cromwell's troops in 1660. In gatehouse, museum with memorabilia of journalist H. M. Stanley who was born in Denbigh and tracked down the explorer Livingstone in Africa ('Dr Livingstone, I presume').

Castle: May–Sept. daily 9.30–6.30, Oct.–April daily 9.30–4, Sun. 2–4.

Brookhouse pottery: studio of David Frith, ∅ 0745 812805.

Whitchurch (1 mile east of Denbigh): late Gothic parish church with hammerbeam roof.

Gwaenynog Park (2 miles south-west of Denbigh): Dr Johnson's Cottage, recording his visit in 1774.

Llanrhaeadr Dyffryn (A525, south of Denbigh): parish church with Jesse east window, 1533, finest medieval stained-glass window in North Wales.

Dolgellau: Tal-y-Waen Farm, Cader Road (⅔ mile outside town): Welsh hill farm with tourist attractions: May–Oct. daily except Sat. 10–5.

Dolwyddelan Castle (A470, south-west of Betws-y-Coed): at foot of Moel Siabod, 1170, rebuilt after English conquest of 1283, presumed birthplace of Llywelyn the Great (1173). May–Sept. daily 9.30–6.30, Sun. 2 6.30, Oct.–April daily 9.30–4, Sun. 2–4. 16th century village church with Gothic rood screen.

Erddig (2 miles south of Wrexham, A525): country house (1684 ff.), dining room by Thomas Hopper (1826) rebuilt in Neo-Classical style; Chinese Room with hand-painted wallpaper; State Bedroom with exquisite chinoiserie (18th and 19th century). Garden in William and Mary style, with straight paths, supported trees, box-tree hedges, and canal-like lake at the end of which are wrought iron park gates by Robert Davies, 1721. NT. April–Oct. daily except Thurs. & Fri. 12–5.30, last admission 4.

Felin Isaf Water Mill (Llansantffraid, east of Conwy, A470): early 18th century. April–Oct. Tues.–Sat. 10.30–5, Sun. 2.30–5.

Fort Belan (nr. Dinas Dinlle, 6 miles south of Caernarfon): at entrance to Menai Strait, built in 1776 to defend the Strait, and might be called the only fortress of the American War of Independence on this side of the Atlantic.

Glyn-Ceiriog (south of Llangollen, A5/B4500): Ceiriog Memorial Institute, High Street: in memory of local hymn-writer John Hughes, called Ceiriog. Mon.–Sat. 1–9.

Gwydir Castle (nr. Llanrwst, B5106): Tudor country home of Wynnes' family, with garden and over 50 peacocks. Easter–mid Oct. daily, except Sat., 10 5.

Gwydir Uchaf Chapel (2 miles south-west of Llanrwst): the Wynnes' chapel, 1673, with painted wooden ceiling.

Harlech: Castle of Edward I, 1283–89. Mid March–mid Oct. daily 9.30–6.30, mid Oct.–mid March Mon.–Sat. 9.30–4, Sun. 2–4.

Coleg Harlech Arts Centre with Theatr Ardudwy, ∅ 0766 780667: changing exhibitions, films, concerts, Welsh and English speaking plays. Mon.–Sat. 10–5.

Old Llanfair Quarry Slate Caverns (1 mile south of Harlech, A496). Easter–Oct. daily 10–5.30.

Hawarden (6 miles west of Chester, A55): home of Victorian Prime Minister W. E. Gladstone, Hawarden Castle (1752–1809). House private, but park with ruined Norman castle open to public. Gladstone's estate is responsible for St Deiniol's Library, which he donated and which, with over 120,000 volumes, is one of the most important Victorian study centres in Great Britain (conferences, seminars, room for 30 guests, ∅ 0244 532350).

Parish church of St Deiniol, founded in 13th century, restored by Sir George Gilbert Scott in 1859 after fire; stained glass windows by Burne-Jones; Gladstone monument.

Holt (north-east of Wrexham, A534): Bridge

over border river Dee, 1343, painted by Richard Wilson c.1761 (National Gallery, London).

Holyhead (Anglesey): Ferry port to Dun Laoghaire, Ireland. Ruins of Roman camp Caer Gybi, 3–4th century; within its walls, late medieval parish church with Norman choir and stained glass windows by Burne-Jones and William Morris.

Holyhead Mountain, west of town: remains of prehistoric hill fort on peak, and remains of Celtic hut settlement on slopes (2–4th century AD).

South Stack Lighthouse, 1808 by David Alexander, who built Princetown Prison on Dartmoor.

Holywell (north-west of Chester, A55): St Winifred's Well, pilgrims' chapel c.1500, with ancient healing spring. Daily 9–5. Closed Mon. in winter.

Panton Place: former industrial settlement, 1816.

The Grange Cavern Military Museum (Holway, A55, ⅔ mile west of town centre): in cavern of former limestone quarry. Easter–Oct. daily 9.30–5. Feb. & March.

Textile Mills, ∅ 0352 712022: 1777, tweed from wool of valuable Jacob's sheep.

Llanbedr, see Rhinog Nature Reserve.

Llanberis (east of Caernarfon, A4086): Welsh Slate Museum, ∅ 0286 870630, on site of Dinorwic Quarry, which closed in 1969. Authentic, fully preserved workshops together with old machinery and tools in granite building of 1870 like a British fortress of 19th century. Easter–Sept. daily 9.30–6.30.

Oriel Eryri: branch of National Museum at Llyn Padarn, changing exhibitions of art, nature and history of Snowdonia.

Llandudno: Mostyn Art Gallery, 12 Vaughan Street, ∅ 0492 79201: excellent changing exhibitions of historical and contemporary British or Welsh art. Mon.–Sat. 10–5.

Rapallo House Museum, Fferm Bach Road, Craig-y-don: Villa and art collection of Victorian bachelor, millionaire and amateur painter. April–Nov. Mon.–Fri. 10–1, 2–5.

Great Orme Cable Tramway: opened 1902 – only others are in Lisbon and San Francisco – on 675 feet high Great Orme.

Ebeneser, 1909: Methodist Chapel of late period, interior with cupola and cast iron columns.

The Rabbit Hole, 384 Trinity Square: grotto with 'Alice in Wonderland' effects and curios. ∅ 0492 860082 for opening hours.

Llangollen: Canal Museum, The Wharf: history of Llangollen Canal with trips on horsedrawn barges. Easter–Oct. 11–5.

Castell Dinas Bran: hill with traces of hill fort from Iron Age and ruined 13th-century Welsh castle painted by Richard Wilson, 1770–71, and others.

Dee Bridge: c.1345, extended several times; the parapet still contains old passing-places.

Plas Newydd: home of the 'Ladies of Llangollen'. Easter–Sept. daily, except Sat., 12–4.30, Oct. Fri. & Sun. only.

St Collen: church of name-saint of Llangollen, richly carved Gothic wooden ceiling, monument to Ladies and their maidservant.

Llanystumdwy (1¼ mile west of Criccieth, A497, Llyn): Lloyd George Memorial Museum. May–Sept. daily 10–5.

Maesgwm Forest Visitor Centre (10 miles north of Dolgellau, A470): information centre in Coed-y-Brenin Forest, survey of forestry and history of goldmining in Mawddach Valley. Delightful forest walks, and don't forget your pans for panning gold (obtainable in Dolgellau).

Marford (north of Wrexham, A483): picturesque village with Neo-Gothic cottages, 1805, by George Boscawen.

Menai Bridge (Anglesey): Museum of Childhood, 1 Castle Street, Beaumaris, ∅ 0248 712498, with antique toys, dolls etc. Easter–Oct. Mon.–Sat. 10–6, Sun. 1–5.

Tegfryn Art Gallery, Cadnant Road, ∅ 0248 712437: changing exhibitions of contemporary North Welsh artists. Daily 10–1, 2–5. Closed Mondays Oct.–May.

Mold (west of Chester, A494/A541): Daniel Owen Centre, Earl Road: literary museum of Welsh novelist. Mon.–Fri. 9.30–7, Sat. 9.30–12.30.

Theatr Clwyd: opera, theatre, concerts, exhibitions, ∅ 0352 55111.

St Mary Church, 15th century, tower 1773, memorial window and grave of Richard Wilson.

Tri Thy Craft Centre, Coed Talon (A541 south-east of Mold), ∅ 0352 771359: studios and holiday courses (with B&B) on 17th-century farm.

Nant Gwrtheyrn (Llyn, B4417, nr. Llithfaen): Welsh language centre in restored former stone quarry on coast of peninsula. ∅ 075885 334.

Penmachno Woollen Mill (south of Betws-y-Coed, A5/B4406): 17th century, on Conwy Falls. Easter–Nov. Mon.–Fri. 9.30–5.30.

Penmon (4 miles north-east of Beaumaris, Anglesey): St Seiriol's Well: retreat of 6th century Celtic saint. Penmon Cross: Celtic cross c.1000. Penmon Priory: ruined 12th-century abbey. Dovecote with stone cupola, c.1600, for about 1,000 doves.

Penrhyn Castle (3½ miles east of Bangor, A5/A55): Neo-Norman, built by Thomas Hopper,

1827–40; collection of dolls; Industrial Railway Museum. NT. April–May and October daily 2–5, June–Sept. daily 11–5.

Plas Newydd (Anglesey, south of Menai Bridge, A4080): home of Marquess of Anglesey, rebuilt by James Wyatt end of 18th century, with murals by Rex Whistler. Portraits by Van Dyck, Lawrence, Hoppner, Romney etc. NT. 20 April–Sept. daily except Sat., 12–5, Oct. 2–5.

Plas Teg (Pontblyddyn, between Mold and Wrexham, A541): former country house of Trevor-Ropers, c.1610, attributed to Inigo Jones or Robert Smythson, earliest Renaissance house in Wales. Interiors with parrots etc. Mon.–Sat. 11–5, Sun. 12–5.

Plas-yn-Rhiw (Llyn, 10 miles from Pwllheli in direction of Aberdaron): small, picturesque country house with garden overlooking Hell's Mouth Bay. NT. End April–Sept. daily, except Sat., 12–5, Oct. Sun. only 12–4.

Porthmadog: Ffestiniog Railway Museum, Harbour Station, ∅ 0766 512340. End March–Oct.

Portmeirion (east of Porthmadog, A487): 'Italian' village on Cardigan Bay, designed by Sir Clough Williams-Ellis. March–Nov. daily 9.30–5.30.

Pwllheli (Llyn): Llen Llyn, Y Maes, ∅ 0758 612907: excellent Welsh bookshop, owned by writer Alun Jones.

Rhinog National Nature Reserve (east of Harlech off A496): 1,500 acres unspoilt countryside in centre of 'Harlech Dome'. Narrow road from Llanbedr through Artro Valley to Llyn Cwm Bychan. From there the 'Roman Steps' go past peak of Rhinog Fawr to the east: these steps are of Cambrian rock, probably built in early Middle Ages as a track for packhorses across the moor to Bala. Beautiful footpaths to Llyn Bodlyn, the dark Llyn Hywel, and the mysterious Llyn Dulyn, the legendary 'Black Lake', one of the loveliest mountain lakes in Wales.

Rhuddlan (A547, south of Rhyl): birthplace of 'Magnum' photographer Philip Jones Griffiths ('Vietnam Inc.', 1971). Castle of Edward I at mouth of the Clwyd, built by his fortress-builder James of St George, 1277–82; first concentric castle in Wales, surrounded by double wall, and with round towers. It was from here that Edward I issued his notorious Statutes of Rhuddlan (1284), the laws by which he intended to govern the conquered country. The castle was razed in 1648 by Cromwell's troops. May–Sept. daily 9.30–6.30, Sun. 2–6.30, Oct.–April daily 9.30–4, Sun. 2–4.

Ruthin (A494/A525): till 1974 county town of Denbighshire. Castle of Edward I (1281) on red sandstone rock, now Castle hotel (medieval banquets with harp music). Owain Glyndwr's rebellion began in Ruthin in 1400. St Peter's Church: splendid Late Gothic ceiling with 480 carved oak panels, a gift from Henry VII. Wrought-iron churchyard gates by Robert Davies, 1727. Half-timbered houses, 14–17th century, in Castle Street and St Peter's Square.

Sarn (B4413 south-west of Pwllheli, Llyn): Sarn Pottery, shop selling ceramics by Czech émigré Oldrich Asenbryl (workshop: Rhiw Awel, Bryncroes nr. Sarn, Ø 075883 427).

Tal-y-Llyn (north-west of Machynlleth, B4405): hamlet on mountain lake of same name at foot of Cader Idris. St Mary's: old church with painted wooden panels of 12 apostles in choir (5–7th century?).

Trefriw Woollen Mills (south of Conwy, B5106): 1859, visit to mill and goods for sale. Mon.–Fri. 9–5.30, Sat. and Sun. afternoons.

Ty Mawr (Gwybrnant, 4 miles south-west of Betws-y-Coed, A5/B4406): birthplace of Bishop Morgan, translator of the Bible into Welsh. NT. End April–Sept. daily except Mon. & Sat., 12–5. Open Bank Holiday. October Fri. & Sun. 12–4. By appointment Fri. evenings 6.30–8. May–end Aug.

Valle Crucis Abbey (2 miles north of Llangollen, A542): Ruined Cistercian monastery c.1201. Grave of bard Iolo Goch. 15 March–15 Oct. daily 9.30–6.30, 16 Oct.–14 March 9.30–4, Sun. 2–4. Eliseg's Pillar (in field north of abbey): famous early 9th-century cross for Eliseg, Prince of Powys. The faded Latin inscription indicates that his ancestor was the Roman general Macsen (Magnus Maximus) – a popular belief since the withdrawal of the Romans.

Y Ffor (A499 north of Pwllheli, Llyn): Gwynedd Pottery, Glyddyn Mawr, Ø 0758 612932: workshop of John Davies; mail order for cassettes of old and contemporary Welsh vocal and instrumental music (Adlonni Recordings).

Eating and Drinking

H = hotel   R = restaurant   GF = good food restaurant (reservation advisable)
B&B = bed and breakfast

How one enjoys one's
supper at one's inn after
a good day's walk!
George Borrow

South Wales

Boncath (south of Cardigan, A478/B43332): Pantyderi Farm, 16th century, with pony trekking, B&B, ∅ 0239 227.

Brecon: Castle of Brecon Hotel, H+R, ∅ 0874 2551 and 2942.

Broad Haven (north-west of Milford Haven): Druidstone Hotel, Druidstone, H+R, ∅ 0437 781221.

Capel-y-Ffin (between Hay-on-Wye and Abergavenny, B4423): The Monastery, later Eric Gill's studio. 2 self-catering apartments, ∅ 0873 890379.
   The Grange, neighbouring farm with pony trekking, B&B, ∅ 0873 890215.

Cardiff: Quayles, 8 Romilly Crescent, Canton: GF, ∅ 0222 341264.
   Riverside, 44 Tudor Street: Chinese food, ∅ 0222 372163.
   Angel Hotel, Castle Street: H+R, ∅ 232633.
   Park Hotel, Park Place: H+R, ∅ 383471
   The Old Arcade: pub with rugby memorabilia (off St Mary Street).
   Blas ar Gymru, 48 Crwys Road: Welsh cooking with Welsh wine (from John Bevan's Croffta Vineyard nr. Cardiff), ∅ 0222 382132.
   Le Cassoulet, 5 Romilly Crescent, Canton: French cuisine. ∅ 0222 221905.

Crickhowell: Gliffaes Country House Hotel (3 miles outside Crickhowell), H+R, ∅ 0874 730371.

Glasbury (west of Hay-on-Wye, A438): Three Cocks, H+R, ∅ 04974 215.

Gower (peninsula south-west of Swansea).
Langland Bay: Langland Court Hotel, Langland Court Road, H+R, ∅ 0792 68505.
   Osborne Hotel, Rotherslade Road, H+R, ∅ 0792 66274.
Bishopston: Winston Private Hotel, 11 Church Lane, H, ∅ 044128 2074.
Port Eynon: Ship Inn, R (laverbread!), ∅ 0792 390201

Haverfordwest: Pembroke House Hotel, Chez Gilbert Restaurant, H+GF, ∅ 0437 3652.

Hay-on-Wye: Black Lion, Cromwell slept here, H+R, ∅ 0497 820841.

Lamphey (1 mile east of Pembroke): The Court Hotel, country house hotel, H+R, ∅ 0646 672273.

Llanddewi Skirrid (3 miles north-east of Abergavenny, B4521): Walnut Tree Inn, GF, Italian-owned, speciality: seafood and fresh pasta; 'the best place to eat in Wales' (Observer), ∅ 0873 2797.

Llangranog (north-east of Cardigan, A487/B4334): Pigeonsford Mansion, Georgian country house, 2 self-catering apartments, ∅ 0239 223.

Llangynidr (west of Crickhowell, B4558): Red Lion, H+GF, ∅ 0874 730223.

Llanthony (north of Abergavenny, B4423): Abbey Hotel, in wing of former 12th-century monastery, H, ∅ 0873 89047.

Llechryd (nr. Cardigan, A484): Castell Malgwyn Hotel, country house hotel on Teifi (1780), H+R, ∅ 023987 382.

Marloes (west of Milford Haven, B4321) Ty Gwyn, H+R, ∅ 0646 415.

Monmouth: King's Head, Agincourt Square: 17th-century inn, stucco portrait of Charles I (a frequent guest) in bar, H+R, ∅ 0600 712177.

Raglan: Beaufort Arms, H+R, ∅ 0291 690412.

Robeston Wathen (8 miles east of Haverfordwest, A40): Robeston House, country house hotel, H+GF, ∅ 0834 860392.

St David's: Warpool Court Hotel, on edge of city, with about 3,000 painted tiles that belonged to the eccentric Lady Williams at the turn of the century, H+GF, ∅ 043788 300.
Whitesands Bay Hotel, H+R, ∅ 043788 403.

Swansea: Mermaid Hotel, 688 Mumbles Road, Mumbles: Dylan Thomas Pub, H+R, ∅ 0792 368125.
Norton House Hotel, Mumbles: H+GF, ∅ 0792 404849.

Tenby: Four Croft Hotel, Croft Terrace, H+R, ∅ 0834 2516.

Wolf's Castle (6½ miles north of Haverfordwest, A40): Wolfscastle Country Hotel, H+R, ∅ 043787 225.

Mid Wales

Abergwesyn (5 miles north-west of Llanwrtyd Wells): Llwynderw Hotel, H+GF, ∅ 05913 238.

Aberystwyth: Belle Vue Royal, Marine Terrace, H+R, ∅ 0970 617558.
Cooper's Arms, Northgate Street: pub with Welsh folk music and jazz.
Conrah Country House Hotel, Chancery: small hotel 3 miles south of town, H+R, ∅ 0970 617941.

Eglwysfach (6 miles south of Machynlleth, A487): Ynyshir Hall, little country house hotel, GF, ∅ 065474 209.

Lake Vyrnwy Hotel (10 miles west of Llanfyllin, B4393): H+GF, ∅ 069173 244.

Llandeilo: Cawdor Arms, H+R, ∅ 0558 823500.

Llandovery (A40/A483): Castle Hotel where Nelson slept in 1802, and George Borrow in 1854 (his 4-poster bed is still in use), H+R, ∅ 0550 20343.

Llangamarch Wells (south-west of Builth Wells): Lake Hotel with golf course, H+R, ∅ 05912 202.

Llangoed Hall (nr. Llyswen, south-east of Builth Wells, A470): Jacobean manor, 17th century, rebuilt 1913–19 by Sir Clough Williams-Ellis. Since 1990 luxury country house hotel (owned by Laura Ashley's widower, Sir Bernard and known as 'Sir Bernie Inn'), H+GF, ∅ 0874 754525.

Llanwrtyd Wells: Dol-y-Coed Hotel, picturesquely situated on Irfon (trout-fishing), H+R, ∅ 059 13 215.

Newcastle Emlyn (east of Cardigan, A484): Felin Geri Flour Mill, first Japanese restaurant in Wales, opened 1988, GF, ∅ 0239 710810. With falconry.

Penarth Farm (1 mile north of Newtown, A483): half-timbered farmhouse, 15–16th century, B&B, ∅ 0686 25760.

Pencerrig Country House Hotel (north of Builth Wells, A483): 18th century. Home of painter Thomas Jones, H+R, ∅ 0982 553226.

Ponterwyd (12 miles east of Aberystwyth, A44): George Borrow Hotel, above Rheidol waterfall, the noise of which disturbed George Borrow during his stay in 1854, H+R, ∅ 097085 230.

Presteigne: Radnorshire Arms, High Street, historical half-timbered house, home of Christopher Hatton, a favourite of Elizabeth I, inn since 1792, H+R, ∅ 0544 267406.

Trelydan Hall (2 miles north of Welshpool): beautifully restored half-timbered country house, 16–19th century. Home of flower arranger Iona Trevor-Jones, Welsh evenings with harp music (a member of the family was royal harpist; Prince Albert's harp is here). H+GF, ∅ 0938 2773.

Welshpool: Moat Farm (2 miles south of Welshpool, off A483), 17th-century farmhouse, H+R, ∅ 0938 3179.

North Wales

Anglesey: The Bulkeley Arms, H+R, ∅ 0248 410.
Badorgau (south-west of Llangefni, B4422): Glantraeth Restaurant and Welsh Entertainment Centre, R, ∅ 0248 840401.
Rhosneigr: Honeypot, Morfa Hill, R, ∅ 0248 810302.
Holyhead: Presaddfed, Bodedern, old family home (since 1184), H, ∅ 0407 740227.

Betws-y-Coed (A5/A470): Craig y Dderwen, angling and pony trekking, H+R, ∅ 069 02 293.

Bodysgallen Hall (south of Llandudno, B5115): 17th-century country home of the Mostyns, luxury hotel with historic garden, H+GF, ∅ 0492 84466.

Bontddu (north-west of Dolgellau, A496): Bontddu Hall, Victorian luxury hotel with view of Mawddach Estuary, former home of Neville Chamberlain's sister, H+R, ∅ 034149 661.

Caernarfon: Plas Bowman, 5 High Street: H+R, ∅ 0286 5555.
The Bakestone, 26 Hole in the Wall Street, Bistro.

Corwen: Valentine's, London Road, H+R, ∅ 0490 2350.

Dolgellau: Dylanwad Da, 2 Smithfield Street, R, ∅ 0341 422870.
Glyn Farm Guest House: old farmhouse, B&B, ∅ 0341 286.
Gwernan Lake Hotel: anglers' hotel on small mountain lake south-west of town, H+R, ∅ 0341 288.

Glyn-Ceiriog (south of Llangollen, B4500): Golden Pheasant, angling and riding, H+R, ∅ 0341 281.

Harlech: Castle Cottage, family guesthouse, H+R, ∅ 0766 780479.

The Cemlyn, High Street: GF, ∅ 0766 780425.

Llanarmon Dyffryn Ceiriog (10 miles west of Chirk, B4500): The West Arms, remote village inn in Berwyn Mountains, H+R, ∅ 069176 665.

Llanberis (east of Caernarfon, A4086): Y Bistro, 43 High Street, GF, ∅ (0286) 871278.

Llandudno: St George's Hotel, St George's Place: Victorian hotel on Promenade, where Bismarck stayed in 1854, H+R, ∅ 0492 77544.

Plas Fron Deg, Church Walk: Victorian family hotel, H+GF, ∅ 0492 77267.

Lanterns, Church Walk: R, ∅ 0492 877924.

Llangollen: Hand Hotel, Bridge Street: H+R, ∅ 0978 860303.

The Royal, Bridge Street: 19th-century hotel on Dee, H+R, ∅ 0978 860331.

Llanrwst (A470/A548): Meadowsweet Hotel, H+GF, ∅ 0492 640733.

Ca'er Berllan, Betws-y-Coed Road: small hotel in 16th century manor, H+R, ∅ 0492 640027.

Llyn: Bronheulog Hotel, Lon Garmon (8 miles south-west of Pwllheli, A499): H+GF, ∅ 075881 2177.

Deucoch Hotel, Abersoch, overlooking bay: H+R, ∅ 075881 2680.

Porth Tocyn Hotel (2 miles south of Abersoch): on cliffs overlooking Cardigan Bay, H+GF, ∅ 075881 2966.

Carreg Plâs (2 miles north of Aberdaron): 17th-century house, B&B+EM, ∅ 075886 308.

Plas Bodegroes (nr. Pwllheli): Georgian country house hotel, H+GF, ∅ 0758 612363.

Maenan (nr. Llanrwst, A470): Gwesty Plas Maenan, country house, H+R, ∅ Dolgarrog 049 269 232.

Maes-y-Neuadd (B4573, between Harlech and Talsarnau): country house hotel, H+GF, ∅ 0766 780200.

Nant Gwynant (A498/A4086): Pen-y-Gwryd Hotel, excellent mountaineers' hotel at foot of Snowdon, H+R, ∅ 0286 211.

Northop (nr. Chester): Soughton Hall Hotel, 18th century country house, H+R, ∅ 035286 811.

Penmaenpool (2 miles south-west of Dolgellau, A493): George III Hotel, picturesquely situated country house on mouth of Mawddach, H+GF, ∅ 0341 422525.

Portmeirion (east of Porthmadog, A487): Italianate fantasy village designed by Sir Clough Williams-Ellis, H+R, self-catering apartments, ∅ 0766 770228.

Ruthin (A494/A525): Ruthin Castle Hotel: medieval banquets, H+R, ∅ 08242 2664.

Pentre Coch Manor (3 miles south of Ruthin): 16th century country house hotel, H+R, ∅ 08242 3287.

Tal-y-Llyn (south of Dolgellau, A487): Tynycornel Hotel, picturesquely situated on Talyllyn Lake, fishing and sailing, H+R, ∅ 065 477 282.

Minffordd Hotel, at foot of Cader Idris, H+GF, ∅ 065473 665.

List of Illustrations
All photographs by Peter Sager unless otherwise stated

Colour Plates

Black and White Plates

Text Illustrations

NL = National Library of Wales, Aberystwyth
NM = National Museum of Wales, Cardiff

p. 21 Welsh heads
King Henry VII. Bust in Westminster Abbey probably based on death mask, 1509 (The Dean and Chapter of Westminster Abbey)
William Roos: Reverend Christmas Evans, oil, undated (NL)
William Williams Pantycelyn (NL)
Alvin Langdon Coburn: David Lloyd George, photo, 1918 (NL)
Neil Kinnock (Photo: dpa Düsseldorf)
Gwynfor Evans (Photo: Peter Sager)
Jonah Jones: John Cowper Powys, bronze (NL)
Saunders Lewis (Photo: Oriel, Welsh Arts Council, Cardiff)
R. S. Thomas (Photo: Peter Sager)

p. 32 Chapel elevations, from John B. Hilling: The Historic Architecture of Wales. Cardiff 1976, figs. 102, 104–106

p. 35 S. & N. Buck: The South-East View of Caerphilly Castle, 1740, copper engraving (NL)

p. 37 Thomas Jones: The Bard, 1774, oil (NM)

p. 41 Turner: Conwy Castle, 1802, watercolour (Whitworth Art Gallery, University of Manchester)

p. 46 Rebecca attacking a tollgate, 19th-century etching (NL)

p. 73 Turner: Tintern Abbey, 1794, watercolour (By courtesy of the Trustees of the Victoria and Albert Museum, London)

p. 75 King Henry V (National Portrait Gallery, London)

p. 77 C. S. Rolls, c.1900 (Monmouth Museum)

p. 83 Tragic mask with Phrygian cap, probably from lady's case, ivory, 2nd or 3rd century AD (Caerleon, Legionary Museum)

p. 84 The Romans in Wales, map based on: 'Caernarvon-Segontium', Bulletin of the NM, 1974.

p. 87 The Duke of York (George VI) on the Newport Transporter Bridge, 1925 (Newport Museum and Art Gallery)

p. 88 J. C. Wilson: Chartists' Riot in Newport, November 4 1839, lithograph after W. Howel (NM)

p. 89 Augustus John: W. H. Davies, 1918, drawing (National Portrait Gallery, London)

p. 92 Cardiff Town Plan, based on AA Touring Guide to Wales, 1975.

p. 114 S. & N. Buck: The North-West View of Cardiff Castle, 1741, copper engraving (NL)

p. 115 W. Burges: Capital design for Summer Smoking Room, Cardiff Castle, from: The Architect, September 14 1872 (NM)

p. 116 William Burges (Illustrated London News, April 30 1881)

p. 117 W. Burges: Cupola of Arab Salon in Cardiff Castle, 1880–81, detail (Photo: Welsh Arts Council, City of Cardiff)

p. 118 W. Burges: Cabinet, 1858 (Victoria & Albert Museum, London)

p. 120 J. C. Ibbetson: A Party of Welsh Damsels, on one horse, under the ruins of Castell Coch, c.1792, watercolour (NM)

p. 121 W. Burges: Castell Coch, frontispiece drawing for his 'Report', 1875

p. 126 T. H. Shepherd: Berw Rhondda, 1831, copper engraving after drawing by Henry Gastineau (NM)

p. 127 Paul Sandby: Landscape with a Coalmine, c.1770, watercolour (NM)

p. 128 L. S. Lowry: Hillside in Wales, 1962, oil (Tate Gallery, London/Mrs Carol Ann Danes)

p. 134 Peter Charles Canot: The Great Bridge over the Taff at Pontypridd, 1775, etching after painting by Richard Wilson (British Museum, London)

p. 135 Dr William Price, 1822 (Welsh Folk Museum St Fagans, Cardiff)

Index

bold type: detailed description
italics: illustration

Places

C = Clwyd
D = Dyfed
Gw = Gwent
Gd = Gwynedd
MG = Mid Glamorgan
SG = South Glamorgan
WG = West Glamorgan
P = Powys

Persons

dates given only for people who
were born or died in Britain

Subjects